ADVERTISING, PROMOTION,

& Supplemental Aspects of Integrated Marketing Communications

Sixth Edition

Terence A. Shimp

University of South Carolina

THOMSON
™
SOUTH-WESTERN

Australia · Canada · Mexico · Singapore · Spain · United Kingdom · United States

THOMSON

SOUTH-WESTERN

Advertising, Promotion, and Supplemental Aspects of Integrated Marketing Communications, 6e

Terence A. Shimp

Editor-in-Chief:
Jack W. Calhoun

Team Leader:
Melissa S. Acuña

Acquisitions Editor:
Steven W. Hazelwood

Developmental Editor:
Erin McGraw

Marketing Manager:
Nicole C. Moore

Production Editor:
Amy A. Brooks

Manufacturing Coordinator:
Diane Lohman

Compositor:
Pre-Press Company, Inc.

Printer:
Quebecor World Versailles
Versailles, KY

Design Project Manager:
Casey Gilbertson

Internal Designer:
Casey Gilbertson

Cover Designer:
Casey Gilbertson

Cover Image:
Casey Gilbertson

Photography Manager:
Deanna Ettinger

Photo Researcher:
Terri Miller / E-Visual Communications

Library of Congress Cataloging-in-
Publication Data

Shimp, Terence A.
    Advertising & promotion : supplemen-
tal aspects of integrated marketing
communications / Terence A. Shimp.—
6th ed.
    p. cm.
    Rev. ed. of: Advertising, promotion &
supplemental aspects of integrated
marketing communications. 5th ed.
c2000.
    Includes bibliographical references
and index.
    ISBN 0-03-035271-1
    1. Communication in marketing.
2. Sales promotion. 3. Advertising.
4. Direct marketing. I. Title: Advertising
and promotion. II. Shimp, Terence A.
Advertising, promotion & supplemental
aspects of integrated marketing communications. III. Title.

HF5415.123 .S54 2003
658.8'2—dc21   2002071957

BRIEF CONTENTS

CONTENTS

CONTENTS

CONTENTS

CONTENTS

CONTENTS

CONTENTS

PREFACE

RESPONDING TO A CHANGING WORLD

The field of marketing communications MarCom has changed dramatically since the conception of this textbook nearly two decades ago. Indeed, changes have been considerable since the prior edition was written three years ago. That edition, written during the height of the dot-com craze and a raging bull market, is replaced by the sixth edition that has been constructed during a period that witnessed a terrorist attack on the World Trade Center and the Pentagon, the dot-com crash, the Enron scandal, and the biggest one-year proportionate reduction in advertising expenditures since the Great Depression some 70 years ago.

Within this milieu, brand managers realize now more than ever that advertising and other MarCom investments must be held financially accountable. Companies are continuously seeking better ways to communicate effectively and efficiently with their targeted audiences. The competition is more intense than ever, and the marketplace is filled with communications clutter. Marketing communicators are challenged to use communication methods that will break through this clutter, reach audiences with interesting and persuasive messages that enhance brand equity, and assure that MarCom investments yield an adequate return on investment. In meeting these challenges, companies are increasingly embracing a strategy of integrated marketing communications (IMC).

FOCUS OF THE TEXT

Whether a student is taking this course simply to learn more about the dynamic nature of this field or has plans for making a career in advertising, promotions, or another aspect of marketing, this textbook continues to provide a contemporary view of the role and importance of marketing communications. The text emphasizes the importance of integrated marketing communications concepts in enhancing the equity of brands and provides thorough coverage of all aspects of an IMC program: advertising, promotions, packaging, and branding strategies, point-of-purchase communications, marketing-oriented public relations, and event-and-cause-oriented sponsorships. These topics are made even more accessible in this edition through expanded use of examples and applications. The text continues to cover appropriate academic theories and concepts to provide formal structure to the illustrations and examples.

This textbook is intended for use in undergraduate or graduate courses in marketing communications, advertising, promotion strategy, promotion management, and in other courses with similar concentrations. Professors and their students should find this book substantive but highly readable, eminently current but also appreciative of the evolution of the field. Above all, this textbook thoroughly blends marketing communications practice in its varied forms with research and theory.

In order to provide your students with the latest information on the industry and academic environment of marketing, the text has been updated with new material, new box features, and current examples. Major changes include the following:

◆ The text provides state-of-the-art coverage of major academic literature and practitioner writings on all aspects of marketing communications. These writings are presented at an accessible level to students and illustrated with copious examples and special inserts – Opening Vignettes, IMC Focus boxes, Global Focus inserts, and Online Focus boxes.

- **Online Focus** – Brand New to this edition! Just as the Internet has increased in importance in our lives, so has its importance increased in the world of advertising and promotions. The *Online Focus* boxes provide coverage of the concepts covered in the chapter and their impact on Internet marketing. Students learn about a variety of interesting topics, such as new technology, the myths of the Internet, and foreign companies designed to entice new Internet users.

- **IMC Focus** – These features have been updated to further emphasize key IMC concepts within each chapter by using real-company situations that illustrate how Integrated Brand Communications is put into practice everyday.

- **Global Focus** – These updated boxed features enhance the text's global marketing perspective and spotlight the International impact of IMC by reviewing how companies, such as, Procter & Gamble or the Lipton tea company have applied these concepts when marketing products overseas.

- **Opening Vignettes** – Opening Vignettes have been updated and revised. Each chapter begins with a current issue and a well-known company. These vignettes illustrate how chapter topics relate to advertising strategies that work to make campaigns and products successful. Some of the companies and brands featured are Viagra, Absolut Vodka, Saab, and Mountain Dew.

The Marketing Communications Process and Brand Equity Enhancement   Chapter Two   25

IMC
focus

Levi's Effort to Reinvent Itself

There was a time when Levi's was the brand virtually synonymous with jeans. Now the competitive situation is wide open with many brands competing for the consumer's loyalty. In a study of 1,800 high school and college students conducted by the New York–based Zandl Group, respondents were asked to name the one brand of jeans they were most likely to purchase. If this study had been conducted in 1990 instead of 2000, it is probable that as many as one-third of the respondents would have named Levi's as their likely purchase choice. However, only 9 percent of high school and 12 percent of college students named Levi's as the brand they would likely purchase. Considering college students, other brands that fared better include Gap (7 percent), Old Navy (3%), Express (3%), Calvin Klein (3%), Jnco (2%), and Abercrombie & Fitch (2%). And 27 percent of respondents dictated intentions to purchase brands other than these, which included such purchase loyalties in the teen market are widely divided. This drop in purchase loyalties comes as no surprise when considering the substantial fragmentation of the jeans market, with new brands regularly being introduced, such as Sixty USA and cutting-edge brands Diesel (from Italy) and François Girbaud (from France).

These survey results indicate the likelihood that Levi's sales performance has declined along with its once-supreme brand image. In fact, Levi's worldwide sales (not just jeans) fell from a high of

and reinvent [Levi's] through communication and great product development."

Levi's Engineered Jeans—a radical-looking style designed to accommodate the body's contour and to combine strength with softness—is the first evidence of Levi's effort to reinvent the brand. Engineered Jeans achieved super success when first introduced in Europe and Asia and now are widely distributed in U.S. specialty and department stores. In addition to print ads and exciting TV spots, Levi's backed the launch of Engineered Jeans with a sweepstakes offer that consumers could enter when visiting

---

Online Focus

The Fundamentals of Consumers' Use of MarCom Information   Chapter Four   97

The Challenge of Capturing Attention Online

Banner ads on the Internet are ubiquitous. Ads, and more ads. But who pays attention? Jupiter Media Metrix estimated that the average Internet user was exposed to more than 700 banner ads per day in 2002 and that this will increase to 950 banner ads daily by 2005. The majority of these ads never receive our attention, however. According to Nielsen/NetRatings, the average click rate in 2001 was a paltry 0.49 percent; in other words, online users pay attention to and solicit information from only a small percentage of all the Internet banner ads to which they are exposed. (Remember: Exposure is necessary for but is not equivalent to attention. Exposure merely indicates that the consumer has a chance to see an advertisement.)

Because click rates are trivially small, online advertisers have turned to new technology and larger ad sizes to grab the online surfer's attention. Many of these changes and the standardization of banner sizes have been facilitated by the efforts of the Internet Advertising Bureau (IAB), a trade association that is a leader in the Internet advertising industry. In early 2001

the IAB endorsed seven new Internet ad formats, labeled Internet marketing units (IMUs). These seven new IMUs compare with the earlier full banner, the size of which was 468 x 60 pixels (28,080 square pixels). The following table compares the new IMUs against this original full banner.

This table makes it clear that the new (as of 2001) IMUs are considerably larger than the original full banner ad. It is likely that these larger ad sizes increase attention and thus click rates. Pop-up ads, though often a source of irritation, are especially effective attention getters. Internet advertisers, like advertisers in all other media, have to fight through the clutter to find ways to attract the online user's attention. Bigger ads, ads popping up, and ads that offer sound and visuals are just some of the ways that have been devised to attract and hold the Internet user's attention.

Sources: Adapted from Dana Blankenhorn, "Bigger, Richer Ads Go Online," Advertising Age, June 18, 2001, T10; Sarah J. Heim, "IAB Establishes New Guidelines for Banners," Brandweek, February 26, 2001, 48; Stephanie Miles, "Advertisers Plan Flashier Ads to Make an Online Impression," Wall Street Journal Interactive Edition, March 1, 2001 (http://interactive.wsj.com).

Type and Size of IMU (pixel size)	Square Pixels	Percent Change Compared to Full Banner (480 x 60 pixels)
Skyscraper (120 x 600)	72,000	156%
Wide Skyscraper (160 x 600)	96,000	242%
Rectangle (180 x 150)	27,000	–4%
Medium Rectangle (300 x 250)	75,000	167%
Large Rectangle (336 x 280)	94,080	235%
Vertical Rectangle (240 x 400)	96,000	242%
Square Pop-Up (250 x 250)	62,500	123%

---

308   Part Four   Advertising Management

Worldwide Concern About Sex and Decency in Advertising

People worldwide are troubled by advertising considered indecent. But, of course, what is indecent in one country may not necessarily be seen the same way in another. The International Chamber of Commerce (ICC) Code of Advertising Practice insists that "advertising should be decent"—that is, "prepared with a due sense of social responsibility ...[and] not be such as to impair public confidence in advertising."

Three categories of advertising indecency that are matters of concern around the world include advertisements that are sexist, sexy, or that sexually objectify their models. Sexist ads are those that demean one sex in comparison with the other, particularly through sex-role stereotyping; sexy ads use sexual imagery or suggestiveness; and *sex-ual objectification* occurs when ads use women (or men) as decorative or attention-getting objects with little or no relevance to the product category. France's Truth in Advertising Bureau released a recent report that criticized advertisers for portraying women in a degrading way. The report especially criticized European fashion houses such as Christian Dior and the Benetton Group. New French standards prohibit violent advertisements and those that convey images of submission or objectify women. For example, the French ad bureau forced the withdrawal of one ad that featured an attractive woman wearing only underwear in a kneeling position beside a sheep with the tagline "I'd like a sweater."

The nature and extent of government regulation of indecent sex-oriented advertising varies considerably, from a relatively laissez-faire attitude in

the United States and Western Europe to stringent controls in various Muslim countries. Following are some examples of government regulations of advertising in different countries:

- In Malaysia, the Ministry of Information's Advertising Code states that women should not be the principal objects of an advertisement or other medium intended to attract sales unless the advertised product is relevant to women.
- The Ministry of Information in Saudi Arabia prevents any advertising depicting veiled or unveiled women.
- Indian law forbids the depiction of a woman's figure or any female body part if the depiction is derogatory to women or immoral.
- Portuguese law prohibits sex discrimination or the subordination or objectification of women in advertising.
- Norway requires that advertising not portray men or women in an offensive manner or imply any derogatory judgment of either sex.

The regulation of advertising (on grounds of decency or otherwise) is complex and controversial, because regulation curtails the rights of advertisers to communicate with their publics and impinges on the rights of people to receive information and images in any form they consider unobjectionable. Regulators in all countries are placed in a tricky position when attempting to balance the rights and interests of advertisers, consumers, and society at large.

Sources: Alessandra Galloni, "Clampdown on 'Porno-Chic' Ads Is Pushed by French Authorities," Wall Street Journal Interactive Edition, October 25, 2001 (http://interactive.wsj.com); Jean J. Boddewyn, "Controlling Sex and Decency in Advertising around the World," Journal of Advertising 20 (December 1991), 25–36.

GLOBAL FOCUS

◆ The new edition continues to include the same number of chapters as covered in the prior edition, but some of the chapters have been updated and rewritten to reflect the changes and dynamics in the marketplace. The updated chapters include:

- Chapter 3, "Positioning and Targeting for MarCom Efforts," adds a major section on positioning, and features expanded coverage of demographics and other targeting issues.

- A Brand New Chapter 13, "Online and Alternative Advertising Media," focuses attention on the importance and use of online and alternative offline media. Coverage includes banner advertising, interstitial, and wireless advertising.

- In the sixth edition, the measurement of message effectiveness is covered primarily in Chapter 11, "Assessing Ad Message Effectiveness." This chapter immediately follows the chapters that cover ad creativity and message formats.

- Whereas Chapter 15 in the previous edition treated both the measurement of message and media effectiveness, in this sixth edition the measurement of message effectiveness is covered in Chapter 11 immediately after the two chapters that deal with ad creativity and message formats.

- The measurement of ad media is integrated throughout Chapter 12, "Traditional Advertising Media," providing an analysis of the traditional forms advertising.

- A vastly expanded treatment of direct advertising and database marketing is presented in Chapter 14, "Direct Advertising Media." This chapter devotes in-depth coverage to opt-in, or permission, and e-mail advertising.

- Regulatory, Ethical, and "Green" Issues in Marketing Communications" has been moved to Chapter 20, as a fitting conclusion to the aspects of marketing agencies, and other MarCom suppliers.

A PREMIER INSTRUCTIONAL RESOURCE PACKAGE

The Learning Package provided with *Advertising, Promotion, and Supplemental Aspects of Integrated Marketing Communications,* sixth edition, was specifically designed to meet the needs of instructors who face a variety of teaching conditions and to enhance students' experience with the subject. We have addressed both the traditional and the innovative classroom environment by providing an array of high quality, and technologically advanced items to bring a contemporary, real world feel to the study of advertising, promotion, and integrated marketing communications.

◆ **CD-ROM PowerPoint Presentation Software.** The sixth edition includes an updated and improved CD-ROM PowerPoint presentation. The amount of audio and video is expanded from the CD-ROM that accompanied the previous edition; the presentation now contains nearly two hours of video and hundreds of still pictures as well as animations, build slides, and viewers. Designed by John H. Lindgren, Jr., at the University of Virginia, the CD-ROM covers all of the material found in the textbook in addition to providing supplemental examples and materials found in radio, television, and print media.

An entire course can be developed around this presentation tool. The CD-ROM has been prepared in a PowerPoint format to be easily supplemented by instructors who wish to introduce additional material.

◆ **Video Package.** The Video Package has been prepared to provide a relevant and interesting visual teaching tool for the classroom. Each video segment gives students the opportunity to apply what they are learning to real-world situations and enables instructors to better illustrate concepts to students. Companies such as Timberland, Tower Records, Pfizer, and Radio Shack are featured. Additional television commercials and video footage can be found on the CD-ROM PowerPoint Presentation Software.

◆ **ExamView.** The Test Bank is available in a computerized format, allowing instructors to select problems at random by level of difficulty or type, customize or add test questions, and scramble questions to create up to 99 versions of the same test. This is available in DOS, Mac, or Windows formats.

◆ **Test Bank.** This valuable resource provides testing items for instructors' reference and use. The test bank contains over 1,500 multiple choice, true/false, and short answer questions in levels of varying difficulty.

◆ **Instructor's Manual.** This comprehensive and valuable teaching aid includes a list of chapter objectives, chapter summaries, detailed chapter outlines, and answers to discussion questions.

Visit the text website at **http://shimp.swcollege.com** to find instructor's support materials and study resources that will help your students practice and apply the concepts they have learned in class.

◆ **Student Resources.**
- The *Chapter Objectives* are listed for each chapter so that students can go to the website and review.
- *Online Quizzes* for each chapter are available to those students who would like extra study material. After each quiz is submitted, automatic feedback tells the students how they scored and what the correct answers are to the questions they missed. Students are then able to email their results directly to their instructor.
- *Crossword Puzzles* pulled from the key terms in the text help students study the vocabulary covered in the text.
- *Internet Exercises* are available to students who would like extra practice applying the concepts in the text to what is happening on the web. Instructors can also use these exercises as supplemental homework material.
- *PowerPoint Presentations* done by John H. Lindgren, Jr. are available for students to download (only available for download without the imbedded videos).

◆ **Instructor Resources.**
- Downloadable *Instructor's Manual* files available in Microsoft Word an Adobe Acrobat format.
- Downloadable *PowerPoint Presentations* by John H. Lindgren, Jr. (only available for download without the imbedded videos).

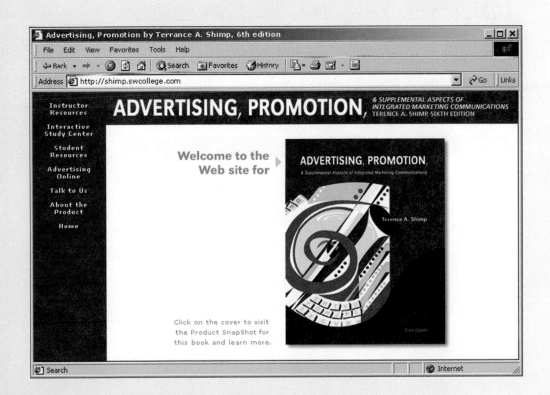

ABOUT THE AUTHOR

Terence A. Shimp received his doctorate from the University of Maryland and taught for four years at Kent State University before moving to the University of South Carolina where he has been a faculty member for the past 25 years. He is Professor of Marketing, Distinguished Foundation Fellow, and Chair of the Marketing Department in the Moore School of Business, University of South Carolina, Columbia. Professor Shimp teaches courses in marketing communications and research philosophy and methods. He has earned a variety of teaching awards, including the Amoco Foundation Award that named him the outstanding teacher at the University of South Carolina in 1990.

He has published widely in the areas of marketing, consumer behavior, and advertising. His work has appeared frequently in outlets such as the *Journal of Consumer Research, Journal of Marketing Research, Journal of Marketing, Journal of Advertising, Journal of Advertising Research, Journal of Consumer Psychology,* and the *Journal of Public Policy and Marketing.* "Endorsers in Advertising: The Case of the Negative Celebrity Information," co-authored with Brian Till, was named the outstanding article published in the *Journal of Advertising* in 1998. "A Critical Appraisal of Demand Artifacts in Consumer Research" published with Eva Hyatt and David Snyder in the *Journal of Consumer Research* received that journal's award for the top article published during the period 1990–1992. In 2001, he was the recipient of the American Academy of Advertising's Lifetime Award for outstanding contributions to research in advertising.

Professor Shimp is past president of the Association for Consumer Research and past president of the *Journal of Consumer Research* policy board. He serves on the editorial policy boards of the *Journal of Consumer Research, Journal of Consumer Psychology, Journal of Marketing, Marketing Letters, Journal of Public Policy & Marketing,* and *Journal of Marketing Communications.* He has represented the Federal Trade Commission and various state agencies as an expert witness in issues concerning advertising deception and unfairness.

DEDICATION

To my wonderful and changing family. My dear brother Jack is gone, but thankfully we have his daughter, Karen, and her family as part of the extended family. Two more grandsons are on the way to form yet another basketball team. (My brothers know what I mean.) I especially thank my wife Judy for being my best friend and understanding why I must spend so many hours away from her. I love all of you.

ACKNOWLEDGEMENTS

My friend and colleague, Professor John H. Lindgren, Jr. (Jack) of the University of Virginia, deserves special recognition and sincere appreciation for his contributions to this sixth edition. Jack developed the multi-media supplements that will serve to create an exciting, dynamic, and enjoyable teaching environment for classroom presentation of the material contained in Advertising, Promotion, and Supplemental Aspects of Integrated Marketing Communications, sixth edition.

I am grateful to a number of people for their assistance in this project. I sincerely appreciate the thoughtful comments from the following people who critiqued the fifth edition and recommended changes:

Craig Andrews - Marquette University	Charles S. Areni - Texas Tech University
Guy R. Banville - Creighton University	M. Elizabeth Blair - Ohio University
Barbara M. Brown - San Jose State University	Gordon C. Bruner II - Southern Illinois University
Newell Chiesl - Indiana State University	Robert Dyer - George Washington University

Prior editions have benefited from the many useful comments from the following friends and acquaintances, whose affiliations may have changed since the time of reviewing a prior edition of this text:

Craig Andrews - Marquette University	Charles S. Areni - Texas Tech University
Guy R. Banville - Creighton University	M. Elizabeth Blair - Ohio University
Barbara M. Brown - San Jose State University	Gordon C. Bruner II - Southern Illinois University
Newell Chiesl - Indiana State University	Robert Dyer - George Washington University
Denise Essman - Drake University	P. Everett Fergenson - Iona College
James Finch - University of Wisconsin, LaCrosse	Linda L. Golden - University of Texas, Austin
Clayton Hillyer -American International College	Stephen Grove - Clemson University
Robert Harmon - Portland State University	Ronald Hill - Villanova University
Stewart W. Husted - Lynchburg College	Patricia Kennedy - University of Nebraska, Lincoln
Russell Laczniak - Iowa State University	Geoffrey Lantos - Bentley College
Monle Lee - Indiana University, South Bend	J. Daniel Lindley - Bentley College
John McDonald - Market Opinion Research	Therese A. Maskulka - Lehigh University
John Mowen - Oklahoma State University	Darrel D. Muehling - Washington State University
Kent Nakamoto - Virginia Tech University	D. Nasalroad - Central State University
Edward Riordan - Wayne State University	Alan Sawyer - University of Florida
Stanley Scott - Boise State University	Douglas Stayman - Cornell University
Jeff Stoltman - Wayne State University	Linda Swayne - University of North Carolina, Charlotte
John A. Taylor - Brigham Young University	Carolyn Tripp - Western Illinois University
Josh Wiener - Oklahoma State University	

My appreciation extends to a number of former Doctoral students who have shared their experiences in using the textbook and have provided valuable suggestions for change:

Avery Abernethy - Auburn University	Craig Andrews - Marquette University
Paula Bone - West Virginia University	Ken Manning - Colorado State University
David Sprott - Washington State University	Elnora Stuart - Winthrop University
Newell Chiesl - Indiana State University	Robert Dyer - George Washington University

I also appreciate the work of several MBA students who provide considerable assistance on the sixth edition: Yenseob (Cklio) Lee, Barbara Yale, and Yun J. Yang. I am grateful to Tracy Dunn and Scott Swain for their valuable assistance on the fifth edition.

Special appreciation is extended to my friend and colleague, Satish Jayachandran, for his invaluable suggestions regarding chapter sequencing and material coverage. I appreciate as well my other colleagues at the University of South Carolina for their understanding, that when I was under writing pressure I may have neglected some administrative duties or not been quite the friend and colleague they deserve.

My great appreciation goes out to my many friends at the Dryden Press who I worked with over the past 20 years during the first five editions. I am especially grateful to: Mary Fisher, Rob Zwettler, Lyn Hastert, Lise Johnson, and Bill Schoof.

I am grateful as well to my new friends at South-Western/Thomson for their outstanding efforts in bringing this sixth edition to fruition. I especially appreciate the support and guidance of Erin McGraw, the professional editing by Barbara McGowran, the work in gaining permissions by Deanna Ettinger, and the extensive work in production by Amy Brooks to help us meet deadline.

Terence A. Shimp
University of South Carolina, February 2002

Integrated
Marketing
Communications
and Its Role in
Brand Equity
Enhancement

PART ONE

Part One introduces the student to the fundamentals of integrated marketing communications (IMC). *Chapter 1* overviews the topic and discusses the importance of marketing communications. The chapter emphasizes the necessity of integrating the various marketing communications elements to "speak with a single voice" rather than treating them as separate and independent tools. Chapter 1 describes in detail the five key IMC features: (1) starting the communications process with the customer or prospect; (2) using any form of relevant contact for reaching customers/prospects; (3) speaking with a single voice; (4) building relationships with customers; and (5) ultimately affecting behavior.

Chapter 2 explains how integrated marketing communications accomplishes the objective of enhancing brand equity through a systematic process of elevating brand awareness and creating strong, favorable, and unique brand associations. The chapter is based on an integrative framework that postulates the MarCom program as consisting of a set of fundamental decisions (regarding brand positioning, targeting, objective setting and budgeting) and a set of implementation decisions (in terms of mixing communications elements, creating messages, selecting media, and establishing momentum). These crucial MarCom decisions determine program outcomes with regard to enhancing brand equity and affecting behavior. The final component of the model is program evaluation, which entails measuring the results of communications activities, providing feedback, and taking corrective action. The chapter includes an especially in-depth discussion of the concept and practice of brand-equity enhancement.

OVERVIEW OF INTEGRATED MARKETING COMMUNICATIONS

Chapter Objective

This chapter introduces the topic of marketing communications and suggests why it is such a critical component of modern marketing. First overviewed is the nature and importance of different elements of marketing communications. Next examined are the features and advantages of integrated marketing communications (IMC). It is argued that all communication elements (advertising, personal selling, sales promotions, packaging, point-of-purchase materials, and so on) must be tightly interwoven to achieve communication objectives and enhance brand equity.

Opening Vignette: Mountain Dew— Staying True to the Brand

Consider this dilemma: The soft drink beverage Mountain Dew is often thought of as a fringe brand consumed only by teenagers who participate in skateboarding and other "alternative" sports. In actuality, Mountain Dew, or Dew for short, is the number three selling soft drink in the United States with a market share exceeding 7 percent. Though teenagers do in fact represent the brand's primary market, 20- to 39-year-olds make up a substantial secondary market for the brand. And the dilemma: How do the brand managers of Dew continue to increase the brand's revenues and share without alienating the core market that considers the brand to be theirs alone? In other words, how can the brand continue to grow and at the same time remain hip among its primary market without appearing to have "sold out," to have become just another Coke or Pepsi for the masses?

As a matter of fact, Dew's managers have masterfully handled this delicate balance by effectively integrating Mountain Dew's marketing communications program and staying true to the brand's heritage and positioning. On the market for more than 30 years, Dew remains positioned as a brand that stands for fun, exhilaration, and energy—FEE for short. Brand managers have been consistent over time and across communication media in maintaining the FEE theme that represents the brand's core meaning, its positioning. Various advertising media, event sponsorships, and consumer promotions have been recruited to trumpet and preserve the brand's core meaning. The holiday-like excitement of Super Bowl advertising reaches millions of viewers around the world. Heralding the brand's exciting and high-energy image, one Super Bowl commercial depicted a guy racing against a cheetah to retrieve a can of Dew from inside the animal's mouth. Local TV and radio spots are used to appeal to the brand's primary and secondary targets as well as to reach African American and Hispanic consumers who represent a major growth opportunity for the brand.

Event sponsorships provide a major communication medium for Mountain Dew, which sponsors two of the leading alternative sports competitions: ESPN's X Games and NBC's Gravity Games. In addition to these prominent sponsorships, Mountain Dew also hosts a variety of smaller events that draw audiences as small as 5,000 people. Appealing giveaway items (T-shirts, videos, branded snowboards and mountain bikes, etc.) are distributed at these events to generate excitement and foster positive connections between the Dew brand and its loyal consumers.

Urban marketing techniques also are employed in the quest for more African American and Hispanic consumers. Vans and trucks loaded with 20-

---

Source: Adapted from Theresa Howard, "Being True to Dew," *Brandweek*, April 24, 2000, 28–31; Kate MacArthur and Hillary Chura, "Urban Warfare," *Advertising Age*, September 4, 2000, 16–17.

ounce bottles of Mountain Dew have toured major American cities and the schools, parks, and basketball courts where inner-city youth often congregate. Disk jockeys play hip-hop music and workers distribute free bottles of Mountain Dew with under-the-cap offers for another free bottle. Dew's brand managers have effectively practiced what this chapter refers to as integrated marketing communications, or IMC for short.

THE NATURE OF MARKETING COMMUNICATIONS

The term *marketing communications* can be understood best by examining its two constituent elements, marketing and communications. **Marketing** is the set of activities whereby businesses and other organizations create transfers of value (*exchanges*) between themselves and their customers. Of course, marketing is more general than marketing communications per se, but much of marketing involves communications activities. **Communications** is the process whereby thoughts are conveyed and meaning is shared between individuals or between organizations and individuals. Taken together, **marketing communications** represents the collection of all elements in a brand's marketing mix that facilitate exchanges by targeting the brand to a group of customers, positioning the brand as somehow distinct from competitive brands, and sharing the brand's meaning—its point of difference—with the brand's target audience. It was emphasized in the *Opening Vignette*, for example, that Mountain Dew's brand managers have targeted primarily teens; positioned the brand as standing for fun, exhilaration, and energy; and communicated the brand using a diversity of advertising media, event sponsorships, sales promotions, and urban marketing techniques. By maintaining a consistent message over time and across communication media, the brand has achieved the number three market share position among soft drink brands marketed in the United States—and sales are growing worldwide using similar methods in Europe, South America, and elsewhere.

Marketing communications is a critical aspect of a company's overall marketing mission and a major determinant of its success. The importance of the marketing communications component of the marketing mix has increased dramatically in recent decades. Indeed, it has been claimed that marketing and communications are virtually inseparable: Marketing is communication and communication is marketing.[1] All organizations—whether firms involved in business-to-business exchanges (B2B), companies engaged in business-to-consumer marketing (B2C), or organizations delivering not-for-profit services (museums, symphony orchestras, charitable organizations, etc.)—use various forms of marketing communications to promote their offerings and achieve financial and nonfinancial goals.

The primary forms of marketing communications include traditional mass media advertising, online advertising, sales promotions (such as samples, coupons, rebates, and premium items), store signage, point-of-purchase displays, product packages, direct-mail literature, opt-in e-mailing, publicity releases, event and cause sponsorships, presentations by salespeople, and various other communication devices. Collectively, these communication tools and media constitute what traditionally has been termed the **promotion** component of the marketing mix. (As you will recall from an introductory marketing course, the so-called marketing mix includes four sets of interrelated decision spheres: *product, price, place (or distribution), and promotion.*) Although the "4P" characterization has led to widespread use of the term *promotion* for describing communications with prospects and customers, the term *marketing communications* is preferred by most marketing practitioners as well as many educators. In this text we use *marketing communications* to refer to the collection of advertising, sales promotions, public relations, event marketing, and other communication devices and use the term *promotions* only as a shorthand reference to sales promotions. (I hope the student appreciates this brief terminology excursion and realizes that the author's intent is to clarify rather than obfuscate.)

The Marketing Communicator's Tools

At this point some brief definitions of the major types of marketing communications are in order. Before reviewing these definitions, it will be useful to evaluate an actual marketing situation. Consider the line of salted snacks marketed by Frito-Lay under the brand name Wow! (The exclamation point is part of the name.) Frito-Lay introduced Wow! in the late 1990s. These fat-free chips are fried in a substance called olestra, which is a soybean-based product invented by scientists at Procter & Gamble. Frito-Lay used an aggressive advertising and sales promotion program to introduced Wow! Media advertising exceeded $40 million in the introductory year.[2] Because consumers were expected to be skeptical that a fat-free snack product could really taste good, it was critical that the product be extensively sampled so that people could learn for themselves that Wow! tastes virtually identical to the widely available fat-laden and higher-calorie snack products. Bins with trial-size bags priced at three for 99 cents were available in stores and were supported with displays that featured the theme "Wow! All the taste and half the calories." To further generate an opportunity for consumers to try Wow! , coupons for free trial-size packages were distributed nationally as free-standing inserts (FSIs) in Sunday newspapers. Frito-Lay also launched an Internet site as an additional means of communicating Wow! and building a positive brand image.

Using the Wow! brand introduction as a frame of reference, let's now briefly examine the major forms of marketing communications.

Personal selling involves person-to-person communication whereby salespeople inform, educate, and persuade prospective buyers to purchase the company's products or services. Frito-Lay's sales force called on hundreds of retail buyers in an effort to convince them to add Wow! products to their existing lines of salted snacks. These selling efforts were simplified by providing retailers with introductory discounts and assuring them that heavy advertising, sampling, and couponing initiatives would successfully move Wow! products out of their stores.

Advertising, such as Frito-Lay's $40 million campaign to introduce Wow! , involves either mass communication via newspapers, magazines, radio, television, and other media (billboards, the Internet, etc.) or *direct* communication pinpointed to each business-to-business customer or ultimate consumer. Both forms of advertising are paid for by an identified sponsor (the advertiser) but are considered to be nonpersonal because the sponsoring firm is simultaneously communicating with multiple receivers, perhaps millions, rather than with a specific person or small group. Direct advertising consisting of traditional (postal) mail and opt-in, or permission, e-mailing has experienced huge growth in recent years due to the effectiveness of targeted communications and the computer technology that has made it possible.

Sales promotions consist of all marketing activities that attempt to stimulate quick buyer action or immediate sales of a product. In comparison, advertising is designed to accomplish other objectives, such as creating brand awareness and influencing customer attitudes. Sales promotions are directed both at the trade (wholesalers and retailers) and to consumers. *Trade-oriented sales promotions* include the use of various types of allowances to encourage wholesaler and retailer response. *Consumer-oriented sales promotions* involve the use of coupons, premiums, free samples, contests/sweepstakes, rebates, and other devices. Frito-Lay used both trade-oriented promotions (off-invoice and display allowances) and consumer-oriented promotions (sampling and couponing) to successfully introduce Wow!

Sponsorship marketing is the practice of promoting the interests of a company and its brands by associating the company and its brands with a specific *event*, such as Mountain Dew's sponsorship of the X Games and Gravity Games and other companies' sponsoring major events such as the World Cup in soccer.

Publicity, like advertising, involves nonpersonal communication to a mass audience; but unlike advertising, the company does not pay for media time or space. Publicity usually assumes the form of news items or editorial comments about a company's products or services. These items or comments receive free print space or broadcast time because media representatives consider the information pertinent and newsworthy for their audiences. It is in this sense that publicity is "not paid for" by the company receiving its benefits. Frito-Lay's public relations department spun out voluminous press releases that provided magazines and other news media with stories about Wow! snack foods and the remarkable fat substitute, olestra, that made it possible to develop a low-calorie and no-fat salty snack food.

Point-of-purchase communications encompass displays, posters, signs, and other materials that are designed to influence buying decisions at the point of purchase. In-store displays played a critically important role in attracting consumers' attention to trial-size samples of Wow!

In sum, marketing communication managers have an assortment of communication tools at their disposal. The relative importance and specific application of these tools depends on the circumstances confronting a brand at any point in time. As will be developed throughout the text, each marketing communication tool has its own unique role to play. However, overall effectiveness usually results from combining the assorted tools in a careful, integrated fashion so as to effectively influence customers and move them to action that is favorable to the brand communicator. That is, the partnering of communication tools—for example, advertising along with promotions—generally yields better results than using the tools in isolation.

Marketing Communications at the Brand Level

Marketing communicators in their various capacities (as advertisers, sales promotion specialists, salespeople, public relations professionals, etc.) develop and deliver messages regarding different types of objects: products, services, stores, events, and even people. Although these terms capture different forms of marketing "objects," one term will suffice as a summary means for describing *all* forms of marketing objects. That term is *brand*. Wow! is a brand. Mountain Dew is a brand. So are Red Bull, Evian, McDonald's, Levi's, Motorola, Sony, Intel, Microsoft, MasterCard, Amazon.com, Kodak, IBM, Dell, Honda, Mercedes-Benz, Lexus, and the list goes on. The point that deserves particular emphasis is that most marketing communications occurs at the brand level.

Discussion throughout this text focuses on *brand-level* marketing communications. It is critical for students to fully appreciate that the term *brand* is a convenient (and appropriate) label for describing any object of concerted marketing efforts. It could be a product, a service, a retail outlet, a media company, or even a person. Even *you* can be thought of as a brand. In fact, marketing consultant and author Tom Peters (of *In Search of Excellence* fame) has written about marketing the brand called you.[3]

A well-known and respected brand is an invaluable asset. Brands perform several roles for the organizations that market them.[4] An important economic role is to enable a firm to achieve economies of scale by producing a brand in mass quantities. Another invaluable economic role is that a successful brand can create barriers to entry for competitors who might want to introduce their own brands. Brands also perform a critical strategic role by providing a key means for differentiating one company's offering from competitive brands. A strong brand image enables a manufacturer to gain leverage vis-à-vis retailers and other marketing intermediaries. From the consumer's perspective, respected brands offer an assurance of consistent performance and provide a signal of whatever benefits consumers seek when making purchase decisions in particular product categories. More than this, a brand is a covenant with the consumer whereby the mere mention of the name triggers expectations about what the brand will deliver in terms of quality, convenience, status, and other critical buying considerations.[5]

A senior marketing executive responsible, until recently, for advertising and marketing research for Procter & Gamble—historically one of the world's best marketing organizations—provides keen insight about the roles performed by several of P&G's venerable brands:

> When you [the consumer] have a brand like Tide [detergent], you don't have to think a lot about it. You know that it's going to give you the best performance, the best value and get the job done without question. Great brands bring an element of simplicity to what is a very complex world. I believe as strongly as I possibly could that we're [i.e., P&G] going to be selling Tide and Crest and Pampers and Folgers and Downy 50 years from now, and they're going to be bigger and better than they are today.[6]

The *Global Focus* insert provides more of the P&G executive's views on the role of brands.

THE INTEGRATION OF MARKETING COMMUNICATIONS

The *Opening Vignette* described Mountain Dew's marketing communication activities and emphasized that Dew's brand managers are dedicated to presenting a consistent message about the brand both over time and across communication media. Many companies, however, treat the communication elements—advertising, sales promotions, public relations, and so on—as virtually separate activities rather than integrated tools that work together to achieve a common goal. For example, personnel responsible for advertising sometimes fail to coordinate their efforts with individuals in charge of sales promotions or publicity. The lack of integration was more prevalent in the past than currently, but many brands still suffer from poorly integrated marketing communications programs.

Current marketing philosophy holds that integration is absolutely imperative for success. *Integrated marketing communications*, or simply IMC, is the philosophy and practice of carefully coordinating a brand's sundry marketing communications elements. The following quotes capture the spirit of IMC:

> The marketer who succeeds in the new environment will be the one who coordinates the communications mix so tightly that you can look from [advertising] medium to medium, from program event to program event, and instantly see that the brand is speaking with one voice.[7]

> The basic reason for integrated marketing communications is that marketing communication will be the only sustainable competitive advantage of marketing organizations in the 1990s and into the twenty-first century.[8]

The logic underlying the integration of the various communications elements seems so crystal clear and compelling that the student may be wondering: Why is this such a big deal? Why haven't firms practiced IMC all along? Why is there reluctance to integrate, and what are the impediments to integration? Good questions all, but what sounds good in theory is not always easy to implement into practice.[9] Organizations traditionally have handled advertising, sales promotions, point-of-purchase displays, and other communication tools as virtually separate practices because different units within organizations have specialized in a single aspect of marketing communications—advertising *or* sales promotions *or* public relations—rather than having generalized knowledge and experience with all communication tools. Furthermore, outside suppliers (such as advertising agencies, PR firms, and sales promotion providers) also have tended to specialize in a single facet of marketing communications rather than possess expertise across the board.

There has been a reluctance to change from this single-function, specialist model due to managerial parochialism (e.g., advertising people sometimes view the world exclusively from an advertising perspective and are blind to other communication traditions) and for fear that change might lead to budget cutbacks in their areas of control (such as advertising) and reductions in their authority and

Global Brands and a Global Fiasco

Many observers consider Procter & Gamble to be the world's leading packaged goods company. P&G operates in more than 70 countries and offers dozens of brands in many product categories. Robert Wehling, a senior VP of advertising and marketing research at P&G who held this position for many years prior to his retirement in 2001, defines a global brand as "One that has a clear and consistent equity—or identity—with consumers across geographies. It is generally positioned the same from one country to another. It has essentially the same product formulation, delivers the same benefits and uses a consistent advertising concept."

Interestingly, Mr. Wehling believes that only three of P&G's many famous brands truly have achieved global brand stature. These are Pringles (chips), Pantene (shampoo and conditioner), and Always/Whisper (a feminine product that is marketed under two names in different countries). One of the major obstacles to accomplishing global brand status is that Asian consumers are extremely diverse and require unique brands and brand positioning customized to each culture.

On the humorous side, efforts to globalize a brand can meet with unexpected resistance and unanticipated re-sults. A near-disastrous experience occurred with one P&G marketing effort in Japan. American managers in Japan thought that P&G's diaper brand, Pampers, should be advertised in that country using the same television commercial that was running for that brand in the United States. That commercial depicted an animated stork delivering Pampers to consumers' homes. The same commercial, when dubbed with Japanese and aired on Japanese television, was a flop. With surprise and dismay, research was undertaken to determine the problem. Interviews with Japanese consumers quickly revealed that they were confused as to why a stork would be delivering diapers. Unlike American custom, which includes the myth that babies are delivered by storks, Japanese folklore presents the story that babies are delivered to deserving parents in giant peaches that float on the river. Needless to say, the commercial was quickly pulled from the Japanese airways and replaced with more culturally appropriate advertising. By reverse logic, imagine how American consumers (or consumers in other countries that share the stork myth) would respond to a TV commercial for disposable diapers showing a baby floating on a river in a giant peach.

Source: Robert L. Wehling, "Even At P&G, Only 3 Brands Make Truly Global Grade So Far," *Advertising Age*, January 1998, 8.

power. Advertising agencies, PR firms, and sales promotion specialists also have resisted change due to reluctance to broaden their function beyond the one aspect of marketing communications in which they have developed expertise and built their reputations.

However, in recent years a number of advertising agencies have expanded their roles by merging with other companies or creating new departments that specialize in the growth areas of sales promotions, marketing-oriented public relations, event sponsorship, and direct marketing. Consider, for example, the award-winning Minneapolis advertising agency Fallon McElligott. This agency realized that achieving its success and that of its clients required more than just a dependence on advertising. The agency's founder and chairman recognized that the agency needed managers with marketing experience broader than just advertising and accordingly hired an integrated marketing manager. Fallon McElligott was thus transformed from an agency known primarily for its print advertising to one that could assist its clients in most any aspect of marketing communications. This integrated approach has enabled the agency to attract notable clients such as McDonald's Arch Deluxe, United Airlines, Holiday Inn, the USA Network, and Miller Lite Beer.[10]

Many firms, including suppliers of marketing communication services along with their brand-manager clients, have increasingly adopted an integrated approach to their communication activities.[11] This growth is not restricted to North America but has spread to the United Kingdom, elsewhere in Europe, and Latin America.[12] Although IMC received its primary initial acceptance by manufacturers of consumer packaged goods, the practice has also been adopted by numerous retail and service marketers.[13]

Some skeptics have suggested that IMC is little more than a management fashion that is short lived,[14] but evidence to the contrary suggests that IMC is not fleeting but rather has become a permanent feature of the marketing communications landscape around the world and in many different types of marketing organizations.[15] As one IMC pioneer puts it, "Integration just plain makes sense for those planning to succeed in the 21st-century marketplace. Marketers, communicators, and brand organizations simply have no choice."[16] In the final analysis, the key to successfully implementing IMC is that brand managers, who represent the client side, must closely link their efforts with outside suppliers of marketing communications services (such as ad agencies), and both parties must be committed to assuring that all communication tools are carefully and finely integrated.[17]

Although there is movement toward increased implementation of IMC among brand managers and communication suppliers, not all firms are equally likely to have adopted IMC. A recent study found the following characteristics of firms that are most likely to have adopted IMC:[18] (1) Smaller firms are more likely to have adopted IMC, perhaps because smaller firms use less diverse marketing communications tools, which thus simplifies integration efforts; (2) firms involved in marketing services (rather than products) also are more likely to adopt IMC, again perhaps because they use fewer and less diverse communication tools; (3) B2C companies are more likely to practice integration than B2B firms — this because B2C companies typically practice more sophisticated marketing communications than do those firms marketing to other businesses rather than to consumers; (4) firms whose marketing communications budgets are allocated predominantly to advertising (versus trade promotions) are more likely to practice IMC; (5) firms enjoying higher market shares and realizing greater profits are more likely to employ IMC than are their less-successful counterparts. (A cautionary note is appropriate in this regard: Do not interpret this correlation between product success and IMC adoption as necessarily indicating that adopting IMC causes firms to become more successful; rather, it may simply be that firms having achieved past success are inclined to adopt IMC to sustain that success. Heed the statistician's advice: Correlation does not imply causation.) And finally (6) experienced managers are more likely than novice managers to practice IMC.

Let us now explore in some detail the nature of IMC and its key features.

A Definition of IMC

Proponents of integrated marketing communications have provided slightly different perspectives on this management practice. The following definition captures a widely accepted viewpoint and reflects this text's particular position on the topic.

> **IMC** is a communications process that entails the planning, creation, integration, and implementation of diverse forms of marketing communications (advertisements, sales promotions, publicity releases, events, etc.) that are delivered over time to a brand's targeted customers and prospects. The goal of IMC is ultimately to influence or directly affect the behavior of the targeted audience. IMC considers all sources of contact that a customer/prospect has with the brand as potential delivery channels for messages and makes use of all communications methods that are relevant to customers/prospects and to which they might be receptive. IMC requires that all of a brand's communication media and messages deliver a consistent message. The IMC process further necessitates that the customer/prospect is the starting point for determining the types of messages and channels (media) that will serve best to inform, persuade, and induce action.[19]

Key Features of IMC

This definition suggests five features that provide the philosophical foundation for the practice of integrated marketing communications. These features are listed in Table 1.1 and discussed hereafter. It is important to note before proceeding that these features are interdependent and that there is no particular order of importance suggested by the ordering in Table 1.1 and discussed hereafter.

I. Start with the Customer or Prospect.

An initial key feature of IMC is that the process should *start with the customer or prospect* and then work back to the brand communicator in determining the most appropriate messages and media for informing, persuading, and inducing customers and prospects to act favorably toward the communicator's brand. The IMC approach avoids an "inside-out" (from company to customer) approach in identifying contact methods and communication vehicles and instead starts with the customer ("outside-in") to determine those communication methods that will best serve the customers' information needs and motivate them to purchase the brand. The following discussion of IMC element number 2 is a natural extension of being customer focused.

2. Use Any Form of Relevant Contact.

IMC uses all forms of communication and *all sources of appropriate contacts* as potential message delivery channels. The term **contact** is used here to mean any message medium capable of reaching target customers and presenting the brand in a favorable light. The key feature of this IMC element is that it reflects a willingness on the part of the brand communicator to use any communication outlets (contacts) that are appropriate for reaching the target audience. Marketing communicators who practice this principle are not precommitted to any single medium or subset of media, such as television advertising. Rather, the objective is to surround customers/prospects with the brand message at every possible opportunity and allow them to use whatever information about the brand they deem most useful.[20] An established advertising practitioner has referred to this as "360-degree branding," an apt phrase indeed.[21]

Brand message contacts include a virtually endless list of possibilities. For example, the author once observed a sticker for Jell-O pudding affixed to bananas—one product (bananas) was being used as a contact channel for reaching consumers about another (Jell-O). Brand managers at Procter & Gamble placed the Tide detergent logo on napkin dispensers in pizza shops and cheese steak shops in a test conducted in Boston and Philadelphia. These napkin dispensers held napkins imprinted with the Tide logo and the message "Because napkins are never in the right place at the right time." In the fine spirit of using all appropriate contact points, a P&G spokesman justified the use of napkin dispensers as a communication medium by saying that the company is constantly evaluating new ways to reach consumers.[22]

Mountain Dew's brand managers, as described in the *Opening Vignette*, rely on alternative sport venues and urban settings to reach the intended audience. In a particularly clever effort to reach teenagers, who are difficult to contact via traditional mass media, the brand managers of Mountain Dew used beepers to transmit messages every week for a six-month period to over 250,000 teenagers. Teens were encouraged to listen to messages that were

---

Five Key Features of IMC   Table 1.1

1. **Start with the customer or prospect.**
2. **Use any form of relevant contact.**
3. **Achieve synergy (speak with a single voice).**
4. **Build relationships.**
5. **Affect behavior.**

delivered by sports stars and other celebrities. As inducement to give their attention to Mountain Dew messages, teens had an opportunity to win desirable products such as Burton snowboards, Killer Loop sunglasses, and other items.[23] Beepers represented an appropriate source of contact for a teenage audience that is notoriously difficult to reach on a regular basis using traditional mass media.

The introduction of Smirnoff's premium brand of vodka, Smirnoff Black, provides another illustration of a unique form of contact. In introducing this brand, Smirnoff wanted to create excitement as well as to dramatize Smirnoff's Russian connection. Toward this end, Smirnoff officials employed the services of a firm—BFG Communications of Hilton Head, South Carolina—that specializes in conducting on-premises sampling programs. BFG put together a production in which troupes of actors, who were dressed in 19th-century Russian outfits and played the roles of czar, czarina, and Rasputin, went to bars and generated attention and enthusiasm for Smirnoff Black by exciting and entertaining patrons. In markets such as Philadelphia, Dallas, Atlanta, and Denver, the troupes visited as many trendy bars as possible, giving out free samples of Smirnoff Black and explaining the distillation intricacies of the brand.[24] The Russian entertainment motif served to attract bar attendees' attention and helped build an appropriate association in consumers' minds between the Smirnoff Black brand and its Russian heritage. Bars thus served as an appropriate point of contact for delivering Smirnoff Black's brand message.

Another example of an unusual form of contact comes from the marketing of rap music. A newcomer on the national rap scene, Master P. Pushed, came out with an album titled *MP Da Last Don*. The album sold nearly 500,000 copies in its first week and became number one in the country. This smashing success was due in large part to the use of "street teams" that distributed free tapes at schools, in housing projects, and elsewhere.[25] These teams talked up the "brand" (i.e., the album) and generated a groundswell of enthusiasm among potential rap music purchasers.

The marketers of Bayer Select—the brand name for a line of aspirin-free pain relievers, each designed to attack a specific symptom: sinus, menstrual, nighttime, and general pain and headache—required creative ways to reach prospective consumers with messages about this new brand. The objective was to reach millions of consumers with the message that Bayer stands for more than just aspirin. Television was a useful medium for conveying this message, but the product manager for Bayer Select recognized that TV alone would not be sufficient because many people do not watch much TV, especially during the times when it is less expensive to advertise.

Strategies were devised for reaching consumers in as many productive ways as possible. Ads were prepared for placement in doctors' waiting rooms and to run in various special interest magazines. One billion coupons were distributed during the course of the first-year campaign (an average of four coupons for every man, woman, and child in the United States). Bayer arranged with Emergency Medical Services (EMS) to contribute financial assistance to volunteers and to distribute telephone procedures for emergencies. This agreement effectively amounted to a free public-service campaign for EMS and created a favorable association for Bayer Select by aligning its name with a worthy cause. A special advertising campaign also was developed to appeal specifically to Hispanic consumers. All told, Sterling invested $116 million to introduce this new product line, with all messages communicating the concept that Bayer Select "puts the help where it hurts."[26]

For a final illustration of using multiple contact methods, see the *IMC Focus* about Cheese Whiz.

The foregoing illustrations have made it clear that adherents to IMC are not tied to any single communication method (such as mass media advertising) but instead use whatever media and methods of contact that best enable the communicator to deliver the brand message to the targeted audience. Direct-mail advertising, promotions at sporting and entertainment events, advertisements on packages of other brands, slogans on T-shirts, in-store displays, and Internet banner

IMC
focus

Surrounding the College Student with Cheez Whiz Messages

Most American college students are familiar with Cheez Whiz, a whipped cheese product that is packaged in glass jars and used primarily as a spread for bread or as a key ingredient in making nachos. Students like the product because it is easy to use, convenient, and relatively inexpensive. Cheez Whiz is not, however, one of those products that is a top-of-mind item for most people. In other words, consumers typically think about the brand only when they see an advertisement for it or spot it at the point of sale. Hence, the challenge confronting Kraft Foods and Cheez Whiz's brand managers was to reach college students in an effective and inexpensive manner. How is this accomplished?

For starters, college students are not an easy-to-reach target audience. Their TV viewing habits are variable, and the programs they do regularly watch are expensive to advertise on; they are not avid newspaper or magazine readers; and their radio listening habits are, like television viewing, highly variable. Cheez Whiz's brand managers hired the J. Walter Thompson agency to develop a marketing communications program that would be effective in encouraging students to increase consumption of the brand. JWT created a tongue-in-cheek character named Cheezy Guy as a humorous way of appealing to students by spoofing the "cheesy" image of Cheez Whiz. Cheezy Guy is portrayed as the host of a film festival, which includes a series of wacky five-minute films (e.g., "When Lawn Deer Attack") that are made available to students via the Internet. Employing the technique of viral marketing that has been effective in launching many products in recent years (e.g., the Blair Witch movie), Kraft sent e-mail messages to 250,000 college students urging them to watch the films and to forward the e-mail to friends. The objective was to steer students to the Cheez Whiz Web site (http://www.cheezyguy.com) and create a connection with the brand. At the Web site students could access the short films and also view recipes featuring multiple uses for Cheez Whiz.

In addition to the Web site, Kraft outfitted a fleet of vans that, in keeping with Cheezy Guy's image, were outfitted with faux-retro décor. The vans visited over 60 college campuses. At each stop characters wearing Cheezy Guy heads generated enthusiasm for the brand and distributed free Cheez Whiz samples. Limited print and radio advertising supplemented the viral marketing and on-campus sampling efforts. Kraft Foods used multiple methods of contact to reach college students with humorous messages and subtle encouragement to purchase and use more of this versatile, lifestyle-fitting product.

Source: Adapted from Kate Fitzgerald, "Kraft's Movie Whiz," *Advertising Age*, November 27, 2000, 44, 46.

---

ads are just some of the contact methods for reaching present and prospective customers. The IMC objective is to reach the target audience efficiently and effectively using whatever contact methods are appropriate. Television advertising, for example, may be the best medium for contacting the audience for some brands, while less traditional (and even unconventional) contact methods may best serve other brands' communication and financial needs. The chairman and CEO of Young & Rubicam, a major Madison Avenue ad agency, succinctly yet eloquently captured the essence of the foregoing discussion when stating, "At the end of the day, we [i.e., ad agencies] don't deliver ads, or direct mail pieces, or PR and corporate identity programs. We deliver results."[27]

Many brand managers have concluded that traditional mass media advertising often is too costly and ineffective. European managers have been particularly likely to use contact methods other than advertising to build brand awareness and enhance brand image.[28] For example, the high-end clothier Hugo Boss created its exclusive image primarily by sponsoring events such as tennis, golf, and ski competitions.[29]

3. Achieve Synergy.

Inherent in the definition of IMC is the need for *synergy*. A brand's assorted communication elements (advertisements, point-of-purchase signage, sales promotions, event sponsorships, etc.) must all strive to present the same brand message and convey that message consistently across diverse message channels, or points of contact. Marketing communications for a brand must, in other words, "speak with a single voice." Coordination of messages and media is absolutely critical to achieving a strong and unified brand image and moving consumers to action.[30] The failure to closely coordinate all communication elements can result in duplicated efforts or—worse yet—contradictory brand messages. A VP of marketing at Nabisco fully recognized the value of speaking with a single voice when describing her intention to integrate all the marketing communication contacts for Nabisco's Oreo brand of cookies. This executive captured the essential quality of synergy when stating that under her leadership, "Whenever consumers see Oreo, they'll be seeing the same message."[31] A general manager at Mars Inc., maker of candy products, expressed a similar sentiment when stating, "We used to look at advertising, PR, promotion plans, each piece as separate. Now every piece of communication from package to Internet has to reflect the same message."[32] See the *Online Focus* insert for another example of the synergy principle.

In general, the single-voice, or synergy, principle involves selecting a specific *positioning statement* for a brand. A **positioning statement** is the key idea that encapsulates what a brand is intended to stand for in its target market's mind and then consistently delivers the same idea across all media channels. True IMC practitioners, such as Oreo's VP of marketing and Mars Inc.'s general manager, know that it is critical that they continuously convey the same message, or positioning statement, on every occasion where the brand comes into contact with the target audience. Chapter 3 will cover the topic of positioning in some detail.

4. Build Relationships.

A fourth characteristic of IMC is the belief that successful marketing communication requires building a *relationship between the brand and the customer*. It can be argued, in fact, that relationship building is the key to modern marketing and that IMC is the key to relationship building.[33] A relationship is an enduring link between a brand and its customers.[34] Successful relationships between customers and brands lead to repeat purchasing and perhaps even loyalty toward a brand. The importance of relationship building has spawned the growth of an entire industry of consultants and software suppliers who are involved in the practice of customer relationship management, or CRM. Companies that hire these consultants and use their software programs have learned that it is more profitable to build and maintain relationships than it is to continuously search for new customers. The value of customer retention has been compared to a "leaky bucket," the logic of which is nicely captured in the following quote:

> As a company loses customers out of the leak in the bottom of the bucket, they have to continue to add new customers to the top of the bucket. If the company can even partially plug the leak, the bucket stays fuller. It then takes fewer new customers added to the top of the bucket to achieve the same level of profitability. It's less expensive and more profitable to keep those customers already in the bucket. Smart business people realize that it costs five to 10 times more to land a new customer than to keep a customer they already have. They also recognize that increasing the number of customers they keep by a small percentage can double profits.[35]

There are myriad ways to build brand/customer relationships. One, perhaps overused, method is the use of frequent-flyer and other so-called frequency, loyalty, or ambassador programs. All these programs are dedicated to retaining existing customers and encouraging them to satisfy most of their product or service needs from offering organizations. Airlines, hotels, supermarkets, and many other businesses provide customers with bonus points for their continued patronage.

Relationships between brand and customer also are nurtured by creating brand experiences that make positive and lasting impressions. This is done

Think Oxy, Think Oxygen. Get It?

SmithKline Beecham, marketers of the Oxy brand of acne medication, developed an integrated marketing communications campaign that delivered a branding message consistently across all media. A senior brand manager stated, "We wanted to give a seamless look to the audience regardless of media." Because Oxy uses an oxygen-based formula to kill acne-causing bacteria, the branding message, or positioning statement, became "Think Oxy, think oxygen. Get it?" This same message was delivered via TV and radio, in magazines, and on the Internet. Two animated characters, Angela—a skeptical but hip shaggy-haired blond—and Chip—a quintessential nerd (see Figure 1.1)—became the centerpiece of the campaign. Every execution, whether off- or online, included these animated characters to convey the same consistent message. The campaign developers chose animated characters and cartoon situations rather than real people and events as an entertaining way to portray a brand that is part of a product category stigmatized with teenage embarrassment and even humiliation.

The integrated campaign for Oxy started with television advertising, followed with radio and print advertising, and then turned to online advertising. Starting the campaign with TV advertising familiarized members of the target audience with the Angela and Chip characters. Banner ads and interstitials were subsequently launched on Web sites such as MTV.com and Seventeen.com. A promotional contest allowed viewers to go online at MTV.com and submit song requests on MTV's *Total Request Live.* Oxy's Web site (http://www.oxyoxygen.com) featured a product information section with descriptions of acne-related products that reinforced the branding message that Oxy's oxygen is formulated to kill acne-causing bacteria. The major draw of the site was a video game featuring attacking bacteria called Oxygenator. Playing the role of either Angela or Chip, visitors to the site used their mouses to discharge electronic "bullets" that unclogged and then killed bacteria exiting the opened pores. The developer of the Oxygenator game commented, "We specifically designed the game to illustrate the equity of the brand in the most entertaining way possible. We counted on the fact that teens are driven by interactive games. This one embodies the branding message."

Source: Adapted from Karl Greenberg, "Zit Drive," *Brandweek,* September 11, 2000, 78–86.

with the creation of special events—called *experiential programs*—that attempt to create the sensation that a sponsoring brand is relevant to the consumer's life and lifestyle. For example, Toronto-based Molson beer conducted the Molson Outpost campaign that took 400 sweepstakes winners on a weekend escapade of outdoor camping and extreme activities such as mountain climbing. Another illustration is Lincoln automobiles, a sponsor of the U.S. Open tennis tournament, that converted an unused building at the USTA Tennis Center into a complex that immersed visitors into the history of tennis. The building featured soundstages, faux docks with real water, and images of the evolution of tennis around the world. Some 30,000 leads were obtained from people interested in Lincoln automobiles, prompting Lincoln's marketing communications coordinator to comment that "Experiential marketing is permeating our entire marketing mix."[36]

A final illustration of relationship building comes from Connecticut-based bicycle retailer, Zane's Cycles.[37] This business is built on trust between retailer and customer and outstanding customer service. Zane's offers every bicycle purchaser a 90-day price protection (i.e., assurance that it will match lower prices at a competitive store), lifetime free service, and a lifetime parts warranty. Another relationship-building offering at Zane's is the practice of not charging customers for any purchase under $1. Christopher Zane explains: "I decided a long time ago

Figure 1.1

The Animated Characters Used in Oxy's Advertising

to develop programs that are good for the customers first and then figure out how to make the long-term relationship profitable."[38]

5. Affect Behavior.   A final IMC feature is the goal to *affect the behavior* of the communications audience. This means that marketing communications must do more than just influence brand awareness or enhance consumer attitudes toward the brand. Instead, successful IMC requires that communication efforts be directed at encouraging some form of behavioral response. The objective, in other words, is to move people to action. We must be careful not to misconstrue this point. An integrated marketing communications program *ultimately* must be judged in terms of whether it influences behavior; but it would be simplistic and unrealistic to expect an action to result from every communication effort. Prior to purchasing a new brand, consumers generally must be made aware of the brand and its benefits and influenced to have a favorable attitude toward it. Communication efforts directed at accomplishing these intermediate, or prebehavioral, goals are fully justified. Yet eventually—and preferably sooner rather than later—a successful marketing communications program must accomplish more than encouraging consumers to like a brand or, worse yet, merely familiarizing them with its existence. This partially explains why sales promotions and direct-to-consumer advertising are used so extensively—both practices yield quicker results than other forms of marketing communications.

To better understand IMC's behavior-affecting objective, consider the situation faced by the U.S. dairy industry. Throughout most of the 1980s and into the 1990s, the industry touted milk as the drink that "does the body good." Research by the dairy industry revealed that most consumers got the message and perceived milk as a nutritious drink. The problem, however, was that average per capita consumption dropped by more than 14 percent. Consumers had positive attitudes toward milk, but they simply were not drinking it as much as in the past. Hence, a new communications campaign was initiated with the theme,

"Milk. Help Yourself." The advertising was designed to influence behavior—that is, to get people to drink milk more often. The J. Walter Thompson ad agency prepared eight different commercials to present milk with different meals and snacks throughout the day. In a morning commercial, for example, milk was shown being poured into a glass with surrounding shots of a waffle oozing with syrup and a powdered doughnut descending from a bag.[39]

The predicament faced by producers of natural food products is another instance in which a behavior-oriented communications program was needed. Research conducted to gauge consumers' feelings about 10 natural products (free-range chickens, organic fruits, and so on) revealed that natural products have a good image, but not many people were buying them. Only 6 percent of the sampled consumers had purchased free-range chickens during the year preceding the survey, yet 43 percent thought that free-range chickens were superior to conventional chickens.[40] This is a classic illustration of buyer behavior not following directly from attitudes. In a case such as this, the goal of marketing communications would be to convert these good feelings toward natural products into product consumption—it does little good to have consumers like your product but not buy it!

A similar challenge confronts antismoking proponents. Although most people understand intellectually that smoking causes cancer, emphysema, and other ailments, these same people often think that cancer and other problems will happen to other smokers but not them. Hence, antismoking ads may serve to make people aware of the problems associated with smoking, but such campaigns are ineffective if people continue to smoke. The IMC goal in such a case is to develop more compelling advertisements that influence smokers to discontinue this practice. A creative approach other than the standard smoking-is-bad-for-you message is needed to redirect behavior. Appeals to normative influences (e.g., "smoking is uncool" or "only losers smoke") may represent a far superior tack in the antismoking initiative to reduce this unhealthy practice, particularly among teenagers.

Changes in Marketing Communication Practices

The adoption of an IMC mind-set necessitates some fundamental changes in the way marketing communications have traditionally been practiced. The following interrelated changes are particularly prominent.

Reduced Dependence on Mass Media Advertising.   Many marketing communicators now realize that communication methods other than media advertising often better serve the needs of their brands. As noted previously, the objective is to contact customers and prospects effectively; media advertising is not always the most effective or cost-efficient medium for accomplishing this objective. But of course this does not mean that media advertising is unimportant or in threat of extinction. The point instead is that other communication methods should receive careful consideration before mass media advertising is automatically assumed to be *the* solution.

Increased Reliance on Highly Targeted Communication Methods.
Direct mail, opt-in (permission) e-mailing, specialty interest magazines, cable TV, and event sponsorships are just some of the contact methods that enable pinpointed communications that often are less expensive and more effective than mass media advertising. Targeting messages is especially feasible today with the large, up-to-date databases of customers that are maintained by many organizations.

Heightened Demands on Suppliers.   Marketing communication suppliers such as advertising agencies, sales promotion firms, and public relations agencies have historically offered a limited range of services. Now it is increasingly important for suppliers to offer multiple services—which explains why some major advertising agencies have expanded their offerings beyond just advertising services to include sales promotion assistance, public relations, direct marketing, and event marketing support.

Increased Efforts to Assess Communications' Return on Investment.   A final key feature of IMC is that it demands systematic efforts be undertaken to determine whether communication programs yield a reasonable return on their investment. All managers—and marketing communicators are no exception—must increasingly be held financially accountable for their actions. The investment in marketing communications must be assessed in terms of the profit-to-investment ratio to determine whether changes are needed or whether other forms of investment might be more profitable.[41]

Obstacles to Implementing IMC

Brand managers typically use outside suppliers, or specialized services, to assist them in managing various aspects of marketing communications. These include advertising agencies, public relations firms, sales promotion agencies, direct advertising firms, and special event marketers. Herein is a major reason why marketing communication efforts often do not meet the ideals described in this chapter. Integration requires tight coordination among all elements of a communications program. However, this becomes complicated when different specialized services operate independently of one another.[42]

Perhaps the greatest obstacle to integration is that few providers of marketing communication services have the far-ranging skills to plan and execute programs that cut across all major forms of marketing communications. Advertising agencies, which traditionally have offered a greater breadth of services than do other specialists, are well qualified to develop mass media advertising campaigns; most, however, do not also have the ability to conduct direct-to-customer advertising, and even fewer have departments for sales promotions, special events, and publicity campaigns. Although many advertising agencies have expanded their services, integrated marketing communications awaits major changes in the culture of marketing departments and service providers before it becomes a reality on a large scale.[43] It has been suggested that firms might need to create a key organizational position responsible for all forms of marketing communication, and that the position might be headed by an executive with a title such as marcom director.[44] Whatever the title, it is certain that the successful practice of IMC requires top-level organizational commitment.

SUMMARY

This chapter overviews the fundamentals of integrated marketing communications (IMC). IMC is an organization's unified, coordinated effort to promote a consistent brand message through the use of multiple communication tools that "speak with a single voice." One of several key features of IMC is the use of all sources of brand or company contacts as potential message delivery channels. Another key feature is that the IMC process starts with the customer or prospect rather than the brand communicator to determine the most appropriate and effective methods for developing persuasive communications programs. The use of database marketing and highly pinpointed communication methods (such as direct mail and opt-in, or permission, e-mailing) to affect behavioral responses, along with attempts to measure the impact of marketing communications, are significant developments associated with the growing practice of integrated marketing communications.

As author of this text for two decades, it is my sincere hope that this introductory chapter has piqued your interest and provided you with a basic understanding of the many topics you will be studying throughout this course along with the reading of my text. Marketing communications truly is a fascinating and dynamic subject. It combines art, science, and technology and allows the practitioner considerable latitude in developing effective ways to skin the proverbial cat. It will serve you well throughout your studies and into your marketing or perhaps advertising career to remain vigilant of the five key elements of IMC described in this chapter. Organizations that truly succeed in their marketing communication pursuits must accept and practice these key elements.

Because the field of marketing communications involves many forms of practice, a number of specialty trade associations have evolved over time. The following appendix provides, in alphabetical order, an overview of a subset of some of the more influential associations in the United States.[45] Internet sites are provided to facilitate your search for additional information about these organizations. (Many countries other than the United States have similar associations. Interested students might want to conduct an Internet search to identify similar associations in a country of interest.)

Find more resources to help you study at http://shimp.swcollege.com!

APPENDIX

Some Important Trade Associations in the Marketing Communications Field

Advertising Research Foundation (ARF, http://www.arfsite.org) — ARF is a nonprofit association dedicated to increasing advertising effectiveness by conducting objective and impartial research. ARF's members consist of advertisers, advertising agencies, research firms, and media companies.

American Association of Advertising Agencies (AAAA, http://www.aaaa.org) — The Four As, as it is referred to in speaking, has the mission of improving the advertising agency business in the United States by fostering professional development, encouraging high creative and business standards, and attracting first-rate employees to the advertising business.

Association of Coupon Professionals (ACP, http://www.couponpros.org) — This coupon-redemption trade association strives to ensure coupons as a viable promotional tool and to improve coupon industry business conditions.

Association of National Advertisers (ANA, http://www.ana.net) — Whereas the AAAA serves primarily the interests of advertising agencies, ANA represents the interests of business organizations that advertise regionally and nationally. ANA's members collectively represent over 80 percent of all advertising expenditures in the United States.

Association of Promotion Marketing Agencies Worldwide (APMAW, http://www.apmaw.org) — This worldwide industry association represents full-service sales promotion agencies and serves to educate members of the promotion agency's strategic role in distinction from that of advertising and direct marketing agencies.

Direct Marketing Association (DMA, http://www.the-dma.org) — DMA is dedicated to encouraging and advancing the effective and ethical use of direct marketing. The association represents the interests of direct marketers to the government, media, and general public.

Incentive Manufacturers and Representatives Association (IMRA, http://www.imra1.org) — Members of IMRA are suppliers of premium merchandise. The association serves these members by promoting high professional standards in the pursuit of excellence in the incentive industry.

International Prepaid Communications Association (IPCA, http://www.i-pca.org) — IPCA promotes the professional and ethical use of prepaid communications, or telephone cards, by educating businesses and policy officials about prepaid phone cards.

Point-of-Purchase Advertising International (POPAI, http://www.popai. org)—This trade association serves the interests of advertisers, retailers, and producers/suppliers of point-of-purchase products and services.

Promotional Products Association International (PPAI, http://www.ppa. org)—PPAI serves the interests of producers, suppliers, and users of promotional products. The businesses PPAI represents used to be referred to as the specialty advertising industry, but promotional products is the term of current preference.

Promotion Marketing Association, (PMA, http://www.pmalink.org)—PMA's mission is to foster the advancement of promotion marketing and facilitate better understanding of promotion's role and importance in the overall marketing process.

DISCUSSION QUESTIONS

1. Assume that your college or university is currently undertaking a huge marketing communications campaign targeted to high school students. Explain how your school might "partner" advertisements and sales promotions to increase enrollment.

2. Offer your views on the following statement: "The basic reason for integrated marketing communications is that marketing communication will be the only sustainable competitive advantage of marketing organizations in the 1990s and into the twenty-first century."

3. One key characteristic of IMC discussed in this chapter is the belief that marketing communications requires building a relationship between the brand and the customer. Visit a Web site for an automobile brand of your choice and do the following:
   a. Identify the characteristics of the consumers you think the brand is targeting for relationships.
   b. Provide specific examples of attempts to build enduring links to these consumers.
   c. Describe the *actions* encouraged by the Web site, and relate these actions to the sustenance of a relationship with the brand's consumers.

4. Given your understanding of IMC and its fundamental characteristics, describe the probable outcome of practicing nonintegrated, rather than integrated, marketing communications.

5. One key feature of IMC is the emphasis on affecting behavior and not just its antecedents (such as brand awareness or favorable attitudes). For each of the following situations, indicate the specific behavior(s) that marketing communications might attempt to affect: (a) your university's advertising efforts; (b) a professional baseball team's promotion for a particular game; (c) a not-for-profit organization's efforts to recruit more volunteers; and (d) Gatorade's sponsorship of a volleyball tournament.

6. IMC also emphasizes using all economically effective contact methods as potential message delivery channels. Assume you are advertising a product that is marketed specifically to high school seniors. Identify seven contact methods (include no more than two forms of mass media advertising) you might use to reach this audience.

7. Explain how the managers of Mountain Dew (*Opening Vignette*) have used the principles of IMC.

8. Early in the chapter it was claimed that the partnering of communication tools—for example, advertising along with promotions—generally yields better results than using the tools in isolation. Provide an explanation of what this claim means to you, and support your explanation with an example of a specific brand of your choosing.

9. When discussing the characteristics of firms that are more (or less) likely to practice integrated marketing communications, point number 4 (see page 8) asserted that those firms whose marketing communications budgets are allocated predominantly to advertising (versus trade promotions) are more likely to practice IMC. Provide an explanation as to why this is the case.

ENDNOTES

1. Don E. Schultz, Stanley I. Tannenbaum, and Robert F. Lauterborn, *Integrated Marketing Communications* (Lincolnwood, Ill.: NTC Publishing Group, 1993), 46.

2. This and other facts are based on Stephanie Thompson, "Frito Looks to *Wow!* 'Em with Sample Blitz," *Brandweek*, March 9, 1998, 1, 6.

3. Tom Peters, "The Brand Called You," *Fast Company*, August/September 1997, 83–94.

4. This discussion follows Leslie De Chernatony and Francesca Dall'Olmo Riley, "Expert Practitioners' Views on Roles of Brands: Implications for Marketing Communications," *Journal of Marketing Communications* 4 (June 1998), 87–100.

5. Jacques Chevron, "Of Brand Values and Sausage," *Brandweek*, April 20, 1998, 22.

6. Robert Wehling, cited in *Marketing Science Institute Review* (spring 1998), 7.

7. Quoting Spencer Plavoukas, chairman of Lintas (New York), and cited in Laurie Petersen, "Pursuing Results in the Age of Accountability," *Adweek's Marketing Week*, November 19, 1990, 21.

8. Schultz, Tannenbaum, and Lauterborn, *Integrated Marketing Communications*, 47.

9. For further discussion of problems inherent with implementing IMC, see Bob Hartley and Dave Pickton, "Integrated Marketing Communications Requires a New Way of Thinking," *Journal of Marketing Communications* 5 (June 1999), 97–106.

10. Richard A. Melcher, "Hot Ship in the Heartland," *Business Week*, January 13, 1997, 51.

11. Fred Beard, "IMC Use and Client-Ad Agency Relationships," *Journal of Marketing Communications* 3 (December 1997), 217–230.

12. Patricia B. Rose, "Practitioner Opinions and Interests Regarding Integrated Marketing Communications in Selected Latin American Countries," *Journal of Marketing Communications* 2 (September 1996), 125–140.

13. Glen J. Nowak, Glen T. Cameron, and Denise Delorme, "Beyond the World of Packaged Goods: Assessing the Relevance of Integrated Marketing Communications for Retail and Consumer Service Marketing," *Journal of Marketing Communications* 2 (September 1996), 173–190.

14. Joep P. Cornelissen and Andrew R. Lock, "Theoretical Concept or Management Fashion? Examining the Significance of IMC," *Journal of Advertising Research* 40 (September/October 2000), 7–15. For counter positions, see Don E. Schultz and Philip J. Kitchen, "A Response to 'Theoretical Concept or Management Fashion?,'" *Journal of Advertising Research* 40 (September/October 2000), 17–21; Stephen J. Gould, "The State of IMC Research and Applications," *Journal of Advertising Research* 40 (September/October 2000), 22–23.

15. Don E. Schultz and Philip J. Kitchen, "Integrated Marketing Communications in U.S. Advertising Agencies: An Exploratory Study," *Journal of Advertising Research* 37 (September/October 1997), 7–18; Philip J. Kitchen and Don E. Schultz, "A Multi-Country Comparison of the Drive for IMC," *Journal of Advertising Research* 39 (January/February 1999), 21–38.

16. Don E. Schultz, "Integration Is Critical for Success in 21st Century," *Marketing News*, September 15, 1997, 26.

17. Stephen J. Gould, Andreas F. Grein, and Dawn B. Lernan, "The Role of Agency-Client Integration in Integrated Marketing Communications: A Complementary Agency Theory-Interorganizational Perspective," *Journal of Current Issues and Research in Advertising* 21 (spring 1999), 1–12.

18. These findings are based on research by George S. Low, "Correlates of Integrated Marketing Communications," *Journal of Advertising Research* 40 (May/June 2000), 27–39.

19. This definition is the author's adaptation of one developed by members of the marketing communications faculty at the Medill School, Northwestern University. The original definition was reprinted in Don E. Schultz, "Integrated Marketing Communications: Maybe Definition Is in the Point of View," *Marketing News*, January 18, 1993, 17.

20. David Sable, "We're Surrounded," *Agency* (Spring 2000), 50–51.

21. The practitioner is Shelly Lazarus, whose career at Ogilvy & Mather advertising agency has extended over a quarter century. Lazarus was quoted by Laurie Freeman, "Internet Fundamentally Changes Definition," *Marketing News*, December 6, 1999, 15.

22. Christine Bittar, "P&G's Tide Rolls into Pizza Shops," *Brandweek*, July 26, 1999, 9.

23. Bruce Orr, "Dew Gets Personal: Brand-Building with Beepers," *Marketing News*, July 6, 1998, 13.

24. Elaine Underwood, "Dramatic Entrance," *Brandweek*, December 2, 1996, 26–27.

25. Patrick M. Reilly, "Phat Sales: 'Street Teams' Create Rap Stars with Curbside Technique," *The Wall Street Journal Interactive Edition*, June 25, 1998.

26. Patricia Winters, "$116M Intro for Bayer Select Isn't Just Ads," *Advertising Age*, November 23, 1992, 37.

27. Peter A. Georgescu, "Looking at the Future of Marketing," *Advertising Age*, April 14, 1997, 30.

28. This argument is made particularly well by Erich Joachimsthaler and David A. Aaker in "Building Brands Without Mass Media," *Harvard Business Review* (January/February 1997), 39–50.

29. Ibid., 44.

30. This one-voice perspective is widely shared by various writers on the topic of IMC. See Schultz, Tannenbaum, and Lauterborn, *Integrated Marketing Communications*; Tom Duncan, "Integrated Marketing? It's Synergy," *Advertising Age*, March 8, 1993, 22; and Glen J. Nowak and Joseph Phelps, "Conceptualizing the Integrated Marketing Communications' Phenomenon: An Examination of Its Impact on Advertising Practices and Its Implications for Advertising Research,"

Journal of Current Issues and Research in Advertising 16 (spring 1994), 49–66.

31. Judann Pollack, "Nabisco's Marketing VP Expects 'Great Things,'" *Advertising Age*, December 2, 1996, 40.

32. Stephanie Thompson, "Busy Lifestyles Force Change," *Advertising Age*, October 9, 2000, s8.

33. See Schultz, Tannenbaum, and Lauterborn, *Integrated Marketing Communications*, 52–53.

34. For an insightful discussion of different forms of consumer-brand relationships, see Susan Fournier, "Consumers and Their Brands: Developing Relationship Theory in Consumer Research," *Journal of Consumer Research* 24 (March 1998), 343–373.

35. This quote is from author Vicki Lenz as cited in Matthew Grimm, "Getting to Know You," *Brandweek*, January 4, 1999, 18.

36. Dan Hanover, "Are You Experienced?" *Promo*, February 2001, 48.

37. This discussion is based on Christopher J. Zane, "Creating Lifetime Customers," *Retailing Issues Letter* 12 (September 2000) — a publication of the Center for Retailing Studies, Texas A&M University.

38. Ibid., 3.

39. Based on Skip Wollenberg, "Dairy Industry Ads Touting Milk As Complement to Favorite Foods," *The State*, October 12, 1994, B12.

40. Leah Rickard, "Natural Products Score Big on Image," *Advertising Age*, August 8, 1994, 26.

41. For discussion of how to assess the ROI for marketing communications, see Don E. Schultz, "Trying to Determine ROI for IMC," *Marketing News*, January 3, 1994, 18; and Don E. Schultz, "Spreadsheet Approach to Measuring ROI for IMC," *Marketing News*, February 28, 1994, 12.

42. Kim Cleland, "Few Wed Marketing, Communications," *Advertising Age*, February 27, 1995, 10.

43. Ibid.

44. Schultz, Tannenbaum, and Lauterborn, *Integrated Marketing Communications*.

45. Adapted from "Directory of Marketing Industry Associations," *Promo's 8th Annual Sourcebook 2001*, 255–256.

THE MARKETING COMMUNICATIONS PROCESS AND BRAND EQUITY ENHANCEMENT

Chapter Two

Chapter Objective

This chapter's purpose is to provide a framework that integrates the various aspects of managerial decision making related to marketing communications (MarCom) strategy and tactics. This framework provides a useful model for both thinking about and discussing the role of marketing communications as a means of enhancing brand equity and affecting desired behavior from the target audience. The chapter devotes a major section to explaining the concept of brand equity from the customer's perspective. By enhancing brand equity, firms can increase brand loyalty, augment market shares, charge relatively higher prices, and enjoy other benefits that result from being well known and respected.

Opening Vignette: How Does a Korean Company Known for Consumer Electronics Compete in the Automobile Business?

You probably are familiar with Korean automobile models manufactured by Hyundai and maybe even Kia, but have you ever heard of Daewoo cars? Daewoo is a huge Korean conglomerate that markets consumer electronics, heavy equipment, and now automobiles. Three Daewoo models were introduced to the United States in the late 1990s—the Lanos, Leganza, and Nubira—and then in 2000 Daewoo launched the Korando, a sports utility vehicle. Daewoo's dealer network consists of over 400 outlets located in most every U.S. state.

Big deal, another car company, so what? Well, the interesting thing about Daewoo's automobile introduction in the United States is the manner in which the cars were originally marketed. The company recruited about 2,000 college students from hundreds of colleges and universities to become Daewoo Campus Advisors (DCAs). Students selected as DCAs received free trips to Korea, where they toured Daewoo auto plants and dealerships to gain in-depth product knowledge. Back on campus, DCAs were hired to work about 10 hours per week passing out information about Daewoo cars, giving presentations to student groups, and promoting what were called "ride-and-drive events." The DCAs received commissions of up to $400 on referrals and got the opportunity to purchase Daewoo cars at significant discounts.

Several reasons buttressed Daewoo's choice of this interesting means of marketing its cars in the United States. First, it provided a way of building Daewoo's brand equity with young people, who are said to have more brand-preference flexibility when choosing an automobile than older consumers who have already owned multiple cars. Second, it was a less expensive method for Daewoo to get its cars noticed quickly compared with the mass media advertising favored by most automobile marketers. Finally, by focusing on college students, Daewoo realized an opportunity to reach budding professionals who, if favorably impressed, would spread the word about Daewoo on leaving campuses.

Daewoo started its college-oriented marketing efforts in university towns such as Atlanta, Boston, Philadelphia, Orlando, Chicago, and San Diego. Daewoo's campus advisors at colleges and universities in these cities promoted the various Daewoo models, and some were given free use of Daewoo vehicles for several months to demonstrate them to friends and acquaintances and to drive prospects to local Daewoo showrooms. Daewoo also made extensive use of the

Sources: Jean Halliday, "Daewoo's Ambitious Push: First National Ad Campaign," *Advertising Age*, January 17, 2000, 8; "Daewoo Sales Continue to Rise," Daewoo News Release, May 4, 2000 (http://www.daewoomotor.com/cgi-bin/news/news.asp?postno=20000304001); Al Urbanski, "The Old College Try," *Promo*, July 1998, 48–50.

Internet to promote its cars with banner ads on frequently visited sites that appeal to college-age young adults. The only other media that accompanied the launch of Daewoo were local newspaper and radio ads.

How successful was this creative and original strategy for marketing automobiles? Actually, it was anything but a smashing success. Without national advertising support, Daewoo sold only around 2,400 automobiles in the United States in 1998 and about 31,000 in 1999. Starting in 2000 the company began a national advertising campaign after discontinuing the college-student program, with aspirations of selling at least 100,000 automobiles annually in the United States. Advertising will be key to this success. A marketing consultant familiar with Daewoo's strategy commented that a national ad campaign will help create more brand equity than the tried-but-rejected college program.

Daewoo faces an uphill battle, to say the least. The brand is virtually unknown in the United States and confronts an image problem associated with being an upstart brand from a country that is not as yet known for producing high-quality and reliable automobiles. Daewoo has limited brand equity and little prospect for market share growth in the absence of sustained advertising spending and impeccable product performance. Indeed, it is possible that Daewoo may no longer be marketing automobiles in the United States by the time the newest edition of this text is published. If that in fact is the denouement, the moral will be clear: Building positive brand equity is essential to success in competitive markets, and this requires a commitment to product quality, customer service, and sustained advertising spending along with other forms of supportive marketing communications.

A MODEL OF THE MARKETING COMMUNICATIONS DECISION-MAKING PROCESS

Chapter 1 introduced the various forms of marketing communications (advertisements, sales promotions, events, etc.) and discussed the importance of tightly integrating all forms such that a unified message is delivered wherever the customer or prospect comes into contact with the brand. This chapter now develops a framework that will provide a useful conceptual and schematic structure for thinking about the types of decisions marketing communicators make. The framework is presented in Figure 2.1 and described hereafter. It is very important at this time that you scan and achieve a basic understanding of the model components in preparation for the following discussion, which fleshes out the model's skeleton.

Figure 2.1 offers a conceptualization of the various types of brand-level marketing communications decisions and the outcomes desired from those decisions. It will be noted that the model consists of a set of *fundamental decisions* (relating to positioning, targeting, setting objectives, and budgeting), a set of *implementation decisions* (involving the mixture, or integration, of communications elements and the choice of messages, media, and momentum), and *program evaluation* (measuring MarCom results, providing feedback, and taking corrective action).

The objective of marketing communications, or MarCom for short, is to enhance **brand equity** as a means of moving customers to *favorable action toward the brand* — that is, trying it, repeat purchasing it, and, ideally, becoming loyal toward the brand. Enhancing equity and affecting behavior depend, of course, on the suitability of all marketing-mix elements. MarCom efforts nonetheless play a pivotal role by informing customers about new brands and their relative advantages and by elevating brand images. As will be fully developed in a later section, brand equity is enhanced when consumers become *familiar* with the brand and hold *favorable, strong,* and perhaps *unique* associations in memory about the brand.[1] A brand has no equity if consumers are unfamiliar with it. Once consumers have become aware of a brand, the amount of equity depends on how favorably they perceive the brand's features and benefits as compared to competitive brands and how strongly these views are held in memory.

Figure 2.1

Making Brand-Level Marketing Communications Decisions and Achieving Desired Outcomes

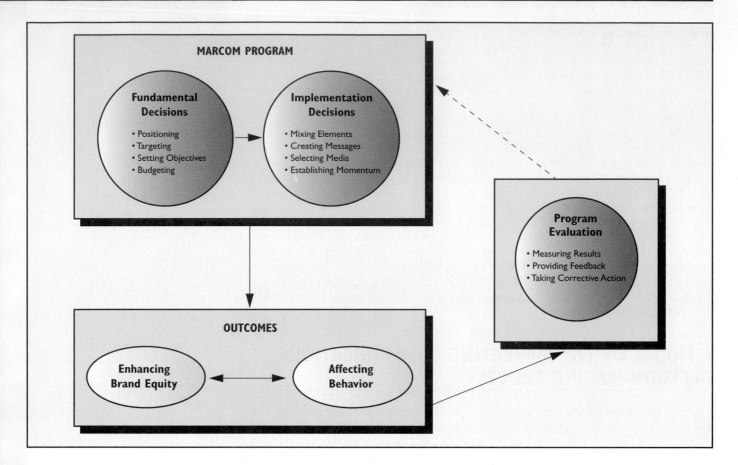

MAKING BRAND-LEVEL MARCOM DECISIONS

The model in Figure 2.1 shows that *fundamental decisions* (positioning, targeting, setting objectives, and budgeting) influence *implementation decisions* regarding the mixture of communications elements and the determination of messages, media, and momentum. The expected outcomes from these decisions are shown in Figure 2.1 as *enhancing brand equity* and *affecting behavior.* Subsequent to the implementation of the MarCom decisions, *program evaluation*—in the form of measuring the results from MarCom efforts, providing feedback (see dashed arrow in Figure 2.1), and taking corrective action—is essential to determining whether outcomes match objectives. Corrective action is required when performance falls below expectations.

Fundamental MarCom Decisions

Positioning.   A brand's position represents the key feature, benefit, or image that it stands for in the target audience's collective mind. Brand communicators and the marketing team in general must decide on a brand positioning statement, which, as noted in the previous chapter, is the central idea that encapsulates a brand's meaning and distinctiveness vis-à-vis competitive brands in the product category. This topic is detailed in the following chapter, which focuses on the interrelated topics of positioning and targeting. The *IMC Focus* describes the decline of Levi's jeans and efforts to reinvent the brand through new product introductions and creative communications. Engineered Jeans is a Levi's brand in the vanguard of this revitalization move. Levi's brand managers apparently have positioned Engineered Jeans as a hip yet uncharacteristically comfortable pair of jeans.

IMC
focus

Levi's Effort to Reinvent Itself

There was a time when Levi's was the brand virtually synonymous with jeans. Now the competitive situation is wide open with many brands competing for the consumer's loyalty. In a study of 1,800 high school and college students conducted by the New York–based Zandl Group, respondents were asked to name the one brand of jeans they were most likely to purchase. If this study had been conducted in 1990 instead of 2000, it is probable that as many as one-third of the respondents would have reported Levi's as their likely purchase candidate. However, only 9 percent of high schoolers and 12 percent of college students indicated Levi's as the brand they most likely would purchase. Considering just college students, other brands they lean toward include Gap (7 percent), Hilfiger (6%), LEI (3%), Express (3%), Calvin Klein (3%), Jnco (2%), and Abercrombie & Fitch (2%). And 27 percent of respondents indicated intentions to purchase a brand other than these, which suggests that purchase loyalties in the jean category are widely divided. This division of purchase loyalties comes as little surprise when considering the unparalleled fragmentation of the jeans industry with new brands regularly being introduced, brands such as Sixty USA and trendy European brands Diesel (from Italy) and Marithé + François Girbaud (from France).

These survey results intimate the likelihood that Levi's sales performance has declined along with its deteriorating brand image. In fact, Levi's corporate sales (not just jeans) fell from a high of $7.1 billion in 1996 to $5.1 billion by 1999. What has Levi's done to stop the hemorrhaging? A major move has been the introduction of youth-oriented jean styles in an appeal to teens and consumers in their twenties. A marketing director expressed Levi's imperative in these terms: "Our top challenge is to attract the youth generation back to the Levi's brand and stabilize our share with that group." Another marketing director stated that our goal "is to rejuvenate and reinvent [Levi's] through communication and great product development."

Levi's Engineered Jeans—a radical-looking style designed to accommodate the body's contour and to combine strength with softness—is the first evidence of Levi's effort to reinvent the brand. Engineered Jeans achieved super success when first introduced in Europe and Asia and now are widely distributed in U.S. specialty and department stores. In addition to print ads and exciting TV spots, Levi's backed the launch of Engineered Jeans with a sweepstakes offer that consumers could enter when trying on the jeans at participating retailers. Winners received trips to destinations such as the Guggenheim Museum in Spain. Levi's also sent tractor-trailers equipped with interactive games, karaoke, and cameras to dozens of events, including concerts by Christina Aguilera, Santana, and Dave Matthews. Consumers visiting the Levi's trailers could pose for a chance to be featured in a Levi's commercial, thereby enhancing their involvement with the brand.

Only time will tell whether Levi's can regain its past icon status in the jeans category. It is certain, however, that efforts to enjoy past glory will not be without complications. For example, Levi Strauss had an extended legal battle before the European Court of Justice to preclude Tesco, a large British supermarket chain, from selling Levi's brands at discounted prices. Levi's concern is that its brand image is damaged when the brand is made available at discounted prices in a supermarket rather than in clothing outlets more appropriate for Levi's desired image. (At the time of this writing, the European Court of Justice has not ruled on whether Tesco will be permitted to continue selling Levi's jeans.)

Sources: Sandra Dolbow, "Assessing Levi's Patch Job," *Brandweek*, November 6, 2000, 34–44; Alessandra Galloni, "Levi's Battles Supermarket Chain as It Struggles to Rebuild Brand," *Wall Street Journal Interactive Edition*, April 10, 2001 (http://interactive.wsj.com); Sandra Dolbow, "Fashion, Fabric, Freshness in Focus as Jean Companies Vie for Attention," *Brandweek*, July 2, 2001, 19.

Targeting.   Targeting allows marketing communicators to deliver messages more precisely and to prevent wasted coverage to people falling outside the intended audience. Hence, selection of target segments is a critical step toward effective and efficient marketing communications. It should be obvious that positioning and targeting decisions go hand in hand: Positioning decisions are made with respect to intended targets, and targeting decisions are based on a clear idea of how brands are to be distinguished from competitive offerings.

Companies identify potential target markets in terms of demographics characteristics, lifestyles, product usage patterns, and geographic considerations. It is important to recognize, however, that most profitable segments are not based on a single characteristic (such as gender, age, ethnicity, etc.). Rather, meaningful market segments generally represent consumers who share a *combination of characteristics* and demonstrate similar behavior.

Consider, for example, the segmentation implications of a new brand of premium-priced nonfat ice cream. The market segment for this new brand is not just women, not just men, not just younger people or older people, and, in general, not any group of people sharing any single characteristic. Rather, a meaningful segment would possess several or more shared characteristics—for example, people who live in urban or suburban areas, earn annual incomes in excess of $50,000, are older than 35, and are health and weight conscious.

Business-to-business (B2B) marketing communicators also make targeting decisions. Illustrative of this is an advertising effort by the National Cattlemen's Beef Association that was designed to increase sales of veal. Beef ranchers faced rapidly declining sales of veal as a result of advertising by animal rights activists that had convinced many consumers to bypass veal because, according to the activists' claims, calves are raised in cruel circumstances.

The activists' argument is not without merit, but the cattle ranchers believe they have a legitimate right to raise calves. The trade association's challenge was to counter antiveal sentiment that had been created by the activist advertising effort. But the association had a budget of only slightly more than $1 million. Surely such a small budget could not reach many consumers nor allow sufficient momentum (as discussed later in the chapter) to have much impact. What to do? The decision was made to best use the small ad budget by targeting advertising efforts at chefs rather than toward consumers. Attractive ads were placed in magazines read by chefs, magazines such as *Restaurant Business Magazine* and *Bon Appetit*. This campaign increased veal consumption by 20 percent, which is a substantial increase under the circumstances.[2]

Setting Objectives.   Marketing communicators' decisions are grounded in the underlying goals, or objectives, to be accomplished for a brand. Of course, the content of these objectives varies according to the form of marketing communications used. For example, whereas mass media advertising is ideally suited for creating consumer awareness of a new or improved brand, point-of-purchase communications are perfect for influencing in-store brand selection, and personal selling is unparalleled when it comes to informing business-to-business customers and retailers about product improvements.

Specific chapters later in the text detail the objectives that each component of the MarCom mix is designed to accomplish; for present purposes it will suffice merely to list a set of nonexhaustive objectives that communicators hope to accomplish using different forms of marketing communications.

- Facilitate the successful introduction of new brands.
- Build sales of existing brands by increasing the frequency of use, the variety of uses, or the quantity purchased.
- Inform the trade (wholesalers, agents/brokers, retailers) and consumers about brand improvements.
- Enhance a brand's image.
- Generate sales leads.
- Persuade the trade to handle the manufacturer's brands.
- Stimulate point-of-purchase sales.
- Develop brand awareness, acceptance, and insistence.
- Increase customer loyalty.

- Improve corporate relations with special interest groups.
- Offset bad publicity about a brand.
- Generate good publicity.
- Counter competitors' communications efforts.
- Provide customers with reasons for buying immediately instead of delaying a purchase choice.

Budgeting.   Financial resources are budgeted to specific MarCom elements to accomplish desired objectives. Companies use different budgeting procedures in allocating funds to marketing communications managers and other organizational units. At one extreme is *top-down budgeting (TD),* in which senior management decides how much each subunit receives. At the other extreme is *bottom-up budgeting (BU),* in which managers of subunits (such as at the product category level) determine how much is needed to achieve their objectives; these amounts are then combined to establish the total marketing budget.

Most budgeting practices involve a combination of top-down and bottom-up budgeting. For example, in the *bottom-up/top-down process (BUTD),* subunit managers submit budget requests to a chief marketing officer (say, a vice president of marketing), who coordinates the various requests and then submits an overall budget to top management for approval. The *top-down/bottom-up process (TDBU)* reverses the flow of influence; top managers first establish the total size of the budget and then divide it among the various subunits.

Research has shown that combination budgeting methods (BUTD and TDBU) are used more often than the extreme methods (TD or BU).[3] The BUTD process is by far the most frequently used, especially in firms where marketing departments have greater influence than finance units.[4]

A Concluding Mantra.   *Mantra* is a Hindu word meaning incantation or recitation (of a song, word, statement, or passage). The following statement serves as a mantra to summarize the preceding discussion of fundamental MarCom decisions:

> *All marketing communications should be: (1) clearly **positioned,** (2) directed to a particular **target market,** (3) created to achieve a **specific objective,** and (4) undertaken to accomplish the objective **within budget constraint.***

Figure 2.2 graphically illustrates this mantra. The position/target, objective, and budget are displayed as three interconnected circles. The point at which the circles intersect represents the **guiding structure** for the implementation decisions that remain to be made. That is, decisions about the mixture of MarCom tools,

Guiding Structure for MarCom Implementation Decisions   Figure 2.2

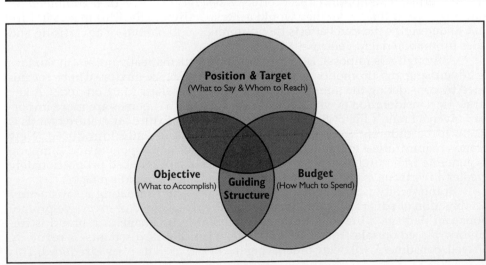

message design, and media placement are guided by more fundamental determinations about brand positioning, targeting, objective setting, and budgeting.

MarCom Implementation Decisions

The fundamental decisions just described are conceptual and strategic. Comparatively, the implementation decisions are practical and tactical. Here is where the proverbial rubber hits the road. MarCom managers must make a variety of implementation decisions in the pursuit of accomplishing brand-level objectives and achieving the brand's positioning and targeting requirements. Initially they must choose how best to integrate, or mix, the various communications elements to achieve objectives toward the target market and within budget constraint. Then they must decide what types of messages will accomplish the desired positioning, which media are appropriate for delivering messages, and what degree of momentum is needed to support the media effort. Please refer again to Figure 2.1 to obtain a view of the "forest" prior to examining specific trees.

Mixing Elements.   A fundamental issue confronting all companies is deciding exactly how to allocate resources among the various marketing communications tools that were outlined in Chapter 1—advertising, sales promotion, events, and so on.

For B2B companies, the mixture typically emphasizes personal selling with supplementation from trade advertising, technical literature, and trade shows.[5] For consumer goods manufacturers, mixture decisions are, in many respects, more complicated because greater options are available. Personal selling is important in a consumer goods company's *push efforts*, but the real difficulty and controversy arises when deciding how best to *pull* a product through the channel.[6] The issue boils down in large part to a decision of how much to allocate to advertising and to promotions. (Note: In keeping with practitioner convention, the word *promotion* hereafter will be used interchangeably with *sales promotion*.) The trend during the past two decades has been toward greater expenditures on promotions and less on advertising. Promotion's share of the total marketing communications budget has grown from less than 60 percent in the late 1970s to approximately 70 percent today.

Is there an *optimum mixture* of expenditures between advertising and promotion? There is not, unfortunately, because the marketing communications-mix decision constitutes an *ill-structured problem*.[7] This means that for a given level of expenditure, there is no way of determining the mathematical optimum allocation between advertising and promotion that will maximize revenue or profit. Two major factors account for this inability to determine a mathematically optimum mix.[8] First, advertising and promotions are somewhat interchangeable—both tools can accomplish some of the same objectives. Hence, it is impossible to know exactly which tool or combination of tools is better in every situation. Second, advertising and promotions produce a *synergistic effect*—their combined results are greater than what they would achieve individually. This makes it difficult to determine the exact effects that different combinations of advertising and sales promotion might generate.

Although it is impossible to determine a mathematically optimum mixture of advertising and promotion expenditures, a satisfactory mixture can be formulated by considering the differing purposes of each of these MarCom tools. A key strategic consideration is whether short- or long-term schemes are more important given a brand's life-cycle stage. An appropriate mixture for mature brands is likely to be different from the mixture for brands recently introduced. New brands require larger investment in promotions such as couponing and sampling to generate trial purchases, whereas mature brands might need proportionately greater advertising investment to maintain or enhance a brand's image.

Brand equity considerations also play a role in evaluating a satisfactory combination of advertising and promotions. Poorly planned or excessive promotions can damage a brand's equity by cheapening its image. If a brand is frequently placed on sale or if some form of deal (price-offs, discounts) is regularly offered, consumers will delay purchasing the brand until its price is reduced. This can cause the brand to be purchased more for its price discount than for its non-price attributes and benefits.

The matter of properly mixing advertising and promotion is aptly summarized in the following quote:

> As one views the opportunities inherent in ascertaining the proper balance between advertising and promotion, it should be quite clear that both should be used as one would play a pipe organ, pulling out certain stops and pushing others, as situations and circumstances change. Rigid rules, or continuing application of inflexible advertising-to-promotion percentages, serve no real purpose and can be quite counterproductive in today's dynamic and ever-changing marketing environment. A short-term solution that creates a long-term problem is no solution at all.[9]

The "short-term solution" refers to spending excessive amounts on promotion to create quick sales while failing to invest sufficiently in advertising to build a brand's long-term equity. That is, excessive promotions can rob a brand's future. An appropriate mixture involves spending enough on promotions to ensure sufficient sales volume in the short term while simultaneously spending enough on advertising to ensure the growth or preservation of a brand's equity position.

Creating Messages.   A second implementation decision is the creation of messages in the form of advertisements, publicity releases, promotions, package designs, and any other form of MarCom message. Subsequent chapters will address specific message issues relating to each MarCom tool. Suffice it to say at this point that systematic (versus ad hoc) decision making requires that message content (in advertisements, promotions, on packages, or at events) be dictated by the brand's positioning strategy and aligned with the communications objective for the designated target audience.

Selecting Media.   All marketing communications messages require an instrument, or medium, for transmission. Though the term *media* is typically applied to advertising (television, magazines, radio, Internet, etc.), the concept of *media* is relevant to all MarCom tools. For example, personal sales messages can be delivered via face-to-face communications or by telemarketing; these media alternatives have different costs and effectiveness. Point-of-purchase materials are delivered via in-store signs, electronically, musically, and otherwise. Each represents a different medium.

Detailed discussions of media are reserved for specific chapters that follow. Advertising media are discussed in particular detail, and considerable attention also is devoted to the media of consumer promotions. At the risk of redundancy it is important to again note that media decisions are determined in large measure by the fundamental decisions previously made regarding positioning strategy, choice of target audience, type of objectives to be achieved, and how much is to be budgeted to a brand during each budgeting period.

Establishing Momentum.   The word *momentum* refers to an object's force or speed of movement—its impetus. A train has momentum as it races down the tracks; a spacecraft has momentum as it is launched into orbit; a hockey player has momentum when skating past the defensive opposition. Marketing communications programs also have, or lack, momentum. Simply developing an advertising message, personal sales presentation, or publicity release is insufficient. The effectiveness of each of these message forms requires both a sufficient amount of effort and continuity of that effort. This is the meaning of momentum as it relates to marketing communications. Insufficient momentum is ineffective at best and a waste of money at worst.

As is the case with almost every decision faced by MarCom managers, momentum is a relative matter: No level of momentum is equally appropriate for all situations. For example, small-share automobile brands such as Hyundai, Daewoo, and Mazda must spend a much larger portion of their sales on advertising than their larger competitors such as Toyota, Honda, and Ford. Also, newer (versus mature) brands must spend a larger proportion of their sales to get established and to create strong, favorable, and perhaps unique brand images.

Critical to the concept of momentum is the need to sustain an effort rather than starting advertising for a while, discontinuing it for a period, reinstating the advertising, stopping it again, and so on. In other words, some companies never create nor sustain momentum because their marketplace presence is inadequate. "Out of sight, out of mind" is probably more relevant to brands in the marketplace than to people. We generally do not forget our friends and family, but today's brand friend is tomorrow's stranger unless it is kept before our consciousness. Because consumers make hundreds of purchase decisions in many different product categories, they require continuous reminders of brand names and their benefits if these brands are to stand a strong chance of becoming serious purchase candidates.

At one point in the late 1990s, Toyota Motor Corporation had only a 16-day supply of the fast-selling Camry. Yet it launched a major advertising campaign aggressively encouraging consumers to purchase Camrys. Some marketing observers were critical of this campaign, saying that it was unwise to advertise when insufficient product was available to fulfill orders. In response, the vice president of Toyota Sales USA asserted that even when demand is strong, it is important "to keep your momentum in the marketplace going."[10] This executive obviously appreciates the value of achieving and maintaining a brand's momentum! Many marketing communicators and higher-level managers don't. For example, advertising is one of the first items cut during economic downturns.

MarCom Outcomes

Referring back to our conceptual framework for marketing communications decisions (Figure 2.1), it can be seen that the outcomes from a MarCom program are twofold: enhancing brand equity and affecting behavior. Figure 2.1 displays a double-headed arrow between these outcomes, which signifies that each outcome influences the other. If, say, an advertising campaign for a new brand generates brand awareness and creates a positive brand image, consumers may be inclined to try the new brand. In such a situation, the brand's equity has been enhanced, and this in turn has affected consumer behavior toward the brand. In similar fashion, a promotion for the new brand, such as a free sample, may encourage consumers to initially try and then subsequently purchase the brand. A positive experience in using the brand may lead to positive brand perceptions. In this situation, a promotion affected consumer behavior, which in turn enhanced the promoted brand's equity.

As established in Chapter 1, a fundamental IMC principle is that MarCom efforts must ultimately be gauged by whether they affect behavior. Sales promotion is the MarCom tool most capable of directly affecting consumer behavior. However, excessive reliance on promotions can injure a brand's reputation by creating a low-price and perhaps low-quality image. It is for this reason that marketing communicators often seek to first enhance a brand's equity as a foundation to influencing behavior. It indeed can be argued that much if not most MarCom efforts are designed to enhance brand equity. We thus need to fully explore the concept of brand equity and understand what it is and how it can be influenced by MarCom efforts. We will turn to this topic after briefly describing the essential nature of program evaluation.

Program Evaluation

After marketing communications objectives are set, elements selected and mixed, messages and media chosen, and programs implemented and possibly sustained, program evaluation must take place. This is accomplished by measuring the results of MarCom efforts against the objectives that were established at the outset. For a local advertiser—say, a sporting goods store that is running an advertised special on athletic shoes for a two-day period in May—the results are the number of Nike, Reebok, Adidas, and other brands sold. If you tried to sell an old automobile through the classified pages, the results would be the number of phone inquiries you received and whether you ultimately sold the car. For a national manufacturer of a branded product, results typically are not so quick to occur. Rather, a company invests in point-of-purchase communications, promotions, and advertising and then waits, often for weeks, to see whether these programs deliver the desired sales volume.

Regardless of the situation, it is critical to evaluate the results of MarCom efforts. Throughout the business world there is increasing demand for *accountability*, which requires that research be performed and data acquired to determine whether implemented MarCom decisions have accomplished the objectives they were expected to achieve. Results can be measured in terms of behavioral impact (such as increased sales) or based on communication outcomes.

Measures of *communication outcomes* include brand awareness, message comprehension, attitude toward the brand, and purchase intentions. All of these are communication (rather than behavioral) objectives in the sense that an advertiser has attempted to communicate a certain message argument or create an overall impression. Thus, the goal for an advertiser of a relatively unknown brand may be to increase brand awareness in the target market by 30 percent within six months of starting a new advertising campaign. This objective (a 30 percent increase in awareness) would be based on knowledge of the awareness level prior to the campaign's debut. Postcampaign measurement would then reveal whether the target level was achieved.

It is essential to measure the results of all MarCom programs. Failure to achieve targeted results prompts corrective action (see the dashed arrow in Figure 2.1). Corrective action might call for greater investment, a different combination of communications elements, revised creative strategy, different media allocations, or a host of other possibilities. Only by systematically setting objectives and measuring results is it possible to know whether MarCom programs are working as well as they should and how future efforts can improve on the past.[11]

THE CONCEPT OF BRAND EQUITY

Appreciating the concept of brand equity requires first that we have a clear understanding of the term *brand*. The American Marketing Association defines a **brand** as a "name, term, sign, symbol, or design, or a combination of them intended to identify the goods and services of one seller or group of sellers and to differentiate them from those of competition."[12] A brand thus exists when a product, retail outlet, or service receives its own name, term, sign, symbol, design, or any particular combination of these elements.

More Than Just a Name

But a brand is much more than *just* a name, term, symbol, and so on. A brand is everything that one company's particular offering stands for in comparison to other brands in a category of competitive products. For example, "Volvo stands for safety. Perdue [poultry products] stands for freshness. Nike is about the athlete within all of us. BMW is performance driving. Robitussin is 'Dr. Mom,' the remedy your mother would give you if she was there. Miller Lite stands for fun that's unexpected."[13] A brand that has a clear-cut identity is known for the features it possesses, the benefits it provides, and the emotions and experiences it promises. (See the *Global Focus* insert for further comments about brand identity.)

Just like people, brands even have their own unique personalities. Research has identified five dimensions that seem to capture the personalities of a variety of consumer brands.[14] These dimensions and associated characteristics are as follows:

1. **Sincerity** — This dimension includes brands that are down-to-earth, honest, wholesome, and cheerful. The advertisement in Figure 2.3 for Betty Crocker cookies illustrates a brand that has a "sincere" personality — that is, a brand noted for its wholesomeness and ability to put kids (large and small) in a good mood.
2. **Excitement** — Brands with an exciting personality are perceived as daring, spirited, imaginative, and up-to-date. The illustration in Figure 2.4

The "Glocalization" of European Brands

Some brands are identified with a particular country and have no identity, or image, that extends beyond that country. Other brands have a less country-specific identity and are, in fact, considered local brands in many different countries. McDonald's fast-food restaurants operate in dozens of countries around the world, but most consumers identify this brand as quintessentially American. Ikea on the other hand, though Swedish in origin, is regarded as a pan-European brand rather than just Swedish. (In the event you are unfamiliar with Ikea, it is a Swedish furniture retailer that merchandises inexpensive but well-designed furniture and accessories.) Why is one brand considered global (or, in the case of Ikea, pan-European), whereas another, such as McDonald's, is available virtually worldwide but is considered strictly American?

A recent study by the Intelligence Factory, a New York–based research organization, provides some hint to an answer. In a survey of 250 businesspeople across Europe, researchers at the Intelligence Factory investigated which companies have built pan-European brands—that is, brands considered European in general rather than strictly German, British, Swedish, and so on. Study results determined that the top pan-European brands are Ikea, Virgin, Adidas, DaimlerChrysler, Heineken, L'Oreal, LVMH, Nokia, Philips, and Telefonica. What do these brands have in common? All have local appeal in each European country where they are marketed while at the same time have maintained consistent images across Europe. The president of the Intelligence Fac-

tory commented that ""glocalization"— a combination of a global perspective with a local (country-specific) approach to marketing communications—is the key. For example, Ikea positions itself consistently across Europe as a democratic company that produces well-designed but inexpensive furniture. Adidas associates the brand with sporting excellence by sponsoring world-class athletes with whom consumers throughout Europe can identify.

The Intelligence Factory offered several suggestions for how companies and their advertising agencies can develop pan-European brands. First, it is important to create advertising campaigns that either target common lifestyle groups across countries (e.g., European football/soccer enthusiasts, environmentalists) or appeal to strictly local tastes. Second, appeals to nationalism combined with a consistent message across Europe can be effective at this time because Europeans are trying to assert their own identities. (Keep in mind that in 2002 the euro became a common currency across 12 European countries after a prolonged and heated debate throughout Europe.) Third, it is important to inform consumers about a company's politics and social philosophies insofar as consumers are forming more holistic views of brands. Finally, branding is growing in importance throughout Europe as consumers are increasingly time pressured and thus dependent on brand reputation as a means of both simplifying and improving product choice.

Adapted from Margarete McKegnay, "Y&R Unit Research Reveals Top Pan-European Brands," *Advertising Age*, July 24, 2000, 11. ©2000 by Crain Communications, Inc. Reprinted by permission.

for Sony cameras represents a brand that is indeed daring, spirited, and so on.
3. **Competence**—Brands scoring high on this personality dimension are considered reliable, intelligent, and successful. Figure 2.5 for the Maytag Accellis range represents such a brand.
4. **Sophistication**—Sophisticated brands are upper class and charming, as perhaps exemplified by the Rolex advertisement in Figure 2.6.
5. **Ruggedness**—Rugged brands are thought of as tough and outdoorsy. Timberland (Figure 2.7) represents such a brand.

Illustration of a Sincere Brand   **Figure 2.3**

The Nature and Importance of Brand Equity

We live in a world of brands. It just so happens that some brands are better known and more respected than others. For example, the American Marketing Association was previously mentioned. As someone who is studying marketing, you may belong to a student chapter of that organization or at least have heard of it, but most people probably have never heard of this brand. By way of comparison, consider another organization whose identifying letters also are AMA, the American Medical Association. This latter AMA is undoubtedly better known to a much larger percentage of the American population and even throughout the world. In the context of the present discussion, it is suggested that the American Medical Association has greater brand equity than does the American Marketing Association. Let us now explore the meaning of brand equity.

Brand equity has been defined in many ways, and numerous approaches have been developed to measure it.[15] The concept of brand equity can be considered both from the firm's perspective and from the consumer's.[16] The firm-based viewpoint of brand equity focuses on outcomes extending from efforts to enhance a brand's equity, such as achieving a higher market share, increasing brand loyalty, and being able to charge premium prices.[17]

We will focus more on describing brand equity from the perspective of the consumer. From this perspective, a brand possesses equity to the extent that consumers are familiar with the brand and have stored in their memory warehouses favorable, strong, and unique brand associations.[18] That is, brand equity from the consumer's perspective consists of two forms of brand knowledge: *brand awareness* and *brand image*. For example, Adidas, the German brand of athletic shoes

Figure 2.4   **Illustration of an Exciting Brand**

and apparel, substantially increased its advertising budget one year in the late 1990s by a whopping 25 percent over the previous year's ad budget. Adidas' director of sales and marketing explained that this increase was designed to raise consumer awareness of the Adidas name and pound home the message that Adidas is an authentic and high-performance athletic shoe.[19] You will note that he does not refer to brand equity per se, but this is precisely what he's talking about in reference to raising awareness and conveying a desired performance image for the Adidas brand.

Figure 2.8 on page 38 graphically portrays two dimensions of brand knowledge—awareness and image—and the subsequent discussion describes each dimension in some detail. Please review Figure 2.8 before reading on.

Brand Awareness.   Brand awareness is an issue of whether a brand name comes to mind when consumers think about a particular product category and the ease with which the name is evoked. Stop reading for a moment and consider all the brands of toothpaste that come immediately to your mind. Probably Crest and Colgate came to mind, because these brands are the market share leaders among American brands of toothpaste. Perhaps you also thought of Aquafresh, Mentadent, and Arm & Hammer insofar as these brands also obtain a large share of toothpaste purchases. But did you consider Close-Up, Pepsodent, or Aim? Maybe so; probably not. These brands are not nearly as widely known or frequently purchased as are their more successful counterparts. As such, they have less brand equity than, say, Colgate and Crest.

Illustration of a Competent Brand   **Figure 2.5**

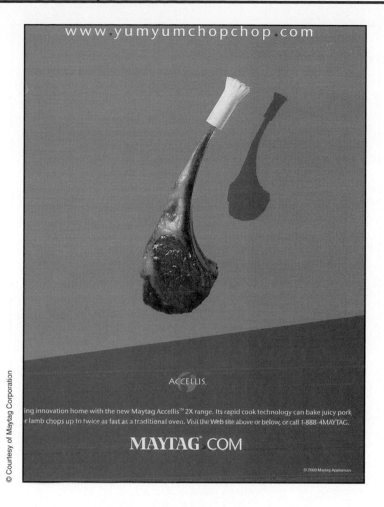

Brand awareness is the basic dimension of brand equity. From the vantage point of an individual consumer, a brand has no equity unless the consumer is at least aware of the brand. Achieving brand awareness is the initial challenge for new brands. Maintaining high levels of brand awareness is the task faced by all established brands.

Figure 2.8 shows two levels of awareness: brand recognition and brand recall. *Brand recognition* reflects a relatively superficial level of awareness, whereas *brand recall* reflects a deeper form of awareness. Consumers may be able to identify a brand if it is presented to them on a list or if hints or cues are provided. However, fewer consumers are able to retrieve a brand name from memory without any reminders or cues. It is this deeper level of brand awareness—recall—to which marketers aspire. Through effective and consistent MarCom efforts, some brands are so well known that virtually every living person of normal intelligence can recall the brand. For example, most people who are conscious of computers would likely mention the name Windows if asked to name a computer operating system. Asked to name brands of athletic footwear, most people would mention Nike, Reebok, and perhaps Adidas. Levi's surely would come to mind for most people of baby-boomer age or younger, but many (most) have never heard of the Daewoo brand mentioned in the *Opening Vignette.* The MarCom imperative is thus to move brands from a state of unawareness, to recognition, on to recall, and ultimately to top-of-mind awareness (TOMA). This pinnacle of brand-name awareness (i.e., TOMA status) exists when your company's brand is the first brand that consumers recall when

Figure 2.6   Illustration of a Sophisticated Brand

thinking of a particular product category. Figure 2.9 on page 39 illustrates this brand-awareness progression.

It is important to note that it is not just consumer-oriented (B2C) firms that must be concerned with building brand awareness. A survey of B2B marketing personnel determined that the vast majority of these practitioners consider the major goal of B2B advertising to be creating awareness of a new product or brand. These same practitioners also believe that building brand image is another goal of B2B MarCom efforts.[20]

As a concluding statement about the importance of building brand awareness, it is useful to be reminded of the dot-com advertising fiasco around the turn of the 21st century. Many upstart dot-com companies invested heavily in advertising to build brand awareness, thinking that this alone would ensure huge flows of revenues and profits. Unfortunately (perhaps especially for individuals who invested in these companies), success is not enjoyed so easily. Please read the *Online Focus* for more details.

Brand Image.   The second dimension of consumer-based brand knowledge is a brand's image. *Brand image* can be thought of in terms of the types of associations that come to the consumer's mind when contemplating a particular brand. An *association* is simply the particular thoughts and feelings that a consumer has about a brand, much in the same fashion that we have thoughts and feelings about other people. For example, what thoughts/feelings come immediately to mind when you think of your best friend? You undoubtedly associate your friend with certain physical characteristics, features, strengths,

Illustration of a Rugged Brand   Figure 2.7

and perhaps frailties. Likewise, brands are linked in our memories with specific thought-and-feeling associations. As shown in Figure 2.8, these associations can be conceptualized in terms of type, favorability, strength, and uniqueness.

To illustrate these points, it will be helpful to return to Chapter 1's discussion of Frito-Lay's Wow! chips and the associations one consumer, Henry, has for this brand. Henry is a life-long lover of potato chips. (It will be instructive to refer back to Figure 2.8 before reading the following description.) He, like so many other consumers, has to be careful about his eating habits both for appearance and health reasons. After skeptically trying Wow! chips and doubting that they would taste as good as regular chips, Henry learned that Wow! chips taste virtually the same as regular chips. He further learned from media reports and his own observations that Wow! chips are made by Frito-Lay, cooked in olestra, lower in calories than regular chips, free of saturated fat, available in ridged as well as smooth versions, and perhaps are slightly higher priced than other potato chip brands. All these thoughts represent *types of associations* in Henry's memory about Wow! All these thoughts, with the exception of Wow!'s higher price, represent *favorable brand associations* as far as Henry is concerned. Insofar as Wow! was the pioneer brand of chips to be cooked with olestra, Henry considers the brand and the product subcategory virtually synonymous, and, as such, his thoughts, or associations, about Wow! are held *strongly*. Because olestra represents a new form of fat substitute, unique thoughts about Wow! are evoked when Henry thinks of this brand. In other words, in Henry's mind Wow! and olestra are linked inextricably because he associates olestra only with Wow!

Figure 2.8

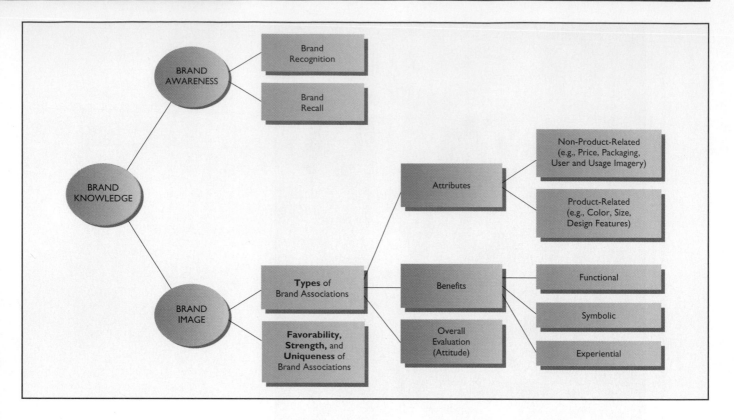

Source: Adapted from Kevin Lane Keller, "Conceptualizing, Measuring, and Managing Customer-Based Brand Equity," *Journal of Marketing* 57 (January 1993), 7.

We can see from this illustration that Henry associates Wow! potato chips with various *attributes* (e.g., made with olestra), *benefits* (e.g., less fattening, healthier, good tasting), and that he possesses an overall favorable evaluation, or *attitude*, toward this brand. These associations for Henry are held strongly and are favorable and somewhat unique. Frito-Lay, the makers of Wow!, would love to have millions of Henrys in its market. To the extent that Henry is prototypical of other consumers, it can be said that Wow! has high brand equity.

In contrast to Wow!, many brands have relatively little equity. This is because consumers are (1) only faintly aware of these brands or, worse yet, are completely unaware of them or (2) even if aware, do not hold strong, favorable, and unique associations about these brands.

Enhancing Brand Equity

In general, efforts to enhance a brand's equity are accomplished through the initial choice of positive brand identity (that is, the selection of a good brand name or logo) but mostly through marketing and MarCom programs that forge favorable, strong, and unique associations in the consumer's mind about a brand. It is impossible to overstate the importance of efforts to enhance a brand's equity. Products that are high in quality and represent a good value potentially possess high brand equity. But effective and consistent MarCom efforts are needed to build on and maintain brand equity.

A favorable brand image does not happen automatically. Sustained marketing communications are generally required to create favorable, strong, and perhaps unique associations about the brand. For example, it could be claimed that

The Brand Awareness Pyramid

Figure 2.9

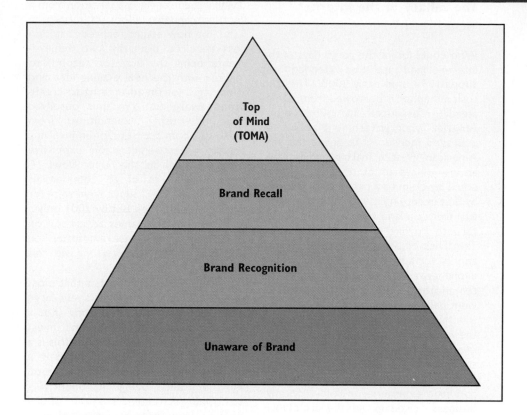

Source: David A. Aaker, *Managing Brand Equity* (New York: Free Press, 1991), 62.

one of the world's greatest brands, Coca-Cola, is little more than colored sugar water. This brand, nevertheless, possesses immense brand equity because its managers are ever mindful of the need for continuous advertising executions that sustain the Coca-Cola story and build the image around the world. In the United States alone, the Coca-Cola Company commanded approximately 44 percent of the nearly $55 billion carbonated soft-drink market in a recent year.[21] Consumers don't buy this "colored sugar water" merely for its taste; they instead purchase a lifestyle and an image when selecting Coca-Cola over other available brands. It is effective advertising, exciting sales promotions, creative sponsorships, and other forms of marketing communications that are responsible for Coca-Cola's positive image and massive market share.

One major by-product of efforts to increase a brand's equity is that consumer *brand loyalty* might also increase.[22] Indeed, long-term growth and profitability are largely dependent on creating and reinforcing brand loyalty. The following quote from two respected marketing practitioners sums up the nature and importance of brand loyalty:

> While marketers have long viewed brands as assets, the real asset is brand loyalty. A brand is not an asset. Brand loyalty is the asset. Without the loyalty of its customers, a brand is merely a trademark, an ownable, identifiable symbol with little value. With the loyalty of its customers, a brand is more than a trademark. A trademark identifies a product, a service, a corporation. A brand identifies a promise. A strong brand is a trustworthy, relevant, distinctive promise. It is more than a trademark. It is a trustmark of enormous value. Creating and increasing brand loyalty results in a corresponding increase in the value of the trustmark.[23]

The Fallacy of the Internet "Land Rush"

Who could forget the go-go days of the Internet "land rush" that extended from about 1998 until early 2000. (The land rush metaphor is borrowed from home-steading practices in 19th-century America when government policy encouraged individuals to settle the vast American West by making land available at low prices or at no cost. Settlers could lay claim to a parcel of land simply by first occupying it, which inspired a virtual frenzy, a land rush.) During the Internet's heyday, it seemed that every Tom, Dick, Harry, and Jane came up with an idea for a new form of etailing. Thus evolving was one dot-com company after another, most of which eventually went belly up.

What was the model for forming these dot-com businesses? At the risk of oversimplification, it was something like the following. A businessperson—or, as likely, a businessperson wanna-be who had little experience in "old-economy" business—came up with the idea of marketing on the Internet a product or service that heretofore was available only from a brick-and-mortar retailer. This in-

dividual then sought capitalization from a venture capitalist. Gobs of money in hand, the new etailer realized that success required primarily two achievements: being the first (or second) to market with the new etailing idea and spending a lot on advertising to create brand awareness. We thus observed huge advertising expenditures from these dot-com start-ups, often involving placing advertisements on expensive programs such as the Super Bowl. (A large percentage of all commercials placed on the 2000 Super Bowl were for dot-com companies. But by 2001 only a few dot-com companies advertised on this hugely expensive extravaganza.) You might be thinking, what's wrong with this approach?

The problem, in short, is that most of the dot-com companies spent large sums of money on advertising (not a problem per se), but they didn't invest adequately in building a brand (this *is* a problem). Investing in and building a brand is a matter of identifying a reason for the brand's being—its underlying positioning statement and point of distinction from competitive offerings—and then promoting that point of distinction on a consistent basis. In other

Research has shown that when firms communicate unique and positive messages via advertising, personal selling, promotions, events, and other means, they are able to differentiate their brands effectively from competitive offerings and insulate themselves from future price competition.[24]

Marketing communications plays an essential role in creating positive brand equity and building strong brand loyalty. However, this is not always accomplished with traditional advertising or other conventional forms of marketing communications. For example, Starbucks, the virtual icon for upscale coffee, does very little advertising, yet this brand has a near cultlike following. The average Starbucks consumer visits a Starbucks outlet an estimated 18 times a month, a situation of nearly unparalleled brand loyalty.[25] The same can be said for Red Bull energy drink. With worldwide sales exceeding $1 billion, the marketers of Red Bull rely more on word-of-mouth buzz and events than advertising for brand-building purposes.[26]

Roger Enrico, who served as CEO and chairman of PepsiCo from 1996 to 2001, provides us with a fitting section conclusion in the following implicit description of the importance of PepsiCo efforts to build brand equity:

> In my mind the best thing a person can say about a brand is that it's their favorite. That implies something more than simply they like the package, or the taste. It means they like the whole thing — the company, the image, the value, the quality, and on and on. So as we think about the measurements of our business, if we're only looking at this year's bottom line and profits, we're missing the picture. We should be looking at market share, but also at where we stand vis-à-vis our competitors in terms of consumer awareness and regard for our brands. You always know where you stand in the [profit and loss

words, many of the dot-com companies spent heavily on advertising, but they failed to build brands. A spokesman from Briefing.com, an investment site, characterized a fatal flaw that he observed with most dot-coms' approach to business:

> Because the marketing budget is only driving short-term name recognition and site traffic rather than building an established brand, sales growth is highly correlated with growth in the marketing budget. But a marketing budget cannot remain at a dollar of ads for each dollar of sales indefinitely. The business model assumes that the initial marketing drive builds self-sustaining growth in sales, which eventually overtake the marketing budget.

The failed brand-building efforts by dot-com companies is stated even more compellingly by marketing consultant Kevin Clancy in the following passage:

> For a long time, etailers believed that marketing and brand building were relatively easy. Go "first to market" with a rave new Internet concept and "grab land." Cre-

ate a site so cool that the viral marketing—efforts that spread information about a company like a virus—goes wild. Then mix it up with requisite brand juice— edgy brand names, beautiful logos, clever tag lines, big-ticket promotions to lure people to Web sites, rave launch parties, nonstop publicity, and lots and lots of advertising.

But drinking brand juice gets you about as close to building a brand as reading bumper stickers gets you to spiritual enlightenment.

Style over substance cannot build a brand. Simply put, a brand is ultimately based on more than marketing communications alone. Product quality, customer service, employee communications, management vision and leadership, and social responsibility all influence a brand's reputation.

Sources: Gregory A. Jones, "The Big Lie," from Briefing.com's subscriber service, June 29, 2000; Kevin J. Clancy, "Getting Serious about Building Profitable Online Retail Brands," *Retailing Issues Letter* 12 (November 2000)—a publication of Texas A&M University's Center for Retailing Studies.

statement] because you see it every month. But what you need to know, with almost the same sense of immediacy, is where you stand with consumers and your customers.[27]

Characteristics of World-Class Brands

Some brands have such exceptional brand equity that they deserve the label "world class." A recent online survey of more than 27,000 consumers aged 15 and older was conducted by the Total Research Corporation employing its EquiTrend survey.[28] This survey asked respondents to rate a number of brands in terms of two dimensions: quality and salience. Respondents are asked to rate a brand's *quality* by selecting a score ranging from 0 to 10, where 0 equals unacceptable/poor quality and 10 equals outstanding/extraordinary quality. *Salience*, which is one measure of brand awareness, represents the percentage of people who feel sufficiently well informed about a brand to rate it. A brand's salience score thus ranges between 0 percent to 100 percent. An *equity* score is determined merely by multiplying the quality and salience scores. Brands receiving high equity scores are both well known and perceived as high quality, whereas those receiving lower scores are either less known or are well known but have received low quality scores.[29]

The EquiTrend online survey identified seven world-class brands based on their exceptionally high equity scores: Waterford crystal, Craftsman tools, Discovery Channel, M&M's candies, Crayola crayons and markers, Bose stereo and speaker systems, and WD-40 spray lubricant. A spokesperson for the research firm commented that the common denominator among all these brands is that they "have a very straightforward promise of what they will deliver and they have consistently delivered it over a long period of time."[30] In other words, these brands are well known, possess strong and favorable associations in consumers' memories, and thus possess high brand equity.

Beyond these particular survey results, a thought leader in the area of branding and brand equity has identified 10 traits shared by the world's strongest brands:[31]

1. **The brand excels at delivering the benefits customers truly desire.** Consumers buying crystal want flawless quality, attractive designs, and prestige. It is little wonder that Waterford crystal obtained a world-class rating in the EquiTrend survey.

2. **The brand stays relevant.** "Relevant" brands stay in touch with consumers' changing tastes, desire for change and excitement, and need for product improvements. For example, M&M candies and Crayola crayons are continuously introducing new colors, and the Discovery Channel regularly produces creative and exciting programs.

3. **The pricing system is based on consumers' perceptions of value.** Bose stereo and speaker systems are not inexpensive, but the product price is justified in light of the high quality delivered.

4. **The brand is properly positioned.** M&M's candies are positioned well against other candies. Only M&M's come in a variety of colors and have the unique shape. M&M's virtually stands for fun, and it is for this reason that children of all ages (from 3 to 83) love this simple little product.

5. **The brand is consistent.** A consistent brand is one that is not continuously changing its positioning and always reinventing itself. Consumers learn to depend on the brand because it remains unchanged—a dependable old friend. All seven brands in the EquiTrend survey personify consistency.

6. **The brand portfolio and hierarchy make sense.** Most brands are part of a company's brand portfolio. For example, automobile manufacturers market multiple models of BMWs, Toyotas, Fords, and so on. Successful brands are well coordinated such that the various offerings under the brand umbrella are not inconsistent with one another or in conflict.

7. **The brand makes use of and coordinates a full repertoire of marketing activities to build equity.** The essential point in this regard is that successful brands employ whatever MarCom tools are needed in order to satisfy the brand's positioning strategy. This characteristic is very much in harmony with the IMC principles established in Chapter 1.

8. **The brand's managers understand what the brand means to consumers.** "If it's clear what customers like and don't like about a brand, and what core associations are linked to the brand, then it should also be clear whether any given action will dovetail nicely with the brand or create friction."[32] In other words, knowing the customer is essential to knowing your brand and determining what MarCom efforts are needed to best position the brand. The managers of WD-40 spray lubricant know what consumers like about this brand and what they expect from it; thus, they are able to maximize sales volume primarily by simply advertising the brand as having innumerable household uses.

9. **The brand is given proper support, and that support is sustained over the long run.** In a word, world-class brands maintain their *momentum*! (Recall the prior discussion of momentum in context of the various implementation decisions.)

10. **The company monitors sources of brand equity.** Ongoing studies (brand audits, tracking studies) are essential for monitoring a brand's health. The need for such studies can be likened to the importance of middle-aged and older individuals having annual medical examinations. Annual exams determine whether changes have occurred in, say, one's heart condition compared to baseline measures from prior exams. An attending physician can thus determine whether a problem exists and whether corrective action is needed. Brand managers must in similar fashion expose

their brands to annual exams to detect potential problems and identify needed changes.

CO-BRANDING AND INGREDIENT BRANDING

Products typically carry a single brand, and MarCom efforts for that brand are designed to exclusively enhance the brand's equity. However, in recent years there have been a number of occurrences where two brands enter into an alliance that potentially serves to enhance both brands' equity and profitability.[33] You need only look at your bank card (e.g., Visa) to see that it likely carries the name of an organization such as your college or university. The two have entered into an alliance for their mutual benefit. This is known as **co-branding.** Rayovac (flashlights) is in partnership with Harley-Davidson (motorcycles) with a line of flashlights carrying the Harley-Davidson logo.[34] Ocean Spray, the well-known marketer of cranberry products, has entered into branding alliances with a number of other famous branded products, including Post's Cranberry Almond Crunch cereal, Nabisco's Cranberry Newtons (cookies), and Kraft's Stove Top Stuffing with Cranberries.[35] Tyson (of chicken fame) has allied with Pillsbury's Green Giant to offer fully cooked chicken and beef items intended specifically for Pillsbury's Create a Meal! vegetable and sauce blends.[36]

The examples are virtually endless, but the common theme is that brands that enter into alliances do so on the grounds that their images are similar, that they appeal to the same market segment, and that the co-branding initiative is mutually beneficial. The most important requirement for successful co-branding is that the brands possess a common fit and that the combined MarCom efforts maximize the advantages of the individual brands while minimizing the disadvantages.[37]

Ingredient branding is a special type of alliance between branding partners. For example, my Dell computer has a sticker on it that reads "Intel Inside." Intel, the well-known maker of disk drives, microchips, and other computer "ingredients," built incredible brand equity for its brand through the use of clever, aggressive, and continuous advertising. Now computer manufacturers are willing to attach the "Intel Inside" sticker to their "boxes" because the equity of Intel holds potential for enhancing their own brand equity.

Lycra, a brand of spandex from DuPont, initiated a $10 million to $12 million global advertising effort to increase consumer ownership of jeans made with Lycra. Along the lines of the "Intel Inside" campaign, Lycra's advertising featured Lycra jeans by Levi Strauss, Diesel, DKNY, and other jean manufacturers. DuPont began this campaign in an effort to differentiate itself from cheaper unbranded spandex from Asia.[38]

You also regularly see the NutraSweet logo on popular brands such as Diet Coke and Crystal Light, which in turn benefit from the improved taste that NutraSweet provides.[39] Other well-known instances of ingredient branding include various ski-wear brands that make prominent note of the Gore-Tex fabric from which they are made and cookware makers that tout the fact that their skillets and other cookware items are made with DuPont's Teflon nonstick coating.[40] Although ingredient branding is in many instances beneficial for both the ingredient and "host" brands, a potential downside for the host brand is that it runs the risk of being turned into a mere commodity. For example, the equity of the ingredient brand might be so great that it overshadows the host brand.[41] This situation would arise, for example, if skiers knew that their ski jacket was made of Gore-Tex fabric but they had no awareness of the company that actually manufactured their jacket.

SUMMARY

This chapter has provided a model of the MarCom process to serve as a useful integrative device for better structuring and understanding the topics covered throughout the remainder of the text. The model (Figure 2.1) includes three components: a MarCom program consisting of fundamental and implementation decisions, outcomes (enhancing brand equity and affecting behavior), and program evaluation.

Fundamental decisions include establishing a brand positioning, choosing target markets, setting objectives, and determining a MarCom budget. Implementation decisions involve determining a mixture of marketing communications tools (advertising, promotions, events, point-of-purchase efforts, etc.) and establishing message, media, and momentum plans. These decisions are evaluated by comparing measured results against brand-level communications objectives.

This chapter discussed in detail the nature and importance of brand equity. The concept of brand equity is described as the value in a brand resulting from high brand-name awareness and strong, favorable, and perhaps unique associations that consumers have in memory about a particular brand. MarCom efforts play an important role in enhancing brand equity. Enhanced equity, in turn, bolsters consumer brand loyalty, increases market share, differentiates a brand from competitive offerings, and permits charging relatively higher prices.

Find more resources to help you study at http://shimp.swcollege.com!

DISCUSSION QUESTIONS

1. From a brand equity perspective, what associations come to mind when you see or think about Levi's brand of Engineered Jeans? (Please refer to the *IMC Focus* on page 25.)
2. Select a brand of your choice from the automotive industry. Then based on what you know about this brand and in view of the guiding structure in Figure 2.2, explain how this brand's positioning and targeting (don't worry about objectives and budget) likely guided brand managers' decisions about message design and media placement.
3. Objectives and budgets are necessarily interdependent. Explain this interdependency and provide an example to support your point.
4. Brand positioning and targeting also are necessarily interdependent. Explain this interdependency and provide an example to support your point.
5. What is the distinction between top-down (TD) and bottom-up (BU) budgeting? Why is BUTD used in companies that are more marketing oriented, whereas TDBU is found more frequently in finance-driven companies?
6. Marketing communications has been described as an ill-structured problem. Explain what this means.
7. Why do you think that marketing communications budgets have been reallocated in recent years to increased expenditures on promotions and reduced advertising spending?
8. Explain the concept of *momentum,* and offer an account as to why momentum is important for a brand such as Red Bull.
9. Assume you are in charge of fund-raising for an organization on your campus—a social fraternity or sorority, a business fraternity, or any other suitable organization. It is your job to identify a suitable project and to manage the project's marketing communications. For the purpose of this exercise, identify a fund-raising project idea and apply the subset of the model involving fundamental decisions. In other words, explain how you would position your fund-raising project, whom you would target, what objective(s) you would set, and how much (ballpark figure) you would budget for MarCom efforts.
10. Tom Peters, author and management consultant, describes a brand as "passion made palpable."[42] What do you think he means by this expression. Provide a couple of personal examples that support Peters's characterization of brands.
11. Using the framework in Figure 2.8, describe all personal associations that the following brands hold for you: (a) the VW Beetle, (b) Mountain Dew, (c) Red Bull energy drink, (d) *The Wall Street Journal,* and (e) movie star Tom Cruise.
12. Roger Enrico, CEO of PepsiCo, was quoted in the text as saying: "In my mind the best thing a person can say about a brand is that it's their favorite." Identify two brands that you regard as your favorites. Describe the specific associations that each of these brands holds for you and thus why they are two of your favorites.
13. Provide examples of brands that in your opinion are positioned in such a way as to reflect the five personality dimensions: sincerity, excitement, competence, sophistication, and ruggedness.
14. Provide several examples of co-branding or ingredient branding other than those presented in the chapter.

ENDNOTES

1. Kevin Lane Keller, "Conceptualizing, Measuring, and Managing Customer-Based Brand Equity," *Journal of Marketing* 57 (January 1993), 2.
2. "Veal Industry Focuses on Chefs in Countering Animal-Rights Ads," *The Wall Street Journal Interactive Edition,* March 18, 1998 (http://interactive.wsj.com).
3. Nigel F. Piercy, "The Marketing Budgeting Process: Marketing Management Implications," *Journal of Marketing* 51 (October 1987), 45–59.
4. Ibid. See 55, fig. 2

5. Donald W. Jackson, Jr., Janet E. Keith, and Richard K. Burdick, "The Relative Importance of Various Promotional Elements in Different Industrial Purchase Situations," *Journal of Advertising* 16, no. 4 (1987), 25–33.

6. The terms *push and pull* are physical metaphors that attempt to capture how marketing communication funds should be allocated. *Push* suggests a forward thrust from a manufacturer to the trade (wholesalers or retailers) on to the consumer; personal selling to the trade is the primary push technique. *Pull* means that a manufacturer promotes directly to consumers, who it is hoped will pressure retailers to stock the promoted product. In actuality, manufacturers use a combination of pull and push techniques. These techniques complement one another and are not perfectly substitutable.

7. Thomas A. Petit and Martha R. McEnally, "Putting Strategy into Promotion Mix Decisions," *The Journal of Consumer Marketing* 2 (winter 1985), 41-47.

8. Ibid.

9. Joseph W. Ostrow, "The Advertising/Promotion Mix: A Blend or a Tangle," *AAAA Newsletter*, August 1988, 7.

10. Quoted in Sally Goll Beatty, "Auto Makers Bet Campaigns Will Deliver Even If They Can't," *The Wall Street Journal Interactive Edition*, October 13, 1997 (http://interactive.wsj.com).

11. For more detailed discussion of the necessity and virtues of measuring MarCom effectiveness, see Tim Ambler, *Marketing and the Bottom Line: The New Metrics of Corporate Wealth* (London: Pearson Education Limited, 2000), especially Appendix A.

12. Cited in Kevin Lane Keller, *Strategic Brand Management: Building, Measuring, and Managing Brand Equity* (Upper Saddle River, NJ: Prentice Hall, 1998), p. 2.

13. David Martin, "Branding: Finding That 'One Thing,'" *Brandweek*, February 16, 1998, p. 18.

14. Jennifer L. Aaker, "Dimensions of Brand Personality," *Journal of Marketing Research* 34 (August 1997), 347–356.

15. Highly readable and insightful discussions of brand equity are provided in two excellent books written by David A. Aaker: *Managing Brand Equity* (New York: The Free Press, 1991) and *Building Strong Brands* (New York: Free Press, 1996).

16. This straightforward distinction has been observed by Arjun Chaudhuri and Morris B. Holbrook, "The Chain of Effects from Brand Trust and Brand Affect to Brand Performance: The Role of Brand Loyalty," *Journal of Marketing* 65 (April 2001), 90.

17. Ibid.

18. Keller, "Conceptualizing, Measuring, and Managing Customer-Based Brand Equity," 2.

19. Terry Lefton, "Adidas Goes to Image Pitch with '98 $$ Boost," *Brandweek*, January 26, 1998, 37.

20. Matthew Martinez, "Reed Study Sees Where Ad Dollars Go," *Advertising Age's Business Marketing*, October 1997, 46.

21. "Coke's Market Share Rises to 43.9% as PepsiCo Slips," *The Wall Street Journal Interactive Edition*, February 13, 1998 (http://interactive.wsj.com).

22. For sophisticated discussions of the relationship between brand equity and brand loyalty, consult the following sources: Tülin Erdem and Joffre Swait, "Brand Equity as a Signaling Phenomenon," *Journal of Consumer Psychology* 7 (number 2, 1998), 131–158; Chaudhuri and Holbrook, "The Chain of Effects from Brand Trust and Brand Affect to Brand Performance: The Role of Brand Loyalty."

23. Larry Light and Richard Morgan, *The Fourth Wave: Brand Loyalty Marketing* (New York: Coalition for Brand Equity, 1994), 11.

24. William Boulding, Eunkyu Lee, and Richard Staelin, "Mastering the Mix: Do Advertising, Promotion, and Sales Force Activities Lead to Differentiation?" *Journal of Marketing Research* 31 (May 1994), 159–172.

25. Bill McDowell, "Starbucks Is Ground Zero in Today's Coffee Culture," *Advertising Age*, December 9, 1996, 1, 49.

26. Kenneth Hein, "A Bull's Market," *Brandweek*, May 28, 2001, 21–24.

27. "The PepsiCo Empire Strikes Back," *Brandweek*, October 7, 1996, 60.

28. Kenneth Hein, "Can't Buy Me Love," *Brandweek*, June 4, 2001, S20–S23.

29. Ibid., S23.

30. Ibid., S22.

31. Kevin Lane Keller, "The Brand Report Card," *Harvard Business Review*, January/February 2000, 147–157.

32. Ibid., 154.

33. For an informative treatment of how one brand's reputation affects consumers' attitudes toward a partnering brand, see Bernard L. Simonin and Julie A. Ruth, "Is a Company Known by the Company It Keeps? Assessing the Spillover Effects of Brand Alliances on Consumer Brand Attitudes," *Journal of Marketing Research* 35 (February 1998), 30–42.

34. Cara Beardi, "Rayovac's Flashlight Line Hitches a Ride with Harley," *Advertising Age*, May 29, 2000, 89.

35. Ibid.

36. Ibid., 28.

37. Keller, *Strategic Brand Management*, 285. For excellent theoretical treatments of this issue, see C. Whan Park, Sung Youl

Jun, and Allan D. Shocker, "Composite Branding Alliances: An Investigation of Extension and Feedback Effects," *Journal of Marketing Research* 33 (November 1996), 453–466; and Simonin and Ruth, "Is a Company Known by the Company It Keeps?"

38. Sandra Dolbow, "DuPont Lycra Stretches Out Into Jeans," *Brandweek*, July 2, 2001, 8.

39. Stephanie Thompson, "Branding Bud-dies," February 23, 1998, 26.

40. Sally Goll Beatty, "Intel Wannabes Unleash a Flood of New Ads on TV," *The Wall Street Journal Interactive Edition*, January 14, 1998 (http://interactive.wsj.com).

41. Ibid.

42. "Great Age of the Brand," *Advertising Age*, November 8, 1999, s10.

IMC from the Customer's Perspective: Targeting, Communicating, and Persuading

PART TWO

Part Two builds a foundation for better understanding the nature and function of marketing communications by providing a practical and theoretical overview of communication principles, consumer information processing, and persuasion processes and practices. *Chapter 3* introduces brand positioning and targeting as key elements in effective marketing communications. The section on positioning describes the value and necessity of formulating a distinct communication strategy that enables marketing communicators to distinguish their brand from competitive offerings and to imprint this difference—this positioning—prominently and distinctively in customers' memories. The section on targeting examines the demographic, psychographic, and geodemographic factors used in targeting the recipients of MarCom efforts. Major emphasis is devoted to important demographic developments such as (1) population growth and geographical dispersion, (2) the changing age structure of the population, (3) the growth of the singles market, and (4) ethnic population developments. Psychographic targeting is discussed with emphasis on the VALS 2 classification scheme. A final section describes geodemographic targeting and overviews the Claritas PRIZM service that is in wide use for this purpose.

Chapter 4 provides further foundation for targeting efforts by examining the nature of meaning creation, the communication process, and the fundamentals of consumer behavior. Behavioral foundations of marketing communications are approached from two perspectives: first, the logical thinking person as embodied in the consumer information processing approach, and, second, the hedonic-experiential perspective of the pleasure-seeking, feeling person. Particular detail is devoted to describing the marketing communication activities necessary to promote consumer attention, comprehension, and learning of marketing messages.

Chapter 5 continues the overview of buyer behavior by discussing the central concepts of attitudes and persuasion. These topics are important because marketing communications represents an organized effort to influence and persuade customers to make choices that are compatible with the communicator's interests while simultaneously satisfying the customer's needs. A major section examines practical marketing communication efforts to influence the consumer's motivation, opportunity, and ability to process marketing messages. Another major section examines applications of persuasion principles (e.g., reciprocity, scarcity, liking) used by MarCom practitioners.

Chapter Three

POSITIONING AND TARGETING FOR MARCOM EFFORTS

Chapter Objectives

After studying this chapter, you should be able to:

1. Explain the concept of positioning and the role it plays in directing the implementation of MarCom decisions.
2. Discuss the importance of targeting marketing communications to specific consumer groups.
3. Understand the role of demographics, psychographics, and geodemographics in targeting consumer groups.
4. Appreciate major demographic developments such as changes in the age structure of the population and ethnic population growth.
5. Describe the nature of psychographic targeting and the VALS 2 system.
6. Explain the meaning of geodemographics and understand the role for this form of targeting.

Opening Vignette: New Products and a New Target Market for Polaroid

Polaroid is a famous name in photography dating back to the 1950s when the Massachusetts-based company introduced self-developing photograph technology. This technology was widely adopted for well over a quarter century and the company prospered, but then consumers' photographic tastes and preferences changed and Polaroid fell on hard times. In an effort to regain its lost momentum, Polaroid Corporation in 1999 introduced new consumer products for the first time in over two decades.

The i-Zone Pocket Camera and the JoyCam are Polaroid's new instant cameras targeted to consumers from Generations X and Y. The i-Zone delivers postage-stamp-size photos or photo stickers and is directed primarily at 12- to 17-year-olds—mostly girls because they are more likely than boys to own a camera. The JoyCam is aimed at a slightly older target consisting primarily of teens and adults younger than 25.

This "youth movement" represents a rather dramatic repositioning of Polaroid's marketing thrust, which historically has been aimed at commercial markets and older consumers. Slow growth in these areas encouraged the company to pursue other avenues for sales gains. Targeting teens and young adults has required Polaroid to depart from the ways it traditionally has marketed cameras. In addition to a major increase in its ad budget, Polaroid has invested in sponsoring tours of teen pop stars—first the Backstreet Boys and then Britney Spears. The company also is sponsoring the mall tour of the all-female group Nobody's Angels. This sponsorship has enabled Polaroid to gain distribution in stores such as Toys "R" Us and Tower Records. In an Apple Computer–type effort, Polaroid has produced i-Zone cameras in a variety of colors that appeal to its teenage target: red, green, blue, sorbet, silver, and wasabi green.

Though Polaroid has experienced rapid and substantial sales growth with its focus on youth, financial analysts and other observers doubt that the sales trajectory can be sustained. The concern is that teens are highly fickle and will eventually shift their interest to the next fad that follows on Polaroid's innovative thrust. In fact, competitor Kodak is hot on Polaroid's tail with its own Kodak Max and Advantix cameras aimed at the same teen market. Kodak has committed $75 million in marketing dollars over a five-year period to reach girls aged 9 to 15 based on research results showing that teenage girls are, by a margin of 75 percent to 49 percent, more likely to own a camera than boys.

The *Opening Vignette* alludes to two topics, positioning and targeting, that represent the purpose and content of this chapter. As touched on in the previous

---

Sources: Adapted from Todd Wasserman, "Kodak, Polaroid to Duel in Malls Over Gen Y Girls," *Brandweek*, January 31, 2000, 10; Cara Beardi, "Targeting Teens Pays Off for Polaroid," *Advertising Age*, March 6, 2000, 16.

chapter, positioning and targeting are two of MarCom's fundamental decisions that serve to direct subsequent implementation decisions such as designing messages and selecting media. All sophisticated MarCom efforts must start with a clear brand positioning and a definite target in mind.

BRAND POSITIONING

Brand positioning is an essential preliminary activity, or fundamental decision, to developing successful MarCom programs. It is only by having a clear positioning statement that we know to whom our brand should be targeted, what we should say about the brand, and what media and message vehicles should be selected for contacting target customers.

Positioning is both a useful conceptual notion and an invaluable strategic tool. Conceptually, the term *positioning* suggests two interrelated ideas: First, the marketing communicator wishes to create a specific meaning for the brand and have that meaning clearly lodged in the consumer's memory (think of this as "positioned in"). Second, the brand's meaning in consumers' memories stands in comparison to what they know and think about competitive brands in the product/service category (think of this as "positioned against").

Strategically and tactically, positioning is a short statement—even a word— that represents the message you want to "imprint in the minds of customers and prospects."[1] This statement tells how your brand differs from and is superior to competitive brands. It gives a reason why consumers should buy your brand rather than a competitor's and promises a solution to the customer's needs or wants. A good positioning statement should satisfy two requirements: (1) reflect a brand's competitive advantage and (2) motivate customers to action.[2] In sum, a *positioning statement* for a brand represents how we want customers and prospects to think and feel about our brand. These thoughts and feelings should stand out in comparison to competitive offerings and motivate the customer or prospect to want to try our brand.

To make this idea of positioning even more concrete, let us call on the customer-based brand equity framework that was presented in the previous chapter as Figure 2.8. For present purposes, it will be useful to reproduce the *brand image* part of the brand equity framework as a useful graphic device for expanding our discussion of brand positioning. As can be seen in Figure 3.1, a brand's image consists of types, favorability, strength, and uniqueness of brand associations. Our focus for present purposes will be limited to the *types* of brand associations. Please notice in Figure 3.1 that types of associations include brand attributes, benefits, and an overall evaluation, or attitude toward the brand.

Let us talk more about brand attributes and benefits. Notice carefully in Figure 3.1 that brand *attributes* include product-related and non-product-related attributes. For example, the size and color features of the i-Zone camera described in the *Opening Vignette* represent product-related attributes. Non-product-related attributes would include, for example, the i-Zone's price and consumer perceptions of the type of people who use the camera (user imagery) and the occasions when such a camera is used (usage imagery). Brand *benefits* consist of ways by which a brand satisfies customers' needs and wants and can be classified as functional, symbolic, or experiential.

With Figure 3.1 and the above terminology in mind, we now can pursue the options available to marketing communicators for positioning their brands. Generally speaking, we can position a brand by focusing on product attributes or on functional, symbolic, or experiential benefits.

Positioning via Product Attributes

A brand can be positioned in terms of a product feature or attribute, provided that the attribute represents a competitive advantage and can motivate customers to purchase that brand rather than a competitive offering. Product attributes, as shown in Figure 3.1, can be distinguished as either product-related or non-product-related features.

Figure 3.1   **A Framework for Brand Positioning**

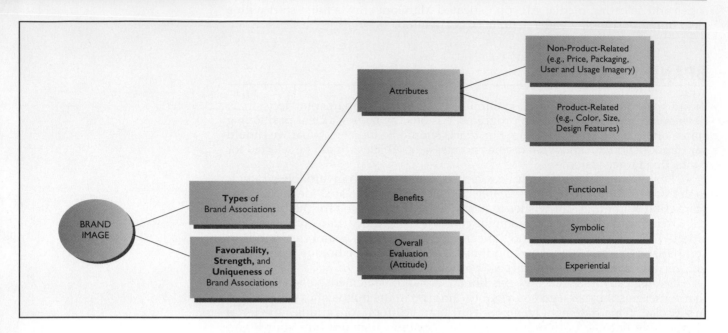

Source: Adapted from Kevin Lane Keller, "Conceptualizing, Measuring, and Managing Customer-Based Brand Equity," *Journal of Marketing* 57 (January 1993), 7.

Product-related Features.   Sleeker product design, superior materials, and more color options are just a few of the virtually endless list of attributes that can provide the foundation for positioning a brand. If your brand has a product advantage, flaunt it, especially if the advantage is something that consumers truly desire in the product category.

Usage and User Imagery.   Brands can be positioned in terms of their unique usage symbolism or with respect to the kinds of people who use them. A brand positioned according to the image associated with how it is used, its *usage imagery*, depicts the brand in terms of specific, and presumably unique, usages that become associated with it. For example, advertisers sometimes position sport utility vehicles (SUVs) and passenger trucks in terms of their seemingly unique ability to traverse rough terrain. Such advertisements create the impression that only the advertised brand is capable of forging streams, climbing hills, and navigating other tough-to-travel areas. The Jeep Grand Cherokee (Figure 3.2) is positioned in terms of its unique agility—as the ad claims, "more agile than some of the mountains' own residents."

Similarly, brands can be positioned in terms of the kind of people who use them. This *user imagery* thus becomes the brand's hallmark; the brand and the people who are portrayed as using it become virtually synonymous. Positioning a brand via user imagery thus amounts to associating the brand with iconlike representations of the kind of people who are portrayed in advertisements as typical users of the brand. Consider for example an advertisement for Acqua Di Gio cologne marketed by Giorgio Armani. The ad, which is not displayed here, simply mentions the brand name along with the name of the retailer where it is available (Nordstrom) and presents a bottle of the product. But the main feature of the ad is a prominent facial portrayal of an attractive man in his early twenties. The ad says absolutely nothing about brand benefits. Rather, the ad associates this brand with the prominently featured user, who himself is symbolic of the brand's target class. Plain and simple, Acqua Di Gio's meaning (what it stands for) is inseparable from the user who serves to signify the brand's desired users. Hence, this brand is being positioned *not* in terms of what it has (its features) or what needs it satisfies (its benefits) but in terms of the type of man who uses the brand (its user imagery).

Illustration of Positioning via Usage Imagery   Figure 3.2

Positioning via Brand Benefits

Positioning with respect to brand benefits can be accomplished by appealing to any of three categories of basic consumer needs: functional, symbolic, or experiential.[3] Upon a quick review of the consumer-based brand equity framework presented earlier (Figure 3.1), you will see that these three categories are shown as a specific type of association termed *benefits*. The distinction between benefits and needs should not trouble us insofar as it simply involves a matter of perspective. That is, consumers have needs and brands have attributes or features that satisfy those needs. Brand benefits are then the need-satisfying features provided by brands. So as you can see, needs and benefits can be thought of, metaphorically speaking, as flip sides of the same coin.

A brand positioned in terms of **functional needs** attempts to provide solutions to consumers' current consumption-related problems or potential problems by communicating that the brand possesses specific benefits capable of solving those problems. The advertisement for the Gillette Mach3 (Figure 3.3) appeals to the consumer's need for an easy-to-use razor that provides a close shave (see ad wording). In general, appeals to functional needs are the most prevalent form of brand benefit positioning. In business-to-business (B2B) marketing, for example, salespeople typically appeal to their customers' functional needs for higher-quality products, faster delivery time, or better service. Consumer goods marketers also regularly appeal to consumers' needs for convenience, safety, good health, cleanliness, and so on, all of which are functional needs that can be satisfied by brand benefits.

Other brands are positioned in terms of their ability to satisfy *psychological desires*. Appeals to **symbolic needs** include those directed at consumers' desire for

Figure 3.3

Illustration of Positioning via Appeal to Functional Needs

self-enhancement, group membership, affiliation, and belongingness. Brand positioning in terms of symbolic needs attempts to associate brand use with a desired group, role, or self-image. Marketers of brands in categories such as personal beauty products, jewelry, alcoholic beverages, cigarettes, and motor vehicles frequently appeal to symbolic needs.

An advertisement for Harley-Davidson motorcycles illustrates an exemplary appeal to symbolic needs. This ad depicts a driver-less Harley-Davidson motorcycle on an open-road in the American West in a fashion reminiscent of a wild mustang in a similar scene. The ad's headline declares, "Even Cows Kick Down the Fence Once in a While." The headline is supported with copy points stating, "It's right there in front of you, Road, wind, country. A Harley-Davidson motorcycle. In other words, freedom. A chance to live on your own terms for a while . . . Anyone who's been there knows: Life is better on the outside". This ad does not tout product features for which the Harley-Davidson is known or functional benefits such as power and performance. It rather simply represents the sense of freedom, independence, and even rebelliousness ("Life is better on the outside") that a prospective purchaser might desire in owning this brand and driving the open roads. The message is subtle but clear: If you cherish freedom, independence, and perhaps a sense of being a kindred spirit with others of like mind, then Harley-Davidson is the brand of motorcycle for you. The cowboy spirit is encapsulated in this positioning, which tacitly equates Harley motorcycles with horses. (Harley-Davidson equals "iron horse.") Potential purchasers of Harley motorcycles probably as youngsters envisioned themselves riding horses in America's Old West.

Illustration of Positioning via Appeal to Experiential Needs

Figure 3.4

The last time you had this much fun driving a car
it cost a quarter and gyrated in front of the supermarket.

The six-speed, 240-horsepower, 0-60 in less than six seconds Honda S2000.   HONDA

Consumers' **experiential needs** represent their desires for products that provide sensory pleasure, variety, and, in a few product circumstances, cognitive stimulation. Positioning directed at experiential needs promotes brands as being out of the ordinary and high in sensory value (looking elegant, feeling wonderful, tasting or smelling great, sounding divine, being exhilarating, and so on) or rich in the potential for cognitive stimulation (exciting, challenging, mentally entertaining, and so on). Look at the ad in Figure 3.4 for the Honda S2000. The experience of driving this car is likened to a child's exhilaration when riding in a gyrating toy car. This brand's positioning is an unadorned promise of excitement—not an unwise appeal to a target audience of baby boomers who are seeking to relive some of the joys of an earlier life when times were perhaps more exciting and less stressful.

It is important to recognize that brands often offer a mixture of functional, symbolic, and experiential benefits or some combination of any two of these benefits. In the case of the Honda S2000, for example, the brand offers a 240-horsepower engine and goes from 0 to 60 miles per hour in less than six seconds (functional benefit), while at the same time promising exhilaration (experiential benefit). However, the Honda S2000 ad (Figure 3.4) does not devote equal attention to both types of benefits but rather appeals primarily to prospective consumers' symbolic needs. Generally speaking, successful brand positioning requires a communication strategy that entices a *single type* of consumer need (functional, symbolic, or experiential) rather than attempting to be something for everyone—that is, a *generic* brand image. A brand with a generic (multiple-personality) image is difficult to manage because it (1) competes against more brands (those with purely functional, purely symbolic, purely experiential, and mixed images) and (2) may be difficult for consumers to readily understand what it stands for and what its defining characteristics are.[4]

TARGETING CUSTOMERS AND PROSPECTS

This section's purpose is to expand the discussion of *targeting* that was introduced in Chapter 2. At that point it was emphasized that the targeting of customers and prospects allows marketing communicators to deliver more precisely their messages and prevent wasted coverage to people falling outside the targeted market. Meaningful and profitable market segmentation efforts typically require that segment members share demographic and lifestyle characteristics. Hence, selection of target segments is a critical first step toward effective and efficient MarCom efforts. In the remainder of this chapter we will focus on three sets of consumer characteristics that singularly or in combination influence what people consume and how they respond to marketing communications: *demographic, psychographic,* and *geodemographic* characteristics.

Targeting MarCom efforts is critical to avoiding wasted efforts and better satisfying the particular group of customers for whom a brand is intended. Targeting thus implies precision and efficiency of effort. Not to target is equivalent to shooting a basketball wildly in the air without directing it toward the hoop. It is difficult enough to connect on a shot from a 20-foot distance when that is one's intent. Imagine how unlikely you are to make a shot if you don't consciously concentrate on a specific target. Such is the case when MarCom efforts fail to focus on a specific target!

Demographic variables include characteristics such as age, income, and ethnicity. By monitoring demographic shifts, marketers are better able to (1) identify and select market segments, (2) forecast product sales, and (3) select media for reaching target customers.[5] Aspects of consumers' lifestyles—their activities, interests, and opinions—comprise **psychographic** characteristics. Purchasing patterns often are influenced more by our lifestyles than our demographic backgrounds. **Geodemographics** include a combination of demographic and lifestyle characteristics of consumers within geographic clusters such as zip code areas and neighborhoods. Knowing that consumers who share similar demographic and psychographic profiles tend to reside in geographic proximity to one another offers marketing communicators, particularly direct mailers and telemarketers, an especially effective and efficient means for reaching consumers who are most receptive to marketing messages. Marketing research firms have developed classification, or clustering, systems that identify relatively distinct geodemographic segments of consumers. (These will be discussed in a concluding section.)

Separate sections are devoted to all three groups of "-graphics" (demographics, psychographics, and geodemographics), but major emphasis in this chapter is devoted to demographic characteristics insofar as the demographic landscape is particularly dynamic. As a matter of necessity, the focus is on demographic characteristics of the U.S. population. Although the same variables are relevant elsewhere, the particulars are country specific. Thus, interested readers in countries outside the United States will certainly want to perform a similar analysis of your country's demographics.

DEMOGRAPHIC TARGETING

Three major demographic topics are examined in this section: (1) the age structure of the U.S. population (e.g., the baby boom, Generations X and Y); (2) the changing American household (e.g., the increase in the number of single-person households); and (3) ethnic population developments. It will be helpful to place these topics in context by first examining population growth and geographic distribution of the world and U.S. populations.

Population Growth and Geographic Dispersion

At the time of this writing, the total population of human beings on the earth was estimated to be 6.16 billion people.[6] (For a daily update on the projected world population, go to http://www.census.gov/cgi-bin/ipc/popclockw.) The world population is expected to grow to just less than 8 billion people by the year 2025 and to reach slightly more than 9 billion people by 2050. Table 3.1 provides a list of the world's 15 largest countries as of 2001.

The U.S. Census Bureau more recently estimates the U.S. population at closer to 281 million.[7] This size represents almost an exact doubling of the U.S. population at the end of World War II in 1945 when there were approximately 140 million Americans. The U.S. population is projected to reach approximately 346 million by 2025.[8]

A particularly interesting aspect of the U.S. population is the shifts that have taken place in its *geographical distribution*. Historically, the population was concentrated in the industrial Northeast and Midwest, but by 2000 a solid majority of Americans lived in the South or West. Population increases have been modest in the Northeast and Midwest but explosive in the warm-weather climes of the South and West; in fact, projections indicate that 70 percent of foreseeable U.S. population growth will take place in these two regions.[9]

The Changing Age Structure

One of the most dramatic features of the American population is its *relentless aging*. The median age of Americans was 28 in 1970, 30 in 1980, and 33 in 1990; it rose to its present level of nearly 36 in 2000 and is expected to increase to 38.5 by 2025.[10] Table 3.2 presents 2000 population figures distributed by age group. The following sections examine major age groupings of the U.S. population and the implications these hold for MarCom efforts. Discussion starts with the so-called baby-boom generation and also includes separate sections devoted to middle-aged and mature consumers, children and teenagers, and the much-touted Generations X and Y.

The Baby-Boom Generation. The changing age structure in the United States is attributable in large part to what demographers term the **baby boom** — the birth of 76 million Americans between 1946 and 1964. This population-boom period followed the end of World War II (in 1945) and persisted for nearly two

World's 15 Largest Countries in 2001

Table 3.1

Rank	Country	Population (millions)
1	China	1,273
2	India	1,033
3	United States	285
4	Indonesia	206
5	Brazil	172
6	Pakistan	145
7	Russia	144
8	Bangladesh	134
9	Japan	127
10	Nigeria	127
11	Mexico	100
12	Germany	82
13	Vietnam	79
14	Philippines	77
15	Egypt	70

Source: Population Reference Bureau (http://www.prb.org/pubs/wpds2000).

Table 3.2   Population of the United States by Age Group, as of 2000

Age	Population (millions)
Children and Teens	
Under 5	19.18
5–9	20.55
10–14	20.53
15–19	20.22
Total	80.48
Young Adults	
20–24	18.96
25–34	39.89
Total	58.85
Middle-Agers	
35–44	45.15
45–54	37.68
Total	82.83
Olders	
55–59	13.47
60–64	10.81
Total	24.28
Elders	
65–74	18.39
The Very Old	
75–84	12.36
85+	4.24
Total	16.60
Total U.S. Population	281.43

Source: Profiles of General Demographic Characteristics, *2000 Census of Population and Housing*, Table DP-1 (May 2001).

decades. Using 2000 as a point of reference, the oldest baby boomer was 54 years old at the start of the new millennium, whereas age 36 was the youngest person to be classified as a "boomer." The effects of the baby boom (and subsequent bust) have been manifested in the following major population developments:

1. The original baby boomers created a *mini baby boom* as they reached child-bearing age. As shown in Table 3.2, the number of children and teenagers in the United States totaled 80.48 million in 2000.
2. Due to a low birthrate from the mid-1960s through the 1970s (prior to the time when most baby boomers were of childbearing age), relatively few babies were born. There now are proportionately fewer young adults (ages 20 to 34) than there were in prior generations.
3. The number of middle-agers (people aged 35 to 54) has increased dramatically, totaling nearly 83 million Americans as of 2000. This maturing of the baby boomers has been one of the most significant demographic developments faced by marketers.

The baby-boom generation offers tremendous potential for many marketers. Boomers are an attractive market for a variety of products ranging from breath mints and gums to high-tech products such as computers and personal digital assistants. For example, Eclipse gum (see Figure 3.5) is marketed specifically to baby-boomer consumers.[11] What makes boomers such an attractive target is that

A Product Marketed to Baby Boomers   **Figure 3.5**

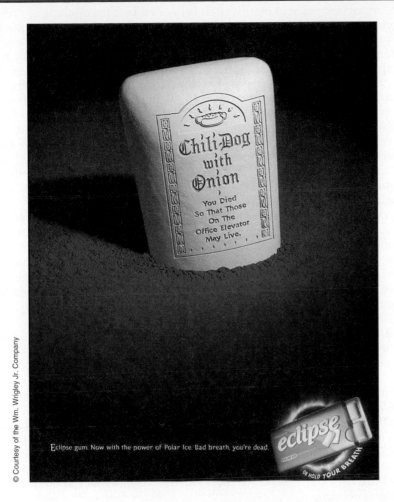

this age category is relatively affluent and thus represents a good general target for quality automobiles, investments (insurance, real estate, and securities), and "grown-up toys" like Harley-Davidson motorcycles. Interestingly, the median age of a Harley rider in 1987 was 34.7, but as of 1999 the median age had increased to 44.6—a clear reflection of baby-boomer influence in the purchase of this product.[12] Baby boomers represent an attractive target for a variety of "luxury" goods. For example, appliance maker Whirlpool appeals to affluent boomers who want the very best appliance quality with a line of items named Whirlpool Gold. And luxury skin-care marketers have experienced fabulous revenue growth by introducing high-priced antiaging products. L'Oreal's Absolue sells for $90 for a 1.7-ounce jar, and even this is lower priced than some other brands on the market.[13]

Moreover, just because baby boomers are aging does not necessarily mean they are getting psychologically old or are significantly altering their consumption patterns from a younger age. Rather, there are indications that baby boomers are retaining many of their more youthful consumption habits and, in a sense, are taking longer to grow up or are unwilling to change.[14] For example, the rather dramatic increase in purchases of hair-color products by baby boomers reflects this tendency for boomers to prolong youth and to gravitate toward products that support their youth obsession.[15] Manufacturers of health-care items, exercise machines, and food products have actively appealed to baby boomers' passion for remaining in youthful shape. Because boomers represent the "epicenter of society," advertisers will march in lockstep with this group and continue to reflect their characteristics and appeal to their purchase interests and needs.[16] For example, athletic-footwear makers cater to baby boomers by offering shoes that come in wider widths than just the medium-size option offered in the past.

An important point of clarification is needed before concluding this section and moving on to the next age group. In particular, it is tempting to think of baby boomers as a monolithic group of people who think alike, act the same, and purchase identical products. Such an impression would be erroneous. Baby boomers do *not* represent a true market segment in the strictest sense of this term. That is, just because millions of Americans share one commonality (being born between 1946 and 1964), this does not mean they are virtual clones of one another. Within this age cohort, there are distinct differences among people with respect to age, income, ethnicity, lifestyle choices, and product/brand preferences. Hence, although it is convenient to speak of baby boomers as a single group, it would be a mistake to conclude that they represent an actionable market segment. It is important to appreciate the fact that meaningful and profitable market segmentation efforts typically require that segment members share a combination of demographic, lifestyle, and possibly geographical characteristics; broad groupings such as "baby boomers" are much too crude to satisfy the characteristics of a meaningful market segment.

In sum, baby boomers are a significant age cohort and en masse represent a powerful economic force, but they do *not* constitute a specific market segment. Thus, for example, the marketers of L'Oreal Absolue should not consider their target to be all boomers but rather only the subset of people in this age category who have indulgent personalities and sufficient incomes to afford a product that costs $90 for 1.7 ounces.

Mature Consumers. With an aging U.S. population, the 1990s was the decade of marketing to middle-aged baby boomers and mature consumers. Although somewhat arbitrary, we can think of **middle age** as starting at age 35 and ending at age 54, at which point maturity is reached. Actually, there is some disagreement over the dividing point between middle age and maturity.[17] Sometimes a 65-and-over classification is used, because age 65 normally marks retirement. In this text we will use the U.S. Bureau of the Census's designation, which classifies **mature people** as those who are 55 *and older*. As of 2000 there were roughly 83 million Americans between the middle ages of 35 and 54 (see Table 3.2). Because most of these individuals constitute the previously described baby boomers born between 1946 and 1964, no further commentary about middle-aged consumers is needed.

Turning to mature consumers (also called seniors), in 2000 there were approximately 59 million U.S. citizens aged 55 or older, representing about 21 percent of the total U.S. population. Historically, many marketers have ignored mature consumers or have treated this group in unflattering ways by focusing on "repair kit products" such as dentures, laxatives, and arthritis remedies.[18] Not only are mature consumers numerous, but they also are wealthier and more willing to spend than ever before. Mature Americans control nearly 70 percent of the net worth of all U.S. households.

People aged 65 and older are particularly well off, having the highest *discretionary income* (i.e., income unburdened by fixed expenses) and the most assets of any age group.[19] The number of people in this 65-plus age category is huge, totaling about 35 million in 2000, which represents approximately 12 percent of the total population.

A variety of implications accompany MarCom efforts directed at mature consumers. In advertising aimed at this group, it is advisable to portray them as active, vital, busy, forward looking, and concerned with looking attractive and being romantic.[20] The Viagra advertisement (Figure 3.6) perhaps exemplifies advertisers' recognition that romance is not the sole province of youth. Advertisers now generally appeal to seniors in a flattering fashion as typified by the use of attractive models to represent clothing, cosmetics, and other products that had been the exclusive advertising domain of youthful models.

Advertisers that use the Internet cannot neglect appeals to seniors, who represent one of the fastest growing groups on the Web. In fact, seniors represent a greater number of online users (at 20 percent of total online users) than 18-to-24-

Recognition of Senior Citizens' Romantic Inclinations   Figure 3.6

© Courtesy of Pfizer Consumer Group, Pfizer, Inc.

year-olds (17.5 percent)![21] Investments, health and travel research, genealogy, and (sadly) gambling are the most popular online activities with seniors.[22] Seniors spend an average 700 minutes online per month, which exceeds any other group's use of the Internet.[23]

It is important to point out again that just because mature consumers share a single commonality (i.e., aged 55 or older), they by no means represent a homogeneous market segment. Indeed, the Census Bureau divides people aged 55 and older into four distinct age segments: 55 to 64 (*olders*); 65 to 74 (*elders*); 75 to 84 (*the very old*); and 85 and over (see Table 3.2). On the basis of age alone, consumers in each of these groups differ—sometimes dramatically—in terms of lifestyles, interest in the marketplace, reasons for buying, and ability to spend. Moreover, it is important to realize that age alone is not the best indicator of how an individual lives or what role consumption plays in that lifestyle. In fact, research has identified four groups of mature consumers based on a combination of health and self-image characteristics. Based on a national mail survey of over 1,000 people aged 55 and older, respondents were classified into the following groups: Healthy Hermits, 38 percent; Ailing Outgoers, 34 percent; Frail Recluses, 15 percent; and Healthy Indulgers, 13 percent.[24] Brief descriptions follow.

Healthy Hermits, though in good health, are psychologically withdrawn from society. They represent a good market for various services such as tax and legal advice, financial services, home entertainment, and do-it-yourself products. Direct mail and print advertising are the best media for reaching this group. *Ailing Outgoers* are diametrically opposite to Healthy Hermits. Though in poor health, they are socially active, health conscious, and interested in learning to do new things. Home health care, dietary products, planned retirement communities, and entertainment services are some of the products and services most desired by this group. They can be reached via promotions and through select mass media tailored to their positive self-image and active, social lifestyle. *Frail Recluses* are withdrawn socially and are in poor health. Various health and medical products and services, home entertainment, and domestic assistance services (e.g., lawn care) can be successfully marketed to this group via mass media advertising. *Healthy Indulgers* are vigorous, relatively wealthy, and socially active. They are independent and want the most out of life. Mature consumers in this group represent a good market for financial services, leisure/travel entertainment, clothes, luxury goods, and high-tech products and services. They are accessible via in-store promotions, direct mail, specialized print media, and the Internet.

Children and Teenagers.

At the other end of the age spectrum are children and teenagers. The group of young Americans aged 19 and younger has fallen dramatically from 40 percent of the population in 1965 (during the baby-boom heyday) to approximately 29 percent of the population in 2000. Yet this is still a substantial group, with 80.5 million occupants in 2000. (See Table 3.2 for specific breakouts by age group—i.e., under 5, 5 to 9, 10 to 14, and 15 to 19.)

Marketers typically refer to children aged 4 through 12 as "kids" to distinguish this cohort from toddlers and teenagers. It is estimated that children in this broad grouping either directly spend or influence the spending of billions of dollars worth of purchases each year. Aggregate spending by children aged 4 through 12 or in behalf of this age group roughly doubled every decade in the 1960s, 1970s, and 1980s. Spending in the 1990s tripled. Spending by or for this age group in 1997 alone totaled more than $24 billion.[25]

Preschoolers.

Children of *preschool age* represent a cohort that has grown substantially in recent years. More babies were born in the United States in 1990 (4.2 million) than at any time since the baby boom peak of 4.3 million babies born in 1957.[26] Toys, furniture items, and other products and services appealing to the family and home have increased to cater to this mini baby boom. For example, 5 million LeapPads—the educational toy that allows specially designed books to speak at the touch of small antennae disguised as a pen—were sold in 2000 at a price of $49.99.[27]

Elementary-school-age children.

This group includes children aged 6 to 11. These children directly influence product purchases (e.g., toys, records) and indirectly influence what their parents buy.[28] Children in this group are influential in their parents' choice of clothing and toys and even the brand choice of products such as toothpaste.[29] Advertising and other forms of marketing communications aimed at young children, or their families, have increased substantially in recent years. Numerous new products annually hit the shelves to cater to kids' tastes. (For a sophisticated but readable treatment of how children are socialized as consumers and learn to understand advertising, the reader is encouraged to examine two articles identified in this endnote.[30])

Tweens.

A category of children that marketers have dubbed "tweens"—not quite kids nor yet teenagers—is an age cohort actively involved in consumption. *Tweens* are usually classified as children between the ages of 8 and 12.[31] One specialist in the area of marketing to children estimates that tweens in 2000 had a weekly average income of $22.68 or, collectively, a total annual income of around $23 billion.[32] Retailers such as Limited Too and even Abercrombie & Fitch gear their MarCom efforts at garnering tweens' growing desire for fashionable clothing items.

Teenagers.

Consumers in this age group, totaling in the United States over 25 million 13- to 19-year-olds, have tremendous earning power and considerable influence in making personal and household purchases.[33] Teenagers often are referred to as the *Millennial Generation* or *Generation Y* (in contrast to the generation that preceded it, *Generation X*). Technically speaking, Gen Y consists of individuals born between the years 1979 and 1994. Thus, as of 2002, Gen Yers include all people between the ages of of 8 and 23, approximately 60 million Americans. The present discussion focuses just on the subset of teenagers who comprise this generation.

A study by Teenage Research Unlimited, which follows teen trends and attitudes, estimated that American teenagers spent $155 billion in 2000.[34] Teenagers have purchasing influence and power far greater than ever before, which accounts for the growth of MarCom programs aimed at this group.

Teenagers are noted for being highly conformist, narcissistic, and fickle consumers. These characteristics pose great opportunities and yet challenges for marketing communicators. An accepted product can become a huge success when the teenage bandwagon selects a brand as a personal mark of the in-crowd. However, today's accepted product or brand can easily become tomorrow's passé item. As described in Chapter 1, the Levi brand of jeans, for example, has lost some of its prior appeal to teenagers, who seem to favor, at least for the time being, brands such as Tommy Hilfiger, Paris Blues, and Mudd. Purchasing brands that are considered "cool" is important to teenagers. Table 3.3 lists the 10 coolest brands based on a large-scale (2,030 respondents) nationally representative sample of 12-to-19-year-olds.

It is said that teenagers don't like to be "marketed to." As with all consumers, it is important that marketing communicators provide useful information, but teens would rather acquire the information themselves—such as on the Internet or from friends—rather than having it imposed on them. MarCom personnel thus walk a precarious plank in communicating useful information to teens while at the same time avoiding being overbearing. The Internet is an obvious communication medium for reaching teens, who, it is estimated, will be an 11-million-strong force on the Internet by 2002.[35] The *Online Focus* describes a solution to teenagers' purchasing online when they don't own a credit card.

Young Adults. Scholarly treatment of this age cohort, commonly referred to as *Generation X*, identifies it as Americans born between 1961 and 1981.[36] However, to avoid overlap with the baby boomer generation (1946 to 1964), it is convenient to define this age cohort as people born between 1965 and 1981. Hence, as of 2000, Generation X constituted over 50 million Americans in the age category 19 to 35. Because Gen X'ers were born immediately after the baby boom, which ended in 1964, this group also is referred to as *baby busters* and *twentysomethings*—the latter label reflecting the fact that most people in this cohort are in their 20s. The labels do not end there, however; indeed, Generation X has been subjected to more clichés than any group in history, most of which are deprecatory: slackers, cynics, whiners, grunge kids, and hopeless. As is typically the case when a group is stereotyped, these labels characterize only a subset of Gen Xers and are much too general to begin to capture the complexity of this group and the differences among its occupants.[37]

Top 10 Coolest Brands	Table 3.3

1. Nike
2. Sony
3. Abercrombie & Fitch
4. Tommy Hilfiger
5. Old Navy
6. Adidas
7. American Eagle
8. Gap
9. Pepsi
10. Coke

Source: Coolest Brand Meter. Teenage Research Unlimited (http://www.teenresearch.com). Cited in Dan Lippe, "It's All in Creative Delivery," *Advertising Age*, June 25, 2001, s8.

Purchasing Online Without a Credit Card

How do you purchase something over the Internet if you are only 15 years old and don't have a credit card? The fact is that a teenager can't unless he or she uses a parent's card. A dot-com company named Rocketcash.com was launched in 1999 to solve this problem. Here is how it works: Parents or other relatives deposit money into an account held in the teenager's name. The teenage user contacts the Rocketcash.com site, which is linked to well over 100 Web merchants such as Jcrew.com, the online Disney store, and other popular online merchants. Kids thus have the freedom to shop online and gain a sense of fiscal responsibility, and parents don't have to worry about their children running up excessive credit card bills.

Seventeen is the average age of Rocketcash's customers, who have few limits on what teens can buy from the online merchants that are affiliated with Rocketcash's service. Rocketcash's revenue source is commissions from its merchant partners ranging from 5%-to-15% of the purchase amount.

Rocketcash has signed up nearly a half-million customers, but this is a pittance compared with the more than 35 million preteens and teenagers who are estimated to have spent over $1 billion online in 2002. Several competitors have attempted to wrest business from Rocketcash.com, but this pioneer appears to have the best business model and greatest odds at succeeding in the lucrative but risky online business.

Source: Adapted from Adam Bryant, "Where's My E-llowance?" Grok (www.thestandard.com/grok), February-March 2001, pp. 58–59. www.thestandard.com. ©2001 and reprinted with permission from International Data Group.

One well-known marketing research firm has classified Gen Xers into four groups based on their attitudinal profiles: Yup & Comers, Bystanders, Playboys, and Drifters. *Yup & Comers* have the highest levels of education and income and account for 28 percent of Gen Xers. They tend to focus on intangible rewards rather than material wealth and are confident about themselves and their futures. This clearly is not a group of people who fit the stereotypical labels attached to Gen X. *Bystanders* represent 37 percent of Gen Xers and consist predominantly of female African Americans and Hispanics. Although their disposable income is relatively low, this subsegment of Gen Xers has a flair for fashion and loves to shop. *Playboys* is a predominantly white, male group accounting for 19 percent of the Generation X cohort. Playboys adhere to a "pleasure before duty" lifestyle and are self-absorbed, fun loving, and impulsive. *Drifters* constitute the smallest subset at 16 percent of Gen Xers. This group is closest to the Generation X stereotype. They are frustrated with their lives, are among the least educated, seek security and status, and choose brands that offer a sense of belonging and self-esteem.[38]

These groupings make it apparent that contrary to their stereotypical portrayal, Gen Xers are not monolithic. The generalizations are incorrect and generally unfair. As a group they are no more cynical, disenfranchised, or inclined to whine than most people. Marketing communications directed to twentysomethings must use appeals targeted to specific subgroups such as Yup & Comers rather than stereotypes that do not adequately reach any subsegment.

Once again it is important to emphasize that the Gen X age cohort, however labeled, is not a unified group in terms of demographics or lifestyle preferences and should not be misconstrued as a single market segment. Indeed, the four groupings just described are themselves simplifications, but they do offer some refinement of the general differences among the over 50 million Americans who have been simplistically collapsed into a single category.

The *IMC Focus* describes one marketer's attempt to appeal to Gen X and, to a lesser extent, Gen Y consumers. The *Global Focus* insert illustrates a major screwup in a direct mail campaign aimed at German Gen Xers.

IMC
focus

No Longer Just Your Mother's Skin-Care Brand

Oil of Olay, a line of skin-care products on retail shelves for decades, was first marketed by a company called Richardson-Vicks. Though created in World War II as a lotion to treat burns, Richardson-Vicks advertised the product as a "beauty fluid." Procter & Gamble subsequently acquired Richardson-Vicks in 1985 and became the new owner of the Oil of Olay brand. With various product line extensions to the original moisturizer, P&G developed Oil of Olay into a major line of skin-care products with revenue exceeding $500 million.

The brand eventually became a bit outdated over the years. P&G's consumer research revealed that many young women consider the brand more appropriate for older women than for themselves. Young women also do not like the idea of using what they erroneously consider to be a greasy skin-care product. Although in actuality Oil of Olay is not greasy, apparently the word "oil" in the Oil of Olay brand name suggested just such an unpleasant product characteristic to young women who had never actually tried the brand.

Based on this invaluable research evidence, P&G's brand management team decided to reposition Oil of Olay to make it more appealing to younger women. Several steps were undertaken: First, without any fanfare so as not to bring attention to the change, P&G changed the brand name from Oil of Olay to simply Olay. They also altered the logo to look more modern and reduced the amount of writing on the package to make it more appealing to younger consumers. The new name and look clearly have potential to appeal to younger women without alienating baby boomers and older women who have been Oil of Olay's core consumers.

The moral of this story is that brands sometimes must be repositioned in order to grow and prosper. Oil of Olay's mature image was unappealing to millions of younger consumers who also were turned off by the thought of using what they imagined to be a greasy, oily product. By dropping Oil from the name and updating the packaging, Procter & Gamble breathed new life into this old, successful brand. Interestingly, the name Olay, which originally was made up by the chemists who developed the product, is a surprisingly good name when marketing the product globally. The word is easily pronounced in most languages and hints at being of Spanish origin with its similar pronunciation to the Spanish word *olé*, which means a shout of approval to a bullfighter or other performer.

Source: Adapted from Emily Nelson, "Procter & Gamble Tries to Hide Wrinkles in Aging Beauty Fluid," *Wall Street Journal Online*, May 16, 2000. Copyright 2000 by DOW JONES & CO INC. Reproduced with permission of DOW JONES & CO INC. in the format Textbook via Copyright Clearance Center.

The Ever-Changing American Household

A household represents an independent housing entity, either rental property (e.g., a single room or an apartment) or owned property (a mobile home, condominium, or house). As of 2000, there were *105.5 million* households in the United States, of which 71.8 million (68.1 percent) were family households (i.e., two or more related people occupying the household) and 33.7 million (31.9 percent) nonfamily households.[39] The average household size across all 105.5 million American households was 2.6 people. Family households had an average of 3.1 family members.[40]

Households are growing in number, shrinking in size, and changing in character. The traditional American family—that is, married couples with children younger than 18—represents less than one-fourth (23.5 percent) of all U.S. households, whereas in 1960 such families constituted 45 percent of all households.[41] The number of new households has grown twice as fast as the population, while household size has declined. In 1950, families constituted 90 percent of all households, whereas in 2000 fewer than 70 percent of all households were family units.

"Every Time I See Them, I Think About You. Your Sweetie."

Sometimes the best intentions go awry, as illustrated by the following case involving the advertising of flowers in Germany. Funding for the campaign was made available in large part by German taxpayers, though the European Union actually discharged most of the 15 million euros ($13 million) to support the advertising effort.

A direct-mail advertising campaign was designed to persuade young men in the age category 20 to 32 that flowers can be an exciting gift. A creative effort was needed to accomplish this task. Accordingly, the advertising agency in charge developed the idea of sending multiple, handwritten-appearing postcards to select men in the targeted age group. The first card was posted with this wording: "Dear (recipient's name), Thanks for the wonderful flowers! Every time I see them, I think about you. Your

Sweetie." A following card read: "Hello (recipient's name), it could have been so nice if you had really given your Sweetie flowers. But you didn't. So do it. She'll certainly be happy!"

Not a bad idea, don't you agree? In actuality, this creative execution was disastrous. Problem is, the postcards were more-than-occasionally intercepted by recipients' wives or girlfriends. Thinking the "Your Sweetie" postcard was legitimate, jealous wives and girlfriends accused their husbands/boyfriends of being unfaithful. After receiving numerous complaints from angry couples, the agency changed the campaign. Fortunately, the initial campaign was mailed to a test sample of only 7,000 homes, so the damage was limited.

Source: Adapted from Dagmar Aalund, "Say It with Flowers: EU Criticized for Funding Offbeat Ad Campaign," *Wall Street Journal Online*, October 9, 2000. Copyright 2000 by DOW JONES & CO INC. Reproduced with permission of DOW JONES & CO INC. in the format Textbook via Copyright Clearance Center.

The changing composition of the American household has tremendous implications for marketing communicators, especially advertisers. Advertising will have to reflect the widening range of living situations that exist. This is particularly true in the case of households with a single occupant. Singles and unrelated couples or friends living together re present a large and ever-growing group, with more than 30 million nonfamily households as of 2000.

Many advertisers make special appeals to the buying interests and needs of singles, appealing in food ads, for example, to such needs as ease and speed of preparation, maintenance simplicity, and small serving sizes. Reaching singles requires special media-selection efforts because singles (1) tend not to be big prime-time television viewers but are skewed instead toward the late fringe hours (after 11 p.m.), (2) are disproportionately more likely than the rest of the population to view cable television, and (3) are disproportionately heavy magazine readers.

Ethnic Population Developments

America has always been a melting pot. It became even more so in recent decades. The largest ethnic groups in the United States are Hispanics and African Americans. Ethnic minorities now represent nearly one of three people in the United States. In recognition of the growing role of ethnic groups, the following sections examine population developments and MarCom implications for African, Hispanic, and Asian Americans.

A few background statistics will be helpful to set the stage for these discussions. First, as of 2000 the population of approximately 281 million Americans was distributed in roughly the following fashion:[42]

White, not Hispanic	71 percent
Black, not Hispanic	12 percent
Hispanic, of any race	12 percent
Asian and Pacific Islanders	4 percent
American Indians, Eskimos, and Aleut	1 percent

Non-Hispanic whites' share of the U.S. population is projected to decline from 71 percent to 67.3 percent of the total population by the year 2010.[43] The implication is obvious: Marketers and marketing communicators need to do a better job in developing products and MarCom strategies that are designed to meet the unique needs of ethnic groups because ethnicity plays an important role in directing consumer behavior.[44]

African Americans. Non-Hispanic African Americans totaled approximately 34.7 million individuals, or slightly more than 12 percent of the U.S. population. African Americans are characterized more by their common heritage than by skin color. This heritage "is conditioned by an American beginning in slavery, a shared history of discrimination and suffering, confined housing opportunities, and denial of participation in many aspects of the majority culture."[45] Although many black Americans share a common culture in that they have similar values, beliefs, and distinguishable behaviors, African Americans do not represent a single market any more than whites do.

Several notable reasons explain why African Americans are attractive consumers for many companies: (1) The average age of black Americans is considerably younger than that for whites; (2) African Americans are geographically concentrated, with approximately three-fourths of all blacks living in just 16 states (California, Texas, Illinois, Louisiana, Alabama, Georgia, Florida, South Carolina, North Carolina, Maryland, Michigan, Ohio, Pennsylvania, Virginia, New York, and New Jersey)[46]; and (3) African Americans tend to purchase prestige and name-brand products in greater proportion than do whites.

These impressive figures notwithstanding, many companies make no special efforts to communicate with African Americans. This is foolish, for research indicates that blacks are responsive to advertisements placed in black-oriented media and to advertisements that make personalized appeals by using African-American models and advertising contexts with which blacks can identify. Major corporations are developing effective programs for communicating with black consumers. For example, Sears, Roebuck & Co. in the late 1990s launched its first ad campaign that specifically targeted African Americans.[47] Jaguar Cars North America embarked on a major direct marketing effort to African Americans in 2000. Approximately 1 million advertising brochures were mailed to middle-aged African Americans (i.e., ages 35 to 54) who had annual incomes of $75,000 or more.[48]

Although greater numbers of companies are realizing the importance of directing special marketing communications efforts to African Americans, it is important to emphasize that black consumers do *not* constitute a homogeneous market. African Americans exhibit different purchasing behaviors according to their lifestyles, values, and demographics. Therefore, companies must use different advertising media, distribution channels, advertising themes, and pricing strategies as they market to the various subsegments of the African-American population.

Hispanic Americans (Latinos).[49] The U.S. Hispanic population grew from only 4 million in 1950 to approximately 35.3 million in 2000 and now is America's largest minority with a slight edge over African Americans in share of the total U.S. population (12.5 percent versus 12.3 percent).[50] The U.S. Census estimates that the Latino population will grow to 43.7 million by 2010.[51] It is estimated that by 2025 Hispanics will constitute 43 percent of the California population, 38 percent of Texas, and 24 percent of Florida.[52] The largest percentage of Hispanics are Mexican Americans, but large numbers of Puerto Rican Americans, Latin Americans from Central and South America, and Cuban Americans also reside in the United States.

Hispanic Americans have historically been concentrated in a relatively few states such as California, Texas, New York, Florida, Illinois, Arizona, and New Jersey. However, Latinos are becoming increasingly mobile and have begun to fan out from the few states in which they originally concentrated. Table 3.4 provides information pertinent to the top five Hispanic markets in the U.S.

Marketing communicators in the past did not devote sufficient attention to Hispanic Americans; however, marketers have been "clambering aboard the

Table 3.4   Top Five Latino Markets

Market	Hispanic Population (millions)	Primary Ethnic Group
Los Angeles	6.2	Mexican
New York	3.5	Puerto Rican
Miami/Fort Lauderdale	1.4	Cuban
San Francisco/ Oakland/San Jose	1.3	Mexican
Chicago	1.3	Mexican

Source: Adapted from "Top Ten Hispanic Markets," *Brandweek Special Multicultural Media Report*, November 13, 2000. ©2000 VNU Business Media, Inc.

Latino bandwagon" since the Census Bureau announced a 58 percent increase in the number of Hispanic Americans between 1990 and 2000.[53] Yet companies advertise to Latinos much less than their market size would justify. Research has shown that the frequency of Hispanics' appearances in television advertising is considerably less than their proportion of the population.[54] Marketing communicators need to be aware of several important points when attempting to reach Hispanic consumers:

1. A large percentage of Hispanic Americans speak only Spanish or just enough English to get by; consequently, many Hispanics can be reached only via Spanish-language media. The following statistics indicate the percentages of Hispanics who speak Spanish and/or English at home:[55]
   - Only Spanish   21 percent
   - Spanish and English   15 percent
   - Only English   13 percent
   - Mostly Spanish   28 percent
   - Mostly English   23 percent

2. Because a large percentage of Hispanics use primarily Spanish media, it is important to target messages to some (but not all) Hispanics using Spanish-speaking media.

3. It appears that a key in designing effective advertising for Hispanics is to advertise to them in their *dominant language*.[56] As the percentages listed in point 1 indicate, approximately half of Hispanic Americans speak only or mostly Spanish at home. Hence, reaching these consumers requires the use of Spanish. However, for Hispanics who are English dominant, it makes greater sense to use English in advertising copy that reflects Hispanic values and culture.

4. Advertisers must be very careful in using the Spanish language. A number of snafus have been committed when advertisers translated their English campaigns to Spanish. For example, Frank Perdue, an East Coast marketer of chickens, had his famous slogan ("It takes a strong man to make a tender chicken") translated into Spanish so he could read it to Hispanics. Amusingly (probably to everyone except Frank), the Spanish version erroneously substituted "a sexually excited man" for "a strong man."[57]

5. It is absolutely critical to recognize that Latinos do *not* represent a single, unified market. There are strong intraethnic differences among Cubans, Mexicans, and Puerto Ricans, which thus necessitates unique appeals be directed to each Latino group. Moreover, as with all general groupings, there are huge differences within each group in terms of English-speaking ability, length of residence in the United States (and thus degree of acculturation), level of income, and so on. It is erroneous to speak of a Hispanic market, a Mexican market, or any other crude lumping of people who share their descent as a single defining factor.

Prominent marketers—Coca-Cola, Pepsi, Procter & Gamble, AT&T, MCI/WorldCom, Sears, and McDonald's, to name a few—are now investing heavily in Hispanic-oriented advertising and event sponsorships that reach Latinos in their local communities and often in joyous moods. Sponsoring Cinco de Mayo events, for example, is beginning to take on the same proportion as putting commercial support behind St. Patrick's Day celebrations.[58]

Asian Americans.   Asians in the United States include many nationalities: Asian Indians, Chinese, Filipino, Japanese, Korean, Vietnamese, and others. Asian Americans have been heralded as the newest "hot ethnic market." The demographics support this optimistic outlook. As of the year 2000, approximately 11 million Asians were living in the United States. By 2025 the U.S. Census Bureau has projected that nearly 22 million Asians will reside here. Though the 2.4 million Chinese are the largest group of Asians leaving in the United States, Asian Indians grew the fastest during the decade from 1990 to 2000, with that population doubling and now totaling 1.7 million in the United States.[59]

Asian Americans on average are better educated, have higher incomes, and occupy more prestigious job positions than any other segment of American society. The median household income for Asian Americans in one recent year was $46,700 compared with median incomes of $40,600, $30,300, and $25,900 for whites, Hispanics, and African Americans, respectively.[60]

It is important to emphasize that just as there is no single black or Hispanic market, there certainly does not exist a single Asian market. Moreover, unlike other ethnic groups, such as Hispanics, who share a similar language, Asian Americans speak a variety of uniquely different languages. Among Asian nationalities there are considerable differences in product choices and brand preferences. Even within each nationality there are variations in terms of English-language skills and financial well-being. Indeed, it is estimated that over 50 percent of all Asian Americans over the age of 5 do not speak English fluently, and many are "linguistically isolated" insofar as they live in homes where no adults speak any English.[61]

Some firms have been successful in marketing to specific Asian groups by customizing marketing programs to their values and lifestyles rather than merely translating Anglo programs. For example, Metropolitan Life, an insurance company, conducted research that determined that Asian parents' top priority was their children's security and education. Metropolitan translated this finding into a successful campaign targeted to Korean and Chinese Americans. An advertisement portrayed a baby in a man's arms with the heading "You protect your baby. Who protects you?" This ad, along with the hiring of Asians for Metropolitan Life's sales force, resulted in a substantial increase in insurance sales to Asians.[62] Reebok's sales among Asian Americans increased substantially after that company used tennis star Michael Chang in its advertisements.[63]

Mainstream marketers have greater media options than before for reaching Asian Americans: Asian-language radio stations are now burgeoning in areas where large concentrations of Asians live, and direct marketing via the mail is an outstanding medium for micromarketing to specific groups of Asian Americans.[64] The Internet is a valuable medium for reaching Asians inasmuch as 49 percent of Asians had Net access in 2000, compared to 50 percent of whites, and 30 percent of African Americans, and 24 percent of Hispanics.[65]

PSYCHOGRAPHIC TARGETING

The preceding discussion has described demographic factors and the implications they hold for marketing communicators. Demographics tell only part of the story, however. It is for this reason that marketing communicators also investigate consumers' lifestyles, or *psychographic* characteristics. When marketers first began to segment markets, they relied on the various demographic variables described earlier. More sophisticated marketers came to realize that demographics generally provide an insufficient basis for identifying and catering to differences in consumer demand. Some three decades ago, marketers turned to using psychographic data in conjunction with demographic characteristics as a means of obtaining a richer understanding of marketplace dynamics and differences in consumer behavior.[66]

For example, PowerBar, a brand of energy bar, is marketed primarily to young males (demographic variable) who are dedicated to exercise (a psychographic factor).[67] Nabisco Biscuit Company undertook a concerted marketing effort to reach the roughly one million U.S. consumers who maintain kosher dietary habits or believe that kosher products are of higher quality. Nabisco's Oreo cookie advertisements, for example, displayed a separated Oreo with a large U carved out of the white filling. The two parts of the separated cookie thus formed OU, which is the trademark of the Union of Orthodox Jewish Congregations, a kosher certification agency.[68] Although, demographically, there are approximately 6 million Jews living in the United States, only the one-sixth who practice kosher, a psychographic trait, are the targets of Nabisco's MarCom efforts.

In general, psychographics represents a combination of consumers' *a*ctivities, *i*nterests, and *o*pinions. Marketing researchers customize measures of these **AIO** items to suit the needs of their particular product categories and brands. For example, a maker of a mountain board, snowboard, or other form of equipment intended for "alternative athletes" might design a study to determine the particular activities, interests, and opinions—collectively, lifestyles—that best characterize the users of its brand and the competition. This information would be useful in designing advertising messages and selecting appropriate media vehicles. Table 3.5 lists illustrative AIO components.

Numerous marketing research firms conduct psychographic studies for individual clients. These studies are typically customized to the client's specific product category. In other words, AIO items included in a psychographics study are selected in view of the unique characteristics of the product category. Consider, for example, a study investigating the psychographic characteristics of purchasers of sport utility vehicles (SUVs). With reference to Table 3.5, such research undoubtedly would include questions relating to consumers' work, hobbies, entertainment, and sports activities along with items that tap into family, recreation, and community activities and social, political, and cultural opinions. It likely would be determined from such a study that purchasers of the Jeep Grand Cherokee and the Toyota Land Cruiser are similar demographically (i.e., nearly equivalent in terms of age and income) but differ psychographically.

In addition to psychographic studies that are customized to a client's particular needs, available also are "off-the-shelf" services that develop psychographic profiles of people that are independent of any particular product or service. Perhaps the best known of these is the Values and Lifestyles (VALS) classification model developed by the Stanford Research Institute, or SRI. In the most recent model, known as *VALS 2*, eight categories are identified based on a combination of demographic and lifestyle factors such as age, income, education, level of self-confidence, health, and interest in consumer issues.

Table 3.5   Illustrative AIO Components

Activities	Interests	Opinions
Work	Family	About themselves
Hobbies	Home	Social issues
Social events	Job	Politics
Vacation	Community	Business
Entertainment	Recreation	Economics
Club membership	Fashion	Education
Community	Food	Products
Shopping	Media	Future
Sports	Achievement	Culture

Source: Del I. Hawkins, Roger J. Best, and Kenneth A. Coney, *Consumer Behavior: Implications for Marketing Strategy*, 6th ed. (Chicago: Irwin, 1995), p. 329. Reprinted by permission from McGraw-Hill, a division of The McGraw-Hill Companies.

Figure 3.7 portrays the eight VALS 2 categories in a two-dimensional format. The horizontal dimension represents three self-orientations: (1) *principle-oriented* consumers are guided by their views of how the world should be; (2) *status-oriented* consumers are influenced by the actions and opinions of others; and (3) *action-oriented* consumers are directed by a desire for social or physical activity, variety, and risk taking. The vertical dimension is based on consumers' resources (income, education, intelligence, health, etc.), and ranges from minimal resources at the bottom to abundant resources at the top. The eight VALS 2 categories can be summarized as follows.[69]

Principle-oriented consumers are guided by their views of how the world should be.

1. *Fulfillers* (11 percent of population; median age 48) are mature, responsible, well-educated professionals who are informed about current affairs. They have high incomes but are practical, value-oriented consumers. Their leisure activities center on their homes. Fulfillers are a potential target for manufacturers of health-conscious products featured as low in cholesterol, salt, sugar, and fat. The Lean Cuisine advertisement in Figure 3.8 represents an appropriate appeal to Fulfillers.

2. *Believers* (16 percent of population; median age 58) are conservative and predictable consumers who favor established brands and American-made products. They have more modest incomes than Fulfillers, and their lives are centered around their families, churches, communities,

VALS 2 Groupings   Figure 3.7

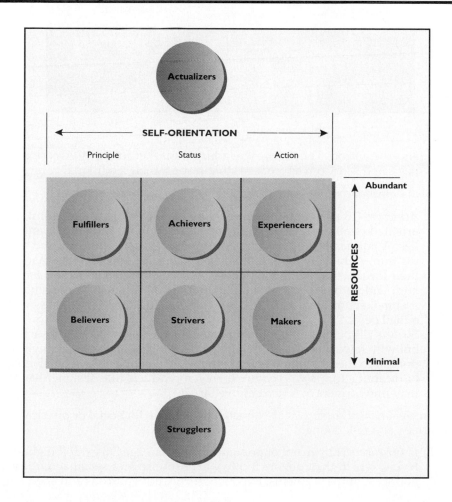

Figure 3.8

and the nation. They represent a target market for "buy American" appeals and MarCom approaches that respect their traditional values.

Status-oriented consumers are motivated by the actions and opinions of others.

3. *Achievers* (13 percent of population; median age 36) are successful, work-oriented people who mainly derive satisfaction from their jobs and families. A politically conservative group who respects authority and the status quo, Achievers favor established products and services that reflect their level of success to their peers. Achievers are an attractive target for high-end automobile and clothing marketers, expensive specialty shops, and makers of high-tech "luxury" items such as the Blackberry wireless e-mail device.

4. *Strivers* (13 percent of population; median age 34) are similar to Achievers but with fewer economic, social, and psychological resources. Style is important to them as they strive to emulate the people they wish they could be. Manufacturers who copy expensive products like designer handbags may find Strivers to be a receptive target.

Action-oriented consumers are directed by a desire for social or physical activity, variety, and risk taking.

5. *Experiencers* (12 percent of population; median age 26) exhibit high energy levels, which they devote to physical exercise and social activities. The youngest of the segments, Experiencers are adventurous and spend heav-

ily on clothing, fast food, music, and other youthful activities. Experiencers are a promising target for fast-food restaurants, clothing manufacturers/retailers, and health clubs.

6. *Makers* (13 percent of population; median age 30) are practical, self-sufficient consumers who focus on family, work, and physical recreation. Makers have little interest in the broader world and are only interested in those material possessions that have a practical or functional purpose. Sporting goods manufacturers and companies offering family-oriented activities and products might find Makers to be an attractive target market.

Two other groups of consumers are characterized by resource levels either below or above the other six categories.

7. *Strugglers* (14 percent of population; median age 61) have the lowest incomes and too few resources to be included in any consumer self-orientation. They do tend to be brand-loyal consumers within their limited means. They represent a market for manufacturers of products emphasizing value within the household products and food categories.

8. *Actualizers* (8 percent of population; median age 43) enjoy the highest incomes, strongest self-esteems, and abundant resources. Image is important as they buy the finer things in life. They represent a potential market for manufacturers of high-end products like luxury automobiles, expensive watches, lavish vacations, sumptuous dining, and splendid home furnishings.

Marketers use the detailed information from the VALS 2 model to position their brands, select media vehicles, and determine the sizes of the various potential market segments and their corresponding product needs. Moreover, as shown in Table 3.6, various buyer behaviors are related to VALS 2 lifestyle groupings. With 100 representing the base rate, or average level of consumption, Table 3.6 reveals distinct differences among the eight groups in terms of their consumption behaviors. Considering exercise activity, for example, it can be seen that Actualizers (index 145) and Experiencers (index 143) are the most likely to exercise, whereas Strugglers (index 39) and Believers (index 69) are the least likely to engage in this activity. Actualizers and Experiencers also are disproportionately more likely than all other groups to drink imported beer (indices of 238 and 216, respectively)—perhaps this is why they feel the need to exercise!

Although psychographic variables provide useful marketing information for segmentation purposes, these characteristics, compared to demographic variables, are more difficult to identify and measure. Secondary research of published data can tell a marketer how many male consumers aged 25 to 34 live in a particular market; however, secondary research cannot tell a marketer how many male Achievers aged 25 to 34 live in a particular market. Often marketers use psychographic variables along with other variables when segmenting markets. (You can take an online test of which VALS 2 category you fall into by going to the following Web site: http://future.sri.com/vals/surveynew.shtml.)

GEODEMOGRAPHIC TARGETING

The word geodemographic is a conjunction of *geography* and *demography*, which beautifully describes this form of targeting. The premise underlying geodemographic targeting is that people who reside in similar areas, such as neighborhoods or postal zip code zones, also share demographic and lifestyle similarities. Hence, knowing where people live also provides some information regarding their general marketplace behaviors. Several companies have developed services that delineate geographical areas into common groups, or clusters, wherein reside people with similar demographic and lifestyle characteristics. These companies (and their services, in parentheses) include CACI (ACORN), Donnelly Marketing

Table 3.6

Activities of the Eight VALS 2 Groups

Activity	Actualizers	Fulfillers	Believers	Achievers	Strivers	Experiencers	Makers	Strugglers
Buy hand tools	148	65	105	63	59	137	170	57
Barbecue outdoors	125	93	82	118	111	109	123	50
Do gardening	155	129	118	109	68	54	104	80
Do gourmet cooking	217	117	96	103	53	133	86	47
Drink coffee daily	120	119	126	88	87	55	91	116
Drink domestic beer	141	88	73	101	87	157	123	50
Drink herbal tea	171	125	89	117	71	115	81	68
Drink imported beer	238	93	41	130	58	216	88	12
Do activities with kids	155	129	57	141	112	89	116	32
Play team sports	114	73	69	104	110	172	135	34
Do cultural activities	293	63	67	96	45	154	63	14
Exercise	145	114	69	123	94	143	102	39
Do home repairs	161	113	85	82	53	88	171	58
Camp or hike	131	88	68	95	84	156	158	33
Do risky sports	190	48	36	52	59	283	171	7
Socialize weekly	109	64	73	90	96	231	94	62

Note: Table entries are index numbers. For example, the number 148 under Actualizers for "Buy hand tools" means that this group is 48 percent more likely to buy this product than are all groups on average.

Source: SRI International.

(ClusterPlus), National Decision Systems (Vision), Experian (MOSAIC), and Claritas (PRIZM). The following section describes Claritas's PRIZM system of geodemographic profiling.[70]

PRIZM, which stands for Potential Rating Index by Zip Markets, is a classification system that delineates every neighborhood in the United States into 62 clusters based on their unique demographic and lifestyle characteristics. The idea of geodemographic clustering is not restricted to the United States. Cluster systems have been developed for at least 25 countries, including Canada, most countries in Western Europe, some African countries, Australia, and Japan.[71] These clusters are labeled with colorful and descriptive names such as Blue Blood Estates, Bohemian Mix, Greenbelt Families, Boomers & Babies, Latino America, Towns & Gowns, Military Quarters, Shotguns & Pickups, Southside City, Norma Rae-ville, Mines & Mills, and Back Country Folks. Let us briefly characterize two of these clusters.[72]

Bohemian Mix, for example, describes intercity singles neighborhoods representing the most liberal lifestyle type in America. Bohemian Mixers are overwhelmingly single or divorced and many are gay. Illustrative neighborhoods are Dupont Circle (Washington, D.C.), Greenwich Village (New York, New York), and Broadway (Seattle, Washington). Bohemian Mix neighborhoods represent progressive, multiracial mixtures of students, artists, writers, executives, aging hippies, and so on. Foreign videos, espresso makers, European travel, imported beer and wine, *GQ* and *Mademoiselle* magazines, and *Nightline* on TV are just some of the lifestyles, products, and media enjoyed by Bohemian Mixers.

Towns & Gowns is the name given to America's college towns, places like Boulder (Colorado University), Berkeley (University of California), Gainesville (University of Florida), Stillwater (University of Oklahoma), and Bowling Green, Ohio (Bowling Green State University). Foreign videos, pool, tequila, DoveBars, *Cosmopolitan*, *Sports Illustrated*, *Saturday Night Live*, and *Friends* are a few of the products, lifestyles, and media liked by many students residing in the dorms and neighborhoods in these college towns.

Many major marketers use PRIZM, Donnelly's ClusterPlus, or other geodemographic clustering services to help them with important MarCom decisions. Selecting geographical locales for spot television advertising and identifying candidates for direct mailing are just two of the decisions facilitated by the availability of geodemographic data. Interested students are strongly encouraged to read the works of Michael Weiss, who has popularized geodemographic clustering via his books, such as the one cited in endnote 70.

SUMMARY

This chapter has emphasized the importance of two interrelated topics: positioning and targeting. Positioning involves developing a short description of what a brand stands for and what it is intended to mean to the target audience in comparison to competitive brands. Positioning is undertaken by emphasizing a brand's features or attributes, its user or usage imagery, and the functional, symbolic, or experiential needs that it satisfies. Targeting communication efforts to specific demographic, psychographic, or geodemographic groups is an aspect of a brand's MarCom program that goes hand in hand with the brand's positioning strategy.

Three major demographic developments were reviewed in this chapter: (1) the age structure of the U.S. population, (2) the changing American household, and (3) ethnic population developments. Some of the major demographic developments discussed included (1) the continuous shifting of the U.S. population to the South and West, (2) the progressive aging of the U.S. population from an average age of 33 in 1990 to nearly 36 years old in 2000 and to an expected average age of 38.5 by 2025, (3) the dramatic increase in the percentage of single American adults in the past two decades, and (4) the explosive growth of ethnic minorities, particularly Hispanics.

Marketing communicators have in recent decades targeted customers using knowledge about their activities, interests, and opinions (or, collectively, their lifestyles) to better understand what people want and how they respond to advertising, direct mail, and other forms of marketing communications. The term *psychographics* describes this form of targeting effort. Many customized studies are conducted to identify psychographic segments directly applicable to the marketer's product category and brand, but syndicated research systems such as SRI's VALS 2 system also provide useful information for making important MarCom decisions. The VALS 2 system classifies people into one of eight groups based on a combination of their self-orientation and resources: Fulfillers, Believers, Achievers, Strivers, Experiencers, Makers, Strugglers, and Actualizers.

A final section of the chapter reviewed the role of geodemographic targeting. This form of targeting basically identifies clusters of consumers who share similar demographic and lifestyle characteristics. Donnelly's ClusterPlus and Claritas's PRIZM are two well known and respected clustering systems that identify meaningful groupings of geographical units such as zip code areas.

Find more resources to help you study at http://shimp.swcollege.com!

DISCUSSION QUESTIONS

1. Imagine that you are in the market for a job after graduation. Develop a positioning statement for yourself that will help you land the "job of your dreams." Of course, be sure to read the section on positioning prior to writing your personal positioning statement.

2. Consider your favorite brand of nonalcoholic beverage. Now, within the product subcategory in which this brand competes, come up with a new competitive brand (name and all) that would compete against your favorite beverage brand. Develop two positioning statements for this brand: one based on user imagery and the other based on usage imagery.

3. Consider your favorite brand of snack food, whether salted or sweetened. As with question 2, come up with a new competitive brand that would compete against your favorite snack food. Develop three positioning statements for your new snack food: functional, symbolic, and experiential.

4. Demographers tell us that households in the United States are growing in number, shrinking in size, and changing in character. Assume that you are the vice president of marketing for a corporation that manufactures chairs and sofas, say La-Z-Boy Corporation. What specific implications do these changes hold for your company?

5. As a percentage of the total population, Americans aged 19 and younger represent a much smaller percentage of the population today (approximately 29 percent) than they did a quarter of a century ago (approximately 40 percent in 1965). In light of this development, what would you do if you were the CEO of a firm that markets exclusively youth-oriented products?

6. African American, Hispanic American, and Asian American consumers do not signify three homogeneous markets; rather, they represent many markets composed of people who merely share a common race and/or language. Explain.

7. Explain the reasons for the relentless aging of the U.S. population, and discuss some implications this will have on marketing and marketing communications into the first decade of the 21st century.

8. Due to rather dramatic changes in the population composition of the United States, one could argue that advertising in earlier decades, say the 1970s and 1980s, was a lot easier than it is today. From your reading of the chapter, provide three or four reasons to support this argument.

9. Assume you are brand manager of a food product that is consumed by all Americans—blacks, whites, Hispanics, Asians, and others. You are considering running an extended advertising campaign on prime-time television that uses Hispanic actors and appeals to Hispanic consumers. Aside from cost considerations, what reservations might you have about this type of campaign?

10. When the mature market was discussed, it was noted that advertising aimed at this group should portray them as vital, busy, forward looking, and attractive or romantic. Interview several mature consumers and coalesce their views on how they perceive advertising directed at them and their peers. Your interview results along with those from fellow students should lead to an interesting class discussion.

11. What are your views on the targeting of products to children? Aside from your personal views, discuss the issue of targeting to children from two additional perspectives: first, that of a brand manager who is responsible for the profitability of a child-oriented product, and second, from the viewpoint of an ethicist. Imagine what each of these parties might say about the practice of targeting products to children.

12. Based on your personal background and using the VALS 2 system, how would you categorize most of the adults with whom you and your family associate? Complete the survey at the following URL from the perspective of your father or mother: http://future.sri.com/vals/surveynew.shtml.

13. Identify magazine advertisements that reflect appeals to at least five of the eight VALS 2 groups.

14. Describe in as much detail as possible the neighborhood in which you were raised. Come up with a label (similar to the PRIZM cluster names) that captures the essence of your neighborhood.

ENDNOTES

1. Kevin J. Clancy and Peter C. Krieg, *Counter-Intuitive Marketing: Achieve Great Results Using Uncommon Sense* (New York: Free Press, 2000), 110.

2. Ibid., 111.

3. C. Whan Park, Bernard J. Jaworski, and Deborah J. MacInnis, "Strategic Brand Concept-Image Management," *Journal of Marketing* 50 (October 1986), 136. The following discussion of functional, symbolic, and experiential needs/benefits adheres to Park et al.'s conceptualizations.

4. For further discussion of this point, see ibid.

5. Thomas S. Robertson, Joan Zielinski, and Scott Ward, *Consumer Behavior* (Glenview, Ill.: Scott, Foresman and Company, 1984), 340.

6. Based on projection from the U.S. Census Bureau's World POPClock Projection (http://www.census.gov/cgi-bin/ipc/popclockw).

7. "Profiles of General Demographic Characteristics, *2000 Census of Population and Housing*, Table DP-1 (May 2001).

8. http://www.census.gov/population/projections/nation/summary/np-t1.txt.

9. Tom Morganthau, "The Face of the Future," *Newsweek*, January 27, 1997, 58.

10. http://www.census.gov/population/projections/nation/summary/np-t4-f.txt.

11. Stephanie Thompson, "'Die, Bad Breath,' Eclipse Proclaims in $15 Mil Ad Push," *Advertising Age*, October 9, 2000, 103.

12. Bob Woods, "Growing Old and Loving It," *Promo*, August 2000, 27.

13. Emily Nelson, "Baby Boomers Help Boost Sales of Luxury Skin-Care Products," *Wall Street Journal Interactive Edition*, June 12, 2001 (http://interactive.wsj.com/articles/SB992281782459263841.htm).

14. Ken Dychtwald and Greg Gable, "Portrait of a Changing Consumer," *Business Horizons*, January/February 1990, 62–73.

15. Yumiko Ono, "Some Hair-Color Sales Get Boost As Baby Boomers Battle Aging," *The Wall Street Journal*, February 3, 1994, B7; Joe Schwartz, "Boomer," *Brandweek*, October 1996, 42.

16. The "epicenter of society" expression is attributed to Fred Elkind, an executive with the Ogilvy & Mather advertising agency, and cited in Christy Fisher, "Boomers Scatter in Middle Age," *Advertising Age*, January 11, 1993, 23.

17. William Lazer, "Dimensions of the Mature Market," *The Journal of Consumer Marketing* 3 (summer 1986), 24.

18. The expression "repair kit" is from Charles D. Schewe, "Marketing to Our Aging Population: Responding to Physiological Changes," *The Journal of Consumer Marketing* 5 (summer 1988), 61–73.

19. Chris Kelly, "Active Lifestyles Central to Targeting," *Advertising Age*, July 10, 2000, s8.

20. Rick Adler, "Stereotypes Won't Work with Seniors Anymore," *Advertising Age*, November 11, 1996.

21. John Dodge, "Seniors Often Are Overlooked by Web Sites, Hardware Firms," *Wall Street Journal Interactive Edition*, October 3, 2000 (http://interactive.wsj.com/articles/SB970499405528507648.htm); Sara Teasdale Montgomery, "Senior Surfers Grab Web Attention," *Advertising Age*, July 10, 2000, s4.

22. Dodge, "Seniors Often Are Overlooked by Web Sites, Hardware Firms."

23. Ibid.

24. The research was performed by George P. Moschis and is reported in "Survey: Age Is Not Good Indicator of Consumer Need," *Marketing Communications*, November 21, 1988, 6. See also George P. Moschis and Anil Mathur, "How They're Acting Their Age," *Marketing Management* 2, no. 2 (1993), 40–50.

25. Lisa Bannon, "For Toys and Clothes, the Six-to-12 Set Is Showing Teenage Purchasing Habits," *The Wall Street Journal Interactive Edition*, October 13, 1998.

26. Christy Fisher, "Wooing Boomers' Babies," *Advertising Age*, July 22, 1991, 3, 30.

27. Miguel Helft, "Leapfrogging the Competition," *The Industry Standard*, April 9, 2001, 68–75.

28. Horst H. Stipp, "Children As Consumers," *American Demographics*, February 1988, 27–32; Ellen Graham, "As Kids Gain Power of Purse, Marketing Takes Aim at Them," *The Wall Street Journal*, January 19, 1988, 1; John Schwartz, "Portrait of a Generation," *Newsweek* Special Issue, summer 1991, 6–9; and Monte Williams, "'Parental Guidance' Lost on This Crop," *Advertising Age*, July 30, 1990, 1, 28.

29. Youth Monitor (winter 1987), Yankelovich, Skelly and White/Clancy, Shulman, Inc.

30. Deborah Roedder John, "Consumer Socialization of Children: A Retrospective

Look at Twenty-Five Years of Research," *Journal of Consumer Research* 26 (December 1999), 183–213; Elizabeth S. Moore and Richard J. Lutz, "Children, Advertising, and Product Experiences: A Multimethod Inquiry," *Journal of Consumer Research* 27 (June 2000), 31–48.

31. James U. McNeal, "It's Not Easy Being Tween," *Brandweek*, April 16, 2001, 22.

32. Ibid.

33. For an academic treatment on the topic, see Sharon E. Beatty and Salil Talpade, "Adolescent Influence in Family Decision Making: A Replication with Extension," *Journal of Consumer Research* 21 (September 1994), 332–341; and Kay M. Palan and Robert E. Wilkes, "Adolescent-Parent Interaction in Family Decision Making," *Journal of Consumer Research* 24 (September 1997), 159–169. A provocative treatment on teenagers' work, study, and spending behaviors is available in Steven Waldman and Karen Springen, "Too Old, Too Fast?" *Newsweek*, November 16, 1992, 80–87.

34. Dan Lippe, "It's All in Creative Delivery," *Advertising Age*, June 25, 2001, s8.

35. Carrie LaFerle, Steven M. Edwards, and Wei-Na Lee, "Teens' Use of Traditional Media and the Internet," *Journal of Advertising Research* 40 (May/June 2000), 55.

36. William Strauss and Neil Howe, *Generations: The History of America's Future, 1584–2069* (New York: William Morrow and Company, Inc., 1991). For a less technical treatment written by an advertising person, see Karen Ritchie, *Marketing to Generation X* (New York: Lexington Books, 1995).

37. For an intelligent critique of the stereotypical treatment of the Gen X label, see David Ashley Morrison, "Beyond the Gen X Label," *Brandweek*, March 17, 1997, 23–25.

38. Yankelovich Partners, cited in "Don't Mislabel Gen X," *Brandweek*, May 15, 1995, 32, 34.

39. "Profiles of General Demographic Characteristics, *2000 Census of Population and Housing*, Table DP-1 (May 2001).

40. Ibid.

41. Vanessa O'Connell and Jon E. Hilsenrath, "Madison Avenue Is Cautious As U.S. Households Change," *Wall Street Journal Interactive Edition*, May 15, 2001 (http://interactive.wsj.com/articles/SB989878428619130075.htm).

42. http://www.census.gov/population/estimates/nation/intfile3-1.txt.

43. http://www.census.gov/population/projections/nation/summary/np-t5-c.txt.

44. See Douglas M. Stayman and Rohit Deshpande, "Situational Ethnicity and Consumer Behavior," *Journal of Consumer Research* 16 (December 1989), 361–371; and Cynthia Webster, "Effects of Hispanic Ethnic Identification on Marital Roles in the Purchase Decision Process," *Journal of Consumer Research* 16 (September 1994), 319–331.

45. James F. Engel, Roger D. Blackwell, and Paul W. Miniard, *Consumer Behavior*, 8th ed. (Fort Worth: The Dryden Press, 1995), 647.

46. Bob Woods, "Urban Sprawl," *Promo*, September 2000, 29.

47. Alice Z. Cuneo, "New Sears Label Woos Black Women," *Advertising Age*, May 5, 1997, 6.

48. Jean Halliday, "Spike Lee's Jaguar Ads Begin First Test Mailing," *Advertising Age*, December 18, 2000, 18.

49. Hispanic is a government-invented term that encompasses people of Spanish or Latin American descent or Spanish-language background. Many people of Latin American descent prefer to be referred to as Latinos.

50. Michael Barone, "The Many Faces of America," *U.S. News & World Report*, March 19, 2001, 18.

51. http://www.census.gov/population/projections/nation/summary/np-t5-c.txt.

52. http://www.census.gov/population/projections/state/9525rank/caprsrel, txprsrel,flprsrel.txt.

53. Marci McDonald, "Madison Avenue's New Latin Beat," *U.S. News & World Report*, June 4, 2001, 42.

54. Thomas H. Stevenson and Patricia E. McIntyre, "A Comparison of the Portrayal and Frequency of Hispanics and Whites in English Language Television Advertising," *Journal of Current Issues and Research in Advertising* 17 (spring 1995), 65–74.

55. Christy Fisher, "Marketing to Hispanics," *Advertising Age*, January 23, 1995, 29, 37.

56. Sigfredo A. Hernandez and Larry M. Newman, "Choice of English vs. Spanish Language in Advertising to Hispanics," *Journal of Current Issues and Research in Advertising* 14 (fall 1992), 35–46.

57. "Snafus Persist in Marketing to Hispanics," *Marketing News*, June 24, 1983, 3.

58. Joel Millman, "U.S. Marketers Turn Cinco de Mayo into Pan-Ethnic National Celebration, *Wall Street Journal Interactive Edition*, May 1, 2001 (http://interactive.wsj.com/articles/SB98866644876206943.htm.

59. Nicholas Kulish, "U.S. Asian Population Increased and Diversified," *Wall Street Journal Interactive Edition*, May 15, 2001 (http://interactive.wsj.com/articles/SB989876964229972690.htm.

60. Bob Woods, "Asian Persuasion," *Promo*, April 2000, 33.

61. Christy Fisher, "Marketers Straddle Asia-America Curtain," *Advertising Age*, November 7, 1994, S2.

62. John Schwartz, Dorothy Wang, and Nancy Matsumoto, "Tapping into a

Blossoming Asian Market," *Newsweek*, September 7, 1987, 47–48.

63. Cyndee Miller, "'Hot' Asian-American Market Not Starting Much of a Fire Yet," *Advertising Age*, January 21, 1991, 12.

64. "Targeting the Asian-American Market in Direct Mail," *Asian Connection* 1, no. 1 (1995), 3.

65. Genia Jones, "Digital Divide Persists," *The Industry Standard*, November 6, 2000, 224.

66. Joseph T. Plummer, "The Concept and Application of Life Styles Segmentation," *Journal of Marketing* 38 (January 1974), 33–37.

67. Stephanie Thompson, "PowerBar Budget Gets Healthy Hike to $20 Mil," *Advertising Age*, September 25, 2000, 8.

68. Stephanie Thompson, "Nabisco Keeps Kosher in New Ad Push," *Advertising Age*, September 25, 2000, 58.

69. The following discussion is based on Martha Farnsworth Riche, "Psychographics for the 1990s," *American Demographics*, July 1989, 24–31, 53.

70. Michael J. Weiss, *The Clustered World: How We Live, What We Buy, and What It All Means About Who We Are* (Boston: Little, Brown and Company, 2000).

71. Ibid., 5.

72. Based on ibid., 212–213 for the Bohemian Mix and 240–241 for Towns & Gowns.

Chapter Four

THE COMMUNICATION PROCESS, MEANING CREATION, AND THE FUNDAMENTALS OF CONSUMERS' USE OF MARCOM INFORMATION

Chapter Objectives

After studying this chapter, you should be able to:

1. Appreciate the elements of the communications process.
2. Understand the nature of meaning in marketing communications using a perspective known as semiotics.
3. Describe marketing communicators' usage of three forms of figurative language (simile, metaphor, and allegory).
4. Discuss two models of consumer behavior: the consumer processing model (CPM) and the hedonic, experiential model (HEM).
5. Describe the eight stages of consumer information processing.
6. Explain the fundamental features of the hedonic, experiential model.

Opening Vignette: Hamburger Helper and "Doing Enough"

Time is a precious commodity to women and men throughout the world, perhaps especially in countries such as the United States where work weeks regularly extend beyond 40 hours and, in married-couple households, both husband and wife often are employed outside the home. Also, many single people work long hours and return home after a long day's work tired, hungry, and not particularly motivated to spend time preparing a nice meal. Eating out is always an option, but this grows old and can be expensive. Millions of consumers throughout the world thus confront the challenge of preparing an evening meal that is quick yet still good tasting and psychologically involving.

The answer for many American consumers is products such as Hamburger Helper, or Helper for short—a precooked dry mix that requires the consumer to simply heat the product in a skillet along with adding an item such as cooked hamburger. In fact, it is estimated that more than 40 percent of evening meals in American households are prepared in less than 30 minutes. For well over a generation, Helper has been the leading brand of convenient-dinner products—a $15 billion product category that includes dry mixes (such as Hamburger Helper), frozen meals, and prepared foods. The CEO of General Mills, makers of Hamburger Helper, expresses the brand's success this way: "Hamburger Helper was once thought to be something you did instead of cooking. Now it *is* cooking."

Hamburger Helper has become a symbol of American dining. During the 1990s sales of Helper increased by an incredible average of 7 percent a year, which compares to a population growth of approximately only 2 percent per year. Helper's growth was fostered by the increasingly time-pressured household and facilitated by the continuous addition of new and popular flavors to the product line—Pizza Pasta, Double Cheese Pizza, Beef Taco, Zesty Mexican, and so on.

What is the secret to Hamburger Helper's success? The continual addition of new flavors to overcome boredom is part of the answer, but beyond this it seems that the product nicely accommodates consumers' needs to simultaneously prepare a meal quickly and remain suitably involved in the process so as to avoid a tinge of guilt over a sense of being lazy. Hamburger Helper's brand manager explains it this way when comparing the preparation of Helper with the mere warming of frozen pizza: "With a frozen pizza, you're bringing it out of a cold state, you're bringing it out of the morgue. There's not that much aroma. You don't feel great about it. Mom didn't really do much. With Helper, she's taking

Source: Adapted from Jonathan Eig, "Hamburger Helper Faces New Rivals in the Race to Offer Homemade Feel," *Wall Street Journal Online*, March 7, 2001 (http://interactive.wsj.com/articles/SB98391 5943536949337.htm). Copyright 2001 by DOW JONES & CO INC. Reproduced with permission of DOW JONES & CO INC. in the format Textbook via Copyright Clearance Center.

the meat, taking the protein, and transforming it into a meal. You're stirring. You're browning. You're doing enough."

The quest for speedy meal solutions while simultaneously allowing Mom (or Dad) to feel involved in the process has spawned a host of new products attempting to steal share from Hamburger Helper. For example, Birds Eye developed Voila!, which is a frozen product containing precooked meat, starch, and vegetables. People simply throw the whole mess into a skillet—which research demonstrates is overwhelmingly preferred to the microwave for "quicky" cooking—and in minutes they have a finished dinner. Stouffer's Skillet Sensations and Green Giant Complete Skillet Meals are brands that are similar to Birds Eye's Voila! Consumers apparently prefer these new offerings because they don't have to think ahead about thawing out, say, ground beef or purchasing the meat prior to preparing a Hamburger Helper dinner. Yet because buying and preparing their own meat is more psychologically involving, it might be that these new, no-work-required alternatives to Hamburger Helper are mere novelties and that Helper will recap lost market share in a matter of time.

The *Opening Vignette* touches on various aspects of the content of this chapter, which addresses the communication process, the nature of meaning and meaning transfer, and fundamentals of consumer behavior. All these topics are essential to an appreciation of marketing communications. The chapter begins with a formal description of the communication process; considers then the nature of meaning and the semiotics of marketing communications; and concludes with a detailed description of how consumers receive, process, and respond to MarCom information.

THE COMMUNICATION PROCESS

The word *communication* is derived from the Latin word *communis*, which means "common." In other words, communication can be thought of as the process of establishing a commonness, or oneness, of thought between a message sender, such as an advertiser, and a receiver, such as consumer.[1] The key point in this definition is that there must be a commonness of thought developed between sender and receiver if communication is to occur. Commonness of thought implies that a *sharing* relationship must exist between, say, an advertiser and the consumer.

Consider a situation in which a salesperson is delivering a presentation to a consumer who appears to be listening to what the salesperson is saying but who actually is thinking about a personal problem. Contrary to what an observer might perceive, communication is *not* occurring because thought is not being shared. The reason for the lack of communication in this instance is, of course, the inattentiveness of the intended receiver. Although sound waves are bouncing against receiving eardrums, the consumer is not actively hearing and thinking about what the salesperson is saying.

An analogy can be drawn between a human receiver and a television set. A television set is continuously bombarded by electromagnetic waves from different stations; yet it will only receive the station to which the channel selector is tuned. Human receivers also are bombarded with stimuli from many sources, and, like the television set, people are selective in what information they choose to process.

Both sender and receiver must be active participants in the same communicative relationship for thought to be shared. Communication is something one does *with* another person, not *to* another person. A British advertising researcher conveys the same idea when she reminds us that the question for advertisers is not "What does advertising do to people?" but rather "What do people do with advertising? What do people use advertising for?"[2]

Elements in the Communication Process

All communication activities involve the following elements: (1) a *source*, who has a (2) *communication objective*, which is transformed into a (3) *message*, which is delivered via a (4) *message channel* to a (5) *receiver*, which experiences a (6) *communication outcome.* That outcome represents (7) *feedback* to the message source. And the entire process is subject to interference, interruptions, or, in general, (8) *noise.* Figure 4.1 displays this process. Each element is briefly described.

Source.   In marketing communications, the **source** is a communicator in some MarCom capacity—an advertiser, salesperson, sales promoter—who has thoughts (ideas, sales points, etc.) to share with an individual customer or prospect or an entire target audience. The source *encodes* a message to accomplish a communication objective. **Encoding** is the process of translating thought into symbolic form. The source selects specific *signs* from a nearly infinite variety of words, sentence structures, symbols, and nonverbal elements to design a message that will communicate effectively with the target audience.

Communication Objective.   As established in Chapter 2, the objectives of MarCom efforts include creating brand awareness, implanting positive associations in the consumer's memory as a basis for a positive brand image, and affecting behavior. Creative, effective marketing communications requires that the advertiser (or communicator in any other MarCom capacity) have a crystal clear idea of what should be accomplished.

Message.   The **message** itself is a symbolic expression of what the communicator intends to accomplish. Advertisements, sales presentations, package designs, and point-of-purchase signs are some of the various forms of MarCom messages.

Message Channel.   The **message channel** is the path through which the message moves from source to receiver. Television, radio, newspapers, magazines, the Internet, billboards, T-shirts, packages, point-of-purchase displays, signs painted on automobiles, and advertisements at movie theaters are just some of the more notable channels for delivering brand messages. Messages also are transmitted to customers directly via salespeople and indirectly via word-of-mouth communication from friends and family members.

Figure 4.1   Elements in the Communication Process

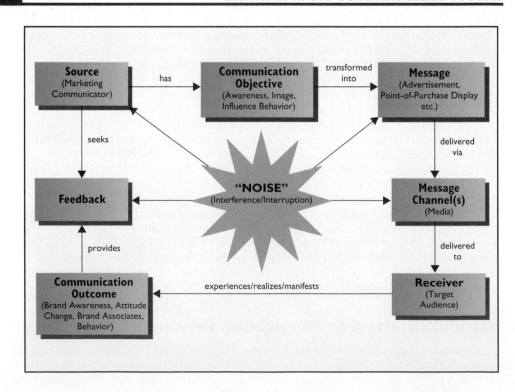

Receiver.   The **receiver** is the person or group of people (target audience) with whom the source attempts to share ideas. In marketing communications, receivers are the prospective and present customers of an organization's product or service. **Decoding** involves activities undertaken by receivers to interpret—or derive meaning from—marketing messages. (Because the meaning formation process plays such a crucial role in all marketing communications, the following section discusses the nature of meaning in detail.)

Communication Outcome.   The target audience experiences, realizes, or manifests an outcome(s) in response to the message (or, more likely, a stream of messages) received from a brand communicator. It is hoped that the outcome matches the communicator's general objective and results in increased levels of brand awareness, more positive attitudes, or greater purchasing of the brand.

Feedback.   **Feedback** affords the source a way of monitoring how accurately the intended message is being received and whether it is accomplishing its intended objective(s). As suggested in Figure 4.1, feedback allows the source to determine whether the original message hit the target accurately or whether it needs to be altered. Thus, the feedback mechanism offers the source some measure of control in the communication process. Using research-based feedback from their markets, management can reexamine and often correct ineffective or misdirected MarCom messages.

Noise.   A message moving through a channel is subject to the influence of extraneous and distracting stimuli. These stimuli interfere with or interrupt reception of the message in its pure and original form. Such interference and distortion is called **noise.** Noise may occur at any stage in the communication process (see Figure 4.1). For example, at the point of message encoding, the sender may be unclear about what the message is intended to accomplish. A likely result is a poorly focused and perhaps even contradictory message rather than a message that is clear-cut and integrated. Noise also occurs in the message channel—a fuzzy television signal, a crowded magazine page on which an advertisement is surrounded by competitive clutter, or a personal sales interaction that is interrupted repeatedly by telephone calls. Noise also can be present at the receiver/decoding stage of the process. An infant might cry during a television commercial and block out critical points in the sales message; passengers in an automobile might talk and not listen to a radio commercial; or the receiver simply may not possess the knowledge base needed to understand fully the promotional message.

MARKETING COMMUNICATIONS AND MEANING

Fundamental to the communication process is the concept of *meaning.* Marketers attempt to accomplish certain brand-related objectives when designing MarCom messages, whereas consumers construct meanings from messages that may or may not be the same as that intended by the marketing communicator. This section discusses the nature of meaning in marketing communications using a perspective known as *semiotics.* **Semiotics,** broadly speaking, is the study of signs and the analysis of meaning-producing events.[3]

Before proceeding, it is important to emphasize that our interest in semiotics is purely practical rather than theoretical or philosophical. The important point to appreciate is that the semiotics perspective sees meaning as a *constructive process.* That is, meaning is determined both by the message source's choice of signs and, just as importantly, by the receiver's unique social-cultural background and mind-set at the time he or she is exposed to a message. In other words, meaning is not thrust upon the consumers as if they are automatons that understand MarCom messages precisely as intended by the communicator. Rather, the consumer is actively involved in constructing meaning from MarCom messages, meaning that may or may not be equivalent to what the communicator intended to convey. The MarCom goal is, of course, to do everything possible to increase the odds that consumers will interpret messages exactly as they are intended.

The Nature of Signs

The fundamental concept in semiotics is the *sign*. Marketing communications in all its various forms uses signs in the creation of messages. When you read the word *sign*, you probably think of its everyday usages—such as road signs (stop, yield, danger, or directional signs), store signs, signs announcing a car or home for sale, and signs of abstract concepts such as happiness (the happy face sign). The general concept of sign encompasses these everyday notions but includes many other types of signs. That is, the concept of sign is an all-inclusive notion that comprises words, visualizations, tactile objects, olfactory sensations, and anything else that is perceivable by the senses and has the potential to communicate meaning to the receiver, or interpreter. By definition, a **sign** is something physical and perceivable that signifies something (the *referent*) to somebody (the *interpreter*) in some *context*.[4] The dollar sign ($), for example, is understood by many people throughout the world as signifying the currency of the United States (as well as the currencies of Australia, Canada, Hong Kong, New Zealand, and several other countries). The *Global Focus* describes another sign—the # mark on the telephone and above the 3 key on a keyboard—and how this sign means different things in different countries.

It is important to understand that the same sign can mean different things to different people at different times and in different contexts. That is, all meaning is somewhat *idiosyncratic* and *contextually dependent*.[5] To illustrate this point, consider the concept of a pickup truck. The primary and explicit, or *denotative*, meaning of pickup truck is straightforward: a vehicle with a cab compartment for passengers and space in the rear for hauling objects. The secondary and implicit, or *connotative*, meaning of pickup truck is more diverse. To some people, a pickup truck connotes a functional vehicle, and the owner of such a vehicle may be perceived as "cool" for owning a truck rather than a more conventional automobile. To others, a pickup truck might suggest a crude, undignified lifestyle. Some people might consider a jacked-up pickup with huge tires and a gun rack in the back as the ultimate in style, whereas others would perceive such a vehicle as a sign of low-class, "redneck" behavior.

In other words, the same sign (a pickup truck in this illustration) means different things to different people. Moreover, over time, meaning is subject to change. The director of the University of Michigan's Office for the Study of Automotive Transportation had this to say about the modern meaning of the pickup (in contrast to the meaning of this consumption object to previous generations): "You can take it almost anywhere and it's almost viewed as a status symbol. It isn't a view that people driving these things are clods, but risk takers."[6] It must be recognized, of course, that the positive, status-symbol meaning of the pickup is uniquely American. It is difficult to imagine pickup trucks achieving the level of stature in European or Asian countries that they have achieved in the United States, which further highlights the point that all meaning is meaning in context.

The Meaning of Meaning

Although we use signs to share meaning with others, the two terms (*signs* and *meanings*) should not be construed as synonymous.[7] Signs are simply stimuli that are used to evoke an intended meaning within another person. But words and nonverbal signs do not have meanings per se; instead, *people have meanings for signs*. Meanings are internal responses people hold for external stimuli. Many times people have different meanings for the same words, as the prior discussion of pickup trucks illustrated.

It follows from these points that meanings are *not* in a MarCom message per se but rather are in the message receiver.[8] Marketing communication is most effective when signs are common to both the sender's and the receiver's fields of experience. A field of experience, also called the *perceptual field*, is the sum total of a person's experiences during his or her lifetime. The larger the overlap, or commonality, in their perceptual fields, the greater the likelihood that signs will be decoded by the receiver in the manner intended by the sender. Effective communication is severely compromised when, for example, marketing communicators use words, visualizations, or other signs that customers do not understand. This

GLOBAL FOCUS

What Word Do You Use in Referring to the # Sign?

Telephones, in addition to having buttons, or keys, for digits 0 through 9, also include buttons for two nondigit signs: a star sign (*) and a sign that people in the United States refer to as a pound sign (#). Interestingly, fellow speakers of English in Australia, Britain, Canada, and South Africa have a different name for the # sign. What Americans know as a pound sign, people in Canada refer to as a number sign and those in the other English-speaking countries call a hash or hash mark.

Why hash or hash mark? The English verb *hatch* is a derivative of the French word *hatcher*, which means to cut or draw lines and gave rise to the term *cross-hatch*, a reference to crossed parallel lines. Hence, the # sign to people in Australia, Britain, and South Africa visually represents crossed parallel lines. Because the phrase *pound sign* in Britain is reserved for their currency symbol (£), it is necessary to use *hash* or *hash mark* in reference to the # sign.

Americans also use the term *hash mark*, but it refers to the yardage markers on a football field. The word *hash* used by Americans refers to food made with chopped ingredients such as potatoes, onions, and ground beef or as slang reference to hashish. So, although Americans might consider strange the British use of *hash mark* for the # sign, Brits regard the American/Canadian reference to "pound/number mark" as equally peculiar. Which takes us back to the original point: Signs mean different things to different people in different contexts!

is especially problematic when developing communication programs for consumers in other cultures.

Up to this point we have referred to meaning in the abstract. Now a definition is in order. **Meaning** can be thought of as *the perceptions (thoughts) and affective reactions (feelings) to stimuli evoked within a person when presented with a sign, such as a brand name, in a particular context.*[9] It should be clear at this point that meaning is internal, rather than external, to an individual. Meaning, in other words, is subjective.

Imagine, for example, two consumers seated in front of their respective television sets watching a commercial for a new brand of cat food. For one consumer, the commercial represents a charming display of adorable animals consuming a brand possibly worth buying for the cat purring on the sofa. The other consumer, who is not a cat lover, sees the commercial as a disgusting portrayal of unappealing creatures eating an unappetizing product. Clearly the identical message has decidedly different meanings for these two consumers. (For an interesting advertising effort to attract attention of cats (yes, cats, not cat owners!), please read the *IMC Focus*.)

Meaning Transfer: From Culture to Object to Consumer

The culture and social systems in which marketing communications take place are loaded with meaning. Through socialization, people learn cultural values, form beliefs, and become familiar with the physical manifestations, or artifacts, of these values and beliefs. The artifacts of culture are charged with meaning, which is transferred from generation to generation. For example, the Lincoln Monument and Ellis Island are signs of freedom to Americans. To Germans and many other people throughout the world, the now-crumbled Berlin wall signified oppression and hopelessness. Comparatively, yellow ribbons signify crises and hopes for hostage release and the safe return of military personnel. Pink ribbons signal support for breast cancer victims. Red ribbons have grown into an international symbol of solidarity on AIDS. The Black Liberation flag with its red, black, and green

Luring Those Feline Eyeballs

Cat food sales in the United States amount to $2.3 billion annually. The challenge: How do you, as brand manager of a cat food, get cat owners to buy your brand rather than a competitive option? Owners have no way of knowing whether their cats will like a new brand prior to actually buying it and putting it in front of them to eat; hence, purchasing a new brand is a risky proposition. The cat-food advertiser thus has a challenge in getting consumers to try new brands. It is a challenge worth accepting, because each share point of business amounts to $23 million in revenue (i.e., 1 percent of $2.3 billion).

Here is what the managers of one brand, Whiskas, and its ad agency did to convert triers to the brand. They created a 30-second TV spot that included sights and sounds that would attract feline attention: rustling leaves, a ball of yarn, floating fish, and other appealing sights, sounds, and colors. Copy-testing research revealed that 60 percent of tested cats responded in the intended manner by perking up their ears, turning their heads toward the TV screen, or pawing at the screen when the commercial was aired.

The marketing VP for Kal-Kan, the company that makes Whiskas cat food, had this to say in justifying the commercial: "[We hope it will pique owners' interest in Whiskas] so that they basically say 'someone who understands my cat well enough to devise a commercial with stimulants that my cat actually responds to probably understands my cat well enough to provide us with a food my cat will like.'"

A slightly different version of this commercial had run previously in the United Kingdom and France. Sales in the United Kingdom supposedly shot up by 20 percent after the feline-attention-grabbing commercial was aired. As will be discussed subsequently in the chapter, gaining the consumer's attention is essential to the success of any MarCom effort. This application is a particularly clever way of attracting a consumer's attention. Specifically, owners observing their cats reacting to a commercial are themselves increasingly likely to attend what they observe their pets attending.

Source: Adapted from Hillary Chura, "Whiskas Woos Finicky Felines with Offbeat Ad," *Advertising Age*, May 24, 1999, 16.

---

stripes—representing blood, achievement, and the fertility of Africa—symbolizes civil rights.

Marketing communicators draw meaning from the *culturally constituted world* (i.e., the everyday world filled with artifacts such as the preceding examples) and transfer that meaning to consumer goods. Advertising is an especially important instrument of meaning transfer. The role of advertising in transferring meaning has been described in this fashion:

> *Advertising works as a potential method of meaning transfer by bringing the consumer good and a representation of the culturally constituted world together within the frame of a particular advertisement. . . . The known properties of the culturally constituted world thus come to reside in the unknown properties of the consumer good and the transfer of meaning from world to [consumer]good is accomplished.*[10]

When exposed to an advertisement, the consumer is not merely drawing information from the ad but is actively involved in assigning meaning to the advertised brand.[11] Stated alternatively, the consumer approaches advertisements as texts to be interpreted.[12] (Note that the term *text* refers to any form of spoken or written words and images, which clearly encompasses advertisements.) To demonstrate the preceding points, take into account the following advertising illustrations. Consider first an advertisement for the Honda Accord that was created to convey the point that four out of five Accords sold in America are manufactured in the United States. Beyond stating this fact in the ad copy, the two-page advertisement presented large photos of five icons of American culture: a hamburger, cowboy boots, an oversized bicycle (not like the sleek, European racing bikes), a baseball, and a jazz ensemble. By associating itself with these well-known symbols of American consumer culture, Honda pulled meaning from the "culturally constituted world" of the consumers in its target audience, most of whom would immediately recognize the five icons as uniquely American. The obvious intent was to persuade consumers that the Accord, embedded as it was among the five icons of American popular culture, is made in America and thus is itself American. If Honda's advertising agency had made such a claim in stark, verbal form ("Honda *is* an American automobile!"), most readers likely would have challenged the claim, fully realizing that the Honda is of Japanese origin. But by presenting the message at a nonverbal level and merely via association with Americana icons, consumers probably were somewhat inclined to accept the Honda Accord as at least quasi-American.

Consider also the advertisement for the Chrysler Sebring convertible in Figure 4.2 which embeds this brand in the context of a swimming pool and lounge chairs. The suggestion is that the driving a Sebring with the top down will, like lounging alongside a glistening pool, enable the owner to release stress and unwind (see body copy). Thus, once again the advertiser is drawing meaning from the "culturally constituted world" (lounging by a swimming pool equates with stress release) and attempting to transfer that meaning to the advertised automobile.

Drawing Meaning from the Culturally Constituted World

Figure 4.2

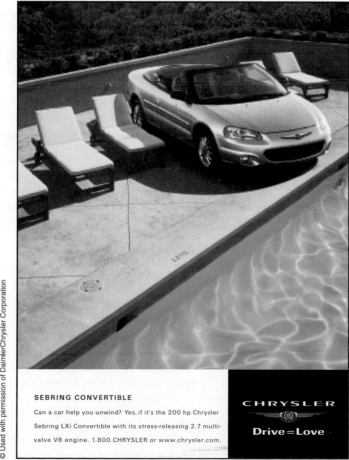

SEBRING CONVERTIBLE

Can a car help you unwind? Yes, if it's the 200 hp Chrysler Sebring LXi Convertible with its stress-releasing 2.7 multi-valve V6 engine. 1.800.CHRYSLER or www.chrysler.com.

CHRYSLER

Drive = Love

The Use of Figurative Language in Marketing Communications

Symbol usage is widespread in marketing communications. A symbol relation is formed when an object (such as a brand) becomes a **symbol** of something else, called the referent, and the object and referent have no prior intrinsic relationship but rather are arbitrarily or metaphorically related.[13] Prudential Insurance advertises itself as *The Rock* and portrays the company in the context of the Rock of Gibraltar. The rock metaphor symbolizes strength and security, which are good traits for an insurance company. Merrill Lynch features a bull in its advertising, undoubtedly because in financial circles the bull is a symbol of growth and prosperity. Nike has made famous the "swoosh" symbol to identify its brand and impart the notion of speed — a key performance attribute, especially when this brand was introduced in the heyday of the jogging and road-running craze.

When establishing symbolic relations, marketing communicators often use *figurative*, or nonliteral, language. Figurative language involves expressing one thing (such as a brand) in terms normally used for denoting another thing (such as an idea or object) with which it may be regarded as analogous.[14] Three forms of figurative language used by marketing communicators are simile, metaphor, and allegory.[15]

Simile. **Simile** uses a comparative term such as *like* or *as* to join items from different classes of experience. "Love is like a rose" exemplifies the use of simile.[16] For many years, viewers of the soap opera *Days of Our Lives* have listened to the program open with the intonation of the simile: "Like sands through an hourglass, so are the days of our lives." A tourist advertisement for Jekyll Island, a popular resort on the coast of Georgia, illustrates one advertiser's use of simile in proclaiming: "Jekyll Island, Georgia. Like the tide, it draws you back again and again." Of course, the suggestion being made is that satisfied tourists return again and again to Jekyll Island, the same way that the drifting tide returns inexorably to the shore. Advertising slogans sometimes use simile, as illustrated in the advertisement in Figure 4.3, which likens the Trailblazer to a rock ("Trailblazer . . . Like a Rock").

Metaphor. Metaphor differs from simile in that the comparative term (*as, like*) is omitted (e.g., "love is a rose," "she has a heart of gold"). **Metaphor** applies a word or a phrase to a concept or object that it does not literally denote to suggest a comparison and to make the abstract more concrete. With metaphor, the qualities of one object or idea are transferred to another object, such as a brand. Metaphors are widely used in advertising because they arouse and enliven the consumer's imagination, represent an effective yet economical (in terms of print space or broadcast time) way to create brand associations and enhance persuasion.[17] When used in advertising, metaphors create a picture in consumers' minds and tap into meaning shared both by the advertiser and the consumer.[18] Metaphors may not accomplish their desired objective, however, if the metaphor is complicated or too abstract.[19]

Metaphors abound in advertisements. Advertising metaphors occur in verbal form, through visual representations, or by combining verbal and visual presentation. For example, all the following advertising slogans have been used or are now being used: Jaguar XJ-S is claimed to be "the stuff of legends"; Wheaties is the "cereal of *everyday* champions" (the insertion of "everyday" is of recent origin, possibly to avoid the impression that this cereal brand is just for superstars); Budweiser is the "king of beers"; and Chevrolet is "the heartbeat of America." The advertiser in using metaphor hopes that by repeatedly associating its brand with a well-known and symbolically meaningful referent, the meaning contained in the referent will eventually transfer to the brand.

Consider the following illustrative uses of metaphor in advertisements. An advertisement for Castrol Syntec (a synthetic motor oil) associates the brand metaphorically with Rolaids, the well-known antacid product. The ad's headline states, "Think of it as Rolaids for your engine." The body copy in the ad goes on to compare a motor's engine with a person's stomach, which thus validates the metaphorical comparison of this product to the better known Rolaids. Figure 4.4 for Cheer laundry detergent uses a visual metaphor in comparing its ability to preserve clothes from fading with a Mason jar's widely understood capacity for preserving food products from spoiling.

The Use of Simile in an Advertising Slogan

Figure 4.3

Allegory.   Allegory, a word derived from a Greek term meaning "other-speak," represents a form of *extended metaphor*. Allegorical presentation equates the objects in a particular text (such as the advertised brand in a television commercial) with meanings outside the text itself.[20] In other words, "allegory conveys meaning in a story-underneath-a-story, where something other than what is literally represented is also occurring."[21] In addition to the use of metaphor, another determining characteristic of allegorical presentation is *personification*.[22]

Through personification, the abstract qualities in a brand (its attributes or benefits) assume positive human characteristics. Current or past examples of allegorical characters in advertising include

- Mr. Clean, who personifies heavy-duty cleaning ability in the brand of cleaner whose package he adorns.
- Mr. Goodwrench (Chevrolet), who exemplifies professional, efficient car service.
- The Pillsbury dough boy, who signifies the joy of making (and eating) cookies and fond remembrances.
- The koala bear (Figure 4.5), which personifies the CEO-type treatment one can expect to receive when flying Qantas business class. This advertisement's body copy mentions several attractive features of flying business class, but the "story beneath the story" is that the business-class passenger will be pampered in a fashion that CEOs of major corporations are accustomed to. The ad doesn't say this, but the allegorical representation suggests it.

Allegory often is used in promoting products that are difficult to advertise without upsetting or boring some audience members. Advertisers have found

Figure 4.4   The Use of Metaphor

There's a better way to preserve your clothes.
Cheer helps prevent fading by neutralizing the chlorine in tap water so your clothes come out looking bright wash after wash after wash. We love what you're wearing.

that using personifications (e.g., humanlike animals or personlike product characters) makes advertising of these potentially offensive or mundane products more palatable to audiences. For example, the successful, albeit much-criticized and now retired, advertising campaign for Camel cigarettes employed the camel personification known as Old Joe. Joe was the embodiment of hip. In the many executions of this campaign, Joe was always portrayed as a cool, adventurous, swinging-single-type character. The subtle implication was that smoking Camels was itself the with-it thing to do. Although there are distinct ethical issues associated with this campaign, there is no questioning its effectiveness. Two years after Old Joe's introduction, Camel shipments rose 11.3 percent and market share increased from 3.9 percent to 4.3 percent.[23] This may seem a pittance, but every share point in the cigarette industry amounts to sales in the hundreds of millions of dollars. The critics of smoking, especially concerning youth, were outraged by R.J. Reynolds' advertising of Camel cigarettes; indeed, Joe Camel in its allegorical splendor became the rallying point around which criticism of tobacco advertising was based and restrictions were eventually imposed.[24]

Budweiser's advertising with frogs and lizards represents another application of allegory in advertising a product category that is subject to criticism, particularly as it relates to drinking by underage consumers. You may remember the television commercials that included disaffected lizard character (Louie) and his straight man sidekick (Frank). What is the allegorical representation, or story underneath a story, in these humorous lizard executions? Could it be that Louie and Frank represent competitors envious of Budweiser's success, and could it be that

The Use of Allegory

Figure 4.5

the frogs (who exclaimed "Bud-Weis-Er") personify Budweiser itself, the good guy in this allegory? An interesting class discussion might debate these questions as well as the ethics of this particular ad campaign, which is said to have had great appeal to teens and preteens.

Allegory certainly is not restricted to taboo products. Consider the two advertisements for Chevron gasoline with its Techron additive, one for a green station wagon (Figure 4.6) and the other for a blue pickup truck (Figure 4.7). In both executions the vehicle is made to look human (called anthropomorphizing) and in fact serves to personify the lifestyle of the intended market segment. The ad with the green station wagon is aimed at young mothers ("soccer moms") who constantly are on the go, and the blue pickup ad is directed at macho males who want a high-performing pickup truck. On the surface, both ads are entertaining ways of advertising a mundane gasoline product. Slightly below the surface, however, both ads are attempting to persuade consumers that the choice of Chevron gasoline reflects good judgment ("She uses her head"; and, for him, "Keep all your horses happy").

Summary of Meaning Within Marketing Communications

This section has described the nature of meaning in marketing communications and the elements involved in meaning transfer. Perhaps the most important lesson to learn is that marketers use a variety of different signs, nonverbal as well

Figure 4.6   **Allegorical Personification**

as verbal, in their efforts to accomplish communication objectives. In the final analysis, marketing communicators hope to manage brand concepts by creating desired meanings for their brands. Meaning is the fundamental concept in all marketing communications. It is the foundation of the brand image component of brand equity that was introduced in Chapter 2 as a core concept throughout the text.

Because meaning resides in the minds of people and not in messages per se, it is important to understand the psychological factors that determine how consumers derive meaning from messages. Accordingly, the following sections elaborate on some of the issues only alluded to so far.

BEHAVIORAL FOUNDATIONS OF MARKETING COMMUNICATIONS

Marketing communicators direct their efforts toward influencing consumers' brand-related *beliefs, attitudes, emotional reactions,* and *choices.* Ultimately, the objective is to encourage consumers to choose "our" brand rather than competitive offerings. To accomplish this goal, marketing communicators design advertising messages, promotions, packaging cues, brand names, sales presentations, and other forms of brand-related messages. Because a fundamental understanding of consumer behavior is essential to appreciate fully the intricacies of marketing communications, the ideas presented in this section lay an important foundation for subsequent topical chapters.

Allegorical Personification

Figure 4.7

This section examines how consumers process and respond to marketing communications stimuli and make choices among brands. The discussion focuses on two models—the *consumer processing model (CPM)* and the *hedonic, experiential model (HEM)*—that describe how consumers process MarCom information and ultimately use this information to choose from among the many alternatives available in the marketplace. From a consumer-processing perspective, behavior is seen as rational, cognitive, systematic, and reasoned.[25] The hedonic, experiential perspective, on the other hand, views consumer behavior as driven by emotions in pursuit of "fun, fantasies, and feelings."[26]

A very important point needs to be emphasized before moving on to discussions of each model. In particular, it must be recognized that consumer behavior is much too complex and diverse to be captured perfectly by two extreme models. Rather, you should think of these models as bipolar perspectives that anchor a continuum of possible consumer behaviors—ranging, metaphorically speaking, from the "icy-blue cold" CPM perspective to the "red-hot" HEM perspective (see Figure 4.8). At one end of the continuum is consumer behavior that is based on *pure reason*—cold, logical, and rational—the behavior best described by the CPM perspective. At the other end is consumer behavior that is based on *pure passion*—hot, spontaneous, and perhaps even irrational—the behavior best described by the HEM perspective. Between these extremes rests the bulk of consumer behavior, most of which is not based on pure reason or pure passion and is neither icy-blue cold nor red-hot. Rather, most behavior ranges, again in metaphorical terms, from cool to warm. In the final analysis, we will examine the rather extreme perspectives of consumer behavior but recognize that often both perspectives are applicable to understanding how and why consumers behave as they do.

Figure 4.8 — Comparison of the CPM and HEM Models

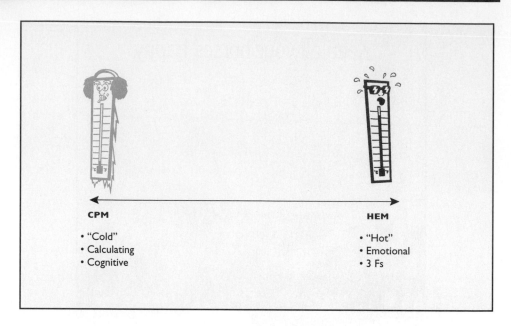

CPM
- "Cold"
- Calculating
- Cognitive

HEM
- "Hot"
- Emotional
- 3 Fs

The Consumer Processing Model (CPM)

The information-processing situation faced by consumers and the corresponding communication imperatives for marketing communicators have been described in these terms:

> *The consumer is constantly being bombarded with information which is potentially relevant for making choices. The consumer's reactions to that information, how that information is interpreted, and how it is combined or integrated with other information may have crucial impacts on choice. Hence, [marketing communicators']decisions on what information to provide to consumers, how much to provide, and how to provide that information require knowledge of how consumers process, interpret, and integrate that information in making choices.*[27]

The following sections discuss consumer information processing in terms of eight interrelated stages.[28] Although MarCom efforts play an important role in affecting all stages of this process, we will focus primarily on the first six stages because as the last two (decision making and action) are determined by all marketing-mix elements and not marketing communications per se.

Stage 1:   *Exposure* to information.
Stage 2:   Selective *attention*.
Stage 3:   *Comprehension* of attended information.
Stage 4:   *Agreement* with comprehended information.
Stage 5:   *Retention* in memory of accepted information.
Stage 6:   *Retrieval* of information from memory.
Stage 7:   *Decision making* from alternatives.
Stage 8:   *Action* taken on the basis of the decision.

Stage 1: Exposure to Information.   The marketing communicator's fundamental task is to deliver messages to consumers, who, it is expected, will process the messages and be persuaded to undertake the course of action advocated by the marketer. By definition, **exposure** simply means that consumers come in contact with the marketer's message (they see a magazine ad, hear a radio commercial, spot an Internet banner, and so on). Although exposure is an essential preliminary step to subsequent stages of information processing, the mere fact of exposing consumers to the marketing communicator's message does not ensure that the message will have any impact. Gaining exposure is a *necessary* but *insufficient* condition for communication success. Ultimate success (i.e., influencing action as discussed in Chapter 1), generally depends upon message quality and frequency, or momentum, as discussed in Chapter 2. The preceding sentence added a qualifier in saying that ultimate success "generally" depends on message quality along with frequency. The reason for this qualification is that there is some evidence that the mere fact of being repeatedly exposed to a message increases the likelihood that the receiver will judge that message to be true. This is called the "truth effect."[29]

In practical terms, exposing consumers to a brand's message is a function of two key managerial decisions: (1) setting the MarCom budget, and (2) selecting media and vehicles in which to present a brand message. In other words, a high percentage of a targeted audience will be exposed to a brand's message if sufficient funds are allocated and wise choices of media outlets are made; insufficient budget and/or poor media selection invariably result in low levels of exposure.

Stage 2: Selective Attention.

Laypeople use the expression "paying attention" in reference to whether someone is really listening to and thinking about what a speaker (such as a teacher) is saying, or whether his/her mind is wondering off into its own world of thought. For psychologists, the term *attention* means fundamentally the same thing. **Attention,** in its formal use, means to focus cognitive resources on and think about a message to which one has been exposed. Actually, consumers pay attention to only a small fraction of MarCom stimuli. This is because demands placed on attention are great (we are virtually bombarded with advertisements and other commercial messages), but information-processing *capacity is limited*. It therefore is necessary for attention to be highly *selective*. That is, effective utilization of limited processing capacity requires that consumers allocate mental energy (processing capacity) to only messages that are *relevant and of interest to current goals*.[30]

For example, once their initial curiosity is satisfied, most people who do *not* suffer allergies would, on exposure to the ad in Figure 4.9, pay relatively little attention to the detailed comments about Flonase nasal spray because the product has little relevance to them. On the other hand, allergy sufferers could be expected to devote *conscious attention* to the advertisement because it holds a high level of relevance to their interests. Please notice that "conscious attention" is emphasized in the previous sentence. This is to distinguish this deliberate, controlled form of attention from an *automatic* form of relatively superficial attention that occurs due to factors such as stimulus novelty even when a message holds little personal relevance to the consumer.[31] The Flonase ad is likely to grab the initial attention of magazine readers due to the eye-catching graphic of a golfer equipped with a life-support oxygen system; however, nonallergy sufferers would have little reason to do anything other than quickly scan this visual and bypass reading the rather detailed body copy.

How can attention selectivity be avoided?

We have explained what selective attention is and why it exists, but we haven't examined what marketing communicators can do to gain the consumer's attention and to prevent being "selected out." The short-version answer is that marketing communicators can most effectively gain the consumers' attention by creating messages that truly appeal to their needs for product-relevant information. The likelihood that consumers' will pay attention to an advertisement or other form of MarCom message also is increased by creating messages that are novel, spectacular, aesthetically appealing, eye catching, and so forth.

At the present time we will not further discuss these attention-gaining strategies. We will instead delay this discussion until the subsequent chapter, at which point we will describe in detail ways to augment consumers' motivation to attend to "our" brand message. This description will take place in the context of a detailed explanation of how marketing communicators can enhance consumers' motivation, opportunity, and ability to process brand information.

In sum, attention involves allocating limited processing capacity in a selective fashion. Effective marketing communications are designed to activate

Figure 4.9

Illustration of Selective Attention

consumer interests by appealing to those needs that are most relevant to a market segment. This is no easy task; MarCom environments (stores, advertising media, noisy offices during sales presentations) are inherently cluttered with competitive stimuli and messages that also vie for the prospective customer's attention. Research shows that advertising *clutter*, whether real or perceived, reduces advertising effectiveness.[32] Television commercials appearing later in a stream of multiple commercials and those for low-involvement products are particularly susceptible to clutter effects.[33] The *Online Focus* describes efforts to better capture Internet users' attention to online advertisements.

Stage 3: Comprehension of What Is Attended.   To comprehend is to understand and create meaning out of stimuli and symbols. Communication is effective when the meaning a marketing communicator intends to convey matches what consumers actually extract from the messages. The term **comprehension** often is used interchangeably with *perception*; both terms refer to *interpretation*. Because people respond to their perceptions of the world and not to the world as it actually is, the topic of comprehension, or perception, is one of the most important subjects in marketing communications.[34]

The perceptual process of interpreting stimuli is called **perceptual encoding.** Two main stages are involved.[35] **Feature analysis** is the initial stage whereby a receiver examines the basic features of a stimulus (such as size, shape, color, and angles) and from this makes a preliminary classification. For example, we are able to distinguish a motorcycle from a bicycle by examining features such as size, presence of an engine, and the number of controls. Lemons and oranges are distinguishable by their colors and shapes.

The Challenge of Capturing Attention Online

Banner ads on the Internet are ubiquitous. Ads, ads, and more ads. But who pays attention? Jupiter Media Metrix estimated that the average Internet user was exposed to more than 700 banner ads per day in 2002 and that this will increase to 950 banner ads daily by 2005. The majority of these ads never receive our attention, however. According to Nielsen/NetRatings, the average click rate in 2001 was a paltry 0.49 percent; in other words, online users pay attention and solicit information from only a small percentage of all the Internet banner ads to which they are exposed. (Remember: Exposure is necessary for but is not equivalent to attention. Exposure merely indicates that the consumer has a chance to see an advertisement.)

Because click rates are trivially small, online advertisers have turned to new technology and larger ad sizes to grab the online surfer's attention. Many of these changes and the standardization of banner sizes have been facilitated by the efforts of the Internet Advertising Bureau (IAB), a trade association that is a leader in the Internet advertising industry. In early 2001 the IAB endorsed seven new Internet ad formats, labeled Internet marketing units (IMUs). These seven new IMUs compare with the earlier full banner, the size of which was 468 x 60 pixels (28,080 square pixels). The following table compares the new IMUs against this original full banner.

This table makes it clear that the new (as of 2001) IMUs are generally considerably larger than the original full banner ad. It is likely that these larger ad sizes increase attention and thus click rates. Pop-up ads, though often a source of irritation, are especially effective attention getters. Internet advertisers, like advertisers in all other media, have to fight through the clutter to find ways to attract the online user's attention. Bigger ads, ads popping up, and ads that offer sound and visuals are just some of the ways that have been devised to attract and hold the Internet user's attention.

Sources: Adapted from Dana Blankenhorn, "Bigger, Richer Ads Go Online," *Advertising Age*, June 18, 2001, T10; Sarah J. Heim, "IAB Establishes New Guidelines for Banners," *Brandweek*, February 26, 2001, 48; Stephanie Miles, "Advertisers Plan Flashier Ads to Make an Online Impression," *Wall Street Journal Interactive Edition*, March 1, 2001 (http://interactive.wsj.com/).

Type and Size of IMU (pixel size)	Square Pixels	Percent Change Compared to Full Banner (480 x 60 pixels)
Skyscraper (120 x 600)	72,000	156%
Wide Skyscraper (160 x 600)	96,000	242%
Rectangle (180 x 150)	27,000	−4%
Medium Rectangle (300 x 250)	75,000	167%
Large Rectangle (336 x 280)	94,080	235%
Vertical Rectangle (240 x 400)	96,000	242%
Square Pop-Up (250 x 250)	62,500	123%

The second stage of perceptual encoding, **active synthesis,** goes beyond merely examining physical features. The *context* or situation in which information is received plays a major role in determining what is perceived and interpreted, or, in other words, what meaning is acquired. Interpretation results from combining, or synthesizing, stimulus features with expectations of what should be present in the context in which a stimulus is perceived. For example, a synthetic fur coat placed in the window of a discount clothing store (the context) is likely to be perceived as a cheap imitation; however, the same coat, when attractively merchandised in an expensive boutique (a different context) might now be considered a high-quality, stylish garment.

A humorous way to better understand the difference between feature analysis and active synthesis is by examining cartoons. Witty cartoonists often use humor in subtle ways. They insert characters and props in cartoons that require the reader to draw from his or her own past experiences in order to perceive (comprehend) the

Figure 4.10   Humorous Illustration of Active Synthesis

humor. Before reading on, consider the cartoon in Figure 4.10 from Gary Larson's "The Far Side." The readily recognized features in this cartoon (feature analysis) are three Neanderthal characters, a mammoth, and a spear that has fallen short of the mammoth. These features are not humorous per se; rather, humor is *comprehended* by active synthesis on the reader's part. Some students immediately comprehend the humor, whereas others see no humor at all. Understanding the cartoon requires that one generalize to the situation in the cartoon from what happens in a basketball game when a player fires up a shot that completely misses the basket. At that instance fans from the opposing team spontaneously hoot in unison "Airrrr ball . . . airrrr ball." Gary Larson has generalized to the plight of the Neanderthal man who has failed to reach the mammoth with his spear and is then ridiculed by his chums: "Airrrrr spearrrr . . . airrrrr spearrrr! . . ."

The important point in the preceding discussion is that consumers' comprehension of marketing stimuli is determined by stimulus features and by characteristics of the consumers themselves. Expectations, needs, personality traits, past experiences, and attitudes toward the stimulus object all play important roles in determining consumer perceptions.[36] Due to the subjective nature of the factors that influence our perceptions, comprehension is oftentimes idiosyncratic, or peculiar to each individual. Figure 4.11 provides a humorous, albeit revealing, illustration of the idiosyncrasy of perception. "The Investigation" illustrates that each individual's personal characteristics and background influence how he or she perceives the man in the middle. A classic statement regarding the idiosyncratic nature of perception/comprehension is offered in the following quote:

We do not simply "react to" a happening or to some impingement from the environment in a determined way (except in behavior that has become reflex-

Humorous Illustration of Selective Perception

Figure 4.11

ive or habitual). We [interpret und] behave according to what we bring to the occasion, and what each of us brings to the occasion is more or less unique.[37]

This quote is from an analysis of fan reaction to a heatedly contested football game between Dartmouth and Princeton universities way back in 1951. The game was highly emotional and arguments, fights, and "dirty play" broke out on both sides. Interestingly, fan reaction to the dirty play divided along team loyalties. Dartmouth fans perceived Princeton players as the perpetrators, and vice versa. That is, what fans experienced and how they interpreted events depended on their view of who the "good guys" were prior to the game. In short, our individual uniqueness conditions what we see!

An individual's *mood* also can influence his or her perception of stimulus objects. Research has found that when people are in a good mood they are more likely to retrieve positive rather than negative material from their memories; are more likely to perceive the positive side of things; and, in turn, are more likely to respond positively to a variety of stimuli.[38] These findings have important implications for both advertising strategy and personal selling activity. Both forms of marketing communications, especially personal selling, are capable of placing consumers in positive (or negative) moods and may enhance (or mitigate) consumer perceptions and attitudes toward marketers' offerings.

Miscomprehension. People sometimes *misinterpret* or *miscomprehend* messages so as to make them more consistent with their existing beliefs or expectations. This typically is done without conscious awareness; nonetheless, distorted perception and message miscomprehension are common.

A dramatic but tragic case that points out the consequences of misperception occurred in 1988, when the crew of the USS *Vincennes* shot down an Iranian commercial airliner in the Persian Gulf. The stressed-out crew had been alerted that Iranian F-14 warplanes were in the area; therefore, they expected to see an F-14 warplane attacking their ship. They saw what they thought to be a warplane and shot it down. The "warplane" actually was a commercial airliner, and 290 innocent passengers were killed—a tragic case of human error.[39]

Research also has revealed a high rate of consumer miscomprehension of television commercials, perhaps as high as 30 percent.[40] Miscomprehension of TV commercials and other forms of MarCom messages occurs primarily for three reasons: (1) Messages sometimes are misleading or unclear, (2) consumers' are biased by their own preconceptions and thus "see" what they choose to see, and (3) processing of advertisements and other MarCom messages often takes place under time pressures and noisy circumstances. The moral is clear: Marketing communicators cannot assume that consumers interpret messages in the manner intended. It is for this reason that message testing (also called copy testing) is absolutely imperative before investing in print space, broadcast time, or other media outlets.

Stage 4: Agreement with What Is Comprehended.

A fourth information-processing stage involves the matter of whether the consumer *agrees with* (i.e., accepts) a message argument that he or she has comprehended. It is crucial from a MarCom perspective that consumers not only comprehend a message but that they also agree with the message (as opposed to countering it or rejecting it outright). Comprehension by itself does not ensure that the message will change consumers' attitudes or influence their behavior. Understanding a marketer's selling points is not tantamount to accepting those points.

Agreement depends on whether the message is *credible* (i.e., believable, trustworthy) and whether it contains information and appeals that are *compatible with the values* that are important to the consumer. For example, a consumer who is more interested in the symbolic implications of consuming a particular product than in acquiring functional value is likely to be persuaded more by a message that associates the advertised brand with a desirable group than one that talks about mundane product features. Using endorsers who are perceived as trustworthy is one means by which to enhance message credibility. Credibility also can be boosted by structuring believable messages rather than making bamboozle-type claims of the used-car-advertisement variety.

Stages 5 and 6: Retention and Search/Retrieval of Stored Information.

These two information processing stages, *retention* and information *search and retrieval*, are discussed together because both involve *memory* factors related to consumer choice. The subject of memory is a complex topic, but these complexities need not concern us here, because our interest in the topic is considerably more practical.[41]

From a MarCom perspective, memory involves the related issues of what consumers remember (recognize and recall) about marketing stimuli and how they access and retrieve information in the process of choosing among product alternatives. The subject of memory is inseparable from the process of learning, so the following paragraphs first discuss the basics of memory, then examine learning fundamentals, and finally, emphasize the practical application of memory and learning principles to marketing communications.

Elements of memory. Memory consists of long-term memory *(LTM)*; short-term, or working, memory *(STM)*; and a set of sensory stores *(SS)*. Information is received by one or more sensory receptors (sight, smell, touch, and so on) and passed to an appropriate SS, where it is rapidly lost (within fractions of a second) unless attention is allocated to the stimulus. Attended information is then transferred to STM, which serves as the center for current processing activity by integrating information from the sense organs and from LTM. *Limited processing capacity* is the most outstanding characteristic of STM; individuals can process only a finite amount of information at any one time. An excessive amount of information will result in reduced recognition and recall. Furthermore, information in STM that is not thought about or rehearsed will be lost from STM in about 30 seconds or less.[42] (This is what happens when you get a phone number from a telephone directory but then are distracted before you have an opportunity to dial the number. You must refer to the directory a second time and then repeat the number to yourself—rehearse it—so that you will not forget it again.)

Information is transferred from STM to LTM, which cognitive psychologists consider to be a virtual storehouse of unlimited information. Information in LTM is organized into coherent and associated cognitive units, which are variously called *schemata, memory organization packets,* or *knowledge structures.* All three terms reflect the idea that LTM consists of associative links among related information, knowledge, and beliefs.[43] The concept of a knowledge structure is illustrated in Figure 4.12. This representation captures one baby boomer's schema for the Volkswagen Beetle, a car she first owned during her college years in the late 1960s and repurchased in 2002 to celebrate her double-nickel birthday (age 55). (Historical note: The VW Beetle had its heyday in the United States in the 1960s and 1970s but then lost its brand equity and market share. But like phoenix ascending from the ashes, the new VW Beetle was reintroduced in the late 1990s to stunning consumer acceptance.)

The marketing communicator's challenge is to provide positively valued information that consumers will store in LTM and that will be used at some point in time in influencing the consumer's choice of "our" brand over competitive options. There is a good reason why information communicated about a brand *must* achieve long-term memory storage and be readily retrievable from memory. The reason is that the point at which a consumer is exposed to information about a brand typically is separated in time—sometimes by months—from the occasion at which the consumer needs to access and use the information to make a purchase decision.

Consumer's Knowledge Structure for the VW Beetle   Figure 4.12

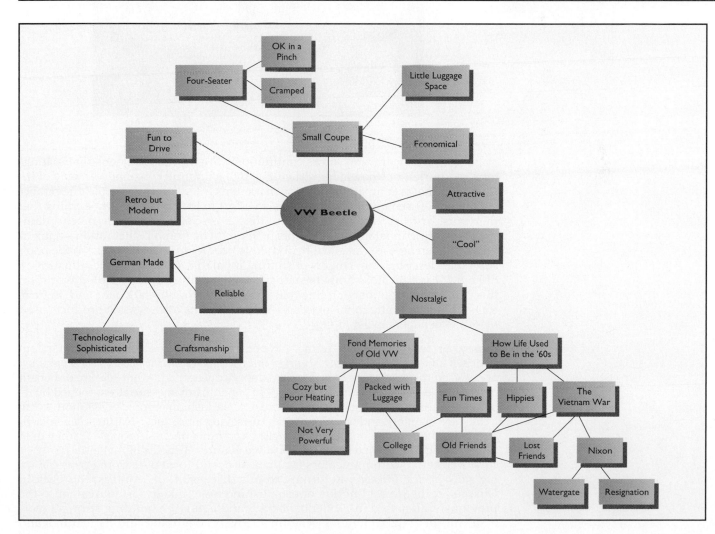

Figure 4.13   **Facilitating Learning**

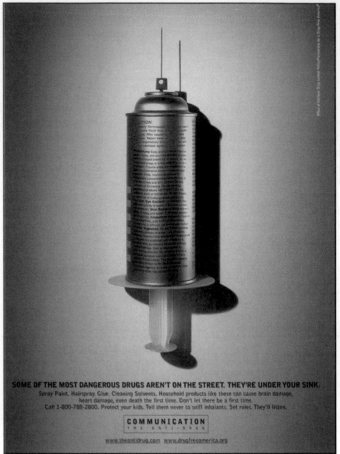

Marketing communicators continuously attempt to alter consumers' long-term memories, or knowledge structures, by facilitating consumer *learning* of information that is compatible with the marketer's interest. For example, the public-service advertisement in Figure 4.13 is an effort to facilitate parents' learning that they must instruct their children about the adverse effects (brain and heart damage) of sniffing inhalants to get a cheap "high." The graphic illustration—a juxtaposition of an aerosol can and a hypodermic needle—cleverly buttresses the body copy that describes the dangers of sniffing inhalants. (This is another illustration of how communicators draw meaning from the culturally constituted world [in this case, parents' understanding that needles for drug use are bad] and, in turn, transfer that meaning to the object advertised [in this case, aerosol products used by some teenagers to get high.])

Types of learning. Two primary types of learning are relevant to MarCom efforts.[44] One type is the *strengthening of linkages among specific memory concepts,* such as between the marketer's brand (one memory concept) and some feature or benefit of that brand (another memory concept). In general, linkages are strengthened by *repeating* claims, presenting them in a more *concrete* fashion (a topic given more detail in the next chapter), and being *creative* in conveying a product's features. Metaphorically, the marketing communicator wishes to build mental "ropes" (rather than flimsy strings) between a brand and positive features/benefits of that brand.

Marketing communicators facilitate a second form of learning by *establishing entirely new linkages.* Returning to our discussion of brand equity back in Chapter 2, the present notion of establishing new linkages is equivalent to the previously discussed idea of enhancing brand equity by building strong, favorable, and perhaps unique associations between the brand and its features and

Establishing a Linkage Between a Brand and Its Benefits   Figure 4.14

benefits. Hence, the terms *linkage* and *association* are interchangeable in this context. Both involve a relation between a brand and its features/benefits that are stored in a consumer's memory.

The advertisement in Figure 4.14 for Danimals (Dannon's drinkable lowfat yogurt) illustrates a rather typical effort to establish a new linkage in consumers' minds via advertising—in this case, linking in parents' minds the belief that Danimals means "healthy snacking." The clever visual (a container of Danimals augmented with faux training wheels) together with the headline and body copy combine to suggest that Danimals is to children's healthy snacking what training wheels are to their safety in learning to ride a bicycle.

Search and retrieval of information. Information that is learned and stored in memory only impacts consumer choice behavior when it is searched and retrieved. Precisely how retrieval occurs is beyond the scope of this chapter.[45] Suffice it to say that retrieval is facilitated when a new piece of information is linked, or associated, with another concept that is itself well known and easily accessed. This is precisely what the Danimals' brand management/ad agency team has attempted to accomplish by using the training-wheel analogy. It is much easier for parents to retrieve the concrete idea of training wheels, which represent a well-known device for safely transitioning young children from tricycles to bicycles, than it is to salvage from memory the abstract semantic concept of "healthy snacking." *Dual-coding theory* offers an explanation.

According to **dual-coding theory,** pictures are represented in memory in verbal as well as visual form, whereas words are less likely to have visual representations.[46] In other words, pictures and visuals (versus words) are better remembered because pictures are especially able to elicit mental images. The advertisement for

Figure 4.15

Illustration of the Dual-Coding Principle

Millstone coffee (Figure 4.15) nicely illustrates an advertising effort to exploit the benefits of visual imagery and dual coding. Here the advertiser wants simply to convey the notion that this coffee brand has a "taste for adventure." The tiger-appearing coffee mug conveys visually this concept of adventure, and thus Millstone and adventure can be stored in consumers' memories in two ways, both verbally and visually.

Research has shown that information about product attributes is better recalled when the information is accompanied with pictures than when presented only as prose.[47] The value of pictures is especially important when verbal information is itself low in imagery.[48] Consumer researchers have found that people remember significantly greater numbers of company names when the names are paired with meaningful pictorials. For example, the name "Jack's Camera Shop" is better remembered when the store name is presented along with a jack playing card shown holding a movie camera to its eye.[49] Many marketing communicators use similar pictorials, as can be proven by perusing the yellow pages of any city telephone directory and by surfing the Internet.

Stage 7: Deciding Among Alternatives.

The six preceding stages have examined how consumers receive, encode, and store information that is pertinent to making consumption choices. Stored in consumers' memories are numerous information packets for different consumption alternatives. This information is in the form of bits and pieces of *knowledge* (e.g., Adidas is a brand of athletic shoes) and specific *beliefs* (e.g., Danimals is for healthy snacking)

The issue for present discussion is this: When contemplating a purchase from a particular product category, how does a consumer decide which brand to choose? The simple answer is that she or he simply selects the "best" brand. However, it is not always clear what the best brand is, especially when considering that the consumer likely has stored in long-term memory a wide variety of information (facts, beliefs, etc.) about each brand in his or her consideration set. Some of the information is positive, and some negative; occasionally the information is contradictory; often the information is incomplete.

The following discussion provides some insight into how consumers react in this situation. It will become clear that consumers often resort to simplifying strategies, or *heuristics,* to arrive at decisions that are at least satisfactory if not perfect. Before we describe specific heuristics, it should be instructive to review a decision that all of us have made and that, in many respects, is one of the most important decisions we will ever make, namely, which college or university to attend.

For some of you, there really was no choice—you went to a school you had always planned on attending, or perhaps your parents insisted on a particular institution. Others, especially those of you who work full or part time or have family responsibilities, may have selected a school purely as a matter of convenience or affordability; in other words, you really did not seriously consider other institutions. But some of you actively evaluated several or many colleges and universities before making a final choice. The process was probably done in the following manner: You received information from a variety of schools and formed preliminary impressions of these institutions; you established criteria for evaluating schools (academic reputation, distance from home, cost, curricula, availability of financial assistance, quality of athletic programs, etc.); you formed weights regarding the relative importance of these various criteria; and you eventually integrated this information to arrive at the all-important choice of which college to attend. Now, let's use this example to understand better the different types of heuristics and the terminology that follows.

The simplest of all decision heuristics is what is called **affect referral.**[50] With this strategy the individual simply calls from memory his or her attitude, or affect, toward relevant alternatives and picks that alternative for which the affect is most positive. In the college decision, for example, you may have always liked most the school that you chose to attend—your affect for it was much stronger than was that for other institutions. In general, this type of choice strategy would be expected for frequently purchased items where risk is minimal.

Consider, by comparison, the use of a **compensatory heuristic.** To understand how and why compensation operates, it is important to realize that rarely is a particular alternative completely superior or dominant over other consumption alternatives. Although a brand may be preferable with respect to one, two, or several benefits, it is unlikely that it is superior to its alternatives in terms of all attributes or benefits that consumers are seeking. (If you're having trouble appreciating the idea that alternatives are rarely dominant, consider this question: Have you ever known another person who is more intelligent, more honest, more attractive, more athletic, more caring, and who has a better sense of humor than anyone else you have ever known? If the answer is yes, do your best to marry him or her!)

When making choices under *nondominant* circumstances, consumers must give something up to get something else. That is, *trade-offs* must be made. If you want more of a particular benefit, you typically have to pay a higher price; if you want to pay less, you often give something up in terms of performance, dependability, prestige, or durability. Returning to the university choice decision, illustrative trade-offs concern tuition cost versus the quality of education, the size of school versus the quality of athletic programs, or the desirability of the school versus its proximity or distance from home.

In general, when applying principles of compensation, the chosen alternative probably is not the best in terms of all criteria; rather, its superiority on some criteria offsets, or compensates for, its lesser performance on other criteria. In short, the consumer typically cannot have it all unless she or he is willing to pay super-premium prices to obtain *crème de la crème* brands.

In addition to compensatory choice behavior, consumers use a variety of so-called noncompensatory heuristics. Because a discussion of these heuristics would take us beyond our primary purpose in this text, which focuses on MarCom activities rather than consumer psychology per se, we will dismiss further discussion of this topic and turn to the last stage of the consumer processing model.

Stage 8: Acting on the Basis of the Decision.   It might seem that consumer-choice behavior operates in a simple lockstep fashion. This, however, is not necessarily the case. *People do not always behave in a manner consistent with their preferences.*[51] A major reason is the presence of events, or *situational factors,* that disrupt, inhibit, or otherwise prevent a person from following through on his or her intentions. Situational factors are especially prevalent in the case of low-involvement consumer behavior. Stock-outs, price-offs, in-store promotions, and shopping at a different store are just some of the factors that lead to the purchase of brands that are not necessarily the most preferred and that would not be the predicted choice based on some heuristic, such as affect referral.

What all this means for marketing communicators is that all aspects of marketing (as discussed in Chapter 1) must be coordinated and integrated to get consumers to act favorably toward the marketer's offering.

A CPM Wrap-Up.   A somewhat detailed account of consumer information processing has been presented. As noted in the introduction, the CPM perspective provides an appropriate description of consumer behavior when the behavior is deliberate, thoughtful, or, in short, highly cognitive.

Much consumer behavior and perhaps especially the behavior of business-to-business buyers is of this nature. On the other hand, buyer behavior also is motivated by emotional, hedonic, and experiential considerations. Therefore, we need to consider the HEM perspective and the implications this model holds for marketing communicators.

The Hedonic, Experiential Model (HEM)

It again is imperative to emphasize that the *rational* consumer processing model (CPM) and the *hedonic, experiential* model (HEM) are *not* mutually exclusive. Indeed, there is impressive evidence that individuals comprehend reality by these rational and experiential processes operating interactively with one another, with their relative influence contingent on the nature of the situation and the amount of emotional involvement—the greater the emotional involvement, the greater the influence of experiential processes.[52] Hence, the HEM model probably better explains how consumers process information and make decisions when they are carefree and happy and confronted with positive outcomes.[53]

Whereas the CPM perspective views consumers as pursuing such objectives as "obtaining the best buy," "getting the most for the money," and "maximizing utility," the HEM perspective recognizes that people often consume products for the sheer fun of it or in the pursuit of amusement, fantasies, or sensory stimulation.[54] Product consumption from the hedonic perspective results from the *anticipation* of having fun, fulfilling fantasies, or having pleasurable feelings. Comparatively, product choice behavior from the CPM perspective is based on the thoughtful evaluation that the chosen alternative will be more functional and provide better results than will alternatives.

Thus, viewed from an HEM perspective, products are more than mere objective entities (a bottle of perfume, a stereo system, a can of soup) and are, instead, subjective symbols that precipitate *feelings* (love, pride) and promise *fun* and the possible realization of *fantasies*. Products most compatible with the hedonic perspective include the performing arts (opera, modern dance), the so-called plastic arts (photography, crafts), popular forms of entertainment (movies, rock concerts), fashion apparel, sporting events, leisure activities, and recreational pursuits.[55] It is important to realize, however, that any product—not just these examples—may have hedonic and experiential elements underlying its choice and consumption. For example, a lot of pleasant feelings and fantasizing are attached to contemplation of purchasing products such as new skis, an automobile, a bicycle, and furniture. Even Procter & Gamble, which is noted for its matter-of-fact advertising style, altered its historical emphasis on performance claims for Tide detergent and focused more on the emotions associated with clean, fresh laundry.[56]

The differences between the HEM and CPM perspectives hold meaningful implications for MarCom practice. Whereas verbal stimuli and rational arguments designed to affect consumers' product knowledge and beliefs are most appropriate in the CPM-oriented MarCom efforts, the HEM approach emphasizes nonverbal content or emotionally provocative words and is intended to generate images, fantasies, and positive emotions and feelings.

A vivid contrast between the CPM and HEM orientations is illustrated in the differences in the advertisements for the Srixon golf ball (Figure 4.16) and Russell Stover candy (Figure 4.17). The former ad uses verbal content to explain in some detail why the Srixon Hi-Spin ball is allegedly superior to the better-known Titleist Pro V1. (Parenthetically, note the subtle superiority claim via the ball-numbering distinction: Srixon is given a 1 and Titleist a 2. Nongolfers may not be aware that golf balls always are numbered, typically with numerals from 1 to 4.) The ad exemplifies the CPM approach in that it attempts to move the consumer through all the CPM stages discussed previously—create *attention* via the eye-catching image of balls being severely compressed; achieve *comprehension* via clearly worded claims; accomplish *agreement* through reference to scientific testing and identification of pros who play with the Srixon ball; and so forth. That is, Srixon's ad agency expects the consumer to attend to the message arguments, agree with them, retain them in memory, and to use this information in ultimately choosing the Srixon brand over the Pro V1 from Titleist.

Comparatively, the Russell Stover ad (Figure 4.17) provides no information about product attributes and functional benefits such as taste, caloric content, and flavors. Rather, the ad in its striking simplicity (though some may consider it exploitative of the female body) appeals directly to the emotions of romance and passion. Emotion and fantasy are front and center in this ad; thought and rationale need not be expended.

Advertisement Exemplifying the CPM Approach	Figure 4.16

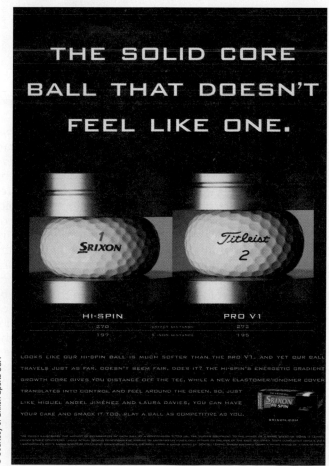

THE SOLID CORE BALL THAT DOESN'T FEEL LIKE ONE.

© Courtesy of Srixon Sports USA

Figure 4.17

Advertisement Exemplifying the HEM Approach

As a side comment (and in anticipation of the discussion in the following chapter of ways to motivate attention), please note how this ad cleverly draws attention to the candy box and the Russell Stover name. To appreciate this cleverness, one must realize that the advertiser's imperative in this advertisement is straightforward—namely, to create name and box recognition. Russell Stover's brand management/ad agency team know that men buy candy for their wives and girlfriends on Valentine's Day but that the candy-buying choice is made infrequently. As such, candy brands typically are not top-of-mind considerations. Hence, for Russell Stover's advertising to succeed, it must at minimum create brand name awareness and familiarity with the candy box that later will be seen at the point of purchase. The ad in Figure 4.17 naturally directs eye movement along a scan of the legs to the *coup de grâce* statement ("A man who remembers" in response to "What does a woman want") and then to the candy box and brand name. Thus, the advertiser's objective is accomplished if viewers of this ad now incorporate Russell Stover into their brand consideration sets and recognize the brand name when encountering it among other brands in a retail outlet.

The prior discussion and examples have emphasized advertising, but it should be apparent that the differences between CPM and HEM perspectives apply as well to other forms of marketing communications. A salesperson, for example, may emphasize product features and tangible benefits in attempting to make a sale (CPM approach), or he or she may attempt to convey the fun, fantasies, and pleasures that prospective customers can enjoy with product ownership. Successful salespersons employ both approaches and orient the dominant approach to the consumer's specific personality and needs. That is, successful salespersons know how to adapt their presentations to different customers—it is hoped, of course, doing it honestly and maintaining standards of morality.

Finally, no single marketing communications approach, whether aimed at CPM or HEM processing, is effective in all instances. What works best depends on the specific nature of the product category, the competitive situation, and the character and needs of the target audience. Returning to the discussion on *positioning* in Chapter 3, brands can be positioned to appeal to *functional* needs, which is congenial with the CPM perspective, or to *symbolic/experiential* needs, which is harmonious with the HEM approach.

SUMMARY

Communication is the process of establishing a commonness or oneness of thought between sender and receiver. The process consists of the following elements: a source that encodes a message to achieve a communication objective; a channel that transmits the message; a receiver who decodes the message and experiences a communication outcome; noise, which interferes with or disrupts effective communication at any of the previous stages; and a feedback mechanism that affords the source a way of monitoring how accurately the intended message is being received and whether it is accomplishing its objective.

Signs are used to share meaning, but signs and meaning are not synonymous. Meaning represents people's internal responses toward signs. Meaning is acquired through a process whereby stimuli (signs in the form of words, symbols, etc.) become associated with physical objects and evoke within individuals responses that are similar to those evoked by the physical objects themselves. Marketing communicators use a variety of techniques to make their brands stand for something, to embellish their value, or, in short, to give them meaning. This can be accomplished by relating the brand to a symbolic referent that has no prior intrinsic relation to the brand (forging a symbol relation). Simile, metaphor, and allegory are forms of figurative language that perform symbolic roles in marketing communications.

This chapter also described the fundamentals of consumer choice behavior. Two relatively distinct perspectives on choice behavior were presented: the consumer processing model (CPM) and the hedonic, experiential model (HEM). The CPM approach views the consumer as an analytical, systematic, and logical decision maker. According to this perspective, consumers are motivated to achieve desired goals. The CPM process involves attending to, encoding, retaining, retrieving, and integrating information so that a person can achieve a suitable choice among consumption alternatives.

The HEM perspective views consumer-choice behavior as resulting from the pursuit of fun, fantasy, and feelings. Thus, some consumer behavior is based predominantly on emotional considerations rather than on objective, functional, and economic factors.

The distinction between the CPM and HEM views of consumer choice is an important one for marketing communicators. The techniques and creative strategies for affecting consumer-choice behavior clearly are a function of the prevailing consumer orientation. Specific implications and appropriate strategies are emphasized throughout the chapter.

Find more resources to help you study at http://shimp.swcollege.com!

DISCUSSION QUESTIONS

1. Discuss the nature and importance of feedback. In what ways do marketing communicators receive feedback from present and prospective customers?

2. A reality of communication is that the same sign often means different things to different people. The red ribbon, for example, means different things to different groups. Provide a good example from your own personal experience in which the same sign might have various meanings for diverse people. What are the general implications for marketing communications?

3. Some magazine advertisements show a picture of a product, mention the brand name, but have virtually no verbal content except, perhaps, a single statement about the brand. Locate an example of this type and explain what meaning you think the advertiser is attempting to convey. Ask two friends to offer their interpretations of the same ad, and then compare their responses to determine the differences in meaning that these ads have for you and your friends. Draw a general conclusion from this exercise.

4. How can a marketing communicator (such as an advertiser or salesperson) reduce noise when communicating a product message to a customer?

5. The famous California Raisins commercial humanized raisins by using claymatic characterizations. Raisins dressed in sunglasses and sneakers were shown dancing to "I Heard It Through the Grapevine." Explain how this ad illustrates allegorical presentation in advertising.

6. Provide two examples of the use of metaphor in magazine advertisements.

7. In the late 1980s Seven-Up introduced a line extension called 7Up Gold, a caffeinated drink with a ginger-ale taste, a cinnamon-apple overtone, and a reddish caramel hue. 7Up Gold was not a cola or a lemon-lime drink; in fact, it fit no established soft-drink category. Seven-Up executives had high hopes that 7Up Gold would capture around a 1 percent share of the annual U.S. soft-drink market. Unfortunately, after Seven-Up invested millions of dollars advertising and promoting 7Up Gold, the brand had gained only one-tenth of 1 percent of the market. 7Up Gold was dumped from the company's product line. Using concepts presented in this chapter, offer your explanation of why 7Up Gold failed.

8. When discussing exposure as the initial stage of information processing, it was claimed that gaining exposure is a necessary but insufficient condition for success. Explain.

9. Explain why attention is highly selective and what implication selectivity holds for brand managers and their advertising agencies.

10. All marketing communications environments are cluttered. Explain what this means and provide several examples. Do not restrict your examples just to advertisements.

11. Explain each of the following related concepts: perceptual encoding, feature analysis, and active synthesis. Using a packaged good of your choice (i.e., a product found in a supermarket, drug store, or mass merchandise outlet), explain how package designers for your brand have used concepts of feature analysis in designing the package.

12. In what sense would attending a Saturday afternoon college football game represent an hedonic- or experiential-based behavior?

13. Figure 4.12 presents one consumer's knowledge structure for the VW Beetle. Construct your knowledge structure for this vehicle. Then illustrate your knowledge structure for the one automobile that you most covet owning.

14. When discussing allegory, the text suggested that Budweiser's television commercials with lizards (Frank and Louie) represent an application of allegory. What is your interpretation of the Frank and Louie ads? What story is being told underneath the superficial commercial story?

15. Internet advertisements must draw attention away from consumers' primary goals for using the Internet—namely, entertainment and informational pursuits. Expose yourself to some current Web ads and then identify and describe at least three specific techniques that Web advertisers use to grab attention. What are the strengths and limitations of each technique?

ENDNOTES

1. Wilbur Schramm, *The Process and Effects of Mass Communication* (Urbana: University of Illinois Press, 1955), 3.

2. Judie Lannon, "New Techniques for Understanding Consumer Reactions to Advertising," *Journal of Advertising Research* 26 (August/September 1986), R6–9.

3. For in-depth treatments of semiotics in marketing communications and consumer behavior, see David Glen Mick, "Consumer Research and Semiotics: Exploring the Morphology of Signs, Symbols, and Significance," *Journal of Consumer Research* 13 (September 1986), 196–213; Eric Haley, "The Semiotic Perspective: A Tool for Qualitative Inquiry," in *Proceedings of the 1993 Conference of the American Academy of Advertising*, ed. Esther Thorson (Columbia, Mo.: The American Academy of Advertising, 1993), 189–196; and Birgit Wassmuth et al., "Semiotics: Friend or Foe to Advertising?" in *Proceedings of the 1993 Conference of the American Academy of Advertising*, ed. Esther Thorson (Columbia, Mo.: The American Academy of Advertising, 1993), 271–276. For interesting applications of a semiotic analysis, see Morris B. Holbrook and Mark W. Grayson, "The Semiology of Cinematic Consumption: Symbolic Consumer Behavior in *Out of Africa*," *Journal of Consumer Research* 13 (December 1986), 374–381; Edward F. McQuarrie and David Glen Mick, "On Resonance: A Critical Pluralistic Inquiry into Advertising Rhetoric," *Journal of Consumer Research* 19 (September 1992), 180–197; Linda M. Scott, "Understanding Jingles and Needledrop: A Rhetorical Approach to Music in Advertising," *Journal of Consumer Research* 17 (September 1990), 223–236; Teresa J. Domzal and Jerome B. Kernan, "Mirror, Mirror: Some Postmodern Reflections on Global Advertising," *Journal of Advertising* 22 (December 1993), 1–20. For an insightful treatment on "deconstructing" meaning from advertisements and other marketing communications, see Barbara B. Stern, "Textual Analysis in Advertising Research: Construction and Deconstruction of Meanings," *Journal of Advertising* 25 (fall 1996), 61–73.

4. This description is based on John Fiske, *Introduction to Communication Studies* (New York: Routledge, 1990); and Mick, "Consumer Research and Semiotics," 198.

5. Robert E. Klein III and Jerome B. Kernan, "Contextual Influences on the Meanings Ascribed to Ordinary Consumption Objects," *Journal of Consumer Research* 18 (December 1991), 311–324. See also Mary Jo Bitner, "Servicescapes: The Impact of Physical Surroundings on Customers and Employees," *Journal of Marketing* 56 (April 1992), 57–71.

6. Jean Halliday, "Pickups Gather Momentum As Status Symbols," *Advertising Age*, June 24, 1996, 20.

7. The subsequent discussion is influenced by the insights of David K. Berlo, *The Process of Communication* (San Francisco: Holt, Rinehart & Winston, 1960), 168–216.

8. Berlo, *The Process of Communication*, 175. On this point, see also Stern, "Textual Analysis in Advertising Research: Construction and Deconstruction of Meanings."

9. This interpretation is adapted from Roberto Friedmann and Mary R. Zimmer, "The Role of Psychological Meaning in Advertising," *Journal of Advertising* 17, no. 1 (1988), 31; and Klein and Kernan, "Contextual Influences on the Meanings Ascribed to Ordinary Consumption Objects."

10. Grant McCracken, "Culture and Consumption: A Theoretical Account of the Structure and Movement of the Cultural Meaning of Consumer Goods," *Journal of Consumer Research* 13 (June 1986), 74.

11. For further discussion, see Grant McCracken, "Advertising: Meaning or Information," in *Advances in Consumer Research*, vol. 14, ed. Melanie Wallendorf and Paul F. Anderson (Provo, Utah: Association for Consumer Research, 1987), 121–124.

12. Edward F. McQuarrie and David Glen Mick, "Visual Rhetoric in Advertising: Text-Interpretive, Experimental, and Reader-Response Analyses," *Journal of Consumer Research* 26 (June 1999), 37–54; Linda M. Scott, "The Bridge from Text to Mind: Adapting Reader-Response Theory to Consumer Research," *Journal of Consumer Research* 21 (December 1994), 461–480.

13. Jeffrey F. Durgee, "Richer Findings from Qualitative Research," *Journal of Advertising Research* 26 (August/September 1986), 36–44.

14. Kristine Bremer and Moonkyu Lee, "Metaphors in Marketing: Review and Implications for Marketers," *Advances in Consumer Research* 24 (Provo, Utah: Association for Consumer Research, 1997), 419. For additional discussion of figurative language and its role in persuasion, see William J. McGuire, "Standing on the Shoulders of Ancients: Consumer Research, Persuasion, and Figurative Language," *Journal of Consumer Research* 27 (June 2000), 109–114.

15. The following discussion is based on writings by Barbara B. Stern: "Figurative Language in Services Advertising: The Nature and Uses of Imagery," in *Advances in Consumer Research*, vol. 15, ed. Michael J. Houston (Provo, Utah: Association for Consumer Research, 1987),

185–190; "How Does an Ad Mean? Language in Services Advertising," *Journal of Advertising* 17, no. 2 (1988), 3–14; "Medieval Allegory: Roots of Advertising Strategy for the Mass Market," *Journal of Marketing* 52 (July 1988), 84–94; and "Other-Speak: Classical Allegory and Contemporary Advertising," *Journal of Advertising* 19, no. 3 (1990), 14–26.

16. Stern, "Figurative Language in Services Advertising."

17. Donna R. Pawlowski, Diane M. Badzinski, and Nancy Mitchell, "Effects of Metaphors on Children's Comprehension and Perception of Print Advertisements," *Journal of Advertising* 27 (summer 1998), 86–87. See also McGuire, "Standing on the Shoulders of Ancients."

18. Nancy A. Mitchell, Diane M. Badzinski, and Donna R. Pawlowski, "The Use of Metaphors As Vivid Stimuli to Enhance Comprehension and Recall of Print Advertisements," in *Proceedings of the 1994 Conference on the American Academy of Advertising*, ed. Karen Whitehall King (Athens, GA: The American Academy of Advertising, 1994), 198–205.

19. Susan E. Morgan and Tom Reichert, "The Message Is in the Metaphor: Assessing the Comprehension of Metaphors in Advertisements," *Journal of Advertising* 28 (winter 1999), 1–12.

20. Stern, "How Does an Ad Mean? Language in Services Advertising," 186.

21. Stern, "Other-Speak: Classical Allegory and Contemporary Advertising," 15.

22. Stern, "Medieval Allegory: Roots of Advertising Strategy for the Mass Market," 86. (Stern also recognizes moral conflict as an additional characteristic but notes that moral conflict is less relevant to the use of allegory in advertising than in its historical application. See Stern, "Other-Speak: Classical Allegory and Contemporary Advertising.")

23. Laura Bird, "Joe Smooth for President," *Adweek's Marketing Week*, May 20, 1991, 20–22.

24. For discussion of issues related to tobacco advertising effectiveness and subsequent ad restrictions, see Richard W. Pollay et al., "The Last Straw? Cigarette Advertising and Realized Market Shares Among Youths and Adults, 1979–1993," *Journal of Marketing* 60 (April 1996), 1–16; Sandra E. McKay, Mary Jane Dundas, and John W. Yeargain, "The FDA's Proposed Rules Regulating Tobacco and Underage Smoking and the Commercial Speech Doctrine," *Journal of Public Policy & Marketing* 15 (fall 1996), 296–302.

25. What is being called the consumer processing model (CPM) is more conventionally called the consumer information processing (CIP) model. CPM is chosen over CIP for two reasons: (1) It is nominally parallel to the HEM label and thus simplifies memory; and (2) the term "information" is too limiting inasmuch as it implies that only verbal claims (information) are important to consumers and that other forms of communications (e.g., nonverbal statements) are irrelevant. This latter point was emphasized by Esther Thorson, "Consumer Processing of Advertising," *Current Issues & Research in Advertising* 12, ed. J. H. Leigh and C. R. Martin, Jr. (Ann Arbor: University of Michigan, 1990), 198–199.

26. Elizabeth C. Hirschman and Morris B. Holbrook, "Hedonic Consumption: Emerging Concepts, Methods, and Propositions," *Journal of Marketing* 46 (summer 1982), 92–101; Morris B. Holbrook and Elizabeth C. Hirschman, "The Experiential Aspects of Consumption: Consumer Fantasies, Feelings, and Fun," *Journal of Consumer Research* 9 (September 1982), 132–140.

27. James B. Bettman, *An Information Processing Theory of Consumer Choice* (Reading, Mass.: Addison-Wesley, 1979), 1.

28. William J. McGuire, "Some Internal Psychological Factors Influencing Consumer Choice," *Journal of Consumer Research* 4 (March 1976), 302–319.

29. Scott A. Hawkins and Stephen J. Hoch, "Low-Involvement Learning: Memory without Evaluation," *Journal of Consumer Research* 19 (September 1992), 212–225.

30. Bettman, *An Information Processing Theory of Consumer Choice*, 77.

31. For an excellent treatment of this distinction as well as a broader perspective on factors determining consumer attention, comprehension, and learning of advertising messages, see Klaus G. Grunert, "Automatic and Strategic Processes in Advertising Effects," *Journal of Marketing* 60 (October 1996), 88–102.

32. Peter H. Webb, "Consumer Initial Processing in a Difficult Media Environment," *Journal of Consumer Research* 6 (December 1979), 225–236; Peter H. Webb and Michael L. Ray, "Effects of TV Clutter," *Journal of Advertising Research* 19 (June 1979), 7–12.

33. Paul Surgi Speck and Michael T. Elliott, "The Antecedents and Consequences of Perceived Advertising Clutter," *Journal of Current Issues and Research in Advertising* 19 (fall 1997), 39–54. In addition to being disliked by consumers, advertising clutter has also been shown to have undesirable effects for the advertising community, at least in the case of magazine circulation. See Louisa Ha and Barry R. Litman, "Does Advertising Clutter Have Diminishing and Negative Returns?" *Journal of Advertising* 26 (Spring 1997), 31–42.

34. A thorough discussion of comprehension processes is provided by David Glen Mick, "Levels of Subjective Comprehension in Advertising Processing and Their

Relations to Ad Perceptions, Attitudes, and Memory," *Journal of Consumer Research* 18 (March 1992), 411–424.

35. Bettman, *An Information Processing Theory of Consumer Choice*, 79.

36. For discussion of the effects of attitudes on perception, see Russell H. Fazio, David R. Roskos-Ewoldsen, and Martha C. Powell, "Attitudes, Perception, and Attention," in *The Heart's Eye: Emotional Influences in Perception and Attention*, ed. Paula M. Niedenthal and Shinobu Kitayama (San Diego: Academic Press, 1994), 197–216.

37. Albert H. Hastorf and Hadley Cantril, "They Saw a Game: A Case Study," *Journal of Abnormal & Social Psychology* 49 (1954), 129–134.

38. Alice M. Isen, Margaret Clark, Thomas E. Shalker, and Lynn Karp, "Affect, Accessibility of Material in Memory, and Behavior: A Cognitive Loop," *Journal of Personality and Social Psychology* 36 (January 1978), 1–12; Meryl Paula Gardner, "Mood States and Consumer Behavior: A Critical Review," *Journal of Consumer Research* 12 (December 1985), 281–300.

39. "A Case of Human Error," *Newsweek*, August 15, 1988, 18–19.

40. Jacob Jacoby and Wayne D. Hoyer, "Viewer Miscomprehension of Televised Communication: Selected Findings," *Journal of Marketing* 46 (fall 1982), 12–26. It is relevant to note that the Jacoby and Hoyer research has stimulated considerable controversy. See Gary T. Ford and Richard Yalch, "Viewer Miscomprehension of Televised Communications—A Comment," *Journal of Marketing* 46 (fall 1982), 27–31; Richard W. Mizerski, "Viewer Miscomprehension Findings Are Measurement Bound," *Journal of Marketing* 46 (fall 1982), 32–34; and Jacob Jacoby and Wayne D. Hoyer, "On Miscomprehending Televised Communications—A Rejoinder," *Journal of Marketing* 46 (fall 1982), 35–43.

41. Several valuable sources for technical treatments of memory operations are available in the advertising and marketing literatures. See Bettman, "Memory Functions," *An Information Processing Theory of Consumer Choice*, chap. 6; James B. Bettman, "Memory Factors in Consumer Choice: A Review," *Journal of Marketing* 43 (spring 1979), 37–53; Andrew A. Mitchell, "Cognitive Processes Initiated by Advertising," in *Information Processing Research in Advertising*, ed. R. J. Harris (Hillsdale, N.J.: Lawrence Erlbaum Associates, 1983), 13–42; Jerry C. Olson, "Theories of Information Encoding and Storage: Implications for Consumer Research," in *The Effect of Information on Consumer and Market Behavior*, ed. A. A. Mitchell (Chicago: American Marketing Association, 1978), 49–60; Thomas K. Srull, "The Effects of Subjective Affective States on Memory

and Judgment," in *Advances in Consumer Research*, vol. 11, ed. T. C. Kinnear (Provo, Utah: Association for Consumer Research, 1984); and Kevin Lane Keller, "Advertising Retrieval Cues on Brand Evaluations," *Journal of Consumer Research* 14 (December 1989), 316–333.

42. Richard M. Shiffrin and R. C. Atkinson, "Storage and Retrieval Processes in Long-Term Memory," *Psychological Review* 76 (March 23, 1969), 179–193.

43. See Mitchell, "Cognitive Processes Initiated by Advertising."

44. Mitchell, "Cognitive Processes Initiated by Advertising."

45. A good discussion is provided by Darlene V. Howard, "General Knowledge," *Cognitive Psychology* (New York: Macmillan, 1983), chap. 6.

46. Allan Paivio, "Mental Imagery in Associative Learning and Memory," *Psychological Review* 76 (May 1969), 241–263; John R. Rossiter and Larry Percy, "Visual Imaging Ability as a Mediator of Advertising Response," in *Advances in Consumer Research*, vol. 5, ed. H. Keith Hunt (Ann Arbor: Association for Consumer Research, 1978), 621–629.

47. Michael J. Houston, Terry L. Childers, and Susan E. Heckler, "Picture-Word Consistency and the Elaborative Processing of Advertisements," *Journal of Marketing Research* 24 (November 1987), 359–369.

48. H. Rao Unnava and Robert E. Burnkrant, "An Imagery-Processing View of the Role of Pictures in Print Advertisements," *Journal of Marketing Research* 28 (May 1991), 226–231.

49. Kathy A. Lutz and Richard J. Lutz, "The Effects of Interactive Imagery on Learning: Application to Advertising," *Journal of Applied Psychology* 62 (August 1977), 493–498.

50. Peter L. Wright, "Consumer Choice Strategies: Simplifying vs. Optimizing," *Journal of Marketing Research* 11 (February 1975), 60–67.

51. Martin Fishbein and Icek Ajzen, *Beliefs, Attitude, Intention, and Behavior: An Introduction to Theory and Research* (Reading, Mass.: Addison Wesley, 1975).

52. Veronika Denes-Raj and Seymour Epstein, "Conflict between Intuitive and Rational Processing: When People Behave against Their Better Judgment," *Journal of Personality and Social Psychology* 66, no. 5 (1994), 819–829.

53. Ibid.

54. Hirschman and Holbrook, "Hedonic Consumption."

55. Ibid., 91.

56. Pat Sloan and Judann Pollack, "P&G Preparing for New Tide Approach," *Advertising Age*, January 19, 1998, 3.

Chapter Five

PERSUASION IN MARKETING COMMUNICATIONS

Chapter Objectives

After studying this chapter, you should be able to:

1. Understand the nature and role of attitudes in marketing communications.
2. Appreciate the role of persuasion in marketing communications.
3. Understand the elaboration likelihood model (ELM) and its implications for marketing communications.
4. Explain basic attitude change strategies.
5. Understand practical marketing communications efforts that enhance consumers' motivation, opportunity, and ability to process messages.
6. Explain tools of persuasion from the marketing communicator's perspective.

Opening Vignette: Will American Consumers Accept Recycling Kiosks?

Tomra Systems is a Norwegian company that specializes in recycling. After conducting an intensive analysis of American recycling practices (or, perhaps more appropriately, lack of recycling), Tomra launched a chain of 200 recycling kiosks in a test market in southern California. Tomra has ambitious plans to expand its rePlanet kiosks across the United States. The rePlanet kiosks have several features that should appeal to Americans: They are conveniently located (in supermarket parking lots), clean, and brightly lit to provide the user a sense of safety. Plus, the recycler gets paid for depositing used recyclable cans and bottles. Attendants are available at the kiosks during daytime hours and are trained to be friendly, accommodating, and efficient. But even when daytime attendants are not available, a "reverse vending machine" accepts containers deposited by the recycler and then issues a machine-printed receipt the recycler can later redeem for cash.

Tomra has its sights on a huge recycling market in the United States. Fewer than one-half of Americans have access to curbside recycling services, and hence bottles and cans often end up in landfills. Bottles and cans in landfills have no value to anyone and thus represent a huge environmental problem both in occupying landfill space and requiring energy expenditures to produce replacement containers. Tomra has plans to convert millions of people, who now deposit cans and bottles in their curbside trash, into enthusiastic recyclers. The hook? First, there is an economic incentive: Users receive anywhere from 2 to 10 cents per recycled container. Plus, the convenient, efficient, and safe kiosks simplify the act of recycling. These benefits would seem to have the potential to attract millions of Americans to become regular users of Tomra's services.

What will it take for Tomra to succeed? The basic business model requires annual revenue from each kiosk of approximately $100,000. The rePlanet kiosks cost the company about $50,000 each to install and another $25,000 annually for payroll and pickup expenses. Tomra's plan is to process about 150,000 containers per month at each kiosk. This volume is essential to achieve reasonable profitable goals. Tomra is expanding its operation into northern California and has tested the viability of the concept in metropolitan areas such as Atlanta, Orlando, and Tampa.

An executive of Tomra's North American operation claims that the company hopes to market recycling as an "experience" rather than an unpleasant chore. "We want to be the Starbucks of the recycling business." Though this aspiration is perhaps a bit pie-in-the-skyish, it nonetheless represents a worthwhile goal both in terms of environmental benefits and profit opportunities for the company. The reservation, however, is whether the masses can be persuaded to

Source: Adapted from Jim Carlton, "Norway's Tomra Redefines Recycling with Bright, Clean, Accessible Kiosks," *Wall Street Journal Online*, March 6, 2001 (http://interactive.wsj.com/). Copyright 2001 by DOW JONES & CO INC. Reproduced with permission of DOW JONES & CO INC. in the format Textbook via Copyright Clearance Center.

change their attitudes and behavior toward recycling. Will Tomra's attractive and convenient kiosks provide people with sufficient reason to slightly complicate their lives in return for environmental enrichment and a relatively small economic incentive? Let us hope that Tomra's kiosks spread like wildfire and that it does indeed become the Starbucks of recycling!

The *Opening Vignette* touches on the two interrelated topics treated in this chapter, attitudes and persuasion. To understand one topic requires an understanding of the other. *Attitude* is a mental property of the consumer, whereas *persuasion* is an effort by a marketing communicator to influence the consumer's attitude and behavior in a manner that benefits the communicator and, in relationship-oriented marketing, the consumer. This chapter first describes the core concept of attitude and then discusses several frameworks that explain how attitudes are formed and changed and how persuasion occurs. In effect, we will be studying marketing communications from the consumer's perspective. The chapter builds on the fundamentals treated in the previous chapter and provides insight into why MarCom messages sometimes succeed and at other times fail to influence consumers' attitudes and behavior.

THE NATURE AND ROLE OF ATTITUDES

What Is an Attitude?

Attitudes are *hypothetical constructs*; they cannot be seen, touched, heard, or smelled. Because attitudes cannot be observed, a variety of perspectives have developed over the years in attempting to describe them.[1] The term **attitude** will be used here to mean a general and somewhat enduring positive or negative feeling toward, or evaluative judgment of, some person, object, or issue.[2] Of course, for our purposes, brands are the attitude object of primary interest.

Beyond this basic definition are three other notable features: Attitudes (1) are *learned*, (2) are *relatively enduring*, and (3) *influence behavior*.[3] Consider the following examples of people's attitudes that express feelings and evaluations with varying degrees of intensity: "I like Diet Pepsi"; "I really like the initiatives undertaken by Mothers Against Drunk Driving (MADD)"; "I don't very much like Jesse Ventura" (the ex-wrestler who by some incredible twist of fate became governor of Minnesota); "I favor recycling and really like the idea of Tomra's kiosks"; and "I very much like David Gray" (British singer who has recorded *White Ladder* and other albums). All these attitudes are learned and likely will be retained until there is some strong reason to change them. Moreover, it can be expected that the holders of these attitudes would behave consistently with their evaluations—drinking Diet Pepsi, supporting MADD with perhaps a financial contribution, questioning Jesse Ventura's actions as governor, recycling aluminum cans, purchasing a new album by David Gray or attending a concert, and so on.

The preceding description focuses on feelings and evaluations, or what is commonly referred to as the **affective component**; this is generally what is referred to when people use the word *attitude*. However, attitude theorists recognize two additional components, *cognitive* and *conative*.[4] The **cognitive component** refers to a person's *beliefs* (i.e., knowledge and thoughts) about an object or issue ("the euro should greatly simplify currency transactions while traveling throughout Europe"; "talking on cell phones is dangerous while driving"; "BMW automobiles are well engineered"). The **conative component** represents one's *behavioral tendency*, or *predisposition* to act, toward an object. In consumer behavior terms, the conative component represents a consumer's intention to purchase a specific item. Generally speaking, attitudes predispose people to respond to an object, such as a brand, in a consistently favorable or unfavorable way.[5] Thus, for example, people who like the idea of recycling kiosks (as described in the *Opening Vignette*) are more likely to engage in recycling than are their fellow citizens who do not favorably embrace this concept.

A clear progression is implied: from initial cognition to affection to conation. An individual becomes aware of an object, such as a new brand, then acquires information and forms beliefs about the brand's ability to satisfy consumption needs (cognitive component). Beliefs are integrated, and feelings toward and evaluations of the product are developed (affective component). On the basis of these feelings and evaluations, an intention is formed to purchase or not to purchase the new product (conative component). An attitude, then, is characterized by progressing from thinking (cognitive) to feeling (affective) to behaving (conative). (The view that this strict progression applies to every behavior and that cognition must necessarily precede affect is not uncontested. Various alternative "hierarchies of effect" have been postulated, but such intricacies need not concern us here.)[6]

An illustration will help clarify the notion of attitude progression. Consider the case of Doug, who recently purchased a new sport utility vehicle (SUV), the Jeep Grand Cherokee (see Figure 5.1). When in the process of making a brand choice decision, Doug knew precisely what he wanted in a new SUV: a lot of passenger and luggage space, the ability to drive off-road during hunting and fishing trips, an attractive but rugged vehicle, unpretentious status, and good resale value. He acquired information about the Grand Cherokee and other models from friends and acquaintances, from advertisements, from online searching, and from dealer visitations. He formed beliefs about product features and about specific SUV models as a result of this information search-and-processing activity. These beliefs (representing the cognitive component) led Doug to form specific feelings toward and evaluations of various SUV models (affective component). He also liked the Land Rover Discovery, but that model lost a little luster

Figure 5.1   The Jeep Grand Cherokee

after a friend commented to Doug that some people consider Land Rover a "pretentious" brand name. In the final analysis, Doug's most positive affect was toward the Jeep Grand Cherokee, and his intention to purchase this model (conative component) finally materialized when he drove the new SUV away from the DaimlerChrysler dealership.

PERSUASION IN MARKETING COMMUNICATIONS

The foregoing discussion of attitudes provides us with useful concepts as we turn now to the strategic issue of how marketing communicators influence customers' attitudes and behaviors through persuasive efforts. Salespeople attempt to convince customers to purchase one product rather than another. Advertisers appeal to consumers' intellect (the CPM approach from prior chapter) or to their fantasies and feelings (the HEM approach) in attempting to create desired images for their brands so that consumers will someday purchase them. Brand managers use coupons, samples, rebates, and other types of promotions to induce consumers to try their products and to purchase them now rather than later.

Persuasion is the essence of marketing communications. Marketing communicators—along with people in other persuasion-oriented roles (e.g., theologians, parents, teachers, politicians)—attempt to guide people toward the acceptance of some belief, attitude, or behavior by using reasoning and emotional appeals.[7] The actual process by which this occurs is examined later in the chapter. First, however, it will be useful to provide some brief discussion on the ethics of persuasion inasmuch as the word *persuasion* may suggest to you something manipulative, exploitative, or unethical.

The Ethics of Persuasion

At times, marketing communicators' persuasion efforts are undeniably unethical. Shrewd operators bamboozle the unsuspecting and credulous into buying products or services that are never delivered. Elderly consumers, for example, are occasionally hustled into making advance payments for household repairs (e.g., roof repairs) that are never performed.[8] Unscrupulous realtors sell useless swampland in Florida to unsuspecting retirees who think they are acquiring prized real estate. Telemarketers sometimes get our attention under the pretense that they are conducting marketing research or representing a charitable cause and then try to sell us something.

Yes, persuasion by *some* marketing communicators is unethical. Of course, so sometimes are persuasive efforts by government officials, the clergy, teachers, your friends, and even you. Persuasion is a part of daily life in all its facets. The practice of persuasion can be noble or deplorable. There is nothing wrong with persuasion per se; it is the practitioners of persuasion who sometimes are at fault. To adapt an old adage: Don't throw the persuasion baby out with the bath water; just make sure the water is clean.

Multiple Forms of Persuasion

It would be erroneous to think that persuasion is a single method, practice, or technique. Rather, there are as many persuasion methods in theory as there are persuasion practitioners. This is a bit of an exaggeration, but it serves to emphasize that persuasion practices are highly diverse.

Another important point is that the topic of persuasion can be viewed from two perspectives. The first involves examining persuasion from the perspective of the *persuadee* (qua consumer) by exploring what factors cause a person to be persuaded. The other looks at persuasion from the perspective of the *persuader* (qua marketing communicator) and examines the techniques practitioners use to influence attitudes and encourage action. We will examine persuasion first from the persuadee's perspective and then from that of the persuader.

THE INFLUENCE PROCESS: THE PERSUADEE'S PERSPECTIVE

The persuasive efforts by two advertisers will serve to illustrate the following discussion. In the advertisement for the Dodge Grand Caravan (see Figure 5.2), reason after reason, argument upon argument is presented to convince consumers that this van is superior to competitive models. Of course, the "scorecard" comparison format portrays the Grand Caravan as having the lowest price yet possessing unparalleled features. On the other hand, a Discover Card advertisement says virtually nothing (at least in words) about this credit card brand. The ad contains minimal text and simply states that this card is "accepted at 1000 new locations every day including Godiva Chocolatier." Figure 5.3 depicts such a purpose. A prominent and attractive picture cleverly connects the Discover Card with Godiva by displaying the card in the form of a piece of fine Godiva chocolate. Perhaps the advertisement's real message—its subtext—is that the Discover Card has a prestige brand image similar to that of the famous brand, Godiva, with which the card is associated.

These contrasting persuasive efforts highlight the fact that there are many different ways in which to use persuasion. The following sections identify four factors fundamental in the persuasion process. Two factors (message arguments and peripheral cues) deal with persuasion vehicles under the marketing communicator's control. The other two (receiver involvement and initial position) apply to persuadee characteristics.

Figure 5.2   An Argument-Based Persuasive Effort

© Used with permission of DaimlerChrysler Corporation

Discover Card and Godiva Chocolate   **Figure 5.3**

© Terri Miller/e-visual communications

Message Arguments

The *strength or quality of message arguments* (e.g., the reasons given in Figure 5.2 to encourage consumer interest in the Dodge Grand Caravan) is often the major determinant of whether and to what extent persuasion occurs. Consumers are much more likely to be persuaded by convincing and believable messages than by weak arguments. It may seem strange, then, that much advertising fails to present substantive information or compelling arguments. One reason is that the majority of advertising, particularly television commercials, is for product categories (like soft drinks) in which interbrand differences are modest or virtually nonexistent. Another reason for advertising that promotes images rather than presents facts is that emotion, as discussed in Chapter 4, plays a key role in driving consumer choice.

Peripheral Cues

A second major determinant of persuasion is the presence of cues that are *peripheral to the primary message arguments*. These include such elements as background music, scenery, and graphics. As will be explained in a later section, under certain conditions these cues may play a more important role than message arguments in determining the outcome of a persuasive effort.

Receiver Involvement

The *personal relevance* that a communication has for a receiver is a critical determinant of the extent and form of persuasion. Highly involved consumers (i.e., those for whom an advertisement is most relevant) are motivated to process message arguments when exposed to marketing communications, whereas uninvolved consumers are likely to exert minimal attention to message arguments and perhaps to process only peripheral cues. The upshot is that involved and uninvolved consumers have to be persuaded in different ways. This will be detailed fully in a following section that presents an integrated model of persuasion.

Receiver's Initial Position

Scholars agree that persuasion results not from external communication per se but from the *self-generated thoughts* that people produce in response to persuasive efforts. Persuasion, in other words, is self-persuasion, or, stated poetically, "thinking makes it so."[9] These self-generated thoughts include both cognitive and emotional responses. These responses are directed at message arguments and executional elements or may involve emotional reactions and images related to using the advertised brand (e.g., "Coca-Cola *is* like family").[10]

There are two primary forms of cognitive responses: supportive arguments and counterarguments.[11] These responses are subvocal rather than vocalized; they are the thoughts elicited spontaneously in response to advertisements and other persuasive efforts. **Supportive arguments** occur when a receiver *agrees* with a message argument. For example, a person reading the Dodge Grand Caravan advertisement might respond favorably to all of the "exclusive features" possessed by this van. **Counterarguments** arise when the receiver *challenges* a message claim. Another person reading the same Grand Caravan ad might react that it doesn't seem possible that this van could be lower priced than five competitive vans (see Figure 5.2) yet possess numerous exclusive features. This "counterarguer," in other words, does not agree with the message arguments despite fully comprehending the advertiser's claims. (If you recall from the previous chapter the concept of *agreement*—stage 4 in the CPM process—you now understand that counterarguing represents a form of subvocal *dis*agreement. You also realize that a MarCom message's effectiveness is seriously compromised if message receivers counterargue, or disagree with, message claims. On the other hand, supportive arguments represent agreement with the claims, thereby facilitating message effectiveness.)

Whether a persuasive communication accomplishes its objectives depends on the balance of cognitive and emotional responses. If counterarguments outnumber supportive arguments, it is unlikely that many consumers will be convinced to undertake the course of action advocated. On the other hand, marketing communications can successfully persuade consumers if more supportive than negative arguments are registered or if emotional responses are predominantly positive.

AN INTEGRATED MODEL OF PERSUASION

The various factors overviewed are now combined into a coordinated theory of persuasion. Figure 5.4 presents a model of alternative mechanisms, or "routes," by which persuasion occurs.[12] This explanation is based on psychologists Petty and Cacioppo's **elaboration likelihood model (ELM)** and on marketing scholars MacInnis and Jaworski's integrative framework.[13]

It should be clear by this point in the chapter that there is no single mechanism by which persuasion occurs. Instead, there are a variety of possibilities. Understanding why this is so requires that you understand the concept of elaboration. **Elaboration** deals with mental activity in response to a message such as an advertisement. People elaborate on a message when they think about what the message is saying, evaluate the arguments in the message, engage in mental imagery when viewing pictures, and perhaps react emotionally to some of the claims. In other words, elaboration involves an application of cognitive resources in response to a MarCom message. To merely look at a TV commercial with a blank stare, for example, does not involve elaboration. However, elaboration *is* engaged when one views, say, a different commercial—a commercial that is personally relevant—and thinks about the people in the commercial and their simi-

An Integrated Model of Persuasion

Figure 5.4

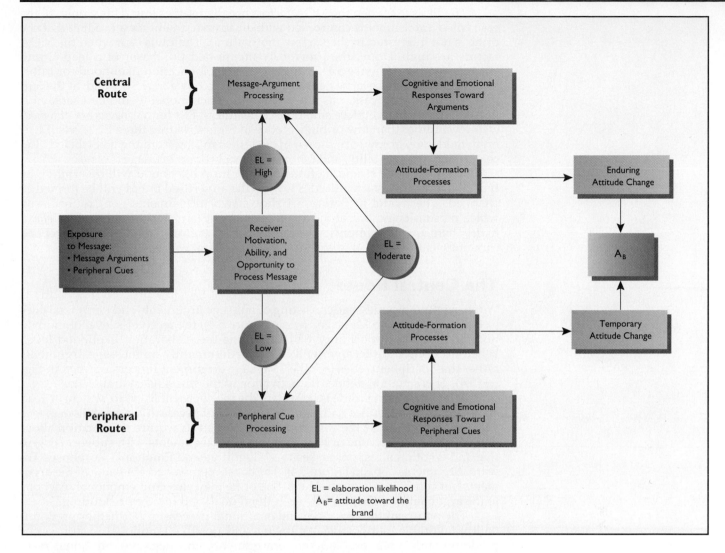

larity to one's own family or friends and how the advertised product may indeed fit into one's consumption lifestyle.

Whether and to what extent a person engages in elaboration depends on that person's *motivation, ability,* and *opportunity* to process (i.e., to attend to and comprehend) a marketing message's selling claims. **Motivation** is high when a message relates to a person's present consumption-related goals and needs and is thus relevant to that individual. Generally speaking, consumers are more motivated to process messages the more involved they are in the subject matter of a message. **Opportunity** involves the matter of whether it is physically possible for a person to process a message; opportunity is restricted when, among other reasons, a message is presented too quickly, the sound is too low, or an individual is distracted. **Ability** concerns whether a person is familiar with message claims and is capable of comprehending them. Consumers, on occasion, are motivated but unable to process message claims.

Together, motivation, opportunity, and ability, or **MOA** for short, determine each individual's *elaboration likelihood* for a particular message. **Elaboration likelihood (EL)** represents the chance or prospect that a message receiver will elaborate on a message by thinking about and reacting to it and comparing it with his or her preexisting thoughts and beliefs regarding the product category, the advertised brand, and perhaps competitive brands. (Please note the close similarity between elaboration likelihood and the concept of *active synthesis* that was discussed in the previous chapter.) We can envision an elaboration likelihood continuum ranging from a low likelihood at one end to a high likelihood at the other.

The EL is *low* when the MOA factors are themselves low. This would be the case when a consumer is confronted with an advertisement for a product that she or he is not interested in (hence low motivation). The EL is *high* when the MOA factors are high. Doug, the previously mentioned purchaser of a Jeep Grand Cherokee vehicle (Figure 5.1), exhibited a high elaboration likelihood for information about SUVs because he was determined to buy a new SUV and, at the outset of the buying process, was uncertain as to which model would best satisfy his needs. In many marketplace situations, consumers' ELs for messages are at a *moderate* level rather than low or high. Notice in Figure 5.4 that three EL levels (EL = high, moderate, or low) are shown in circles extending from the box labeled "Receiver Motivation, Ability, and Opportunity to Process Message."

In general, the strength of one's elaboration likelihood will determine the type of process by which attitudes toward the advertised brand will be formed or changed. The model in Figure 5.4 shows two mechanisms—or "routes"—by which persuasion occurs: at the top, a *central route*, and at the bottom, a *peripheral route*. There is also an implicit *dual route* that results from a moderate EL level and combines features of both the central and peripheral routes.

The Central Route

When exposed to a message consisting of message arguments and peripheral cues (see the "Exposure to Message" box in Figure 5.4), the receiver's level of motivation, ability, and opportunity will determine the elaboration likelihood level. When EL is *high*, the receiver will focus predominantly on message arguments rather than peripheral cues (see the "Message-Argument Processing" box in Figure 5.4). This situation defines the activation of the so-called central route.

When the central route is activated, the receiver will listen to, watch, or read about a brand's attributes and benefits but will not necessarily accept them at face value. Rather, because the consumer is motivated to acquire information about the product category, she or he will react to the arguments with subvocal cognitive and emotional responses (see the "Cognitive and Emotional Responses Toward Arguments" box in Figure 5.4). The consumer may accept some of the arguments but counterargue with others. She or he may also emit emotional reactions to the arguments—"That's a lie!" or "Whom do they think they're kidding?"

The nature of the cognitive and emotional processing—whether predominantly favorable (supportive arguments and positive emotional responses) or predominantly unfavorable (counterarguments and negative emotional reactions)—will determine whether the persuasive communication influences attitudes and also the direction of that influence. This takes us to the box labeled "Attitude-Formation Processes" in Figure 5.4, which addresses how attitudes under the central route are formed or changed. There are, in fact, several possibilities, two of which are discussed in the following sections: *emotion-based* persuasion and *message-based* persuasion.[14]

Emotion-Based Persuasion.   When a consumer is highly involved in a marketing communications message, say, a TV commercial, there is a tendency to relate aspects of the message to his or her personal situation. The consumer may vicariously place himself or herself into the commercial, relate to the product and people in the commercial, and *empathically* experience positive emotions (e.g., a sense of pride, romantic feelings, nostalgia) or negative emotions (e.g., anguish, fear). Under these circumstances, attitudes toward the advertised brand (depicted as A_B in Figure 5.4) stand a good chance of being changed in the direction of the experienced emotion—positive emotional reactions leading to positive brand attitudes and negative reactions leading to negative attitudes. Moreover, because the consumer's elaboration likelihood is high, it is to be expected that any attitude change experienced under the central route will be relatively enduring (see the "Enduring Attitude Change" box in Figure 5.4).

Consider, for example, an award-winning advertising campaign undertaken by the South Carolina Department of Highways. This ongoing campaign is directed at persuading people (especially teenagers and young adults) not to drink and drive. Commercials graphically depict the aftermath of accidents and the personal tragedy suffered by the driver and the victims of his or her drunken driving. Many viewers of these commercials find themselves emotionally involved with the people and situations depicted. They vicariously experience the anguish that the drama presents. Research indicates that the campaign has successfully influenced many people in the target audience to hold negative attitudes toward driving after drinking or riding with someone who has been drinking. (Of course, the real advertising challenge in this situation is to get teenagers, and other people who often drive an automobile after drinking, not just to have more negative attitudes toward this practice but to *change their behavior*—to absolutely not drive after drinking. This comment should remind you of our discussion back in Chapter 1, which emphasized that IMC's ultimate objective is to *affect behavior*.)

Message-Based Persuasion. The second central-route attitude-formation process results from processing message arguments. When consumers are sufficiently motivated and able to process a message's specific arguments or selling points, their cognitive responses may lead to changes in *beliefs* about the advertised brand or changes in *evaluations* of the importance of brand attributes and benefits. In either or both cases, the result is a change in attitudes toward the brand.

The process just described has been fully developed in the well-known theory of reasoned action (TORA). This theory proposes that all forms of planned and reasoned behavior (versus unplanned, spontaneous, impulsive behavior) have two primary determinants: attitudes and normative influences.[15] Many of you have learned about this theory in a psychology or consumer behavior course, so rather than explain the entire theory, the present discussion describes just the attitudinal component.[16]

Attitude formation according to TORA can best be described in terms of the following equation:

$$A_{Bj} = \sum_{i=1}^{n} b_{ij} \cdot e_i$$

Equation 5.1

where:

A_{Bj} = *attitude* toward a particular brand (brand *j*)
b_{ij} = the *belief*, or expectation, that owning brand *j* will lead to outcome *i*
e_i = the positive or negative *evaluation* of the *i*th outcome

A consumer's attitude toward a brand (or, more technically, toward the act of owning and consuming the brand) is determined by his or her beliefs regarding the *outcomes*, or consequences, of owning the brand weighed by the evaluations of those outcomes. **Outcomes** (expressed in Equation 5.1 as $i = 1$ through n, where n is typically fewer than 7) involve those aspects of product ownership that the consumer either desires to obtain (e.g., safety, attractive styling, and good gas mileage with an automobile) or to avoid (e.g., frequent breakdowns). Outcomes involve both brand-related *benefits* (positive outcomes) and *detriments* (negative outcomes). The term *outcomes* thus encompasses the good (benefits) and the bad (detriments) with respect to purchasing and consumption. Consumers approach benefits and avoid detriments.

Beliefs (the b_{ij} term in Equation 5.1) are the consumer's subjective probability assessments, or expectations, regarding the likelihood that performing a certain act (e.g., buying the brand *j* automobile) will lead to a certain outcome. In theory, the consumer who is in the market for a product has a separate belief associated with each potential outcome for each brand he or she is considering buying, and it is for this reason that the belief term in Equation 5.1 is subscripted with both an *i* (referring to a particular outcome consideration) and *j* (referring to a specific brand). Doug, the previously mentioned purchaser of a Jeep Grand Cherokee, considered outcomes such as passenger and luggage space, the ability to drive off-road during hunting and fishing trips, an attractive but rugged vehicle, unpretentious status, and good resale value to be the most important factors in choosing an SUV. Doug formed, or already had in memory, specific beliefs

IMC
focus

Faster Than a Microwave Oven, Better Than a Conventional Oven

Imagine that you want to bake a potato and have a choice of a conventional or microwave oven. The conventional oven will take a long time (at least an hour), but the potato will come out well cooked on the inside and crisp on the outside. Prepared in a microwave oven, on the other hand, the potato will be baked in less than 10 minutes but it won't have that crisp, scrumptious exterior. In other words, the choice of oven in which to prepare the potato requires a trade-off between speed of cooking (the microwave oven wins hands down) and delectability of the finished potato (the conventional oven is the clear winner). What if there were an alternative, an oven that provides the quick-cooking ability of a microwave and the better-tasting result from a conventional oven.

Too good to be true? Well that is the challenge faced by the General Electric company (GE) in its marketing of the Advantium oven, which has been on the market now for several years. The Advantium oven uses white-hot halogen bulbs in combination with microwave energy to cook foods as much as eight times faster than conventional ovens. The food tastes as good as if it were cooked in a conventional oven (in comparison to what one gets with microwave cooking) and comes out beauti-fully browned. GE somehow has to convince consumers that they can "have their cake and eat it too"—that is, that the Advantium oven cooks in microwave time but the food is as good as from a conventional oven. GE's VP of marketing described the company's challenge in these terms: "The microwave oven made the same promise of speed and quality, and it delivered on half the equation."

GE thus has to convince consumers—that is, to change their beliefs—that it is technologically feasible to prepare good-tasting food in microwave time. To alter beliefs, it is critical that consumers experience products cooked in an Advantium oven so they can learn for themselves that fast cooking and good taste are not mutually exclusive benefits. Cooking demonstrations by retailers (followed by taste testing by consumers) are critical to assure people that it is possible to prepare items quickly that taste great. GE's greatest fear is that consumers will not be convinced that these dual benefits are possible and that it might therefore take a decade or more, as in the case of microwave ovens, before the Advantium is widely adopted.

Sources: Adapted from Steve Kruschen, "Speedcooking Now Easier Than Ever with GE Profile Advantium 120 Oven" (http://www.mrgadget.com/hitechhome01/advantium120.html); Matt Murray, "Marketing Fast and Costly Oven Poses a Tricky Challenge for GE," October 18, 1999 (http://interactive.wsj.com/).

---

about each of these attributes for each SUV model that he seriously considered. See the *IMC Focus* insert for a discussion of GE's challenge in changing consumers' beliefs for a new oven product.

Because all outcomes are not equally important or determinant of consumer choice, we need to introduce a term that recognizes this influence differential. This term is the evaluation component, e_i, in Equation 5.1. **Evaluations** represent the *value*, or importance, that consumers attach to consumption outcomes. For example, Doug may have considered ruggedness to be the most important consideration in selecting an SUV, followed by resale value and then passenger and luggage space. It is important to note that outcome evaluations apply to the product category in general and are *not* brand specific. It is for this reason that we need only a single subscript, i, to designate evaluations and not also a j, as in the case of beliefs.

Hence, Equation 5.1 and the corresponding discussion represent the attitude-formation process that results from the integration (see the summation symbol in the equation) of beliefs regarding individual outcomes of brand ownership weighed by their evaluation. Attitudes toward a brand are more positive when a brand is perceived favorably with respect to valued outcomes and less positive when a brand is perceived unfavorably on these outcomes.

Attitude Change Strategies.   With Equation 5.1 in mind, we can identify three strategies that marketing communicators employ in attempting to change consumer attitudes.[17] These three strategies are (1) to change beliefs, (2) to alter outcome evaluations, or (3) to introduce a new outcome into the evaluation process.

The first attitude change strategy attempts to bolster attitudes by influencing brand-related beliefs, which thus explains the term *belief change* to characterize this strategy. The marketing communicator's objective is to create (in the case of new brands) or change (for established brands) consumer beliefs regarding outcomes that are valued by consumers. In other words, this strategy "operates" on the b_{ij} term from Equation 5.1. Consider the following MarCom efforts to influence consumers' beliefs:

- Many American consumers consider the BMW to be an automobile that is excessively expensive to maintain. Accordingly, a campaign was introduced to advertise BMW as "the car that tunes itself."[18]
- When you think of safety, what automobile comes to mind? If you're like most people, the car that occurred to you is a Volvo. Knowing this fact, marketers at Swedish-made Saab undertook a major ad campaign to put Saab in a safety class with Volvo. In an effort to enhance consumers' beliefs regarding Saab's safety, print ads included copy lines such as "Safety marries performance. They elope"; "If there were elephants in Sweden, we'd have a safety test for that, too"; "If Saab makes the safest cars in Sweden, and Sweden makes the safest cars in the world. . . ."[19]
- Many automobile owners are of the mind-set that they should have their motor oil changed approximately every 3,000-miles. The advisability of the 3,000-mile oil changes was inculcated in earlier generations of drivers who drove less efficient automobiles than those of the current era, and this questionable wisdom is reinforced today by oil-change retail chains that instruct customers to have oil changes at 3,000-mile intervals. In context of the fact (or fiction) of a 3,000-mile oil change interval, the STP Products Company attempted to convince consumers that it has an oil extender product that will allow automobiles to travel safely for up to 6,000 miles between oil changes. To accentuate this point, the headline in a magazine advertisement for STP oil extender proclaimed "Introducing the 3000/6000-mile oil change" with the 3000 amount shown with a big X drawn through it. It is obvious that the STP Products Company wanted customers to form the belief that STP oil extender, when added to an engine's motor oil, will virtually double the amount of mileage a car can travel before another oil change is required. Consumers surely would be responsive to such a benefit if indeed they can be convinced that STP oil extender will deliver on its promise.

A second attitude change strategy is to influence existing evaluations (the e_i term in Equation 5.1). This *evaluation change* strategy involves getting consumers to reassess a particular outcome associated with brand ownership and to alter their evaluations of the outcome's value. For example, Tylenol advertised the fact that it, unlike some competitive brands of pain reliever, contains no caffeine. Tylenol's advertising objective was to get consumers to place a negative value on the presence of caffeine in pain relievers and by doing so to have a more favorable attitude toward Tylenol and less favorable attitudes toward brands that are not caffeine free. In general, an evaluation change strategy involves MarCom efforts to get consumers to place more weight or value on product outcomes on which "our" brand performs especially well.

A third strategy used by marketing communicators to change attitudes is what we might call an *add-an-outcome strategy.* The objective, in other words, is to get consumers to judge brands in a product category in terms of a product benefit on which "our" brand fares especially well. Consider for example some marketing efforts by Tropicana Products. First, in the late 1990s Tropicana reformulated its Pure Premium orange juice with a newly patented calcium source called FruitCal—a highly soluble form of calcium. The advertising campaign that trumpeted this product reformulation attempted to modify the way consumers evaluate orange juice by focusing on a purchase consideration—calcium—that most consumers had never before considered when making a brand selection from the orange juice category. In other words, Tropicana wanted consumers to begin thinking of orange juice as a source of calcium.[20]

A number of other food product companies touted the same source-of-calcium benefit as did Tropicana, so eventually this product feature lost some its differentiating luster. To regain a health claim advantage over other food products, Tropicana several years later began an advertising campaign claiming that orange juice is a natural source of potassium, a mineral that can reduce the risk of high blood pressure and strokes. Hence, reducing the risk of high blood pressure and strokes represents a potent new outcome that consumers typically do not think of when considering a product such as orange juice. Nutrition claims such as these have enabled Tropicana to build its premium orange juice into the number 3–selling grocery brand in the United States, behind only Coca-Cola and Pepsi.[21]

An advertisement for Neutrogena No-Stick Sunscreen further illustrates an effort to introduce a new outcome into consumers' set of choice criteria. All brands in this category can claim to block the sun, so Neutrogena's advertising encouraged consumers to evaluate brands in terms of a new consideration—whether sunscreen is nongreasy and eliminates sticking sand. Of course, competitive brands could not, at the time of Neutrogena's introductory advertising campaign, make a comparable claim, and, as such, Neutrogena gained an advantage in the minds of those consumers bothered by sticking sand.

The Peripheral Route

When the MOA factors—motivation, opportunity, and ability (see Figure 5.4)—are at low levels, a different form of persuasion is involved. Specifically, when the consumer is not motivated to attend and comprehend message arguments, she or he may nonetheless attend a message's *peripheral* features. The peripheral route is shown at the bottom of Figure 5.4, where attention focuses on processing peripheral cues rather than message arguments.

As previously noted, peripheral cues involve elements of a message that are unrelated (and hence peripheral) to the primary selling points in the message. For example, a TV commercial's peripheral cues might include the background music, the scenery, or attractive models. In the case of a presentation by a salesperson, peripheral cues could include that individual's physical appearance, how he or she is dressed, his or her accent, and so on.

The consumer, having attended to a peripheral cue, may experience thoughts or emotions in response to the cue ("The music is exhilarating"; "What a beautiful dress"; "The scenery is gorgeous"). These responses (labeled "Cognitive and Emotional Responses Toward Peripheral Cues" in Figure 5.4) might produce an attitude toward the advertisement itself and/or the advertised brand.[22] Classical conditioning provides one account of how attitudes toward a brand (A_B) are formed via the peripheral route.

Classical Conditioning of Attitudes.
Perhaps you are familiar with the experiments in which the famous Russian scientist, Ivan Pavlov, trained dogs to salivate on hearing a bell ring. Pavlov accomplished this canine response by establishing a systematic *contingency relation* between the bell and a desirable object (to dogs) such as meat powder, which itself was able to make dogs salivate. Trial after trial, dogs would hear a bell ring and then would be presented with meat powder. In this situation, meat powder was an *unconditioned stimulus (US)*, and salivation was an *unconditioned response (UR)*. By repeatedly pairing the bell (a *conditioned stimulus,* or *CS*) with the meat powder, the bell by itself eventually caused the dog to salivate. The dog, in other words, had been trained to emit a *conditioned response (CR)* on hearing the bell ring. The dog had learned that the bell regularly preceded meat powder, and thus the ringing bell caused the dog to predict that something desirable—the meat powder—was forthcoming.

Something analogous to this happens when consumers process peripheral cues. For example, brand advertisements that include adorable babies, sexy people, and majestic scenery can elicit positive emotional reactions. (Think of these peripheral cues as analogous to meat powder [the US], the emotional reactions as analogous to the dog's salivation [the UR], and the advertised brand as analogous to the bell in Pavlov's experiments [the CS].) The emotion contained in the cue may become associated with the brand, thereby influencing consumers to like the brand more than they did prior to viewing the commercial. In other words, through their repeated association, the CS (advertised brand) comes to elicit a CR similar to the UR evoked by the US itself (the peripheral cue).[23]

Temporary Versus Enduring Attitude Change. According to the ELM theory on which the foregoing discussion is based, people experience only *temporary* attitude change when persuaded via the peripheral route in comparison to the relatively *enduring* change experienced under the central route. Thus, in circumstances in which receivers think about and process message arguments (i.e., when the elaboration likelihood is high and the central route is invoked), attitudes that are formed will be relatively enduring compared to attitudes formed via the peripheral route. Moreover, these attitudes will be comparatively stronger, more accessible, and more resistant to change.

On the other hand, when the elaboration likelihood is low (because the communication topic is not particularly relevant to the message recipient), attitude change may nevertheless occur (by virtue of receivers' processing peripheral cues) but will be only temporary unless consumers are exposed continuously to the peripheral cue. There is some evidence, however, that the use of peripheral cues in advertising can influence attitudes and even shape choice behavior so long as the advertised brand is *not* dominated by a competitive brand that is superior with respect to all pertinent choice criteria.[24]

Dual Routes

The central and peripheral paths represent end points on a continuum of persuasion strategies and are not intended to imply that persuasion is an either-or proposition. In other words, in many cases there is a combination of central and peripheral processes operating simultaneously.[25] This is shown in Figure 5.4 when the MOA factors produce a *moderate* elaboration likelihood level. In this instance, which no doubt captures the majority of situations in marketing communications, consumers can be expected to process both message arguments and peripheral cues. As such, attitudes toward the brand result from a combination of central- and peripheral-route attitude-formation processes.

PRACTICAL IMPLICATIONS: ENHANCING CONSUMERS' PROCESSING MOTIVATION, OPPORTUNITY, AND ABILITY

In recognizing alternative paths to attitude formation and thus to persuasion, the ELM points out that the form of persuasion will depend both on consumer *characteristics* (their motivation, opportunity, and ability to process marketing messages) and on the relative *strengths* of the brand. If consumers are interested in learning about a product, and a company's brand has clear advantages over competitive brands, then the persuasion tactic to be taken is obvious: *Design a message telling people explicitly why our brand is superior.* The result should be equally clear: Consumers likely will be swayed by our arguments, which will lead to relatively enduring attitude change and a strong chance they will select our brand over its competitors.

However, the reality is that most brands in a product category are similar, and, because of this, consumers generally are not anxious to devote mental effort toward processing messages that provide little new information. Thus, the marketing communicator, faced with this double whammy (only slightly involved consumers and a me-too brand), has to find ways to enthuse consumers sufficiently such that they will listen to and/or read the communicator's message. Hence, anything a marketing communicator can do to enhance the MOA factors likely will result in increased communication effectiveness. This is because increases in motivation, opportunity, or ability result in greater message elaboration; greater elaboration, in turn, facilitates central-route processing and the possibility for more enduring attitude change and attitudes that are more resistant to attacks from competitors.

Figure 5.5 provides a framework for the following discussion of how marketing communicators can enhance each of the MOA factors.[26] Each of six strategies will be systematically discussed and illustrated with appropriate examples. At the risk of redundancy, it is important once again to emphasize that it cannot be assumed that consumers will attend MarCom messages and process them just because they are printed, broadcast, or disseminated through some other medium. Rather, it is essential that special efforts be made to increase consumers' motivation, opportunity, and ability to process MarCom messages.

Enhancing Motivation to Attend to Messages

Figure 5.5 shows, under Roman numeral I, that the communicator's objective is to increase the consumer's motivation to *attend to* the message and *process* brand information. This section discusses just the attention component; the following section will consider the processing element.

Figure 5.5   Enhancing Consumers' Motivation, Opportunity, and Ability to Process Brand Information

I. **Enhance Consumers' MOTIVATION to . . .**

A. *Attend to the message by . . .*
- Appealing to hedonic needs (appetite appeals, sex appeals)
- Using novel stimuli (unusual pictures, different ad formats, large number of scenes)
- Using intense or prominent cues (action, loud music, colorful ads, celebrities, large pictures)
- Using motion (complex pictures; edits and cuts)

B. *Process brand information by . . .*
- Increasing relevance of brand to self (asking rhetorical questions, using fear appeals, using dramatic presentations)
- Increasing curiosity about the brand (opening with suspense or surprise, using humor, presenting little information in the message)

II. **Enhance Consumers' OPPORTUNITY to . . .**

A. *Encode information by . . .*
- Repeating brand information
- Repeating key scenes
- Repeating the ad on multiple occasions

B. *Reduce processing time by . . .*
- Creating Gestalt processing (using pictures and imagery)

III. **Enhance Consumers' ABILITY to . . .**

A. *Access knowledge structures by . . .*
- Providing a context (employing verbal framing)

B. *Create knowledge structures by . . .*
- Facilitating exemplar-based learning (using concretizations, demonstrations, and analogies)

Source: Adapted from Deborah J. MacInnis, Christine Moorman, and Bernard J. Jaworski, "Enhancing and Measuring Consumers' Motivation, Opportunity, and Ability to Process Brand Information from Ads," *Journal of Marketing* 55 (October 1991), p. 36. Reprinted with permission from Journal of Marketing, published by the American Marketing Association.

There are two forms of attention: voluntary and involuntary.[27] **Voluntary attention** is engaged when consumers devote attention to an advertisement or other MarCom message that is perceived as *relevant to their current purchase-related goals*. In other words, messages are voluntarily attended if they are perceived as pertinent to our needs. Marketing communicators attract voluntary attention by appealing to consumers' informational or hedonic needs. **Involuntary attention**, on the other hand, occurs when attention is captured by the use of attention-gaining techniques rather than by the consumer's inherent interest in the topic at hand. Novel stimuli, intense or prominent cues, complex pictures, and, in the case of broadcast ads, edits and cuts of the sort one sees with MTV-like videos are some of the techniques used to attract attention that otherwise would not be given.

Appeals to Informational and Hedonic Needs. Consumers are most likely to attend to messages that serve their informational needs and those that make them feel good and bring pleasure (hedonic needs). Regarding **informational needs,** consumers are attracted to those stimuli that supply relevant facts and figures. A student who wants to move out of a dormitory and into an apartment, for example, will be on the lookout for information pertaining to apartments. Classified ads and overheard conversations about apartments will be attended even when the apartment seeker is not actively looking for information. As another illustration, consider also the advertisement in Figure 5.6 for Toppik, a product for thinning hair. People experiencing thinning hair and who are concerned about that condition are likely to attend this ad when exposed to it while

An Appeal to Consumers' Informational Needs

Figure 5.6

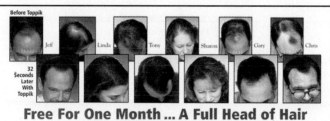

Figure 5.7   An Appeal to Hedonic Needs

reading a magazine in which it appears. Whether the product actually "works" is incidental to the present discussion. The point stands, however, that such an advertisement is capable of attracting the attention of people experiencing hair loss.

Hedonic needs are satisfied when consumers attend to messages that make them feel good and serve their pleasure needs. People are most likely to attend those messages that have become associated with good times, enjoyment, and things we value in life. For example, the use of babies (Figure 5.7), warm family scenes (Figure 5.8), and sex/romance appeals are just some of the commonly used attention-gaining techniques widely used in advertisements. Similarly, advertisements for appetizing food products are especially likely to be noticed when people are hungry. For this reason, many restaurant and fast-food marketers advertise on the radio during the after-work rush hour. Fast-food advertisers also promote their products on late-night television for the same reason. Needless to say, the best time to reach consumers with a message is just at the time they are experiencing a need for the product category in which the brand resides.

Use of Novel Stimuli.   There are innumerable ways marketing communicators use novelty to attract involuntary attention. In general, **novel messages** are *unusual, distinctive,* or *unpredictable.* Such stimuli tend to produce greater attention than those that are familiar and routine. This can be explained by the behavioral concept of *human adaptation.* People adapt to the conditions around them: As a stimulus becomes more familiar, people become desensitized to it. Psychologists refer to this as *habituation.* For example, if you drive past a billboard on the way

Another Appeal to Hedonic Needs   Figure 5.8

Many admirable qualities. A variety of colors. Sort of like people.

CAMRY

Toyota Camry is the #1 selling car in America for the second year in a row." Looks like we all share more in common than we think

TOYOTA | *everyday*

© Courtesy of Camry — Toyota Motor North America, Inc.

to school or work each day, you probably notice it less on each occasion. If the billboard were removed, you probably would notice it was no longer there. In other words, we notice by exception.

Examples of novelty abound. Consider, for example, an advertisement for Sauza Conmemorativo tequila. This incredibly eye-catching magazine advertisement, which is not shown here because the company denied permission, simply shows an old, full-bearded man wearing a brimmed hat. Most conspicuous, however, is the fact that the broadly smiling man has a mouth with only a single tooth! Imprinted above his mouth is the statement, "This man has one cavity." The ad personifies novelty insofar as most ads show "beautiful people." This eye-catching ad and its use of an old, virtually toothless man is a humorous attempt to catch attention and make a point that is accentuated below the old man's face, "Life is Harsh—Your tequila shouldn't be." Figure 5.9 for Ginsana, a dietary supplement, further illustrates the use of novelty to gain the reader's attention. Notice again that the ad layout "forces" the reader's eye flow from the unusual, and thus novel, portrayal of a leaning man directly down to the package and brand name. Both examples represent a key point: The effective use of novelty involves not just attracting attention but also *directing* that attention to key visual and verbal information.

Use of Intense Stimuli.   **Intense stimuli** (those that are louder, more colorful, bigger, brighter, etc.) increase the probability of attracting attention. This is because it is difficult for consumers to avoid intense stimuli, thus leading to involuntary

Figure 5.9

attention. One need only walk through a shopping mall, department store, or supermarket and observe the various packages, displays, sights, sounds, and smells to appreciate the special efforts marketing communicators take to attract attention.

Advertisements, too, utilize intensity to attract attention. For example, an advertisement for the Ericsson mobile phone, which is not shown here because the company denied permission, attracts attention through intensity by using splendid colors. Specifically, the ad shows the body of a well-conditioned man painted in the colors of the flags representing various nations. This colorful visualization further serves the purpose of pictorially representing the ad copy, which explains that the advertised mobile phone works in 120 countries around the world. The flag-painted man is thus symbolic of the global road warrior who carries his or her mobile phone everywhere.

Using Motion. Advertisers sometimes employ motion to both attract and direct consumer attention to the brand name and to pertinent ad copy. (Motion obviously is used in TV commercials, which is an inherently dynamic medium. However, the issue is more germane in the case of print advertising—magazines and newspapers—which is a static form of advertising display. Hence, artistic and photographic techniques are employed that produce a semblance of movement, though nothing is of course actually moving.) Falling objects (e.g., a flipping coin), people appearing to be running, and automobiles in motion are some of the techniques used in print ads to attract attention. The Jaguar automobile (Figure 5.10) seems to be moving, and this movement attracts the reader's attention and then directs it to the body copy and on to the brand name.

Using Motion to Attract Attention

Figure 5.10

0–60 in 5.4 seconds.

Now, about the rest of the ride.

The Jaguar XJR is also engineered to handle like a dream. With a racing-inspired suspension. Road-gripping 18" Pirelli tires. And a supercharged, 370 horsepower engine that will steal your heart in a matter of seconds.

JAGUAR

THE ART of PERFORMANCE

© Courtesy of FORD MOTOR COMPANY

Enhancing Motivation to Process Messages

Enhanced processing motivation means that the ad receiver has increased interest in reading and/or listening to the ad message to determine what it has to say that might be of relevance. Among other desirable outcomes, increased processing motivation has been shown to strengthen the impact of brand attitudes on purchase intentions.[28] To enhance consumers' motivation to process brand information, marketing communicators do two things: (1) enhance the *relevance* of the brand to the self and (2) enhance *curiosity* about the brand. Methods for enhancing brand relevance include the use of *rhetorical questions* (see Figure 5.11—Multiple Cats?), *fear appeals* (to be discussed in Chapter 10), and *dramatic presentation* to increase the significance of the brand to consumers' self-interests.

Enhancing curiosity about a brand can be accomplished by using *humor*, presenting *little information* in the message (and thereby encouraging the consumer to think about the brand), or opening a message with *suspense* or *surprise*. The American Express ad (Figure 5.12 on page 136) reflects a combination of suspense and surprise to draw attention to the depiction of the AE card and the ad copy. What is this? What's going on here? (Notice how your attention flows directly from the great white shark, along the female body grasped in its mouth, on then to the green AE card [bingo!], and perhaps up to the ad copy.) Figure 5.13, on page 137, for Honda cars uses surprise (the head of a dog on the body of a woman!) to provoke curiosity. You will note that a dog has nothing to do with the advertising content per se, which is a safety appeal to mothers who are concerned about protecting their children. The juxtaposition of a dog's head on "mom's" body is merely a clever device to increase the readers' curiosity and thus their processing motivation.

Figure 5.11   Using a Rhetorical Question to Enhance Processing Motivation

Enhancing Opportunity to Encode Information

Marketing messages have no chance of effectiveness unless consumers comprehend information about the brand and incorporate it with information related to the product category in their existing memory structure. Hence, the communicator's goal is to get consumers to *encode* information and, toward this end, to make it as simple and quick as possible for them to do so. The secret to facilitating encoding is *repetition*: The marketing communicator should repeat brand information, repeat key scenes, and repeat the advertisement on multiple occasions. Through repetition consumers have increased opportunity to encode the important information the communicator wishes to convey. Please see the *Global Focus* insert, which discusses repetition of a different sort—namely, the long-standing use of a brand icon for Lipton tea that served simultaneously to make the brand immediately recognizable yet terribly outdated.

Enhancing Opportunity to Reduce Processing Time

Opportunity to process is further enhanced if the communicator goes to extra measure to *reduce the time* required of the consumer to read, listen to, and ultimately to discern the meaning of a MarCom message. The use of pictures and imagery create a form of total-message processing (or Gestalt processing) whereby the consumer can readily encode the totality of the message rather than having to process information bit by bit. This is in line with the old aphorism that a picture

A Brand with a Rich but Irrelevant Heritage

When you awaken in the morning, which of the following beverages do you generally drink: coffee, hot tea, iced tea, a Coke or Pepsi, water, an energy drink, or something else? Lipton, the largest tea marketer in the United States, wants to encourage more consumers than ever to switch to tea—not just in the morning but anytime throughout the day. In fact, Lipton spent $100 million in 2001 alone to persuade people to begin thinking of tea as an alternative to traditional soft drinks, which command about 30 percent share of all beverage consumption.

In initiating this ambitious program to change beverage preferences, Lipton's MarCom people faced a major challenge: The icon of Lipton tea—a white-mustachioed British gentlemen dressed in a blue uniform—has adorned Lipton tea boxes since the late 19th century. This mascot is not just any old Brit but is in fact the Lipton founder himself, Sir Thomas J. Lipton. The Lipton brand is world famous, but consumers associate the brand with older people. (In other words, Lipton's *user imagery*, as that term was discussed in Chapter 2 in context of the brand equity model, is that of an older person.) For example, a participant in one focus-group study compared the Lipton box to something that aged actress Katharine Hepburn might want to purchase. Lipton's marketing VP, distressed by such perceptions, acknowledged that Lipton's image is rich but no longer relevant.

What to do? The answer may seem obvious, but it took considerable courage on the part of Lipton's marketing strategists to relinquish the heritage of the Sir Thomas J. Lipton emblem and to change the box that had carried his image for more than a century. After dumping Sir Thomas and otherwise modernizing the famous Lipton tea box, research revealed that consumers' perceptions of Lipton were quickly refreshed and in line with a 21st-century rather than 19th-century image. The incentive for change was great. Although Americans consume 182.5 gallons of liquid on average per year, tea consumption (hot and iced) averages only 7 gallons. In other words, tea represents only about 4 percent of total liquid consumption in the United States. A modernized image and an aggressive advertising campaign were exactly what the image-revitalization doctor called for in the case of Lipton tea. After the package-modernization move, younger consumers now believe that Lipton is an up-to-date brand and hold more favorable attitudes toward it. On the other hand, some older consumers who grew up with Sir Thomas emblazoning the Lipton box are not happy with the move. With no disrespect intended, Lipton's marketing executives are understandably more concerned with recruiting new, younger consumers to the Lipton brand—consumers who will be around for 40 or more years—rather than merely catering to the nostalgia whims of the "old loyals."

Source: Adapted from Vanessa O'Connell, "Lipton Tea Overhauls Its Image by Eliminating Sir Thomas Mascot," *Wall Street Journal Online*, May 21, 2001 (http:// interactive.wsj.com/). Copyright 2001 by DOW JONES & CO INC. Reproduced with permission of DOW JONES & CO INC. in the format Textbook via Copyright Clearance Center.

is worth a thousand words. The Camry Solara advertisement (Figure 5.14 on page 138) "says" it all with the imagery conveyed by the Hawaiian shirt. Similarly, the Norelco ad (Figure 5.15 on page 139) readily conveys its intent with a suggestive graphic illustration and minimal body copy.

Enhancing Ability to Access Knowledge Structures

In general, people are most able to process new information that relates to something they already know or understand. If one knows a lot about computers, then information presented in computer language is readily comprehended. The marketing communicator's task is to enable consumers either to *access* existing

Figure 5.12   Using Suspense/Surprise to Enhance Processing Motivation

knowledge structures or to *create* new knowledge structures. As described in Chapter 4, a brand-based knowledge structure represents the associative links in the consumer's long-term memory between the brand and information, knowledge, and beliefs about that brand.

To facilitate consumer accessing of knowledge structures, marketing communicators need to *provide a context* for the text or pictures. *Verbal framing* is one way of providing a context. This means that pictures in an ad are placed in the context of, or framed with, appropriate words or phrases so ad receivers can better understand brand information and the key selling point of the MarCom message. The two advertising executions for Bankrate.com—an online service for securing low interest rates for mortgages, car loans, and other forms of borrowing—illustrate perfectly, albeit disgustingly, the role of verbal framing. The first ad (Figure 5.16 on page 141) overlays this statement on top of a man with spoon to mouth: "The government ensures that no more than .0009% of your food is rodent feces." The second ad (Figure 5.17 on page 142) exclaims (over the full-busted man) that "Less than .5% of performance-enhancing chemicals have any noticeable side effects." The two quoted statements are essential in conveying Bankrate.com's selling point, specifically, that even a small reduction in interest rates can provide a meaningful savings.

Enhancing Ability to Create Knowledge Structures

Sometimes marketing communicators need to *create* knowledge structures for information they want consumers to have about their brands. This is accomplished by facilitating *exemplar-based learning.* An *exemplar* is a specimen or model of a particular concept or idea. By using concretizations, demonstrations, or analogies, the marketing communicator can facilitate learning by appealing to exemplars. Consider, for example, the concept of freshness. We all know what freshness means, but it is a rather abstract concept that is difficult to verbalize. That is, it is

Using Surprise to Enhance Processing Motivation

Figure 5.13

difficult to explain what freshness means without resorting to an example. Diet Pepsi's brand managers faced this situation when introducing to consumers the practice of "freshness dating"—that is, printing on the soft-drink container the final date up to which the beverage remained fresh. If you were Diet Pepsi's brand manager, what grocery products might you use to exemplify freshness? Their choice was to use pictures of products that people routinely inspect for freshness (squeeze an orange, pinch a loaf of bread) and, by analogy, communicate the idea that consumers should check arrows on Diet Pepsi cans to ensure that the contents are not outdated.[29] The advertisement for the Jeep Grand Cherokee (Figure 5.18 on page 143) uses the analogy of snowshoes in promoting its Quadra-Drive feature.

Concretizations.   Concretizing is used extensively in marketing communications to facilitate both consumer learning and retrieval of brand information. **Concretizing** is based on the straightforward idea that it is easier for people to remember and retrieve *tangible* rather than abstract information. Claims about a brand are more concrete (versus abstract) when they are made perceptible, palpable, real, evident, and vivid. Concretizing is accomplished by using concrete words and examples. Here are some illustrations:

1. An advertisement for Johnson's baby powder positioned the brand to be capable of making the user's body feel "as soft as the day you were born." To concretize this claim, a series of age-regression scenes revealed, first, a shot of a woman in her 30s, then a shot as she looked in her 20s, next as an early teenager, and finally as a baby. Accompanying music was played

Figure 5.14

Using a Picture and Imagery to Create Gestalt Processing

throughout to the lyrics "make me, make me your baby." This beautiful and somewhat touching ad made concrete Johnson's claim that its baby powder will make the user feel "as soft as the day you were born."

2. The makers of Anacin tablets needed a concrete way to present that brand as "strong pain relief for splitting headaches." The idea of a splitting headache was concretized by showing a hard-boiled egg splitting with accompanying sound effects.

3. Tinactin, a treatment for athlete's foot, concretized its relief properties by showing a person's pair of feet literally appearing to be on fire (representing the fiery sensation of athlete's foot), which is "extinguished" by an application of Tinactin.

4. To convey the notion that Purina brand Hi Pro dog food will recharge an active dog and keep it running, a magazine ad portrayed the brand in the form of a battery, which is a widely recognized apparatus for charging electrical objects. In effect, the battery in this symbolic concretization conveyed pictorially the more abstract claim contained in the ad's body copy.

5. To establish in consumers' minds that Tums E-X is "twice as strong as Rolaids," the commercial showed a sledgehammer behind Tums and a regular-sized hammer behind Rolaids. The commercial then showed the sledgehammer driving in a nail twice as quickly as the regular hammer, thus concretizing Tums' claim.

6. Another Tums advertisement claimed in its headline that "scientific studies find Tums to be the purest form of calcium available." This claim was concretized with the visual display of a package of Tums inside an empty

Another Example of Using a Picture and Imagery to Create Gestalt Processing

Figure 5.15

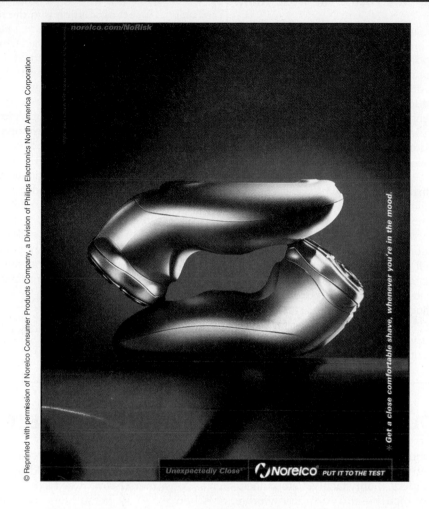

milk bottle, an exemplar of calcium, and with the juxtaposed words "cal-cium" and "Tums" forming the new word Calciums.

7. Finally, the York candy advertisement (Figure 5.19 on page 144) uses the water-faucet exemplar of hot and cold in an effort to concretize the fea-ture/benefit of cool-mint candy.

This concludes our discussion of practical ways of enhancing consumers' MOA factors, but please read the *Online Focus*, which briefly describes appeals to the olfactory sense of smell.[30]

Section Summary

The foregoing discussion has emphasized that advertisers and other marketing communicators benefit from enhancing consumers' motivation, opportunity, and ability to process marketing messages. A variety of communication devices enable marketing communicators to achieve their goals in the hopes of influencing con-sumers' brand-related attitudes, purchase intentions, and, ultimately, their be-havior. Marketing communications do not just happen; rather, sophisticated com-munications are planned, orchestrated, and engineered toward the objective of accomplishing specific persuasion goals. Anything that can be done to enhance consumers' MOA factors—motivation, opportunity, and ability to attend and process MarCom messages—will benefit "our" brand's equity and increase the odds that consumers will purchase "our" brand rather than a competitive offering.

Online Focus: The Nose Knows

Marketing practitioners appeal to the sense of smell, *olfaction*, with a variety of point-of-purchase displays and advertising practices. Store environments are filled with smells, including the use of aromatic discs that emit pleasant and purchase-enhancing odors. Packages and magazine advertisements sometimes are encapsulated with scents that are emitted when scratch-and-sniff patches are rubbed; and sales promotions and point-of-purchase materials embody the scents contained in the products they are designed to promote. Smells can evoke strong images of products, product usage, and consumption situations. Moreover, olfactory stimuli are able to attract attention, motivate information processing, influence memories, affect store and product evaluations, and activate behavior.

The effectiveness of olfactory stimuli is widely appreciated by marketing practitioners, but how does a brand avail itself of the sense of smell when it is marketing online? A sort of solution is in the making. A company called DigiScents offers a small, speaker-like peripheral (named iSmell) that plugs into a computer. An online site can code a smell (such as that of cookies, candy, or the fragrance of a new automobile) into a Web page, and the iSmell unit will waft it out. Another company, TriSenx, has developed a printer-like machine that produces aromatic wafers embedded with government-approved chemicals to simulate the taste and smell of food products. Will these new devices work? Will consumers use them? Will they be effective? Only time will tell, but these developments suggest that online marketers are attempting to make the Internet medium as life-like as the in-store environment.

Source: Adapted from Jesse Oxfeld, "See. Touch. Taste. Click. Buy." *Grok*, December 2000–January 2001, pp. 57–60. www.thestandard.com. © 2001 and reprinted with permission from International Data Group.

TOOLS OF INFLUENCE: THE PERSUADER'S PERSPECTIVE

Persuaders in all capacities of life use various persuasion tools, which have evolved throughout the millennia to influence people. They are widely understood by many persuaders, if only tacitly. Persuadees, such as consumers, learn these tactics—again, if only tacitly—and form knowledge, or schemas, about persuaders' persuasive intent. A well-known persuasion researcher coined the catchy phrase *schemer schema* to capture the idea that people form rather strong and stable intuitive theories about marketers' efforts to influence their actions.[31]

A social psychologist, Robert Cialdini, has spent much of his professional career studying the persuasive tactics used by car dealers, insurance salespeople, fund-raisers, waiters, and other persuasion practitioners. His studies, involving both fieldwork (as car salesperson, fund-raiser, etc.) and laboratory research, have identified six tools of influence that cut across persuasion practices. These are: (1) reciprocation, (2) commitment and consistency, (3) social proof, (4) liking, (5) authority, and (6) scarcity.[32]

Before discussing these influence tools, it is important to note that these tactics work because much of our behavior occurs in a somewhat mindless, automatic, and uncontrolled fashion. In other words, due to limitations on our information processing capacities (as discussed in the previous chapter) and time pressures, we often make judgments and choices without giving a great deal of thought to the matter. Cialdini refers to this as *click, whirr behavior*. He uses this term in reference to patterns of behavior (called *fixed-action patterns*) that appear throughout the animal kingdom. Many animal species (including Homo sapiens) will, under special circumstances, engage in patterns of scripted behavior in response to some trigger feature. For example, mother hens will automatically act motherly on hearing the sound *cheep-cheep*.[33] That single sound activates maternal behavior. If a football could emit the sound *cheep-cheep*, a mother turkey would act motherly toward it, taking it under her wing and nurturing it; however, she will not nurture her own offspring if they are unable to make that sound.

Employing Verbal Framing to Provide a Context   Figure 5.16

The government ensures that no more than .0009% of your food is rodent feces.

Every percent counts.
ⓦbankrate.com℠

A complete, unbiased listing of the best rates on mortgages, car loans, credit cards, CDs and more. Come and get it.

© Courtesy of Bankrate.com

Humans sometimes also operate in a click, whirr fashion. Something triggers a response (click), and then an automatic, scripted pattern of behavior follows (whirr). We are not fully aware of this happening (if we were, it would not happen), but, as we will see, persuaders know how to click on, or trigger, our behavior. Out whirrs a response that results in our purchasing a product, making a donation, or doing something else that favors the persuader's interests (but not necessarily the persuadee's).

Reciprocation

As part of the socialization process in all cultures, people acquire a *norm of reciprocity*. As children we learn to return a favor with a favor, to respond to a nicety with another nicety. Knowing this, marketing communicators sometimes give gifts or samples with hopes that customers will reciprocate by purchasing products. We see this with in-store sampling of food items in supermarkets. Anyone who has ever attended a Tupperware party (or other product party of this sort) knows that the hostess often distributes free gifts at the beginning with designs that attendees will reciprocate with big purchases. College students are encouraged to apply for a credit card after being baited by an offer for a free T-shirt emblazoned with their university's logo. (You've never fallen for this, have you?)

This happens not only with individual consumers but also in business-to-business marketing interactions. For example, pharmaceutical companies hold

Figure 5.17

A Related Example of Employing Verbal Framing to Provide a Context

Less than .5% of performance-enhancing chemicals have any noticeable side effects.

Every percent counts.
bankrate.com™

bankrate.com has the straight dope on mortgage rates, car loans, credit cards, CDs and more. Totally objective information. No artificial ingredients.

dinner meetings with physicians. A sales rep invites a small group of physicians to dinner at an expensive restaurant; exposes them to a product presentation before dinner; wines and dines them; then, afterward, presents them with, say, a $100 "honorarium" for having given their time and attention. Research shows that 80 percent of dinner meetings produce increased sales of the presented brand. Click, whirr: "Something nice was done for me; I should return the favor."[34]

You would be correct if you are thinking that reciprocation tactics do not always work. Sometimes we "see through" the tactic and realize that the nicety is not really a sincere offering but rather a come-on to get us to respond in kind. In saying this, an important theme carries through the entire discussion of influence tactics: No influence tactic is equally effective under all circumstances. Rather, the effectiveness of a tactic is *contingent on the circumstances*: Whether and when a tactic is effective depends on the persuasion circumstances and the characteristics of the persuader and persuadee. As a student of marketing communications, it is critical that you incorporate this "it depends" thinking into your understanding of marketing practices. *No influence tactic is universally effective.* Rather, the situation or circumstances determine whether and when a tactic might be successful.

With regard to reciprocation, this tactic is most effective when the persuadee perceives the gift giver as honest and sincere. Party plans like the Tupperware parties typify this situation in that the persuader (the host or hostess) is often friendly with the persuadees who attend.

Using Analogy to Create a Knowledge Structure   **Figure 5.18**

Commitment and Consistency

After people make a choice (a commitment), there often is a strong tendency to remain faithful to that choice. Consistency is a valued human characteristic. We admire people who are consistent in their opinions and actions. We sometimes feel ashamed of ourselves when we say one thing and do something different. Hence, the marketing communicator might attempt to click-whirr the consumer by getting him or her to commit to something (commitment is the click, or trigger) and then hope that the consumer will continue to act in a manner consistent with this commitment.

Consider the tactic often used by automobile salespeople. They get the consumer to commit to a price and then say they have to get their sales manager's approval. At this point the consumer has psychologically committed to buying the car. The salesperson, after supposedly taking the offer to the sales manager, returns and declares that the manager would not accept the price. Nevertheless, the consumer, now committed to owning the car, will often increase the offer. In the trade this is referred to as *lowballing* the consumer, a tactic that is widespread because it is effective (albeit not entirely ethical).

When would you expect commitment and consistency to be most effective in marketing communications? (Think first before reading on.) Again, the apparent sincerity of the persuader would play a role. The tactic is unlikely to work when it is obviously deceitful and self-serving. From the persuadee's perspective it would be expected that consumers are most likely to remain consistent when

Figure 5.19

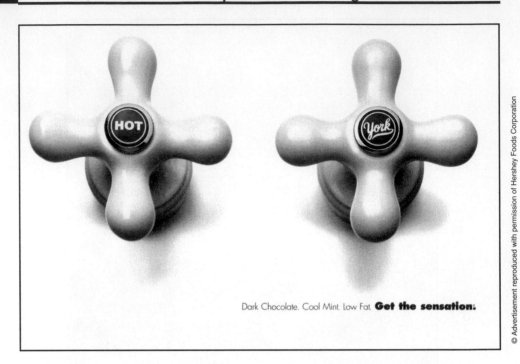

Dark Chocolate. Cool Mint. Low Fat. **Get the sensation.**

they are *highly ego involved* in their choices. In other words, it is hard not to be consistent when a great amount of thought and psychological energy have gone into a choice.

Social Proof

What do I do? How should I behave? The principle of social proof is activated in circumstances where *appropriate behavior is somewhat unclear*. Not knowing exactly what to do, we take leads from the behavior of others; their behavior provides *social proof* of how we should behave. For example, suppose someone asks you for a charitable donation. The appropriate amount to give is unclear, so you might ask the fund-raiser what amount others are giving and then contribute a similar amount. As discussed in the following chapter, new-product developers sometimes encourage widespread adoption by giving new products to opinion leaders and trendsetters, who, it is expected, will provide social proof for others to adopt the same behavior. In general, we are most likely to accept the actions of others as correct "when we are unsure of ourselves, when the situation is unclear or ambiguous, when uncertainty reigns."[35]

Liking

This influence tactic deals with the fact that we are most likely to adopt an attitude or undertake an action when a likable person promotes that action. There are various manifestations of likability. Two of the more prominent in marketing communications are physical attractiveness and similarity. Research (described in detail in Chapter 11) has shown that people respond more favorably to others whom they perceive to be like themselves and physically attractive. This explains why models in advertising, individuals on magazine covers, and celebrity endorsers are typically attractive people to whom consumers can relate and like. The montage presented as Figure 5.20 shows a small sampling of celebrities who have been used in the ongoing "Milk Mustache" advertising campaign under-

A Montage of Milk-Mustache Celebrities   Figure 5.20

taken by the National Fluid Milk Processing Promotion Board. These individuals (including the animated Kermit and the late Curly Howard of the Three Stooges) represent various demographic categories and appeal to different consumer groups.

Authority

Most people are raised to respect authority figures (parents, teachers, coaches, etc.) and to exhibit a sense of duty toward them. It therefore comes as no surprise that marketing communicators sometimes appeal to authority. Because marketers cannot invoke the same types of sanctions as real authority figures (e.g., parents withholding allowances), appeals to authority in the marketplace typically use surrogates of real authority figures. For example, advertisers sometimes use medical authorities to promote their products' virtues. Broadcasters often air *infomercials* that devote 30-minute programs to weight-loss, skin-care, and hair-restoration products, exercise equipment, and other items of the sort. Frequently, these products are endorsed by medical doctors, entertainers, and athletes, on whose authority the consumer is promised the product will perform its function.

Scarcity

This influence tactic is based on the principle that things become more desirable when they are in great demand but short supply. Simply put, an item that is rare or becoming rare is more valued. Salespeople and advertisers use this tactic when encouraging people to buy immediately with appeals such as "only a few are left," "we won't have any more in stock by the end of the day," and "they're really selling fast."

The theory of **psychological reactance** helps explain why scarcity works.[36] This theory suggests that people react against any efforts to reduce their freedoms or choices. Removed or threatened freedoms and choices are perceived as even more desirable than previously. Thus, when products are made to seem less available, they become more valuable in the consumer's mind. Of course, appeals to scarcity are not always effective. But if the persuader is credible and legitimate, then an appeal may be effective. (Click, whirr: "Not many of this product remain, so I better buy now and pay whatever it takes to acquire it.")

Perhaps nowhere in the world is scarcity more used as an influence tactic than in Singapore. In the Hokkien dialect of Chinese, the word *kiasu* means the "fear of losing out." Singaporeans, according to a lecturer in the philosophy department at the National University, will take whatever they can secure, even if they are not sure they really want it.[37] The majority of Singaporeans apparently share a herd mentality—no one wants to be different, and most conform to what others do. Marketers, needless to say, have exploited this cultural characteristic of Singaporeans to sell all types of products. For example, a Singapore automobile dealership, announced that it was moving its location and offered for sale 250 limited-edition BMW 316i models, priced at $78,125 for a manual transmission and $83,125 for automatic. All 250 models were sold within four days, and the dealer was forced to order another 100, which were quickly sold even though delivery was unavailable for months.

The *kiasu* mentality makes Singaporeans virtually "sitting ducks" for users of the scarcity tactic. However, Singapore consumers, like consumers everywhere, are only susceptible to such a persuasion tactic in those situations in which there is in fact scarcity. Singapore consumers otherwise would become skeptical of such transparent attempts to mislead them and reject such blatant efforts to sell products by using deceit.

SUMMARY

Marketing communications in its various forms (advertising, personal selling, point-of-purchase displays, and so on) involves efforts to persuade consumers by influencing their attitudes and ultimately their behavior. This chapter described the role and nature of attitudes and different mechanisms by which they are formed and changed. From the marketing communicators' perspective, attitude formation and change represent the process of persuasion.

The nature of persuasion was discussed with particular emphasis on an integrated framework called the elaboration likelihood model (ELM). Two alternative persuasion mechanisms were described: a central route, which explains persuasion under conditions when the receiver is involved in the communication topic, and a peripheral route, which accounts for persuasion when receivers are not highly involved. In this context, three attitude-formation processes were described: emotion-based persuasion, message-based persuasion, and classical conditioning. The first two are mechanisms for attitude change under the central route, whereas classical conditioning is a peripheral-route process.

In-depth treatment was given to practical efforts to enhance consumers' motivation, opportunity, and ability to process marketing messages. This section included descriptions and illustrations of MarCom efforts to heighten consumers' motivation to attend and process messages, measures to augment consumers' opportunity to encode information and reduce processing time, and techniques used to increase consumers' ability to access knowledge structures and create new structures.

A final topic covered was persuasion efforts on the part of the persuader. Six influence tactics were described and illustrated: reciprocity, commitment and consistency, social proof, liking, authority, and scarcity.

Find more resources to help you study at http://shimp.swcollege.com!

DISCUSSION QUESTIONS

1. Explain the cognitive, affective, and conative attitude components. Provide examples of each using your attitude toward the idea of personally pursuing a career in selling and sales management.

2. Distinguish between message arguments and peripheral cues as fundamental determinants of persuasion. Provide several examples of each from actual television commercials or other advertisements.

3. Receiver involvement is the fundamental determinant of whether people may be persuaded through a central or a peripheral route. Explain.

4. There are three general strategies for changing attitudes. Explain each, using, for illustration, consumers' attitudes toward a fast food chain of your choice (McDonald's, Burger King, KFC, etc.).

5. Assume that your target audience is composed of people who can afford to purchase a "hybrid" automobile such as Honda's Insight or Toyota's Prius. (Note: Hybrid automobiles are high-mileage cars that combine efficient gasoline engines with electric motors powered by batteries.) Assume that your target audience is composed of people who have negative attitudes toward hybrid vehicles. Using material from the chapter, explain how you would attempt to change their attitudes if you were the advertising agency responsible for this campaign. Be specific.

6. Have you personally experienced unethical persuasive efforts from marketing communicators? Under what circumstances would you most expect to find unethical marketing communications, and when would unethical communications most likely be effective in marketing? Draw on the elaboration likelihood model (Figure 5.4) in forming your answer.

7. In the discussion of the influence tactic of reciprocation, you were introduced to the concept of contingency, or "it-depends," thinking. What it-depends factors best explain when the scarcity tactic would and would not be effective?

8. Assume that you are on the fund-raising committee for a social or professional fraternity or sorority. Explain how in this situation you could use each of the six influence tactics discussed in the text. Be specific.

9. Describe the similarity between the concept of elaboration and active synthesis, which was explained in the prior chapter.

10. Locate two advertisements (along the lines of those in Figures 5.16 and 5.17) that illustrate exemplar-based learning and provide detailed explanations as to how specifically your chosen advertisements facilitate exemplar-based learning.

11. Pretend you are in charge of advertising for an online retailer. You know that consumers have positive evaluations for the convenience of online shopping, but many are distrustful of unknown retailers and of giving out credit card numbers online. Using material from this chapter, explain how you would attempt to change consumers' attitudes about the risks of online shopping. Visit several actual online retailers and describe instances where the retailers have addressed consumers' risk perceptions.

12. Visit the Internet sites of approximately five brands that appeal to you. Based on the framework in Figure 5.5, identify at least one example of each of the following efforts to enhance consumers' MOA factors: (a) Locate an effort to increase consumers' motivation to process brand information. (b) Identify an Internet advertisement that attempts to enhance consumers' opportunity to encode information. (c) Find an advertisement that uses an exemplar to assist consumers in either accessing or creating a new knowledge structure.

13. The *Opening Vignette* posed this question: Will Americans accept recycling kiosks? What is your viewpoint on this matter? Please back up your position with appropriate content from the chapter.

14. Identify two magazine advertisements of your choice, presumably involving brands/products that hold some interest for you. With each advertisement indicate what you consider to be its message arguments and periph-

eral cues. Then explain why you regard these as message arguments or peripheral cues.

15. Construct an illustration to demonstrate your understanding of Equation 5.1. Identify three brands in a product category that is personally relevant. Then specify four "outcomes" (i.e., benefits and detriments) pertinent to that category. Next, assign a numerical value from 1 to 5 to each outcome, where 1 equals "virtually no importance" and 5 equals "extreme importance." Then assign a value from 1 to 5 to represent your beliefs regarding how well each of the three brands satisfies each of the four outcomes. In assigning your beliefs, treat 1 as indicating that the brand performs very poorly on this outcome, 5 as indicating the brand performs extremely well, and 2 through 4 reflecting increasingly positive performance.

16. Assume that all outcomes ($i = 1 \ldots n$ outcomes) are equally important to consumers in a particular product category. If this were so, how would you adjust the attitude model in Equation 5.1 to capture the attitude-formation process?

ENDNOTES

1. A number of major theories of attitudes and attitude-change processes have developed over the last half-century. Seven particularly significant theories are reviewed in Richard E. Petty and John T. Cacioppo, *Attitudes and Persuasion: Classic and Contemporary Approaches* (Dubuque, Iowa: Wm. C. Brown Company, 1981). For another review, see Richard E. Petty, Rao H. Unnava, and Alan J. Strathman, "Theories of Attitude Change," in *Handbook of Consumer Behavior*, ed. T. S. Robertson and H. H. Kassarjian (Englewood Cliffs, N.J.: Prentice Hall, 1991), 241–280.

2. This definition adheres to Petty and Cacioppo, *Attitudes and Persuasion*, 7, and also reflects the concept of attitude popularized by Fazio and his colleagues. See, for example, Russell H. Fazio, Jeaw-Mei Chen, Elizabeth C. McDonel, and Steven J. Sherman, "Attitude Accessibility, Attitude-Behavior Consistency, and the Strength of the Object-Evaluation Association," *Journal of Experimental Social Psychology* 18, 1982, 339–357. On a technical note, the definition makes no distinction between what some authors properly consider to be the distinct constructs of *affect* (or feeling states) and *attitude* (or evaluative judgments). For discussion, see Joel B. Cohen and Charles S. Areni, "Affect and Consumer Behavior," in *Handbook of Consumer Behavior*, ed. T. S. Robertson and H. H. Kassarjian (Englewood Cliffs, N.J.: Prentice Hall, 1991), 188–240.

3. Daniel J. O'Keefe, *Persuasion: Theory and Research* (Newbury Park, Calif.: Sage Publications, 1990), 18.

4. See, for example, Richard P. Bagozzi, Alice M. Tybout, C. Samuel Craig, and Brian Sternthal, "The Construct Validity of the Tripartite Classification of Attitudes," *Journal of Marketing Research* 16 (February 1979), 88–95; and Richard J. Lutz, "An Experimental Investigation of Causal Relations among Cognitions, Affect, and Behavioral Intention," *Journal of Consumer Research* 3 (March 1977), 197–208.

5. This is the classic viewpoint of attitude popularized by Gordon W. Allport, "Attitudes," in *A Handbook of Social Psychology*, ed. C. A. Murchinson (Worcester, Mass.: Clark University Press, 1935), 798–844.

6. For further discussion, see Thomas E. Barry, "The Development of the Hierarchy of Effects," in *Current Issues and Research in Advertising*, ed. James H. Leigh and Claude R. Martin, Jr. (Ann Arbor: Division of Research, Graduate School of Business, University of Michigan, 1987), 251–296.

7. A similar account is offered by Kathleen Kelley Reardon, *Persuasion in Practice* (Newbury Park, Calif.: Sage Publications, 1990), 2.

8. For discussion of how elderly consumers are particularly vulnerable to being deceived, see Jeff Langenderfer and Terence A. Shimp, "Consumer Vulnerability to Scams, Swindles, and Fraud: A New Theory of Visceral Influence on Persuasion," *Psychology & Marketing* 18 (July 2001), 763–783.

9. Richard M. Perloff and Timothy C. Brock, "'And Thinking Makes It So': Cognitive Responses to Persuasion," in *Persuasion: New Directions in Theory and Research*, ed. M. E. Rioloff and G. R. Miller (Beverly Hills, Calif.: Sage Publications, 1980), 67–99. See also Robert E. Burnkrant and H. Rao Unnava, "Effects of Self-Referencing on Persuasion," *Journal of Consumer Research* 22 (June 1995), 17–26.

10. Deborah J. MacInnis and Bernard J. Jaworski, "Information Processing from Advertisements: Toward an Integrative Framework," *Journal of Marketing* 53 (October 1989), 8.

11. Peter L. Wright, "The Cognitive Processes Mediating the Acceptance of Advertising," *Journal of Marketing Research* 10 (February 1973), 53–62. Also see Amitava Chattopadhyay and Joseph W. Alba, "The Situational Importance of Recall and Inference in Consumer Decision Making," *Journal of Consumer Research* 15 (June 1988), 1–12.

12. Readers familiar with Petty and Cacioppo's ELM model may wonder why it is not presented. Although it is suitable for guiding academic research and graduate study, my own experience in teaching the ELM has revealed that students often have some difficulty in following the model. The reworking of Petty and Cacioppo's model is intended to provide a more accessible structure for students without doing disservice to their theory.

13. Petty and Cacioppo, *Attitudes and Persuasion*; MacInnis and Jaworski, "Information Processing from Advertisements." For an excellent application of ELM predictions, see Paul W. Miniard, Sunil Bhatla, Kenneth R. Lord, Peter R. Dickson, and H. Rao Unnava, "Picture-Based Persuasion Processes and the Moderating Role of Involvement," *Journal of Consumer Research* 18 (June 1991), 92–107. Another impressive integrative framework is provided by Joan Meyers-Levy and Prashant Malaviya, "Consumers' Processing of Persuasive Advertisements: An Integrative Framework of Persuasion Theories," *Journal of Marketing* 63 (Special Issue 1999), 45–60.

14. The discussion of what is termed here "emotion-based persuasion" is guided by the presentation in MacInnis and Jaworski, "Information Processing from Advertisements."

15. Martin Fishbein and Icek Ajzen, *Belief, Attitude, Intention, and Behavior: An Introduction to Theory and Research* (Reading, Mass.: Addison-Wesley, 1975); Icek Ajzen and Martin Fishbein, *Understanding Attitudes and Predicting Social Behavior* (Englewood Cliffs, N.J.: Prentice Hall, 1980).

16. The normative component of the theory concerns the influence that important others (also called referent groups) have on our intentions and behavior.

17. Richard J. Lutz, "Changing Brand Attitudes through Modification of Cognitive Structure," *Journal of Consumer Research* 1 (March 1975), 49–59.

18. Fara Warner, "BMW Ads Challenge Maintenance Myth," *Advertising Age*, June 20, 1994, 5.

19. Jim Henry, "Saab Takes on Volvo, BMW in First Campaign Via Martin," *Advertising Age*, August 18, 1997, 4.

20. Elizabeth Jensen, "New Juice Ad Touts Calcium without the Chalky Undertaste," *Wall Street Journal Interactive Edition*, August 15, 1997.

21. Betsy McKay, "PepsiCo's Tropicana to Claim Its Juice Has Cardiac Benefit," *Wall Street Journal Interactive Edition*, October 31, 2000 (http://interactive.wsj.com/).

22. For a thorough review of research involving the attitude toward the ad construct, see Scott B. MacKenzie and Richard J. Lutz, "An Empirical Examination of the Structural Antecedents of Attitude Toward the Ad in an Advertising Pretesting Context," *Journal of Marketing* 53 (April 1989), 48–65.

23. For a more detailed account of classical conditioning, see Terence A. Shimp, "Neo-Pavlovian Conditioning and Its Implications for Consumer Theory and Research," in *Handbook of Consumer Behavior*, ed. T. S. Robertson and H. H. Kassarjian (Englewood Cliffs, N.J.: Prentice Hall, 1991), 162–187.

24. Paul W. Miniard, Deepak Sirdeshmukh, and Daniel E. Innis, "Peripheral Persuasion and Brand Choice," *Journal of Consumer Research* 19 (September 1992), 226–239.

25. Indirect demonstration of this is provided in a series of experiments conducted by Michael Tuan Pham, "Cue Representation and Selection Effects of Arousal on Persuasion," *Journal of Consumer Research* 22 (March 1996), 373–387.

26. The ensuing discussion is based on the work of Deborah J. MacInnis, Christine Moorman, and Bernard J. Jaworski, "Enhancing and Measuring Consumers' Motivation, Opportunity, and Ability to Process Brand Information from Ads," *Journal of Marketing* 55 (October 1991), 32–53.

27. James R. Bettman, Mary Frances Luce, and John W. Payne, "Constructive Consumer Choice Processes," *Journal of Consumer Research* 25 (December 1998), 193; Daniel Kahneman, *Attention and Effort* (Englewood Cliffs, NJ: Prentice Hall, 1973).

28. Scott B. MacKenzie and Richard A. Spreng, "How Does Motivation Moderate the Impact of Central and Peripheral Processing on Brand Attitudes and Intentions?" *Journal of Consumer Research* 18 (March 1992), 519–529.

29. Marcy Magiera and Emily DeNitto, "Pepsi Takes Fresh Angle in New Ad Effort," *Advertising Age*, April 4, 1994, 8.

30. Marketing and consumer researchers have generally neglected the study of olfactory stimuli. For exceptions, see

Pam Scholder Ellen and Paula Fitzgerald Bone, "Does It Matter If It Smells? Olfactory Stimuli As Advertising Executional Cues," *Journal of Advertising* 27 (winter 1998), 29–40; Paula Fitzgerald Bone and Swati Jantrania, "Olfaction as a Cue for Product Quality," *Marketing Letters* 3 (July 1992), 289–296; Eric R. Spangenberg, Ayn E. Crowley, and Pamela W. Henderson, "Improving the Store Environment: Do Olfactory Cues Affect Evaluations and Behaviors?" *Journal of Marketing* 60 (April 1996), 67–80. For the role of olfaction in influencing memory, refer to Frank R. Schab, "Odors and the *Remembrance of Things Past*," *Journal of Experimental Psychology: Learning, Memory, and Cognition* 16, no. 4 (1990), 648–655; and Frank R. Schab, "Odor Memory: Taking Stock," *Psychological Bulletin* 109, no. 2 (1991), 242–251.

31. Peter Wright, "Schemer Schema: Consumers' Intuitive Theories about Marketers' Influence Tactics," in *Advances in Consumer Research* 13, ed. Richard J. Lutz (Provo, Utah: Association for Consumer Research, 1985), 1–3. An elaborate and thorough discussion of consumers' persuasion knowledge is provided by Marian Friestad and Peter Wright, "The Persuasion Knowledge Model: How People Cope with Persuasion Attempts," *Journal of Consumer Research* 21 (June 1994), 1–31. An empirical demonstration of consumers' persuasion knowledge vis-à-vis that of advertising researchers is available in Marian Friestad and Peter Wright, "Persuasion Knowledge: Lay People's and Researchers' Beliefs about the Psychology of Advertising," *Journal of Consumer Research* 22 (June 1995), 62–74.

32. Cialdini actually discusses seven influence tactics, but the seventh, instant influence, cuts across all the others and need not be discussed separately. Also, he refers to influence tactics as "weapons" of influence. Because the term *weapons* implies that the persuadee is an adversary, I prefer instead the term *tools* insofar as many modern marketing practitioners view their customers as participants in a long-term relation-building process and not as adversaries or victims. The following sections are based on Cialdini's insightful work. See Robert B. Cialdini, *Influence: Science and Practice*, 2d ed. (Glenview, Ill.: Scott, Foresman, 1988).

33. Ibid., 2.

34. "Pushing Drugs to Doctors," *Consumer Reports*, February 1992, 87–94.

35. Cialdini, *Influence: Science and Practice*, 123.

36. Jack W. Brehm, *A Theory of Psychological Reactance* (New York: Academic Press, 1966). See also Mona Clee and Robert Wicklund, "Consumer Behavior and Psychological Reactance," *Journal of Consumer Research* 6 (March 1980), 389–405.

37. Ian Stewart, "Public Fear Sells in Singapore," *Advertising Age*, October 11, 1993, I8. Singaporeans even make fun of themselves regarding their *kiasu* behavior. "Mr. Kiasu" is a popular comic book character, and a small cottage industry has sprung up around the character.

Communicating
New Products,
Brand Naming,
Packaging, and
Point-of-Purchase
Advertising

PART THREE

The chapters in Part Three deal with the role of marketing communications in successfully introducing new products and the functions of brand names, packages, and point-of-purchase communications in introducing new products and facilitating the growth of mature products. *Chapter 6* looks at the adoption and diffusion processes and examines the role of marketing communications in facilitating these processes and achieving acceptance for new products. Particular attention is devoted to how marketing communicators facilitate product adoption and diffusion by establishing a new product's relative advantages, showing how the product is compatible with the consumer's past behavior and consumption values, removing perceptions of product complexity, and facilitating product trial. Also receiving extensive treatment in this chapter is the role of marketing communications in stimulating word-of-mouth influence and creating "buzz."

Chapter 7 describes the initial elements responsible for a brand's image, namely the brand name, logo, and package. The chapter investigates requirements for a good brand name, the steps involved in arriving at a good name, the role of logos, and the systematic steps implicated in designing an effective package.

The other major topic covered in Chapter 7 is the ever-growing practice of point-of-purchase (P-O-P) communications. The point-of-purchase is the critical point where the brand name, logo, and package come face to face with the customer. Marketing communicators are increasingly appreciative of P-O-P's importance. Expanded investment in this marketing communications component is explained in terms of the valuable functions that P-O-P performs for consumers, manufacturers, and retailers. The chapter devotes considerable attention to the various forms of P-O-P communications, presents results from the POPAI Consumer Buying Habits Study, and provides evidence regarding the impact that displays can have in increasing a brand's sales volume, especially in interaction with advertising and dealing activity.

MARCOM'S ROLE IN FACILITATING PRODUCT ADOPTION

Chapter Six

Chapter Objectives

After studying this chapter, you should be able to:

1. Appreciate the role of marketing communications in facilitating the introduction of new products.
2. Explain the innovation-related characteristics that influence consumers' adoption of new products.
3. Describe the diffusion process and the various groups of adopters.
4. Understand efforts employed by marketing communicators to manage the diffusion process.
5. Appreciate word-of-mouth communications in facilitating new-product adoption.
6. Use "buzz" to heighten the rate of product adoption.

Opening Vignette: Adoption of the Internet Follows TV Pattern

By 2001, 63 percent of all U.S. households owned a computer. As of this same year, 57 percent of U.S. households were connected to the Internet. How long do you think it will it take for the remaining 43 percent of homes to have Internet access? Examining the rate at which American households adopted television sets provides a glimpse at what the continued adoption of Internet access might look like. According to the Consumer Electronics Association, it took eight years (between 1947 and 1955) for 63 percent of American households to buy TV sets. However, following this rapid rate of initial adoption it then required another 30 years after 1955 for television to reach its current penetration rate of 98 percent of all U.S. households.

Would you expect the Internet to reach a penetration level as high as 98 percent or something less than this? Would you anticipate that penetration level, whatever it might be (80 percent, 90 percent?), to be achieved in about the same time as television (30 years), faster, or slower than that period? Let's examine some relevant considerations that might shed light on this question.

First, buying a TV in the late 1940s and early 1950s was a pretty simple thing for consumers to do. If you had enough money and could plug in a TV, you instantaneously become a proud television owner. Internet adoption, on the other hand, is far more involved; indeed, many older people consider owning a computer or other Internet-access medium too complicated. A second factor that likely will slow Internet adoption is that many people have Internet access at work and don't consider it necessary to have access also at home. A third factor that might slow the rate of Internet adoption is the increasing cost of Internet access. America Online, which dominates the industry with about 30 million subscribers, increased its monthly rate in August 2001 by 9 percent (from $21.95 to $23.90).

As a matter of fact, the Internet has grown faster than many other technologies, and the availability of high-speed Internet access should further accelerate the growth rate. With high-speed access, the Internet will eventually be able to compete with the traditional broadcast media as a delivery vehicle for movies, music, and other forms of live or prerecorded entertainment. For example, Intertainer, an Internet entertainment company, has raised $100 million from well-known companies such as NBC, Sony, and Microsoft to deliver high-speed Internet entertainment via so-called streaming video.

Source: Adapted from Julia Angwin, "Consumer Internet Adoption Rate Slows Mimicking Patterns of Past Technologies," *Wall Street Journal Interactive Edition*, July 16, 2001 (http://interactive.wsj.com); also, Robert La Franco, "The Longest Last Mile," *Red Herring*, January 2, 2001, 71–74.

All said, adoption and diffusion of the Internet is not unlike the patterns for many other high-tech products. This chapter explores those factors that determine product adoption for low- as well as high-tech products and describes actions MarCom players can take to manage the diffusion of new product adoption.

Introducing a stream of new products is absolutely essential to most companies' success and long-term growth. Despite the huge investments and concerted efforts to introduce new products and services, many are never successful. Though it is impossible to pinpoint the exact percentage of new ideas and products that eventually flop, failure rates typically range between 35 percent and 45 percent, and the rate may be increasing.[1] This chapter's purpose is to explain MarCom's role in facilitating successful new-product introductions and reducing the product failure rate.

NEW PRODUCTS AND MARKETING COMMUNICATIONS

An organization's marketing communications specialists have a number of responsibilities to ensure new-product success. This perhaps can best be appreciated by conceptualizing the process by which consumers become *trial* and *repeat* purchasers of new products.[2] The notions of trial and repeat purchase are particularly apt for inexpensive consumer packaged goods, but even expensive durable goods like automobiles are tried via test drives and then repeat purchased when the consumer is in the market for another new car.

The model in Figure 6.1 indicates with circles the three main stages through which an individual becomes an adopter of a new product. These stages are the awareness, trier, and repeater classes. The blocks surrounding the circles are mostly MarCom tools that play a role in moving consumers from initial awareness, through product trial, and ultimately to becoming a repeat purchaser. The advertisement in Figure 6.2 for the Sony Mavica MVC-CD1000 digital camera will facilitate the subsequent discussion. Before proceeding, please notice that this camera, when introduced in 2000, was the first camera that enabled users to burn

New-Product Adoption Process Model   **Figure 6.1**

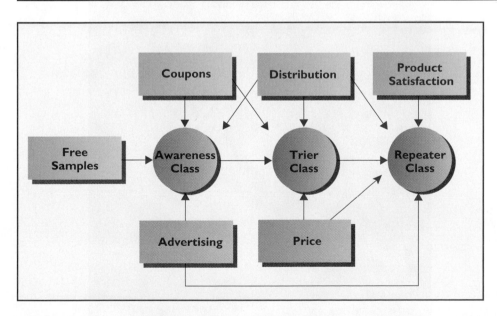

Adapted from Chakravarthi Narasimhan and Subrata K. Sen, "New Product Models for Test Market Data," *Journal of Marketing* 47 (winter 1983). pp. 13 & 14. Reprinted with permission from *Journal of Marketing Research*, published by The American Marketing Association.

pictures directly onto a compact disc and store up to 1,000 images with 156 MB of memory—hence the name CD 1000.

The first step in facilitating adoption is to make consumers aware of a new product's existence. Figure 6.1 illustrates four determinants of the **awareness class:** free samples, coupons, advertising, and distribution. The first three of these are distinctly MarCom activities, and the fourth, distribution, is closely allied in that the sales force is responsible for gaining distribution, providing reseller support, and making point-of-purchase materials available to the trade. Successful introduction of new products typically requires an effective advertising campaign (as with the attention-getting and captivating ad for the Sony Mavica in Figure 6.2), widespread product distribution backed up with point-of-purchase materials, and, in the case of inexpensive package goods, extensive couponing and sampling. Though not shown in the new-product adoption process model (Figure 6.1), word-of-mouth communication, a form of free advertising, also plays a significant role in facilitating product awareness. A later section of the chapter will describe in detail efforts by marketing communicators to build "buzz" surrounding the introduction of new products.

Once consumers becomes aware of a new product or brand, there is an increased probability that they will actually try the new offering. Coupons, distribution, and price are the factors that affect the **trier class** (see Figure 6.1). That is, the availability of cents-off coupons, wide product distribution on retailer shelves (distribution), and lower prices (such as introductory, low-price offers) all facilitate consumer trial of new products. For durable goods, trial may involve test driving a new automobile or visiting an electronics store to acquire hands-on experience with, say, a product such as the Sony Mavica MVC-CD1000 digital camera.

Figure 6.2   Introduction of the Sony Mavica MVC-CD1000 Digital Camera

In the case of inexpensive packaged goods, trial more likely involves purchasing a new brand to test its performance characteristics—its taste, cleaning ability, or whatever attributes and benefits are pertinent to the product category.

Repeat purchasing, demonstrated by the **repeater class,** is a function of four primary forces: advertising, price, distribution, and product satisfaction. That is, consumers are more likely to continue to purchase a particular brand if advertising reminds them about the brand, if the price is considered reasonable, if the brand is accessible in retail outlets, and if product quality is deemed satisfactory. On this last point, it is undeniable that MarCom efforts are critical to boosting repeat purchasing but cannot substitute for poor product performance. In other words, consumer satisfaction with a brand is *the* major determinant of repeat purchasing. Consumers typically will not stick with brands that have failed to live up to expectations.

Product Characteristics That Facilitate Adoption

Discussion to this point has identified several MarCom activities that affect new-product adoption, factors such as advertising, couponing, and sampling. Explanation now turns to five product-related characteristics that influence consumers' attitudes toward new products and hence their likelihood of adopting innovative products. These are a product's (1) relative advantage(s), (2) compatibility, (3) complexity, (4) trialability, and (5) observability.[3] Each of these characteristics is discussed in detail in the following sections, but first it will be useful to provide an example (in the *IMC Focus*) of an actual product introduction that illustrates these adoption-influencing factors.

Relative Advantage.   The degree to which consumers perceive a product innovation as better than existing alternatives is called relative advantage. **Relative advantage** is a function of consumer perception and is *not* a matter of whether a product is actually better by objective standards. Consider the case of round tea bags. Tetley was the number two brand of tea in the United Kingdom with little prospect of increasing that position. The company researched ways to physically differentiate its brand but with little success until it developed the idea of a *round* tea bag. Marketing research revealed that consumers perceive the round bag (versus the traditional square bag) to make a better cup of tea. Armed with these results, Tetley introduced round bags in England and quickly earned sales increases of 40 percent and the number one market position. Success with the round tea bag also has been achieved in Canada and the United States. In test marketing in the northeastern United States, Tetley's market share jumped from 15 percent to over 20 percent.[4] Round tea bags are *perceived* as making a better cup of tea, but consumers may not actually be able to discern any difference from tea brewed in square bags in a blind taste test.

Relative advantage is positively correlated with an innovation's adoption rate—the greater an innovation's relative advantage(s) compared to existing offerings, the more rapid the rate of adoption to be expected. (Conversely, a new brand's relative *dis*advantage(s)—high price, poor performance, etc.—will retard the rate of adoption.) In general, a relative advantage exists to the extent that a new product offers (1) better performance compared to other options, (2) increased comfort, (3) savings in time and effort, or (4) immediacy of reward.

Consider the following illustrations of relative advantages provided by several new brands. Unilever introduced a line of Ragu Express microwaveable pasta meals directed at young consumers (teens and tweens) for snack or dinner preparation when parents aren't around. Introductory advertising appealed to the youth audience by emphasizing the quick and easy preparation time.[5] Pfizer Consumer Health Care launched Listerine PocketPaks, which are portable dissolving mouthwash strips. In addition to the advantage of portability, PocketPaks kill germs that cause bad breath (unlike breath mints and gum).[6] The sweetener product Splenda affords consumers the distinct relative advantage of tasting like sugar but being calorie free. The advertisement for the Toyota Prius in Figure 6.3 (page 159) illustrates another product innovation offering a meaningful relative advantage in the form of being a fuel-efficient, hybrid automobile that is more environmentally friendly than conventional, fully gasoline-fueled automobiles.

IMC focus

Big Success Comes in a Small Package—Yoplait's Go-Gurt

Here's the challenge: How do you get children and teens to regularly eat yogurt, especially when they are away from home, such as at school? Eating yogurt from a standard container minimally requires the availability of a spoon. For adults working in an office, that's no big deal, but kids and teens don't want to bother with a spoon when taking a lunch or snack to school. Hence, standard yogurt packaging has essentially restricted sales of yogurt to adults and to the relatively few children/teens willing to take a spoon to school. Marketing executives at General Mills' Yoplait division developed a fascinatingly simple but profitable solution to this problem when it introduced the Go-Gurt brand of yogurt in a tube—*yogurt* for kids on the *go*!

In its first year after introduction, Go-Gurt garnered national sales in excess of $100 million and nearly doubled the proportion of yogurt users under the age of 19 to about one in six. The inspiration for the idea of a tube-delivered yogurt product came from a French product called Fromage Frais, a creamy cheese in a tube. After two years working on product formulation and package design, the R&D staff at General Mills devised a three-sided sealed tube measuring nine inches in length that ensures the integrity of the frozen yogurt product. With flavors such as Strawberry Splash, Berry Blue Blast, and Watermelon Meltdown, Go-Gurt was a near-instantaneous hit with its youthful target audience.

The choice of Go-Gurt as the brand name facilitated product adoption by signifying that the tube contained yogurt and suggesting that the brand was to be consumed on the go. With portability as the key positioning statement, Yoplait's ad agency—Saatchi & Saatchi Kid Connection—devised a "Lose the Spoon" campaign advertising that Go-Gurt could be consumed on the go without bothering with a spoon. For example, in one spot a skateboarder holding a Go-Gurt was shown whizzing by a bored-looking teenager who was eating yogurt with a spoon from a traditional yogurt container. In addition to the clever advertising, Go-Gurt was sampled extensively in major U.S. markets. Fleets of teenagers on skateboards and scooters were equipped with shoulder packs that handled up to 150 cold Go-Gurt samples. Refrigerated trucks were parked near distribution areas so the shoulder packs could be quickly reloaded for further distribution. More than a million samples were distributed. Kids quickly accepted the new Go-Gurt product, and sales accelerated rapidly. Based on Go-Gurt's success, Yoplait developed a similar yogurt-in-a-tube product for adults called Yoplait Express.

Adapted from Sonia Reyes, "Groove Tube." *Brandweek's* Marketers of the Year insert, October 16, 2000, M111–M116. © 2000 VNU Business Media, Inc.

Compatibility. The degree to which an innovation is perceived to fit into a person's way of doing things is termed **compatibility.** In general, a new product or brand is more compatible to the extent that it matches consumers' needs, personal values, beliefs, and past consumption practices. Incompatible products are those that are perceived as incongruent with how consumers have learned to satisfy their consumption needs. For example, although horse meat is an alternative to beef in European countries such as Belgium, France, Italy, and Spain, it is hard to imagine that North American consumers would convert to this lean, sweet-tasting alternative to the deeply ingrained preference for beef.

Generally speaking, adoption rapidity is increased with greater compatibility. Innovations that are compatible with consumers' existing situation are less risky, more meaningful, and require less effort to incorporate into one's consumption lifestyle. Hybrid automobiles such as Toyota's Prius (Figure 6.3) and Honda's Insight (Figure 6.4 on page 160) probably will experience a relatively slow rate of adoption because the idea of a gasoline-electric hybrid automobile is somewhat incompatible with consumers' concept of how an automobile should be energized.

Another Illustration of Relative Advantage

Figure 6.3

Sometimes the only way to overcome perceptions of incompatibility is through heavy advertising to convince consumers that a new way of doing things truly is superior to an existing solution. Consider the case of ultra-high-temperature (UHT) milk, which is a heat-treated product that lasts up to six months on the shelf and tastes the same as "regular" milk. Shelf-stable milk is standard fare throughout much of Europe and Latin America. For example, market shares of UHT milk are 95 percent in France, 90 percent in Belgium, 80 percent in Spain, 55 percent in Germany, and 55 percent in Italy.[7] In the United States, however, sales of UHT are negligible. Italy's Parmalat entered the massive U.S. market in the 1990s with plans of changing America's preference to shelf-stable milk. However, after nearly a decade on the U.S. market, Parmalat's market share pales in comparison to sales of refrigerated milk. The problem is one of incompatibility: Americans are wedded to refrigerated milk. Parmalat will have to advertise heavily to stand any chance of large numbers of American consumers regularly purchasing UHT milk instead of the conventional refrigerated variety.[8] Of course, because success breeds further success, products that suffer from images of incompatibility often do not have sufficient funds to overcome their status.

In the same situation as Parmalat, makers of soy "milk" have recognized that they must advertise aggressively to overcome incompatibility problems. Although soy drinks possess the relative advantage of being healthier than traditional cow's milk, many consumers eschew purchasing soy drinks due to thoughts that a product made from a vegetable would probably taste strange and

Figure 6.4   A Compatibility Problem?

ruin, rather than enhance, the taste of milk-related products such as cereal. In an attempt to overcome incompatibility problems, makers of soy drinks substantially increased their ad budgets for brands such as Silk and Great Awakenings in the hopes of attracting new users to the category.[9]

Complexity. Complexity refers to an innovation's degree of perceived difficulty. The more difficult an innovation is to understand or use, the slower the rate of adoption. Home computers were adopted slowly because many homeowners perceived them too difficult to understand and use. Advertisers confronted this by creating subtle (and not-so-subtle) television commercials to convey the idea that anyone can easily learn to use a computer, even little kids. Companies also redesigned their products and introduced new computers that are easier to use.

The success of Apple's iMac in the late 1990s attests to the value of making product use simple. The iMac was virtually an instant success upon its introduction, selling about a quarter million units in the first six weeks after launch and becoming one of the hottest products on the market during the holiday season. Although a very good PC, the iMac's retail price at $1,299 was, if anything, at a premium level compared to functionally competitive PCs. Indeed, in terms of specifications, the original iMac was nothing exceptional, with only 32MB of RAM, a 4GB hard drive, and a 233-MHz processing chip. However, the iMac's design *was* special. With a choice of five novel colors (for computers), translucent case, one-piece unit, rounded (versus angular) shape, and preinstalled software, the iMac was unlike any personal computer that consumers had seen. Beyond its unique design, the iMac was perhaps the most user-friendly computer to ever hit the market. Essentially, the user simply had to plug it in and turn it on—no setup, no hassle. This perhaps explains why nearly one-third of the iMac buyers were first-time computer owners who apparently believed that the iMac did not exceed their threshold level for complexity.[10]

Trialability.   The extent to which an innovation can be used on a limited basis prior to making a full-blown commitment is referred to as **trialability**. In general, products that lend themselves to trialability are adopted at a more rapid rate. Trialability is tied closely to the concept of *perceived risk*. Test drives of new automobiles, free items of food products at local supermarkets, and mail-delivered samples of new grocery products all permit the consumer to try a new brand on an experimental basis. The trial experience serves to reduce the risk of a consumer's being dissatisfied with a product after having permanently committed to it through an outright purchase. As will be discussed in detail in Chapter 18, sampling is an incomparable promotional method for encouraging trial by reducing the risk that accompanies spending money on a new, untried product.

Facilitating trial is typically more difficult with durable products than with inexpensive packaged goods. Automobile companies allow consumers to take test drives, but what do you do if you are, say, a computer manufacturer or a lawnmower maker? If you are creative, you do what companies like Apple Computer and John Deere did in novel efforts to give people the opportunity to try their products. Apple developed a "Test Drive a Macintosh" promotion that gave interested consumers the opportunity to try the computer in the comfort of their own homes for 24 hours at no cost. John Deere offered a 30-day free test period during which prospective mower purchasers could try the mower and then return it, no questions asked, if not fully satisfied. Ford Motor Company, the owner of British-based Land Rover, initiated a unique money-back offer to encourage purchases of Land Rover's Discovery Series II model of sport utility vehicle. Prospective buyers could drive the new SUV for 30 days or 1,500 miles and then return it for a full refund if they were dissatisfied with its performance.[11]

Observability.   **Observability** is the degree to which the product user or other people can observe the positive effects of new-product usage. The more a consumption behavior can be sensed (seen, smelled, etc.), the more observable, or *visible*, it is said to be. Thus, wearing a new perfume fragrance is less "visible" than adopting an *avant-garde* hairstyle, and driving an automobile with a new type of engine is less visible than driving one with a unique body design such as the PT Cruiser in Figure 6.5 or the Honda Insight shown previously in Figure 6.4. In general, innovations that are high in observability/visibility lend themselves to rapid adoption if they also possess relative advantages, are compatible with consumption lifestyles, and so on. Products whose benefits lack observability are generally slower in adoptability.[12]

The important role of product observability/visibility is illustrated by Nike's longstanding use of showing the technology in its athletic shoes. The most recent version of this practice is the Nike Shox. These highly visible inserts in the heel section of Nike shoes convey the product benefits of stability, cushioning, and increased lift through tiny shock absorbers ("Shox") that provide spring.[13] Nike could have designed its shoes so that the Shoxs were concealed from observation; instead, the company decided to make the feature conspicuous by "exposing the technology" and in so doing provided itself with the easily communicable point that Nike shoes enable greater leaping ability than do competitive brands. Nike's exposing-the-technology practice recognizes the basic fact that consumers are more likely to adopt a new product when its advantages are observable.

Because status from brand ownership is one form of consumption advantage, albeit an advantage high in symbolism rather than functionality, it perhaps is not surprising that many well-known brands of fashion wear (e.g., Tommy Hilfiger, Polo by Ralph Lauren) plaster the outside of clothing with prominent brand names observable to the world. Consumers have become walking billboards for designer brands, a case of observability incarnate.

Figure 6.5

An Automobile Design High in Visibility

Boldly go.

PT CRUISER®

Presenting the new Chrysler PT Cruiser. Ingenious functionality.

Stand-out styling. Surprising affordability. Guaranteed to recharge

any road. Get details at 1.800.CHRYSLER or www.chrysler.com

CHRYSLER

© Used with permission of DaimlerChrysler Corporation

Breathe Right was a product introduced in the mid-1990s to allow easier breathing during exercise or while sleeping. Sales were slow when first introduced, so the company sent a case of Breathe Right to all National Football League team trainers. While wearing the highly visible Breathe Right, running back Herschel Walker scored two touchdowns during a game when his Philadelphia Eagles played the Washington Redskins. Almost immediately thereafter sales increased dramatically.[14]

THE DIFFUSION PROCESS

The foregoing discussion examined MarCom activities and product characteristics that facilitate the adoption process. The focus was on the individual consumer. Emphasis now is directed at the broader issue of how an innovation is communicated and adopted *throughout the marketplace*. This marketplace adoption is termed the **diffusion process** in contrast to the individual-level adoption process just described. In simple terms diffusion is the process of spreading out. In a MarCom sense this means that as time passes a new product is adopted by increasingly greater numbers of people. By analogy consider what happens when gas is released into a small room: The fumes eventually spread throughout the entire room. Similarly, product innovations spread ideally to all parts of a potential market. The word *ideally* is used because, unlike the physical analogy, the communication of an innovation in the marketplace often is impeded by factors such as unsuitable communication channels, competitive maneuverings, and other imperfect conditions.

This section deals with the *aggregate behavior* of groups of customers who adopt products at different points in time following a product's introduction. Examined are the characteristics that typify each group.[15] It should be noted that the classification scheme discussed hereafter is insightful but also somewhat simplified, which typically is the case when complex human behavior is categorized into a small set of categories.[16]

Adopter Categories

As a product spreads through the marketplace over time, it is adopted by different types of consumers. Five general groups have been identified: (1) innovators, (2) early adopters, (3) early majority, (4) late majority, and (5) laggards. As a matter of convention, these five categories are presumed to follow a normal (bell-shaped) statistical distribution with respect to each group's average (mean) time of adoption following the introduction of an innovation (see Figure 6.6). That is, in accordance with the properties of a normal distribution, approximately two-thirds of all people who ultimately adopt an innovation fall within plus (late majority) or minus (early majority) one standard deviation of the mean time of adoption. The other adopter categories are interpreted in a similar manner. Although the categorization is arbitrary, it represents a useful metaphor for thinking about and discussing the "typical" diffusion process.

Innovators. The small group of **innovators,** constituting less than 3 percent of all adopters, are the first people to accept a new idea or product. Innovators are extremely *venturesome* and are more willing to take risks—a requirement of innovation. That is, the first people to adopt a new product, especially if it is expensive, incur the risk that the product will not work as well as expected, that money will be lost, and possibly that they will be embarrassed by a bad decision. Consider, for example, the risk of being among the very first people in a community to own a hybrid automobile such as the Toyota Prius or Honda Insight. Not many people are willing to be the first to invest over $25,000 in a product that may turn out to have relatively low resale value and even to be the butt of jokes.

Another characteristic of innovators is that they are willing to seek social relationships outside their local peer group—that is, they are *cosmopolites.* Innovators also tend to be younger, higher in social status, and better educated than later

Classification of Adopter Groups   **Figure 6.6**

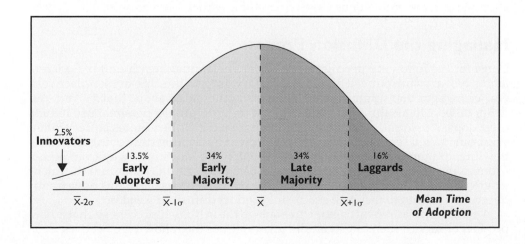

adopter groups. Innovators interact mostly with other innovators and rely heavily on *impersonal* informational sources (e.g., media reports, online searches, salespeople) rather than other people to satisfy their information needs. Innovators generally have been found to display a broader range of interests than noninnovators.[17]

Early Adopters.

Early adopters are the second group (see Figure 6.6) to adopt an innovation. The size of this group is defined statistically as 13.5 percent of all potential adopters. (Please note that this percentage is the area under the normal curve between one and two standard deviations from the mean.) Early adopters are *localites*, in contrast to innovators, who were described as cosmopolites. The early adopter is well integrated within his or her community and is respected by his or her friends.[18] Because of this respect, the early adopter is often sought for advice and information about new products and services. The respect he or she commands among peers makes the early adopter a very important determinant of the success or failure of an innovation. Opinion leaders come primarily from the early adopter group. Their characteristics and role in the diffusion process are discussed later in the chapter.

Early Majority.

Approximately one-third of all potential adopters of an innovation fall into the **early majority** group. As shown in Figure 6.6, the early majority adopt the product prior to the mean time of adoption. Members of this group are deliberate and cautious in their adoption of innovations.[19] They spend more time in the innovation decision process than the two earlier groups. Though the group displays some opinion leadership, it is well below that shown by early adopters. This group is slightly above average in education and social status but below the levels of the early adopter group.

Late Majority.

As shown in Figure 6.6, the **late majority** also consists of approximately one-third, or 34 percent, of potential adopters; however, unlike the early majority, consumers in the late majority category are below average in the time at which they finally adopt a new product. The key word that characterizes the late majority is *skepticism*.[20] By the time they adopt an innovation, the majority of the market has already done so. Peers are the primary source of new ideas for consumers in the late majority, who make little use of mass media. Demographically, they are below average in education, income, and social status.

Laggards.

The final group to adopt an innovation is referred to as **laggards**; they represent the bottom 16 percent of potential adopters. These people are bound in tradition.[21] As a group, laggards focus on the past as their frame of reference. Their collective attitude may be summarized as, "If it was good enough for my parents, it's good enough for me." Laggards are tied closely to other laggards and to their local communities and have limited contact with the mass media. This group, as might be expected, has the lowest social status and income of all adopter groups. If and when laggards adopt an innovation, it usually occurs after one or more innovations have replaced the earlier innovation.

Managing the Diffusion Process

Consider the following product innovation. The animal health unit of Switzerland's Novartis introduced an antidepressant drug to the U.S. marketplace several years ago. You might think, "What's so innovative about that?" Well, the drug, called Clomicalm, was marketed not for individuals' personal use but for their dogs. Apparently, about 7 million dogs in the United States suffer from a syndrome called separation anxiety, manifested by the dog destroying furniture, howling, or inappropriate elimination when their owners are away from home. Clomicalm is a meat-flavored pill priced at $1 per day for the minimum treatment length of two to three months.[22] What did Novartis, the maker of this doggy antidepressant pill, do to facilitate successful product diffusion? Read on.

Firms such as Novartis hope to manage the diffusion process so that a new product or service such as Clomicalm accomplishes the following objectives:[23]

1. Secure initial sales as quickly as possible (*a rapid takeoff*).
2. Achieve cumulative sales in a steep curve (*rapid acceleration*).
3. Secure the highest possible sales potential in the targeted market segment (*maximum penetration*).
4. Maintain sales for as long as possible (*a long-run franchise*).

Figure 6.7 displays the *desired* diffusion pattern that satisfies the preceding conditions and compares it with the *typical* diffusion pattern. The typical pattern involves a relatively slow takeoff, a slow rate of sales growth, maximum penetration below the full market potential, and a sales decline sooner than what would be desired.

What can marketing communicators do to make the typical pattern more like the desired pattern? First, *rapid takeoff* can be facilitated by having a MarCom budget that is sufficiently large to permit (1) the aggressive sales-force efforts needed to secure trade support for new products, (2) intensive advertising to create high product-awareness levels among the target market, and (3) sufficient sales promotion activity to generate desired levels of trial-purchase behavior. Novartis embarked on a major marketing campaign to persuade pet owners to take their anxious dogs to see a veterinarian. Millions of dollars were invested in radio and magazine advertising, including ad placements in *Parade, Reader's Digest*, and *People*. Advertisements portrayed a sad-looking dog with an emotional appeal in the headline reading "Some dogs just hate to be alone" (see Figure 6.8). In addition to the consumer-oriented advertising, a major promotional campaign was aimed at training vets and encouraging them to prescribe Clomicalm to the owners of separation-anxious dogs. All in all, this was an earnest effort to secure a rapid takeoff.

Second, *rapid acceleration* may be accomplished by (1) ensuring that product quality is suitable and will promote positive word-of-mouth communication, (2) continuing to advertise heavily to reach later adopter groups, (3) ensuring that the sales force provides reseller support, and (4) using sales promotion creatively so that incentives are provided for repeat-purchase behavior. Following the introduction of Clomicalm, Novartis continued supporting its resellers' (i.e., vets)

Desired and Typical Diffusion Patterns   **Figure 6.7**

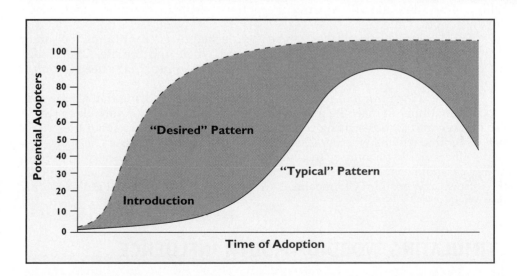

Figure 6.8

Clomicalm Advertisement

selling efforts and offered attractive promotional deals to consumers to accelerate the adoption rate.

Third, *maximum penetration* can be approached by (1) continuing the same strategies that stimulated rapid acceleration and, where appropriate, (2) revising the product and advertising strategies as necessary to appeal to the needs of later adopters.

Finally, a *long-run franchise* can be maintained by ensuring that (1) the old product continues to meet the market's needs, (2) distribution is suitable to reach the market, and (3) advertising continues to remind the market about the product. Only time will tell whether Clomicalm achieves a long-run franchise. Its success will assuredly encourage the introduction of new brands from competitors and necessitate continued advertising and promotional effort to offset competitive efforts and position Clomicalm as the best brand for treating Fido's separation anxiety.

STIMULATING WORD-OF-MOUTH INFLUENCE

People in all buying capacities—consumers buying automobiles, industrial purchasing agents buying maintenance materials, physicians ordering drug products, hospitals ordering supplies, athletic teams purchasing equipment, and so on—rely on two major sources of information to assist them in making decisions: impersonal and personal sources. *Impersonal sources* include information received from television, magazines, the Internet, and other mass media sources. *Personal sources*, the subject of this section, include word-of-mouth influence from friends and acquaintances, and from business associates in the case of organizational buying decisions.[24] Research has shown that the more favorable information a potential product adopter has received from peers, the more likely that individual is to adopt the new product or service.[25] This section begins with some theoretical ideas about word-of-mouth influence, or WOM, and then discusses the practice of "buzz building"—also referred to as viral marketing, guerilla marketing, diffusion marketing, and street marketing. (Marketing practitioners like to label their practices, often with clever terms, an observation you undoubtedly already have made!)

Strong and Weak Ties

People are connected in what can be referred to as a network of interpersonal relationships. Family members and friends interact on a regular basis, and people also intermingle with work associates daily. There also are interaction patterns that are less frequent and less strong. We thus can think of social relations in terms of "tie strength." Consumers' interpersonal relations range along a continuum from very strong ties (such as frequent and often intimate communications between friends) to weak ties (such as rare interactions between casual acquaintances).[26] It is through these ties, both weak and strong, that information flows about new products, new restaurants, recently released movies and albums, and the myriad of other new products and services.

Research has shown that both weak- and strong-link interpersonal relations play key word-of-mouth roles in the dissemination of product and service information.[27] A recent study detected several interesting, indeed surprising, findings regarding WOM, among which are the following:[28]

1. Weak social ties have virtually as much influence as strong ties in accelerating information dissemination.
2. MarCom efforts such as advertising initially influence information dissemination about new products, but this effect diminishes quickly, and thereafter it is WOM influence that propels information dissemination.
3. As the level of advertising increases, the effect of strong ties in speeding information dissemination also increases, whereas the effect of weak ties decreases.

The important point to conclude from this brief discussion is that MarCom efforts (especially through traditional advertising media) are critical for getting the information-dissemination ball rolling, but thereafter it is social interactions via both strong and weak ties between consumers that drives the flow of information about new products. Hence, marketing communicators need to orchestrate the flow of information about products using advertising and "buzz" efforts (as discussed in a later section) and then the information ball will be propelled at an accelerating rate by social networks of people interacting with one another—via online chat rooms or through more traditional venues of social intercourse. Opinion leaders play a crucial role in this process.

Opinion Leadership

An **opinion leader** is a person who frequently influences other individuals' attitudes and behavior.[29] Opinion leaders perform several important functions: They inform other people (followers) about new products, they provide advice and reduce the follower's perceived risk in purchasing a new product, and they offer positive feedback to support or confirm decisions that followers have already made. Thus, an opinion leader is an informer, persuader, and confirmer. Consider the phenomenon of movie critiques and the role of the critic. These individuals preview movies before the general public and write reviews, which then are aired on TV or printed in newspapers. The critics' comments serve to influence moviegoers' choice of movies and possibly confirm their own opinions about the movies they have seen.[30]

Opinion leadership influence is typically restricted to one or several consumption topics rather than applying universally across many consumption domains. That is, a person who is an opinion leader with respect to issues and products in one consumption area—such as, movies, computers, skiing, or cooking—is not generally influential in other unrelated areas. It would be very unlikely, for example, for one person to be respected for his or her knowledge and opinions concerning all four of the listed consumption topics. Moreover, opinion leaders are found in every social class. In most instances, opinion leadership influence moves *horizontally* through a social class instead of vertically from one class to another.

Opinion leader profiles are distinctly different from others. In general, opinion leaders (1) are more *cosmopolitan* and have greater contact with the mass media than do followers; (2) are usually more *gregarious* than the general population and have more social contacts—and thus more opportunity for discussing and conveying information—than followers; (3) have slightly *higher socioeconomic status* than followers; (4) are more *innovative* than followers; and (5) are willing to act differently than other people, can withstand criticism and rejection, and have a *need to be unique*.[31]

What motivates opinion leaders to give information? It seems that opinion leaders are willing to participate in word-of-mouth communications with others because they derive satisfaction from sharing their opinions and explaining what they know about new products and services. Opinion leaders thus continually strive (and often feel obligated) to keep themselves informed.

What's the Motivation?

Prestige is at the heart of WOM. "We like being the bearers of news. Being able to recommend gives us a feeling of prestige. It makes us instant experts."[32] Being an expert in marketplace matters does bring prestige. Researchers have referred to the marketplace expert as a *maven*. (In dictionary terms, a *maven*, or mavin, is considered an expert in everyday matters.) **Market mavens** are characterized as "individuals who have information about many kinds of products, places to shop, and other facets of markets, and initiate discussions with consumers and respond to requests from consumers for market information."[33] In other words, the market maven is looked upon as an important source of information and receives prestige and satisfaction from supplying information to friends and others. Opinion leaders are mavens!

The key to generating good WOM is by finding *cheerleaders*—that is, consumers who will "get the talk started."[34] Usually this is a carefully selected target group that is most likely to love a new movie, a new book, or other product or service. In the publishing industry, cheerleading is stimulated by giving free copies of a new book to a select group of opinion leaders. Converse successfully introduced its All Star 2000 basketball shoe by going into 10 markets prior to the brand's launch and supplying advance pairs to local hero basketball players, a practice suitably referred to as "seeding" the market.[35] Teenage girls in Japan play an extremely important cheerleading role (called *kuchikomi*) that has been recognized and cultivated by Japanese firms.

Kuchikomi is a word that refers to the swift network of word-of-mouth advertising that connects teenage girls in Japan. Never was *kuchikomi* more apparent than in the success of the Tamagotchi craze that first hit Japan and then spread globally. Because there is little space in Japan for people to own pets, the Tamagotchi toy provided a substitute outlet for the desire to own an animal. Meaning "cute little egg," Tamagotchi is a plastic toy with an embedded electronic chip that emits chirps of affection based on the owner's behavior. After an extraterrestrial creature hatches from the toy "egg," the owner presses select buttons on a tiny screen to feed, clean, and care for the virtual pet. Proper care is rewarded with affectionate chirps. Bandai Company Ltd., the innovator of this product, estimated initial sales of about 300,000 Tamagotchies at $16 each. However, without any advertising and relying primarily on the WOM generated by teenage girls and other owners, sales volume reached 23 million units in Japan in slightly over one year. Since then Bandai has exported the Tamagotchi to over 25 other countries.

The Tamagotchi is just one example of the *kuchikomi* power of Japan's teenage girls. Many Japanese consumer product companies do not just wait for Japanese girls to engage in word-of-mouth behavior but solicit their opinions during new-product development. "Girl guides," as they are called, are recruited by Japanese companies to test proposed new products and also provide feedback on preliminary television commercials. They also are paid to "cheerlead" new products. For example, Dentsu Eye, a marketing consultancy, paid schoolgirls to talk up a previously unknown product at their schools. Brand awareness quickly grew to 10 percent of high-school students. Dentsu Eye's executives estimated that using television advertising to achieve a comparable level of brand awareness would have cost at least $1.5 million compared with less than $100,000 actually paid to the schoolgirls.[36]

Avoid Negative Information

Positive word-of-mouth communication is a critical element in the success of a new product or service. Unfavorable WOM, on the other hand, can have devastating effects on adoption, because consumers seem to place more weight on negative information in making evaluations than on positive information.[37]

Marketing communicators can do several things to minimize negative word of mouth.[38] At a minimum, companies need to show customers that they are responsive to legitimate complaints. Manufacturers can do this by providing detailed warranty and complaint-procedure information on labels or in package inserts. Retailers can demonstrate their responsiveness to customer complaints through employees with positive attitudes, store signs, and inserts in monthly billings to customers. Companies also can offer toll-free numbers and e-mail addresses to provide customers with an easy way to voice their complaints and provide suggestions. By being responsive to customer complaints, companies can avert negative—and perhaps even create positive—WOM.[39]

CREATING "BUZZ"

The preceding section applied traditional concepts such as opinion leadership to describe the process of word-of-mouth communication. The section may have given the impression that WOM is something that just happens and that marketing communicators are like spectators in a sporting event who passively enjoy the action but are not involved in its creation. The present section makes it clear that marketing communicators—now more than ever—are active participants in the WOM process rather than merely idle spectators.

Because interpersonal communications plays such a key role in affecting consumers' attitudes and actions, brand marketers have found it essential to proactively influence what is said about their brands rather than merely hoping that positive word of mouth is occurring. Marketing practitioners refer to this proactive effort as creating the buzz. The terms *guerrilla marketing*, *viral marketing*, *diffusion marketing*, and *street marketing* also are used to refer to proactive efforts to spread positive WOM information and to encourage product usage. Let's explore these practices and understand why they are being extensively used, even now to the point that major advertising agencies have created buzz-generating units.[40]

Some Anecdotal Evidence

Buzz creation, guerrilla marketing, and similar notions can best be appreciated by examining the following illustrations of these practices.

1. Perhaps you have seen *Crouching Tiger, Hidden Dragon*—the Chinese-language martial arts film directed by Ang Lee. It was a sensation during the movie season of 2000–2001 and an Academy Award winner as best foreign film. With a limited budget for promoting the film, the studio decided

that word of mouth would be critical to the film's box-office success. In an effort to generate "cheerleading" by movie aficionados, special screenings of the film were presented to a variety of audiences deemed likely to spread positive commentary about the film. These screenings included audiences such as graduates of a women's leadership institute, an assemblage of female athletes, advertising agency executives, and representatives of magazines and television. It was expected that these various groups would subsequently share their delight with others and thus get the WOM "ball" rolling for the movie.[41]

2. Hebrew National (HN), a unit of ConAgra Foods, has traditionally been thought of as an ethnic hot dog. In an effort to extend beyond its niche-market status, HN used a WOM guerrilla marketing campaign to reach families who might think the brand is not for them. So-called Mom Squads were employed in key markets such as New York, Los Angeles, and Tampa to create buzz for the brand. "Moms" drove SUVs embossed with HN logos to supermarkets, church fairs, and other community events and also hosted backyard barbecues where they distributed coupons and invited other women to join the Mom Squad.[42]

3. The ad agency for Lee jeans, Fallon McElligott, needed a way to encourage consumers to visit stores where they might try on and purchase the Lee brand. Toward this end, the agency created an online game that featured characters from an accompanying ad campaign. To move to level 2 of the game, consumers needed a special code they could obtain only by checking out a price tag for Lee jeans. To generate enthusiasm for the game, Fallon sent e-mail messages to 200,000 consumers who were targeted with the intent of directing them to a video clip designed to interest them in the game characters. These messages, described as "hip" and "intriguing," were widely disseminated by the original recipients to their friends, who in turn, in the best spirit of viral marketing passed the messages along to their friends, who forwarded it to their friends, and so on.[43]

4. In an effort to generate enthusiasm for new brands *prior* to their national launches, Procter & Gamble tested the use of interactive kiosks in suburban shopping malls. Touch-screen computers at the kiosks enabled interested consumers to acquire information about new P&G brands and even to purchase them before they appeared on store shelves. P&G's objective was to have these early users "cheerlead" the new brands, which appeared in P&G's Innovation Location kiosks anywhere from 6 to 12 months before their national launch.[44]

5. New York-based JetBlue Airways began operations in 2000. This innovative airline features attractive planes with leather seats, live television, and low prices. In an effort to establish Long Beach, a suburb of Los Angeles, as a hub for West Coast flights, the marketing personnel at JetBlue undertook a buzz-building campaign. The campaign was designed to reach influential customers such as bartenders and hotel concierges in hopes that they would spread the word about JetBlue Airways and its flights from the Long Beach airport. College interns were employed to visit bars, hotels, and other locales and to talk up JetBlue and provide "influentials" with bumper stickers, buttons, and tote bags that served as visible reminders of JetBlue's daily flights from the Long Beach airport. To generate further interest in JetBlue and initiate buzz, interns drove Volkswagen Beetles painted in JetBlue's signature blue color around the streets of Long Beach.[45]

6. For a final illustration of buzz creation efforts, see the *Online Focus* about "Vic Ladies" in Spain.

Formal Perspectives on Buzz-Building Practices

This section describes two perspectives on buzz-building efforts. One is based on the insightful observations of a journalist that became popularized in a book titled *The Tipping Point*. The other originates from principles derived by the

Boosting Internet Usage in Spain with "Vic Ladies"

Internet usage in Spain is among the lowest in Europe, yet telephone usage is among the highest. An enterprising businessman and CEO of Vic Telephone devised an innovative way to augment Internet usage. His approach? Use middle-aged women, who represent one of the *least* likely segments of the Spanish population to use the Internet, to recruit homemakers and retired people into Internet usage. A staff of "Vic Ladies" was trained to become Internet savvy themselves and in turn to teach their neighbors how to navigate the Web and to eventually sign up for Internet service—from Vic Telephone, of course. The strategy was to "go after people who might never have used the Internet if Vic hadn't entered their lives."

After acquiring Internet navigation ability, Vic Ladies are assigned to Vic Centers from which their relationship-building efforts take place. After new customers are recruited, Vic installs necessary equipment, provides the Internet service and phone link, and, via the Vic Ladies, provides requisite assistance when the new user encounters problems. It is too soon to know whether this highly personalized approach will become a profitable endeavor, but the "human touch" and a sympathetic ear are critical components when attempting to convert tech-phobics to new technology such as Internet usage. Vic's CEO has ambitious plans to expand Vic Centers globally.

Adapted from Carlta Vitzthu, "Vic Telephone Hopes 'Ladies' Will Bring the Internet to Their Neighbors," *Wall Street Journal Online*, November 9, 2000 (http://interactive.wsj.com/). Carlta Vitzthu, "Spanish Women Get Web-Savvy, Selling Access to the Internet," *Wall Street Journal Online*, November 9, 2000 (http://interactive.wsj.com/). Copyright 2001 by DOW JONES & CO INC. Reproduced with permission of DOW JONES & CO INC. in the format Textbook via Copyright Clearance Center.

renowned consulting firm McKinsey & Company and is called "explosive self-generated demand." Frankly, there is some redundancy in these two perspectives. Yet the author of your text considers each perspective sufficiently unique to warrant separate treatment.

Creating an Epidemic.   Marketplace buzz can be compared to an epidemic. By analogy, consider how common influenza spreads. A flu epidemic starts with a few people, who interact with other people, who in turn spread it to others until eventually, and generally quickly, thousands or even millions of people have the malady. Needless to say, flu epidemics could not occur unless people were in close contact with one another. For an epidemic to occur there must be a "tipping point," which is the "moment of critical mass" at which enough people are infected that the epidemic diffuses rapidly throughout the social system.[46]

It has been conjectured that epidemics in a social context, including the spread of information about new products and their adoption, can be accounted for by three straightforward rules: the "law of the few," the "stickiness factor," and the "power of context."[47] The first rule, the "law of the few," suggests that it only takes a few well-connected people ("connectors," opinion leaders, market mavens) to start an epidemic. In a social context, connected people start epidemics—such as the widespread adoption of new ideas and products—because they know a lot of people and are innately persuasive. Hebrew National's Mom Squads were enlisted to perform this role, as were JetBlue's college interns.

In short, buzz-building efforts for new products (new product epidemics!) require *messengers* who are willing to talk about a new product and share their product usage experience with others and who, by virtue of their inherent persuasiveness, influence others to also become product users. Paid advertising could never accomplish the results that informal social networks achieve! Advertising might inform, but it is common people who legitimize new product usage.

The second rule, the "stickiness factor," deals with the nature of the *message*, whereas the first rule involves the messenger. In short, messages about new products that are attention catching and memorable (i.e., messages that stick) enable more rapid diffusion. This explains why rumors and urban legends fly through the social system. Such messages are inherently interesting and thus are passed along with lightning speed.

Do you remember Anheuser-Busch's "Wassup" campaign for Budweiser? For a short period of time in 2000 it seemed like everyone was saying "Wassup?" This is a memorable, or sticky, expression that caught consumers' imaginations and thus spread rapidly after it first aired on television. Similarly, new products that possess observable/visible relative advantages (recall the earlier discussion of adoption-influencing factors) spread via word-of-mouth communication from consumer to consumer. Viagra (see Figure 6.9), the pharmaceutical product for men suffering erectile dysfunction, "buzzed" through society, helped in part by the jokes from late-night talk show hosts and further propelled by a frequently aired television commercial featuring a product endorsement by ex-presidential candidate Bob Dole. Also, the *Blair Witch Project* spread rapidly due to this film's fascinating subject matter and unique home-movie-like cinematography.

The take-away point from this discussion is that not all messages will diffuse rapidly, just those that are innately interesting and memorable. People must want to talk about a product or brand-related idea if it is to spread. Hence, it is through clever advertising and viral-marketing efforts that otherwise mundane

Figure 6.9   **Viagra Advertisement**

news can be made interesting, even exciting and thus worthy of sharing with other people who are connected via strong or weak social ties.

The third rule of epidemics, the "power of context," simply indicates that the circumstances and conditions have to be right for a persuasive message conveyed by a connector to have its impact and initiate an epidemic. It doesn't sound very scientific to say it, but sometimes the "stars have to be properly aligned" for epidemics to occur. In other words, there is a luck factor involved that is difficult to predict or control, or even to explain.

Igniting Explosive Self-Generated Demand. The famous management consulting firm McKinsey & Company has formulated a set of principles for igniting positive WOM momentum for new brands. McKinsey's associates refer to word-of-mouth momentum as explosive self-generated demand, or ESGD for short.[48] Key principles underlying ESGD are as follows:[49]

1. *Designing the product.* Products and brands that are most likely to experience ESGD have two distinguishing characteristics: First, they are *unique* in some respect—in terms of appearance (e.g., the PT Cruiser in Figure 6.5), functionality (e.g., Viagra), or in any other attention-gaining manner (e.g., Yoplait's Go-Gurt with the catchy name and unique package). Second, they are *highly visible* and/or *confer status* on opinion leaders and connectors who talk about product hipness and thus are themselves seen as hip via association. The *Global Focus* discussion of DaimlerChrysler's Smart car offers another illustration of a product that lends itself to ESGD.

2. *Selecting and seeding the vanguard.* Every new product/service has a group that is out in front of the crowd in terms of the speed at which the group adopts the product. This group, earlier termed innovators, is called the *vanguard* by McKinsey & Company. The challenge for the marketer of a new brand is identifying which consumer group will have the greatest influence over other consumers and then doing whatever it takes to get your brand accepted by that group, the vanguard. As noted earlier, Converse successfully introduced its All Star 2000 basketball shoe by going into 10 markets prior to the brand's launch and supplying advance pairs to local hero basketball players, the vanguard for this product. Vanguards include basketball stars, Hollywood divas, the most popular kids in high schools, the coolest kids in the 'hood, and so on. Abercrombie & Fitch, for example, recruits college students from popular fraternities and sororities to work in its stores and wear that retailer's clothing items.[50]

3. *Rationing supply.* As discussed in the previous chapter, scarcity is a powerful force underlying influencers' efforts to persuade. This is because people often want what they can't have. Automobile companies frequently exploit this reality by not producing sufficient supplies to meet immediate demand when the product is launched. The BMW Z3, the DaimlerChrysler PT Cruiser, and Ford's 2002 retro Thunderbird roadster all experienced demand far outstripping supply.

4. *Using celebrity icons.* Perhaps there is no better means to generate excitement about a new product than to first get it into the hands of a celebrity. If Nike golf balls are good enough for Tiger Woods, then Mack the Hack wants this brand also. The examples are numerous, and the reader undoubtedly has several examples in mind. (Don't you?) As I write this chapter (August 2001), I recall seeing a recent back-to-school commercial that included, among other items, a tartan skirt similar to the ceremonial kilts worn by Scottish men. I suspect this unlikely wardrobe item was inspired by Madonna's 2001 concert tour in which she regularly appeared wearing a kilt.

This section hopefully has provided you with an appreciation that WOM momentum can be managed in a proactive fashion rather than accepted as a *fait accompli.* Also, it should be clear that not all products and brands are appropriate for buzz-creation efforts. The "principles" identified here offer insight into when and why buzz creation is particularly likely and most effective.

A Highly Visible Product— DaimlerChrysler's Smart Car

DaimlerChrysler introduced its Smart car to the streets of Europe and Japan in 1998. This tiny car (see Figure 6.10), at only eight feet in length, is perfect for city conditions where parking space is at a premium and drivers must scurry for any available parking spot. The Smart car, though having sold only slightly more than 100,000 units in 2000, has created considerable buzz and achieved celebrity-like status. (As an American touring the streets of Berlin and Munich, I know it caught my attention and interest. I entertained thoughts such as, Why isn't such a car available in cities such as New York and Boston? Would urban Americans adopt such a midget vehicle?)

Interestingly, a German company, Wolf-Garten, is experimenting with the prospect of converting Smart cars into high-tech lawn mowers for use on golf courses and large corporate and residential lawns. A Wolf-Garten spokesperson describes the Smart car as having the perfect motor and transmission for large-area lawn cutting, and the car's short front would enable drivers to see exactly what and where they are cutting.

Executives at Wolf-Garten became interested in converting the car to a mower as a means of substantially re-ducing the noise and emissions from a conventional riding lawn motor. (Operating a conventional rider mower for just one hour produces as much emissions as driving an automobile for 10 hours!) The only problem prior to Wolf-Garten's going into full production is coming up with a suitable cutting device. The company is experimenting with a laser cutter. Obstacles to overcome include developing a laser cutter that will not cut shrubs and ornamental trees when the cutting platform tilts going over hills and assuring that laser cutting will not have long-term negative effects on grass.

This prospective new lawn mower would have an obvious relative advantage over conventional riding mowers if in fact laser cutting is a feasible procedure. On the downside, the Smart car riding lawn mower (to be named Zero, for its low noise and emissions) would be an expensive proposition, costing perhaps $25,000 or more. If the Zero ever reaches full-scale production, the buzz undoubtedly will be vigorous.

SUMMARY

The continual introduction of new products and services is critical to the success of most business organizations. The concepts of adoption and diffusion explain the processes by which new products and services are accepted by increasing numbers of customers as time passes. Marketing communications can facilitate the process by communicating a new product's relative advantages, showing how it is compatible with consumers' existing purchase preferences and values, reducing real or perceived complexity, enhancing the product's communicability, and making it easy to try.

The diffusion process is concerned with the broader issue of how an innovation is communicated and adopted throughout the marketplace. Diffusion, in simple terms, is the process of spreading out. Diffusion scholars have identified five relatively distinct groups of adopters. These groups, moving from the first to adopt an innovation to the last, are innovators, early adopters, early majority, late majority, and laggards. Research has shown that these groups differ considerably in terms of such variables as socioeconomic status, risk-taking tendencies, and peer relations.

Opinion leadership and word-of-mouth influence are important elements in facilitating more rapid product adoption and diffusion. Opinion leaders are

A Smart Car on the Streets of Berlin   **Figure 6.10**

Photo by Terence A. Shimp

individuals who are respected for their product knowledge and opinions. Opinion leaders inform other people (followers) about new products and services, provide advice and reduce the follower's perceived risk in purchasing a new product, and confirm decisions that followers have already made. Compared with followers, opinion leaders are more cosmopolitan, more gregarious, have higher socioeconomic status, and are more innovative. Positive word-of-mouth influence is often critical to new-product success. It appears that people talk about new products and services because they gain a feeling of prestige from being the bearer of news. Marketing communicators can take advantage of this prestige factor by stimulating cheerleaders, who will talk favorably about a new product or service.

Buzz creation—also called viral marketing, guerrilla marketing, and street marketing—is a relatively recent phenomenon as a proactive marketing practice. Firms employ the services of buzz-creation units to generate new product adoption by recruiting the efforts of connected people (opinion leaders, market mavens) who will both adopt and talk about new products. Indeed, buzz creation can be compared to a social epidemic.

Find more resources to help you study at http://shimp.swcollege.com!

Fournier, "Paradoxes of Technology: Consumer Cognizance, Emotions, and Coping Strategies," *Journal of Consumer Research* 25 (September 1998), 123–143, especially at 140.

17. Thomas S. Robertson and James N. Kennedy, "Prediction of Consumer Innovators: Application of Discriminant Analysis," *Journal of Marketing Research* 5 (February 1968), 64–69, citing *America's Tastemakers, Research Reports Nos. 1 and 2* (Princeton, N.J.: Opinion Research Corporation, 1959).

18. Rogers, *Diffusion of Innovations.*

19. Ibid.

20. Ibid.

21. Ibid.

22. Elyse Tanouye, "When It Looks Like a Dog's Life, Novartis May Help with a Canine Antidepressant," *The Wall Street Journal Interactive Edition*, January 5, 1999.

23. This section is adapted from Thomas S. Robertson, Joan Zielinski, and Scott Ward, *Consumer Behavior* (Glenview, Ill.: Scott, Foresman and Company, 1984), 380–382.

24. R. Bruce Money, Mary C. Gilly, and John L. Graham, "Explorations of National Culture and Word-of-Mouth Referral Behavior in the Purchase of Industrial Services in the United States and Japan," *Journal of Marketing* 62 (October 1998), 76–87. Rogers, *Diffusion of Innovations.*

25. Johan Arndt, "Role of Product-Related Conversation in the Diffusion of a New Product," *Journal of Marketing Research* 4 (August 1967), 291–295; Dorothy Leonard-Barton, "Experts as Negative Opinion Leaders in the Diffusion of a Technological Innovation," *Journal of Consumer Research* 11 (March 1985), 914–926.

26. For further discussion, see Jacqueline Johnson Brown and Peter H. Reingen, "Social Ties and Word-of-Mouth Referral Behavior," *Journal of Consumer Research* 14 (December 1987), 350–362.

27. In addition to Brown and Reingen's findings, ibid., see also Jacob Goldenberg, Barak Libai, and Eitan Muller, "Talk of the Network: A Complex Systems Look at the Underlying Process of Word-of-Mouth," *Marketing Letters* 12 (August 2001), 211–224.

28. Goldenberg, Libai, and Muller, "Talk of the Network."

29. Rogers, *Diffusion of Innovations.*

30. Jehoshua Eliashberg and Steven M. Shugan, "Film Critics: Influencers or Predictors?" *Journal of Marketing* 61 (April 1997), 68–78.

31. This fifth point is based on research that has detected a dimension of opinion leadership termed *public individuation*. In a study of college students' wine-consumption attitudes and behavior, the researchers obtained support that opinion leaders in this category are more publicly individuated. See Kenny K. Chan and Shekhar Misra, "Characteristics of the Opinion Leader: A New Dimension," *Journal of Advertising* 19, no. 3 (1990), 53–60.

32. This quote is from the famous motivational researcher Ernest Dichter, in Eileen Prescott, "Word-of-Mouth: Playing on the Prestige Factor," *The Wall Street Journal*, February 7, 1984, 1.

33. Lawrence F. Feick and Linda L. Price, "The Market Maven: A Diffuser of Marketplace Information," *Journal of Marketing* 51 (January 1987), 83–97.

34. Prescott, "Word-of-Mouth."

35. Steve Gelsi and Matthew Grimm, "Marketing by Seed," *Brandweek*, October 7, 1996, 20.

36. Aki Maita, "Tamagotchi," *Ad Age International*, December 1997, 10; Norihiko Shirouzu, "Japan's High-School Girls Excel in the Art of Setting Trends," *The Wall Street Journal Interactive Edition*, April 24, 1998 (http://interactive. wsj.com).

37. Paul M. Herr, Frank R. Kardes, and John Kim, "Effects of Word-of-Mouth and Product-Attribute Information on Persuasion: An Accessibility-Diagnosticity Perspective," *Journal of Consumer Research* 17 (March 1991), 454–462; Richard J. Lutz, "Changing Brand Attitudes through Modification of Cognitive Structure," *Journal of Consumer Research* 1 (March 1975), 49-59; and Peter Wright, "The Harassed Decision Maker: Time Pressures, Distractions, and the Use of Evidence," *Journal of Applied Psychology* 59 (October 1974), 555–561.

38. Marsha L. Richins, "Negative Word-of-Mouth by Dissatisfied Consumers: A Pilot Study," *Journal of Marketing* 47 (winter 1983), 76.

39. Ibid.

40. Ellen Neuborne, "Ambush," *Agency*, Spring 2001, 22-25; Wendy Davis, "Y&R Buzz-Builder Partilla Takes on Sony's Account," *Advertising Age*, March 5, 2001, 25.

41. John Lippman, "Sony's Word-of-Mouth Campaign Creates Buzz for 'Crouching Tiger,'" *Wall Street Journal Interactive Edition*, January 11, 2001 (http://interactive.wsj.com/).

42. Sonia Reyes, "Hebrew Nat'l Rolls Out 'Mom Squad,'" *Brandweek*, May 28, 2001, 6.

43. Neuborne, "Ambush," 25.

44. Jack Neff, "P&G Goes Viral with Test of Innovation Locations," *Advertising Age*, September 4, 2000, 4.

45. Chris Woodyard, "JetBlue Turns to Beetles, Beaches, Bars," *USA Today*, August 22, 2001, 3B.

46. The idea of a "tipping point" is based on the popular book by journalist Malcolm Gladwell, *The Tipping Point* (Boston: Little, Brown and Company, 2000).

47. Ibid.

48. Renée Dye, "The Buzz on Buzz," *Harvard Business Review* (November/December 2000), 139–146.

49. Based on ibid.

50. Ibid.

BRAND NAMES, LOGOS, PACKAGES, AND POINT-OF-PURCHASE MATERIALS

Chapter Objectives

After studying this chapter, you should be able to:

1. Understand the role of brand naming and the requirements for developing effective brand names.
2. Explain the activities involved in the brand-naming process.
3. Appreciate the role of logos.
4. Describe the various elements underlying the creation of effective packages.
5. Explain the VIEW model for evaluating package effectiveness.
6. Describe a five-step package design process.
7. Appreciate the role of point-of-purchase advertising.
8. Discuss the Consumer Buying Habits Study and its implications for point-of-purchase advertising.
9. Describe the role of displays in influencing brand sales.

Opening Vignette: Absolut Wanna-Be Becomes Absolute Flop

First, a little history lesson. Vodka is a distilled spirit that traditionally has been associated with eastern European countries such as Poland and Russia. Many brands, often with brand names that are unpronounceable to English speakers, have been available on retail shelves for years, and most are relatively inexpensive. Until the late 1970s the famous Russian brand Stolichnaya was the only premium-priced vodka brand that most non–eastern European consumers considered buying. But then, around 1980, an unknown brand from Sweden, Absolut, literally revolutionized vodka marketing. This brand had a radical package design (clear bottle with blue lettering) compared with traditional vodka brands. Moreover, it was considerably higher priced than all brands except the classic Stoli. On top of this, it was from a country—Sweden—not known for vodka! Yet largely driven by an excellent brand name (Absolut, which sounds and reads like the word *absolute*, suggesting a product that is complete, perfect, pure, and supreme), a unique and memorable package design, and an outstanding advertising campaign (see Figure 7.1 for a montage of Absolut advertisements), Absolut became a category leader. And it held this position for nearly two decades.

An interesting development in the vodka category started in the mid-1990s. Around this time a number of vodka companies began stealing market share from Absolut. They did this by developing quality products that had interesting brand names (e.g., Belvedere, Grey Goose, Ketel One), appealing and eye-catching bottles, and super-premium prices as much as twice that of Absolut. Some of Absolut's loyal users began switching to the new brands. Executives at Swedish-based V&S Vin & Sprit AB (the parent company of Absolut Vodka Company) and its North America distributor, Seagrams, knew it was time to develop a new brand to capture lost sales and profits.

In the late 1990s the V&S-Seagram team launched a new brand that sold at retail for $30 a bottle. Executives knew that the brand name and package design for this new brand would play instrumental roles in its successful launch and profitability. A series of focus-group tests was conducted to determine an appropriate brand name. Numerous English and Swedish words were placed before focus group participants. The name ultimately selected was Sundsvall, a small town in Sweden. The packaging decision entailed numerous meetings conducted over several months and high-level give-and-take sessions between the V&S and Sea-

A Montage of Absolut Magazine Advertisements

Figure 7.1

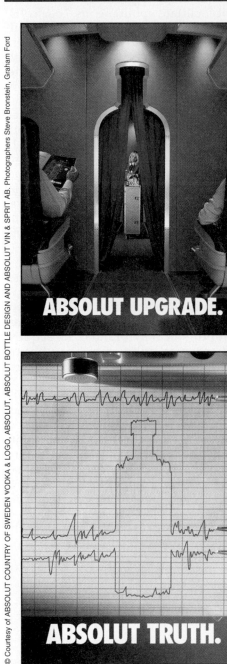

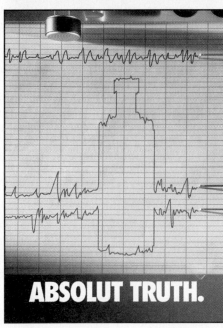

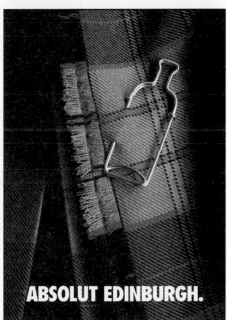

gram participants. V&S executives favored an understated, clear-bottle design, whereas Seagram's representatives preferred a sleek, frosted bottle. The eventual selection was a bottle with a clear barrel and an orange shrink-wrapped top.

With the name and package selected and price strategy determined, Sundsvall was ready for launch. This required generating buzz for the brand (as discussed in the previous chapter) by seeding the vanguard (e.g., entertainment celebrities, food and beverage writers) and gaining the support of influential bartenders in major markets who determine where on shelves to place different brands and which brands to recommend to customers. Unfortunately for the V&S-Seagram team, a "tipping point" (see the previous chapter) never occurred for Sundsvall. In addition to not achieving adequate retail distribution and having to compete in an overcrowded product category at the time of launch, could it be that the brand name, Sundsvall, simply did not register positively with either bartenders or consumers and thus did not facilitate spontaneous "bar calls" ("I'll have a Sundsvall vodka") or resonate positively with customers while making brand selection decisions from retail outlets? And was the bottle sufficiently eye-catching and appealing to attract attention and generate positive brand associations? Perhaps not. One executive characterized the package design as "difficult to see. It wasn't invisible, but it was too discrete where it was competing."

After months of disappointing sales, Sundsvall was eventually yanked from the market. As with many other new-product failures (see the previous chapter), no single factor can fully explain why the brand did not achieve the financial objectives that had been established for it. However, it is more than a remote possibility that the brand name and package may have been poorly chosen. Because hindsight always is better than foresight, it is only fair to conclude that the rationale underlying the introduction of the Sundsvall brand probably was sound but that the marketing execution was perhaps not up to the challenging requirements for product success in a somewhat saturated and highly competitive product category.

This chapter provides a critical link between the previous six chapters and the chapters that follow. To this point in the text, we have discussed integrated marketing communications (IMC), developed the importance of brand equity enhancement, examined the fundamentals of communicating with consumers and the role of persuasion, and described efforts undertaken by marketing communicators to facilitate the adoption of new brands. Subsequent chapters will focus on advertising, promotions, marketing-oriented public relations, and sponsorship/event marketing. Brand names, logos, and packages are critical to all these efforts, and the point-of-purchase is the point where all of the components of an IMC program ultimately come together. Sundsvall's failure (*Opening Vignette*) can be largely attributed to problematic brand naming and packaging decisions.

The marketing communicator's intermediate goal is enhancing brand equity with the ultimate goal of channeling consumer behavior toward the marketer's brand. That is, the goal, as established in Chapter 1, is to influence customers' behavior. We want people to buy our brand rather than competitors' brands. We want them to purchase sooner rather than later, more rather than less, frequently rather than intermittently, and so on. Having a good brand name, a good logo, an appealing package, and an eye-catching point-of-purchase display enables the brand marketer to achieve the ultimate goal of influencing consumer behavior. We now turn our attention to each of these topics.

BRAND NAMING

A brand is a company's unique designation, or trademark, which distinguishes its offering from other product category entries.[1] Many marketing executives regard brand naming to be one of the most important aspects of marketing management.[2] Product and brand managers consider it critical to choose an appropriate brand name, largely because that choice can influence early trial of a brand and affect sales volume.[3] The brand name identifies a company's offering and differentiates it from others on the market. The brand name and package graphics work together to communicate and position the brand's image. In short, a brand's name is crucially important—indeed, a name is "the cerebral switch that activates an image in the mind of the audience."[4]

A good brand name can evoke a feeling of trust, confidence, security, strength, durability, speed, status, and many other desirable associations. The name chosen for a brand (1) affects the speed with which consumers become aware of the brand, (2) influences the brand's image, and (3) thus plays a major role in brand equity formation.[5] Achieving consumer awareness of a brand name is the critical initial aspect of brand equity enhancement. Brand name awareness has been characterized as the "gateway" to consumers' more complicated learning and retention of associations that constitute a brand's image.[6]

Through brand names, a company can create excitement, elegance, exclusiveness, and influence consumers' perceptions and attitudes.[7] For example, 99 percent of the customers of Polo brand clothing have never seen nor will ever play a match of polo, yet Ralph Lauren, through the wise choice of the Polo name, was able to endow this brand with a high-status cachet. Pizza Hut selected the name Big New Yorker when introducing its New York–style product in the late 1990s to suggest, in addition to size, an "attitude" for which New York is known. This product was the most successful in Pizza Hut's history, with 40 million consumers trying the product within three months of its introduction.[8] The name JetBlue (*IMC Focus*) provides this company with a memorable name unlike any other in the airline industry.

What Constitutes a Good Brand Name?

What determines whether a brand name is a good name? This is a complex question that precludes a straightforward answer. To gain perspective, let's twist the question around and pose it in these terms: What determines whether a person's name is a good name? (Please think about this for a moment before reading on.) As you pondered this question, you likely arrived quickly at the conclusion that people's names differ dramatically and that no simple rule can answer whether a person's name is good. Perhaps you also entertained the notion that whether a person's name is "good" depends in large part on whether it "fits" the person's size, personality, and demographic characteristics. In short, there are many ways to have a good name, either for a person or for a brand.

Complexity aside, researchers have attempted to specify the factors that determine brand name quality. Although the accumulated knowledge is nowhere close to the point of specifying scientific principles, there is general agreement that brand names should satisfy several fundamental requirements: (1) distinguish the brand from competitive offerings, (2) describe the brand and its attributes or benefits, (3) achieve compatibility with the brand's desired image and with its product design or packaging, and (4) be memorable and easy to pronounce and spell.[9]

Requirement I: Distinguish the Brand from Competitive Offerings.
It is desirable for a brand to have a unique identity, something that clearly differentiates it from competitive brands. Failure to distinguish a brand from competitive offerings creates consumer confusion and increases the chances that consumers will not remember the name or mistakenly select another brand. Clinique selected the name Happy to suggest precisely that feeling for its perfume brand, a name choice that is striking in its differentiation from the usually sexually suggestive names chosen for perfumes such as Passion, Allure, and Obsession.[10] This brand quickly achieved the top market share in the category.

Some marketers attempt to hitchhike on the success of other brands by using names that are similar to better-known and more respected brands. However, the Federal Trademark Dilution Act of 1995 protects owners of brand names and logos from other companies using the identical or similar names. (In legal terms, brand names and logos are referred to as trademarks.) The objective of this legislation is to protect trademarks from losing their distinctiveness.[11] Trademark infringement cases occur with some regularity in the United States, and stealing well-known brand names is widely practiced in some newly emerging market economies. Chinese marketers have been accused of using facsimiles of famous brand names on their own domestically manufactured products. For example, a toothpaste is packaged under the Colgate-sounding name Cologate, and a Chinese brand of sunglasses is named Ran Bans, which is obviously similar to Bausch & Lomb's well-known Ray Ban brand.[12]

IMC
focus

Selecting a Name for a New Airline

The previous chapter mentioned a buzz-building effort in Long Beach, California, by the new airline, JetBlue Airways. Let's learn a little more about this company and how it selected its interesting name. The company's CEO is a guy named David Neeleman, who had been involved in the early 1990s with a successful start-up airline that eventually was sold to Southwest Airlines. Neeleman described his new JetBlue Airways in these terms: "We're a new kind of low-fare airline, with deep pockets, new planes, leather seats with more legroom, great people, and innovative thinking. With our friendly service and hassle-free technology, we're going to bring humanity back to air travel." JetBlue is based at New York's JFK International Airport. The airline is positioned as being both less expensive and providing greater comforts compared with established airlines. In short, JetBlue wants to be known as a low-fare but classy airline.

But how and why did it select the name JetBlue? Initially, Neeleman and his associates were uncertain what they wanted in a name for their new airline, but they were absolutely certain what they did *not* want—namely, they didn't want (1) a geographic destination such as southwest or northeast or (2) a made-up word such as brand names popular in automobile marketing (e.g., Lexus and Acura). The marketing team at "New Air," which was the operating name for the airline while awaiting the selection of a permanent name, considered numerous name possibilities, including New York Air, Gotham, Taxi, the Big Apple, Imagine Air, Yes!, and Fresh Air. Taxi was the name that had the greatest appeal to a top marketing executive, who thought that name had "a New York feel" and would enable a unique plane design with yellow and black checkering on the tails of planes (reminiscent of the look of New York's Checker cabs). The name Taxi eventually was rejected, however, because in its verb usage, *taxi* describes what planes do on runways, and the Federal Aviation Administration rejected this usage for a brand name. Also, some feared that New York taxi cabs had a negative image associated with high prices, poor service, and unsafe rides.

Requirement 2: Describe the Brand and Its Attributes or Benefits.
It is important to note in this regard that a brand name need not state a specific benefit but may rather simply suggest an abstract promise.[13] Post-it (note pads), I Can't Believe It's Not Butter (margarine), I Can't Believe It's Not Chicken (a faux chicken soy-based product), Healthy Choice (low-fat foods), and Huggies (diapers) illustrate brand names that do outstanding jobs in describing their respective products' attributes or benefits.

Transmeta Corp., a manufacturer of computer chips that competes against the much larger Intel and its Pentium class of products, introduced a super-efficient chip designed for laptop computers. This new chip promised to extend laptop usage without battery recharge for many hours beyond the standard two or three hours enabled by conventional chips. Transmeta named the new chip Crusoe after the famous fictional character Robinson Crusoe. This brand name suggests (to anyone familiar with the Robinson Crusoe story) that a laptop powered with a Crusoe chip permits a "stranded" user to continue working for many hours without access to an electrical outlet. Though the name-benefit relation is a bit abstract in this case, it would be expected that Crusoe readily suggests a stranded-usability benefit to most prospective laptop purchasers.

Researchers have carefully examined the issue of brand name suggestiveness. *Suggestive brand names* are those that imply particular attributes or benefits in the context of a product category. Crusoe is a suggestive brand name. So is Healthy Choice for food products, intimating that this brand is low in fat content and calories. The name Outback for Subaru's sport utility vehicle sug-

New Air's marketing executives then considered other name possibilities, such as Blue, It, and Egg (what were they thinking?). All three names were rejected, and as a last resort the company employed the services of Landor Associates, a firm that specializes in brand naming. Landor eventually came up with six candidate names that were presented to CEO Neeleman and his colleagues at a gathering in Landor's San Francisco headquarters. The slate of finalists (and their reasons for rejection) were: Air Avenues (too suggestive of New York's swank Park Avenue, which is an inappropriate association for a budget airline); Hiway Air (a made-up word that Neeleman eschewed, and silly at that); Air Hop (another silly name); Lift Airways (ultimately rejected for being suggestive of the emergency situation embodied in the similar sounding "airlift"); Scout Air (rejected because it implied an adventure destination and suggested the name of scouting organizations such as the Girl Scouts); and True Blue.

True Blue was the name selected at this important meeting in San Francisco. A key member of the marketing team shared these views: "The *blue* has a good visual aspect to it. It's the sky, it's friendship, it's loyalty." A long and arduous process was finally completed, and the new airline was prepared to trumpet its engaging name, True Blue. But just two weeks before launching PR and advertising campaigns, the company learned that the True Blue name was already owned by Thrifty-Rent-A-Car, which had copyrighted the name for use in a customer service program. (Parenthetically, the fact that the name was already owned had escaped Landor's legal analysis, much to the dismay of this respected brand-naming company.) Just one week before announcing the new airline, a member of the marketing team recommended the name JetBlue. Everyone agreed that the name would work, and New Air became JetBlue Airways—a fledgling airline that may become a mainstay of American airline service.

Sources: Adapted from Rebecca Johnson, "Name That Airline," *Travel & Leisure*, October 1999, 159–164; "JetBlue Airways Open for Business" (Company Press Release), January 11, 2000 (http://www.jetblue.com/learnmore/pressDetail.asp?newsId=10); Bonnie Tsui, "JetBlue Soars in First Months," *Advertising Age*, September 11, 2000, 26.

---

gests a product that is durable and rugged—capable of taking on the challenge of the famous Australian outback. Ford Explorer is a name that suggests adventure for prospective purchasers of pickup trucks seeking the thrill of off-road driving.

Research has demonstrated that suggestive brand names facilitate consumer recall of advertised benefit claims that are consistent in meaning with the brand names.[14] Suggestive brand names reinforce in consumers' memories the association between the name and the semantically related benefit information about the brand.[15] On the other hand, these same suggestive names may reduce the recallability of benefit claims after a brand has been repositioned to stand for something different than its original meaning.[16]

Brand names sometimes are created rather than selected from words found in a dictionary. Compaq (a computer brand) is a created name, as are many automobile brand names currently in use or used in the past. This includes names such as Acura, Altima, Geo, Lexus, Lumina, and Sentra. These names were created from *morphemes*, which are the semantic kernels of words. For example, Compaq, which combines two morphemes (com and paq), is an excellent name for suggesting the product's benefits of a computer and compactness. The automobile name Acura indicates precision in product design and engineering.

Requirement 3: Achieve Compatibility with a Brand's Desired Image and with Its Product Design or Packaging.
Again, Healthy Choice is an ideal name for a category of fat-free and low-fat food items that are targeted toward weight- and health-conscious consumers. The name suggests

that the consumer has an alternative and that Healthy Choice is the right choice. Another name that is perfectly compatible with the brand's desired image is Second Nature, which is the brand name for a line of recycled tablets and legal pads. The o in *Second* is formed from three chasing arrows that symbolize recyclability, and the words *Second* and *Nature* are colored in environmentally congruent green against a woodsy-brown background. Second Nature is an excellent name that suggests that writing pads carrying this name are not made from virgin wood but rather are recycled—hence, the rebirth of nature, or Second Nature. The name also serves as a subtle injunction to the consumer that using recycled writing materials should be virtually an automatic decision, as implied by the vernacular expression "it's second nature."

Because marketplaces are dynamic and consumer preferences and desires change over time, some brand names lose their effectiveness and have to be changed to avoid negative images. A case in point is Kentucky Fried Chicken. This name was compatible with the product for well over two decades, but a name change was needed when health consciousness swept the nation. A change from Kentucky Fried Chicken to simply KFC was undertaken with hopes of preventing the negative implications associated with the word *fried*.

Company names are being changed with increasing frequency due to mergers, acquisitions, and other factors. For example, the company name Verizon Communications was created from the merger of Bell Atlantic and GTE. The name Verizon was formed by combining the words *veritas* and *horizon*, the former word suggesting the quality of truth.[17] The company now known as Accenture had to change its name after a split with its sister company. Arthur Andersen introduced the Accenture name and logo in 2001, which features a greater-than sign over the letter *t* (see Figure 7.2). The name is a made-up word that conjoins two real words, *accent* and *future*, thus suggesting an accent on the future. Interestingly, in the process of selecting this new name, the company employed the services of the same San Francisco firm, Landor Associates, that had worked on the JetBlue name (see *IMC Focus*). Landor's name selection process considered 5,500 different names, half of which were generated by Accenture employees who participated in an internal naming initiative. The Accenture name was, in fact, invented by one of its own employees. That employee described his choice in these words:

> Basically, I wanted a word that had a lot of positive associations to it, and that would emphasize accomplishment and accelerated growth—the terms that we have been talking about in the firm—as well as adventure and excitement and also the future. Coupling these words gave me the idea— it just came.[18]

Requirement 4: Be Memorable and Easy to Pronounce.
Finally, a good brand name is one that is easy to remember and pronounce. To facilitate memory and pronunciation, many brand names are short, one-word names (e.g., Tide, Bold, Shout, Edge, Bounce, Cheer, Dips), though shortness is not an essential ingredient for a good name. Probably few words are as memorable as those learned in early childhood, and among the first words learned are animal names. This likely explains marketers' penchant for using animals as brand names; for example, automobile companies are using or have used names such as Mustang, Thunderbird, Bronco, Cougar, Lynx, Skyhawk, Skylark, Firebird, Jaguar, and Ram.

In addition to their memorability, animal names also conjure up vivid images. This is very important to the marketing communicator because, as discussed in Chapter 4, concrete and vivid images facilitate consumer information processing. Dove soap, for example, suggests softness, grace, gentleness, and purity. Ram (for Dodge trucks) intimates strength, durability, and toughness.

Some Exceptions to the "Rules."
The foregoing discussion has identified four guidelines for brand naming. The observant student will note, however, that some successful brand names seem entirely at odds with the above "rules."

The New Name Accenture   **Figure 7.2**

© Courtesy of Accenture

Why is this the case? First, some brands become successful in spite of their names. (Analogously, some people achieve prominence even though their names may not be the ones they personally would have chosen or that a "namemeister" would have selected as more ideal.) The first brand in a new product category can achieve tremendous success regardless of its name if the brand offers customers distinct advantages over alternative solutions to their problems. Second, in all aspects of life there are exceptions to the rules, and this certainly is the case in brand naming. There simply are many ways to "skin a cat."

A third major exception to the above "rules" is that brand managers and their brand name consultants sometimes intentionally select names that, at inception, are virtually meaningless. For example, the word *lucent* in Lucent Technologies was selected because for most people this word has relatively little meaning or associations—the *empty-vessel philosophy* of brand naming. The empty-vessel expression implies that when a name does not have much preexisting meaning, subsequent marketing communications are able to create the exact meaning desired without contending with past associations already accumulated in people's memories. Slates is another brand name selected precisely for this purpose. Slates is the brand name for a line of dress pants marketed by Levi Strauss & Company. The name Slates was selected to be purposefully vague, perhaps only hinting at slate rock and its thin, durable strength. Levi Strauss hired a California company called Lexicon to assist in selecting a name for dress slacks. This naming consultant said that its key criterion in ultimately recommending this name was that it was "an empty vessel into which its marketers could pour their meaning."[19] In other words, rather than selecting a name already rich in meaning and filled with associations, there are advantages to using a relatively neutral name that a MarCom campaign can endow with intended meaning.

The Brand-Naming Process

Brand naming involves a rather straightforward process as determined by a survey of over 100 product and brand managers who represent both consumer and industrial goods products. Figure 7.3 lists the steps, and the following discussion describes each.

Step 1: Specify Objectives for the Brand Name.   As with all managerial decisions, the initial step is to identify the objectives to be accomplished. Most managers are concerned with selecting a name that will successfully position the brand in the minds of the target audience, provide an appropriate image for the brand, and distinguish it from competitive brands.[20]

Step 2: Create Candidate Brand Names.   Brand name candidates often are selected using creative-thinking exercises and brainstorming sessions.

Figure 7.3   **The Brand-Naming Process**

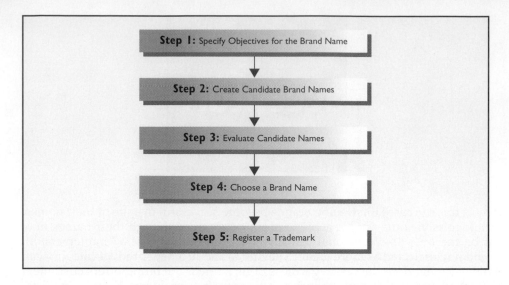

Source: "The Brand-Naming Process," adapted from Chiranjeev Kohli and Douglas W. LaBahn, "Observations: Creating Effective Brand Names: A Study of the Naming Process," *Journal of Advertising Research* 37 (January/February 1997), p. 69. Reprinted by permission.

Companies frequently use the services of naming consultants to generate candidate names, as was the case in the selection of JetBlue, Verizon, Accenture, Lucent, and Slates. The survey of product and brand managers noted above determined that nearly 50 candidate names were created for each brand-naming assignment.[21]

Step 3: Evaluate Candidate Names.   The many names generated are evaluated using criteria such as relevance to the product category, favorability of associations conjured up by the name, and overall appeal. Product and brand managers consider it critical that names be easily recognized and recalled.[22]

Step 4: Choose a Brand Name.   The criteria noted in steps 1 and 3 are used by managers to select a final name from the candidate field. In many firms this choice is a matter of subjective judgment rather than the product of rigorous marketing research.[23] As previously described, JetBlue was chosen subjectively based on hunch and insight.

Step 5: Register a Trademark.   Most companies apply for trademark registration. Some companies submit only a single name for registration, whereas others submit multiple names (on average, five names). One survey found that three names are rejected for every registered name.[24] A brand-naming consultant indicated that the number of rejections is even higher, noting that about 75 percent of the names his firm generates are already taken upon searching federal registrations.[25]

The Role of Logos

Related to the brand name is a graphic design element called a brand *logo*. For purposes of identifying their brands, companies use logos with or without brand names.[26] Not all brand names possess a distinct logo, but many do. For example, the Nike swoosh is virtually as famous as the company name, as are the logos for

Evolution of Cracker Jack's Sailor Jack Logo   **Figure 7.4**

© Courtesy of Frito Lay

| 1910's | 1920's | 1950's | 1970's | 1997 |

Adidas athletic shoes and for automobile brands such as Mercedes, Lexus, BMW, and Infiniti. Consumers learn these logos and easily recognize the brands on which the logos are emblazoned. (To test this, take a moment and visualize the logos for each of the following well-known brands: Pepsi, Ralph Lauren's Polo, Tommy Hilfiger clothing, Starbucks coffee, Mercedes-Benz automobiles, Toyota automobiles, Arm & Hammer baking soda, and Cracker Jack popcorn.) One marketing executive nicely captures the role of logos when claiming, "The logo is nothing but a shorthand way of identifying a brand."[27]

Logo designs are incredibly diverse, ranging from highly abstract designs to those that depict nature scenes and from very simple to complex depictions. Generally, good logos are (1) recognized readily, (2) convey essentially the same meaning to all target members, and (3) evoke positive feelings.[28] The logo for Cracker Jack, the sweetened popcorn snack item, perhaps typifies a readily recognized and feel-good design. What American kid can forget the Sailor Jack logo that has appeared on the Cracker Jack package since the early 1900s? (Figure 7.4 shows the periodic updates in the Sailor Jack design since its inception in 1910.[29])

Although logos undoubtedly perform valuable communication roles and influence brand equity via their effect both on brand awareness and image, published research on logos is surprisingly absent. However, a major study determined that the best strategy for enhancing the likeability of a logo is to choose a design that is *moderately elaborate* rather than one that is too simple or too complex. Also, natural designs (as opposed to abstract illustrations) were found to produce more favorable consumer responses.[30] Cingular's heavily advertised logo perhaps represents an illustration of a logo that achieves the goal of being neither too simple nor too complex. Cingular, a major company in the wireless industry, invested heavily in selecting the simple yet distinct icon shown in Figure 7.5. Company personnel refer affectionately to the Cingular icon as Jack, apparently due to its similarity to the object in the old-fashioned children's game of jacks.

PACKAGING

A brand's package is, of course, the "container" that both protects and sells the product. Products available on store shelves are most always contained, boxed, or packaged in some manner. As the term *package* is used in the present context, a beverage bottle is a package; so are the jewel box for a CD and Gateway Computer's Jersey cow box, and so on. Growing numbers of MarCom specialists appreciate the crucial role performed by brand packaging. The increasingly important communications role of packaging has given rise to expressions such

Figure 7.5

as "Packaging is the least expensive form of advertising"; "Every package is a five-second commercial"; "The package is a silent salesman"; and "The package is the product."[31] The advertising and salesmanship roles of packaging are critical inasmuch as research reveals that shoppers spend an incredibly short amount of time—on the order of 10 to 12 seconds—viewing brands before moving on or selecting an item and placing it in the shopping cart.[32]

The growth of supermarkets, mass merchandisers (such as Wal-Mart, Kmart, and Target) and other self-service retail outlets has necessitated that the package perform marketing functions beyond the traditional role of merely containing and protecting the product. The package also serves to (1) draw attention to a brand, (2) break through competitive clutter at the point of purchase, (3) justify price and value to the consumer, (4) signify brand features and benefits, (5) convey emotionality, and (6) ultimately motivate consumers' brand choices. Packaging is particularly important for differentiating homogenous or unexciting brands from available substitutes. Packaging accomplishes this by working uninterruptedly to say what the brand is, how it is used, and what it can do to benefit the user.[33] In short, packages perform a major role in enhancing brand equity by creating or fortifying brand awareness and building brand images via conveying functional, symbolic, and experiential benefits (recall the brand equity model presented in Chapter 2).

Packaging Structure

There is a tendency for consumers to impute characteristics from a package to the brand itself, a tendency termed *sensation transference*.[34] A package communicates meaning about a brand via its various symbolic components: color, design, shape, size, physical materials, and information labeling. These components taken together represent what is referred to as the *packaging structure*.[35] These structural elements must interact harmoniously to evoke within buyers the set of meanings intended by the brand marketer. The notion underlying good packaging is *gestalt*. That is, people react to the unified whole, the gestalt, not to the individual parts.

The following sections describe various package structure components. Although these descriptions are more anecdotal than scientific, the student should find these characterizations thought provoking though certainly not definitive.

The Use of Color in Packaging.   Colors have the ability to communicate various cognitive and emotional meanings to prospective buyers. Research studies have documented the important role that color plays in affecting our senses. Consider the following study in which researchers tested color's cueing role using vanilla pudding as the experimental product. The researchers altered the color of vanilla pudding by adding food colors to create dark brown, medium brown, and light brown "flavors." The pudding, which actually was identical in all three experimental versions (namely vanilla), was perceived as tasting like chocolate. Moreover, the dark brown pudding was considered to have the best chocolate flavor and to be the thickest. The light brown pudding was perceived to be the creamiest, possibly because cream is white in color.[36] This study, though not conducted in a packaging context per se, certainly holds implications for the use of color in package design.

The strategic use of colors in packaging is effective because colors affect people emotionally. For example, the so-called high-wavelength colors of red, orange, and yellow possess strong excitation value and induce elated mood states.[37] *Red* is often described in terms such as *active, stimulating, energetic,* and *vital*. Brands using this as their primary color include Close-Up (toothpaste), Tylenol (medicine), Coca-Cola (soft drink), Pringles (potato chips), and Diamond (matches). *Orange* is an appetizing color that is often associated with food. Popular food brands using orange packaging include Wheaties (cereal), Uncle Ben's (rice), Sanka (coffee), Stouffer's (frozen dinners), and Kellogg's Mini-Wheats (cereal). *Yellow*, a good attention getter, is a warm color that has a cheerful effect on consumers. Cheerios (cereal), Kodak (film), Prestone (antifreeze), Mazola (corn oil), and Pennzoil (motor oil) are just a few of the many brands that use yellow packages.

Green connotes abundance, health, calmness, and serenity. Green packaging is sometimes used for beverages (e.g., Heineken beer, Seven-Up, Sprite, Mountain Dew), often for vegetables (e.g., Green Giant), most always for mentholated products (e.g., Salem cigarettes, Altoids mentholated breath mints), and for many other products (Irish Spring deodorant soap, Fuji film, etc.). Green also has come to stand for environmentally friendly products and as a cue to consumers of reduced-fat, low-fat, and fat-free products (e.g., Lay's reduced-fat potato chips). *Blue* suggests coolness and refreshment. Blue is often associated with laundry and cleaning products (e.g., Downey fabric softener, Snuggle dryer sheets) and skin products (e.g., Nivea skin lotion, Noxzema skin cream). Finally, *white* signifies purity, cleanliness, and mildness. Gold Medal (flour), Special K (cereal), Dove (body lotion), and Pantene (shampoo) are a few brands that feature white packages.

In addition to the emotional impact that color brings to a package, elegance and prestige can be added to products by the use of polished reflective surfaces and color schemes using white and black or silver and gold.[38] Cosmetic packages often use gold (e.g., Revlon's Moisturestay lip color) or metallic silver packages (e.g., Almay Sheer makeup).

It is pertinent to note that the meaning of color varies from culture to culture. The comments made here are based on North American culture and are not directly applicable elsewhere. Readers from other cultures should identify exceptions to these comments and illustrate packages that do not adhere to North American color usage.

Design and Shape Cues in Packaging.   *Design* refers to the organization of the elements on a package. An effective package design is one that permits good eye flow, provides the consumer with a point of focus, and conveys meaning about the brand's attributes and benefits. Package designers bring various elements together to help define a brand's image. These elements include—in addition to color—shape, size, and label design.

One way of evoking different feelings is through the choice of slope, length, and thickness of lines on a package. *Horizontal lines* suggest restfulness and quiet, evoking feelings of tranquillity. There appears to be a physiological reason for this reaction—it is easier for people to move their eyes horizontally than vertically; vertical movement is less natural and produces greater strain on eye muscles than horizontal movement. *Vertical lines* induce feelings of strength, confidence, and even pride. Energizer (batteries), Aquafresh (toothpaste), and Jif (peanut butter) all feature vertical lines in their package designs. *Slanted lines* suggest upward movement to most people in the Western world, who read from left to right and thus view sloped lines as ascending rather than descending. Armor All (automobile polish), Gatorade (power drink), and Dr. Pepper (soft drink) use slanted lines in their package designs.

Shapes, too, arouse certain emotions and have specific connotations. Generally, round, curving lines connote femininity, whereas sharp, angular lines suggest masculinity. A package's shape also affects the apparent volume of the container. In general, if two packages have the same volume but a different shape, the taller of the two will appear to hold a greater volume inasmuch as height is usually associated with volume.

Packages also can be shaped so as to convey information about their product contents. An interesting example of this is the package for the WhipperSnapple brand of fruit drinks. WhipperSnapple, from Triarc Beverage, is a packaged "smoothie," a fruit drink made from fresh fruit blended and thickened with milk or another dairy product. WhipperSnapple is itself a clever brand name derived from the word *whippersnapper,* which is an expression referring to a young, presumptuous person. Testing revealed that the name appealed to consumers from all age groups and geographic regions of the United States. The packaging objective was to design a container that would signal WhipperSnapple's dairy content in an unmistakable way at the point of purchase. After much deliberation, it was decided to mold an ice-cream-style swirl into the bottle to convey the impression that WhipperSnapple mixes fruit and dairy products in a smoothie-drink fashion. [39]

Packaging Size.   Many product categories are available in several product sizes. Soft drinks, for example, come in 8- and 12-ounce bottles, 1- and 2-liter containers, and in 6-, 12-, and 24-unit packs. Manufacturers offer different-sized containers to satisfy the unique needs of various market segments, to represent different usage situations, and to gain more shelf space in retail outlets. An interesting issue arises from the consumer's perspective with regard to the size of the container. In particular, does the amount of product consumption vary depending on the size of the container? For example, do consumers consume more content from a large package than a smaller version? Preliminary research on this matter reveals a tendency for consumers to indeed consume more content from larger packages. One reason for this behavior is that consumers perceive they gain lower unit prices from larger than smaller packages.[40] This finding is not universal across all products, however, because consumption for some products (such as laundry bleach or vitamins) is relatively invariant.

Physical Materials in Packaging.   Another important consideration is the materials that make up a package. Increased sales and profits often result when upgraded packaging materials are used to design more attractive and effective packages. Packaging materials can arouse consumer emotions, usually subconsciously. Packages constructed of *metal* evoke feelings of strength, durability, and, perhaps undesirably, coldness. *Plastics* connote lightness, cleanliness, and perhaps cheapness. Materials that are *soft,* such as velvet, suede, and satin are associated with femininity. *Foil* can be used to convey a high-quality image and provoke feelings of prestige.[41] Beverage products such as beers and sparkling wines often use foil with apparently the intent of appearing "high class." Finally, *wood* sometimes is used in packages to arouse feelings of masculinity. For example, the Body Shop's Snow Soap brand is packaged in a wooden container.

Evaluating the Package: The VIEW Model

A number of individual features have been discussed in regard to what a package communicates to buyers, but what exactly constitutes a good package? Although, as always, no single response is equally suitable across all packaging situations, four general features can be used to evaluate a particular package. These are visibility, information, emotional appeal, and workability, which are conveniently remembered with the acronym **VIEW**.[42]

V = Visibility.   *Visibility* signifies the ability of a package to attract attention at the point of purchase. The objective is to have a package stand out on the shelf yet not be so garish that it detracts from a brand's image. Brightly colored packages are especially effective at gaining the consumer's attention. For example, the bright orange package for Kellogg's Mini-Wheats (Figure 7.6) illustrates a highly visible package that is easily spotted at the point of purchase. Novel packaging graphics, sizes, and shapes also enhance a package's visibility.

Many brands in product categories such as soft drinks, cereal, and candy alternate packages throughout the year with special seasonal and holiday packaging as a way of attracting attention. By aligning the brand with the shopping mood

A Highly Visible Package Design   **Figure 7.6**

fitting the season or holiday, companies provide consumers with an added reason for selecting the specially packaged brand over more humdrum brands that never vary their package design. The heart-shaped package for Reese's peanut butter cups (Figure 7.7) is an attractive, attention-gaining, and romance-conveying package design that is perfect for Valentine's Day.

I = Information.   The second consideration, *information,* deals with various forms of product information (e.g., ingredients, product-usage instructions, claimed benefits, and warnings) that are presented anywhere on the package. Package information is useful for (1) stimulating trial purchases, (2) encouraging repeat purchase behavior, and (3) providing correct product usage instructions.[43] The objective is to provide the right type and quantity of information without cluttering the package with excessive information that could interfere with the primary information or cheapen the look of the package. An example of the effectiveness of information included on packages comes from a field experiment that measured weekly sales of bread. When a "Made with 100 percent natural ingredients: No artificial additives" statement was affixed to the package, sales volume increased. When the message was removed, sales returned to their prior level.[44]

The words *new, improved*, and *free* frequently appear on packages. These words sometimes can stimulate immediate trial purchases or restore a brand purchase pattern for past brand users who have switched to other brands. Furthermore, these key words presumably offer consumers change, novelty, and excite-

---

Figure 7.7   **An Effective Seasonal Package Design**

ment. Some observers contend that words such as these have been overworked in the marketplace and do not significantly affect consumer evaluations of certain products.[45] More research is necessary to support or refute this point. Perhaps there is a need for new motivating words. Some examples may be the use of numerals, as in Gleem II (toothpaste) and Clorox 2 (laundry bleach). These names inform consumers that there is a new and improved version of an old brand without directly employing overused words such as new and improved.[46]

In some instances, putting a short, memorable slogan on a package is a good marketing tactic. Slogans on packages are best used when a strong association has been built between the brand and the slogan through extensive and effective advertising. The slogan on the package, a concrete reminder of the brand's advertising, can facilitate the consumer's retrieval of advertising content and thereby enhance the chances of a trial purchase. (When discussing point-of-purchase advertising later in the chapter, we will refer to this practice of putting an advertising slogan on a package as utilizing the encoding specificity principle.)

E = Emotional Appeal.

The third component of the VIEW model, *emotional appeal*, is concerned with the ability of a package to evoke a desired feeling or mood. Package designers attempt to arouse specific feelings (elegance, prestige, cheerfulness, fun, nostalgia, etc.) through the use of color, shape, packaging materials, and other devices. Packages for some brands contain virtually no emotional content and emphasize instead informational content, while packages of other brands emphasize emotional content and contain very little information. The emotional value of packaging is well illustrated by the relatively new packaging of Heinz ketchup. Heinz, like other brands in this category, had always been packaged in glass bottles. Then the company began packaging ketchup in plastic containers. Both the bottles and the plastic containers were relatively blah, however. In an appeal to children, who consume 55 percent of all ketchup in the United States, Heinz eventually designed an emotionally appealing, fun-oriented package with bright coloring and a multihued, striped design.[47] Kids love the different ketchup colors (red, green, and purple) and the packages that convey these various hues.

What determines whether information or emotion is emphasized in a brand's package? The major determinant is the nature of the product category and the underlying consumer behavior involved. Recognizing the distinction drawn in Chapter 4 between the consumer processing model (CPM) and the hedonic, experiential model (HEM), it should be expected that greater informational influence in packaging would go along with CPM-oriented consumer behavior, whereas more emotional influence would be associated with HEM-oriented behavior.

In other words, if consumers make brand-selection decisions based on objectives such as obtaining the best buy or making a prudent choice (CPM-type objectives), then packaging must provide sufficient concrete information to facilitate the consumer's selection. When, however, product and brand selections are made in the pursuit of amusement, fantasies, or sensory stimulation (HEM-type objectives), packaging must contain the requisite emotional content to activate purchase behavior.

This discussion should not be taken as suggesting that all packaging emphasizes information or emotion. Although the packaging of brands in some categories does emphasize one or the other, there are many product categories where it is necessary for packaging to blend informational and emotional content so as to simultaneously appeal to consumers' rational and symbolic needs. Cereal is a case in point. Consumers require nutritional information to intelligently select from among the dozens of available brands, and research indicates that consumer choice in the cereal category is indeed influenced by nutritional components such as protein, fat, fiber, sodium, sugar, and vitamins and minerals.[48] Cereal choice also is driven by emotional factors—wholesomeness, nostalgia, excitement, and so on. General Mills, for example, has used pictures of fictitious Betty Crocker on its boxes for over 50 years. This virtual icon on the supermarket shelves symbolizes family values and wholesomeness. Over the years, General Mills has periodically changed the photo of Betty Crocker to keep in step with the times. Several years ago General Mills introduced the most recent Betty Crocker—a digitally

Figure 7.8   The Changing Faces of Betty Crocker

Used with permission of General Mills, Inc.

morphed amalgam of the photos of 75 women in celebration of General Mills's 75th birthday (see Figure 7.8).

An executive with Apple Designsource, a branding and package design firm, explained the emotional appeal that his firm tried to create in packaging for Wow! potato chips (see Figure 7.9). First, the Wow! package was designed to appeal primarily to female, health-oriented shoppers and at the same time be attractive to male, heavy users. Second, to overcome potential skepticism regarding Wow!'s taste, a taste claim was integrated into the Wow! brandmark ("All the taste, fat free"). Third, a rich packaging material (mylar foil) and colorful graphics were chosen to convey a premium product-usage experience.[49] This same design firm also created packages for Tostitos corn chip and salsa items. Figure 7.10 on page 198 is an advertisement from Apple Designsource that was directed at potential clients (not consumers). This ad highlights the various packaging features that were designed to create a desired image for the Tostitos brand.

W = Workability.   The final component of the VIEW model, *workability*, refers to how a package functions rather than how it communicates. Several workability issues are prominent: (1) Does the package protect the product contents? (2) Does it facilitate easy storage on the part of both retailers and consumers? (3) Does it simplify the consumer's task in accessing and using the product? (4) Does it protect retailers against unintentional breakage from consumer handling and from pilferage? (5) Is the package environmentally friendly?

Numerous packaging innovations in recent years have enhanced workability. These include pourable-spout containers for motor oil and sugar, easy-pour containers (such as for Heinz ketchup as previously mentioned), microwaveable containers for many food items, aseptic cartons, zip-lock packaging, less-mess toothpaste containers, single-serving bags and boxes, and plastic beer bottles. Cereal companies introduced one-ounce bags of presweetened cereal products for kids and adults who are on the go and would not otherwise eat cereal during the school or work week. Companies also have developed "smart packages" that include magnetic strips, bar codes, and electronic chips that can communicate with appliances, computers, and consumers. For example, packages of microwaveable foods eventually will be programmed to "tell" microwaves how long the food item should be cooked.[50] Upjohn, maker of the hair-loss product Rogaine, developed packaging to prevent consumer pilferage of the $30 bottles of Rogaine. The new package contains electronic sensors that require deactivation at the store register.[51] Procter & Gamble is testing a smart-package program that is designed to send information about a product sale to a computer database as soon as a customer removes a P&G brand from the shelf. Small computer chips attached to the

Emotional Appeals in the Packaging of Wow!

Figure 7.9

© Courtesy of Frito Lay

package send a signal to the store shelf, which contains printed circuit boards. The objective is, of course, to provide the company with immediate sales data that will facilitate its supply chain management.[52]

A host of environmentally safe packaging innovations have served to increase what might be called societal workability. Many of the changes have involved moves from plastic to recyclable paper packages; for example, many fast-food chains eliminated the use of foam packaging, and other firms have transformed their packages from plastic to cardboard containers. Another significant environmental initiative has been the increase in spray containers as substitutes for ozone-harming aerosol cans.

Workability is, of course, a relative matter. The objective is to design a package that is as workable as possible yet is economical for the retailer and consumer. For example, consumers prefer food packages that completely prevent food from getting stale or spoiling, but the manufacturer's ability to provide this degree of workability is limited by cost. At the other extreme, some marketers skimp in package design and use inexpensive packages that are unsuitable because they are difficult to use and frustrate consumers.

In conclusion, most packages do not perform well on all the VIEW criteria, but packages need not always be exemplary on all four VIEW components because the relative importance of each criterion varies from one product category to another. Emotional appeal dominates for some products (e.g., perfume), information is most important for others (e.g., staple food items), while visibility and workability are generally important for all products. In the final analysis, the

Figure 7.10   Rationale for Tostitos' Packaging Graphics

relative importance of packaging requirements depends, as always, on the particular market and the competitive situation.

Designing a Package

Designing a package is not as simple as what it may seem merely by walking through a supermarket and gazing at the thousands of packages located on the shelves. Because package design is so critical to a brand's success, a systematic approach is recommended. Figure 7.11 provides a five-step package design process. The subsequent discussion describes each of these stages.[53]

Step 1: Specify Brand-Positioning Objectives.   This initial stage requires the brand management team to specify how the brand is to be positioned in the consumer's mind and against competitive brands. What identity or image is desired for the brand? For example, it would appear that Tostitos' brand management team selected a dual positioning strategy for that brand—namely, that it is both an authentic nacho chip and a fun brand (see Figure 7.10).

Step 2: Conduct a Product Category Analysis.   Having established what the brand represents (step 1) and thus what the packaging must convey, it is essential to study the product category and related categories to determine relevant trends or anticipated events that would influence the packaging decision. The point, in other words, is that to be forewarned is to be forearmed.

The Package Design Process   **Figure 7.11**

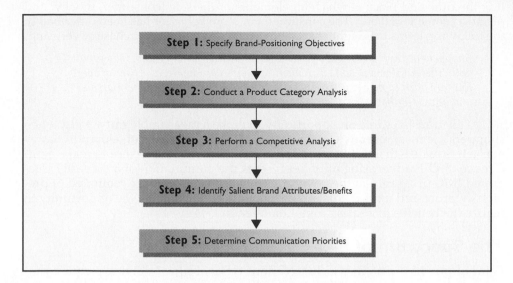

Step I: Specify Brand-Positioning Objectives

Step 2: Conduct a Product Category Analysis

Step 3: Perform a Competitive Analysis

Step 4: Identify Salient Brand Attributes/Benefits

Step 5: Determine Communication Priorities

Step 3: Perform a Competitive Analysis.   Armed with knowledge about competitors' use of packaging colors, shapes, graphical features, and materials, the package designer is thus prepared to create a package that conveys the desired image (step 1) yet is sufficiently unique and differentiating (step 2) to capture consumer attention.

Step 4: Identify Salient Brand Attributes or Benefits.   As noted earlier, research reveals that shoppers spend an incredibly short amount of time—on the order of 10 to 12 seconds—viewing brands before moving on or selecting an item and placing it in the shopping cart.[54] It is imperative, therefore, that the package not be too cluttered with information and that it feature benefits that are most important to consumers. A general rule for identifying packaging benefits is "the fewer, the better."[55]

Step 5: Determine Communication Priorities.   Having identified the most salient brand benefits (step 4), the package designer at this phase of the process must establish verbal and visual priorities for the package. Although perhaps three benefits may have been identified in step 4 as essentially equal in importance, the designer must prioritize which of the three is to capture the greatest visual or verbal attention on the package. This is a very tough decision because it is tempting to devote equal attention to all important brand benefits. It is critical that the package designer acknowledge that the package "advertisement" at the point of purchase occurs in an incredibly cluttered environment for a very short duration. Acknowledging this fact makes it much easier to devote package space to the most important brand benefit.

POINT-OF-PURCHASE ADVERTISING

Brand names and packages, the topics of prior sections in this chapter, confront head on at the point of purchase the ultimate arbiter of their effectiveness, the consumer. The point of purchase, or store environment, provides brand marketers with a final opportunity to affect consumer behavior. Brand managers recognize the value of point-of-purchase (P-O-P) advertising; indeed, Point of Purchase Advertising International (POPAI), the trade association for this form of advertising, estimates that in 2000 marketers in the United States spent $17 billion on P-O-P advertising.[56]

The point of purchase is an ideal time to communicate with consumers because this is the time at which many product and brand choice decisions are made. It is the time and place at which all elements of the sale (consumer, money, and product) come together.[57] The consumer's in-store behavior has been described in the following terms that highlight the importance of point-of-purchase advertising:

> *Shoppers are explorers. They're on safari, hunting for bargains, new products and different items to add excitement to their everyday lives. Three of every four are open to new experiences as they browse the aisles of supermarkets and search for bargains at drugstores and mass merchandisers.*[58]

This translates into an opportunity to make a measurable impact just when shoppers are most receptive to new product ideas and alternative brands. Savvy marketers realize that the store environment is the last best chance to make a difference. P-O-P advertising often represents the culmination of a carefully integrated IMC program—at the point of purchase, consumers are reminded of previously processed mass media advertisements and now have the opportunity to realize the benefits of a sales promotion offer.

The Spectrum of P-O-P Materials

Point-of-purchase materials include various types of signs, mobiles, plaques, banners, shelf ads, mechanical mannequins, lights, mirrors, plastic reproductions of products, checkout units, full-line merchandisers, various types of product displays, wall posters, floor advertisements, in-store radio advertisements, electronic billboard advertising, and other items.[59]

Industry officials classify P-O-P materials into four categories:

- *Permanent displays*: **Permanent displays** are intended for use for six months or more. (Note that the six-month dividing line is an arbitrary convention established by POPAI.) An illustration of one award-winning permanent display is presented in Figure 7.12.[60]

Figure 7.12   **Permanent Display for Brachs Candy**

Semipermanent Display for ChapStick

Figure 7.13

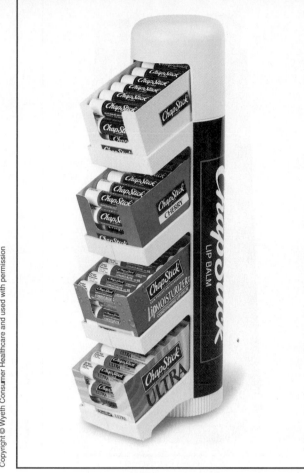

- *Semipermanent displays*: **Semipermanent P-O-P displays** have an intended lifespan of less than six but more than two months. Illustrations of two award-winning semipermanent displays are presented in Figures 7.13 and 7.14.
- *Temporary displays:* **Temporary P-O-P displays** are designed for fewer than two months' usage. Illustrations of two award-winning temporary displays are presented in Figures 7.15 on page 203 and 7.16 on page 204.
- *In-store media:* **In-store media** include advertising and promotion materials, such as in-store radio advertising, shopping cart advertisements, shelf advertisements (called shelf talkers), floor graphics (advertisements placed on store floors), coupon dispensers, and other in-store materials. A third-party company (i.e., a company other than the brand manufacturer or retailer) executes these in-store media. For example, ActMedia, a company well known in the P-O-P industry, provides a variety of in-store services, including (1) POP Radio,—in-store radio programs that carry commercials in thousands of stores nationwide; (2) ActMedia Carts—shopping carts with signs that are available nationwide; and (3) ShelfTalk—shelf extensions that promote brands in stores nationwide. Brand marketers pay ActMedia advertising rates to secure in-store radio time or shopping cart and shelf talker space on a nationwide basis or in specific markets. Another example of shelf talker advertising is the point-of-purchases services

Figure 7.14

© Courtesy of Mars Incorporated

program (POPS) offered by Insignia Systems. (See Figure 7.17 on page 205, which is an advertisement for POPS directed at brand managers). Unlike conventional shelf talkers, which simply identify the advertised brand, a POPS ad presents the brand's image or logo, its major attributes or benefits, the retailer's logo, and the retailer's price. In other words, POPS ads provide consumers with necessary information for making a purchase decision.

What Does P-O-P Accomplish?

Companies are increasingly investing in point-of-purchase advertising materials. As mentioned earlier, annual P-O-P advertising expenditures in the United States exceed $17 billion. This investment in point-of-purchase materials is justified inasmuch as in-store materials provide useful services for all participants in the marketing process: manufacturers, retailers, and consumers.

Accomplishments for Manufacturers.   For *manufacturers*, P-O-P keeps the company's name and the brand name before the consumer and reinforces a brand image that has been previously established through advertising. P-O-P also calls attention to sales promotions and helps stimulate impulse purchasing. Consider, for example, a point-of-purchase effort undertaken by the American Dairy Association (ADA). The ADA, a trade association for producers of cheese and other dairy products, hired the A. C. Nielsen research firm to investigate

Temporary Display for Gillette   **Figure 7.15**

© Courtesy of The Gillette Company

whether stores that use point-of-purchase materials to promote cheese enjoy higher sales levels than do nonparticipants. A football-related promotion was tested ("Kick Off the Season with Cheese"). A. C. Nielsen employees monitored more than 700 grocery stores over a three-week period in 13 major markets in the United States. The ADA's in-store "Kick Off" promotion used a football motif including small banners, varsity letters, case flags, and helmet mobiles—all drawing shopper attention to cheese. Over half the 700 monitored stores used these point-of-purchase materials, while the remaining stores used no in-store advertising. Some of the stores that chose to use ADA's advertising materials also created their own displays to further attract consumer attention.

Test results convincingly established the effectiveness of P-O-P materials in this particular application. In the stores that did not participate in the "Kick Off" event, cheese sales averaged $4,184. Stores that used the ADA in-store advertising package (banners, mobiles, etc.) experienced average sales of $5,392— a 29 percent increase over the nonadvertising stores. Stores that supplemented the ADA's package with their own displays enjoyed 38 percent greater sales than the nonparticipating stores, or average sales of $5,790 per store. These results, according to an ADA marketing executive, prove "beyond a shadow of a doubt" that point-of-purchase materials are an effective way to increase sales volume.[61]

Service to Retailers.   P-O-P serves *retailers* by attracting the consumer's attention, increasing his or her interest in shopping, and extending the amount

Figure 7.16

Temporary Display for Kellogg's Special K Plus

of time spent in the store—all of which lead to increased revenue and profits for retailers. Furthermore, P-O-P helps retailers use available space to the best advantage by displaying various products in the same unit, as is done with the Brachs candy display illustrated in Figure 7.12. P-O-P displays also enable retailers to better organize shelf and floor space and to improve inventory control, volume, stock turnover, and profitability.

Value to Consumers. *Consumers* are served by point-of-purchase units that deliver useful information and simplify the shopping process. Permanent, semi-permanent, and temporary P-O-P units provide this value to consumers by setting particular brands apart from similar items and simplifying the selection process.

In addition to benefiting all participants in the marketing process, point-of-purchase plays another important role: It serves as the capstone for an IMC program. P-O-P by itself may have limited impact, but when used in conjunction with advertisements and promotions, P-O-P can create a synergistic effect. Indeed, research by Information Resources, Inc.—the well-known provider of optical scanning data—has shown that when P-O-P reinforces a brand's advertising message, the increase in sales volume averages more than 100 percent compared to advertising alone.[62]

Functions Performed by P-O-P Materials

The functions performed by P-O-P materials are, in general, fourfold: informing, reminding, encouraging, and merchandising.

The POPS Shelf-Talker Advertising from Insignia Systems   **Figure 7.17**

Informing.   *Informing* consumers is P-O-P's most basic communications function. Signs, posters, displays, and other P-O-P materials alert consumers to specific items and provide potentially useful information.

Motion displays are especially effective for this purpose. Motion displays, though typically more expensive than static displays, represent a sound business investment because they attract significantly higher levels of shopper attention. Evidence from three studies shows that motion displays are often worth the extra expense.[63]

Researchers tested the relative effectiveness of motion and static displays for Olympia beer, a once successful but now bygone brand, by placing the two types of displays in a test sample of Californian liquor stores and supermarkets. Each of the sampled stores was stocked with either static or motion displays. Another sample of stores, serving as the control group, received no displays. More than 62,000 purchases of Olympia beer were recorded during the four-week test period. Static displays in liquor stores increased Olympia sales by 56 percent over stores with no displays (the control group). In supermarkets, static displays improved Olympia sales by a considerably smaller, though nonetheless substantial, amount (18 percent). More dramatic, however, was the finding that motion displays increased Olympia sales by 107 percent in liquor stores and by 49 percent in supermarkets.

A second test of the effectiveness of motion displays used S. B. Thomas' English muffins as the focal product. Two groups of 40 stores each were matched by store volume and customer demographics. One group was equipped with an S. B. Thomas' English muffin post sign that moved from side to side. The other 40 stores used regular floor displays with no motion. Records of product movement revealed that sales in the stores stocked with motion displays were more than 100 percent greater than in stores with static displays.

Researchers conducted a study of motion displays for Eveready batteries in Atlanta and San Diego. Studied in each city were six drugstores, six supermarkets, and six mass merchandise stores. The stores were divided into two groups, like the English muffin study. For mass merchandisers, the static displays increased sales during the test period by 2.7 percent over the base period, but surprisingly, sales in the drug and food outlets using the static displays were slightly less (each 1.6 percent lower) than those not using the static displays. By comparison, the motion displays uniformly increased sales by 3.7 percent, 9.1 percent, and 15.7 percent in the drugstore outlets, supermarkets, and mass merchandisers, respectively.

All three sets of results demonstrate the effectiveness of motion displays. The consumer information-processing rationale (see Chapter 4) is straightforward: Motion displays attract attention. Attention, once attracted, is directed toward salient product features, including recognition of the displayed brand's name. Brand name information activates consumers' memories pertaining to brand attributes previously processed from media advertising. Information on brand attributes, when recalled, supplies a reason for the consumer to purchase the displayed brand. It also is possible that the mere fact of seeing a display suggests the prospect that the displayed brand is on sale, whether in fact it is.[64]

Hence, a moving display performs the critical in-store function of bringing a brand's name to active memory. The probability of purchasing the brand increases, perhaps substantially (as in the case of S. B. Thomas' English muffins), if the consumer is favorably disposed toward the brand. The Eveready display was less effective apparently because the selling burden was placed almost exclusively on the display. Without prior stimulation of demand through advertising, the static display was ineffective, and the motion display was not as effective as it might have been.

Reminding. A second point-of-purchase function is *reminding* consumers of brands they have previously learned about via broadcast, print, or other advertising media. This reminder role serves to complement the job already performed by advertising before the consumer enters a store.

To fully appreciate the reminder role served by point-of-purchase materials, it is important at this point to address a key principle from cognitive psychology: the **encoding specificity principle.** In simple terms, this principle states that information recall is enhanced when the context in which people attempt to *retrieve* information is the same or similar to the context in which they originally encoded the information.[65] (Encoding is the placing of informational items into memory.)

A nonmarketing illustration—one that may bring back some unpleasant memories—will serve to clarify the exact meaning and significance of the encoding specificity principle. Remember back to a time when you were studying for a crucial exam that required problem-solving skills. You may have been up late at night trying to solve a particularly difficult problem, perhaps in accounting, calculus, or statistics. Eventually, the solution came to you, and you felt well prepared for the next day's exam. Sure enough, the exam had a problem very similar to the one you worked on the night before. However, to your dismay, your mind went blank, and you were unable to solve the problem. But after the exam, back in your room, the solution hit you like the proverbial ton of bricks.

Encoding specificity is the "culprit." Specifically, the context (your room) in which you originally encoded information and formulated a solution to the problem was different from the context (your classroom) in which you subsequently were asked to solve a similar problem. Hence, contextual retrieval cues were unavailable in the classroom to readily facilitate your recall of how you originally solved the problem.

Returning to the marketplace, consider the situation in which consumers encode television commercial information about a brand and its unique features and benefits. The advertiser's expectation is that consumers will be able to retrieve this information at the point of purchase and use it to select the advertiser's brand over competitive offerings. It doesn't always work like this, however. Our memories are fallible, especially since we are exposed to an incredible amount of advertising information. Hence, although we may have encoded advertising information at one time, we may not be able to retrieve it subsequently without a reminder cue at the point of purchase.

Consider, for example, the ongoing pink-bunny-pounding-a-drum advertising campaign. Most everyone is aware of this campaign, but many consumers have difficulty remembering the advertised brand. (Think for a moment; which brand is it?) When facing brands of Duracell, Eveready, and Energizer on the shelf, the consumer may not connect the pink-bunny advertising with any specific brand. Here is where point-of-purchase materials can perform a critically important role. Energizer (the pink-bunny brand) can facilitate encoding specificity by using shelf signs or packaging graphics that present the bunny and the Energizer name together (just as they appeared together in advertisements). Accordingly, by providing consumers with encoding-specific retrieval cues, chances are that consumers will recall from earlier advertisements that Energizer is the battery brand that powers the unceasing drum-pounding bunny.

The crucial point is that media advertising and P-O-P communications must be tightly integrated so that in-store reminder cues can capitalize on the background work accomplished by media advertising. Signs, displays, and in-store media provide the culmination for an IMC campaign and increase the odds that consumers will select a particular brand over alternatives.

Encouraging.   *Encouraging* consumers to buy a specific item or brand is P-O-P's third function. Effective P-O-P materials influence product and brand choices at the point of purchase and encourage impulse buying.

Merchandising.   The *merchandising* function is served when point-of-purchase displays enable retailers to use floor space effectively and boost retail sales by assisting consumers in making product and brand selections.

The merchandising role is well illustrated with the information-center displays developed by Clairol to merchandise women's hair-coloring products and to answer consumers' questions concerning these products. Product information appeared on large, colorful header signs above Clairol products that were placed on the display's shelves. The information center made product selection easy: Color-coded labels identified product subcategories, and shelf dividers separated the various products. When the information center displays were first introduced to retail accounts, Clairol's sales increased an average of 32 percent, and shelf space devoted to Clairol products averaged 15 percent more linear feet.[66]

Interactive Displays

Interactive displays are computerized units with liquid crystal displays that allow consumers to answer questions pertaining to their product category needs and help them make well-informed product choices. L'eggs Products, for example, used an interactive unit—called the Pantyhose Advisor—that was available in 2,000 food and drug chains and mass merchandisers. The 14-inch units "asked" shoppers questions about their height, weight, the occasion for which they were buying pantyhose, and the style of shoes they would be wearing. The unit then recommended two styles of pantyhose and the appropriate size from the L'eggs and Just My Size brands of pantyhose. This unit reduced the confusion women face when choosing among a wide variety of styles and shades.

Kal Kan, makers of Expert pet food, introduced the Select-A-Diet interactive unit to assist pet owners in choosing the right nutritional formula of Expert pet food. The unit, attached to supermarket shelves, presented shoppers with a series of questions regarding their pet's age, weight, and activity level. The unit then recommended the best formula of food for the pet.

An interactive unit from Kelly-Springfield presented automobile tire shoppers with questions on car type, driving habits, and tire style performance, and consumers responded via a touch keypad. The unit recommended three tire choices from which the consumer could choose.

Titleist has an interactive display for its various golf balls. The display queries golfers about such matters as whether they are more interested in distance or spin, prefer a hard- or soft-feeling ball, and how far they normally drive the ball. Based on how the consumer answers the queries, the unit recommends a specific Titleist ball that best matches the golfer's interests and needs.

An especially clever interactive display was developed to assist shoppers in choosing the "right" bottle of wine. Consumers used a touch-screen monitor to select wines based on quality, price, type, and food pairing. The display provided reviews and ratings for the wines contained in a particular retailer's inventory. Information in the computerized display was periodically updated via modem with inventory and price changes.

A final illustration is a display for Pantene, a Procter & Gamble line of hair-care products. Pantene had experienced weak distribution and poor in-store visibility. Sales were being lost due to these problems and because retail sales personnel were not always well informed about Pantene's advantages. Procter & Gamble and a display design firm developed an impressive interactive display for Pantene. The display included a video monitor that continuously showed animated graphics to attract customer traffic. After being instructed to touch the screen, customers were guided through a series of multiple-choice questions to find out what products had been designed for their particular hair condition. A printout of Pantene's hair-care prescription was automatically provided. The customer then selected the recommended product directly from the display below the monitor. Tests conducted in two markets revealed sales increases in excess of 400 percent.[67]

A Vital Result of P-O-P:
Increased In-Store Decision Making

Studies of consumer shopping behavior have shown that a high proportion of all purchases are unplanned, especially in supermarkets, drugstores, and mass merchandise outlets (such as Wal-Mart and Target) where packaged goods are carried. *Unplanned purchasing* means that many product and brand choice decisions are made while the consumer is in the store rather than beforehand. Point-of-purchase materials play a role—perhaps the major role—in influencing unplanned purchasing and in increasing sales. The following section discusses research on unplanned purchasing, and a subsequent section then presents impressive evidence on the role of P-O-P displays in increasing sales volume.

The POPAI Consumer Buying Habits Study.   This study, conducted by Point-of-Purchase Advertising International (POPAI), is the most recent of a series of studies conducted by this trade association.[68] The study confirms that in-store media, signage, and displays heavily influence consumers' purchase decisions. In conducting the study, researchers obtained purchase data and other information from 4,200 consumers who were shopping in the stores of 22 leading supermarket chains and four mass merchandisers—Bradlees, Kmart, Target, and Wal-Mart—located in 14 major markets throughout the United States.

The Consumer Buying Habits Study was conducted in the following manner.[69] Shoppers aged 16 or older were screened by researchers to determine that they were on a "major shopping trip." Researchers then interviewed qualified shoppers both before they began their shopping (entry interviews) and after they had completed their shopping trips (exit interviews). During the preshopping entry interviews, researchers used an *unaided* questioning format to ask shoppers about their planned purchases on that particular occasion and probed for brand buying intentions. Then, during postshopping exit interviews, researchers gathered supermarket shoppers' register tapes or physically inventoried shoppers' carts at the mass merchandise stores. Interviews were conducted during all times of the day and every day of the week.

By comparing shoppers' planned purchases obtained during entry interviews with actual purchases during exit interviews, it was possible to classify every brand purchase into one of four types of purchase behaviors:

Table 7.1

Results from the POPAI Consumer Buying Habits Study

Type of Purchase	Supermarket	Mass Merchandising Store
1. Specifically planned	30%	26%
2. Generally planned	6	18
3. Substitute	4	3
4. Unplanned	60	53
In-store decision rate (2 + 3 + 4)	70%	74%

The 1995 POPAI Consumer Buying Habits Study, p. 18 (Washington, D.C.: Point-Of-Purchase Advertising International). Reprinted by permission.

1. *Specifically planned:* This category represents purchases of a brand that the consumer had indicated an intention to buy. For example, the purchase of Diet Pepsi would be considered a specifically planned purchase if during the entry interview a consumer mentioned her or his intention to purchase that brand and in fact bought Diet Pepsi. According to the Consumer Buying Habits Study (see Table 7.1), 30 percent of supermarket purchases and 26 percent of mass merchandise purchases were specifically planned.

2. *Generally planned:* This classification applies to purchases for which the shopper indicated an intent to buy a particular product (say, a soft drink) but had no specific brand in mind. The purchase of Diet Pepsi in this case would be classified as a generally planned purchase rather than a specifically planned purchase. Generally planned purchases constituted 6 percent of those in supermarkets and 18 percent in mass merchandise stores (see Table 7.1).

3. *Substitute purchases:* Purchases where the shopper does not buy the product or brand he or she indicated in the entry interview constitute substitute purchases. For example, if a consumer said she or he intended to buy Diet Pepsi but actually purchased Diet Coke, that behavior would be classified as a substitute purchase. These represented just 4 percent of supermarket purchases and 3 percent of mass merchandise purchases.

4. *Unplanned purchases:* Under this heading are purchases for which the consumer had no prior purchase intent. If, for example, a shopper buys Diet Pepsi without having informed the interviewer of this intent, the behavior would be recorded as an unplanned purchase. Sixty percent of the purchases in supermarkets and 53 percent of those in mass merchandise stores were classified as unplanned.

Notice in Table 7.1 that the summation of generally planned, substitute, and unplanned purchases constitutes the *in-store decision rate*. In other words, the three categories representing purchases that are not specifically planned all represent decisions influenced by in-store factors. The in-store decision rates are 70 and 74 percent for supermarkets and mass merchandise stores, respectively. These percentages indicate that approximately 7 out of 10 purchase decisions are influenced by in-store factors. It is apparent that P-O-P materials represent a very important determinant of consumers' product and brand choice behaviors.

A technical point needs to be addressed at this time. It is important to recognize that not all purchases recorded as unplanned by interviewers are truly unplanned. Rather, some purchases are recorded as unplanned simply because shoppers are unable or unwilling during the entry interview to inform interviewers of their exact purchase plans. This is not to imply that the POPAI research is seriously flawed but rather that the measurement of unplanned purchases probably is somewhat overstated due to the unavoidable bias just described. Other categories may be biased also. For example, by the same logic, the percentage of specifically planned purchases is probably somewhat

Table 7.2

Product Categories with the Five Highest and Five Lowest In-Store Decision Rates: Supermarket Purchases

Category	In-Store Decision Rate
Highest in-store decision rate	
First aid	93%
Toys, sporting goods, crafts	93
Houseware/hardware	90
Stationery	90
Candy/gum	89
Lowest in-store decision rate	
Produce	33
Meat, seafood	47
Eggs	53
Coffee	58
Baby food/formula	58

"Product Categories with the Five Highest and Five Lowest In-Store Decision Rates: Supermarket Purchases," p. 19. The 1995 POPAI Consumer Buying Habits Study (Washington, D.C.: Point-Of-Purchase Advertising International). Reprinted by permission.

understated. In any event, POPAI's findings are important even if they are not precisely correct.

The summary statistics in Table 7.1 represent types of purchases aggregated over literally hundreds of product categories. It should be apparent that in-store decision rates vary greatly across product categories. To emphasize this point, Tables 7.2 and 7.3 present categories with the highest and lowest in-store decision rates for supermarkets (Table 7.2) and mass merchandise stores (Table 7.3).

The data presented in Tables 7.2 and 7.3 make it clear that in-store decision rates vary substantially. Supermarket products that are virtual staples (e.g., produce) and mass merchandise products that are essential and regularly purchased items (e.g., disposable diapers) have the lowest in-store purchase rates because most consumers know they are going to purchase these items when they go to the store. On the other hand, nonnecessities and items that generally do not occupy top-of-the-mind thoughts (e.g., first-aid supplies and garbage bags) are especially susceptible to the influence of in-store stimuli. It is clear that for these types of products, brand marketers must have a distinct presence at the point of purchase if they hope to sway purchase decisions toward their brands.

Factors Influencing In-Store Decision Making. Two academic researchers were provided access to data from POPAI's Consumer Buying Habits Study.[70] The researchers' objective was to determine what effect a variety of shopping-trip factors (e.g., size of shopping party, use of a shopping list, number of aisles shopped) and consumer characteristics (e.g., deal proneness, compulsiveness, age, gender, income) have on unplanned purchasing. Among other findings, they determined that the rate of unplanned purchasing is elevated when consumers are on a major (versus fill-in) shopping trip, when they shop more of a store's aisles, when the household size is large, and when they are deal prone. Perhaps the major practical implication from this research is that retailers benefit from having consumers shop longer and traverse more of the store while shopping, thus increasing the odds of purchasing unintended items. One way of accomplishing this is by locating frequently purchased items (e.g., items such as bread and milk) in locations that require consumers to pass as many other items as possible.[71]

The Brand Lift Index. POPAI and its research collaborator (the Meyers Research Center) have developed a measure—called the **brand lift index**—to gauge the average increase of in-store purchase decisions when P-O-P is present versus

Product Categories with the Five Highest and Five Lowest In-Store Decision Rates: Mass Merchandise Purchases

Table 7.3

Category	In-Store Decision Rate
Highest in-store decision rate	
Apparel accessories	92%
Foils, food wraps	91
Hardware, electric, plumbing	90
Infant/toddler wear	90
Garbage bags	88
Lowest in-store decision rate	
Disposable diapers	35
Baby food	35
Eyedrops and lens care	52
Prerecorded music, videos	54
Coffee, tea, cocoa	55

"Product Categories with the Five Highest and Five Lowest In-Store Decision Rates: Mass Merchandise Purchases," p. 20. The 1995 POPAI Consumer Buying Habits Study (Washington, D.C.: Point-Of-Purchase Advertising International). Reprinted by permission.

when it is not.[72] (The term *lift* is used in reference to increasing, or lifting, sales in the presence of P-O-P materials.) This index simply indicates how in-store P-O-P materials affect the likelihood that customers will buy a product that they had not specifically planned to buy. Table 7.4 shows the products sold in supermarkets and mass merchandise stores that enjoy the highest brand lift indexes from displays. For example, the index of 47.67 for film and photofinishing products in mass merchandise stores indicates that shoppers are nearly 48 times more likely to make in-store purchase decisions for these products when advertised with displays than if there were no displays. (Note very carefully that the index of 47.67 does *not* mean that sales of film and other photofinishing items are over 47 times greater when a display is used. Rather, this index merely reveals that consumers are nearly 48 times more likely to make in-store decisions in the presence versus absence of displays.) And supermarket shoppers are 6.47 times more likely to make in-store decisions to purchase butter or margarine when these items are displayed compared to when they are not displayed. Needless to say, displays can have incredible influence on consumer behavior.

The Impact of Displays on Brand Sales

Practitioners are vitally interested in knowing whether the cost of special P-O-P displays is justified. It has only been in recent years that good research evidence has been available to provide answers to this question. Two particularly important studies have examined the impact of displays on a brand's temporary sales.

The POPAI/Kmart/P&G Study.   This notable study was conducted by a consortium of a trade association (POPAI), a mass merchandiser (Kmart), and a consumer-goods manufacturer (Procter & Gamble).[73] The study investigated the impact that displays have on sales of P&G brands in six product categories: paper towels, shampoo, toothpaste, deodorant, coffee, and fabric softener. The test lasted for a period of four weeks, and P&G's brands were sold at their regular prices throughout this period. Seventy-five Kmart stores in the United States were matched in terms of brand sales, store volume, and shopper demographics and then assigned to three panels of 25 stores each:[74]

> *Control panel.* The 25 stores in this group contained the advertised brands in their normal shelf position with no display or other advertising present.

Table 7.4	Supermarket and Mass Merchandise Product Categories with Highest Average Brand Lifts from Displays

	Brand Lift Index
Supermarket categories	
Butter/margarine	6.47
Cookies	6.21
Soft drinks	5.37
Beer/ale	4.67
Mixers	4.03
Sour cream/cream cheese	3.79
Cereal	3.73
Hand and body soaps	3.62
Packaged cheese	3.57
Canned fish	3.55
Salty snacks	3.50
Mass merchandise categories	
Film/photofinishing	47.67
Socks/underwear/pantyhose	29.43
Cookies/crackers	18.14
Small appliances	8.87
Foils, food wraps, and bags	7.53
Adult apparel	7.45
Pet supplies	5.55
Packaged bread	5.01

"Supermarket and the Mass Merchandise Product Categories with Highest Average Brand Lifts from Displays," p. 24. The 1995 POPAI Consumer Buying Habits Study (Washington, D.C.: Point-Of-Purchase Advertising International). Reprinted by permission.

Test panel 1. These 25 stores carried the advertised brands on display.
Test panel 2. These stores contained the advertised brands either on a different display or on the same display as in test panel 1 but at a different location in the store.

Specific differences in displays/locations between test panels 1 and 2 are shown in Table 7.5. For example, paper towels were displayed in a mass waterfall display at two different (but undisclosed) store locations; shampoo was displayed in either a special shelf unit display or a floorstand display; and coffee was displayed either on a quarter pallet outside the coffee aisle or a full pallet at the end of the coffee aisle—called an endcap display.

The last column in Table 7.5 compares the percentage sales increase in each set of test stores (with displays) against the control stores where P&G brands were sold in their regular (nondisplay) shelf locations. It is readily apparent that positive sales increases materialized for all products and both test conditions; in some instances the increases were nothing short of huge. P&G's brands of shampoo and deodorant experienced modest increases during the four-week test of only about 18 percent (test 1), whereas paper towels and coffee experienced triple-digit increases in both display conditions—sales increases of 773.5 percent for paper towels (test 2) and 567.4 percent for coffee (test 2).

The POPAI/Warner-Lambert Benylin Study.   Another important study extends the POPAI/Kmart/P&G findings obtained from mass merchandise stores in the United States to drugstores in Canada.[75] POPAI and Warner-Lambert Canada jointly investigated the effectiveness of P-O-P displays on sales

Display Information for POPAI/Kmart/P&G Study

Table 7.5

Product Category	Test Panels and Displays	Test Panel Sales versus Control Panel Sales (Percentage Increase)
Paper towels	Test 1: Mass waterfall (MW) display Test 2: MW display in a different location	447.1% 773.5
Shampoo	Test 1: Shelf unit Test 2: Floorstand	18.2 56.8
Toothpaste	Test 1: Floorstand in toothpaste aisle Test 2: ¼ pallet outside toothpaste aisle	73.1 119.2
Deodorant	Test 1: Powerwing Test 2: Powerwing in a different store location	17.9 38.5
Coffee	Test 1: ¼ pallet outside coffee aisle Test 2: Full pallet on endcap of coffee aisle	500.0 567.4
Fabric softener	Test 1: Full pallet on endcap of laundry aisle Test 2: ¼ pallet outside laundry aisle	66.2 73.8

"Display Information for POPAI/Kmart/P&G Study," from POPAI/Kmart/Procter & Gamble Study of P-O-P Effectiveness in Mass Merchandising Stores, p. 20. The 1995 POPAI Consumer Buying Habits Study (Washington, D.C.: Point-Of-Purchase Advertising International). Reprinted by permission.

of health items in drugstores. Eighty stores from four major drugstore chains participated (Shoppers Drug Mart, Jean Coutu, Cumberland, and Pharmaprix), and testing was conducted in three major cities: Toronto, Montreal, and Vancouver. Two brands were involved in the testing: Benylin cough syrup and Listerine mouthwash. This section discusses the Benylin study, and the following section describes the Listerine study.

For the Benylin test, stores were divided into four groups: One group offered regularly priced Benylin in its normal shelf position; a second group merchandised Benylin in the normal shelf position but at a feature (i.e., discounted) price; a third group of stores displayed Benylin at a feature price on endcap displays; and the final group employed in-aisle floorstand displays of Benylin at a feature price. Sales data were captured during a two-week period in each store to gauge display effectiveness.

The effectiveness of both feature pricing and displays is determined simply by comparing sales volume during the test period in store groups 2 through 4 with sales in group 1 — the baseline group. These comparisons reveal the following:

- Stores in group 2 (Benylin located at its regular shelf position but feature priced) enjoyed 29 percent greater sales volume of Benylin than the stores in group 1 (Benylin at both its regular price and shelf location). This 29 percent increment reflects simply the effect of feature pricing inasmuch as both store groups sold Benylin from its regular shelf location.
- Stores in group 3 (Benylin on an endcap display and feature priced) enjoyed 98 percent greater sales of Benylin than did stores in group 1. This increment reflects the substantial impact that the endcap display and

feature price combination had on the number of units sold. The large percentage increase in comparison to group 2 (i.e., 98 percent versus 29 percent) reflects the incremental impact of the endcap display location over the effect of feature pricing per se.

- Stores in group 4 (Benylin displayed in aisle and feature priced) realized 139 percent greater sales volume than the baseline stores, which indicates that this location, at least for this product category, is more valuable than is the endcap location.

The POPAI/Warner-Lambert Listerine Study.

Stores were divided into four groups for this test: One group offered regularly priced Listerine in its normal shelf position; a second group of stores offered Listerine in the normal shelf position but at a feature price; a third group displayed Listerine at a feature price on endcap displays at the *rear* of the store; and the fourth group displayed Listerine at a feature price on endcap displays at the *front* of the store. Sales data were captured during a two-week period in each store to gauge display effectiveness.

Again, the effectiveness of displays can be determined simply by comparing sales volume of groups 2 through 4 with sales in baseline group 1.

- Stores in group 2 (Listerine located at its regular shelf position but feature priced) enjoyed 11 percent greater sales volume of Listerine than the stores in group 1 (where Listerine was regular priced and located in its regular shelf position).
- Stores in group 3 (Listerine at a rear endcap display and feature priced) experienced 141 percent greater sales of Listerine than the stores in group 1.
- Stores in group 4 (Listerine at a front endcap display and feature priced) enjoyed 162 percent greater sales volume than the baseline stores.

Both sets of results reveal that these two drugstore brands, Benylin and Listerine, benefited greatly when feature priced and merchandised from prized locations. The Listerine study results came as a bit of surprise to industry observers, however, who expected the advantage of the front endcap location to be substantially greater in comparison to the rear endcap location. The premium price that manufacturers pay for front endcap placement (versus rear endcap positioning) may not be fully justified in light of these results. Additional research with other product categories is needed before any definitive answer is possible.

The Use and Nonuse of P-O-P Materials

Although P-O-P materials can be very effective for manufacturers and perform several desirable functions for retailers, the fact remains that perhaps as much as 40 to 50 percent of all P-O-P materials supplied by manufacturers are never used by retailers.[76]

Reasons Why P-O-P Materials Go Unused.

Five major reasons explain why retailers choose not to use P-O-P materials. First, there is no incentive for the retailer to use certain P-O-P materials because these materials are inappropriately designed and do not satisfy the retailer's needs. Second, some displays take up too much space for the amount of sales generated. Third, some materials are too unwieldy, too difficult to set up, too flimsy, or have other construction defects.[77] A fourth reason many signs and displays go unused is because they lack eye appeal. Finally, retailers are concerned that displays and other P-O-P materials simply serve to increase sales of a particular manufacturer's brand during the display period, but that the retailer's sales and profits for the entire product category are not improved. In other words, a retailer has little incentive to erect displays or use signage that merely serves to transfer sales from one brand to another but that does not increase the retailer's overall sales and profits for the product category. (The subsequent discussion of category management in Chapter 17 will emphasize that increased pressures have been imposed by retailers on manufacturers to develop merchandising programs that build category growth and profits rather than merely serving the manufacturer's brand needs.)

Encouraging Retailers to Use P-O-P Materials. Encouraging retailers to use P-O-P materials is a matter of basic marketing. Persuading the retailer to enthusiastically use a display or other P-O-P device means that the manufacturer must view the material from the retailer's perspective. First and foremost, P-O-P materials must satisfy the retailer's needs and the needs of the retailer's customers (the consumers) rather than just those of the manufacturer. This is the essence of marketing, and it applies to encouraging the use of P-O-P materials just as much as promoting the acceptance of the manufacturer's own products. Hence, manufacturers must design P-O-P materials to satisfy the following requirements:

- They are the right size and format.
- They fit the store decor.
- They are user friendly—that is, easy for the retailer to attach, erect, or otherwise use.
- They are sent to stores when they are needed (e.g., at the right selling season).
- They are properly coordinated with other aspects of the MarCom program (i.e., they should tie into a current advertising and/or sales promotion program).
- They are attractive, convenient, and useful for consumers.[78]

SUMMARY

The brand name is the single most important element found on a package. The brand name works with package graphics and other product features to communicate and position the brand's image. The brand name identifies the product and differentiates it from others on the market. A good brand name can evoke feelings of trust, confidence, security, strength, durability, speed, status, and many other desirable associations. A good brand name must satisfy several fundamental requirements: It must describe the product's benefits, be compatible with the product's image, and be memorable and easy to pronounce. A major section in this chapter was devoted to a five-step process for selecting a brand name. Another section discussed the nature and role of brand logos.

The second major section of the chapter focused on packaging. The package is perhaps the most important component of the product as a communications device. It reinforces associations established in advertising, breaks through competitive clutter at the point of purchase, and justifies price and value to the consumer. Package design relies on the use of symbolism to support a brand's image and to convey desired information to consumers. A number of package cues are used for this purpose, including color, design, shape, brand name, physical materials, and product information labeling. These cues must interact harmoniously to evoke within buyers the set of meanings intended by the marketing communicator. Package designs can be evaluated by applying the VIEW model, which contains the elements of visibility, informativeness, emotionality, and workability. A concluding section described a five-step process for package design.

The last major section in the chapter was devoted to point-of-purchase advertising. The point of purchase is an ideal time to communicate with consumers. Accordingly, anything that a consumer is exposed to at the point of purchase can perform an important communications function. A variety of P-O-P materials—signs, displays, and various in-store media—are used to attract consumers' attention to particular products and brands, provide information, affect perceptions, and ultimately influence shopping behavior. P-O-P displays, which are distinguished broadly as either temporary or permanent, perform a variety of useful functions for manufacturers, retailers, and consumers.

Research has documented the high incidence of consumers' in-store purchase decision making and the corresponding importance of P-O-P materials in these purchase decisions. POPAI's Consumer Buying Habits Study classified all consumer purchases into four categories: specifically planned, generally planned, substitutes, and unplanned decisions. The combination of the last three categories represent in-store decisions that are influenced by P-O-P displays and other store cues. In-store decisions represent 70 percent of supermarket purchase decisions and 74 percent of the decisions in mass merchandise stores. Research on the effectiveness of displays — such as the joint undertaking by POPAI, Kmart, and Procter & Gamble — provides evidence that displayed brands sometimes enjoy gigantic, triple-digit increases in sales volume during the display period.

DISCUSSION QUESTIONS

1. Assume you operate a company that creates a brand name by using the morpheme, or the combination of morphemes, that best captures the primary selling feature a client wishes to convey with its new product. Your first client is a company that plans to go into business to compete against Dunkin' Donuts. However, the company's unique advantage is that its donuts are made with a fat substitute and hence are fat free. The client wants a name for its future donut shops to convey that its donuts are fat free but tasty. Create two names you consider appropriate and justify the logic underlying each.

2. Perform the same exercise as in question 1, but this time develop a brand name for a new brand of soy milk, a growing product category mentioned in Chapter 6.

3. Select a product category of personal interest and analyze the brand names for three competitive brands in that category. Analyze each brand name in terms of the fundamental requirements that were described in the text. Order the three brands according to which has the best, next best, and worst brand name. Support your ranking with specific reasons.

4. As reported in an issue of *The Wall Street Journal Interactive Edition* (July 8, 1997), two Atlanta entrepreneurs started a retail personal computer business named StupidPC. They arrived at that name during a give-and-take session in which they exchanged possible names for their proposed store. After a period of labeling each other's ideas as "stupid," one of the men suggested that they might as well call their store StupidPC. The name stuck. What are your thoughts on this name? What are its pros and cons? Be specific.

5. According to an article in *The Wall Street Journal Interactive Edition* (June 1, 1998), a Boston diamond wholesaler developed a special way for cutting diamonds that gives diamonds perfect symmetry and extra sparkle. The wholesaler developed a viewing device (called the proportion scope) that allows consumers to see a diamond with eight perfect hearts and eight arrows when they peer through the scope. The inventor of this specially cut diamond gave his gems the brand name Hearts on Fire. Evaluate this name by applying concepts from the chapter. Propose an alternative name.

6. What are your views regarding the Sundsvall brand name for vodka as described in the *Opening Vignette*?

7. Considering the JetBlue brand-naming process described in the *IMC Focus*, present your thoughts on some of the other names that the company considered—particularly the names that suggested a New York base of operation.

8. Sport utility vehicles (SUVs) have names such as the Ford Explorer, Chevy Blazer, Mercury Mountaineer, Lincoln Navigator, Subaru Outback, Mazda Navajo, Infinity QX-4, Honda Passport, Jeep Wrangler, Dodge Dakota, Olds Bravada, and so on. The Ford Motor Company in 1999 purchased the Volvo Motor Company of Sweden. Assume that Ford executives decide to add an upscale Volvo SUV to their expanded product line. What would you name this new vehicle? What is your rationale for this name?

9. One job of packaging is to drive associations established in advertising into the consumer's mind. Discuss specifically what this means, using several marketplace illustrations to support your explanation.

10. What is sensation transference? Provide two specific examples to support your answer.

11. In your opinion, why do so many marketers use the words *new* and *improved* on their product packages? Justify why you think this usage is effective or ineffective.

12. Can you identify any brands that avail themselves of the "power" of the encoding specificity principle with their packaging? (Next time you go to the supermarket, cruise the aisles to identify examples of packages that use advertising slogans or symbols on their packages.)

13. Select a packaged-goods product category, and apply the VIEW model to three competitive brands within that category. Define all four components

of the model, and explain how each applies to your selected product. Then use the following procedures to weigh each component in the model in terms of your perception of its relative packaging importance in your chosen product category:

a. Distribute 10 points among the four components, with more points signifying more importance and the sum of the allocated points totaling exactly 10. (This weighting procedure involves what marketing researchers refer to as a constant sum scale.)

b. Next, evaluate each brand in terms of your perception of its performance on each packaging component by assigning a score from 1 (does not perform well) to 10 (performs extremely well). Thus, you will assign a total of 12 scores: four for each VIEW component for the three different brands.

c. Combine the scores for each brand by multiplying the brand's performance on each component by the weight of that component (from step a) and then summing the products of these four weighted scores.

The summed score for each of your three chosen brands will reflect your perception of how good that brand's packaging is in terms of the VIEW model — the higher the score, the better the packaging in your opinion. Summarize the scores for the three brands for an overall assessment of each brand's packaging.

14. What functions can point-of-purchase materials accomplish that mass media advertising cannot?

15. Explain why the POPAI Consumer Buying Habits Study probably overestimates the percentage of unplanned purchases and underestimates the percentage of specifically planned and generally planned purchases.

16. Although not presented in the chapter, the POPAI Consumer Buying Habits Study revealed that the percentage of in-store decisions for coffee was 57.9 percent, whereas the comparable percentage for salsa, picante sauce, and dips was 87.1 percent. What accounts for the 30.2 percent difference in in-store decision making for these two products? Go beyond these two product categories and offer a generalization as to what product categories likely have high and low proportions of in-store decision making.

17. The POPAI Consumer Buying Habits Study also revealed that the highest average brand lift index from signage (rather than displays) in mass merchandise stores was dishwashing soaps, with an index of 21.65. Provide an exact interpretation of this index value.

18. The discussion of the S. B. Thomas' English muffin study pointed out that in stores using motion displays, sales increased by more than 100 percent. By comparison, sales of Eveready batteries, when promoted with motion displays, increased anywhere from 3.7 percent to 15.7 percent, depending on the type of store in which the display was placed. Provide an explanation that accounts for the tremendous disparity in sales impact of motion displays for English muffins compared with batteries.

19. Why were motion and static displays considerably more effective at increasing Olympia beer sales in liquor stores than in supermarkets?

ENDNOTES

1. For a thorough discussion of the technical and legal aspects of trademarks, see Dorothy Cohen, "Trademark Strategy Revisited," *Journal of Marketing* 55 (July 1991), 46–59.

2. Mark Landler and Zachary Schiller, "What's in a Name: Less and Less," *Business Week*, July 8, 1991, 66–67.

3. Chiranjeev Kohli and Douglas W. LaBahn, "Observations: Creating Effective Brand Names: A Study of the Nam-

ing Process," *Journal of Advertising Research* 37 (January/February 1997), 67–75.

4. Rob Osler, "The Name Game: Tips on How to Get It Right," *Marketing News*, September 14, 1998, 50.

5. Kevin Lane Keller, "Conceptualizing, Measuring, and Managing Customer-Based Brand Equity," *Journal of Marketing* 57 (January 1993), 9.

6. Joseph W. Alba, J. Wesley Hutchinson, and John G. Lynch, "Memory and Deci-

69. This and all following details are according to the 1995 POPAI Consumer Buying Habits Study, ibid.
70. J. Jeffrey Inman and Russell S. Winer, "Where the Rubber Meets the Road: A Model of In-store Decision Making," Marketing Science Institute Report No. 98–122 (October 1998).
71. Ibid., 26.
72. *Measuring the In-Store Decision Making of Supermarket and Mass Merchandise Store Shoppers*, 23.
73. *POPAI/Kmart/Procter & Gamble Study of P-O-P Effectiveness in Mass Merchandising Stores* (Englewood, N.J.: Point-of-Purchase Advertising Institute, 1993).
74. This study is in adherence with POPAI's guidelines for appropriate sales effectiveness research. See POPAI's *Association of In-Store Marketing Guidebook to Research Methodologies for the In-Store Marketing Industry* (Englewood, N.J.: Point-of-Purchase Advertising Institute, 1993), 4.
75. *POPAI/Warner-Lambert Canada P-O-P Effectiveness Study* (Englewood, N.J.: The Point-of-Purchase Advertising Institute, 1992).
76. John P. Murry, Jr. and Jan B. Heide, "Managing Promotion Program Participation within Manufacturer-Retailer Relationships," *Journal of Marketing* 62 (January 1998), 58. *POPAI/Progressive Grocer Supermarket Retailer Attitude Study* (Englewood, N.J.: Point-of-Purchase Advertising Institute, 1994), 2.
77. Don E. Schultz and William A. Robinson, *Sales Promotion Management* (Lincolnwood, Ill.: NTC Business Books, 1982), 279.
78. Adapted from Schultz and Robinson, *Sales Promotion Management*, 278–279. For further insights on gaining retailer participation in P-O-P programs, see Murry, Jr. and Heide (1998), "Managing Promotion Program Participation within Manufacturer-Retailer Relationships."

sion Making," in *Handbook of Consumer Behavior*, ed. Thomas S. Robertson and Harold H. Kassarjian (Englewood Cliffs, NJ: Prentice Hall, 1991), 1–49.
7. France Leclerc, Bernd H. Schmitt, and Laurette Dubé, "Foreign Branding and Its Effects on Product Perceptions and Attitudes," *Journal of Marketing Research* 31 (March 1994), 263–270.
8. Theresa Howard, "Attitude, Not Anchovies," *Brandweek*, August 23, 1999, 24.
9. These requirements represent a summary of views from a variety of sources, including Kevin Lane Keller, *Strategic Brand Management: Building, Measuring, and Managing Brand Equity* (Upper Saddle River, NJ: Prentice Hall, 1998), 136–140; Daniel L. Doden, "Selecting a Brand Name That Aids Marketing Objectives," *Advertising Age*, November 5, 1990, 34; and Walter P. Margulies, "Animal Names on Products May Be Corny, but Boost Consumer Appeal," *Advertising Age*, October 23, 1972, 77.
10. Christine Bittar, "Happy Intro Makes Scents," *Brandweek*, September 6, 1999, 25.
11. For excellent coverage of trademark infringement, review the following sources: Jeffrey M. Samuels and Linda B. Samuels, "Famous Marks Now Federally Protected Against Dilution," *Journal of Public Policy & Marketing* 15 (fall 1996), 307–310; Daniel J. Howard, Roger A. Kerin, and Charles Gengler, "The Effects of Brand Name Similarity on Brand Source Confusion: Implications for Trademark Infringement," *Journal of Public Policy & Marketing* 19 (fall 2000), 250–264.
12. Marcus W. Brauchli, "Chinese Flagrantly Copy Trademarks of Foreigners," *The Wall Street Journal*, June 20, 1994, B1, B2.
13. Doden, "Selecting a Brand Name That Aids Marketing Objectives."
14. Kevin Lane Keller, Susan E. Heckler, and Michael J. Houston, "The Effects of Brand Name Suggestiveness on Advertising Recall," *Journal of Marketing* 62 (January 1998), 48–57. See also J. Colleen McCracken and M. Carole Macklin, "The Role of Brand Names and Visual Clues in Enhancing Memory for Consumer Packaged Goods," *Marketing Letters* 9 (April 1998), 209–226; Richard R. Klink, "Creating Brand Names with Meaning: The Use of Sound Symbolism," *Marketing Letters* 11, no. 1 (2000), 5–20.
15. Sankar Sen, "The Effects of Brand Name Suggestiveness and Decision Goal on the Development of Brand Knowledge," *Journal of Consumer Psychology* 8 (4), 431–454.
16. Keller et al., "The Effects of Brand Name Suggestiveness on Advertising Recall." However, for an alternative perspective see Sen "The Effects of Brand Name Suggestiveness and Decision Goal."
17. Steve Jarvis, "What Changing a Name Involves Today," *Marketing News*, March 26, 2001, 1, 11, 12.
18. Mr. Kim Peterson quoted in Richard Linnett, "Andersen's Accenture Gets $175 Mil Ad Blitz," *Advertising Age*, December 4, 2000, 20.
19. Elaine Underwood, "Levi's New Dress Code," *Brandweek*, August 19, 1996, 26.
20. Kohli and LaBahn, "Observations: Creating Effective Brand Names," 69.
21. Ibid.
22. Ibid., 71.
23. Ibid., 72.
24. Ibid., 73.
25. Osler, "The Name Game."
26. Pamela W. Henderson and Joseph A. Cote, "Guidelines for Selecting or Modifying Logos," *Journal of Marketing* 62 (April 1998), 14–30. This article is must reading for anyone interested in learning more about logos.
27. Laura Bird, "Eye-Catching Logos All Too Often Leave Fuzzy Images in Minds of Consumers," *Wall Street Journal*, December 5, 1991, B1, B3.
28. Ibid., 15.
29. Ian P. Murphy, "All-American Icon Gets a New Look," *Marketing News*, August 18, 1997, 6.
30. Henderson and Cote, "Guidelines for Selecting or Modifying Logos."
31. Some of these phrases were mentioned in Michael Gershman, "Packaging: Positioning Tool of the 1980s," *Management Review* (August 1987), 33–41.
32. Peter R. Dickson and Alan G. Sawyer, "The Price Knowledge and Search of Supermarket Shoppers," *Journal of Marketing* 54 (July 1990), 42–53; John Le Boutillier, Susanna Shore Le Boutillier, and Scott A. Neslin, "A Replication and Extension of the Dickson and Sawyer Price-Awareness Study," *Marketing Letters* 5 (January 1994), 31–42.
33. John Deighton, "A White Paper on the Packaging Industry," Dennison Technical Papers, December 1983, 5.
34. An interesting article about package meaning is available in Robert L. Underwood and Julie L. Ozanne, "Is Your Package an Effective Communicator? A Normative Framework for Increasing the Communicative Competence of Packaging," *Journal of Marketing Communications* 4 (December 1998), 207–220.
35. Herbert M. Meyers and Murray J. Lubliner, *The Marketer's Guide to Successful Package Design* (Chicago: NTC Business Books, 1998), 2.

36. Gail Tom, Teresa Barnett, William Lew, and Jodean Selmants, "Cueing the Consumer: The Role of Salient Cues in Consumer Perception," *The Journal of Consumer Marketing* 4 (spring 1987), 23–27.

37. This comment and parts of the following discussion are based on statements appearing in Joseph A. Bellizzi, Ayn E. Crowley, and Ronald W. Hasty, "The Effects of Color in Store Design," *Journal of Retailing* 59 (spring 1983), 21–45. Some of the brand name examples in this section were suggested in "Color Is Prime 'Silent Communicator,'" *Marketing News*, April 25, 1986, 15.

38. Dennis J. Moran, "Packaging Can Lend Prestige to Products," *Advertising Age*, January 7, 1980, 59–60.

39. Gerry Khermouch, "Triarc's Smooth Move," *Brandweek*, June 22, 1998, 26–32.

40. Brian Wansink, "Can Package Size Accelerate Usage Volume?" *Journal of Marketing* 60 (July 1996), 1–14.

41. Kevin Higgins, "Foil's Glitter Attracts Manufacturers Who Want Upscale Buyers," *Marketing News*, February 3, 1984, 1.

42. Dik Warren Twedt, "How Much Value Can Be Added through Packaging," *Journal of Marketing* 32 (January 1968), 61–65.

43. Kerry J. Smith and Daniel Shannon, "Let Your Package Do the Talking," *Promo* (February 1995), 29–32.

44. William H. Motes and Arch G. Woodside, "Field Test of Package Advertising Effects on Brand Choice Behavior," *Journal of Advertising Research* 24 (February/March 1984), 39–45.

45. Edward H. Asam and Louis P. Bucklin, "Nutrition Labeling for Canned Goods: A Study of Consumer Response," *Journal of Marketing* 37 (April 1973), 36–37.

46. "Packaging Plays Starring Role in TV Commercials," *Marketing News*, January 30, 1987, 6.

47. Sonia Reyes, "Heinz Picks Purple As New EZ Squirt Color," *Brandweek*, June 25, 2001, 7.

48. George Baltas, "The Effects of Nutrition Information on Consumer Choice," *Journal of Advertising Research* 41 (March/April 2001), 57–63.

49. James Steinberg, "Controversial Products Helped by Packaging," *Brandweek*, January 26, 1998, 20.

50. "Packaging 2000," *Brandweek*, October 16, 1995, 40.

51. Terry Lefton, "Whole New Card Game," *Brandweek*, April 28, 1997, 17.

52. Greg Dalton, "If These Shelves Could Talk," *The Industry Standard*, April 2, 2001, 49–51.

53. This discussion is adapted from Meyers and Lubliner, *The Marketer's Guide to Successful Package Design*, 55–67.

54. Dickson and Sawyer, "The Price Knowledge and Search of Supermarket Shoppers"; Le Boutillier, Le Boutillier, and Neslin, "A Replication and Extension of the Dickson and Sawyer Price-Awareness Study."

55. Meyers and Lubliner, *The Marketer's Guide to Successful Package Design*, 63.

56. Cara Beardi, "POP Ups Sales Results," *Advertising Age*, July 23, 2001, 27.

57. John A. Quelch and Kristina Cannon-Bonventre, "Better Marketing at the Point-of-Purchase," *Harvard Business Review* (November/December 1983), 162–169.

58. "Impact in the Aisles: The Marketer's Last Best Chance," *Promo*, January 1996, 25.

59. An inventory of P-O-P advertising materials is provided in Robert Liljenwall and James Maskulka, *Marketing's Powerful Weapon: Point-of-Purchase Advertising* (Washington, DC: Point-of-Purchase Advertising International, 2001), 177–180.

60. This and the following examples are drawn from two *Point-of-Purchase Design Annuals* (No. 7 and No. 8), The 42nd and 43rd Merchandising Awards (New York: Point-of-Purchase Advertising Institute, 2000, 2001).

61. "A. C. Nielsen Research Reveals Cheese Sales Skyrocket with In-Store Promotions," *POPAI News*, Marketplace 1990, 19.

62. Doug Leeds, "Accountability Is In-Store for Marketers in '94," *Brandweek*, March 14, 1994, 17.

63. *The Effect of Motion Displays on the Sales of Beer; The Effect of Motion Displays on Sales of Baked Goods; The Effect of Motion Displays on Sales of Batteries* (Englewood, N.J.: Point-of-Purchase Advertising Institute, undated).

64. J. Jeffrey Inman, Leigh McAlister, and Wayne D. Hoyer, "Promotion Signal: Proxy for a Price Cut," *Journal of Consumer Research* 17 (June 1990), 74–81.

65. Margaret W. Matlin, *Cognition* (New York: Holt, Rinehart & Winston, 1989), 109.

66. Adapted from "Marketing Textbook: Clairol's Haircoloring Information Center," *POPAI News* (1983), 3.

67. This description is based on trade literature from Intermark Corporation, the developers of Procter & Gamble's Pantene merchandising center (1985).

68. *Measuring the In-Store Decision Making of Supermarket and Mass Merchandise Store Shoppers* (Englewood, N.J.: Point-of-Purchase Advertising Institute, 1995). Please note that POPAI recently changed its name from the Point-of-Purchase Advertising Institute to Point-of-Purchase Advertising International.

Advertising
Management

PART FOUR

Part Four includes eight chapters that examine in great detail various facets of advertising management. *Chapter 8* overviews the advertising management process and provides detailed discussions of advertising objective setting and budgeting. *Chapter 9* delves into the creative aspect of the advertising management process. Topics include requirements for effective advertising messages, characteristics of advertising planning, alternative styles of creative advertisements, means-end chains and MECCAS models, and corporate image/issue advertising.

Chapter 10 expands the coverage of advertising message creation by examining the use of endorsers in advertising and the various message appeals. Endorser characteristics and selection receive initial discussion. Coverage then turns to treatment of six types of appeals/formats that are widely used in designing advertising messages.

Chapter 11 deals with the assessment of ad message effectiveness by discussing industry standards for message research and the five general categories of message-based research.

Chapter 12 provides an analysis of traditional advertising media. The chapter devotes primary attention to evaluating the unique characteristics and strengths/weaknesses of five major advertising media: out-of-home, newspapers, magazines, ra-

dio, and television. The chapter also describes media-based research methods.

Chapter 13 covers two general categories of nontraditional ad media: alternative offline media and mass online advertising. Discussion of alternative offline advertising media includes product placements in movies, videos for VCRs, virtual signage at sporting venues, CD-ROM advertising, and yellow pages advertising. Internet advertising receives extensive coverage in the remainder of the chapter.

Chapter 14 focuses exclusively on offline and online direct advertising. After overviewing the fundamentals of database marketing, data mining, and lifetime value analysis, the chapter provides detailed discussions of traditional direct mail advertising (referred to as p-mail advertising) and e-mail advertising.

Chapter 15 provides thorough treatment of the four major activities involved in media planning and analysis: target audience selection, objective specification, media and vehicle selection, and media-buying activities. In-depth discussion focuses on media selection considerations. Also explored are advertising continuity considerations and cost considerations in media planning; cost-per-thousand (CPM and CPM-TM) computations are described and illustrated.

Chapter Eight

OVERVIEW OF ADVERTISING MANAGEMENT

Chapter Objectives

After studying this chapter, you should be able to:

1. Explain why advertising is an investment in the brand equity bank.
2. Describe the functions of advertising.
3. Understand the role for advertisement objectives and the requirements for setting good objectives.
4. Describe the hierarchy-of-effects model and its relevance for setting advertising objectives.
5. Explain the distinction between direct and indirect advertising objectives.
6. Understand the role of sales as an advertising objective and the logic of vaguely right versus precisely wrong thinking.
7. Understand the nature and importance of advertising budgeting.
8. Explain the relation between a brand's share of market (SOM) and its share of voice (SOV).
9. Explain the various rules of thumb, or heuristics, that guide practical advertising budgeting.

Opening Vignette: With Soaring Sales, Why Advertise?

Viagra, the male anti-impotence pill for an ailment labeled ED, for erectile dysfunction, was introduced in the late 1990s. Viagra quickly became one of the most successful prescription drugs ever, with annual revenues exceeding $1 billion. The months following introduction witnessed Viagra as the source of fun and pun on late-night talk shows, in cocktail party chatter, and in jokes shared among employees at work. Believers in Viagra's effectiveness spoke glowingly of Viagra's wonders. With all this free publicity following Viagra's introduction, one might question whether investing in advertising might have been a waste of money.

But this is not how executives at Pfizer, the pharmaceutical company that introduced Viagra, looked at the situation. Indeed, in addition to millions of dollars invested in advertising to physicians, more than $60 million was spent on advertising aimed at consumers. A spokesperson for Pfizer commented, in response to the "why advertise" question, that "there is a risk in not advertising." The risk to which he refers is twofold: One form is the risk that consumers will use Viagra along with other drugs that they shouldn't, which could cause death due to a fatal interaction of drugs that should not be taken together. A second form of risk is the competitive challenge from other pharmaceutical companies that compete against Viagra.

Pfizer's decision to heavily advertise Viagra was supported by advertising agency professionals, who shared the following reactions to Pfizer's advertising decision:

- Penny Hawkey, executive creative director at Medicus Communications, said, "You can never do enough to gain top-of-mind [awareness]. You need to get there and stay there. You have to claim the hill so whoever is coming in behind you doesn't have a shot. The faster the better."
- Ed Rady, president of Medicus Medical Education, commented: "If I were them [Pfizer], I would try to capture as big a share of this market as possible before others come."
- Jerry Lee, managing director of HMC Advertising & Marketing, an ad agency that specializes in drug advertising, proffered that a brand has to control its own image. "If you don't create your own brand image, other people will take it and control it for you, and you can't let that happen."

Source: Adapted from Sally Goll Beatty, "Just What Goes In a Viagra Ad? Early Reports Say Dancing Couples," *Wall Street Journal Online*, June 17, 1998. Copyright 1998 by DOW JONES & CO INC. Reproduced with permission of DOW JONES & CO INC. in the format Textbook via Copyright Clearance Center.

These professionals fully understand and appreciate the value of advertising. They understand the importance of gaining momentum. They know that a successful brand remains successful only by protecting itself from the inroads of competitors. They know that, like Viagra itself, advertising is an "anti-impotence" mechanism—it can be used effectively to build on existing brand strength and to protect against declining strength in the marketplace.

This chapter presents an introduction to fundamentals of advertising management. The initial section indicates the role and importance of advertising. Included is a detailed discussion of the arguments favoring investments in advertising and counterarguments regarding circumstances when it is advisable to disinvest. A subsequent section then describes the functions advertising performs for a brand and the process of managing advertising. Major sections then cover objective setting in advertising and budgeting for advertising.

THE MAGNITUDE OF ADVERTISING AND AD-INVESTMENT CONSIDERATIONS

Advertising is big business, to say the very least. Ad expenditures in the United States alone totaled approximately $230 billion in 2001.[1] This amounts to more than $800 in advertising for each of the nearly 280 million men, women, and children in the United States as of 2001. Advertising spending is also considerable in other major industrialized countries but not nearly to the same magnitude as in the United States.

Some American companies invest more than $2 billion a year on domestic advertising. In 2000, General Motors spent $3.93 billion; Philip Morris, $2.60 billion; Procter & Gamble, $2.36 billion; Ford Motor Company, $2.35 billion; Pfizer, $2.27 billion; and PepsiCo, $2.1 billion.[2] Table 8.1 lists the top 100 U.S. advertisers in 2000. As can be seen, even the U.S. government (ranked number 18) advertised to the tune of $1.25 billion. The government's advertising goes to such efforts as drug control, military recruiting, the Postal Service, Amtrak rail services, and antismoking campaigns.[3]

Advertising is costly and its effects often uncertain. It is for these reasons that many companies think it appropriate occasionally to reduce advertising expenditures or to eliminate advertising entirely. Marketing managers and MarCom personnel sometimes consider it unnecessary to advertise when their brands already are enjoying great success. Companies find it particularly seductive to pull funds out of advertising during economic downturns—every dollar not spent on advertising is one more dollar added to the bottom line. During the economic downturn in 2001 and the impending recession late that year—propelled in part by the economic fallout from the unimaginable terrorist attacks on the World Trade Center and the Pentagon—advertising expenditures in the United States declined between 4 percent and 6 percent. Declines of this magnitude had not been seen in the United States since the Great Depression of the late 1920s and early 1930s.[4]

Such behavior implicitly fails to consider the fact that advertising is not just a current expense (as the term is used in accounting parlance) but rather is an investment. Although businesspeople fully appreciate the fact that building a more efficient production facility or purchasing a new computer system is an investment in their company's future, many of these same people often think advertising is an expense that can be reduced or even eliminated when financial pressures call for cost-cutting measures.

However, an ex-CEO at Procter and Gamble—one of the world's largest advertisers—aptly draws an analogy between advertising and exercise in that both provide long-term benefits. Moreover, like exercise, it is easy to stop advertising or postpone it because there is no immediate penalty for the interruption.

If you want your brand to be fit, it's got to exercise regularly. When you get the opportunity to go to the movies or do something else instead of working out, you can do that once in a while—that's [equivalent to] shifting funds into [sales] promotion. But it's not a good thing to do. If you get off the regimen, you will pay for it later.[5]

Table 8.1

Rank	Company	Total U.S. Ad Spending (in millions)
1	General Motors Corp.	$3,934.8
2	Phillip Morris Cos.	2,602.9
3	Procter & Gamble Co.	2,363.5
4	Ford Motor Co.	2,345.2
5	Pfizer	2,265.3
6	PepsiCo	2,100.7
7	DaimlerChrysler	1,984.0
8	AOL Time Warner	1,770.1
9	Walt Disney Co.	1,757.5
10	Verizon Communications	1,612.9
11	Johnson & Johnson	1,601.2
12	Sears, Roebuck & Co.	1,455.4
13	Unilever	1,453.6
14	AT&T Corp.	1,415.7
15	General Electric Co.	1,310.1
16	Toyota Motor Corp.	1,273.9
17	McDonald's Corp.	1,273.9
18	U.S. government	1,246.3
19	Sprint Corp.	1,227.3
20	Viacom	1,220.9
21	Bristol-Myers Squibb Co.	1,190.7
22	IBM Corp.	1,189.0
23	Federated Department Stores	1,127.6
24	GlaxoSmithKline	1,126.4
25	Diageo	1,112.1
26	Honda Motor Co.	1,035.0
27	Sony Corp.	1,030.0
28	J. C. Penney Co.	1,011.2
29	L'Oreal	987.1
30	Merck & Co.	983.9
31	News Corp.	923.2
32	Coca-Cola Co.	894.9
33	Tricon Global Restaurants	865.2
34	Microsoft Corp.	854.8
35	Target Corp.	826.7
36	Nissan Motor Co.	813.8
37	WorldCom	804.9
38	Hewlett-Packard Co.	791.4
39	SBC Communications	786.0
40	Intel Corp.	772.9
41	Pharmacia Corp.	725.9
42	Estee Lauder Cos.	717.3
43	Anheuser-Busch Cos.	707.6
44	Vivendi Universal	699.8
45	American Home Products Corp.	670.9
46	Mars Inc.	670.8
47	Home Depot	651.6
48	Bayer	648.9
49	General Mills	639.2
50	Nestle	637.7
51	Sara Lee Corp.	617.1

Top 100 Spenders in U.S. Advertising, 2000 *(continued)*

Table 8.1

Rank	Company	Total U.S. Ad Spending (in millions)
52	AT&T Wireless	616.3
53	Nike	613.5
54	ConAgra	578.5
55	Novartis	573.9
56	May Department Stores Co.	570.1
57	Volkswagen	551.3
58	Kroger Co.	551.2
59	Kmart Corp.	542.1
60	Morgan Stanley	539.5
61	American Express	538.2
62	Schering-Plough Corp.	510.5
63	Wal-Mart Stores	497.8
64	Circuit City Stores	479.0
65	Ralston Purina Co.	468.2
66	Gillette Co.	466.0
67	S. C. Johnson & Son	464.8
68	Berkshire Hathaway	455.8
69	Kellogg Co.	455.4
70	Mattel	451.4
71	DreamWorks SKG	450.1
72	Gap Inc.	449.6
73	Best Buy Co.	446.7
74	Adolph Coors Co.	444.2
75	Dell Computer Corp.	429.5
76	Visa International	427.3
77	Cendant Corp.	409.8
78	BellSouth Corp.	399.0
79	Gateway	397.8
80	Safeway	397.7
81	Clorox Co.	397.1
82	Charles Schwab & Co.	379.2
83	The Limited	349.9
84	U.S. Dairy Producers, Processors	348.9
85	Eastman Kodak Co.	343.2
86	Hershey Foods Corp.	338.1
87	Qwest Communications International	336.0
88	Hilton Hotels Corp.	335.6
89	Office Depot	334.5
90	Colgate-Palmolive Co.	331.9
91	Campbell Soup. Co.	331.2
92	Mitsubishi Motors Corp.	317.2
93	MasterCard International	311.1
94	Kimberly-Clark Corp.	297.3
95	Wendy's International	296.3
96	Reckitt Benckiser	289.2
97	Dillard's	288.9
98	Ameritrade Holding Corp.	287.4
99	Apple Computer	285.2
100	Mazda Motor Corp.	283.1

This viewpoint is captured further in the advice of a vice president at Booz, Allen & Hamilton, a major marketing consultant, when asked what great companies such as Procter & Gamble, Kellogg, General Mills, Coca-Cola, and Pepsi-Cola have in common. All these companies, in his opinion, are aware that *consistent investment spending* is the key factor underlying successful advertising. "They do not raid their budgets to ratchet earnings up for a few quarters. They know that advertising should not be managed as a discretionary variable cost."[6] This point should remind you of our discussion back in Chapter 2 where we discussed the importance of momentum. Advertising *momentum* is like exercise. Stop exercising, and you will lose conditioning and probably gain weight. Stop advertising, and your brand likely will lose some of its equity and market share as well.

Putting Matters in Perspective

We can better appreciate the prior discussion by examining a few equations that put things into crisper perspective. These equations deal with the relations among sales volume, sales revenue (or simply revenue), and profit:

$$\text{Profit} = \text{Revenue} - \text{Expenses} \qquad \textbf{Equation 8.1}$$

$$\text{Revenue} = \text{Price} \times \text{Volume} \qquad \textbf{Equation 8.2}$$

$$\text{Volume} = \text{Trial} + \text{Repeat} \qquad \textbf{Equation 8.3}$$

We first see with equation 8.1 that a brand's profit during any accounting period—such as a business quarter or an entire year—is a function of its revenue minus expenses. Because advertising is an expense, total profit during an accounting period can be increased by reducing advertising expenses. At the same time, an undesirable effect of reducing advertising is that revenue may decline because fewer units can be sold or the price per unit has to be reduced in the absence of adequate advertising support (see equation 8.2). We can further note from equation 8.3 that sales volume (i.e., number of units sold) is obtained by a combination of recruiting more trial, or first-time, users to a brand and encouraging users to continue purchasing the brand—that is, to become repeat purchasers.

Whether one chooses to invest or disinvest in advertising a brand depends largely on expectations about how advertising will influence a brand's sales volume (equation 8.3) and revenue (equation 8.2). Let us look first at arguments for investing and then at disinvesting.

Arguments for Investing in Advertising.   In terms of profitability, investing in advertising is justified only if the incremental revenue generated from the advertising effort exceeds the advertising expense. In other words, if the advertising expense is $X, then over the long term (i.e., not immediately) revenue attributable to the advertising must be more than $X to justify the investment. On what grounds might one expect that the revenue will exceed the advertising expense? In terms of equation 8.3, it might be expected that effective advertising will attract new triers to a brand and encourage repeat purchasing. (Obviously, advertising is not the only MarCom tool able to generate trial and repeat purchasing; indeed, sales promotions perform both roles in conjunction with advertising.) Hence, effective advertising should build sales volume by enhancing brand equity—both by increasing brand awareness and by enhancing brand image (recall the discussion in Chapter 2).

Equation 8.2 shows that the other determinant of revenue besides sales volume is the unit price at which a brand is sold. As will be established in a subsequent section, advertising has the power to enhance a brand's perceived quality and thus its ability to charge a higher price; that is, consumers are willing to pay more for brands they perceive as higher quality. Taken together, then, the case for investing in advertising is based on the belief that it can increase profitability by increasing sales volume, enabling higher selling prices, and thus increasing revenue beyond the incremental advertising expense.

Arguments for Disinvesting in Advertising.   As previously noted, firms often choose to reduce advertising expenditures either when a brand is performing well or during periods of economic recession. This is a seductive strategy because a reduction in expenses, everything else held constant, leads to increased profits. But is "everything else held constant" when advertising budgets are cut or even severely slashed? The implicit assumption is that revenue (and revenue's constituent elements, volume and price) will *not* be affected adversely when ad budgets are diminished. However, such an assumption is based on Pollyanna-like thinking that past advertising will continue to positively affect sales volume even when advertising in the current period is curtailed or reduced. The assumption also is somewhat illogical. On the one hand, it presumes that past advertising will carry over into the future to maintain revenue; on the other hand, it neglects to acknowledge that the absence of advertising in the present period will have an adverse effect on revenues in subsequent periods.

Which Position Is More Acceptable?   The profit effect of reducing advertising expenses is relatively certain: For every dollar not invested in advertising, there is a dollar increase in short-term profit—assuming, of course, that advertising does not adversely affect revenue. It is far less certain, however, that maintaining or increasing advertising expenditures will increase profits. This is because it is difficult to know with certainty whether advertising will build brand volume or enable higher prices; either outcome or both will lead to increased revenues. Yet, and it is a big yet, most sophisticated companies are willing to place their bets on advertising's ability to boost revenues and thus enhance profits from the revenue-increase side rather than from the expense-reduction side. Many companies continue to invest in advertising, even during economic downturns, because they believe that advertising is an investment in the brand equity bank. We pursue this line of thinking in the next section, but before moving on it is important to address two forms of elasticity—advertising and price elasticities.

Elasticity, as you will recall from a basic economics or marketing course, is a measure of how responsive quantity demanded is to changes in marketing variables such as price and advertising. We can calculate elasticity coefficients for price (E_P) and advertising (E_A), respectively, based on the following equations:

E_P = **Percent change in quantity ÷ Percent change in price**   **Equation 8.4**

E_A = **Percent change in quantity ÷ Percent change in advertising**   **Equation 8.5**

To illustrate these concepts, consider the situation faced by a recent college graduate, Aubrey, who sells T-shirts imprinted with thematic messages. Let's assume that Aubrey is doing a pretty good business but thinks he can increase revenues and profits by lowering the price at which he sells imprinted T-shirts. (The "law" of inverse demand says that sales volume, or quantity, typically increases when prices are reduced, and vice versa.)

Last week (let's refer to this as week 1) Aubrey priced T-shirts at $10 and sold 1,500 shirts (P1 = $10; Q1 = 1,500). He decided the following week, week 2, to reduce the price to $9, and then sold 1,800 shirts (P2 = $9; Q2 = 1,800). Applying Equation 8.4, we quickly see that the percentage change in quantity is 20 percent. That is, (1,800 − 1,500) ÷ 1,500 = 20 percent. Thus, with an 11 percent decrease in price—that is, (10 − 9) ÷ 9—he realized a 20 percent increase in quantity sold. The price elasticity (E_P) expressed as an absolute value is 1.82 (i.e., 20 ÷ 11). (Refer to equation 8.4 to see how the elasticity coefficient for price, E_P, is calculated.) Aubrey was pleased with this result because total revenue in week 2 was $16,200 (P2 × Q2 = $9 × 1,800 = $16,200) compared with the $15,000 revenue obtained in week 1 ($10 × 1,500). Thus, although he reduced the price of T-shirts, he enjoyed an 8 percent increase in revenue—that is, ($16,200 − $15,000) ÷ $15,000.

Let us now consider the possibility that rather than reducing price, Aubrey decided to increase the amount of advertising from week 1 to week 2. Suppose that in week 1 he had spent $1,000 advertising in the local newspaper. As before, he obtained $15,000 revenue in week 1 from selling 1,500 T-shirts at a price of $10 each. In week 2 suppose he increased the level of advertising to $1,500 (a 50 percent increase over week 1) and sold 1,600 shirts at $10 each. In this case, the percentage change in quantity is 6.67 percent. That is, (1,600 − 1,500) ÷ 1,500 = 6.67 percent. This increase in quantity sold was enjoyed with a 50 percent increase in ad expenditures. Thus, applying equation 8.5, the advertising elasticity (E_A) is 6.67 ÷ 50 = 0.133. Whereas

Aubrey received \$15,000 in week 1 revenue (P1 = \$10; Q1 = 1,500), revenue increased in week 2 by \$1,000 (P2 = \$10; Q2 = 1,600). This increased revenue (\$1,000) was obtained with a \$500 increase in advertising, so Aubrey enjoyed a \$500 increase in profit—not a bad week's work for a young entrepreneur!

You might be thinking, "Where are we going with this?" Well, let's take this simple example and relate it to a more general point that tells us something about how advertising works and whether increases in advertising can be justified, especially when juxtaposed against the alternative possibility of merely reducing prices. We know a lot about advertising and price elasticities.[7] An important study determined that the average price and advertising elasticities for 130 brands of durable and nondurable products were E_P = 1.61 and E_A = 0.11, respectively. (The price elasticity is presented here as an absolute value, though technically it should have a negative sign insofar as price increases result in volume decreases, and vice versa.) Hence, sales volume is about 14.6 times (1.61 ÷ 0.11) more responsive, on average, to changes in price than to changes in advertising. For just *durable* goods, the average price and advertising elacticities are 2.01 and 0.23, which indicates that sales volume for these goods is, on average, 8.7 times more responsive to price discounts than advertising increases. Comparatively, for *nondurable* goods the average price and advertising elasticities are 1.54 and 0.09, respectively, indicating that, on average, sales volume is 17 times more responsive to price cuts than advertising increases.

Do these results indicate that brand managers should always discount prices and never increase advertising? Absolutely not! As you have learned from this text and elsewhere, every situation is unique. Pat answers ("This is how you always should do it") are flat out wrong and misleading! The fact of the matter is that every brand does not experience the same price and advertising elasticities as presented here. "On average," as used in our discussion, means that some brands are at the average, whereas others are above or below the average; there is, in other words, a distribution of elasticity coefficients around the average. In general, we can consider four combinations of advertising and price elasticities. For each situation we will identify the appropriate strategy, whether to increase advertising or reduce price, for increasing profit.[8]

- *Situation 1 (maintain status quo)*: Given a situation where the market is neither very price elastic or advertising elastic, the brand manager should neither discount price nor increase advertising. A situation such as this is likely when consumers have well-established preferences such as during the decline stage of a product's life cycle or in established niche markets. Profits are maximized by basically adhering to the status quo in maintaining the present price and advertising levels.
- *Situation 2 (build image via increased advertising)*: In a situation where the market is more advertising elastic than price elastic, it is advisable to spend relatively more on advertising increases than price discounts. This situation is likely for new products, luxury goods, and products characterized by symbolic imagery (cosmetics, designer labels in apparel and home furnishings, expensive brands of vodka and other distilled spirits, etc.). The profit-increasing strategy in a situation such as this is to use advertising to build a brand's image.
- *Situation 3 (grow volume via price discounting)*: In this situation the market is more price than advertising elastic. Such a situation is to be expected for many mature consumer goods where consumers have complete information about most brands in the category and brand switching is frequent because brands are little differentiated. Profit increases are obtained more from price discounts than advertising investment.
- *Situation 4 (increase advertising and/or discount prices)*: This is a situation where the market is both price elastic and advertising elastic. This would be expected when brands in the product category are inherently differentiable (cereals, automobiles, appliances, etc.) and for products that are seasonal (e.g., lawn products, seasonal clothing, and special holiday gift items). In situations such as these, informative advertising can influence consumers' beliefs about product attributes (e.g., Scott's fertilizer is longer-lasting than competitive brands), but because brands are similar, consumers also are eager to compare prices.

Given knowledge of the price and advertising elasticities that exist in a particular situation, it is possible to mathematically determine whether it is more profitable to increase advertising or discount price. The mathematics are beyond the scope of this text, but the interested reader is referred to the source in the following endnote.[9] It is hoped that this section conveyed the point that the choice to invest (increase) or disinvest (decrease) in advertising can be made only after determining the advertising and price elasticities that confront a brand in a particular market situation. We have provided some general guidelines in the previously mentioned four situations as to when it might be advisable to increase advertising expenditures or discount prices. It is critical to appreciate that every situation is unique. It is important to understand that "on average" applies to all brands in a product category but that particular brands may distinguish themselves by developing really clever advertising that serves to create an appealing advertising image or present functional information in an especially compelling manner.

Your job as a brand manager is to work with your advertising agency and other MarCom suppliers (e.g., PR specialists and event marketers) to develop campaigns that distinguish your brand from the crowd of competitors. Please note, by comparison, that the average major league baseball player hits only around, say, 10 home runs per season. But the Barry Bondses, Mark McGwires, and Sammy Sosas of the baseball world do not perform "on average" but far above the average. Perhaps your brand can also perform above the average with effective advertising. If it cannot, and the average advertising elasticity in your product category is low, then the appropriate strategy is probably *not* to invest in additional advertising but to maintain or even lower prices. In other words, do not waste money on advertising if the circumstances (such as situations 1 or 3 above) dictate against further advertising investment. However, if the market is responsive to advertising (such as situations 2 or 4), then be prepared to invest in developing creative and effective advertising campaigns.

An Investment in the Brand Equity Bank

As established in Chapter 2, the objective of marketing communications is to enhance the equity in a firm's brands. You will recall that MarCom efforts enhance a brand's equity by creating brand awareness and forging favorable, strong, and perhaps unique associations in the consumer's memory between the brand and its features and benefits.[10] When advertising and other forms of marketing communications create unique and positive messages, a brand becomes differentiated from competitive offerings and is relatively insulated from future price competition.[11]

Advertising's long-term role has been described in these terms: "Strong advertising represents a deposit in the brand equity bank."[12] This clever expression nicely captures the advertising challenge. It also correctly notes that not all advertising represents a deposit in the brand equity bank, only advertising that is *strong*—that is, different, unique, clever, and memorable.

ADVERTISING FUNCTIONS AND PROCESS

Advertising Performs Valuable Functions

Many business firms as well as not-for-profit organizations have faith in advertising. In general, advertising is valued because it is recognized as performing five critical communications functions: (1) informing, (2) persuading, (3) reminding, (4) adding value, and (5) assisting other company efforts.[13]

Informing.   Advertising makes consumers *aware* of new brands, *educates* them about brand features and benefits, and facilitates the creation of positive *brand images*. Because advertising is an efficient form of communication capable of reaching mass audiences at a relatively low cost per contact, it facilitates the introduction of new brands and increases demand for existing brands, largely by increasing consumers' *top-of-mind awareness (TOMA)* for established brands in mature product categories.[14] Advertising performs another valuable information role—both for the advertised brand and the consumer—by teaching new uses for existing brands. This practice, termed *usage expansion advertising*, is typified by the following illustrations:[15]

- Campbell's soup, which is typically eaten for lunch and during other informal eating occasions, was advertised as being suitable for eating during formal family dinners or even at breakfast.
- Gatorade, which originally was used during heavy athletic activity, was advertised for use to replenish liquids during flu attacks.
- Special K, a breakfast cereal, was advertised for afternoon or late-night snacking.

Persuading.   Effective advertising influences (persuades) prospective customers to try advertised products and services. Sometimes the persuasion takes the form of influencing *primary demand*—that is, creating demand for an entire product category. More frequently, advertising attempts to build *secondary demand*, the demand for a specific company's brand. Advertising provides consumers with reasons for trying one brand versus another and sometimes offers emotional appeals that have a positive effect on brand attitudes.

Consider Gillette's introduction of the Mach3 razor (Figure 8.1). Gillette invested nearly three-quarters of a billion dollars to develop the Mach3, and corporate success (including maintaining a very attractive stock price) demanded huge sales volume to garner a good return on the investment in Mach3. Gillette executives knew they would have to advertise heavily to convince consumers that the Mach3 was worth its relatively high price. Accordingly, plans were made to spend $300 million on global advertising.[16] See the *Global Focus* insert for another illustration of a global advertising campaign.

Figure 8.1   An Illustrative Persuasion Effort—Gillette's Mach3 Razor

A Global Advertising Campaign for Exxon Mobil

Exxon and Mobil are two major gasoline and oil companies that merged in 1999 to form Exxon Mobil. This huge enterprise markets its portfolio of brands—Exxon, Esso, Mobil, and General—in more than 100 countries around the globe. Success requires effective marketing and advertising that positions these brands in similar fashion throughout the world so as to accomplish Exxon Mobil's objectives for brand equity and market share. All global companies confront a key advertising issue: Should they prepare different advertising campaigns in each country or develop a similar, or even identical, advertising message for use around the globe? Many marketers hold the view that local (versus global) advertising campaigns are most effective. Other marketing and advertising executives are of the viewpoint, however, that local campaigns have the notable disadvantage of creating diverse brand images in different countries rather than building a uniform positioning. Moreover, with local ad campaigns the advertising production expense is compounded compared with producing a uniform (also known as global) campaign.

Exxon Mobil decided on a global advertising campaign for use in all countries. The $150 million campaign includes advertisements with the same look and feel for placement in every country in which Exxon Mobile operates. This may seem a simple task but is actually quite complicated when considering the diversity of language and other cultural differences. To accomplish the task Exxon Mobil and its advertising agency produced five hours of commercial footage that was to be used as a library for unique selection in each local market. Some scenes were videotaped using up to six different casts of actors, with each cast acting out essentially the same story line. Managers in local markets could then pick from the library those vignettes most suitable for their region. As a result, the advertising story line for Exxon Mobil's brands is virtually identical around the globe. The same message is acted out in all commercials, and casting selections reflect local people who act out situations but don't have speaking roles. The audio portion of the commercials is restricted to background statements (voice-over) from an announcer who speaks in one of 25 languages to reflect local language customs.

Reminding.   Advertising keeps a company's brand fresh in the consumer's memory. When a need arises that is related to the advertised product, past advertising impact makes it possible for the advertiser's brand to come to the consumer's mind as a purchase candidate. Effective advertising also increases the consumer's interest in a mature brand and thus the likelihood of purchasing a brand that otherwise might not be chosen.[17] Advertising has been demonstrated, furthermore, to influence *brand switching* by reminding consumers who have not recently purchased a brand that the brand is available and that it possesses favorable attributes.[18]

Adding Value.   There are three basic ways by which companies can add value to their offerings: innovating, improving quality, and altering consumer perceptions. These three value-added components are completely interdependent.

> *Innovation without quality is mere novelty. Consumer perception without quality and/or innovation is mere puffery. And both innovation and quality, if not translated into consumer perceptions, are like the sound of the proverbial tree falling in the empty forest.*[19]

Advertising adds value to brands by influencing perceptions. Effective advertising causes brands to be viewed as more elegant, more stylish, more prestigious, and of higher quality. Indeed, research involving over 100 brands drawn from five nondurable products (e.g., paper towels and shampoo) and five durables (e.g., televisions and 35mm cameras) has demonstrated that greater ad spending influences consumers to perceive advertised brands as higher in quality.[20] Effective advertising, then, by influencing perceived quality and other perceptions can lead to increased market share and greater profitability.[21] Advertising can indeed be an investment in the brand equity bank.

Assisting Other Company Efforts.   Advertising is just one member of the MarCom team. Advertising is at times a scorer that accomplishes goals. At other times advertising's primary role is as an assister that facilitates other company efforts in the MarCom process. For example, advertising may be used as a vehicle for delivering coupons and sweepstakes and attracting attention to these and other promotional tools.

Another crucial role of advertising is to assist sales representatives. Advertising presells a company's products and provides salespeople with valuable introductions prior to their personal contact with prospective customers. Sales effort, time, and costs are reduced because less time is required to inform prospects about product features and benefits. Moreover, advertising legitimizes or makes more credible the sales representative's claims.[22]

Advertising also enhances the effectiveness of other MarCom tools. For example, consumers can identify product packages in the store and recognize the value of a product more easily after seeing it advertised on television or in a magazine. Advertising also can augment the effectiveness of price deals. Customers are known to be more responsive to retailers' price deals when retailers advertised that fact compared to when retailers offer a deal absent any advertising support.[23]

Managing the Advertising Process

Figure 8.2 graphically illustrates the advertising management process. It can be seen that this process consists of formulating advertising strategy, implementing the strategy, and then assessing effectiveness.

Advertising Strategy.   Advertising strategy involves four major activities (see Figure 8.2). The first two, setting objectives and budgeting, are described later in this chapter. Message strategy is a third aspect that is the subject of Chapters 9 and 10. Media strategy, the topic of Chapters 11 through 14, involves the selection of media categories and specific vehicles to deliver advertising messages.

Strategy Implementation.   Strategy implementation deals with the tactical, day-to-day activities that must be performed to carry out an advertising campaign. For example, whereas the decision to emphasize television over other media is a strategic choice, the selection of specific types of programs and times at which to air a commercial is a tactical implementation matter. Likewise, the decision to emphasize a particular brand benefit is a strategic message consideration, but the actual way the message is delivered is a matter of creative implementation. This text focuses more on strategic than tactical issues.

Assessing Advertising Effectiveness.   Assessing effectiveness is a critical aspect of advertising management—only by evaluating results is it possible to determine whether objectives are being accomplished. This often requires that baseline measures be taken before an advertising campaign begins (to determine, for example, what percentage of the target audience is aware of the brand name) and then afterward to determine whether the objective was achieved. Because research is fundamental to advertising control, Chapter 15 is devoted exclusively to evaluating advertising effectiveness.

SETTING ADVERTISING OBJECTIVES

In Chapter 2, which introduced the overall marketing communications process, the relations among brand positioning, target markets, objectives, and budgets were presented with the following mantra:

The Advertising Management Process

Figure 8.2

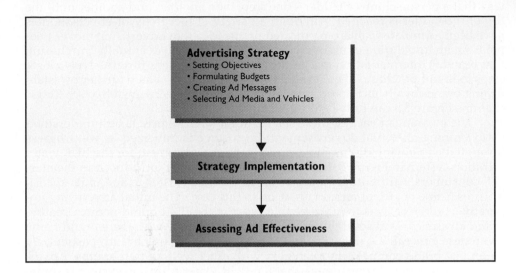

*All marketing communications should be (1) clearly **positioned**, (2) directed to a particular **target market**, (3) created to achieve a **specific objective**, and (4) undertaken to accomplish the objective **within budget constraint**.*

We now continue with this theme as it relates specifically to advertising objective setting and budgeting. These activities, along with positioning (the subject of Chapter 3), are the bedrock of all subsequent advertising decisions. Advertising strategy built on a weak foundation is virtually guaranteed to fail. Intelligent objectives and an adequate budget are critical for advertising success.

Advertising objectives are goals that advertising efforts attempt to achieve. Objectives provide the foundation for all remaining advertising decisions.[24] There are three major reasons why it is essential that advertising objectives be established *prior to* making decisions regarding message selection and media determination, which are the guts of an advertising program:[25]

1. Advertising objectives are an expression of *management consensus*. The process of setting objectives literally forces top marketing and advertising personnel to agree on the course that a brand's advertising will take for the following planning period as well as the tasks it is to accomplish for a specific brand.
2. Objective setting *guides* the budgeting, message, and media aspects of a brand's advertising strategy. Objectives determine how much money should be spent and provide guidelines for the kinds of message strategy and media choice needed to accomplish a brand's marketing communications objectives.
3. Advertising objectives provide *standards* against which results can be measured. As will be detailed later, good objectives set precise, quantitative yardsticks of what advertising hopes to accomplish. Subsequent results can then be compared with these standards to determine whether the advertising accomplished what it was intended to do.

The Hierarchy-of-Effects Framework

A full appreciation of how advertising goals (objectives) are set requires that we first look at advertising from the customer's perspective. That is, advertisers establish objectives that are designed to move customers to purchase the advertiser's brand. A framework called the *hierarchy of effects* is appropriate for accomplishing this understanding.

The **hierarchy-of-effects** metaphor implies that for advertising to be successful it must move consumers from one goal to the next goal, much in the same way that a person climbs a ladder—one step, then another, and another until the top of the ladder is reached. Although a variety of hierarchy-of-effects models have been formulated, all are predicated on the idea that advertising moves people from an initial state of unawareness about a brand to eventually purchasing that brand.[26] Intermediate stages in the hierarchy represent progressively closer steps to brand purchase. The hierarchy in Figure 8.3 goes a step further by establishing brand loyalty as the top step on the ladder of advertising effects.[27] Please examine Figure 8.3 carefully before reading on.

The meaning of each of these stages, or hierarchy steps, is best understood by examining an actual advertisement. Each stage is italicized as we progress through the following discussion. Consider the advertisement for the PŪR water filtration system in Figure 8.4. When this brand was first introduced to the market, consumers were initially *unaware* of the brand's existence and of its special features (some no doubt remain unaware to this day). The initial advertising imperative, therefore, was to make people *aware* of the PŪR brand name. Creating brand awareness is absolutely essential for success; however, mere brand name awareness generally is not sufficient to get people to buy a brand, particularly when that brand competes in a category with other well-known brands. Advertising has to persuade consumers that the PŪR water filtration system is somehow different and better than competitive options, which, in this case, happens to be purchasing bottled water in plastic bottles. The ad, in other words, must influ-

Figure 8.3   Hierarchy-of-Effects Model of Advertising

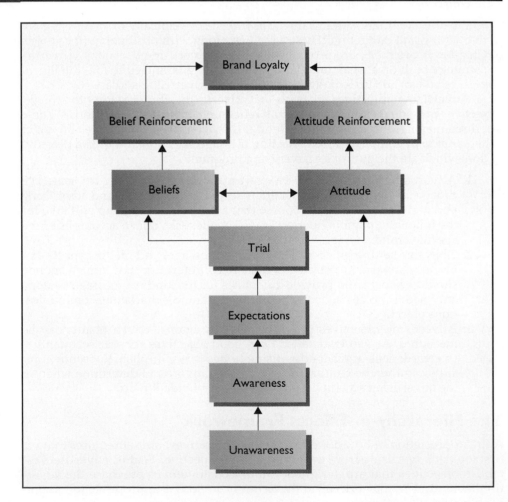

The PŪR Water Filtration System   **Figure 8.4**

ence consumer *expectations* that a PŪR filter attached to a standard water faucet will produce drinking water that is free of impurities and tastes as good as bottled water. To the extent the consumer develops this expectation, she or he may undertake a *trial* purchase of PŪR.

After using the product, the consumer will form *beliefs* about PŪR's performance benefits and an overall *attitude*, or evaluation, toward the brand. Beliefs and attitude are mutually reinforcing, as illustrated by the double-headed arrow linking these two elements in Figure 8.3. To elaborate, as discussed in Chapter 5, the consumer will form an overall evaluation of PŪR along some implicit good-to-bad spectrum. If PŪR lives up to the consumer's expectations about water purity and good taste, the attitude most likely will be positive; on the other hand, the attitude can be expected to be somewhat ambivalent or even negative if the brand fails to meet expectations. Once the attitude is formed, the consumer's additional exposures to PŪR advertisements serve to *reinforce* the attitude. In turn, the consumer can be expected to develop a somewhat resolute belief that PŪR does (or does not) produce good-tasting water that is equivalent to expensive bottled water. This key belief, which the advertising is directed at influencing, also is subject to reinforcement via additional advertising exposures. In Figure 8.3 these are referred to as *belief reinforcement* and *attitude reinforcement*.

As long as the brand continues to satisfy expectations and a superior brand is not introduced, the consumer may become a *brand loyal* purchaser of PŪR. That is, because the PŪR faucet-mount filter must be replaced periodically, some consumers will make multiple purchases of the PŪR system. This indeed is the ultimate advertising objective, because, as has been mentioned in several preceding chapters, it is much cheaper to retain present customers than it is to continuously prospect for new ones.[28]

What Are the Implications for Objective Setting?

Advertising objectives must be set in accordance with the circumstances that characterize the advertiser's particular brand and competitive situation. To understand this more fully, let us continue the discussion of advertising goals alluded to previously. As noted, advertising is undertaken to accomplish goals such as (1) making consumers aware of a new brand, (2) influencing their expectations about a brand's attributes and benefits, and (3) encouraging them to try the brand.

The first goal, awareness, is essential for new or unestablished brands. That is, creating high levels of awareness is an important prerequisite to swaying consumer choice toward the marketer's brand. Unless consumers are aware of a brand, that brand cannot be a member of their *consideration set* of viable purchase alternatives. Getting a brand considered (or, stated another way, moving that brand into consumers' consideration sets) has been demonstrated to influence the odds that it will be chosen—even if it is not more favorably evaluated.[29] Hence, creating awareness toward one's brand is a precondition to accomplishing any subsequent advertising goals.

Advertising must also instill in consumers expectations about brand performance, which, if verified by the outcomes of brand usage experience, will evolve into specific beliefs. Prior to usage one merely *expects* a certain outcome; after usage, one *forms a belief* about the brand's ability to fulfill that expectation. As noted, the PŪR advertisement (Figure 8.4) was designed for consumers to expect that using this device produces good-tasting water that substitutes for expensive bottled water.

All good advertising must inspire some expectation about the brand's capabilities. The two advertisements in Figure 8.5 illustrate efforts to create various forms of expectations. The Allegra ad assures allergy sufferers that taking only one Allegra tablet daily will lead to long-lasting, nondrowsy allergy relief. The Ford Windstar advertisement guarantees soccer moms (and dads) that they will be acquiring a vehicle that is safe and capable of protecting their children.

Much advertising is designed to encourage consumers to undertake a trial purchase, often by encouraging brand switching.[30] For example, the advertisement for St. Joseph aspirin in Figure 8.6 on page 240 offers a free package of this product upon redemption of the manufacturer coupon at checkout. Because most advertisements can simply hope to entice, enthuse, and whet one's appetite—or, in general, create expectations—a more compelling mechanism for generating trial purchases is required. And, indeed, this is the role of the *sales promotions* component of marketing communications. An advertisement is merely the vehicle for a sales promotion offer such as that provided by St. Joseph.

Finally, as clearly indicated in Figure 8.3, the purpose of advertising for mature brands is to *reinforce* beliefs about brand benefits. This objective is accomplished when an advertiser sticks with a particular promise and advertises this point repeatedly over time. There is reason to believe that advertising repetition serves to enhance consumer brand awareness and, to a smaller degree, also to enhance brand preference and market share.[31] To prevent the advertising from becoming stale, it is advisable to periodically refresh executions of the same theme.

Is Brand Loyalty a Guaranteed Outcome?

Brand loyalty is the top rung on the hierarchy-of-effects ladder (Figure 8.3). Loyalty is not, however, a guaranteed outcome. Strong brand loyalty does occasionally develop. Some consumers, for example, always purchase the same brand of cola; others always smoke the same brand of cigarette; and there are those who use the same brand of deodorant, toothpaste, or shampoo. In many other instances, however, the consumer never forms a strong preference for any brand. Rather, the consumer continuously shifts his or her allegiance from one brand to the next, constantly trying, trying, and trying but never developing a strong commitment to any particular brand. Consumer behavior can be like dating; some people continue to "play the field" but never become committed to anyone.

Two Expectation-Creating Advertisements

Figure 8.5

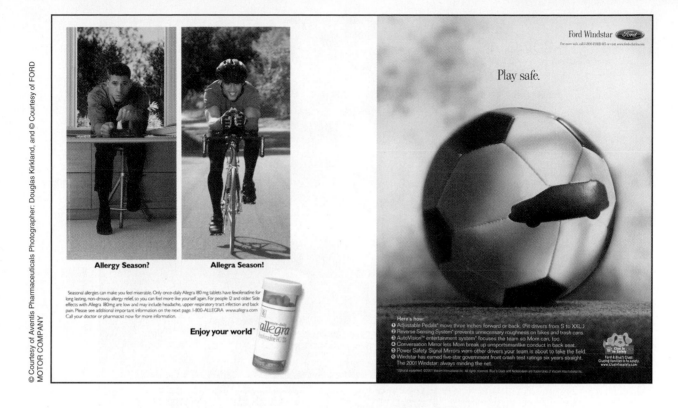

Brand loyalty is a goal that the advertiser aspires to achieve. Obtaining the consumer's loyalty requires (1) providing a brand that meets the consumer's needs, and (2) continuously advertising the brand's merits to reinforce the consumer's brand-related beliefs and attitudes. (See Figure 8.3 as a graphic reminder of this point.) Impressive empirical evidence demonstrates that advertising has the "good" long-run effect of making consumers less price sensitive and more brand loyal, whereas sales promotions have the "bad" long-run effect of reducing loyalty by effectively rewarding consumers for being more price sensitive and less loyal.[32]

Brand marketers and advertisers should do everything economically possible to generate loyal consumers, although most assuredly only a fraction of the target market will become loyalists. Nevertheless, as the 19th-century British poet Robert Browning exclaimed, "A man's reach should exceed his grasp,/Or what's a heaven for?"

Requirements for Setting Good Advertising Objectives

An advertising objective is a specific statement about a planned advertising execution in terms of what that particular advertisement is intended to accomplish. That goal is based on the current, or anticipated, competitive situation in the product category and the problems that the brand must confront or the opportunities that are available.

The specific content of an advertising objective depends entirely on the brand's unique situation. Hence, it is not feasible to discuss objective content without current details (such as market research information) about the advertising context. We can, however, describe the requirements that all good advertising objectives must satisfy. Let us first start by making it clear that not all statements of ad objectives are good. Consider the following examples:

Example A: Brand X's advertising objective this year is to increase sales revenue.

Figure 8.6

A Trial-Inducing Advertisement for St. Joseph Aspirin

Example B: Brand X's advertising objective this year is to increase overall brand awareness from 60 percent to 80 percent.

These extreme examples differ in two important respects. First, example B is obviously more specific. Second, whereas example A deals with a sales objective, example B involves a presales goal. The sections that follow describe the specific criteria that good advertising objectives must satisfy.[33] Figure 8.7 summarizes these criteria.

Objectives Must Include a Precise Statement of Who, What, and When.

Objectives must be stated in precise terms. At a minimum, objectives should specify the target audience (who), indicate the specific goal—such as awareness level—to be accomplished (what), and indicate the relevant time frame (when) in which to achieve the objective. For example, the advertising campaign for the PŪR water filtration system (Figure 8.4) might include objectives such as these: (1) "Within six months from the beginning of the campaign, research should show that 40 percent of all consumers who regularly purchase bottled water are familiar with the PŪR filtering system as an alternative to buying bottled water." (2) "Within six months from the beginning of the campaign, research should show that at least 30 percent of the target audience know that water purified with the PŪR system is good tasting and much cheaper than buying name-brand bottled water." (3) "Within one year from the beginning of the campaign, at least one million PŪR filters should have been sold at retail."

Advertising objectives provide valuable agendas for communication between advertising and marketing decision makers and offer benchmarks against

Criteria That Good Advertising Objectives Must Satisfy

♦ Include a precise statement of who, what, and when
♦ Be quantitative and measurable
♦ Specify the amount of change
♦ Be realistic
♦ Be internally consistent
♦ Be clear and in writing

Figure 8.7

which to compare actual performance. These functions can be satisfied, however, only if objectives are stated precisely.

Example B represents the desired degree of specificity and, as such, would give executives something meaningful to direct their efforts toward as well as a clear-cut benchmark for assessing whether the advertising campaign has accomplished its objectives. Example A, by comparison, is much too general. Suppose sales have actually increased by 2 percent during the course of the ad campaign. Does this mean the campaign was successful since sales have in fact increased? If not, how much increase is necessary for the campaign to be regarded as a success?

Objectives Must Be Quantitative and Measurable. This requirement demands that ad objectives be stated in quantitative terms so as to be measurable, as are the hypothetical objectives given for the PŪR water filter. A nonmeasurable objective for PŪR would be a vague statement such as "Advertising should increase consumers' knowledge of product features." This objective lacks measurability because it fails to specify the product features for which consumers are to possess knowledge.

Objectives Must Specify the Amount of Change. In addition to being quantitative and measurable, objectives must specify the amount of change they are intended to accomplish. Example A (to increase sales) fails to meet this requirement. Example B (to increase awareness from 60 percent to 80 percent) is satisfactory because it clearly specifies that anything less than a 20 percent awareness increase would be considered unsuitable performance.

Objectives Must Be Realistic. Unrealistic objectives are as useless as having no objectives at all. An unrealistic objective is one that cannot be accomplished in the time allotted to the proposed advertising investment. For example, a brand that has achieved only 15 percent consumer awareness during its first year on the market could not realistically expect a small advertising budget to increase the awareness level to, say, 65 percent next year.

Objectives Must Be Internally Consistent. Advertising objectives must be compatible (internally consistent) with objectives set for other components of the MarCom mix. It would be incompatible for a manufacturer to proclaim a 25 percent reduction in sales force size while simultaneously stating that advertising's objective is to increase retail distribution by 20 percent. Without adequate sales force effort, it is doubtful that the retail trade would give a brand more shelf space.

Objectives Must Be Clear and in Writing. For objectives to accomplish their purposes of fostering communication and permitting evaluation, they must be stated clearly and in writing so that they can be disseminated among their users and among those who will be held responsible for seeing that the objectives are accomplished.

Is Sales (Versus Presales) an Appropriate Advertising Objective?

We can broadly distinguish two types of advertising objectives: sales versus presales objectives. (Presales objectives are commonly referred to as *communication objectives*, with the term *communication* derived from efforts to communicate presales outcomes such as increased awareness, enhanced attitudes, etc.) Using sales as the goal of a particular advertising campaign means that the advertising objective literally is to increase sales—stated either in terms of volume (i.e., number of units) or revenue (i.e., number of dollars)—by a specified amount. Advertising practitioners and educators since the early 1960s have traditionally rejected the use of sales as an advertising objective, particularly in the case of advertising by national firms as distinguished from local advertisers.[34] On the other hand, a relatively recent perspective asserts that sales or market share gains should *always* represent the objective of any advertising effort. The following discussions present the traditional view (favoring a presales objective) and then a heretical position (preferring a sales objective) on this matter. In the manner of Hegelian dialectic, we will present the traditional and heretical views as thesis and antithesis, respectively, and follow these with a synthesis of positions.

The Traditional View (Thesis). This point of view asserts that using sales or market share as the objective for a branded product's advertising effort is unsuitable for two major reasons. First, a brand's sales volume during any given period is the consequence of a host of factors in addition to advertising. These include the prevailing economic climate, competitive activity, and all the marketing mix variables used by a brand—its price level, product quality, distribution strategy, personal-selling activity, and so forth. It is virtually impossible, according to the traditional view, to determine precisely the role advertising has had in influencing sales in a given period, because advertising is just one of many possible determinants of sales and profit performance.

A second reason that sales response is claimed to represent an unsuitable objective for advertising effort is that the effect of advertising on sales is typically delayed, or *lagged*. That is, advertising during any given period does not necessarily influences sales in the current period but may influence sales during later periods. This is particularly the case for durable goods. For example, the advertising of a particular automobile model this year may have limited effect on some consumers' purchasing behavior because these consumers are not presently in the market for a new automobile. On the other hand, this year's advertising can influence consumers to select the advertised model next year when they *are* in the market. Thus, advertising may have a decided influence on consumers' brand awareness, product knowledge, expectations, attitudes, and, ultimately, purchase behavior, but this influence may not be evident during the period when advertising's effect on sales is measured.

Advocates of the traditional view thus argue that it is misguided to use sales as the goal for a particular advertising effort. Their view, fundamentally, is that it is idealistic to set sales as the ad objective because the exact impact of advertising on sales cannot be accurately assessed.

A Heretical View (Antithesis). On the other hand, some advertising specialists contend that advertisers should always state objectives in terms of sales or market share gains and that failure to do so is a cop-out. The logic of this nontraditional, or heretical, view is that advertising's purpose is not just to create brand awareness, convey copy points, influence expectations, or enhance attitudes but rather to generate sales. Thus, according to this position it is always possible to measure, if only vaguely and imprecisely, advertising's effect on sales. Presales, or communication, objectives such as increases in brand awareness are claimed to be "precisely wrong," in contrast to sales measures that are asserted to be "vaguely right."[35]

To better understand the logic of this *vaguely right versus precisely wrong* thinking (or VR vs. PW for short), we need to examine closely the constituent oppositional elements: wrong versus right and precise versus vague (see Figure 8.8).

The Logic of Vaguely Right Versus Precisely Wrong Thinking   **Figure 8.8**

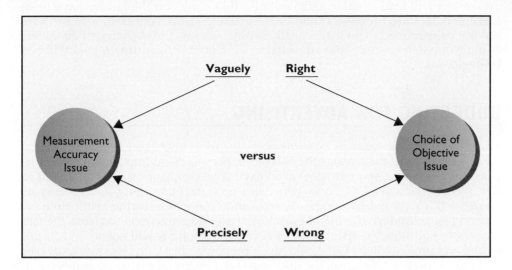

First, the issue of *right* versus *wrong* concerns the advertising objective. The heretical view contends that a sales objective is the right objective and that any other objective is wrong. Second, the issue of *precise* versus *vague* refers to the ability to determine whether advertising has accomplished its objective. With a communication objective such as brand awareness, it can be determined with relative certainty that any registered change in brand awareness since the onset of an ad campaign is due to the advertising effort. Hence, the amount of influence advertising has had on brand awareness can be measured *relatively precisely*. However, as described above, because many factors influence a brand's sales level, the effect that advertising has had on sales can be measured only somewhat crudely, imprecisely, or, in other words, *vaguely*.

Thus, the VR vs. PW perspective makes the very important point that advertisers, and perhaps especially their agencies, might be deceiving themselves into thinking that advertising is effective when it leads to increases in consumer awareness or some other presales objective. Adherents to the vaguely right versus precisely wrong perspective argue that advertising is not accomplishing its job unless sales and market share are increasing. If advertising's sole accomplishment is to create higher awareness levels or bolster brand images, but not to increase sales or market share, then such advertising is ineffective according to this nontraditional viewpoint.

An Accountability Perspective (Synthesis).   Although there is no simple resolution as to whether the traditional or heretical view is more correct, one thing is certain: companies and their chief executives and financial officers are increasingly demanding greater *accountability* from advertising. Increasing pressure has been placed on advertising agencies to develop campaigns that produce bottom-line results—increases in sales, market share, and return on investment (ROI).[36] Although it is difficult to measure the precise effect advertising has on sales, in a climate of increased demands for accountability, it is critical that advertisers and their agencies measure, as best they can, advertising's effect on augmenting a brand's sales, market share, and ROI.

This is not to say that efforts should not also be made to assess whether advertising affects presales goals such as improving brand awareness, driving home copy points, and augmenting attitudes and intentions. The point, instead, is that the measurement of advertising effects should not stop with these measures. Awareness, for example, is a suitable substitute for sales only if there is a direct transformation of increased awareness levels into increased sales. This, unfortunately, is rarely the case. An advertising campaign may increase brand awareness by a substantial amount but have limited impact on sales. As such, brand managers should not permit advertising agencies to mislead them into thinking that an advertising campaign has been successful just because brand awareness has improved. Returning to the hierarchy-of-effects model, increased awareness will lead to sales gains only if other rungs on the ladder have been traversed. In sum, the assessment of advertising effectiveness should include, but not be restricted to, presales goals. Setting sales as the objective of an advertising campaign ensures that advertising's effect on this ultimate goal will not be neglected.

BUDGETING FOR ADVERTISING

The advertising budget is, in many respects, the most important decision made by advertisers. One of the reasons the budgeting decision is so important is that purchasing advertising space or time is an expensive proposition. (As testament to this, please review the *IMC Focus*, which lists costs for purchasing 30-second spots on network TV for two evenings—Sunday and Thursday—during prime time.) A second reason underlying the importance of ad budgeting extends from the fact that if too little money is spent on advertising, sales volume will not achieve its potential and profits will be lost. If too much money is spent, unnecessary expenses will reduce profits. Of course, the dilemma faced by brand managers is determining what spending level is "too little" or how much is "too much." As with most marketing and business decisions, the "devil is in the doing"!

Not only is budgeting one of the most important of all advertising decisions, it also is one of the most complicated decisions. One reason for the complication is that advertising budgets are largely the result of organizational political processes with various organizational units viewing the advertising budget differently.[37]

> *For the accounting department, it's an expense, usually the largest after rent and payroll. For the marketing team, it's the big push that makes the phones ring and it's never big enough. For top management, it's an investment, a speculation formulated to bring in the most revenue for the least amount of cash.*[38]

In general, brand managers are able to obtain larger advertising budgets when the marketing departments in which they function are more powerful relative to other organizational units such as finance and operations.[39]

Another complication in setting the ad budget is the indeterminacy of knowing precisely how effective future advertising might be. To fully appreciate this point we need to introduce the concept of an advertising-sales-response function. The **advertising-sales-response function** is the amount of sales revenue generated at each level of advertising expenditure—that is, X_1 in advertising yields Y_1 in sales, X_2 in advertising produces Y_2 in sales, X_3 in advertising generates Y_3, and so on. Because the advertising-sales-response function is influenced by a multitude of factors (such as quality of advertising execution, intensity of competitive advertising efforts, and customer taste at any point in time) and not solely by the amount of advertising investment, it is difficult to know with any certainty what amount of sales a particular level of advertising expenditure will generate.

Advertising Budgeting in Theory

Aside from practical complications, advertising budgeting in theory is a simple process, provided one accepts the premise that the best (optimal) level of any investment is the level that *maximizes profits*. This assumption leads to a simple rule for establishing advertising budgets: Continue to invest in advertising as long as the marginal revenue from that investment exceeds the marginal cost. As this section describes, this rule extends from the fact that profits are maximized at the point where marginal revenue equals marginal cost.

The reader may recall from basic economics that marginal revenue (MR) and marginal cost (MC) are the changes in total revenue and total cost, respectively, that result from producing and selling an additional item. Thus, the profit-maximization rule is a matter of straightforward economic logic: Profits are maxi-

The Cost of Buying 30-Second Spots During Prime Time on Network TV

The following table details the expense of purchasing a single 30-second spot during prime time on television. Needless to say, it doesn't take that many minutes of airtime to amount to millions of dollars in advertising expenditures.

Program	Network, Time, and Day	Cost per 30-Second Commercial
Wonderful World of Disney	ABC, 7:00 Sunday	$117,200
Alias	ABC, 9:00 Sunday	$173,800
The Practice	ABC, 10:00 Sunday	$263,800
60 Minutes	CBS, 7:00 Sunday	$118,600
The Education of Max Bickford	CBS, 8:00 Sunday	$148,400
CBS Sunday Movie	CBS, 9:00 Sunday	$105,400
Dateline	NBC, 7:00 Sunday	$ 65,200
The Weakest Link	NBC, 8:00 Sunday	$118,200
Law & Order	NBC, 9:00 Sunday	$167,600
UC: Undercover	NBC, 10:00 Sunday	$104,400
Whose Line	ABC, 8:00 Thursday	$ 93,400
Who Wants to Be a Millionaire?	ABC, 9:00 Thursday	$107,800
PrimeTime Thursday	ABC, 10:00 Thursday	$102,800
Survivor	CBS, 8:00 Thursday	$445,000
CSI: Crime Scene Investigation	CBS, 9:00 Thursday	$242,400
The Agency	CBS, 10:00 Thursday	$111,400
Friends	NBC, 8:00 Thursday	$353,600
Inside Schwartz	NBC, 8:30 Thursday	$238,800
Will & Grace	NBC, 9:00 Thursday	$321,200
Just Shoot Me	NBC, 9:30 Thursday	$286,400
ER	NBC, 10:00 Thursday	$425,400

Source: "Fall 2001 Network TV Price Estimates," *Advertising Age*, September 24, 2001, 70.

mized at the point where MR = MC. At any quantity level below this point (where MR > MC), profits are not maximized because at a higher level of output more profit can be earned. Similarly, at any level above this point (where MC > MR), there is a marginal loss.[40]

In practical terms, this means that advertisers should continue to increase their advertising investments as long as it is profitable to do so. For example, suppose a company is currently spending $10 million advertising a particular brand and is considering the investment of another $2 million. Should the additional expenditure be made? The answer is simple: only if the additional advertising generates more than $2 million in additional revenue for the brand. Now say the same company is contemplating a further advertising expenditure of $1 million for this brand later in the same advertising period. Again, the company should go ahead with the advertising if it is confident that the $1 million ad expenditure will yield more than $1 million in additional revenue.

It is evident from this simple exercise that setting the advertising budget is a matter of answering a series of *if-then* questions—*if* $X are invested in advertising, *then* what amount of revenue will be generated? Because budgets are set before the fact, this requires that the if-then questions be answered in advance. To employ the profit-maximization rule for budget setting, the advertising decision maker must know the advertising-sales-response function for every brand for which a budgeting decision will be made. Because such knowledge is rarely available, theoretical (profit maximization) budget setting is an ideal that is generally nonoperational in the real world of advertising decision making.

Budgeting Considerations in Practice

Advertising decision makers must consider three factors when establishing advertising budgets: (1) the ad objective, (2) competitive advertising activity, and (3) the amount of funds available for advertising. It should be obvious that these considerations are not independent of one another. For example, the specific objective for a particular advertising campaign might hinge on competitive advertising activity.

1. What Is the Ad Objective?   A key consideration underlying ad budget determination is the *objective* that advertising is designed to accomplish. That is, the level of the budget should follow from the specific objective established for advertising; more ambitious objectives require larger advertising budgets. If advertising is intended to increase a brand's market share, then a larger budget is needed than would be required if the task were simply to maintain consumer awareness of the brand name.

2. How Much Are Competitors Spending?   *Competitive advertising activity* is another important consideration in setting ad budgets. In highly competitive markets, more must be invested in advertising to increase or at least maintain market position. For example, the 2000 U.S. advertising expenditures for the top six brands in the mobile phone category were as follows: Samsung, $57 million; Nokia, $48.7 million; Motorola, $21 million; Ericsson, $14.6 million; Kyocera/Qualcomm, $800,000; and Audiovox, $100,000.[41] The total amount spent on advertising by these six brands, which collectively commanded 90 percent market share in 2000, was approximately $142.2 million. Taking each company's advertising expenditure as a percentage of this total yields what is called **share of voice,** or **SOV.** Thus, the SOVs for these six brands are, in descending order: Samsung, 40.1 percent; Nokia, 34.2 percent; Motorola, 14.8 percent; Ericsson, 10.3 percent; and Audiovox and Kyocera/Qualcomm, less than 1 percent each.

SOV and **share of market** (**SOM**) generally are correlated: Brands having larger SOVs also generally realize larger SOMs. For example, the SOMs and SOVs for the top 10 fast-food burger brands in the United States for 2000 are reported in Table 8.2. The correlation between the shares of market and shares of voice for these brands is apparent. The relationship between the SOM and SOV is two way: A brand's SOV is partially responsible for its SOM level. At the same time, brands with larger SOMs can afford to achieve higher SOVs, whereas smaller-share brands often are limited to relatively small SOVs in comparison to their better-off competitors.

To further illustrate these points, Table 8.3 presents SOM and SOV data for the top 10 U.S. beer brands in a recent year. It first will be noted that the correspondence between SOM and SOV is far from perfect. The four brands with double-digit SOMs (Budweiser, Bud Light, Miller Lite, and Coors Light) also have double-digit SOVs. However, Budweiser's and Bud Light's SOVs are disproportionately lower than their SOMs, whereas Miller Lite's and Coors Light's SOVs are proportionately higher. The number three and four brands must spend proportionately more to maintain or grow market share, whereas the leading two brands from Anheuser-Busch (Bud and Bud Light) are able to spend proportionately less due to their entrenched positions and high brand equities. Nonetheless, sustained advertising effort at the current levels by Miller Lite and Coors Light would assuredly steal share eventually from Budweiser and Bud Light if these brands continued to spend at the proportionately low levels shown in Table 8.3. The bottom six brands in Table 8.3 are all relatively small market, or *niche*, brands that spend relatively little on advertising to maintain their relatively small market shares. Busch, Natural Light, and Busch Light are products of the Anheuser-Busch brewery. Corporate officials apparently think these brands' market shares can be maintained (but certainly not grown) by virtually renouncing the need for any advertising. It would seem that Anheuser-Busch is willing to retain these brands as niche players while simultaneously committing fully to Bud Light and Budweiser with high ad expenditures and large SOVs. Among the bottom tier of the top 10 beers, only Miller High Life, with a 12.6 SOV, appears poised to steal some market share, perhaps from Budweiser.

The SOM-SOV relationship is a jousting match of sorts between competitors. If large-market-share brands reduce their SOVs to levels that are too low, they are

Shares of Market and Voice for Top 10 Fast Food Burger Brands, 2000   Table 8.2

Brand	Share of Market	Ad Expenditures (in millions)*	Share of Voice
McDonald's	43.1	$664.8	44.0
Burger King	21.1	385.3	25.5
Wendy's	12.7	241.8	16.0
Hardee's	5.3	36.3	2.4
Jack in the Box	4.4	70.6	4.7
Sonic Drive-Ins	4.0	41.9	2.8
Carl's Jr.	2.1	41.6	2.7
Whataburger	1.4	10.4	0.7
Steak 'n Shake	1.1	8.3	0.5
White Castle	1.1	10.8	0.7
Total Top 10	96.3%	$1,512.1	100.0%

*Advertising expenditures in 11 measured media.

Source: "Leading National Advertisers," *Advertising Age*, September 24, 2001, S8. © 2001 by Crain Communications, Inc. Reprinted by permission.

Shares of Market and Voice for Top 10 Beer Brands   Table 8.3

Brand	Total Sales ($Billions)	Share of Market	Media Expenditures ($ Millions)	Share of Voice
1. Budweiser	$ 35.6	29.2%	$ 98.4	20.4%
2. Bud Light	22.8	18.7	55.7	11.5
3. Miller Lite	16.2	13.3	149.0	30.8
4. Coors Light	13.7	11.2	91.9	19.0
5. Busch	7.9	6.5	2.4	0.5
6. Natural Light	7.1	5.8	0.1	0.0
7. Miller Genuine Draft	5.5	4.5	21.5	4.4
8. Miller High Life	4.7	3.9	61.1	12.6
9. Busch Light	4.5	3.7	0.0	0.0
10. Milwaukee's Best	3.9	3.2	3.1	0.6
TOTAL	$121.9	100.0%	$483.2	100.0%

Source: Gerry Khemmouch, "Pockets of Success Tempered by Concern," *Brandweek*, June 15, 1998, S28. © 1998 VNU Business Media, Inc.

vulnerable to losing market share to aggressive competitors. On the other hand, if market followers (such as Miller Lite and Coors Light in Table 8.3) become too aggressive, the leading brands are forced to increase their advertising expenditures to offset the competitive challenge. Figure 8.9 identifies four general situations that compare the advertiser's share of market ("your" share) and the competitor's share of voice.[42] Implications for ad budgeting are now discussed as follows:

- *Cell A:* In this situation, your SOM is relatively low and your competitor's SOV is relatively high. Miller Genuine Draft in Table 8.3 compared with Budweiser exemplifies this situation. The recommendation in such a situation is to *decrease* ad expenditures and find a niche that can be defended against other competitors.

Figure 8.9

The SOV Effect and Ad Spending

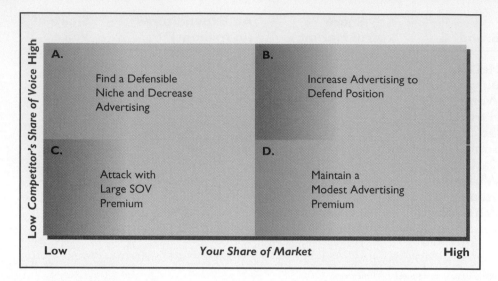

- *Cell B:* Your SOM in this situation is relatively high and your competitor has a high SOV. This characterizes Bud Light in Table 8.3 vis-à-vis Miller Lite and Coors Light. Bud Light probably should *increase* its advertising expenditures to defend its present market share position. Failure to do so likely would result in a share loss to these aggressive competitors.
- *Cell C:* In this situation your SOM is low and your competitor's SOV is also low. (There is no close parallel to this situation in Table 8.3.) The general recommendation in such a situation is to aggressively attack the competitor whose SOV is low with a large SOV *premium* vis-à-vis that competitor. In other words, this is a good opportunity to wrest market share from a moribund or complacent competitor.
- *Cell D:* In this situation you have the attractive position of holding a high market share, but your competitor is nonaggressive and has a relatively low SOV. Hence, it is possible for you to retain your present large share by *maintaining only a modest advertising spending premium* over your competitor.

These simply are guidelines for determining a brand's advertising budget rather than hard-and-fast rules. The general point to be stressed is that advertising budgets must be set with knowledge of what competitors are doing. This is because the opportunity for growth in market share or the challenge to maintain an existing share position depends in large part on the quality and effectiveness of competitive advertising efforts. Moreover, brand marketers should generally set advertising budgets on a market-by-market basis, rather than nationally, because the competitive warfare actually takes place in the individual markets.[43]

It is absolutely essential that advertising budgets be set with an eye to the actions of competitors. This is especially important in view of the fact that a brand's advertising must compete for the consumer's recall with the advertising from competitive brands, a situation of potential competitive interference. If "your" brand were the only one advertising in a particular product category, it probably could get by with a substantially smaller ad budget than what is necessitated when competitors also are aggressively advertising their brands. The mere fact of increasing advertising expenditures is *not* guaranteed to have a substantial impact on augmenting a brand's sales volume.[44]

There are reasons to expect that *familiar brands* are less susceptible to the interference, or clutter, from competitive advertising. Unfamiliar brands that compete in a world of advertising clutter are, in effect, at a competitive disadvantage in conveying their points of uniqueness vis-à-vis established brands.[45] Established brands' market shares tend to exceed their advertising shares of voice.[46] New brands need to avoid heavily cluttered, traditional media and perhaps turn to alternative advertising media—such as by using buzz generation methods (as discussed in Chapter 6) or event marketing (discussed in Chapter 19).

Overcoming competitive interference is not just a matter of spending more but rather one of *spending more wisely*. Researchers have offered a psychological theory called the *encoding variability hypothesis* to explain how advertisers can be smarter spenders.[47] (The term *encoding* refers to transferring information into memory.) The **encoding variability hypothesis,** in its barest details, contends that people's memories for information are enhanced when multiple *pathways*, or connections, are created between the object to be remembered and the information about the object that is to be remembered.

In the case of advertising, the brand represents the object to be remembered, and the brand's attributes and benefits designate the object's information. Advertising can create multiple pathways and thus enhance memory for the advertised information by varying (recall the name *encoding variability hypothesis*) at least two aspects of the advertising execution: (1) the advertising *message* itself and (2) the advertising medium in which the message is placed. That is, altering how the ad is presented (its message) and where the ad is placed (its medium) should enhance memory for the advertised information and hence mitigate the effects of competitive interference. This results because multiple pathways are created when the same brand is advertised with varied messages or in multiple media. In other words, when Brand X is advertised with a single message in a single medium, just a single pathway is established in memory. When, however, Brand X is advertised in two media, there are two potential pathways established in memory whereby consumers can retrieve information about Brand X. Increasing both the number of message executions and the number of media to convey these messages serves to increase the number of pathway permutations. Increased as well is the probability that consumers will be able to retrieve key information about Brand X when they are in the market for the product category in which that brand competes.

3. How Much Money Is Available?   A third major consideration underlying ad budget determination is the *amount of funds available* for advertising. In the final analysis, advertising budgeting is determined in large part by decision makers' perceptions of how much they can afford to spend on advertising. Because top management often views advertising budgets with suspicion and considers them to be inflated, brand managers face the challenge of convincing upper management that proposed budgets are indeed affordable. This is no easy task, especially when hard data on advertising effectiveness are unavailable. It is for this reason that advertising budget setters have tended to use simple decision rules for making budgeting decisions.

Practical Budgeting Methods

In view of the difficulty of accurately predicting sales response to advertising, companies ordinarily set budgets by using judgment, applying experience with analogous situations, and using rules of thumb, or *heuristics*, as guides to setting budgets.[48] Although criticized because they do not provide a basis for advertising budget setting that is directly related to the profitability of the advertised brand, these heuristics continue to be widely used.[49] The practical budgeting methods most frequently used by both industrial advertisers and consumer goods advertisers in the United States and Europe are the percentage-of-sales, objective-and-task, competitive parity, and affordability methods.[50]

Percentage-of-Sales Budgeting.   In using the **percentage-of-sales method,** a company sets a brand's advertising budget by simply establishing the budget as a fixed percentage of *past* (e.g., last year's) or *anticipated* (e.g., next year's) sales volume. Assume, for example, that a company allocates 3 percent of anticipated sales to advertising and that the company projects next year's sales for a particular brand to be $100,000,000. Its advertising budget would be set at $3,000,000.

A survey of the top 100 consumer goods advertisers in the United States found that slightly more than 50 percent employ the percentage-of-anticipated-sales method and 20 percent use the percentage-of-past-sales method.[51] This is to be expected, since budget setting should logically correspond to what a company expects to do in the future rather than being based on what it accomplished in the past.

What percentage of sales revenue do most companies devote to advertising? Actually, the percentage is highly variable. For example, based on the 200 industries that spent the largest percentages of sales on advertising in 2001, the highest percentage of sales devoted to advertising for any of the 200 industries was the miscellaneous publishing industry, with average advertising expenditures of 46.3 percent of sales. Some other industries with double-digit advertising-to-sales ratios were sugar and confectionary products (18.1 percent); cleaners and polish preparations (15.7 percent); wine and brandy (15.6 percent); distilled and blended liquor (15.1 percent); watches, clocks, and parts (15.1 percent); agricultural chemicals (13.7 percent); dolls and stuffed tools (12.9 percent); amusement parks (12.8 percent); and perfume, cosmetics, and toilet preparations (11.2 percent). Most industries average less than 5 percent advertising-to-sales ratios. These, of course, are industry averages, and advertising-to-sales ratios vary considerably across firms within each industry.[52]

The percentage-of-sales method is frequently criticized as being illogical. Criticism is based on the argument that the method reverses the logical relationship between sales and advertising. That is, the true ordering between advertising and sales is that advertising causes sales, or stated alternatively, sales are a function of advertising:

$$Sales = f\ (Advertising)$$

Contrary to this logical relation, implementing the percentage-of-sales method amounts to reversing the causal order by setting advertising as a function of sales:

$$Advertising = f\ (Sales)$$

By this logic and method, when sales are anticipated to increase, the advertising budget also increases; when sales are expected to decline, the budget is reduced. The illogic of the percentage-of-sales method is demonstrated by the fact that this method could lead to potentially erroneous budgeting decisions such as cutting the advertising budget when a brand's sales are expected to decline. For example, many firms reduce advertising budgets during economic downswings. However, rather than decreasing the amount of advertising, it may be wiser during these times to increase advertising to prevent further sales erosion. When used blindly, the percentage-of-sales method is little more than an arbitrary and simplistic rule of thumb substituted for what needs to be a sound business judgment. Used without justification, this budgeting method is another application of precisely wrong (versus vaguely right) decision making.[53]

In practice, most sophisticated marketers do *not* use percentage of sales as the sole budgeting method. Instead, they employ the method as an initial pass, or first cut, for determining the budget and then alter the budget forecast depending on the objectives and tasks that need to be accomplished.

The Objective-and-Task Method. The **objective-and-task method** is generally regarded as the most sensible and defendable advertising budgeting method. In using this method, advertising decision makers must specify what role they expect advertising to play for a brand and then set the budget accordingly. The role is typically identified in terms of a communication objective (e.g., increase brand awareness by 20 percent) but could be stated in terms of expected sales volume or market share (e.g., increase market share from 15 to 20 percent).

The objective-and-task method is the advertising budget procedure used most frequently by both consumer and industrial companies. Surveys have shown that over 60 percent of consumer goods companies and 70 percent of industrial goods companies use this budgeting method.[54] The following steps are involved when applying the objective-and-task method:[55]

1. The first step is to establish specific *marketing objectives* that need to be accomplished, such as sales volume, market share, and profit contribution.

    Consider the marketing and advertising challenge in the United States that faced Volkswagen several years ago. Although this once-vaunted automobile company had achieved huge success in the 1960s and 1970s with its VW "beetle," by the mid-1990s Volkswagen was confronted with what perhaps was its final opportunity to recapture the American consumer, who had turned to other imports and domestic models because VW had not kept up with what Americans wanted.[56] Sales of its two leading brands, the Golf and Jetta, had dropped by about 50 percent each compared with sales in prior years. Volkswagen's marketing objective (not to be confused with its specific advertising objective, which is discussed next) was, therefore, to substantially increase sales of the Golf and Jetta models and its overall share of the U.S. automobile market—from a low of only about 21,000 Golfs and Jettas to a goal of selling 250,000 Volkswagen models in the near future.

2. The second step in implementing the objective-and-task method is to assess the *communication functions* that must be performed to accomplish the overall marketing objectives.

    Volkswagen had to accomplish two communication functions to realize its rather audacious marketing objective: First, it had to substantially increase U.S. consumers' awareness of the Golf and Jetta brand names, and, second, it had to establish an image for Volkswagen as a company that offers "honest, reliable, and affordable cars."[57] In summary, Volkswagen had to enhance brand equities for these brands.

3. The third step is to determine *advertising's role in the total communication mix* in performing the functions established in step 2.

    Given the nature of its products and communication objectives, advertising was a crucial component in Volkswagen's mix.

4. The fourth step is to establish specific advertising goals in terms of the levels of *measurable communication response* required to achieve marketing objectives.

    Volkswagen might have established goals such as (1) increase awareness of the Jetta model from the present level of, say, 45 percent of the target market to 75 percent and (2) expand the percentage of survey respondents who rate Volkswagen products as high quality from, say, 15 percent to 40 percent. Both objectives are specific, quantitative, and measurable.

5. The final step is to establish the *budget* based on estimates of expenditures required to accomplish the advertising goals.

    In view of Volkswagen's challenging objectives, the decision was made to invest approximately $100 million in an advertising campaign in hopes of gaining higher brand awareness levels, enhancing the company's image among American consumers, and, ultimately, substantially increasing sales of VW products. The CEO of Volkswagen's advertising agency explained that the advertising challenge was "to come up with hard, clear, product-focused ads that give car buyers the kind of information they need to make an intelligent choice."[58]

The Competitive Parity Method.   The **competitive parity method** (also called the **match-competitors method**) sets the ad budget by basically following what competitors are doing. A company may learn that its primary competitor is devoting 10 percent of sales to advertising and then decide next year to spend the same percentage advertising its own brand. On the other hand, armed with information on competitors' spending, a company may decide not merely to match but to exceed its expenditures. Consider the case of Minnesota Mining & Manufacturing (3M) when it introduced its new Scotch Brite Never Rust steel wool soap pads to compete against the entrenched S.O.S. and Brillo brands. Based on research that revealed that consumers despised rusty soap pads, 3M introduced its Never

Rust brand as the first major innovation in the soap-impregnated steel wool pad category since Brillo entered the market in 1917. Knowing it had a super product, 3M greatly outspent its rival brands during the product's introductory year by investing an estimated $30 million on advertising in a category that totaled just $120 million in sales potential. The Scotch Brite Never Rust brand quickly acquired a major market share against its competitors who, according to one critic, were essentially doing nothing.[59]

Affordability Method.   In the **affordability method,** only the funds that remain after budgeting for everything else are spent on advertising. Only the most unsophisticated and impoverished firms would be expected to budget in this manner. This method and the competitive parity heuristic are used most frequently by smaller firms that tend to follow industry leaders. However, affordability and competitive considerations influence the budgeting decisions of all companies.

In the final analysis, most advertising budget setters combine two or more methods rather than depending exclusively on any one heuristic. For example, an advertiser may have a fixed percentage-of-sales figure in mind when starting the budgeting process but subsequently adjust this figure in light of anticipated competitive activity, funds availability, and other considerations.

Companies often find it necessary to adjust their budgets during the course of a year in line with sales performance. Many advertisers operate under the belief that they should "shoot when the ducks are flying." In other words, advertisers spend most heavily during periods when products are hot and cut spending when funds are short; however, they should always maintain a decent ad budget even when sales take a downturn.

SUMMARY

This chapter offered an introduction to advertising, an overview of the advertising management process, and detailed discussions of advertising objective setting and budgeting. Advertising is shown to perform five major functions: informing, persuading, reminding, adding value, and assisting other company efforts.

Advertising objective setting depends on the pattern of consumer behavior and information that is involved in the particular product category. Toward this end, an introductory section presented a hierarchy-of-effect model of consumers' responses to advertisements and discussed the implications for setting advertising objectives. Requirements for developing effective advertising objectives also were discussed. A final section described the arguments both promoting and opposing the use of sales volume as the basis for setting advertising objectives.

The chapter concluded with an explanation of the advertising budgeting process. The budgeting decision is one of the most important advertising decisions and also one of the most difficult. The complication arises with the difficulty of determining the sales response to advertising. In theory, budget setting is a simple matter, but the theoretical requirements are generally unattainable in practice. For this reason, advertising practitioners use various rules of thumb (heuristics) to assist them in arriving at satisfactory, if not optimal, budgeting decisions. Percentage-of-sales budgeting and objective-and-task methods are the dominant budgeting heuristics.

DISCUSSION QUESTIONS

1. Of the five advertising functions described in the chapter, which is the most important?
2. Advertising is said to be an "investment in the brand equity bank," but only if the advertising is "strong." Explain.
3. Provide two examples of usage expansion advertising other than those illustrated in the chapter.
4. Using equations 8.1 through 8.3, provide an argument in favor of investing more money in advertising to increase profits.
5. In context of the discussion of price and advertising elasticities, four situations were presented by comparing whether price or advertising elasticity is stronger. Situation 2 was characterized as "build image via increased advertising." In your own terms, explain why it is more profitable to spend relatively more on advertising increases than price discounts.
6. Apply Figure 8.3 (a Hierarchy-of-Effects Model of How Advertising Works) to explain the evolution of a relationship between two people, beginning with dating and culminating in a wedding.
7. Now do the same thing as in question 6, using a relatively obscure brand as the basis for your application of Figure 8.3.
8. What reasons can you give for certain industries investing considerably larger proportions of their sales in advertising than other industries?
9. Why is it so difficult to measure precisely the specific impact that advertising has on sales?
10. Compare the difference between precisely wrong and vaguely right advertising objectives. Give an example of each.
11. Some critics contend that the use of the percentage-of-sales budgeting technique is illogical. Explain.
12. Explain how an advertising budget setter could use two or more budgeting heuristics in conjunction with one another?
13. How do local businesses in your college or university community identify their advertising objectives? Interview three or four local businesses, and investigate whether they set formal ad objectives and, if not, whether they have some rather clear-cut, though implicit, objectives in mind.
14. While interviewing the same businesses from the previous question, investigate their advertising budgeting practices. Determine whether they establish formal ad budgets, and identify the specific budgeting methods they use.
15. Construct a picture to represent your understanding of how the encoding variability hypothesis applies to an advertising context.

ENDNOTES

1. This estimate is based on famed advertising analyst Robert J. Coen's claim that advertising in 2001 would total $249.8 billion, representing an increase of 2.5 percent over 2000 ad expenditures. I deflated the 2000 level of ad expenditures by 5 percent on the assumption of a decline in advertising rather than an increase. For estimates, see Suzanne Vranica, "Industry Forecaster Cuts Projections for U.S. Ad-Spending Growth to 2.5%," *Wall Street Journal Interactive Edition*, June 15, 2001 (http://interactive.wsj.com/). Also, see Laurel Wentz and Mercedes M. Card-ona, "Ad Fall May Be Worst Since Depression," *Advertising Age*, September 3, 2001, 24.
2. "100 Leaders by U.S. Advertising Spending," *Advertising Age*, September 24, 2001, s2.
3. "Uncle Sam, the Advertiser," *Advertising Age*, November 17, 1997, 83.
4. Wentz and Cardona, "Ad Fall May Be Worst Since Depression," 1, 24.
5. Jennifer Lawrence, "P&G's Artzt on Ads: Crucial Investment," *Advertising Age*, October 28, 1991, 1, 53.
6. Bernard Ryan, Jr., *It Works! How Investment Spending in Advertising Pays Off* (New York: American Association of Advertising Agencies, 1991), 11.
7. Raj Sethuraman and Gerard J. Tellis, "An Analysis of the Tradeoff Between Advertising and Price Discounting," *Journal of Marketing Research* 28 (May 1991), 160–174.
8. This discussion is adapted from ibid., especially Figure 1, p. 163, and the surrounding discussion.
9. See ibid., p. 164.

10. David A. Aaker, *Managing Brand Equity* (New York: Free Press, 1991); Kevin Lane Keller, "Conceptualizing, Measuring, and Managing Customer-Based Brand Equity," *Journal of Marketing* 57 (January 1993), 1–22.

11. Willam Boulding, Eunkyu Lee, and Richard Staelin, "Mastering the Mix: Do Advertising, Promotion, and Sales Force Activities Lead to Differentiation?" *Journal of Marketing Research* 31 (May 1994), 159–172.

12. John Sinisi, "Love: EDLP Equals Ad Investment," *Brandweek*, November 16, 1992, 2.

13. These functions are similar to those identified by the noted advertising pioneer James Webb Young. For example, "What Is Advertising, What Does It Do," *Advertising Age*, November 21, 1973, 12.

14. Giles D'Souza and Ram C. Rao, "Can Repeating an Advertisement More Frequently than the Competition Affect Brand Preference in a Mature Market?" *Journal of Marketing* 59 (April 1995), 32–42. See also A. S. C. Ehrenberg, "Repetitive Advertising and the Consumer," *Journal of Advertising Research* (April 1974), 24–34; Stephen Miller and Lisette Berry, "Brand Salience Versus Brand Image: Two Theories of Advertising Effectiveness," *Journal of Advertising Research* 28 (September/October 1998), 77–82.

15. The term *usage expansion advertising* and the examples are from Brian Wansink and Michael L. Ray, "Advertising Strategies to Increase Usage Frequency," *Journal of Marketing* 60 (January 1996), 31–46.

16. Sharon T. Klahr, "Gillette Puts $300 Mil Behind Its Mach3 Shaver," *Advertising Age*, April 20, 1998, 6.

17. Karen A. Machleit, Chris T. Allen, and Thomas J. Madden, "The Mature Brand and Brand Interest: An Alternative Consequence of Ad-Evoked Affect," *Journal of Marketing* 57 (October 1993), 72–82.

18. John Deighton, Caroline M. Henderson, and Scott A. Neslin, "The Effects of Advertising on Brand Switching and Repeat Purchasing," *Journal of Marketing Research* 31 (February 1994), 28–43.

19. *The Value Side of Productivity: A Key to Competitive Survival in the 1990s* (New York: American Association of Advertising Agencies, 1989), 12.

20. Sridhar Moorthy and Hao Zhao, "Advertising Spending and Perceived Quality," *Marketing Letters* 11 (August 2000), 221–234.

21. *The Value Side of Productivity*, 13–15. See also, Larry Light and Richard Morgan, *The Fourth Wave: Brand Loyalty Marketing* (New York: Coalition for Brand Equity, American Association of *Advertising Agencies*, 1994), 25.

22. The synergism between advertising and personal selling does not always equate to a one-way flow from advertising to personal selling. In fact, one study has demonstrated a reverse situation, in which personal sales calls sometimes pave the way for advertising. See William R. Swinyard and Michael L. Ray, "Advertising-Selling Interactions: An Attribution Theory Experiment," *Journal of Marketing Research* 14 (November 1977), 509–516.

23. Albert C. Bemmaor and Dominique Mouchoux, "Measuring the Short-Term Effect of In-Store Promotion and Retail Advertising on Brand Sales: A Factorial Experiment," *Journal of Marketing Research* 28 (May 1991), 202–214.

24. Charles H. Patti and Charles F. Frazer, Advertising: *A Decision-Making Approach* (Hinsdale, Ill.: Dryden Press, 1988), 236.

25. Ibid., 237–239.

26. For thorough discussions, see Thomas E. Barry, "The Development of the Hierarchy of Effects: An Historical Perspective," *Current Issues and Research in Advertising*, vol. 10, ed. James H. Leigh and Claude R. Martin, Jr. (Ann Arbor: Division of Research, Graduate School of Business Administration, University of Michigan, 1987), 251–296; Ivan L. Preston, "The Association Model of the Advertising Communication Process," 11, no. 2 (1982), 3–15; and Ivan L. Preston and Esther Thorson, "Challenges to the Use of Hierarchy Models in Predicting Advertising Effectiveness," in *Proceedings of the 1983 Convention of the American Academy of Advertising*, ed. Donald W. Jugenheimer (Lawrence, Kans.: American Academy of Advertising, 1983).

27. Adapted from Light and Morgan, *The Fourth Wave*, 21.

28. For further reading on the nature and role of brand loyalty, see Richard L. Oliver, "Whence Consumer Loyalty," *Journal of Marketing* 63 (Special Issue 1999), 33–44; Arjun Chaudhuri and Morris B. Holbrook, "The Chain of Effects from Brand Trust and Brand Affect to Brand Performance: The Role of Brand Loyalty," *Journal of Marketing* 65 (April 2001), 81–93.

29. Prakash Nedungadi, "Recall and Consumer Consideration Sets: Influencing Choice without Altering Brand Evaluations," *Journal of Consumer Research* 17 (December 1990), 263–276.

30. For further discussion of advertising's role in encouraging brand switching, see Deighton, Henderson, and Neslin, "The Effects of Advertising on Brand Switching and Repeat Purchasing."

31. D'Souza and Rao, "Can Repeating an Advertisement More Frequently than the Competition Affect Brand Preference in a Mature Market?"

32. Carl F. Mela, Sunil Gupta, and Donald R. Lehmann, "The Long-Term Impact of Promotion and Advertising on Con-

sumer Brand Choice," *Journal of Marketing Research* 34 (May 1997), 248–261.

33. The following discussion is influenced by the classic work on advertising planning and goal setting by Russell Colley. His writing, which came to be known as the DAGMAR approach, set a standard for advertising objective setting. See Colley, *Defining Advertising Goals for Measured Advertising Results.*

34. The traditional view was most compellingly articulated by Russell H. Colley in Defining *Advertising Goals for Measured Advertising Results.*

35. Leonard M. Lodish, *The Advertising and Promotion Challenge: Vaguely Right or Precisely Wrong?* (New York: Oxford University Press, 1986), chap. 5.

36. See Kevin J. Clancy and Peter C. Krieg, *Counter-Intuitive Marketing: Achieve Great Results Using Uncommon Sense* (New York: Free Press, 2000), chap. 18; Kevin J. Clancy, "The Coming Revolution in Advertising: Ten Developments Which Will Separate Winners from Losers," *Journal of Advertising Research* (February/March 1990), 47–52. See also Jon Berry, "Repositioning? Forget It. Sales Are All That Counts," *Brandweek*, August 23, 1993, 13; Gary Stibel, "Investing in Advertising: The Proof Is in the Profit," *Brandweek*, November 8, 1993, 16.

37. Nigel Piercy, "Advertising Budgeting: Process and Structure as Explanatory Variables," *Journal of Advertising* 16, no. 2 (1987), 34–40.

38. Kathleen Weeks, "How to Plan Your Ad Budget," *Sales and Marketing Management*, September 1987, 113.

39. Piercy, "Advertising Budgeting."

40. For further discussion, review any standard economics text. For example, N. Gregory Mankiw, *Principles of Economics* (Fort Worth, TX: Dryden Press, Harcourt Brace College Publishers, 1998).

41. "100 Leaders by U.S. Advertising Spending," s10.

42. Adapted from James C. Schroer, "Ad Spending: Growing Market Share," *Harvard Business Review* 68 (January/February 1990), 48. See also John Philip Jones, "Ad Spending: Maintaining Market Share," *Harvard Business Review* 68 (January/February 1990), 38–42.

43. Ibid.

44. Leonard M. Lodish, Magid Abraham, Stuart Kalmenson, Jeanne Livelsberger, Beth Lubetkin, Bruce Richardson, and Mary Ellen Stevens, "How T.V. Advertising Works: A Meta-Analysis of 389 Real World Split Cable T.V. Advertising Experiments," *Journal of Marketing Research* 32 (May 1995), 125–139.

45. Robert J. Kent and Chris T. Allen, "Competitive Interference Effects in Consumer Memory for Advertising: The Role of Brand Familiarity," *Journal of Marketing* 58 (July 1994), 97–105; Robert J. Kent,

"How Ad Claim Similarity and Target Brand Familiarity Moderate Competitive Interference Effects in Memory for Advertising," *Journal of Marketing Communications* 3 (December 1997), 231–242.

46. Jones, "Ad Spending: Maintaining Market Share."

47. H. Rao Unnava and Deepak Sirdeshmukh, "Reducing Competitive Ad Interference," *Journal of Marketing Research* 31 (August 1994), 403–411.

48. Gary L. Lilien, Alvin J. Silk, Jean-Marie Choffray, and Murlidhar Rao, "Industrial Advertising Effects and Budgeting Practices," *Journal of Marketing* 40 (January 1976), 21.

49. Fred S. Zufryden, "How Much Should Be Spent for Advertising a Brand?" *Journal of Advertising Research* (April/May 1989), 24–34.

50. The extensive use of the percentage-of-sales and objective-and-task methods in an industrial context has been documented by Lilien et al., "Industrial Advertising Effects," while support in a consumer context is provided by Kent M. Lancaster and Judith A. Stern, "Computer-Based Advertising Budgeting Practices of Leading U.S. Consumer Advertisers," *Journal of Advertising* 12, no. 4 (1983), 6. A thorough review of the history of advertising budgeting research is provided in J. Enrique Bigne, "Advertising Budget Practices: A Review," *Journal of Current Issues and Research in Advertising* 17 (fall 1995), 17–32.

51. Lancaster and Stern, "Computer-Based Advertising."

52. All ratios are based on "2001 Advertising-to-Sales Ratios for the 200 Largest Ad Spending Industries," *Advertising Age*, September 17, 2001, 20.

53. See Lodish, *The Advertising and Promotion Challenge*, chap. 6.

54. Charles H. Patti and Vincent J. Blasko, "Budgeting Practices of Big Advertisers," *Journal of Advertising Research* 21 (December 1981), 23–29; Vincent J. Blasko and Charles H. Patti, "The Advertising Budgeting Practices of Industrial Marketers," *Journal of Marketing* 48 (fall 1984), 104–110. See also C. L. Hung and Douglas C. West, "Advertising Budgeting Methods in Canada, the UK and the USA," *International Journal of Advertising* 10, no. 3 (1991), 239–250.

55. Adapted from Lilien et al., "Industrial Advertising and Budgeting," 23.

56. This description is based on Kevin Goldman, "Volkswagen Has a Lot Riding on New Ads," *The Wall Street Journal*, January 31, 1994, B5.

57. Ibid.

58. Ibid.

59. Eben Shapiro, "Minnesota Mining's Wool Pads Grab Sizable Chunk of Business," *The Wall Street Journal*, January 13, 1994, B6.

Chapter Nine

CREATIVE ADVERTISING STRATEGY

Chapter Objectives

After studying this chapter, you should be able to:

1. Understand the role of advertising agencies and the relationship between agency and client.
2. Appreciate the factors that promote creative and effective advertising.
3. Describe a five-step program used in formulating advertising strategy.
4. Describe the features of a creative brief.
5. Explain alternative creative strategies that play a role in the development of advertising messages.
6. Explain the concept of means-end chains and their role in advertising strategy.
7. Understand the MECCAS model and its role in guiding message formulation.
8. Describe the laddering method that provides the data used in constructing a MECCAS model.
9. Describe the role of corporate image and issue advertising.

Opening Vignette: Two of the Greatest Ads in the History of Advertising

Miss Clairol: "Does She . . . or Doesn't She?"   Imagine yourself employed as a copywriter in a New York advertising agency in the year 1955. You have just been assigned creative responsibility for a product that heretofore (as of 1955) had not been nationally marketed or advertised. The product: hair coloring. The brand: Miss Clairol. Your task: Devise a creative strategy that will convince millions of American women to purchase Miss Clairol hair coloring—at the time called Hair Color Bath. This challenge occurred, by the way, in a cultural context where it was considered patently inappropriate for respectable women to smoke in public, wear long pants, or color their hair.

The person actually assigned this task was Shirley Polykoff, a copywriter for the Foote, Cone & Belding agency. Her story of how she came up with the famous line, "Does she . . . or doesn't she?" provides a fascinating illustration of the creative process in advertising. At the time of the Miss Clairol campaign, there was no hair-coloring business. In fact, according to Ms. Polykoff, at-home hair-coloring jobs invariably turned out blotchy. Women were ashamed to color their own hair at home. A product that provided a natural look stood a strong chance of being accepted, but women would have to be convinced that an advertised hair-coloring product would, in fact, give them that highly desired natural look.

Shirley Polykoff explains the background of the famous advertising line that convinced women Miss Clairol would produce a natural look:

> In 1933, just before I was married, my husband had taken me to meet the woman who would become my mother-in-law. When we got in the car after dinner, I asked him, "How'd I do? Did your mother like me?" and he told me his mother had said, "She paints her hair, doesn't she?" He asked me, "Well, do you?" It became a joke between my husband and me; anytime we saw someone who was stunning or attractive we'd say, "Does she, or doesn't she?" Twenty years later [at the time she was working on the Miss Clairol account], I was walking down Park Avenue talking out loud to myself, because I have to hear what I write. The phrase came into my mind again. Suddenly, I realized, "That's it. That's the campaign." I knew that [a competitive advertising agency] couldn't find anything better. I knew that immediately. When you're young, you're very sure about everything.[a]

---

[a]Based on an interview by Paula Champa in "The Moment of Creation," *Agency*, May/June 1991, 32.

The advertising line "Does she . . . or doesn't she?" actually was followed with the tagline "Hair color so natural only her hairdresser knows for sure!" The headline grabbed the reader's attention, whereas the tagline promised a conclusive benefit: The product works so well that only an expert would recognize that the at-home application was not performed at a beauty salon. This brilliant advertising persuaded millions of American women to become product users and led to dramatically increased sales of Miss Clairol.[b]

Macintosh Computer: "1984."   Apple Computer (Figure 9.1) had just developed the world's most user-friendly computer and needed breakthrough advertising to introduce its new Macintosh brand, which was a revolution in computing technology. Steve Jobs, the founder of Apple, who was only 29 at the time of the Macintosh introduction, instructed his advertising agency, Chiat/Day, to create an explosive television commercial that would portray the Macintosh as a truly revolutionary machine. The creative people at Chiat/Day faced a challenging task, especially since Macintosh's main competitor was the powerful and much larger "Big Blue" (IBM). (In 1984, Compaq, Dell, and Gateway were nonexistent. It was only Apple versus IBM in the personal computer business, and IBM was the well-established leader known for its corporate computers.) However, Chiat/Day produced a commercial in which IBM was obliquely caricatured as the much-despised and feared institution reminiscent of the Big Brother theme in George Orwell's book *1984*. (In the book, political power is controlled by Big Brother, and individual dignity and freedom are superseded by political conformity.) The one-minute commercial created in this context, dubbed "1984," was run during the Super Bowl XVIII on January 22, 1984, and was never repeated on commercial television. This was not because it was ineffective; to the contrary, its incredible word-of-mouth-producing impact negated the need for repeat showings.

> *The commercial . . . opens on a room of zombie-like citizens staring at a huge screen where Big Brother is spewing a relentless cant about "information purification . . . unprincipled dissemination of facts" and "unification of thought."*
>
> *Against this ominous backdrop, a woman in athletic wear [a white jersey top and bright red running shorts, which was the only primary color in the commercial] runs in and hurls a sledgehammer into the screen, causing a cataclysmic explosion that shatters Big Brother. Then the message flashes on the TV screen: "On January 24th, Apple Computer will introduce Macintosh. And you'll see why 1984 won't be like '1984.'"*[c]

This remarkable advertising is considered by some to be the greatest TV commercial ever made.[d] It grabbed attention; it broke through the clutter of the many commercials aired during the Super Bowl; it was memorable; it was discussed by millions of people; and, ultimately, it played an instrumental role in selling truckloads of Macintosh computers. Moreover, it created a unique image for the Mac (short for Macintosh) as described adroitly by one observer:

> *The Mac is female. Conversely, IBM must be male. IBM is not just male, it is Big Brother male. And Apple is not just female, but New Female. She is strong, athletic, independent, and, most important, liberated. After all, that's what the young athlete is all about. She is, in terms of the 1980s, empowerment and freedom.*[e]

[b]For additional reading on this famous advertisement, see James B. Twitchell, *20 Ads That Shook the World: The Century's Most Groundbreaking Advertising and How It Changed Us All* (New York: Crown Publishers, 2000), 118–125.

[c]Based on Bradley Johnson, "The Commercial, and the Product, That Changed Advertising," *Advertising Age*, January 10, 1994, 1, 12–14.

[d]Bob Garfield, "Breakthrough Product Gets Greatest TV Spot," *Advertising Age*, January 10, 1994, 14; "The Most Famous One-Shot Commercial Tested Orwell, and Made History for Apple Computer," *Advertising Age*, November 11, 1996, A22.

[e]Twitchell, *20 Ads That Shook the World*, 190.

Figure 9.1   Apple Computer

© AP/Wide World Photo

What is the process by which advertising messages are created? What makes a good advertising message? What are the different types of creative strategies, and when and why are they used? What is the role of corporate advertising?

The present chapter, which is the first of two to examine the message aspect of advertising, surveys these questions. First addressed is the relationship between advertisers and their advertising agencies. Next considered is the matter of what makes effective advertising and the related subject of creative advertising. A third section covers the process underlying the formulation of advertising strategy. A fourth section describes creative strategies used by advertising practitioners. A following topic is the concept of means-end chains as a mechanism for bridging the advertiser's creative process with the values that drive consumers' product and brand choices. Finally, the discussion moves away from brand-oriented advertising to corporate image and issue advertising.

THE RELATIONSHIP BETWEEN CLIENT AND ADVERTISING AGENCY

Message strategies and decisions are most often the joint enterprise of the companies that advertise (the clients) and their advertising agencies. This section examines the role of advertising agencies, describes how agencies are organized, and reviews the issue of agency compensation.

The Role of an Advertising Agency

In general, advertisers have three alternative ways to perform the advertising function. First, a company can choose not to use an advertising agency but rather maintain its own *in-house advertising operation*. This necessitates employing an advertising staff and absorbing the overhead required to maintain the staff's operations. Such an arrangement is unjustifiable unless a company does a large and continuous amount of advertising. Even under these conditions, most businesses choose instead to use the services of advertising agencies.

Rather than having its own in-house advertising operation, brand management may choose to use an ad agency, either by hiring a full-service agency that takes care of all advertising duties or by employing specialists who perform services on an as-needed basis. To appreciate why a company would use an ad agency, it is important to recognize that businesses routinely employ the services of outside specialists: lawyers, financial advisors, management consultants, tax specialists, and advertising agencies. By their very nature, these "outsiders" bring knowledge, expertise, and efficiencies that companies do not possess within their own ranks. Advertising agencies can provide great value to their clients by developing highly effective and profitable advertising campaigns. The

Some Long-Lasting Client-Agency Relationships Table 9.1

Client	Agency	Relationship Length
Unilever	J. Walter Thompson	1902–present
Sunkist Growers	FCB	1907–1999
Exxon	McCann-Erickson	1912–2000
Del Monte	McCann-Erickson	1917–present
Armstrong	BBDO	1917–present
Chevrolet	Campbell-Ewald	1919–present
General Electric	BBDO	1920–present
Kraft	J. Walter Thompson	1922–present
DuPont	BBDO	1929–present
Kellogg's	J. Walter Thompson	1930–present
Kodak	J. Walter Thompson	1930–1999
Hormel	BBDO	1931–present
Mars/Uncle Ben's Rice	DMB&B	1932–present
Pontiac	DMB&B	1934–present
Cadillac	DMB&B	1935–present
Dow Chemical	DMB&B	1935–present
Unilever	BBDO	1939–present
MetLife	Young & Rubicam	1940–present
Campbell Soup	BBDO	1954–present

Source: Ellen Neuborne, "Secrets of Account Longevity," *Agency,* Summer 2001, p. 27. © 2001.

relationship between ad agency and client sometimes lasts for decades, as evidenced by some of the longest-lasting relationships shown in Table 9.1. Of course, client-agency relationships also can be short lived and volatile if the client evaluates the agency as underperforming and failing to enhance the client's brand equity and market share.

Full-service advertising agencies perform research, provide creative services, conduct media planning and buying, and undertake a variety of client services. They also may be involved in the advertiser's total marketing process and, for a fee, may perform other MarCom functions, including sales promotion, publicity, package design, strategic marketing planning, and sales forecasting. Why would an advertiser want to employ the services of a full-service agency? The primary advantages include acquiring the services of specialists with in-depth knowledge of advertising and obtaining negotiating leverage with the media. The major disadvantage is that some control over the advertising function is lost when it is performed by an agency rather than in house.

A third way for a client to accomplish the advertising function is to purchase advertising services *a la carte*. That is, rather than depending on a single full-service agency to perform all advertising and related functions, an advertiser may recruit the services of a variety of firms with particular specialties in creative work, media selection, production, advertising research, and so on. This arrangement's advantages include the ability to contract for services only when they are needed and potential cost efficiencies. On the downside, specialists (so-called *boutiques*) sometimes lack financial stability and may be poor in terms of cost accountability.

Many advertisers actually employ a combination of the different advertising options rather than using one of them exclusively. For example, a firm may have its own in-house agency but contract with boutiques for certain needs. Although in-house agencies and boutiques experienced considerable growth in earlier decades, full-service agencies now are preferred, especially by larger advertisers.

Advertising Agency Organization

A full-service advertising agency performs at least four basic functions for the clients it represents: (1) creative services, (2) media services, (3) research services, and (4) account management. In addition to these functions, many advertising agencies have expanded their offerings to include direct marketing, public relations, and even sales promotion services. This expansion is in response to clients' urging for enhanced integrated marketing communications services, which were detailed in Chapter 1.

Creative Services. Advertising agency copywriters, graphic artists, and creative directors are responsible for developing advertising copy and campaigns to serve their clients' interests. As revealed in the *Opening Vignette*, advertising agencies can create incredibly brilliant advertising campaigns that enhance brand equity and increase a brand's sales volume, market share, and profitability.

Media Services. This unit of an advertising agency is charged with the task of selecting the best advertising media for reaching the client's target market, achieving ad objectives, and meeting the budget. *Media planners* are responsible for developing overall media strategy (where to advertise, how often, when, etc.), and *media buyers* then procure specific vehicles within particular media that have been selected by media planners and approved by clients. The complexity of media buying requires the use of computer analysis and continuous research of changing media costs and availability.

Research Services. Full-service advertising agencies employ research specialists who study their clients' customers' buying habits, purchase preferences, and responsiveness to advertising concepts and finished ads. Focus groups, mall intercepts, ethnographic studies by trained anthropologists, and acquisition of syndicated research data are just some of the services performed by agencies' research specialists.

Account Management. This facet of an advertising agency provides the mechanism to link the agency with the client. Account managers act as liaisons so that the client does not need to interact directly with several different service departments and specialists. In most major advertising agencies, the account management department includes account executives and management supervisors. *Account executives* are involved in tactical decision making and day-to-day contact with brand managers and other client personnel. Account executives are responsible for seeing that the client's interests, concerns, and preferences have a voice in the advertising agency and that the work is being accomplished on schedule. Account executives report to *management supervisors*, who are more involved in actually getting new business for the agency and working with clients at a more strategic level. Account executives are groomed for positions as management supervisors.

Agency Compensation

Ad agencies are compensated for performing the functions described above. There are three basic methods by which clients compensate agencies for services rendered:

1. *Commissions from media* for advertisements aired or printed on behalf of the agency's clients provided the primary form of ad agency compensation in the past. Historically, U.S. advertising agencies charged a standard commission of 15 percent of the gross amount of billings.[1] To illustrate, suppose the Creative Advertising Agency buys $200,000 of space in a certain magazine for its client, ABC Company. When the invoice for this space comes due, Creative would remit payment of $170,000 to the magazine ($200,000 less Creative's 15 percent commission), bill ABC for the full $200,000, and retain the remainder, $30,000, as revenue for services rendered. The $30,000 revenue realized by Creative was, in the past, regarded as a fair amount of compensation to the agency for its creative expertise, media-buying insight, and ancillary functions performed in behalf of its client, ABC Company.

The 15 percent compensation system has, as one may suppose, been a matter of some controversy between company marketing executives and managers of advertising agencies. The primary area of disagreement is the matter of whether 15 percent compensation is too much (the marketing executives' perspective) or too little (the ad agencies' perspective). The disagreement has spurred the growth of alternative compensation systems. Indeed, today only a fraction of advertisers still pay a 15 percent commission. Although there are alternatives to the commission system, it probably will not vanish entirely. Rather, a *reduced commission system*, by which the ad agency is compensated with a flat fee that is less than 15 percent, has experienced increased usage.

2. The most common compensation method today is a *labor-based fee system* by which advertising agencies are compensated much like lawyers, tax consultants, and management consultants. That is, agencies carefully monitor their time and bill clients an hourly fee based on time commitment. This system involves price negotiations between advertisers and agencies such that the actual rate of compensation is based on mutual agreement concerning the worth of the services rendered by the advertising agency.[2]

3. *Outcome-based programs* represent the newest approach to agency compensation. Ford Motor Company, for example, uses a compensation system whereby it negotiates a base fee with its agencies to cover the cost of services provided, and additionally offers incentive payments that are tied to brand performance goals such as targeted revenue levels.[3] Procter & Gamble employs a sales-based model whereby ad agencies are compensated based on a percentage of sales that a P&G brand obtains. The agency's compensation rises with sales increases and falls with declines. Needless to say, this incentive-based system encourages, indeed demands, agencies to use whatever IMC programs are needed to build brand sales. P&G's best interest (growth in brand sales and market share) and the agency's best interest (increased compensation) are joined by this compensation system in a hand-in-glove fashion. In addition to these companies, many others are turning away from the historical commission-based system and toward some form of outcome-based compensation program. The success of outcome-based programs will depend on demonstrating that advertising and other MarCom efforts initiated by agencies do indeed translate into enhanced brand performance—accountability in action, as discussed in the prior chapter.[4]

CREATING EFFECTIVE ADVERTISING

Now that we have overviewed advertising agencies, the creators of advertisements, we turn to the issue of how advertising agency and client work together to develop effective advertising campaigns. No simple answer is possible, but toward this end we first must attempt to understand the meaning of *effective advertising*. It is easy, in one sense, to define effective advertising: Advertising is effective if it accomplishes the advertiser's objectives. This perspective defines effectiveness from the output side, or in terms of what it accomplishes. It is much more difficult to define effective advertising from an input perspective, or in terms of the composition of the advertisement itself. There are many viewpoints on this issue. Practitioners are broadly split on the matter. For example, a practitioner of direct-mail advertising probably has a different opinion about what constitutes effective advertising than does Shirley Polykoff, the creator of the Miss Clairol campaign, or Steve Hayden, the inspirational source behind the "1984" Macintosh commercial.

Although it is impractical to provide a singular, all-purpose definition of what constitutes effective advertising, it is possible to talk about general characteristics.[5] At a minimum, good (or effective) advertising satisfies the following considerations:

1. *It must extend from sound marketing strategy.* Advertising can be effective only if it is compatible with other elements of an integrated and well-orchestrated MarCom strategy.

2. *Effective advertising must take the consumer's view.* Consumers buy product benefits, not attributes. Therefore, advertising must be stated in a way that relates to the consumer's—rather than the marketer's—needs, wants, and values.

3. *Effective advertising is persuasive.* Persuasion usually occurs when there is a benefit for the consumer in addition to the marketer.

4. *Advertising must find a unique way to break through the clutter.* Advertisers continuously compete with competitors for the consumer's attention. This is no small task considering the massive number of print advertisements, broadcast commercials, Internet banners, and other sources of information available daily to consumers. Indeed, the situation in television advertising has been characterized as "audiovisual wallpaper"—a sarcastic implication that consumers pay just about as much attention to commercials as they do to the detail in their wallpaper after seeing it for years.[6]

5. *Good advertising should never promise more than it can deliver.* This point speaks for itself, both in terms of ethics and in terms of smart business sense. Consumers learn quickly when they have been deceived and will resent the advertiser.

6. *Good advertising prevents the creative idea from overwhelming the strategy.* The purpose of advertising is to persuade and influence; the purpose is not to be cute for cute's sake or humorous for humor's sake. The ineffective use of humor results in people remembering the humor but forgetting the selling message.

The following quote aptly summarizes the essentials of effective advertising:

[It] is advertising that is created for a specific customer. It is advertising that understands and thinks about the customer's needs. It is advertising that communicates a specific benefit. It is advertising that pinpoints a specific action that the consumer takes. Good advertising understands that people do not buy products—they buy product benefits. . . . Above all, [effective advertising] gets noticed and remembered, and gets people to act.[7]

The Role of Creativity

Effective advertising is usually *creative*. That is, it differentiates itself from the mass of mediocre advertisements; it is somehow different and out of the ordinary. Advertising that is the same as most other advertising is unable to break through the competitive clutter and grab the consumer's attention. It is easier to give examples of creative advertising than to exactly define it. Many advertising practitioners and observers would consider the following examples to be effective, creative advertising:

- A Holiday Inn television campaign featured various executions of an ensemble of mom, dad, grandma, and a quintessential slacker, who rather than being out on his own gainfully employed instead lives with his family while supposedly attempting to run a dot-com business. The various campaign executions feature the slacker imposing demands on the family for more space (in the kitchen or elsewhere) to run his fledgling business. The *coupe de grace* in every execution is mom exclaiming, "What do you think this is, a Holiday Inn?" The implication from these hilarious executions is clear: Holiday Inn gives its customers special treatment—the sort expected by the slacker but withheld by his family.

- Pepsi-Cola has historically telecast a variety of commercials that poke fun at its competitor, Coca-Cola. None has been more effective than the outstanding commercial in which a security camera captures the antics of a Coke delivery man in a supermarket. While the famous Hank Williams song "Your Cheating Heart" plays in the background, the delivery man approaches a Pepsi cooler that is adjacent to his own Coca-Cola cooler. The security camera catches the delivery man sneaking a look at the Pepsi cooler, opening it, and then removing a can of Pepsi—at which time dozens of Pepsi cans cascade to the floor in a huge noise that catches the attention of shoppers, much to the deliveryman's chagrin. This classic advertisement (key scenes of which are shown in Figure 9.2) is an outstanding attention-getter that subtly conveys the message that perhaps Pepsi *is* better than Coke.

- Consider, also, the stream of creative and effective advertisements for Budweiser beer. Through much of the 1990s the name Budweiser was driven to the point of instant recognition by a trio of frogs chanting "Bud-weis-er!" Then, after the frogs began losing their appeal, Anheuser-Busch's ad agency (Goodby, Silverstein & Partners of San Francisco) extended the campaign by introducing the anthropomorphic lizards Louie and Frank. In these humorous commercials Louie seethes with jealousy that frogs were chosen for the Budweiser gig, while Frank reproves him to "get over it." Then in 2000 another Budweiser ad agency (DDB Worldwide) developed the "Whassup?!" campaign—the various executions of which revealed laid-back men drinking Budweiser beer in comfortable settings and conducting telephone or other conversations opening with "Whassup?" This expression has for years been a staple greeting primarily in African American and Hispanic communities. This award-winning campaign generated an incredible amount of publicity and pass-along value as people everywhere enjoyed the hilarity of the expression, especially as it was dramatized and exaggerated in the TV ads.

Most readers probably remember all these commercials. They appealed to you by making their selling points in an entertaining, creative fashion. But what is creativity? Unfortunately, there is no simple answer to this elusive aspect of advertising.[8] It is beyond the purpose of this text to attempt a thorough explanation of the creative process. Let the following three accounts suffice. First, a vice chairman and creative director of the Leo Burnett advertising agency in Chicago

Key Scenes from Pepsi-Cola's "Security Camera" TV Commercial   Figure 9.2

describes creativity as "a sensitivity to human nature and the ability to communicate it. The best creative [advertising] comes from an understanding of what people are thinking and feeling."[9] A former president of the American Association of Advertising Agencies describes advertising creativity as "a new combination of familiar elements that forces involvement and memorability."[10] Perhaps jazz musician Charlie Mingus said it best: "Creativity is more than just being different. Anybody can play weird, that's easy. What's hard is to be as simple as Bach. Making the simple complicated is commonplace, making the complicated simple, awesomely simple, that's creativity."[11]

In sum, effective, creative advertising must make a relatively lasting impact. This means getting past the clutter from other advertisements, activating attention, and giving consumers something to remember about the advertised product. In other words, advertising *must make an impression*. Based on the perspectives on creativity mentioned here, this means developing ads that are *empathetic* (i.e., that understand what people are thinking and feeling), that are *involving and memorable*, and that are *"awesomely simple."* The following *IMC Focus* describes a brilliant creative advertising campaign for Absolut Vodka.

Achieving Advertising Impact

The foregoing discussion has described general features of effective and creative advertising and presented several illustrative campaigns. It will be useful at this point to provide a conceptual framework that goes beyond mere description. Figure 9.3 offers such a framework.[12] This framework conceptualizes advertising's impact as extending from a combination of message convincingness and execution quality. An advertising message can be thought of as providing the reader/viewer/listener with a *value proposition*. A **value proposition** is the essence of a message and the reward to the consumer for investing his or her time attending an advertisement. The reward may come in the form of needed information about a brand or may simply represent an enjoyable experience, such as I obtain with every viewing of a Holiday Inn ad featuring the slacker character. Having a convincing message is a necessary but insufficient condition for creating an effective advertisement. As shown in Figure 9.3, the ad must be executed effectively. Hence, advertising messages can be conceptualized in terms of a fourfold classification based on whether value propositions are convincing or unconvincing and if agency executions of these propositions are effective or ineffective. Four types of ad outcomes extend from this two-by-two fram-

Figure 9.3   Interaction of Message Convincingness and Execution Quality

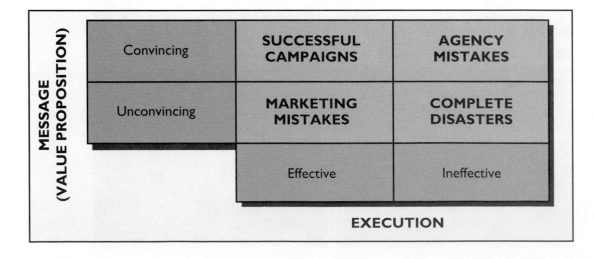

IMC focus

Absolutely Brilliant!

Imported brands of vodka were virtually nonexistent in the United States until the late 1970s. Three brands (Stolichnaya from Russia, Finlandia from Finland, and Wybrowa from Poland) made up less than 1 percent of the total United States vodka market. In 1980 Carillon Importers began marketing Absolut Vodka from Sweden, a brand that at the time was completely unknown in the United States. In addition to having a great name (suggesting the unequivocally best, or *absolute*, vodka), the brand's most distinguishing feature was a unique bottle—crystal clear with an interesting shape.

With a small advertising budget and the capability of advertising only in print media, Carillon's advertising agency, TBWA, set about the task of rapidly building brand awareness. The agency's brilliant idea was to simply feature a full-page shot of the bottle with a two-word headline. The first word would always be the brand name, Absolut, used as an adjective to modify a second word de-

scribing the brand or its consumer. *Advertising Age*, the unofficial bible of the advertising industry, picked this campaign as the seventh best ad campaign of all time. A montage of Absolut advertisements was presented in a previous chapter (see Figure 7.1).

Business grew rapidly from the very beginning, facilitated somewhat by American consumers temporarily boycotting the major competitive brand of imported vodka, Stolichnaya, after Russia invaded Afghanistan. Sales growth has never abated. The advertising budget grew from only $750,000 in 1981 to over $20 million. Absolut has been the most heavily advertised spirits brand anywhere in the world. Although Absolut is now marketed by Seagrams and not Carillon Importers, its advertising remains creative and its sales volume high.

Source: For further reading see "Absolute: The Metaphysics of Wrap," in James B. Twitchell, *20 Ads That Shook the World: The Century's Most Groundbreaking Advertising and How It Changed Us All* (New York: Crown Publishers, 2000), 174–183.

---

ing: (1) successful campaigns, (2) marketing mistakes, (3) agency mistakes, and (4) complete disasters.

Successful Campaigns. Successful advertising campaigns arise from a combination of having a message founded on a convincing value proposition and an effective (i.e., interesting, engaging) execution. In short, successful campaigns communicate meaningful value propositions in an effective way.

Marketing Mistakes. The advertising agency may come up with a good, creative execution, but this cannot make up for the absence of a convincing value proposition. This is referred to as a "marketing mistake" because the fault rests with brand management's failure to identify a meaningful value proposition that distinguishes the brand from competitive offerings. A bad idea well executed is nonetheless unpersuasive.

Agency Mistakes. This form of failed ad campaign is due to the ad agency's inability to design an effective execution, even though its brand management client has presented it with a value proposition that should have represented a convincing message.

Complete Disasters. Poor selling points and mediocre executions are the stuff of advertising disasters. These can be avoided by conducting research that pretests both the selling message and the executional strategy prior to ever printing or airing a final advertisement.

How can an agency or its client know in advance — that is, prior to printing or airing an advertisement — that it is likely to be successful? First, research that examines consumers' product-related needs, expectations, and past experiences should provide the brand manager with a good idea about the likely effectiveness of a particular value proposition. Second, execution effectiveness can be judged by pretesting advertisements before actually initiating an advertising campaign. Chapter 11 will discuss in detail methods to assess message and execution effectiveness.

ADVERTISING PLANS AND STRATEGY

Advertising messages can be developed in an ad hoc fashion without much forethought, or they can be created systematically. Advertising plans provide the framework for the systematic execution of advertising strategies. To appreciate the role of an advertising plan, imagine a soccer team approaching an upcoming game without any idea of how it is going to execute its offense or defense. Without a game plan, the team would have to play in the same spontaneous fashion as do players in a pickup game. Under such circumstances there would be numerous missed assignments and overall misexecution. The team very likely would lose unless they played a badly mismatched opponent.

So it is with advertising. Companies compete against opponents who generally are well prepared. This means that a firm must enter the advertising "game" with a clear plan in mind. An advertising plan evaluates a product or brand's advertising history, proposes where the next period's advertising should head, and justifies the proposed strategy for maintaining or improving a brand's competitive situation.

To put an advertising plan into action requires (1) careful evaluation of customer behavior related to the brand, (2) detailed evaluation of the competition, and (3) a coordinated effort to tie the proposed advertising program to the brand's overall marketing strategy. Because an advertising plan involves a number of steps and details that are beyond the scope of this chapter, attention in this chapter will focus just on the all-important strategy aspect of planning. **Advertising strategy** is what the advertiser says about the brand being advertised. It is the formulation of an advertising message that communicates the brand's value proposition, its primary benefit or how it can solve the consumer's problem.

A Five-Step Program

Formulating an advertising strategy requires that the advertiser and its agency undertake a formal process, such as the following five-step program:[13]

1. Specify the key fact.
2. State the primary marketing problem.
3. State the communications objective.
4. Implement the creative message strategy.
5. Establish mandatory requirements.

Each step in the ad strategy process will be illustrated by considering an advertising campaign undertaken by Florists' Transworld Delivery Association (FTD). FTD, which was founded in 1910, is the largest floral company in the world. It connects approximately 14,000 North American independent retail florists and 50,000 florists in 150 countries. These florists affiliate to enjoy the economic efficiencies of mass marketing and advertising while simultaneously maintaining their ownership and legal independence.[14]

Competition in the retail florist industry has increased rather dramatically in the past decade. Street vendors, supermarkets, and nontraditional retail outlets all compete with conventional retail florists. As a result, the market share of retail florists has fallen from a high of nearly 75 percent to around 50 percent, a loss of several billion dollars in sales.

Step 1: Specify the Key Fact. The **key fact** in an advertising strategy is a single-minded statement from the *consumer's point of view* that identifies why consumers are or are not purchasing the product/service/brand or are not giving it proper consideration.

Research performed for FTD undoubtedly revealed that many North American consumers have found that they can purchase cut flowers at lower prices from supermarkets and other outlets than traditional retail florists. The key fact that underlies FTD's advertising strategy is that many consumers are price conscious when purchasing cut flowers, which leads them to low-price retailers (such as supermarkets) rather than to FTD retail florists.

Step 2: State the Primary Marketing Problem.
Extending from the key fact, this step states the problem from the *marketer's point of view*. The primary marketing problem may be an image problem, a product perception problem, or a competitive problem.

Retail florists are faced with the reality that many consumers, especially young people, are either unaware of or disinterested in whether a florist is an FTD member. FTD-affiliated florists are concerned that they will continue to lose young consumers to low-cost competitors.

Step 3: State the Communications Objective.
This is a straightforward statement about *what effect the advertising is intended to have on the target market and how it should persuade consumers.*

Today's young consumers represent FTD's consumer of the future, so it is imperative that FTD create name awareness and educate consumers about what FTD members have to offer.

Step 4: Implement the Creative Message Strategy.
Creative message strategy, sometimes also called the creative platform, represents the guts of the overall advertising strategy. The *creative platform* for a brand is summarized in a single statement called a *positioning statement*. A **positioning statement** is the key idea that encapsulates what a brand is intended to stand for in its target market's mind and with consideration of how competitors have attempted to position their brands. As discussed back in Chapter 3, a positioning statement for a brand represents how we want customers and prospects to think and feel about our brand. These thoughts and feelings should stand out in comparison to competitive offerings and motivate the customer/prospect to want to try our brand.

Implementing creative message strategy requires (1) defining the target market, (2) identifying the primary competition, (3) choosing the positioning statement, and (4) offering reasons why.

Define the Target Market.
You will recall from the discussion in Chapter 3 that the target market for a brand's advertising strategy and related marketing program is defined in terms of demographics, geodemographics, psychographics, or product-usage characteristics.

FTD's target market consists of all consumers who occasionally or frequently purchase cut flowers, with special emphasis on young consumers, who, on the one hand, are the least concerned about their florists being FTD affiliated and, on the other, are critical to FTD because they represent the core market in the future.

Identify the Primary Competition.
Who are the primary competitors in the segment the brand is attempting to tap, and what are their advantages and disadvantages? Answering this question enables an advertiser to know exactly how to position a brand against consumers' perceptions of competitive brands' advantages and disadvantages.

FTD's primary competitors are supermarkets and other vendors of low-priced cut flowers. Their advantage is lower price, but they are unable to offer extensive services. Also, rather than having to physically visit a supermarket or other brick-and-mortar establishment, consumers can purchase flowers from the convenience of their homes or offices via telephone orders (1-800-SEND-FTD) or by visiting FTD's Web site (http://www.ftd.com).

Choose the Positioning Statement.
This aspect of the creative platform, as previously described, amounts to selecting a brand's primary benefit or major selling idea. In most cases, it is a direct or implicit promise in the form of a consumer benefit or solution to a problem.

The primary benefit to consumers of purchasing from an FTD retail florist is the promise of full services, such as phone or Internet ordering, mailing, attractive wrapping, and knowledgable sales assistance—services one cannot obtain from outlets such as supermarkets.

FTD had its advertising agency design a very sexy magazine ad to appeal to a younger segment of male purchasers. The ad portrayed an attractive young woman holding a vase of flowers and standing in a very provocative pose. Advertising copy matched the model's suggestive pose in simply stating, "Valentine's Day is now available in extra hot and spicy." The ad represents an appeal to young men in hopes they would contact FTD to send flowers on Valentine's Day to their wives or girlfriends. Ads were placed in magazines such as *GQ*, *Men's Health*, and *Sports Illustrated*. FTD justified the use of this advertisement on the grounds that it is attempting to get away from its conservative past because "we don't want to miss the 18- to 25-year-old category who needs to buy last-minute gifts."[15]

Offer Reasons Why.   These are the facts supporting the positioning statement. In some instances advertisers can back up advertising claims with factual information that is relevant, informative, and interesting to consumers. Many times it is impossible to prove or support the promise being made, such as when the promise is symbolic or psychological. In these instances, advertisers turn to authority figures, experts, or celebrities to support the implicit advertising promise.

FTD's promise is that its members are caring and knowledgeable merchants—in other words, they know their business, understand the consumer's needs, and are interested in building long-term relations with their customers. The ability to offer quality and professional service sets FTD-member florists apart from their low-cost competitors.

Step 5: Establish Mandatory Requirements.   The final step in formulating an advertising strategy involves the mandatory requirements that must be included in an ad. This aspect of advertising strategy is relatively technical and uncreative. Basically, it reminds the advertiser to include the corporate slogan or logo (in this case, the Roman god Mercury delivering flowers), a standard tag line, any regulatory requirements (as with food, alcohol, and tobacco advertising), and so on.

In sum, advertising strategy lays out the details for the upcoming advertising campaign. It insists on a disciplined approach to analyzing the product or brand, the consumer, and the competition. A single-minded benefit, or positioning statement, is the outcome. The strategy becomes a blueprint, road map, or guide to subsequent advertising efforts. Every proposed tactical decision is evaluated in terms of whether it is compatible with the strategy.

Constructing a Creative Brief

A systematic approach to creative advertising makes sense in theory, but ultimately the people who write advertising copy and create visual imagery—so-called *creatives* or *copywriters*—must summon their full talents to develop effective advertising. Creatives often complain that marketing research reports and other such directives excessively constrain their opportunities for full creative expression. On the other hand, one cannot forget that advertising is a business with an obligation to sell products. Even though research has shown that advertising copy is based on copywriters' own implicit theories of how advertising works on consumers, they do not have the luxury to create for the mere sake of engaging in a creative pursuit.[16] Their ultimate purpose is to write advertising copy that affects consumers' expectations, attitudes, and eventually purchase behavior (sooner rather than later, it is hoped).

In many advertising agencies, the work of copywriters is directed by a framework known as a **creative brief,** which is a document designed to inspire copywriters by channeling their creative efforts toward a solution that will serve the interests of the client. The creative brief represents an informal pact between client and advertising agency that represents agreement on what an advertising campaign is intended to accomplish. Ogilvy & Mather, a widely acclaimed worldwide advertising agency, offers the following guidelines to its account executives for constructing a creative brief.[17] (It is unnecessary to attempt to memorize the guidelines, but it will be useful to peruse them in order to appreciate the objective they are intended to accomplish.)

1. *What is the background to this job?* The answer to this question requires a brief explanation regarding why the advertising agency is being asked by the client to perform a certain advertising job—such as launching a new brand, gaining back lost sales from a competitor, or introducing a new version of an established product. Part of this explanation would include an analysis of the competitive environment.

2. *What is the strategy?* The response to this question articulates a specific advertising strategy to accomplish the job, a strategy such as based on the process previously described. This strategy statement gives copywriters an understanding of how their creative work must fit into the overall strategy. For example, the strategy statement may indicate that a new brand is to be launched during September using a football motif. Copywriters are required to work within this context but still have freedom to be creative.

3. *What is our task on this job?* Creatives are told exactly what they are being asked to produce—perhaps a series of TV commercials along with supporting magazine inserts.

4. *What is the corporate and/or brand positioning?* Copywriters are reminded that their creative work must reflect the brand's positioning statement. If, for example, an automobile brand is positioned as the most fuel-efficient alternative, then the advertising must creatively express this fact.

5. *What are the client's objectives for this job?* This guideline simply reminds everyone what the client wants the advertising to accomplish. Knowing this, creatives can then design appropriate advertisements to achieve that objective.

6. *Whom are we talking to?* This is a precise description of the exemplary target market. With knowledge of the demographic, geodemographic, or psychographic characteristics of the intended customer (see Chapter 3), creatives have a specific target at which to direct their efforts. This is as essential in advertising as it is in certain athletic events. For example, the late golf sage Harvey Penick offered the following advice to pupils trying to improve their golf games: "Once you address the golf ball, hitting it has got to be the most important thing in your life at that moment. Shut out all thoughts other than picking out a target and taking dead aim at it."[18] His point to golfers about taking "dead aim" is also applicable to advertising creatives: You can't hit a target unless you know where to aim!

7. *What do they currently think/feel about our product/service?* The advice here is for creatives to design research-based advertising that speaks to the target customer in terms of his or her perceptions (thoughts and feelings) about the brand rather than relying on the suppositions of the client or advertising agency.

8. *What do we want them to think/feel about our product/service?* Is there a current perception that needs to be changed? For example, if a large number of consumers in the target market consider the brand to be overpriced, how can we change that perception and convince them that the brand actually is a good value due to its superior quality?

9. *What do we want them to do?* This guideline is reminiscent of the integrated marketing communications mind-set presented in Chapter 1, in which creating specific customer action is a key component of the IMC model. In the present context, creatives must focus on a specific consumer action. The advertising might be designed to get prospects to request further information, to order a videotape containing detailed product information, or to purchase Valentine's Day flowers from FTD within the next five days.

10. *What is the single-minded proposition?* This proposition, or positioning statement, directs the creative idea. It should be the most differentiating and motivating message about the brand that can be delivered to the target market. It should focus on brand benefits rather than product features.

11. *Why should our audience believe this proposition?* Because credibility and believability are key to getting the audience to accept the key proposition, this section of the creative brief supports the proposition with evidence about product features that back up the proposition.

12. *How should we speak to them?* This guideline calls for a short statement about the crucial feelings or thoughts that the advertisement should evoke in its intended audience. For example, the ad might be intended to move the audience emotionally, to make them feel deserving of a better lifestyle, or to get them to feel anxious about a currently unsafe course of behavior.

In sum, the creative brief is a document prepared by an advertising agency's executive on a particular account and is intended both to inspire copywriters and to channel their creative efforts. A truly valuable creative brief requires that the document be developed with a full understanding of the client's advertising needs. It also necessitates the acquisition of market research data that informs the agency about the competitive environment and about consumers' current perceptions of the to-be-advertised brand and its competition.

ALTERNATIVE STYLES OF CREATIVE ADVERTISING

By the very nature of advertising and the creative process that goes into message development and execution, there are innumerable ways to devise creative advertisements.[19] Several relatively distinct creative strategies have evolved over the years and represent the bulk of contemporary advertising.[20] Table 9.2 summarizes six strategies and groups them into three categories: functionally oriented, symbolically/experientially oriented, and product category dominance.

The student may recall the description of brand equity in Chapter 2 and the corresponding discussion of positioning in Chapter 3 in which distinctions were made among functional, symbolic, and experiential needs/benefits. These same distinctions are maintained in the present explanation of different styles of creative advertising. *Functionally oriented* advertising appeals to consumers' needs for tangible/physical/concrete benefits. *Symbolically/experientially oriented* advertising strategies are directed at psychosocial needs. The *category-dominance* strategies (generic and preemptive in Table 9.2) do not necessarily use any particular type of appeal to consumers but are designed to achieve an advantage over competitors in the same product category. Finally, it is important to note that, as is the case with most categorization schemes, the strategies covered in the following sections sometimes have "fuzzy borders" when applied to specific advertising executions. In other words, distinctions are sometimes very fine rather than perfectly obvious, and a particular advertising execution may simultaneously use multiple strategies.

Unique Selling Proposition Strategy

With the **unique selling proposition (USP)** strategy, an advertiser makes a superiority claim based on a unique product attribute that represents a *meaningful, distinctive consumer benefit*. The main feature of USP advertising is identifying an important difference that makes a brand unique and then developing an advertising claim that competitors either cannot make or have chosen not to make. The translation of the unique product feature into a relevant consumer benefit provides the unique selling proposition. The USP strategy is best suited for a company with a brand that possesses a relatively lasting competitive advantage, such as a maker of a technically complex item or a provider of a sophisticated service.

Alternative Styles of Creative Advertising
Table 9.2

Functional Orientation	Symbolic/Experiential Orientation	Category-Dominance Orientation
• Unique selling proposition	• Brand image • Resonance • Emotional	• Generic • Preemptive

The Gillette Sensor razor used a USP when claiming that it is "the only razor that senses and adjusts to the individual needs of your face." The Dodge Caravan had a unique selling proposition, if only temporarily, when it was able to claim that it was "the first and the only minivan with a driver's air bag." Nicoderm CQ's USP is contained in the claim that this product is the only nicotine-substitute patch "you can wear for 24 hours." The Allegra advertisement (Figure 9.4) advertises a USP in its claim that "Only Allegra has fexofenadine for effective nondrowsy relief of seasonal allergy symptoms."

In many respects the unique selling-proposition strategy is *the* optimum creative technique. This is because it gives the consumer a clearly differentiated reason for selecting the advertiser's brand over competitive offerings. The only reason USP advertising is not used more often is because brands in most product categories are pretty much homogeneous. They have no unique physical advantages to advertise and therefore are forced to use strategies favoring the more symbolic, psychological end of the strategy continuum.[21]

Brand Image Strategy

Whereas the USP strategy is based on promoting physical and functional differences between the advertiser's brand and competitive offerings, the **brand image strategy** involves *psychosocial*, rather than physical differentiation. Advertising attempts to develop an image or identity for a brand by associating the product with symbols. In imbuing a brand with an image, advertisers draw meaning from the culturally constituted world (that is, the world of artifacts and symbols) and transfer that meaning to their brands. In effect, the properties of the culturally constituted world that are well known to consumers come to reside in the unknown properties of the advertised brand.[22]

Developing an image through advertising amounts to giving a brand a *distinct identity* or *personality*. This is especially important for brands that compete in product categories where there is relatively little physical differentiation and all brands are relatively homogeneous (beer, soft drinks, cigarettes, blue jeans, etc.). Thus, Pepsi at one time was referred to as the soft drink for the "new generation." Mountain Dew has consistently presented itself as a hip, outrageous brand for teens. The quintessential case of brand image advertising is perhaps the Marlboro campaign, which has been ongoing for virtually a half century. This longstanding advertising campaign is replete with images of cowboys. The cowboy—iconic of open ranges, freedom, and individuality—has by virtue of the advertising campaign become attached to the Marlboro brand, which now has acquired some of the meaning represented in the cowboy image itself. Cowboys are equated with freedom and individuality; Marlboro is equated with cowboys; hence, by association, Marlboro itself has come to represent the qualities of the cowboy life. The reader will recall discussion back in Chapter 4 where meaning was characterized as the process of drawing meaning from the culturally constituted world (i.e., the everyday world filled with artifacts) and transferring that meaning to consumer goods. Marlboro's brand image advertising personifies this meaning-transfer process.

Brand image advertising might also be described as *transformational*. **Transformational advertising** associates the experience of using an advertised brand with a unique set of psychological characteristics that would not

Figure 9.4

typically be associated with the brand experience to the same degree without exposure to the advertisement. Such advertising is transforming (versus informing) by virtue of endowing brand usage with a particular experience that is different from using any similar brand. By virtue of repeated advertising, the brand becomes associated with its advertising and the people, scenes, or events in those advertisements.[23] Transformational advertisements contain two notable characteristics:[24]

1. They make the experience of using the brand richer, warmer, more exciting, or more enjoyable than what would be the case based solely on an objective description of the brand.
2. They connect the experience of using the brand so tightly with the experience of the advertisement that consumers cannot remember the brand without recalling the advertising experience. Marlboro cigarettes and cowboys, for example, are inextricably woven together in many consumers' cognitive structures.

Resonance Strategy

When used in the advertising strategy sense, the term *resonance* is analogous to the physical notion of noise resounding off an object. In a similar fashion, an advertisement resonates *(patterns)* the audience's life experiences. Resonant advertising strategy extends from psychographic research and structures an advertising campaign to pattern the prevailing lifestyle orientation of the intended market segment.

Resonant advertising does not focus on product claims or brand images but rather seeks to present circumstances or situations that find counterparts in the real or imagined experiences of the target audience. Advertising based on this strategy attempts to match "patterns" in an advertisement with the target audience's stored experiences.

The advertisement in Figure 9.5 for Ace Hardware illustrates the use of resonance strategy. The ad essentially requires the reader to imagine the experience of moving into a new apartment or home and fixing it to exactly match one's preferred décor and lifestyle. Ace Hardware hopes, of course, that the reader will consider it as a viable option when purchasing all the items needed for do-it-yourself jobs.

Emotional Strategy

Emotional advertising is the third form of symbolically/experientially oriented advertising. Much contemporary advertising aims to reach the consumer at a visceral level through the use of emotional strategy.[25] Many advertising practitioners and scholars recognize that products often are bought on the basis of emotional factors and that appeals to emotion can be very successful if used appropriately and with the right brands. The use of emotion in advertising runs the

Illustration of Resonance Strategy   **Figure 9.5**

gamut of positive and negative emotions, including appeals to romance, nostalgia, compassion, excitement, joy, fear, guilt, disgust, and regret.[26]

Though the emotional strategy can be used when advertising virtually any brand, emotional advertising seems to work especially well for product categories that naturally are associated with emotions (e.g., foods, jewelry, cosmetics, fashion apparel, soft drinks, and long-distance telephoning).

Generic Strategy

An advertiser employs a **generic strategy** when making a claim that could be made by any company that markets a brand in that product category. The advertiser makes *no* attempt to differentiate its brand from competitive offerings or to claim superiority. This strategy is most appropriate for a brand that *dominates a product category*. In such instances, the firm making a generic claim will enjoy a large share of any primary demand stimulated by advertising.

For example, Campbell's dominates the prepared-soup market in the United States, selling nearly two-thirds of all soup. Any advertising that increases overall soup sales naturally benefits Campbell's. This explains the "Soup is good food" campaign used by Campbell's in the early 1990s. This advertising extolled the virtues of eating soup without arguing why people should buy Campbell's soup. Campbell's subsequently followed this campaign with another one that simply declared, "Never underestimate the power of soup." Along similar lines, AT&T's "Reach out and touch someone" campaign, which encouraged more long-distance calling, was a wise strategy in light of this company's grasp on the long-distance phone market.

Preemptive Strategy

Preemptive strategy, a second category-dominance advertising strategy, is employed when an advertiser makes a generic-type claim but does so with an *assertion of superiority*. This strategy is most often used by advertisers in product or service categories where there are few, if any, functional differences among competitive brands. Preemptive advertising is a clever strategy when a meaningful superiority claim is made because it effectively precludes competitors from saying the same thing. Any branch of the military service could claim that they enable recruits to "be all you can be," but no other branch could possibly make such a claim after the Army adopted this as its unique statement. The huge Chase Bank, which resulted from the merger of Chase Manhattan and Chemical banks, undertook a $45 million advertising campaign shortly after the merger that referred to Chase as "the Relationship Company." In a clear recognition of the value of preemption, the chief marketing officer for Chase justified the campaign by stating "The idea is to stamp that word [*relationship*] on our brand enough to preempt the use of it by anyone else in the category."[27]

The maker of Visine eyedrops advertised that this brand "gets the red out." All eyedrops are designed to get the red out, but by making this claim first, Visine made a dramatic statement that the consumer will associate only with Visine. No other company could subsequently make this claim for fear of being labeled a mimic. An advertisement for Hanes' Smooth Illusions pantyhose used a brilliant preemptive claim in comparing that brand to "Liposuction without surgery." Another clever preemptive campaign was introduced by Nissan Motor Corporation some years ago with its advertising of the Maxima. Preceding the campaign, the Maxima competed against models such as the Ford Taurus and the Toyota Cressida in the upper-middle segment of the industry. To avoid stiff price competition and price rebates, Nissan wanted a more upscale and high-performance image for the Maxima. Based on extensive research, Maxima's advertising agency devised a brilliant preemptive claim touting the Maxima as the "four-door sports car." Of course, other sedans have four doors, but Maxima preempted sports car status for itself with this one clever claim. Its sales immediately increased by 43 percent over the previous year despite a price increase.[28]

A final illustration of the preemptive strategy is the advertising for the luxury Swiss brand of watches named Patek Philippe. Magazine advertisements for this brand portrayed happy scenes of a parent enjoying the company of his or her same-sex child. Corresponding advertising copy simply asserted "You never actually own a Patek Philippe. You merely take care of it for the next generation." Such a claim could be made by any maker of luxury watches, but in appropriating this claim with its implicit assertion of superiority Patek Philippe has preempted competitors from using the heritage tact in advertising their own brands.

In Sum

Six general advertising strategies have been discussed and categorized as functional, symbolic/experiential, or category-dominance oriented. These strategic alternatives provide a useful aid to understanding the different approaches available to advertisers and the factors influencing the choice of creative strategy. It would be incorrect to think of these strategies as pure and mutually exclusive. Because there is some unavoidable overlap, it is possible that an advertiser may consciously or unconsciously use two or more strategies simultaneously.

Some advertising experts contend that advertising is most effective when it reflects both ends of the creative advertising continuum—that is, by addressing both functional product benefits and symbolic/psychosocial benefits. A New York advertising agency provided evidence in partial support of the superiority of combined benefits over using only functional appeals. The agency tested 168 television commercials, 47 of which contained both functional and psychosocial appeals and 121 of which contained functional appeals only. Using recall and persuasion measures, the agency found that the ads containing a combination of functional and psychosocial appeals outperformed the functional-only ads by a substantial margin.[29]

Finally, it is important to recognize that whatever creative strategy is chosen, it must be clearly positioned in the customer's mind. That is, effective advertising must establish a *clear meaning of what the brand is and how it compares to competitive offerings.* Effective positioning requires that a company be fully aware of its competition and exploit competitive weaknesses. A brand is positioned in the consumer's mind relative to competition. The originators of the positioning concept, consultants Jack Trout and Al Ries, contend that successful companies must be "competitors' oriented," must look for weak points in their competitors' positions, and then launch marketing attacks against those weak points.[30] These same management consultants claim that many marketing people and advertisers are in error when operating under the assumption that marketing/advertising is a battle of products. Their contrary position is this:

> There are no best products. All that exists in the world of marketing are perceptions in the minds of the customer or prospect. The perception is the reality. Everything else is an illusion.[31]

This perhaps is a bit overstated, but the important point is that how good (or how prestigious, dependable, sexy, etc.) a brand is depends more on what people think than on objective reality. And what people think is largely a function of effective advertising that creates a unique selling proposition, builds an attractive image, or otherwise differentiates the brand from competitive offerings and lodges the intended meaning securely in the customer's mind.

MEANS-END CHAINING AND THE METHOD OF LADDERING AS GUIDES TO ADVERTISING STRATEGY FORMULATION

The preceding discussion emphasized, if only implicitly, that the consumer (or customer in the case of B2B marketing) should be the foremost determinant of advertising messages. The notion of a means-end chain provides a useful framework for understanding the relationship between consumers and advertising messages. A means-end chain represents the linkages among brand *attributes*, the *consequences* obtained from using the brand, and the *personal values* that the consequences reinforce.[32] These linkages represent a means-end chain because the consumer sees the brand and its attributes as a means for achieving a desired end, namely, the acquisition of desirable consequences (or avoidance of undesirable consequences) and the valued end state resulting from these consequences. Schematically, the means-end chain is as follows:

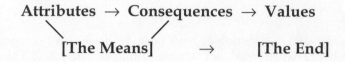

$$\text{Attributes} \rightarrow \text{Consequences} \rightarrow \text{Values}$$

$$\text{[The Means]} \quad\quad \rightarrow \quad\quad \text{[The End]}$$

Attributes are features or aspects of advertised brands. For example, automobile attributes include size, storage capacity, engine performance, aesthetic features, and so on. **Consequences** are what consumers hope to receive (benefits) or avoid (detriments) when consuming brands. Status, convenience, performance, safety, and resale value are positive consequences (benefits) associated with automobiles, whereas breakdowns, mishandling, and poor resale value are negative consequences (detriments) that consumers wish to avoid. In sum, the important thing to appreciate is that attributes reside in brands, whereas consequences are experienced by consumers as a result of brand acquisition and usage.

Values represent those enduring beliefs people hold regarding what is important in life.[33] They pertain to end states that people desire in their lives; they transcend specific situations, and they guide selection or evaluation of behavior.[34] In general, values determine the relative desirability of consequences and serve to organize the meanings for products and brands in consumers' cognitive structures.[35]

Values represent the starting point, the catalyst, and the source of motivation for many aspects of human behavior. Consumer behavior, like other facets of behavior, involves the pursuit of valued states, or outcomes. Brand attributes and their consequences (benefits and detriments) are not sought per se, but rather are desired as means to achieving valued end states. From the consumer's perspective, the *ends* (values) drive the *means* (attributes and their consequences). Let's now examine more fully the values that energize human behavior.

The Nature of Values

Psychologists have conducted extensive research on values and constructed numerous value typologies. This chapter takes the view that 10 basic values adequately represent the important human values that are shared by people in a wide variety of culturally diverse countries. Table 9.3 lists these 10 values.[36] Research identified these values based on studies conducted in 20 culturally diverse countries: Australia, Brazil, Estonia, Finland, Germany, Greece, Holland, Hong Kong, Israel, Italy, Japan, New Zealand, People's Republic of China, Poland, Portugal, Spain, Taiwan, United States, Venezuela, and Zimbabwe. People in these countries shared the same set of values, each of which is now briefly described.[37]

1. *Self-direction.* Independent thought and action is the defining goal of this value type. It includes the desire for freedom, independence, choosing one's own goals, and creativity.
2. *Stimulation.* This value derives from the need for variety and achieving an exciting life.
3. *Hedonism.* Enjoying life and receiving pleasure are fundamental to this value type.
4. *Achievement.* Enjoying personal success through demonstrating competence according to social standards is the defining goal of this value type. Being regarded as capable, ambitious, intelligent, and influential are different aspects of the achievement value.
5. *Power.* The power value entails the attainment of social status and prestige along with control or dominance over people and resources (wealth, authority, social power, and recognition).

10 Universal Values   Table 9.3

1. **Self-Direction**
2. **Stimulation**
3. **Hedonism**
4. **Achievement**
5. **Power**
6. **Security**
7. **Conformity**
8. **Tradition**
9. **Benevolence**
10. **Universalism**

Source: Shalom H. Schwartz, "Universals in the Content and Structure of Values: Theoretical Advances and Empirical Tests in 20 Countries," *Advances in Experimental Social Psychology* 25 (1992), 1–65.

6. *Security.* The essence of this value type is the longing for safety, harmony, and the stability of society. This value includes concern for personal and family safety and even national security. (Especially for people in the United States, the valuation of security increased prominently after the September 11, 2001 terrorist attacks on the World Trade Center and the Pentagon.)

7. *Conformity.* Self-discipline, obedience, politeness, and, in general, the restraint of actions and impulses that are likely to upset or harm others and violate social norms are at the root of this value type.

8. *Tradition.* This value encompasses respect, commitment, and acceptance of the customs that one's culture and religion impose.

9. *Benevolence.* The motivational goal of benevolence is the preservation and enhancement of the welfare of one's family and friends. It includes being honest, loyal, helpful, a true friend, and loving in a mature manner.

10. *Universalism.* Universalism represents a life goal whereby individuals are motivated to understand, appreciate, tolerate, and protect the welfare of all people and nature. It incorporates notions of world peace, social justice, equality, unity with nature, environmental protection, and wisdom.

Which Values Are Most Relevant to Advertising?

The 10 values just presented are apt descriptions of human psychology around the world. It is important to note, however, that they apply to all aspects of life and not to consumer behavior per se. Consequently, all 10 values are not equally important to consumers and thus not equally applicable to advertisers in their campaign-development efforts. Before reading on, take a few moments to review the 10 values and to identify those that you consider most applicable to advertising and consumption.

If you are like me, you will have concluded that the first six values—self-direction through security—apply to many advertising and consumption situations, whereas the last four are not typically the values that drive many aspects of consumer behavior. These latter four values certainly are applicable under select advertising situations (e.g., advertising efforts by nonprofit organizations such as churches and charitable organizations), but they do not typify usual consumer behavior for most products and services. Hence, in concluding our discussion of values, you should realize that self-direction, stimulation, hedonism, achievement, power, and security are the valued end states that drive the bulk of consumer behavior and thus are the goals to which advertisers must appeal.

Advertising Applications of Means-End Chains: The MECCAS Model

The creation of effective advertisements demands that the brand marketer possess a clear understanding of what consumers value from the product category and specific brand. Because consumers differ in what they value from a particular brand, it is meaningful to discuss values only at the market segment level. A brand advertiser, armed with knowledge of segment-level values, is in a position to know what brand attributes and consequences to emphasize to a particular market segment as the means by which that brand can help consumers achieve a valued end state. A formal model, called **MECCAS**—an acronym for *means-end conceptualization of components for advertising strategy*—provides a procedure for applying the concept of means-end chains to the creation of advertising messages.[38]

Table 9.4 presents and defines the various levels of the MECCAS model. Note that the components include a *value orientation, brand consequences,* and *brand attributes,* and a *creative strategy and leverage point* that provides the structure for presenting the advertising message and the means for tapping into or activating the value orientation.[39] The *value orientation* represents the consumer value or end level on which the advertising strategy focuses and can be thought of as the *driving force* behind the advertising execution. Every other component is geared toward achieving the end level. Please study the remaining definitions carefully in Table 9.4 before moving on to the illustrative applications of the MECCAS approach that are described next.

The following sections apply the MECCAS framework in analyzing six advertisements, one for each of the first six values shown in Table 9.3. It is important to note that these applications are the author's post hoc interpretations. It is unknown whether the advertisers in these cases actually performed formal means-end analyses in developing their ads. Nonetheless, these analyses will provide enhanced understanding of how the means-end logic (attributes → consequences → values) can be translated into the design of actual advertisements.

Table 9.4   A MECCAS Model Conceptualization of Advertising Strategy

Component	Definition
Value orientation	The end level (value) to be focused on in the advertising; it serves as the driving force for the advertising execution.
↑	
Brand consequences	The major positive consequences, or benefits of using the brand, that the advertisement verbally or visually communicates to consumers.
↑	
Brand attributes	The brand's specific attributes or features that are communicated as a means of supporting the consequence(s) of using the brand.
↑	
Creative Strategy and Leverage Point	The overall scenario for communicating the value orientation and the manner (leverage point) by which the advertisement will tap into, reach, or activate the key value that serves as the ad's driving force.

Source: Adapted from Thomas J. Reynolds and Jonathan Gutman, "Advertising Is Image Management," *Journal of Advertising Research* 24 (February/March 1984), 27–36

Self-Direction and Cingular.   The self-direction value includes the desire for freedom, independence, and choosing one's own goals. The value orientation serving as the driving force in the Cingular advertisement (Figure 9.6) is an unadorned appeal to consumers' need to "do their own thing" (a form of independence) via self-expression. Indeed, this advertisement appeals to this value without touting any specific service attributes or benefits. It is implied, however, that Cingular's wireless service has features that remove barriers and enable self-expression. The ad's creative strategy simply relates the Cingular jack icon (recall discussion of the icon back in Chapter 7) with the well-established peace and happiness symbols. The value of self-expression is leveraged in this straightforward advertisement by essentially conveying to consumers that Cingular symbolizes self-expression in the same manner that the other two symbols signify similarly abstract qualities of peace and happiness.

Stimulation and the Land Rover Discovery.   The need for variety and achieving an exciting life is the essence of the stimulation value. The advertisement for the Land Rover Discovery (Figure 9.7) appeals to this value by juxtaposing the excited boy in the top scene with the man driving the Land Rover in the bottom scene. (The ad also suggests a boy-gets-girl fantasy with life lived happily ever after in a home with a white picket fence.) The visual of the Land Rover provides information about product attributes, with a reasonable price ("starting at only $33,995") being the only other attribute featured in the copy. The combination of visual and verbal attributes implies desirable consequences of owning this vehicle and its role in achieving variety and excitement. The

MECCAS Illustration for Self-Direction Value   **Figure 9.6**

Figure 9.9

MECCAS Illustration for Achievement Value

that human drivers and their precious cargo of loved ones "both big and small" are the foxes who require protection from the hounds of the world. The advertisement for Chrysler's Town & Country minivan promises this vehicle as the "safe haven" that will afford this protection.

Determining Means-End Chains: The Method of Laddering

Laddering is a research technique that has been developed to identify linkages between attributes (A), consequences (C), and values (V). The method is termed *laddering* because it leads to the construction of a hierarchy, or ladder, of relations between a brand's attributes/consequences (the means) and consumer values (the end). **Laddering** involves in-depth, one-on-one interviews that typically last between 30 minutes to more than one hour. An interviewer first determines what attributes are most important in the product category to the interviewee and from there attempts to identify the linkages in the interviewee's mind from attributes to consequences and from consequences to abstract values.

In conducting a laddering interview, the interviewer refers the interviewee to a specific attribute and then through directed probes attempts to detect how the interviewee links that attribute with more abstract consequences and how the consequences are linked with even more abstract values. After linkages for the first attribute are exhausted, the interviewer moves on to the next salient attribute, and then the next until all important attributes have been explored, which

MECCAS Illustration for Power Value

Figure 9.10

Remember the "Back to Basics" movement?

Neither do we.

Besides, we have our own movement. One for people looking to unwind in a leather- and wood-trimmed cabin. Who want room for six in a whisper-quiet environment. And who enjoy a smooth-riding V-8-powered automobile. Want to join? 1 800 446-8888 or www.lincolnvehicles.com.

Lincoln Town Car. What a luxury car should be.

typically would range between three to seven attributes. Probing is accomplished with questions such as the following:[40]

- "Why is that [particular attribute] important to you?"
- "How does that help you out?"
- "What do you get from that?"
- "Why do you want that?"
- "What happens to you as a result of that?"

With reference to the U.S military advertisement (Figure 9.9), imagine that an interviewer asks potential recruits why it might be important to them to embark on a career that offers "8 different ways to earn college credits." Some recruits might respond that they cannot afford to attend college immediately out of high school but they would like to attend college in the future. A follow-up probe by the interviewer ("Why do you want that?") results in these recruits saying that having a college degree would allow them to have good, well-paying jobs. In response to a "why is that important to you" prompt, they comment that having good jobs would please their parents, who would be very proud to see their children successful in life.

We see in this hypothetical description that a product attribute (the ability to earn college credits while enlisted in the military) is linked in these recruits' minds with the opportunity to get a college degree and obtain a good job. This consequence is, in turn, linked to the achievement value and the resulting satisfaction from having proud parents. The advertisement in Figure 9.9 apparently is based on the view that there is a substantial market segment of high school

Figure 9.11   MECCAS Illustration for Security Value

graduates who see the military as an opportunity to improve their lives and to realize their ambitions.

Practical Issues in Identifying Means-End Chains

In conclusion, the important point to remember about the MECCAS approach is that it provides a systematic procedure for linking the advertiser's perspective (the possession of brand attributes and consequences) with the consumer's perspective (the pursuit of products and brands to achieve desired end states, or values). Effective advertising does not focus on product attributes/consequences per se; rather, it is directed at showing how the advertised brand will benefit the consumer and enable him or her to achieve what he or she most desires in life—self-determination, stimulation, hedonism, and the other values listed in Table 9.3. Products and brands vary in terms of which values they are capable of satisfying; nonetheless, all are capable of fulfilling some value(s), and it is the role of sophisticated advertising to identify and access those values. Advertising and other forms of marketing communications are most relevant to the consumer and thus most effective for the advertised brand when they are based on strong linkages between the right set of attributes, consequences, and values.[41]

All said, it is pertinent to note that the means-end approach and the method of laddering are not without critics. The primary criticisms are several: First, it is claimed that the laddering method "forces" interviewees to identify hierarchies among attributes, consequences, and values that may actually not have existed before the interview and absent the interviewer's directive probes. Second, it is suggested that consumers may possess clear-cut linkages between attributes and consequences but not necessarily between consequences and values. Finally, laddering is criticized on grounds that the ultimate hierarchy constructed is a crude aggregation of $A \rightarrow C \rightarrow V$ chains from multiple individuals into a single chain that represents the input into a MECCAS model.[42]

These criticisms are not unfounded, but the reality is that all methods for creative strategy development in advertising have their imperfections. The value of laddering is that it forces advertisers to identify how consumers relate product attributes to more abstract states such as benefits and values. This systematic approach thereby ensures that advertising emphasis will be placed on communicating benefits and implying valued end states rather than focusing on attributes per se. It is likely for some product categories and particular brands that consumers do not possess clear linkages between brand consequences and values. So, although the means-end chain may entail only $A \rightarrow C$ links rather than the full set of $A \rightarrow C \rightarrow V$ links, the systematic laddering procedure serves its purpose by encouraging creative personnel to focus on product benefits rather than attributes.

CORPORATE IMAGE AND ISSUE ADVERTISING

The type of advertising discussed to this point is commonly referred to as product- or brand-oriented advertising. Such advertising focuses on a product or, more typically, a specific brand and attempts ultimately to persuade consumers to purchase the advertiser's brand.

Another form of advertising, termed **corporate advertising,** focuses not on specific products or brands but on a corporation's overall image or on economic or social issues relevant to the corporation's interests. This form of advertising is prevalent.[43] Consistent spending on corporate advertising can serve to boost a corporation's equity, much in the same fashion that product-oriented advertising is an investment in the brand equity bank. Two somewhat distinct forms of corporate advertising are discussed in the following sections: (1) image advertising and (2) issue, or advocacy, advertising.[44]

Corporate Image Advertising

This type of corporate advertising has been defined as follows:

> Corporate image advertising is aimed at creating an image of a specific corporate personality in the minds of the general public and seeking maximum favorable images amongst selected audiences (e.g., stockholders, employees, consumers, suppliers, and potential investors). In essence, this type of advertising treats the company as a product, carefully positioning and clearly differentiating it from other similar companies and basically "selling" this product to selected audiences. Corporate image advertising is not concerned with a social problem unless it has a preferred solution. It asks no action on the part of the audience beyond a favorable attitude and passive approval conducive to successful operation in the marketplace.[45]

Corporate image advertising attempts to increase a firm's name recognition, establish goodwill for the company and its products, or identify itself with some meaningful and socially acceptable activity. For example, the advertisement for Jaguar cars (Figure 9.12) is not promoting Jaguar cars per se but rather is linking the company with the preservation of wildlife. Like other corporate image advertisements, this ad attempts to enhance the company's image. In general, research has found that executives regard name identity and image building to be the two most important functions of corporate advertising.[46]

Corporate image advertising is directed at more than merely trying to make consumers feel good about a company. Companies are increasingly using the im-

Figure 9.12   Illustration of Corporate Image Advertising

age of their firms to enhance sales and financial performance.[47] Corporate advertising that does not contribute to increased sales and profits is difficult to justify in today's climate of accountability.

Corporate Issue (Advocacy) Advertising

The other form of corporate advertising is **issue,** or **advocacy, advertising.** When using issue advertising, a company takes a position on a controversial social issue of public importance with the intention of swaying public opinion.[48] It does so in a manner that supports the company's position and best interests while expressly or implicitly challenging the opponent's position and denying the accuracy of their facts.[49]

Issue advertising is a topic of considerable controversy.[50] Business executives are divided on whether this form of advertising represents an effective allocation of corporate resources. Critics question the legitimacy of issue advertising and challenge its status as a tax-deductible expenditure. Since further discussion of these points is beyond the scope of this chapter, the interested reader is encouraged to review the sources contained in the last endnote.[51]

SUMMARY

The chapter examined creative advertising, advertising strategy formulation, creative strategies, means-end models, and corporate image and issue advertising. An important initial question asks, What are the general characteristics of effective advertising? Discussion points out that effective advertising must (1) extend from sound marketing strategy, (2) take the consumer's view, (3) be persuasive, (4) break through the competitive clutter, (5) never promise more than can be delivered, and (6) prevent the creative idea from overwhelming the strategy.

Creative advertising formulation involves a multistep process. The strategy is initiated by specifying the key fact advertising should convey to the target market. This key fact is translated, in step 2, into the primary marketing problem. Extending from this problem statement is the selection of specific communications objectives. The guts of advertising strategy consists, in step 4, of designing the creative message strategy. This involves selecting the target market, identifying the primary competition, and choosing the primary benefit to emphasize. The last step in the process involves ensuring that the advertisement meets all corporate/divisional requirements.

The next major subject covered in this chapter were the alternative forms of creative advertising that are in wide use. Six specific strategies — unique selling proposition, brand image, resonance, emotional, generic, and preemptive — were described and illustrated with examples.

The chapter then turned to the concept of means-end chains and the MECCAS framework (means-end conceptualization of components for advertising strategy) that is used in designing actual advertisements and campaigns. Means-end chains and MECCAS models provide bridges between product attributes, the consequences to the consumer of realizing product attributes, and the ability of these consequences to satisfy consumption-related values (the end). MECCAS models provide an organizing framework for developing creative ads that simultaneously consider attributes, consequences, and values.

The final subject discussed was corporate advertising. A distinction was made between conventional product- and brand-oriented strategy and advertising that focuses on facilitating corporate goodwill, enhancing its image, and advocating matters of economic or social significance to a corporation. Two forms of corporate advertising, image and issue (advocacy) advertising, were described.

Find more resources to help you study at http://shimp.swcollege.com!

DISCUSSION QUESTIONS

1. One requirement for effective advertising is the ability to break through competitive clutter. Explain what this means, and provide several examples of advertising methods that successfully accomplish this.

2. Explain the meaning of the MECCAS model, and describe an advertising campaign of your choice in terms of this model—that is, discuss specifically the value orientation, leverage point, and so on.

3. Explain the differences between unique selling proposition and brand image strategies, and indicate the specific conditions under which each is more likely to be used.

4. Positioning strategy is not mutually exclusive of other creative advertising strategies. Explain what this means, and discuss how positioning can be achieved using different types of creative strategies. Provide examples of actual advertisements to buttress your points.

5. What is a resonant advertising strategy? Explain the similarity between resonant advertising and what some advertising practitioners call slice-of-life advertising.

6. A television commercial for Miller Genuine Draft beer started out by showing scenes of people experiencing a stifling summer day while fantasizing about a cold beer. In a subsequent scene, Miller Genuine Draft came into the picture, and, as people opened cans of beer, the urban setting miraculously changed from a hot summer day to snow-covered streets. Describe how this television commercial represents a form of preemptive strategy.

7. Explain the preceding commercial in terms of means-end chain components (attributes, consequences, and values).

8. Some critics contend that advocacy, or issue, advertising should not be treated as a legitimate tax-deductible expenditure. Present and justify your opinion on this matter.

9. Select two advertising campaigns that have been on television for some time, and describe in detail what you think their creative message strategies are.

10. Review magazine advertisements, and locate specific examples of the six creative strategies that were discussed in the chapter. Be sure to justify why each ad is a good illustration of the strategy with which you identify it.

11. Along the lines of the FTD case described in the chapter, select an advertising campaign, and reconstruct in detail your interpretation of all the steps in the campaign's advertising strategy.

ENDNOTES

1. The 15 percent rate was for advertisements placed in newspapers, magazines, and on television and radio. The discount paid to advertising agencies for outdoor advertising has historically been slightly higher at 16.67 percent.

2. Jack Neff, "Feeling the Squeeze," *Advertising Age*, June 4, 2001, 14; Judann Pollack, "ANA Survey: Under 50% Pay Agency Commissions," *Advertising Age*, June 15, 1998, 18.

3. Gregory White, "Ford's Better Idea for Agencies: Incentives Instead of Commissions," *The Wall Street Journal Interactive Edition*, September 10, 1998.

4. A theoretical treatment of outcome-based compensation programs is provided by Deborah F. Spake, Giles D'Souza, Tammy Neal Crutchfield, and Robert M. Morgan, "Advertising Agency Compensation: An Agency Theory Explanation," *Journal of Advertising* 28 (Fall 1999), 53–72.

5. The following points are a mixture of the author's views and perspectives presented by A. Jerome Jewler, *Creative Strategy in Advertising* (Belmont, Calif.: Wadsworth, 1985), 7–8; and Don E. Schultz and Stanley I. Tannenbaum, *Essentials of Advertising Strategy* (Lincolnwood, Ill.: NTC Business Books, 1988), 9–10.

6. Stan Freberg, "Irtnog Revisited," *Advertising Age*, August 1, 1988, 32.

7. Schultz and Tannenbaum, *Essentials of Advertising Strategy*, 75. This quote actually describes what these authors term *creative advertising*, but they use *creative* in the same sense as this text uses *good*, or *effective, advertising*.

8. For an interesting discussion on creativity and the creative process in advertising, see Vincent J. Blasko and Michael P. Mokwa, "Paradox, Advertising and the Creative Process," in *Current Issues and Research in Advertising*, ed. J. H. Leigh and C. R. Martin, Jr. (Ann Arbor: Graduate School of Business Administration, University of Michigan, 1989), 351–366. See also Jacob Goldenberg, David Mazursky, and Sorin Solomon, "Creative Sparks," *Science* 285 (September 1999), 1495–1496.

9. Terence Poltrack, "Stalking the Big Idea," *Agency*, June 1991, 26.

10. Ibid.

11. Lou Centlivre, "A Peek at the Creative of the '90s," *Advertising Age*, January 18, 1988, 62.

12. This framework is borrowed from the world-famous management consulting firm, McKinsey & Company, in an undated document supplied to me by a company that had secured McKinsey's services.

13. The following discussion is an adaptation from Don E. Schultz, Dennis Martin, and William P. Brown, *Strategic Advertising Campaigns* (Lincolnwood, Ill.: NTC Business Books, 1987), 240–245.

14. This discussion is broadly based on Leah Rickard, "FTD Fights Back in $16M Image Ads," *Advertising Age*, September 27, 1993, 12. More current facts are from FTD's Web site (http://www.ftd.com).

15. Kenneth Hein, "FTD Has 'Em Seeing Red in Vampy, V-Day Ads," *Brandweek*, January 15, 2001, 5.

16. Arthur J. Kover, "Copywriters' Implicit Theories of Communication: An Exploration," *Journal of Consumer Research* 21 (March 1995), 596–611.

17. These guidelines are based on an undated document ("How to Write a Creative Brief") from Ogilvy & Mather Worldwide.

18. Harvey Penick with Bud Shrake, *Harvey Penick's Little Red Book* (New York: Simon & Schuster, 1992), 45.

19. A good review of the literature along with the presentation of an insightful message strategy model are provided by Ronald E. Taylor, "A Six-Segment Message Strategy Wheel," *Journal of Advertising Research* 39 (November/December 1999), 7–17.

20. The following discussion is based on Charles F. Frazer, "Creative Strategy: A Management Perspective," *Journal of Advertising* 12, no. 4 (1983), 36–41. For other perspectives on creative strategies, see Henry A. Laskey, Ellen Day, and Melvin R. Crask, "Typology of Main Message Strategies for Television Commercials," *Journal of Advertising* 18, no. 1 (1989), 36–41; and Taylor, "A Six-Segment Message Strategy Wheel."

21. An interesting debate on the issue of whether a USP strategy is appropriate even for parity products is available in the offsetting views of Dennis Chase and Bob Garfield, "Can Unique Selling Proposition Find Happiness in Parity World?" *Advertising Age*, September 21,1992, 58.

22. Grant McCracken, "Culture and Consumption: A Theoretical Account of the Structure and Movement of the Cultural Meaning of Consumer Goods," *Journal of Consumer Research* 13 (June 1986), 74.

23. Christopher P. Puto and William D. Wells, "Informational and Transformational Advertising: The Differential Effects of Time," in *Advances in Consumer Research*, vol. 11, ed. Thomas C. Kinnear (Provo, Utah: Association for Consumer Research, 1984), 638–643. See also David A. Aaker and Douglas M. Stayman, "Implementing the Concept of Transformational Advertising," *Psychology & Marketing* 9 (May/June 1992), 237–253.

24. Ibid., 638.

25. Frazer ("Creative Strategy") refers to this as affective strategy, but emotional strategy is more descriptive and less subject to alternative interpretations.

26. For a variety of perspectives on the use of emotion in advertising, see Stuart J. Agres, Julie A. Edell, and Tony M. Dubitsky, *Emotion in Advertising: Theoretical and Practical Explorations* (New York: Quorum Books, 1990).

27. Terry Lefton, "Cutting to the Chase," *Brandweek*, April 7, 1997, 47.

28. This description is based on "Four-Door Sports Car," *1990 Winners of the Effie Gold Awards: Case Studies in Advertising Effectiveness* (New York: American Marketing Association of New York and the American Association of Advertising Agencies, 1991), 124–131.

29. Kim Foltz, "Psychological Appeal in TV Ads Found Effective," *Adweek*, August 31, 1987, 38. Please note that this research referred to rational rather than functional appeals, but rational is essentially equivalent to functional.

30. Jack Trout and Al Ries, "The Positioning Era: A View Ten Years Later," *Advertising Age*, July 16, 1979, 39–42.

31. Al Ries and Jack Trout, *The 22 Immutable Laws of Marketing* (New York: Harper Business, 1993), 19.

32. A recent book on the topic of mean-end chains summarizes much of the

thinking on this topic. See Thomas J. Reynolds and Jerry C. Olson, *Understanding Decision Making: The Means-End Approach to Marketing and Advertising Strategy* (Mahwah, NJ: Erlbaum, 2001). See also Jonathan Gutman, "A Means-End Chain Model Based on Consumer Categorization Processes," *Journal of Marketing* 46 (spring 1982), 60–72; Thomas J. Reynolds and Jonathan Gutman, "Advertising Is Image Management," *Journal of Advertising Research* 24 (February/March 1984), 27–36; Thomas J. Reynolds and Jonathan Gutman, "Laddering Theory, Method, Analysis, and Interpretation," *Journal of Advertising Research* 28 (February/March 1988), 11–31; and Thomas J. Reynolds and Alyce Byrd Craddock, "The Application of MEC-CAS Model to the Development and Assessment of Advertising Strategy: A Case Study," *Journal of Advertising Research* 28 (April/May 1988), 43–59.

33. For further discussion of cultural values, see Lynn R. Kahle, Basil Poulos, and Ajay Sukhdial, "Changes in Social Values in the United States during the Past Decade," *Journal of Advertising Research* 28 (February/March 1988), 35–41; Sharon E. Beatty, Lynn R. Kahle, Pamela Homer, and Shekhar Misra, "Alternative Measurement Approaches to Consumer Values: The List of Values and the Rokeach Value Survey," *Psychology and Marketing* 2, no. 3 (1985), 181–200; Wagner A. Kamakura and Jose Afonso Mazzon, "Value Segmentation: A Model for the Measurement of Values and Value Systems," *Journal of Consumer Research* 18 (September 1991), 208–218; and Wagner A. Kamakura and Thomas P. Novak, "Value-System Segmentation: Exploring the Meaning of LOV," *Journal of Consumer Research* 19 (June 1992), 119–132.

34. Shalom H. Schwartz, "Universals in the Content and Structure of Values: Theoretical Advances and Empirical Tests in 20 Countries," *Advances in Experimental Social Psychology* 25 (1992), 4.

35. J. Paul Peter and Jerry C. Olson, *Consumer Behavior: Marketing Strategy Perspectives* (Homewood, Ill.: Irwin, 1990).

36. Schwartz, "Universals in the Content and Structure of Values."

37. These descriptions are based on ibid., pp. 5–12.

38. Jerry Olson and Thomas J. Reynolds, "Understanding Consumers' Cognitive Structures: Implications for Advertising Strategy," in *Advertising and Consumer Psychology*, ed. L. Percy and A. Woodside (Lexington, Mass.: Lexington Books, 1983), 77–90.

39. The language used in Table 9.4 is adapted from that employed in the various writings of Gutman, Reynolds, and Olson such as those cited in note 32. It is the author's experience that students are confused with the terminology originally used. The present terminology is more user friendly without doing a disservice to the original MECCAS conceptualization.

40. Thomas J. Reynolds, Clay Dethloff, and Steven J. Westberg, "Advancements in Laddering," in Thomas J. Reynolds and Jerry C. Olson, *Understanding Decision Making*, 91–118.

41. Thomas J. Reynolds and David B. Whitlark, "Applying Laddering Data to Communications Strategy and Advertising Practice," *Journal of Advertising Research* 35 (July/August 1995), 9.

42. See John R. Rossiter and Larry Percy, "The a-b-e Model of Benefit Focus in Advertising," in Thomas J. Reynolds and Jerry C. Olson, *Understanding Decision Making*, 183–213; and Joel B. Cohen and Luk Warlop, "A Motivational Perspective on Means-End Chains," in Thomas J. Reynolds and Jerry C. Olson, *Understanding Decision Making*, 389–412.

43. David W. Schumann, Jan M. Hathcote, and Susan West, "Corporate Advertising in America: A Review of Published Studies on Use, Measurement, and Effectiveness," *Journal of Advertising* 20 (September 1991), 35–56. This article provides a thorough review of corporate advertising and is must reading for anyone interested in the topic. For evidence of the increase in corporate advertising, see Mercedes M. Cardona, "Corporate-Ad Budgets At Record High: ANA Survey," *Advertising Age*, April 27, 1998, 36.

44. This distinction is based on a classification by S. Prakash Sethi, "Institutional/Image Advertising and Idea/Issue Advertising As Marketing Tools: Some Public Policy Issues," *Journal of Marketing* 43 (January 1979), 68–78. Sethi actually labels the two subsets of corporate advertising as "institutional/image" and "idea/issue." For reading ease they are shortened here to image versus issue advertising.

45. Ibid.

46. Charles H. Patti and John P. McDonald, "Corporate Advertising: Process, Practices, and Perspectives (1970–1989)," *Journal of Advertising* 14, no. 1 (1985), 42–49.

47. Lewis C. Winters, "Does It Pay to Advertise to Hostile Audiences with Corporate Advertising?" *Journal of Advertising Research* 28 (June/July 1988), 11–18.

48. Bob D. Cutler and Darrel D. Muehling, "Advocacy Advertising and the Bound-

aries of Commercial Speech," *Journal of Advertising* 18, no. 3 (1989), 40.

49. Sethi, "Institutional/Image Advertising," 70.

50. For discussion of the First Amendment issues surrounding the use of advocacy advertising, see Cutler and Muehling, "Advocacy Advertising and the Boundaries of Commercial Speech"; and Kent R. Middleton, "Advocacy Advertising, The First Amendment and Competitive Advantage: A Comment on Cutler & Muehling," *Journal of Advertising* 20 (June 1991), 77–81.

51. Louis Banks, "Taking on the Hostile Media," *Harvard Business Review* (March/April 1978), 123–130; Barbara J. Coe, "The Effectiveness Challenge in Issue Advertising Campaigns," *Journal of Advertising* 12, no. 4 (1983), 27–35; David Kelley, "Critical Issues for Issue Ads," *Harvard Business Review* (July/August 1982), 80–87; Ward Welty, "Is Issue Advertising Working?" *Public Relations Journal* (November 1981), 29. For an especially thorough and insightful treatment of issue advertising, particularly with regard to the measurement of effectiveness, see Karen F. A. Fox, "The Measurement of Issue/Advocacy Advertising," in *Current Issues and Research in Advertising*, vol. 9, ed. James H. Leigh and Claude R. Martin, Jr. (Ann Arbor: Division of Research, Graduate School of Business Administration, University of Michigan, 1986), 61–92.

Chapter Ten

ENDORSERS AND MESSAGE APPEALS IN ADVERTISING

Chapter Objectives

After studying this chapter, you should be able to:

1. Describe the role of endorsers in advertising.
2. Explain the requirements for an effective endorser.
3. Appreciate the factors that enter into the endorser-selection decision.
4. Discuss the role of Q-ratings in selecting celebrity endorsers.
5. Describe the role of humor in advertising.
6. Explain the logic underlying the use of appeals to fear in advertising.
7. Understand the nature of appeals to guilt in advertising.
8. Discuss the role of sex appeals, including the downside of such usage.
9. Explain the meaning of subliminal messages and symbolic embeds.
10. Appreciate the role of music in advertising.
11. Understand the function of comparative advertising and the considerations that influence the use of this form of advertising.

Opening Vignette: "Who's That Behind Those FosterGrants?"

FosterGrant is a line of sunglasses that has been marketed for more than 70 years. Back in the sixties and seventies, the brand was virtually synonymous with the product category. Then a combination of increased competition and poor marketing resulted in a precipitous decline in brand equity and market share. When the brand's 70th anniversary was approaching, the marketing team at FosterGrant decided it was time to relaunch the famous advertising campaign used in prior decades. In particular, advertising in an earlier era used celebrities bedecked with FosterGrant glasses in magazine ads headed with "Who's That Behind Those FosterGrants?"

The marketing team at FosterGrants concluded that it needed a top-flight celebrity to reinvigorate the brand and launch the new advertising campaign. The team created a list of 50 celebrities, including famous athletes, actors, musicians, and models. Five finalists were selected from the initial list of 50, and Cindy Crawford ultimately was selected to endorse FosterGrant sunglasses. Here is how the company's marketing VP justified the selection of Ms. Crawford to become the celebrity "Behind Those FosterGrants":

> We chose Cindy because she's global, and we're global as well. She appeals to our target audience of women 25–45, but she also skews younger because of House of Style. She's very approachable for a celebrity. In our research, we didn't find anyone who had a bad opinion of her. And, of course, she looked great behind those FosterGrants and could contemporize our image.

The magazine campaign with Cindy Crawford generated near-immediate success. Consumers associated her with the FosterGrant brand, and sales in retail outlets increased substantially over the previous year.

Though enjoying the success of the Cindy Crawford endorsement, FosterGrant's marketing team was concerned that the brand could become so associated with Ms. Crawford herself that consumers might consider FosterGrant just a "female brand." To prevent this from happening, brand management realized the importance of identifying a male celebrity to become a strong complement to Ms. Crawford. Nascar star Jeff Gordon eventually was selected to be this counterpart. The sport of automobile racing is the fastest-growing professional sport in the United States, and Jeff Gordon fits well with FosterGrant's brand image. He matches the brand's male target audience and also scores well with women on

Sources: Adapted from Becky Ebenkamp, "Fostering a Grant Intention," *Brandweek*, January 24, 2000, pp. 26–29; Sandra Dolbow, "NASCAR Sends Gordon Behind Foster Grants," *Brandweek*, April 2, 2001, p. 5. © 2001 VNU Business Media, Inc.

Q-ratings—a metric for selecting celebrity endorsers that is described later in the chapter.

This chapter provides a survey of some of the common approaches that are used in creating advertising messages. First examined is the use of endorsers in advertising. Discussion turns then to five types of advertising messages that are widespread: (1) humor, (2), appeals to fear, (3) appeals to guilt, (4) sex appeals, and (5) subliminal messages. The chapter concludes with reviews of music's role in advertising and the pros and cons of using comparative advertisements.

Where possible, an attempt is made to identify *generalizations* about the creation of effective advertising messages. It is important to realize, however, that generalizations are not the same as scientific laws or principles. These higher forms of scientific truth (such as Einstein's general theory of relativity and Newton's law of gravity) have not been established in the realm of advertising for several reasons: First, the buyer behavior that advertising is designed to influence is complex, dynamic, and variable across situations, which consequently makes it difficult to arrive at straightforward explanations of how advertising elements operate in all situations and across all types of market segments. Second, advertisements are themselves highly varied entities that differ in numerous respects rather than just in terms of their use of humor, or sex, or appeals to fear, or any other single dimension. This complexity makes it difficult to draw specific conclusions about any particular feature of advertising. Third, because products differ in terms of technological sophistication, ability to involve consumers, and in various other respects, it is virtually impossible to identify advertising approaches that are universally effective across all products and services.

Thus, the findings presented and the conclusions drawn should be considered tentative rather than definitive. In accordance with the philosopher's advice, "Seek simplicity and distrust it,"[1] it would be naïve and misleading to suggest that any particular advertising technique will be successful under all circumstances. Rather, the effectiveness of any message format depends on circumstances such as the nature of the competition, the character of the product, the degree of brand equity and market leadership, the advertising environment, and the extent of consumer involvement. Throughout the text we have emphasized the importance of this "it depends" mind-set, and it is important that you bring such an orientation to your reading of the following sections.

THE ROLE OF ENDORSERS IN ADVERTISING

The products in many advertisements receive explicit endorsements from a variety of popular public figures, such as Cindy Crawford's and Jeff Gordon's endorsements of FosterGrant sunglasses (see *Opening Vignette*). In addition to celebrity endorsements, products also receive the explicit or tacit support of noncelebrities.

Celebrity Endorsers

Television stars, movie actors, famous athletes, and even dead personalities are widely used to endorse products. By definition, a celebrity is a well-known personality (actor, entertainer, or athlete) who is known to the public for his or her accomplishments in areas other than the product class endorsed.[2]

Advertisers and their agencies are willing to pay huge salaries to celebrities who are liked and respected by target audiences and who will, it is hoped, favorably influence consumers' attitudes and behavior toward the endorsed brands. For the most part, such investments are justified. Even the investment community recognizes the value of celebrity endorsers. Indeed, stock prices have been shown to increase when companies announce celebrity endorsement contracts.[3] On the downside, there is evidence that a company's stock price declines when negative publicity reaches the media about a celebrity who endorses of one of the company's brands.[4]

Top celebrities receive enormous payments for their endorsement services. For example, golfer Tiger Woods is estimated to earn $54 million annually from endorsement deals with 11 companies.[5] To put this amount in perspective, a person earning a not-so-paltry annual income of $100,000 would have to work 540 years at that salary to earn as much as Tiger Woods receives in a single year from his endorsement activities! One of his endorsement deals is shown in Figure 10.1 (Buick).

Typical-Person Endorsers

A frequent advertising approach is to show regular people—that is, noncelebrities—using or endorsing products. In addition to being much less expensive than celebrities, typical-person endorsers avoid the potential backlash from using "beautiful people" who may be resented for possessing atypical physical attractiveness or other individual traits.[6] Also, real people who have personally experienced the benefits of using a particular brand possess a degree of credibility that likely is unsurpassed. For example, the Subway chain of sandwich shops experienced a sales boom when the product was endorsed by previously unknown Jared, who was advertised to have lost more than 200 pounds while subsisting on a diet of Subway sandwiches.

A magazine advertisement for Allure cologne for men from Chanel featured a noncelebrity in the ad posed as if he were leaning on a larger-than-life

Figure 10.1   **Tiger Woods Endorsing Buick**

bottle of Allure. A caption below the man's face states, "Plastic surgeon Beverly Hills." This typical person, noncelebrity endorser likely was chosen for the ease with which many professional men in the target audience could relate to him compared to, say, a movie star such as Denzel Washington or Brad Pitt. Likewise, the four young women in the Skechers footwear advertisement (Figure 10.2) represent that brand well to the target audience that they mirror.

Many advertisements that portray typical-person users often include *multiple people* rather than a single individual (such as the Skechers footwear ad). Is there any reason why multiple sources should be more effective than a single source? Yes, there is: The act of portraying more than one person seems to increase the likelihood an advertisement will generate higher levels of message involvement and correspondingly greater message elaboration (recall the discussion on involvement and elaboration in the context of the elaboration likelihood model in Chapter 5). In turn, greater elaboration increases the odds that strong message arguments will favorably influence attitudes.[7]

Endorser Attributes: The TEARS Model

Now that a distinction has been made between the two general types of advertising endorsers, it is important to formally describe endorser attributes and the role they play in facilitating communications effectiveness. Extensive research has demonstrated that two general attributes, *credibility* and *attractiveness*,

Another Illustration of a Typical-Person Endorsement   **Figure 10.2**

contribute to an endorser's effectiveness, and that each consists of more distinct subattributes.[8] To facilitate the student's memory with respect to endorser characteristics, we use the acronym TEARS to represent five discrete attributes: *t*rustworthiness and *e*xpertise are two dimensions of credibility, whereas physical *a*ttractiveness, *r*espect, and *s*imilarity (to the target audience) are components of the general concept of attractiveness. Table 10.1 lists and defines all five attributes.

Credibility: The Process of Internalization.

In its most basic sense, credibility refers to the tendency to believe or trust someone. When an information source, such as an endorser, is perceived as credible, audience attitudes are changed through a psychological process called internalization. **Internalization** occurs when the receiver accepts the endorser's position on an issue as his or her own. An internalized attitude tends to be maintained even if the source of the message is forgotten or if the source switches to a different position.[9]

Two important subattributes of endorser credibility are trustworthiness and expertise. **Trustworthiness**, the *T* term in the TEARS model, refers to the honesty, integrity, and believability of a source. Though expertise and trustworthiness are not mutually exclusive, often a particular endorser is perceived as highly trustworthy but not especially expert. Endorser trustworthiness simply reflects the fact that prospective endorsers of a brand vary in the degree to which audience members trust what they have to say. An endorser's trustworthiness rests on the audience's perception of his or her endorsement motivations. If consumers believe that an endorser is motivated purely by self-interest, that endorser will be less persuasive than someone regarded as having nothing to gain by endorsing the brand.

A celebrity earns the audience's trust through the life he or she lives professionally (on the screen, on the sports field, in public office, etc.) and personally as revealed to the general public via the mass media. (To demonstrate this point to yourself, spend a moment and rank four living ex-U.S. presidents–George Bush Sr., Jimmy Carter, Bill Clinton, and Gerald Ford—in terms of how trustworthy you perceive them to be. If President Clinton is not at the top of your list, it is likely due more to his personal life ["I didn't have sex with that woman!"] than

Table 10.1

The Five Components in the TEARS Model of Endorser Attributes

T = Trustworthiness	The property of being perceived as believable, dependable—as someone who can be trusted.
E = Expertise	The characteristic of having specific skills, knowledge, or abilities with respect to the endorsed brand.
A = Physical attractiveness	The trait of being regarded as pleasant to look at in terms of a particular group's concept of attractiveness.
R = Respect	The quality of being admired or even esteemed due to one's personal qualities and accomplishments.
S = Similarity (to the target audience)	The extent to which an endorser matches an audience in terms of characteristics pertinent to the endorsement relationship (age, gender, ethnicity, etc.).

his actual job performance.) Advertisers capitalize on the value of trustworthiness by selecting endorsers who are widely regarded as being honest, believable, and dependable people.

Advertisers sometimes use the *overheard conversation technique* to enhance trustworthiness. A television advertisement might show a middle-aged person overhearing one man explain to another why his brand of arthritis pain relief medicine is the best on the market. In this case, the commercial attempts to have audience members place themselves in the position of the person overhearing the conversation. An experiment tested whether a hidden-camera endorser (one who is presumably extolling the virtues of a product without being aware of it) is more persuasive than a typical-person endorser (one who is aware of his or her spokesperson role). The researchers hypothesized that the hidden-camera endorser should be considered more trustworthy because he or she makes favorable product claims but does not come across as having ulterior motives. The hidden-camera spokesperson was shown, in fact, to be more trustworthy.[10] In general, endorsers must establish that they are not attempting to manipulate the audience and that they are objective in their presentations. By doing so, they establish themselves as trustworthy and, therefore, credible.

The second aspect of endorser credibility is expertise, the *E* component of the TEARS model. **Expertise** refers to the knowledge, experience, or skills possessed by an endorser as they relate to the endorsed brand. Hence, athletes are considered to be experts when it comes to the endorsement of sports-related products. Models are similarly perceived as possessing expertise with regard to beauty-enhancing products and fashion items. Successful businesspeople are regarded as expert in matters of managerial practices. Expertise is a perceived rather than an absolute phenomenon. Whether an endorser is indeed an expert is unimportant; all that matters is how the target audience perceives the endorser. An endorser who is perceived as an expert on a given subject is more persuasive in changing audience opinions pertaining to his or her area of expertise than an endorser who is not perceived as possessing the same charateristic.

Attractiveness: The Process of Identification. The second general attribute that contributes to endorser effectiveness, **attractiveness**, means more than simply physical attractiveness—although that can be a very important attribute—and includes any number of virtuous characteristics that consumers may perceive in an endorser: intellectual skills, personality properties, lifestyle characteristics, athletic prowess, and so on. When consumers find something in an endorser that they consider attractive, persuasion occurs through **identification**. That is, when consumers perceive a celebrity endorser to be attractive, they *identify with* the endorser and are likely to adopt the endorser's attitudes, behaviors, interests, or preferences.

The TEARS model identifies three subcomponents of the general concept of attractiveness: *physical attractiveness*, *respect*, and *similarity*. That is, an endorser is regarded as attractive—in the general sense of this concept—to the extent that she or he is considered physically attractive, is respected for reasons other than physical attractiveness, or is regarded as similar to the target audience in terms of any characteristic that is pertinent to a particular endorsement relationship. Perceived attractiveness can be achieved via any one of these attributes and does *not* require that a celebrity encompass all simultaneously; however, it goes without saying that a celebrity who possesses the entire "package" of attractiveness attributes would represent awesome endorsement potential. Star athletes such as Kobe Bryant (NBA basketball), Marion Jones (Olympic gold medallist in track and field events), Venus Williams (professional tennis), and Tiger Woods (professional golf) would seem to come close to representing the embodiment of all three attractiveness-defining attributes. The student has in mind, no doubt, even better illustrations of celebrities who personify all three attractiveness attributes concurrently. Let us now examine each attractiveness attribute.

First, **physical attractiveness**—the *A* component in the TEARS model—is a key consideration in many endorsement relationships.[11] Perhaps no better illustration of this is possible than tennis player Anna Kournikova's success as an endorser. Ms. Kournikova is estimated to earn around $10 million per year in endorsement deals, which is an incredible feat in view of the fact that she has never won an event on the professional tennis circuit.[12] Swiss watchmaker Omega chose Kournikova because, according to Omega's marketing director, she is "really everything tied into one package."[13] It would seem that Ms. Kournikova is selected for a variety of endorsement deals not because she is particularly credible or respected for exceptional tennis-playing ability but because many people consider her exceptionally physically attractive—and attractiveness goes a long way in a world that often seems to value form over function, appearance over substance. There is a good reason for this: Research has supported the intuitive expectation that physically attractive endorsers produce more favorable evaluations of ads and advertised brands than do less attractive communicators.[14]

Respect, the *R* in the TEARS model, is the second component of the overall attractiveness attribute. **Respect** represents the quality of being admired or even esteemed due to one's personal qualities and accomplishments. Whereas a celebrity's physical attractiveness may be considered the "form" aspect of the overall attractiveness attribute, respect is the "function" or substantive element. Sometimes function trumps form, even in brand-endorser relations.

Celebrities are respected for their acting ability, athletic prowess, appealing personalities, their stand on important societal issues (the environment, political issues, war and peace, etc.), and any number of other qualities. Individuals who are respected also generally are liked, and it is this respect qua likeability factor that can serve to enhance a brand's equity when a respected/liked celebrity endorser enters into an endorsement relationship with the brand. In some sense, the brand acquires some semblance of the characteristics that are admired in the celebrity who endorses the brand. For example, Gatorade and Michael Jordan are inextricably linked in the minds of many consumers. Tiger Woods and Nike golf equipment are somewhat indistinct, and so are Cindy Crawford (*Opening Vignette*) and FosterGrants sunglasses. In sum, when a respected/liked celebrity enters into an extended endorser relationship with a brand, the respect/liking of the celebrity may extend to the brand with which she or he is linked, thus enhancing a brand's equity via the positive effect on consumers' attitudes toward the brand.

Similarity, the third attractiveness component and the *S* term in the TEARS model, represents the degree to which an endorser matches an audience in terms of characteristics pertinent to the endorsement relationship—age, gender, ethnicity, etc. Similarity is an important attribute for the mere fact that people tend to better like individuals who share with them common features or traits. This, of course, is reminiscent of the aphorism that "birds of a feather flock together." In general, an endorser has a greater likelihood of being perceived as trustworthy the more he or she matches the audience in terms of distinct characteristics such as gender and ethnicity. Research with ethnic minorities, for example, reveals that when a spokesperson matches the audience's ethnicity, spokesperson trustworthiness is enhanced, which, in turn, promotes more favorable attitudes toward the advertised brand.[15]

As it applies to the domain of brand-celebrity relationships, the importance of similarity implies that it typically is desirable that a celebrity match his/her endorsed brand's target audience in terms of pertinent demographic and psychographic characteristics. There is some evidence that a matchup between endorser and audience similarity is especially important when the product or service in question is one where audience members are *heterogeneous* in terms of their taste and attribute preferences. For example, because people differ greatly in terms of what they like in restaurants, plays, and movies, a spokesperson perceived to be similar to the audience is expected to have the greatest effect in influencing their attitudes and choices. On the other hand, when preferences among audience members are relatively *homogeneous* (such as might be expected with services such as plumbing, dry cleaning, and auto repair), the matchup between spokesperson and audience similarity is not that important. Rather, it is the spokesperson's *experience or expertise* with the product or service that appears to have the greatest influence in shaping the audience's attitudes and subsequent behavior.[16]

Endorser Selection Considerations: The "No Tears" Approach

The preceding section described in some detail the attributes of celebrities that are important in determining their effectiveness as endorsers. The verbal TEARS model identified five attributes that were grouped under the two general components of credibility and attractiveness. Now let us turn our focus to the issue of how brand managers and their advertising agencies actually select particular endorsers to align with their brands. In a takeoff on the TEARS acronym, endorser selection is described here as the "no-tears" approach. Compared with the prior usage of TEARS, which was merely an acronym combining the first letter of five endorser attributes, the current lowercase usage is applied in the real sense of the word *tears*. In other words, the current discussion is directed at identifying how brand managers and their agencies actually go about selecting celebrities so as to avoid the grief (metaphorically, the tears) from making an unwise decision.

Advertising executives use a variety of factors in selecting celebrity endorsers. The following appear to be the most important: (1) celebrity and audience matchup, (2) celebrity and brand matchup, (3) celebrity credibility, (4) celebrity attractiveness, (5) cost considerations, (6) a working ease/difficulty factor, (7) an endorsement saturation factor, and (8) a likelihood-of-getting-into-trouble factor.[17]

1. Celebrity/Audience Matchup. Perhaps most fundamentally, an endorser must match up well with the endorsed brand's target market. The first question a brand manager must pose when selecting an endorser is, Will the target market positively relate to this endorser? Shaquille O'Neal, Kobe Bryant, Allen Iverson, and other NBA superstars who endorse basketball shoes match up well with the predominantly teenage audience who aspire to slam dunk the basketball, block shots, intercept passes, and sink 25-foot jump shots. Cindy Crawford and Jeff Gordon (*Opening Vignette*) match well with their respective female and male audiences for FosterGrant sunglasses. Can you think of any endorser relations where the match seems inappropriate?

2. Celebrity/Brand Matchup. Advertising executives require that the celebrity's behavior, values, and decorum be compatible with the image desired for the advertised brand. For example, if a brand has a wholesome image or wants to project this particular attribute, then the celebrity endorser should personify wholesomeness. Comparatively, a brand intentionally casting itself with a "bad boy" image would select an entirely different endorser. Suppose a brand manager wished to enhance a brand's equity by portraying the brand as incomparable in terms of durability, dependability, and consistency. Who better to personify these characteristics than, say, Cal Ripken, the Baltimore Orioles baseball player who played in 2,632 consecutive baseball games prior to retiring in 2001.

3. Celebrity Credibility. A celebrity's credibility is a primary reason for selecting a celebrity endorser. People who are trustworthy and perceived as knowledgeable about the product category are best able to convince others to undertake a particular course of action. We discussed the two components of credibility, trustworthiness and expertise, in the TEARS model, so further discussion is unnecessary at this point. Suffice it to say that credibility is a key determinant of endorser effectiveness.

4. Celebrity Attractiveness. In selecting celebrity spokespeople, advertising executives evaluate different aspects that can be lumped together under the general label "attractiveness." As discussed earlier in the TEARS model, attractiveness is multifaceted and does not include just physical attractiveness. It also is important to note that advertising executives generally regard attractiveness as subordinate in importance to credibility and endorser matchup with the audience and with the brand.

5. Cost Considerations.

How much it will cost to acquire a celebrity's services is an important consideration but one that should not dictate the final choice. Everything else held constant, a less costly celebrity will be selected over a more costly alternative. But, of course, everything else is not held constant. Hence, as with any managerial decision when selecting among alternatives, brand managers must perform a cost-benefit analysis to determine whether a more expensive celebrity can be justified in terms of a proportionately greater return on investment. This, unfortunately, is not a simple calculation because it is difficult to project the revenue stream that will be obtained from using a particular celebrity endorser. Difficulty aside, management must attempt to calculate the alternative returns on investment given multiple options of celebrities who would appropriately fit with a brand's desired image and its target market.

6. Working Ease/Difficulty Factor.

Some celebrities are relatively easy to work with, whereas others are simply difficult—stubborn, noncompliant, arrogant, temperamental, inaccessible, or otherwise unmanageable. Brand managers and their advertising agencies would prefer to avoid the "hassle factor" of dealing with individuals who are unwilling to flex their schedules, are hesitant to participate with a brand outside of celebrity-restricted bounds, or are otherwise difficult to work with. At least one advertiser (Reebok) found it difficult to work with basketball player Shaquille O'Neal, which may have diminished this superstar's endorsement value.[18]

7. Saturation Factor.

Another key consideration, certainly not as important as the previous factors but one that nonetheless has to be evaluated, is the number of other brands the celebrity is endorsing. If a celebrity is overexposed—that is, endorsing too many products—his or her perceived credibility may suffer.[19] Tiger Woods, for example, may be somewhat overexposed.

8. The Trouble Factor.

A final consideration is an evaluation of the likelihood that a celebrity will get into trouble after an endorsement relation is established. The potential that a celebrity may get into trouble is a matter of considerable concern to brand managers and ad agencies. Suppose a celebrity is convicted of a crime or has his or her image blemished in some way during the course of an advertising campaign. What are the potential negative implications for the endorsed brand? Frankly, there are no simple answers to this provocative question, and researchers are just beginning to explore the issue in a sophisticated fashion.[20]

In the meantime, many advertisers and advertising agencies are reluctant to use celebrity endorsers. Their concern is not without justification. Consider some of the celebrity-related incidents making news during the 1980s and 1990s: Boxer Mike Tyson—an active endorser before a series of mishaps—was convicted on a rape charge and served a prison sentence. Actress Cybill Shepherd had a lucrative endorsement deal with the beef industry but embarrassed the industry by revealing to the press that she avoided eating beef. Entertainer Michael Jackson was arraigned on child-molestation charges. Tennis player Jennifer Capriati's promising career was sidetracked at an early age with emotional problems and allegations of drug abuse. She later mounted a successful comeback, but her endorsement deals pale in comparison to tennis stars such as Venus Williams. Ex-football player and actor O. J. Simpson was indicted for, but not convicted of, murder.

Due to the risks of such incidents after the consummation of a multimillion-dollar celebrity endorsement contract, there has been increased scrutiny in selecting celebrity endorsers. No selection procedure is fail-safe, however, and it is for this reason that some advertisers and their agencies avoid celebrity endorsements altogether. An alternative is to use the "endorsements" of celebrities who are no longer living: Babe Ruth, Marilyn Monroe, James Dean, and Natalie Wood have all been used in advertisements. Apple Computer used three dead celebrities (Amelia Earhart, Alfred Hitchcock, and Charlie Chaplin) in its "Think different" ad campaign. Dead celebrities are well known and respected by consumers in the target audiences to whom they appeal, and, best of all, their use in advertising is virtually risk free inasmuch as they cannot engage in behaviors that will sully their reputations and resonate adversely to the brands they posthumously endorse.

The Role of Q-Ratings

Needless to say, the selection of high-priced celebrity endorsers is typically undertaken with considerable thought on the part of brand managers and their advertising agencies. Their selection process is facilitated with *Performer Q-Ratings* that are commercially available from a New York–based firm called Marketing Evaluations. For reasons that will shortly become apparent, the *Q* in *Q-rating* signifies *quotient*.

Marketing Evaluations obtains Q-ratings for approximately 1,500 public figures (entertainers, athletes, and other famous personages) by mailing questionnaires to a representative national panel of individuals. Panel representatives are asked two straightforward questions for each person: (1) Have you heard of this person? (a measure of *familiarity*); and (2) if so, do you rate him or her poor, fair, good, very good, or one of your favorites? (a measure of *popularity*). The calculation of each performer's Q-rating, or quotient, is accomplished by determining the percentage of panel members who respond that a particular performer is "one of my favorites" and then dividing that number by the percentage who indicate that they have heard of that person. In other words, the popularity percentage is divided by the familiarity percentage, and the quotient is that person's Q-rating. This rating simply reveals the proportion of a group familiar with a person and who regard that person as one of their favorites.

For example, results from a survey by Marketing Evaluations revealed that Bill Cosby was known by 95 percent of people surveyed and considered a favorite by 45 percent. Hence, his Q-rating (which is expressed without a decimal point) is reported in whole-number form as 47 (i.e., 45 divided by 95 is roughly 47). Comparatively, in this same survey, Roseanne Barr had a Q-rating of only 16, which was obtained by dividing the 15 percent of respondents who considered her one of their favorites by the 93 percent who were familiar with her.[21] It comes as little surprise that advertisers have not flocked to Roseanne to sign her up to endorse their products.

Q-ratings provide useful information to brand managers and advertising agencies, but there is more to selecting a celebrity to endorse a brand than simply scouring through the pages of Q-ratings. Subjective judgment ultimately comes to play in determining whether a prospective celebrity endorser matches well with the brand image and its intended target market.

THE ROLE OF HUMOR IN ADVERTISING

Politicians, actors and actresses, public speakers, professors, and indeed all of us at one time or another use humor to create a desired reaction. Advertisers also turn to humor in the hopes of achieving various communication objectives — to gain attention, guide consumer comprehension of product claims, influence attitudes, enhance recall of advertised claims, and, ultimately, create customer action. The use of humor in advertising is extensive, representing approximately 25 percent of all television advertising in the United States and more than 35 percent in the United Kingdom.[22]

A study based on a sampling of television advertisements from four countries (Germany, Korea, Thailand, and the United States) determined that humorous advertisements in all of these countries generally involve the use of *incongruity resolution*.[23] The use of humor in U.S. magazine advertising also typically employs incongruity resolution.[24] Incongruity exists when the meaning of an ad is not immediately clear. Baffled by the incongruity, the consumer is provoked to understand the ad's meaning. When the meaning is eventually determined — as, for example, when the humor in an ad is detected — the result is a pleasant response and a more favorable attitude toward the advertisement and perhaps toward the advertised brand itself.[25]

Consider, for example, the Eastpak advertisement in Figure 10.3. On encountering this ad in a magazine, the reader likely is initially confused by the incongruity of a skeleton on a dried-out lake surface wearing a backpack. The ad, albeit a bit morbid, serves well to attract attention and encourage the reader to resolve what the ad is all about, what it means. After reading the scant content of the ad ("Guaranteed for life. Maybe longer"), the reader resolves the

Figure 10.3   **The Use of Humor in Magazine Advertising**

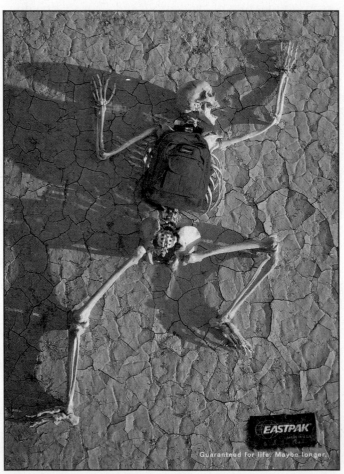

Guaranteed for life. Maybe longer.

EASTPAK

© Courtesy of Eastpak Corporation / Photography by Jim Erickson

incongruity and comprehends the humor. Although humor is used relatively infrequently in magazine advertising compared with TV and radio, the East-pak advertisement illustrates the effective use of humor in the magazine medium.[26]

Whether humor is generally effective and what kinds of humor are most successful are matters of some debate among advertising practitioners and scholars.[27] A survey determined that advertising agency executives consider humor to be especially effective for attracting attention and creating brand awareness.[28] A thorough review of research on the effects of humor leads to the following tentative generalizations:[29]

- Humor is an effective method for attracting attention to advertisements.
- Humor enhances liking of both the advertisement and the advertised brand.
- Humor does not necessarily harm comprehension.
- Humor does not offer an advantage over nonhumor at increasing persuasion.
- Humor does not enhance source credibility.
- The nature of the product affects the appropriateness of using humor. Specifically, humor is used more successfully with established rather than new products. Humor also is more appropriate for products that are more feeling-oriented, or experiential, and those that are not very involving (such as inexpensive consumer packaged goods).

When used correctly and in the right circumstances, humor can be an extremely effective advertising technique. A complication of using humor in advertising is that humorous appeals vary in their effectiveness across demographic groups. For example, men and women are not equally attentive to humorous ads.[30] In addition to demographic differences in responsiveness to humor, research evidence also shows that humorous ads are more effective than nonhumorous ads *only when consumers' evaluations of the advertised brand are already positive*. When prior evaluations are negative toward the advertised brand, humorous ads have been shown to be less effective than nonhumorous ads.[31] This finding has a counterpart in interpersonal relations: When you like someone, you are more likely to consider his or her attempt at humor to be funny than if you do not like that person.

In sum, humor in advertising can be an extremely effective device for accomplishing a variety of marketing communications objectives. Nonetheless, advertisers should *proceed cautiously* when contemplating the use of humor. First, the effects of humor can differ due to differences in audience characteristics — what strikes some people as humorous is not at all funny to others.[32] Second, the definition of what is funny in one country or region of a country is not necessarily the same in another. Finally, a humorous message may be so distracting to an audience that receivers ignore the message content. Thus, advertisers should carefully research their intended market segments before venturing into humorous advertising. Please read the *IMC Focus* for an interesting discussion of how one humorous advertising campaign was created.

THE USE OF APPEALS TO CONSUMER FEARS

In Chapter 5 it was noted that marketing communicators employ a variety of techniques to enhance consumers' information-processing motivation, opportunity, or ability. As would be expected, the appeal to fear is especially effective as a means of enhancing motivation. The unfortunate fact is that consumers in the 21st century live in a world where the threat of terrorism is ever present and crime and health-related problems abound. Advertisers, in attempting to motivate consumers to process information and to take action, appeal to consumers' fears by

IMC focus

Selection of the "Mark" Character in Holiday Inn's Campaign

You may recall the example in the previous chapter of the Holiday Inn advertising campaign, which was presented as an exemplar of clever and creative advertising. That campaign featured various executions of an ensemble of mom, dad, grandma, and quintessential slacker (Mark), who rather than being out on his own gainfully employed lives with his family. In various executions Mark is portrayed imposing various demands on the family—for amenities such as more space, the family TV, and computer data ports. The *coupe de grace* in every execution is mom exclaiming, "What do you think this is, a Holiday Inn?"

To those of us who possess no acting ability or cinematic expertise, the Holiday Inn advertisements may appear to be simple little productions. However, as with creating a great movie, the secret is in having a good script *and* proper casting. The casting of Mark was key to the success of the Holiday Inn campaign. The potential for a successful ad campaign came first from the key phrase, "What do you think this is, a Holiday Inn?" The idea for using this phrase originated with the ad agency's copywriter and art director, who had heard the phrase as kids from their own parents when failing to pick up clothes or toys. Once they had this phrase as the campaign centerpiece, they decided that an ensemble cast with mom, dad, grandma, and slacker Mark would be the constant from one commercial execution to the next.

Casting Mark became an incredible challenge. One candidate after another was rejected because he just didn't seem right for the role. In fact, after many casting failures, there was some question as to whether the concept could be pulled off successfully. Near the point of moving on to another campaign idea, the ad agency's director recalled a guy he had filmed in New Orleans, a downcast street clown named Ross Brockley. After pursuing Brockley, the agency learned that he had given up his stand-up comedy gig and moved back to his native Nebraska. After several phone conversations, the ad agency (Fallon McElligott) was able to convince Ross to consider playing Mark in the Holiday Inn ads. The rest is history: Ross Brockley was offered and accepted the role of Mark and will undoubtedly become one of the comedic legends in advertising lore. His semiconfused mannerisms, slow speech pattern, and he-just-doesn't-get-it demeanor are absolutely perfect for the role of Mark. It is difficult to imagine any other actor who would have been more perfect for this role.

Source: Adapted from Paula Champa, "Wake-Up Calls," *Agency* (Fall 2001), pp. 6–7. © 2001.

---

identifying the negative consequences of either (1) *not using the advertised product* or (2) *engaging in unsafe behavior* (such as drinking and driving, smoking, and using drugs).

Fear-Appeal Logic

The underlying logic is that appeals to consumer fears will stimulate audience involvement with a message and thereby promote acceptance of the message arguments.[33] The appeal to consumer fears may take the form of *social disapproval* or *physical danger*. For example, mouthwashes, deodorants, toothpastes, and other products use threats that appeal to fears when emphasizing the social disapproval we may suffer if our breath is not fresh, our underarms are not dry, or our teeth are not cavity free. Smoke detectors, automobile tires, unsafe sex, driving under the influence of alcohol and other drugs, and being uninsured are a sam-

A Drug Company's Appeal to Fear   Figure 10.4

pling of products and themes used by advertisers to induce fear of physical danger or impending problems. Health-care ads (such as for ARICEPT in Figure 10.4) frequently appeal to fears, and advertising agencies justify the use of such appeals with logic such as, "Sometimes you have to scare people to save their lives."[34]

Appropriate Intensity

Aside from the basic ethical issue of whether fear should be used at all, the fundamental issue for advertisers is determining *how intense* the threat should be. Should the advertiser employ a slight threat merely to get the consumer's attention, or should a heavy threat be used so the consumer cannot possibly miss the point the advertiser wishes to make? Although numerous studies have been performed, the fact remains that there still is no consensus on what threat intensity is optimal. There is, however, some consistency in the demonstration that the more an audience experiences fear from an advertised threat, the more likely it is that they will be persuaded to take the recommended action.[35]

In general, it appears that the degree of threat intensity that is effective in evoking fear in an audience depends in large part on *how much relevance* a topic has for an audience—the greater the relevance, the lower the threat intensity that is needed to activate a response. In other words, people who are highly involved in a topic can be motivated by a relatively "light" appeal to fear, whereas a more intense level of threat is required to motivate uninvolved people.[36]

To illustrate the relation between threat intensity and issue relevance, let us compare a low-threat campaign for Michelin tires with the much more intense appeal of campaigns designed to discourage drinking and driving. As you may recall, the long-standing Michelin campaign contains a series of television commercials that show adorable babies sitting on or surrounded by tires. These commercials are subtle reminders (low levels of threat) for parents to consider buying Michelin tires to ensure their children's safety. A low level of threat is all that is needed in this situation to evoke fear, because safety for their children is the most relevant concern for most parents.

Consider, by comparison, the level of threat needed to reach high school students and other young people who are the targets of public service announcements (PSAs) that attempt to discourage drinking and driving. The last thing many young people want to hear is what they should or should not be doing. Hence, although safety is relevant to most everyone, it is less relevant to young people who consider themselves invulnerable. Consequently, very intense appeals to fear are needed to impress on high schoolers the risk in which they place themselves and their friends when drinking and driving.[37]

THE USE OF APPEALS TO CONSUMER GUILT

Like appeals to fear, appeals to guilt attempt to trigger negative emotions. People feel guilty when they break rules, violate their own standards or beliefs, or behave irresponsibly.[38] Appeals to guilt are powerful because they motivate emotionally mature individuals to undertake responsible action leading to a reduction in the level of guilt. Advertisers and other marketing communicators appeal to guilt and attempt to persuade prospective customers by asserting or implying that feelings of guilt can be relieved by using the promoted product.[39] Consider, for example, the advertisement for life insurance that posed the following situation to readers in three simple sentences that constituted 70 percent of the ad's fullpage space,

IT'S 1999.

YOU'RE DEAD

WHAT DO YOU DO NOW?

This advertisement represents an appeal to anticipatory guilt. That is, the ad attempts to induce a sense of guilt in the reader by suggesting that one would have failed to take proper care of his or her family if she or he would pass away without having an adequate insurance policy

In general, guilt appeals focus on people's past or future transgressions or failure to care for others.[40] An in-depth analysis of a broad spectrum of magazines revealed that about one 1 of 20 ads contains an appeal to guilt.[41]

THE USE OF SEX IN ADVERTISING

Whereas the previous two sets of advertising appeals—to fear and guilt—are fundamentally negative (i.e., people generally avoid these two emotions), the use of sex in advertising appeals to something that people generally approach rather than avoid. Sex appeals in advertising are used frequently and with increasing explicitness. Whereas the use of such explicit sex was unthinkable not many years ago, it now represents part of the advertising landscape.[42] The trend is not restricted to the United States; indeed, sexual explicitness is more prevalent and more overt elsewhere—for example, in Brazil and certain European countries.

What Role Does Sex Play in Advertising?

Actually, it has several potential roles. First, sexual material in advertising acts as an initial *attentional lure* and retains that attention for a longer period, often by featuring attractive models in provocative poses.[43] This is called the *stopping-power role* of sex.[44]

A second potential role is to *enhance recall* of message points. Research suggests, however, that sexual content or symbolism will enhance recall only if it is appropriate to the product category and the creative advertising execution.[45] Sexual appeals produce significantly better recall when the advertising execution has an appropriate relationship with the advertised product.[46]

A third role performed by sexual content in advertising is to *evoke emotional responses*, such as feelings of arousal and even lust.[47] These reactions can increase an ad's persuasive impact, with the opposite occurring if the ad elicits negative feelings such as disgust, embarrassment, or uneasiness.[48] The appeal to lust is typified by a Diet Coke television commercial in which a group of voyeuristic women is shown watching with palpable pleasure from their office building a sexy worker at a nearby construction site taking off his shirt and then opening a Diet Coke.

Whether sexual content elicits a positive or negative reaction depends on the *appropriateness or relevance* of the sexual content to the advertised subject matter. An interesting marketing experiment tested this by varying magazine ads for two products, a ratchet wrench set (a product for which sexual appeal is irrelevant) and a body oil (a relevant sex-appeal product). The study also manipulated three versions of dress for the female model who appeared in the ads: In the *demure* model version, she was shown fully clothed in a blouse and slacks; in the *seductive* model version, she wore the same clothing as in the demure version, but the blouse was completely unbuttoned and knotted at the bottom, exposing some midriff and cleavage; and in the *nude* model version, she was completely undressed. Study findings revealed that the seductive model/body oil combination was perceived most favorably by all respondents, whereas the nude model/body oil combination was perceived as the least appealing advertisement. Females regarded the nude model/ratchet set as least appealing.[49] This study was conducted over two decades ago, and it is uncertain whether the same finding would be obtained in the sexually more explicit society in which we now live.

Sexual content stands little chance of being effective unless it is directly relevant to an advertisement's primary selling point. When used appropriately, however, sexual content is capable of eliciting attention, enhancing recall, and creating a favorable association with the advertised product.

The Downside of Sex Appeals in Advertising

The presentation to this point has indicated that when used appropriately, sex appeals in advertising can be effective. The discussion would be incomplete, however, without mentioning the potential hazards of using sex appeals. There is evidence to suggest that the use of explicit sexual illustrations in advertisements may interfere with consumers' processing of message arguments and reduce message comprehension.[50] Moreover, many people are offended by advertisements that portray

Worldwide Concern About Sex and Decency in Advertising

People worldwide are troubled by advertising considered indecent. But, of course, what is indecent in one country may not necessarily be seen the same way in another. The International Chamber of Commerce (ICC) Code of Advertising Practice states that "advertising should be decent"—that is, "prepared with a due sense of social responsibility ... [and] not be such as to impair public confidence in advertising."

Three categories of advertising indecency that are matters of concern around the world include advertisements that are sexist, sexy, or that sexually objectify their models. *Sexist ads* are those that demean one sex in comparison with the other, particularly through sex-role stereotyping; *sexy ads* use sexual imagery or suggestiveness; and *sex-ual objectification* occurs when ads use women (or men) as decorative or attention-getting objects with little or no relevance to the product category. France's Truth in Advertising Bureau released a recent report that criticized advertisers for portraying women in a degrading way. The report especially criticized European fashion houses such as Christian Dior and the Benetton Group. New French standards prohibit violent advertisements and those that convey images of submission or objectify women. For example, the French ad bureau forced the withdrawal of one ad that featured an attractive woman wearing only underwear in a kneeling position beside a sheep with the tagline "I'd like a sweater."

The nature and extent of government regulation of indecent sex-oriented advertising varies considerably, from a relatively laissez-faire attitude in the United States and Western Europe to stringent controls in various Muslim countries. Following are some examples of government regulations of advertising in different countries:

- In Malaysia, the Ministry of Information's Advertising Code states that women should not be the principal objects of an advertisement or other medium intended to attract sales unless the advertised product is relevant to women.
- The Ministry of Information in Saudi Arabia prevents any advertising depicting veiled or unveiled women.
- Indian law forbids the depiction of a woman's figure or any female body part if the depiction is derogatory to women or immoral.
- Portuguese law prohibits sex discrimination or the subordination or objectification of women in advertising.
- Norway requires that advertising not portray men or women in an offensive manner or imply any derogatory judgment of either sex.

The regulation of advertising (on grounds of decency or otherwise) is complex and controversial, because regulation curtails the rights of advertisers to communicate with their publics and impinges on the rights of people to receive information and images in any form they consider unobjectionable. Regulators in all countries are placed in a tricky position when attempting to balance the rights and interests of advertisers, consumers, and society at large.

Sources: Alessandra Galloni, "Clampdown on 'Porno-Chic' Ads Is Pushed by French Authorities," *Wall Street Journal Interactive Edition*, October 25, 2001 (http://interactive.wsj.com/); Jean J. Boddewyn, "Controlling Sex and Decency in Advertising around the World," *Journal of Advertising* 20 (December 1991), 25–36.

women (and men) as brainless sex objects. For example, an outcry ensued in response to an advertisement for Old Milwaukee beer featuring the so-called Swedish Bikini Team—a boat full of beautiful Scandinavian-looking women wearing blue bikinis who appeared out of nowhere in front of a group of fishermen. Female employees of Stroh's Brewery Company, the makers of Old Milwaukee, sued their employer, claiming that the advertisement created an atmosphere conducive to sexual harassment in the workplace.[51] Regardless of the merits of this particular case, the general point is that sex in advertising can be demeaning to females (and males) and, for this reason, should be used cautiously.

An advertising campaign for Calvin Klein jeans featuring teenagers in provocative poses created a public outcry, and Calvin Klein discontinued the campaign after critics dubbed it kiddie porn.[52] The use of sex in advertising is a matter of concern to people and regulatory bodies throughout the world.[53] For further discussion, see the *Global Focus*.

SUBLIMINAL MESSAGES AND SYMBOLIC EMBEDS

The word *subliminal* refers to the presentation of stimuli at a rate or level that is below the conscious threshold of awareness. One example is self-help audiotapes (such as tapes to help one quit smoking) that play messages at a decibel level indecipherable to the naked ear. Stimuli that cannot be perceived by the conscious senses may nonetheless be perceived subconsciously. This possibility has generated considerable concern from advertising critics and has fostered much speculation from researchers. The reason for the concern is clear: Surveys have shown that a large percentage of American people believe that subliminal methods are used by advertisers.[54] Representatives of the advertising community, however, disavow the widespread use of subliminal advertising.[55]

Original outcry occurred nearly 50 years ago in response to a researcher who claimed to have increased sales of Coca-Cola and popcorn in a New Jersey movie theater by using subliminal messages. At five-second intervals during the movie *Picnic*, subliminal messages saying "Drink Coca-Cola" and "Eat Popcorn" appeared on the screen for a mere 1/3,000 second. Although the naked eye could not possibly have seen these messages, the researcher, James Vicary, claimed that sales of Coca-Cola and popcorn increased 58 percent and 18 percent, respectively.[56] Though Vicary's research is scientifically meaningless because he failed to use proper experimental procedures, the study nonetheless raised public concerns about subliminal advertising and led to congressional hearings.[57] Federal legislation was never enacted, but since then subliminal advertising has been the subject of criticism by advertising critics, a matter of embarrassment for advertising practitioners, and an issue of theoretical curiosity to advertising scholars.[58]

The fires of controversy were fueled again in the 1970s with the publication of three provocatively titled books: *Subliminal Seduction, Media Sexploitation*, and *The Clam Plate Orgy*.[59] The author of these books, Wilson Key, claimed subliminal advertising techniques are used extensively and have the power to influence consumers' choice behaviors.

A Challenge

Many advertising practitioners and MarCom scholars discount Key's arguments and vehemently disagree with his conclusions. Part of the difficulty in arriving at clear answers as to who's right and who's wrong stems from the fact that commentators differ in what they mean by subliminal advertising. In fact, there are three distinct forms of subliminal stimulation. A first form presents *visual stimuli* at a very rapid rate by means of a device called a tachistoscope (say, at 1/3,000 second as in Vicary's research). A second form uses *accelerated speech* in auditory messages. The third form involves the *embedding of hidden symbols* (such as sexual images or words) in print advertisements.[60]

This last form, *embedding*, is what Key has written about and is the form that advertising researchers have studied. However, it is important to remember that embeds (for example, the word *sex* airbrushed into an advertisement) are not truly subliminal since they are visible to the naked eye. Nonetheless, the remaining discussion of subliminal messages is restricted to the practice of embedding.

To better appreciate embedding, consider an advertisement for Edge shaving cream that ran in magazines in the 1980s. This ad featured a picture of a lathered-up man with a look of near ecstasy on his face and a prominent shot of the Edge Gel can grasped in his fingertips. Below his lips were scenes of a nude woman on her back with knees raised, a facial portrayal of an attractive blond woman, and a scene of a sexy male on a surfboard surfing through a water tunnel. Aside from the Freudian symbolism associated with the water tunnel and the look of ecstasy on the man's face, the ad also included three vague nude figures airbrushed into the shaving lather above the man's lip.

Are embedded symbols in advertisements effective? To answer this we first need to examine the process that would have to operate for embedding to influence consumer choice behavior. The Edge shaving gel advertisement provides a useful vehicle for motivating this discussion. The first step in the process requires that the consumer consciously or subconsciously process the embedded symbol (the nude figures in the Edge magazine ad). Second, as the result of processing the cue, the consumer would have to develop a greater desire for Edge shaving gel than he had before seeing the ad. Third, because advertising is done at the brand level and because advertisers are interested in selling their brands and not just any brand in the product category, effective symbolic embedding would require that consumers develop a desire for the specific brand, Edge in this case, rather than just any brand in the category. Finally, the consumer would need to transfer the desire for the advertised brand into actual purchase behavior.

Is there evidence to support this chain of events? Despite a few limited studies on the issue, there are a variety of practical problems that *probably prevent embedding from being effective in a realistic marketing context.*[61] Perhaps the major reason why embedding in advertising has little effect is because the images have to be concealed to preclude detection by consumers. Many consumers would resent such tricky advertising efforts if they knew they existed. Thus, precluding detection from consumers means that embedding is a relatively weak technique compared with more vivid advertising representations. Because the majority of consumers devote relatively little time and effort in processing advertisements, a weak stimulus means that most consumers could not possibly be influenced.[62]

Even if consumers did attend to and encode sexual embeds under natural advertising conditions, there remains serious doubt that this information would have sufficient impact to affect product or brand choice behavior. Standard (supraliminal) advertising information itself has a difficult time influencing consumers. There is no theoretical reason to expect that subliminal information is any more effective. For example, do you really think that men would run out to buy Edge shaving gel just because they consciously or subconsciously spot a nude woman in the advertisement for that product?

In sum, the topic of subliminal advertising (particularly the Wilson Key variety of symbolic embeds) makes for interesting speculation and discussion, but scientific evidence in support of its practical effectiveness is virtually nonexistent. The following quotation appropriately sums up the issue:

A century of psychological research substantiates the general principle that more intense stimuli have a greater influence on people's behavior than weaker ones. While subliminal perception is a bona fide phenomenon, the effects obtained are subtle and obtaining them typically requires a carefully structured context. Subliminal stimuli are usually so weak that the recipient is not just unaware of the stimulus but is also oblivious to the fact that he/she is being stimulated. As a result, the potential effects of subliminal stimuli are easily nullified by other ongoing stimulation in the same sensory channel or by attention being focused on another modality. These factors pose serious difficulties for any possible marketing application.[63]

THE FUNCTIONS OF MUSIC IN ADVERTISING

Music has been an important component of the advertising landscape virtually since the beginning of recorded sound. Jingles, background music, popular tunes, and classical arrangements are used to attract attention, convey selling points, set an emotional tone for an advertisement, and to influence listeners' moods. Well-known entertainers, nonvocal musical accompaniment, and unknown vocalists are used extensively in promoting everything from fabric softeners to automobiles.

Many advertising practitioners and scholars think that music performs a variety of useful communication functions. These include *attracting attention*, putting consumers in a *positive mood*, making them *more receptive to message arguments*, and even *communicating meanings* about advertised products.[64]

Although music's role in marketing has until recently been an incredibly understudied subject, brief commentary on a few studies will convey a sense of the type of research that is being conducted.[65] In one study using classical conditioning procedures, music represented the unconditioned stimulus in an effort to influence experimental subjects' preference for a ballpoint pen, which represented the conditioned stimulus.[66] An *unconditioned stimulus* (US) is one that evokes pleasant feelings or thoughts in people. A *conditioned stimulus* (CS) is one that is emotionally or cognitively neutral prior to the onset of a conditioning experiment. In simple terms, classical conditioning is achieved when the pairing of US and CS results in a transfer of feeling from the US (music in the present case) to the CS (the ballpoint pen).

Experimental subjects in this study were informed that an advertising agency was trying to select music for use in a commercial for a ballpoint pen. Subjects then listened to music while they viewed slides of the pen. The positive US for half the subjects was music from the movie *Grease*, and the negative US for the remaining subjects was classical Asian Indian music. The simple association between music and the pen influenced product preference—nearly 80 percent of the subjects exposed to the *Grease* music chose the advertised pen, whereas only 30 percent of the subjects exposed to the Indian music chose the advertised pen.[67]

Music's Role at the Point of Purchase

Although falling outside of a mass media advertising context, two additional studies of music are noteworthy in that they provide dramatic evidence regarding the potential impact music can have on consumers' buying behavior at retail venues. A first experiment examined the effects of *background music* in a supermarket setting. A supermarket chain was studied over a nine-week period by comparing sales volume during days when slow-tempo background music was played (72 beats per minute or slower) versus days when fast-tempo music was in the background (94 beats per minute or more). The researcher found that daily sales volume averaged approximately $16,740 on days when slow-tempo music was played but only about $12,113 when fast-tempo music was played— an average increase of $4,627, or 38.2 percent per day! The slow-tempo music apparently *slowed the pace* at which customers moved through the store and increased their total expenditures because they had a longer opportunity to purchase more.[68]

In a second field experiment, the same researcher examined the effects of background music on restaurant customers' purchase behavior. A restaurant alternated playing slow- and fast-tempo music on Friday and Saturday nights over a one-month period. Slow music increased the amount of time customers remained seated at their tables—an average of 56 minutes per customer group during slow-music nights compared to an average of 45 minutes during fast-music nights. Also, customers during slow-music nights spent significantly larger amounts on alcoholic beverages (an average of $30.47 per customer group) compared to fast-music nights ($21.62 per customer group).[69]

In the final analysis, music appears to be effective in creating customer moods and stimulating buying preferences and choices. Of course, considerably more research is needed to understand fully the scientific role of music in accomplishing different marketing communications functions. Marketplace wisdom, as manifested by marketing communicators' nearly universal use of music in advertisements and in retail settings, clearly suggests that music is an effective form of nonverbal communication. However, the type of music used in advertising and the specific role music performs undoubtedly varies considerably across cultures inasmuch as music does not mean the same thing to all people around the world.[70]

THE ROLE OF COMPARATIVE ADVERTISING

The practice in which advertisers *directly* or *indirectly* compare their products against competitive offerings, typically claiming that the promoted item is superior in one or several important purchase considerations, is called comparative advertising. Comparative ads vary both with regard to the explicitness of the comparisons and with respect to whether the target of the comparison is named or referred to in general terms.[71]

Salespeople have always used comparative messages in arguing the advantages of their products over competitors'. Likewise, print advertisers (newspapers, magazines) have used comparative claims for decades. It was not until the early 1970s, however, that television commercials in the United States began making direct-comparison claims. Since then all media have experienced notable increases in the use of comparative advertising. In some countries (e.g., Belgium, Hong Kong, and Korea) it is illegal to use comparative advertising; and with exception of the United States and Great Britain, advertising comparisons are used infrequently in those countries where this form of advertising is legal.[72]

To better appreciate comparative advertising, it will be useful to examine a couple of examples. The ad in Figure 10.5 for Tums Ultra compares itself *directly* against competitor Pepcid Complete. This ad uses the "scorecard" approach to portray Tums Ultra as possessing three advantages over its competitive brand. By comparison, consider an illustrative indirect-comparison advertisement for Zest soap. This ad compares itself with "regular soap" without mentioning any specific brand and claims in the body copy, along with visual reinforcement, that Zest does not leave a drying film on the skin when used with hard water but, "regular soap" does.

The questions posed in the following section ask whether and under what conditions comparative advertising is especially effective.

Is Comparative Advertising More Effective?

In deciding whether to use a comparative advertisement rather than a more conventional noncomparative format, an advertiser must confront questions such as the following:

- How do comparative and noncomparative advertisements match up in terms of impact on brand awareness, consumer comprehension of ad claims, and credibility?
- Do comparative and noncomparative ads differ with regard to effects on brand preferences, buying intentions, and purchase behavior?
- How do factors such as consumer brand preference and the advertiser's competitive position influence the effectiveness of comparative advertising?

Illustration of an Direct-Comparison Ad

Figure 10.5

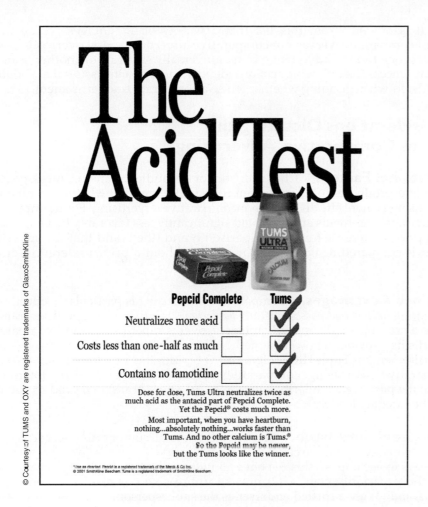

© Courtesy of TUMS and OXY are registered trademarks of GlaxoSmithKline

- Under what specific circumstances should an advertiser use comparative advertising?[73]

Researchers have performed numerous studies that have examined the process by which comparative advertising operates, the results it produces, and how its effects contrast with those from noncomparative ads.[74] Findings are at times inconclusive and even contradictory. Lack of definitive results is to be expected, however, because advertising is a complex phenomenon that varies from situation to situation in terms of executional elements, audience demographics, media characteristics, and other factors. However, a major review of research that has tested comparative versus noncomparative advertising suggests the following conclusions:[75]

- Comparative advertising is better (than noncomparative ads) in enhancing brand awareness (i.e., brand name recall).
- Comparative advertising promotes better recall of message arguments.
- However, comparative advertising is perceived as somewhat less believable than noncomparative advertising.
- Comparative (versus noncomparative) advertising is responsible for generating more favorable attitudes toward the sponsoring brand, especially when the brand is a new (versus established) brand.

- Comparative advertising generates stronger intentions to purchase the sponsored brand.
- Comparative advertising generates more purchases than noncomparative ads.

It is obvious from this list that a variety of advantages accrue to the use of comparative versus noncomparative advertising. However, as is always the case, one form of advertising is *not* universally superior to another under all circumstances. The following sections identify some specific issues that should be considered when deciding whether to use a comparative advertisement.

Considerations Dictating the Use of Comparative Advertising

Situational Factors.   Characteristics of the audience, media, message, company, and product all play important roles in determining whether comparative advertising is more effective than noncomparative advertising. For example, comparative advertisements are evaluated significantly less favorably by people holding a prior preference for the comparison brand (the brand that the advertised brand is compared against) than by those without a prior preference for that brand.[76]

Distinct Advantages.   Comparative advertising is particularly effective for promoting *brands that possess distinct advantages* relative to competitive brands.[77] When a brand has a distinct advantage(s) over competitive brands, comparative advertising provides a powerful method to convey this (these) advantage(s). The advertisement for Tums Ultra (Figure 10.5) typifies this situation. Relative to non-comparative advertising, comparative advertising has also been shown to increase the perceived similarity between a challenger brand in a product category and the category leader.[78]

The Credibility Issue.   The effectiveness of comparative advertising increases when comparative claims are made to appear *more credible*. There are various ways to accomplish this: (1) have an independent research organization support the superiority claims, (2) present impressive test results to back up the claims, and (3) use a trusted endorser as the spokesperson.

Assessing Effectiveness.   Because comparative advertisements make claims for an advertised brand relative to another brand and because consumers encode this comparative information in a relative fashion, *measurement techniques* in assessing the effectiveness of comparative advertising are most sensitive when questions are worded in a relative fashion. This is, for maximal sensitivity, the question context, or wording, should match the consumer's encoding mind-set. For example, with reference to the Zest advertisement, there are two alternative questions that could be framed to ascertain whether consumers perceive Zest as an effective brand in lathering up and rinsing away soap film: (1) How likely is it that Zest is effective when bathing in hard water? (*nonrelative* framing) or (2) How likely is it that Zest is more effective than regular soaps when bathing in hard water? (*relative* framing). Research has shown that relative framing does a better job of assessing consumers' beliefs after their exposure to comparative advertisements.[79]

SUMMARY

This chapter discusses both the role of celebrity endorsers and the nature and effectiveness of specific advertising techniques such as humor, appeals to fear, and the role of sex in advertising. Discussion of celebrity and typical-person endorsers indicates that endorsers have influence on consumers via the attributes of credibility and attractiveness. The TEARS model (trustworthiness, expertise, physical attractiveness, respect, and similarity) provides a convenient acronym for thinking about the endorser attributes that play major roles in determining their effectiveness. The following factors appear to be the most important ones used by brand managers in actually selecting celebrity endorsers: (1) celebrity and audience matchup, (2) celebrity and brand matchup, (3) celebrity credibility, (4) celebrity attractiveness, (5) cost considerations, (6) a working ease/difficulty factor, (7) an endorsement saturation factor, and (8) a likelihood-of-getting-into-trouble factor. Attractiveness operates through an identification mechanism, whereas credibility functions via the process of internalization.

Widely used advertising techniques discussed in this chapter include humor, appeals to fear, appeals to guilt, sex appeals, subliminal messages, the use of music, and comparative advertisements. Discussion covers empirical research and indicates factors involved in selecting each of these message elements.

Find more resources to help you study at http://shimp.swcollege.com!

DISCUSSION QUESTIONS

1. Using the concepts of attractiveness, expertise, and trustworthiness, explain what makes Michael Jordan an effective endorser. Do the same for Tiger Woods.

2. Identify two product categories where Michael Jordan would *not* make an effective endorser. Justify your reasoning, and do not use products that would be ridiculous for Jordan or any other man to endorse.

3. Suppose you are the brand manager for Jell-O and are looking for a celebrity to replace Bill Cosby as the endorser for that brand. What person would you select to replace Mr. Cosby if you were in charge of this account? Fully justify the rationale behind your choice.

4. Infomercials are long commercials that generally last from 30 to 60 minutes. These commercials typically are aired during fringe times and frequently promote products such as diet aids, balding cures, and exercise products. Invariably these infomercials turn to physicians and other health professionals to buttress claims about the promoted brand's efficacy. Using concepts from this chapter, explain why health professionals are used in this form of advertising.

5. You have probably seen a number of public service announcements along the lines described in the fear appeals section to discourage drinking and driving. In your opinion, is this form of advertising effective in altering the behavior of people your age? Be specific in justifying your answer.

6. The fear of getting AIDS should be relevant to many college students. Accordingly, would you agree that a relatively weak fear appeal should suffice in influencing students to either abstain from sexual relations or practice safe sex? If you disagree, then how can you reconcile your disagreement with the degree-of-relevance explanation?

7. Develop a list of products for which you feel appeals to fear might be a viable approach to persuading consumer acceptance of a brand. What kinds of products do not lend themselves to such appeals? Explain why you feel these products would be inappropriate.

8. Consumers occasionally find television commercials to be humorous and enjoyable. Some advertising pundits claim that such commercials may capture attention but are frequently ineffective in selling products. What is your stance on this issue? Justify your position.

9. Distinguish between an attractive and a credible source. Provide two or three examples of well-known product spokespersons who, in your opinion, are high in both attractiveness and credibility. Justify why you consider these individuals to possess both attributes.

10. Provide two or three examples of music in advertisements that you think are particularly effective. For each example, explain precisely why you consider the music to be effective.

11. Photocopy one or two examples of comparative advertisements from magazines. Analyze each ad in terms of why you think the advertiser used a comparative-advertising format and whether you think the advertisement is effective. Justify your position.

12. The article titled "Understanding Jingles and Needledrop: A Rhetorical Approach to Music in Advertising" (see endnote 64), suggests that music in commercials communicates specific meanings to listeners and viewers. In other words, music "speaks" to people by conveying a sense of speed, excitement, sadness, nostalgia, and so on. Identify two commercials in which music communicates a specific emotion or other state or action to consumers, and identify this emotion or state/action.

13. Too much sex is used in advertising. Comment.

ENDNOTES

1. Abraham Kaplan, *The Conduct of Inquiry: Methodology for Behavioral Science* (New York: Intext Educational Publishers/Chandler, 1964).
2. Hershey Friedman and Linda Friedman, "Endorser Effectiveness by Product Type," *Journal of Advertising Research* 19 (October/November 1979), 63–71.
3. Jagdish Agrawal and Wagner A. Kamakura, "The Economic Worth of Celebrity Endorsers: An Event Study Analysis," *Journal of Marketing* 59 (July 1995), 56–62.
4. Therese A. Louie, Robert L. Kulik, and Robert Johnson, "When Bad Things Happen to the Endorsers of Good Products," *Marketing Letters* 12 (February 2001), 13–24.
5. Doug Ferguson, "Woods: $54 Million Man?" *Wall Street Journal Interactive Edition*, September 19, 2000 (http://wsj.totalsports.net/).
6. Amanda Bower, "Highly Attractive Models in Advertising and the Women Who Loathe Them: The Implications of Negative Affect for Spokesperson Effectiveness," *Journal of Advertising* 30 (fall 2001), 51–64; Amanda Bower and Stacy Landreth, "Is Beauty Best? Highly Versus Normally Attractive Models in Advertising," *Journal of Advertising* 30 (spring 2001), 1–12.
7. David J. Moore and Richard Reardon, "Source Magnification: The Role of Multiple Sources in the Processing of Advertising Appeals," *Journal of Marketing Research* 24 (November 1987), 412–417.
8. It is important to note that although the present discussion is framed in terms of endorser characteristics, more general treatment of the topic refers to source characteristics. For a classic treatment of the subject, see Herbert C. Kelman, "Processes of Opinion Change," *Public Opinion Quarterly* 25 (spring 1961), 57–78. For a more current treatment, see Daniel J. O'Keefe, *Persuasion Theory and Research* (Newbury Park, Calif.: Sage, 1990), chap. 8.
9. Richard E. Petty, Thomas M. Ostrom, and Timothy C. Brock, eds., *Cognitive Responses in Persuasion* (Hillsdale, N.J.: Lawrence Erlbaum Associates, 1981), 143.
10. James M. Hunt, Theresa J. Domzal, and Jerome B. Kernan, "Causal Attributions and Persuasion: The Case of Disconfirmed Expectancies," in *Advances in Consumer Research*, vol. 9, ed. Andrew Mitchell (Ann Arbor: Mich.: Association for Consumer Research, 1982), 287–292.
11. For information about how to measure attractiveness, see Roobina Ohanian, "Construction and Validation of a Scale to Measure Celebrity Endorsers' Perceived Expertise, Trustworthiness, and Attractiveness," *Journal of Advertising* 19, no. 3 (1990), 39–52.
12. James Betzold, "Venus Williams, Stephanie Tolleson," *Advertising Age*, October 8, 2001, s25; Terry Lefton, "Kournikova's Big Racket," *Brandweek*, January 31, 2000, 18.
13. Mercedes M. Cardona "Tennis Star Takes Time Out to Pitch Constellation Line," *Advertising Age*, October 30, 2000, 32.
14. W. Benoy Joseph, "The Credibility of Physically Attractive Communicators: A Review," *Journal of Advertising* 11, no. 3 (1982), 15–24; Lynn R. Kahle and Pamela M. Homer, "Physical Attractiveness of the Celebrity Endorser: A Social Adaptation Perspective," *Journal of Consumer Research* 11 (March 1985), 954–961. However, empirical evidence is mixed as to whether an attractive endorser benefits a brand only when there is a good matchup between the endorser and the brand or whether, alternatively, attractive endorsers are more beneficial for a brand regardless of how well the endorser matches with the brand. For discussion, review the following two articles: Brian D. Till and Michael Busler, "The Match Up Hypothesis: Physical Attractiveness, Expertise, and the Role of Fit on Brand Attitude, Purchase Intent and Brand Beliefs," *Journal of Advertising* 29 (fall 2000), 1–14; Michael A. Kamins, "An Investigation into the 'Match-Up' Hypothesis in Celebrity Advertising: When Beauty May Be Only Skin Deep," *Journal of Advertising* 19, no. 1 (1990), 4–13. See also John D. Mittelstaedt, Peter C. Riesz, and William J. Burns, "Why Are Endorsements Effective? Sorting Among Theories of Product and Endorser Effects," *Journal of Current Issues and Research in Advertising* 22 (spring 2000), 55–66.
15. Rohit Deshpande and Douglas Stayman, "A Tale of Two Cities: Distinctiveness Theory and Advertising Effectiveness," *Journal of Marketing Research* 31 (February 1994), 57–64.
16. Lawrence Feick and Robin A. Higie, "The Effects of Preference Heterogeneity and Source Characteristics on Ad Processing and Judgments about Endorsers," *Journal of Advertising* 21 (June 1992), 9–24.
17. Two studies have addressed this issue: B. Zafer Erdogan, Michael J. Baker, and

Stephen Tagg, "Selecting Celebrity Endorsers: The Practitioner's Perspective," *Journal of Advertising Research* 41 (May/June 2001), 39–48; Alan R. Miciak and William L. Shanklin, "Choosing Celebrity Endorsers," *Marketing Management* 3 (winter 1994), 51–59.

18. Jeff Jensen, "Team Reebok-Shaq: Is Big Trouble Afoot?" *Advertising Age*, February 21, 1994, 1, 36.

19. Carolyn Tripp, Thomas D. Jensen, and Les Carlson, "The Effects of Multiple Product Endorsements by Celebrities on Consumers' Attitudes and Intentions," *Journal of Consumer Research* 20 (March 1994), 535–547.

20. See Brian D. Till and Terence A. Shimp, "Endorsers in Advertising: The Case of Negative Celebrity Information, *Journal of Advertising* 27 (spring 1998), 67–82; Louie, Kulik, and Johnson, "When Bad Things Happen."

21. David Finkle, "Q-Ratings: The Popularity Contest of the Stars," *The Wall Street Journal*, June 7, 1992, in special section ("Themes of the Times"), 1.

22. Marc Weinberger and Harlan Spotts, "Humor in U.S. Versus U.K. TV Advertising," *Journal of Advertising* 18, no. 2 (1989), 39–44. For further discussion of differences between American and British advertising, see Terence Nevett, "Differences between American and British Television Advertising: Explanations and Implications," *Journal of Advertising* 21 (December 1992), 61–71.

23. Dana L. Alden, Wayne D. Hoyer, and Chol Lee, "Identifying Global and Culture-Specific Dimensions of Humor in Advertising: A Multinational Analysis," *Journal of Marketing* 57 (April 1993), 64–75.

24. Harlan E. Spotts, Marc G. Weinberger, and Amy L. Parsons, "Assessing the Use and Impact of Humor on Advertising Effectiveness: A Contingency Approach," *Journal of Advertising* 26 (fall 1997), 17–32.

25. For a formal theoretical account, see Dana L. Alden, Ashesh Mukherjee, and Wayne D. Hoyer, "The Effects of Incongruity, Surprise and Positive Moderators on Perceived Humor in Television Advertising," *Journal of Advertising* 29 (summer 2000), 1–16.

26. Differences in the use of humor across advertising media are demonstrated in Marc G. Weinberger, Harlan Spotts, Leland Campbell, and Amy L. Parsons, "The Use and Effect of Humor in Different Advertising Media," *Journal of Advertising Research* 35 (May/June 1995), 44–56.

27. A thorough review of the issues is provided in two valuable reviews: Paul Surgi Speck, "The Humorous Message Taxonomy: A Framework for the Study of Humorous Ads," *Current Issues and Research in Advertising*, vol. 3, ed. J. H. Leigh and C. R. Martin, Jr. (Ann Arbor: Graduate School of Business Administration, University of Michigan, 1991), 1–44; Marc G. Weinberger and Charles S. Gulas, "The Impact of Humor in Advertising: A Review," *Journal of Advertising* 21 (December 1992), 35–59.

28. Thomas J. Madden and Marc G. Weinberger, "Humor in Advertising: A Practitioner View," *Journal of Advertising Research* 24, no. 4 (1984), 23–29.

29. Based on Weinberger and Gulas, "The Impact of Humor in Advertising: A Review," 56–57.

30. Thomas J. Madden and Marc G. Weinberger, "The Effects of Humor on Attention in Magazine Advertising," *Journal of Advertising* 11, no. 3 (1982), 4–14.

31. Amitava Chattopadhyay and Kunal Basu, "Humor in Advertising: The Moderating Role of Prior Brand Evaluation," *Journal of Consumer Research* 27 (November 1990), 466–476.

32. See Yong Zhang, "Responses to Humorous Advertising: The Moderating Effect of Need for Cognition," *Journal of Advertising* 25 (spring 1996), 15–32.

33. Appreciation is extended to Professor Herbert J. Rotfeld, Auburn University, for helpful suggestions in revising this section from the previous edition of the text.

34. This is a quote from the Jerry Della Femina, a well-known advertising agency executive and former copywriter. Cited in Emily DeNitto, "Healthcare Ads Employ Scare Tactics," *Advertising Age*, November 7, 1994, 12.

35. Herbert J. Rotfeld, "Fear Appeals and Persuasion: Assumptions and Errors in Advertising Research," *Current Issues and Research in Advertising*, vol. 11, ed. J. H. Leigh and C. R. Martin, Jr. (Ann Arbor: Graduate School of Business Administration, University of Michigan, 1988), 21–40.

36. Peter Wright, "Concrete Action Plans in TV Messages to Increase Reading of Drug Warnings," *Journal of Consumer Research* 6 (December 1979), 256–269. For an explanation of the psychological mechanism by which fear-intensity operates, see Punam Anand Keller and Lauren Goldberg Block, "Increasing the Persuasiveness of Fear Appeals: The Effect of Arousal and Elaboration," *Journal of Consumer Research* 22 (March 1996), 448–459.

37. For further reading on the use of appeals to fear in antidrinking-and-driving

campaigns, see Karen Whitehill King and Leonard N. Reid, "Fear Arousing Anti-Drinking and Driving PSAs: Do Physical Injury Threats Influence Young Adults?" *Current Issues and Research in Advertising*, vol. 12, ed. J. H. Leigh and C. R. Martin, Jr. (Ann Arbor: Graduate School of Business Administration, University of Michigan, 1990), 155–175. Other relevant articles on fear appeals include John F. Tanner, James B. Hunt, and David R. Eppright, "The Protection Motivation Model: Normative Model of Fear Appeals," *Journal of Marketing* 55 (July 1991), 36–45; Tony L. Henthorne, Michael S. LaTour, and Rajan Natarajan, "Fear Appeals in Print Advertising: An Analysis of Arousal and Ad Response," *Journal of Advertising* 22 (June 1993), 59–70; and James T. Strong and Khalid M. Dubas, "The Optimal Level of Fear-Arousal in Advertising: An Empirical Study," *Journal of Current Issues and Research in Advertising* 15 (fall 1993), 93–99.

38. Carroll E. Izard, *Human Emotions* (New York: Plenum, 1977).

39. Robin Higie Coulter and Mary Beth Pinto, "Guilt Appeals in Advertising: What Are Their Effects?" *Journal of Applied Psychology*, 80 (December 1995), 697–705; Bruce A. Huhmann and Timothy P. Brotherton, "A Content Analysis of Guilt Appeals in Popular Magazine Advertisements," *Journal of Advertising* 26 (summer 1997), 35–46.

40. Huhmann and Brotherton, "A Content Analysis of Guilt Appeals in Popular Magazine Advertisements," 36.

41. Ibid.

42. A content analysis of magazine advertising indicates that the percentage of ads with sexual content had not changed over a two-decade period. What changed, however, was that sexual illustrations had become more overt. Female models were more likely than male models to be portrayed in nude, partially nude, or suggestive poses. See Lawrence Soley and Gary Kurzbard, "Sex in Advertising: A Comparison of 1964 and 1984 Magazine Advertisements," *Journal of Advertising* 15, no. 3 (1986), 46–54.

43. Robert S. Baron, "Sexual Content and Advertising Effectiveness: Comments on Belch et al. (1981) and Caccavale et al. (1981)," in *Advances in Consumer Research*, vol. 9, ed. Andrew Mitchell (Ann Arbor, Mich.: Association for Consumer Research, 1982), 428.

44. B. G. Yovovich, "Sex in Advertising— The Power and the Perils," *Advertising Age*, May 2, 1983, M4.

45. Larry Percy, "A Review of the Effect of Specific Advertising Elements upon Overall Communication Response," in *Current Issues and Research in Advertising*, vol. 2, ed. J. H. Leigh and C. R. Martin, Jr. (Ann Arbor: Graduate School of Business Administration, University of Michigan, 1983), 95.

46. David Richmond and Timothy P. Hartman, "Sex Appeal in Advertising," *Journal of Advertising Research* 22 (October/November 1982), 53–61.

47. Michael S. LaTour, Robert E. Pitts, and David C. Snook-Luther, "Female Nudity, Arousal, and Ad Response: An Experimental Investigation," *Journal of Advertising* 19, no. 4 (1990), 51–62.

48. Baron, "Sexual Content and Advertising Effectiveness," 428.

49. Robert A. Peterson and Roger A. Kerin, "The Female Role in Advertisements: Some Experimental Evidence," *Journal of Marketing* 41 (October 1977), 59–63.

50. Jessica Severn, George E. Belch, and Michael A. Belch, "The Effects of Sexual and Non-sexual Advertising Appeals and Information Level on Cognitive Processing and Communication Effectiveness," *Journal of Advertising* 19, no. 1 (1990), 14–22.

51. Ira Teinowitz and Bob Geiger, "Suits Try to Link Sex Harassment Ads," *Advertising Age*, November 18, 1991, 48.

52. Cyndee Miller, "Sexy Sizzle Backfires," *Marketing News*, September 25, 1995, 1, 2.

53. A study of consumers in Denmark, Greece, New Zealand, and the U.S. revealed consistent criticism of sexist role portrayals. See Richard W. Pollay and Steven Lysonski, "In the Eye of the Beholder: International Differences in Ad Sexism Perceptions and Reactions," *Journal of International Consumer Marketing* 6, vol. 2 (1993), 25–43.

54. Three surveys have demonstrated this fact. For the most recent review of these surveys, see Martha Rogers and Kirk H. Smith, "Public Perceptions of Subliminal Advertising: Why Practitioners Shouldn't Ignore This Issue," *Journal of Advertising Research* 33 (March/April 1993), 10–18.

55. Martha Rogers and Christine A. Seiler, "The Answer Is No: A National Survey of Advertising Industry Practitioners and Their Clients about Whether They Use Subliminal Advertising," *Journal of Advertising Research* 34 (March/April 1994), 36–45.

56. This description is adapted from Martin P. Block and Bruce G. Vanden Bergh, "Can You Sell Subliminal Messages to Consumers?" *Journal of Advertising* 14, no. 3 (1985), 59.

57. Vicary himself acknowledged that the study that initiated the original furor over subliminal advertising was based

on too small an amount of data to be meaningful. See Fred Danzig, "Subliminal Advertising—Today It's Just Historic Flashback for Researcher Vicary," *Advertising Age*, September 17, 1962, 42, 74.

58. For example, see Sharon E. Beatty and Del I. Hawkins, "Subliminal Stimulation: Some New Data and Interpretation," *Journal of Advertising* 18, no. 3 (1989), 4–8.

59. Wilson B. Key, *Subliminal Seduction: Ad Media's Manipulation of a Not So Innocent America* (New York: Signet, 1972); *Media Sexploitation* (New York: Signet, 1976); *The Clam Plate Orgy: And Other Subliminal Techniques for Manipulating Your Behavior* (New York: Signet, 1980). Key has since written *The Age of Manipulation: The Con in Confidence, the Sin in Sincere* (New York: Holt, 1989).

60. For a sophisticated treatment of visual imagery and symbolism in advertising (though not dealing with subliminal advertising per se), see Linda M. Scott, "Images in Advertising: The Need for a Theory of Visual Rhetoric," *Journal of Consumer Research* 21 (September 1994), 252–273.

61. Ronnie Cuperfain and T. K. Clarke, "A New Perspective of Subliminal Perception," *Journal of Advertising* 14, no. 1 (1985), 36–41; Myron Gable, Henry T. Wilkens, Lynn Harris, and Richard Feinberg, "An Evaluation of Subliminally Embedded Sexual Stimuli in Graphics," *Journal of Advertising* 16, no. 1 (1987), 26–31; William E. Kilbourne, Scott Painton, and Danny Ridley, "The Effect of Sexual Embedding on Responses to Magazine Advertisements," *Journal of Advertising* 14, no. 2 (1985), 48–56.

62. For discussion of the practical difficulties with implementing subliminal advertising and the questionable effectiveness of this advertising technique, see Timothy E. Moore, "Subliminal Advertising: What You See Is What You Get," *Journal of Marketing* 46 (spring 1982), 41; and Joel Saegert, "Why Marketing Should Quit Giving Subliminal Advertising the Benefit of the Doubt," *Psychology & Marketing* 4 (summer 1987), 107–120.

63. Moore, "Subliminal Advertising: What You See Is What You Get," 46.

64. Very good reviews of music's various advertising functions are available in Gordon C. Bruner II, "Music, Mood, and Marketing," *Journal of Marketing* 54 (October 1990), 94–104; Linda M. Scott, "Understanding Jingles and Needledrop: A Rhetorical Approach to Music in Advertising," *Journal of Consumer Research* 17 (September 1990), 223–236;

James J. Kellaris, Anthony D. Cox, and Dena Cox, "The Effect of Background Music on Ad Processing: A Contingency Explanation," *Journal of Marketing* 57 (October 1993), 114–125; and Kineta Hung, "Framing Meaning Perceptions with Music: The Case of Teaser Ads," *Journal of Advertising* 30 (fall 2001), 39–50.

65. In addition to those reviewed here, the following studies are recommended reading: Deborah J. MacInnis and C. Whan Park, "The Differential Role of Characteristics of Music on High- and Low-Involvement Consumers' Processing of Ads," *Journal of Consumer Research* 18 (September 1991), 161–173; James J. Kellaris and Robert J. Kent, "The Influence of Music on Consumers' Temporal Perceptions: Does Time Fly When You're Having Fun?" *Journal of Consumer Psychology* 1, no. 4 (1992), 365–376; James J. Kellaris and Robert J. Kent, "An Exploratory Investigation of Responses Elicited by Music Varying in Tempo, Tonality, and Texture," *Journal of Consumer Psychology* 2, no. 4 (1993), 381–402; Michelle L. Roehm, "Instrumental vs. Vocal Versions of Popular Music in Advertising," *Journal of Advertising Research* 41 (May/June 2001), 49–58.

66. Gerald J. Gorn, "The Effects of Music in Advertising on Choice Behavior: A Classical Conditioning Approach," *Journal of Marketing* 46 (winter 1982), 94–101.

67. A replication of this study failed to obtain supporting evidence, thereby calling into question the ability to generalize from Gorn's prior research. See James J. Kellaris and Anthony D. Cox, "The Effects of Background Music in Advertising," *Journal of Consumer Research* 16 (June 1989), 113–118.

68. Ronald E. Milliman, "Using Background Music to Affect the Behavior of Supermarket Shoppers," *Journal of Marketing* 46 (summer 1982), 86–91. For additional insights on the role of music in altering individual's perception of time, see Kellaris and Kent, "An Exploratory Investigation of Responses Elicited by Music Varying in Tempo, Tonality, and Texture."

69. Ronald E. Milliman, "The Influence of Background Music on the Behavior of Restaurant Patrons," *Journal of Consumer Research* 13 (September 1986), 286–289.

70. For a fascinating discussion of cross-cultural differences, see Noel M. Murray and Sandra B. Murray, "Music and Lyrics in Commercials: A Cross-Cultural Comparison Between Commercials Run in the Dominican Republic

and in the United States," *Journal of Advertising* 25 (summer 1996), 51–64.

71. See Darrell D. Muehling, Donald E. Stem, Jr., and Peter Raven, "Comparative Advertising: Views from Advertisers, Agencies, Media, and Policy Makers," *Journal of Advertising Research* 29 (October/November 1989), 38–48.

72. Naveen Donthu, "A Cross-Country Investigation of Recall of and Attitude toward Comparative Advertising," *Journal of Advertising* 27 (summer 1998), 111–122.

73. These questions are adapted from Stephen B. Ash and Chow-Hou Wee, "Comparative Advertising: A Review with Implications for Further Research," in *Advances in Consumer Research*, vol. 10, ed. R. P. Bagozzi and A. M. Tybout (Ann Arbor, Mich.: Association for Consumer Research, 1983), 374.

74. A sampling of significant comparative advertising research includes the following: Cornelia Droge and Rene Y. Darmon, "Associative Positioning Strategies through Comparative Advertising: Attribute versus Overall Similarity Approaches," *Journal of Marketing Research* 24 (November 1987), 377–388; Cornelia Pechmann and David W. Stewart, "The Effects of Comparative Advertising on Attention, Memory, and Purchase Intentions," *Journal of Consumer Research* 17 (September 1990), 180–191; Cornelia Pechmann and S. Ratneshwar, "The Use of Comparative Advertising for Brand Positioning: Association versus Differentiation," *Journal of Consumer Research* 18 (September 1991), 145–160; Cornelia Pechmann and Gabriel Esteban, "Persuasion Processes Associated with Direct Comparative and Noncomparative Advertising and Implications for Advertising Effectiveness," *Journal of Consumer Psychology* 2,

no. 4 (1993), 403–432; Randall L. Rose, Paul W. Miniard, Michael J. Barone, Kenneth C. Manning, and Brian D. Till, "When Persuasion Goes Undetected: The Case of Comparative Advertising," *Journal of Marketing Research* 30 (August 1993), 315–330; Shailendra Pratap Jain, Bruce Buchanan, and Durairaj Maheswaran, "Comparative Versus Noncomparative Advertising: The Moderating Impact of Prepurchase Attribute Verifiability," *Journal of Consumer Psychology* 9, no. 4 (2000), 201–212.

75. Dhruv Grewal, Sukuman Kavanoor, Edward F. Fern, Carolyn Costley, and James Barnes, "Comparative Versus Noncomparative Advertising: A Meta-Analysis," *Journal of Marketing* 61 (October 1997), 1–15.

76. V. Kanti Prasad, "Communications Effectiveness of Comparative Advertising: A Laboratory Analysis," *Journal of Marketing Research* 13 (May 1976), 128–137.

77. Terence A. Shimp and David C. Dyer, "The Effects of Comparative Advertising Mediated by Market Position of Sponsoring Brand," *Journal of Advertising* 7, no. 3 (1978), 13–19.

78. Gerald J. Gorn and Charles B. Weinberg, "The Impact of Comparative Advertising on Perception and Attitude: Some Positive Findings," *Journal of Consumer Research* 11 (September 1984), 719–727.

79. Rose, Miniard, Barone, Manning, and Till, "When Persuasion Goes Undetected: The Case of Comparative Advertising"; Paul W. Miniard, Randall L. Rose, Michael J. Barone, and Kenneth C. Manning, "On the Need for Relative Measures When Assessing Comparative Advertising Effects," *Journal of Advertising* 22 (September 1993), 41–57.

Chapter Eleven

ASSESSING AD MESSAGE EFFECTIVENESS

Chapter Objectives

After studying this chapter, you should be able to:

1. Explain the rationale and importance of message research.
2. Describe the various research techniques used to measure consumers' recognition and recall of advertising messages.
3. Describe measures of physiological arousal to advertisements.
4. Explain the role of persuasion measurement, including pre-post testing of consumer preference.
5. Explain the meaning and operation of single-source measures of advertising effectiveness.

Opening Vignette: More Emotion, More Effect

Procter & Gamble, the huge consumer goods company, spends over $3 billion annually to advertise its many brands around the world. However, P&G officials recently came to the conclusion that the company's internal advertising process probably was too rigid, too time-consuming, and perhaps even too risk adverse, and that the likely result was suboptimal creative advertising from P&G's ad agencies. Part of the problem was that P&G's rigid rules regarding how advertising should be done imposed limitations on the creative product flowing out of its advertising agencies and perhaps even encouraged formulaic advertisements rather than creative ads attuned to the specific needs of P&G's many brands. Moreover, too many P&G personnel were involved in the process, which led to divided accountability and delays in creating new ad campaigns.

Propelled by a passionate desire to improve the advertising process and the quality of creative advertising for its brands, top P&G officials, in concert with high-level ad agency representatives, proposed several major changes in the advertising process: (1) Involve fewer P&G people in the process, (2) have a single P&G representative work with an ad agency on any particular brand advertising assignment (called single-point accountability), and (3) allow ad agencies more discretion in developing advertising concepts.

A result of this paradigm shift at P&G has been the production of more creative, dramatic, and emotional advertisements. The first illustration of this was an ad for Bounty paper towels. Advertising for this brand historically had involved new executions of the same old theme: Mom arriving just in time to mop up her child's spilled juice with Bounty paper towels followed by a side-by-side product demonstration. Under the new system, a new creative execution for Bounty required only about one-quarter of the time that past ad development required. The ad incorporated an emotional scene in which a father knocks over his own glass of juice to make his preschool son feel better about his own juice disaster. Commenting on this emotional advertising execution, an official for Bounty's ad agency stated that consumers don't need to be shown how paper towels work, implying that an emotional execution would do a better job in holding viewer attention and enhancing Bounty's equity.

Having devised a better procedure for developing creative advertisements, the all-important remaining issue is whether P&G's new approach to creating advertisements is effective. Does this advertising provide a good return on P&G's investment? How should P&G measure ad effectiveness? These are questions that the present chapter addresses. As will be seen, there are no simple answers. However, the student will learn about the approaches the advertising community employs in attempting to assess advertising effectiveness and thus to obtain some measure of advertising's ROI.

The two preceding chapters examined the role of advertising creativity (Chapter 9) and explored the role of endorsers and forms of advertising executions—humor, sex appeals, appeals to guilt, and so on (Chapter 10). A well-defined value proposition is the key to advertising effectiveness, but there are "different ways to skin the cat"; that is, different types of creative advertising strategies (e.g., USP, brand image, generic) and different message strategies can accomplish the all-important advertising objectives that were described in Chapter 8. In short, brand managers and their advertising agencies have many options when creating advertising messages.

At the same time, the brand management team is responsible for researching whether proposed advertisements stand a good chance of being successful *prior* to investing money in printing or airing ads in mass media. It would, in other words, be presumptuous at best or even foolhardy to assume that a proposed advertisement will be successful absent any research-based evidence. The demand for accountability that is prevalent throughout business necessitates that ads be tested before they are printed or broadcast and then again during or after the period in which they have been printed or broadcast.

Sound business practice requires that efforts be made to determine whether advertising expenditures are justified, especially considering the amount of money that is invested in advertising both in the United States and worldwide. (See the *Global Focus* for information about advertising dollars spent outside the United States.) Accordingly, a significant amount of time and money are spent on testing message effectiveness. This chapter surveys some of the most important techniques used in the advertising research business.

OVERVIEW OF ADVERTISING RESEARCH

Measuring message effectiveness is a difficult and expensive task. Nonetheless, the value gained from undertaking the effort typically outweighs the drawbacks. In the absence of formal research, most advertisers would not know whether proposed ad messages are going to be effective or whether ongoing advertising is doing a good job, nor could they know what to change to improve future advertising efforts. Advertising research enables management to increase advertising's contribution toward achieving marketing goals and yielding a reasonable return on investment.

Contemporary message research traces its roots to the 19th century, when measures of recall and memory were obtained as indicators of print advertising effectiveness.[1] Today, most national advertisers would not even consider airing a television commercial or placing a magazine advertisement without testing it first. A survey of the largest advertisers and advertising agencies in the United States determined that more than 80 percent of the respondents from each group pretest television commercials before airing them on a national basis.[2] Interestingly, these commercials typically are tested in a preliminary form rather than as finished versions. The *IMC Focus* on page 325 briefly describes the various prefinished forms in which TV commercial typically are tested.

What Does Message Research Involve?

Advertising research encompasses a variety of purposes, methods, measures, and techniques. Effectiveness is measured in terms of achieving awareness, conveying copy points, influencing attitudes, creating emotional responses, and affecting purchase choices. Due to growing calls for advertising accountability, advertising research in its various forms is more prevalent and essential than ever.[3]

Sometimes research is done under natural advertising conditions and other times in simulated or laboratory situations. Measures of effectiveness range from paper-and-pencil instruments (such as attitude scales) to physiological devices (e.g., pupillometers that measure eye movement). It should be clear that there is no single encompassing form of advertising research. Rather, measures of advertising effectiveness are as varied as the questions that advertisers and their agencies want answered.

Message research is undertaken to test the effectiveness of advertising messages. (Message research also is called copy research, or copytesting, but these terms are too limiting inasmuch as message research involves testing all aspects of advertisements, not just the verbal copy material.) Message research involves both *pretesting* messages during developmental stages (prior to actual placement in advertising media) and *posttesting* messages for effectiveness after they have been aired or printed. Pretesting is performed to eliminate ineffective ads before

Table 11.1

Top 25 Advertisers Outside the United States in 2000 (in millions of U.S. dollars)

Rank	Company	Headquarters	Ad Spending
1	Unilever	London/Rotterdam	$2,967
2	Procter & Gamble	Cincinnati	2,610
3	Nestle	Vevey, Switzerland	1,560
4	Toyota Motor Corp.	Toyota City, Japan	1,345
5	Volkswagen	Wolfsburg, Germany	1,290
6	Coca-Cola Co.	Atlanta	1,176
7	Ford Motor Co.	Dearborn, Michigan	1,127
8	General Motors Corp.	Detroit	1,028
9	PSA Peugeot Citroen	Paris	1,004
10	Fiat	Turin, Italy	988
11	Renault	Renault, France	914
12	L'Oreal	Paris	913
13	Kao Corp.	Tokyo	715
14	McDonald's Corp.	Oak Brook, Illinois	694
15	Mars Inc.	McLean, Virginia	692
16	Vodafone Group	Newbury, Berkshire, U.K.	673
17	Nissan Motor Co.	Tokyo	665
18	Henkel	Duesseldorf	654
19	Ferrero	Perugia, Italy	633
20	Sony Corp.	Tokyo	556
21	Phillip Morris Cos.	New York	541
22	Danone Group	Levallois-Peret, France	539
23	France Telecom	Paris	527
24	DaimlerChrysler	Auburn Hills, Mich./Stuttgart	424
25	Telefonica	Madrid	419

IMC
focus

Testing TV Commercials in Prefinished Form

An advertising agency works from a creative brief that has been developed in conjunction with the client-side brand management team. As described in Chapter 9, the creative brief is a document designed to inspire copywriters by channeling their creative efforts toward a solution that will serve the interests of the client. The creative brief represents an informal pact between client and advertising agency that represents agreement on what an advertising campaign is intended to accomplish. Among other features, the creative brief identifies the brand positioning, the overall marketing strategy for the brand, and a statement of the brand's key value proposition. Working from this brief, copywriters and other agency personnel develop two or more creative executions that are considered suitable for accomplishing agreed-on objectives. However, rather than immediately producing a finished commercial, which can easily cost $500,000 or more, it is practical and cost-efficient to test the advertising concept in a prefinished form. There are five prefinished forms that are tested in television commercial research. The form furthest removed from a finished commercial is the storyboard, whereas the other forms become more like a produced commercial as we progress from the animatic form to the livamatic version. Each is briefly described here.

1. *Storyboards:* This prefinished version presents a series of key visual frames and the corresponding script of the audio. The sequence of visual frames is literally pasted on a poster-type board, which thus accounts for the storyboard name. The storyboard version, unlike a dynamic commercial, is completely static. Drawings of

people replace the actual actors or celebrities who ultimately will appear in the finished commercial.

2. *Animatics:* This is a film or videotape of a sequence of drawings with simultaneous playing of audio to represent a proposed commercial. The animatic version maintains the "primitive" nature of the storyboard but incorporates an element of dynamism by videotaping the sequence of drawings.

3. *Photomatics:* A sequence of photographs is filmed or videotaped and accompanied with audio to represent a proposed commercial. This version is increasingly realistic inasmuch as photographs of real people are displayed rather than, as in the case of storyboards, merely shown as drawn renderings of real people.

4. *Ripamatics:* Footage is taken from existing commercials and spliced together to represent the proposed commercial. Hence, the ripamatics version captures the realism of an actual commercial but does not entail the huge expense associated with filming an original commercial.

5. *Liveamatics:* This prefinished version entails filming or videotaping live talent to represent the proposed commercial. This version is the closest to a finished commercial, but it does not fully represent the actual settings or talent who will be used in the actual commercial.

Research has shown that results from testing prefinished commercials closely parallel those from tests performed on finalized commercials—and at significantly lower expense.

Source: Adapted from Karen Whitehill King, John D. Pehrson, and Leonard N. Reid, "Pretesting TV Commercials: Methods, Measures, and Changing Agency Roles," *Journal of Advertising* 22 (September 1993), pp. 85–97. Reprinted by permission.

they are ever run, while posttesting is conducted to determine whether messages have achieved their established objectives.

Idealism Meets Reality in Advertising Research

The role, importance, and difficulty of assessing advertising effectiveness perhaps can best be appreciated by examining what an ideal system of advertising measurement would entail and then comparing this against the reality of advertising research.

First, an ideal measure would provide an *early warning signal*—that is, it would measure ad effectiveness at the earliest possible stage in the ad development process. The sooner an advertisement is found to be ineffective, the less time, effort, and financial resources will be wasted. Early detection of effective advertisements, on the other hand, enables marketers to hasten the development process so that the ads can generate return on investment as quickly as possible.

Second, an ideal measurement system would evaluate advertising effectiveness in terms of the *sales volume generated by advertising*, which is, according to the logic of vaguely right versus precisely wrong objective setting (see Chapter 8), the only bona fide advertising objective.[4] A measure of advertising effectiveness becomes less valuable the further removed it is from an advertisement's potential for generating sales volume. Hence, a measure of preference shift toward a brand is more valuable than a measure of brand recognition, which is less concerned with the act of purchasing the advertised product. Schematically, the sequence of advertising effects—from furthest away from sales to sales itself—can be seen in Figure 11.1. Advertising researchers test specific advertising executions with respect to all these levels. (Please note that "Purchase Behavior" in Figure 11.1 is the consumer response to advertising that equates to brand sales from the brand manager's perspective.)

Third, an ideal measurement system would satisfy the standard research requirements of *reliability and validity*. Advertising measures are reliable when repeated trials yield the same results. Measures are valid when they predict actual marketplace performance.

Finally, an ideal system would permit *quick and inexpensive measurement.* The longer it takes to assess advertising effectiveness and the more it costs, the less valuable is the measuring system.

The ideal conditions just discussed are rarely satisfied. In fact, several are inconsistent. For example, a measurement system capable of predicting sales potential is likely to be expensive. Similarly, one that provides an early warning signal is less likely to be reliable and valid. Advertising research must necessarily deviate from the ideal circumstances described previously. However, the gap between idealism and reality in advertising research is narrowing with advances in technology and greater ingenuity in developing testing procedures.

Literally dozens of methods for measuring message effectiveness have appeared over the years. The following sections discuss some of the more popular methods in use by national advertisers. Message research methods are classified into measures of (1) recognition and recall, (2) physiological arousal, (3) persuasion, and (4) sales response.

Industry Standards for Message Research

Message-based research, or copytesting, is in wide use throughout North America, Europe, and elsewhere. Yet, it may be a bit sobering to note that much message-based research is not of the highest caliber. Sometimes it is unclear exactly what the research is attempting to measure, measures often fail to satisfy basic reliability and validity requirements, and results have little to say about whether copytested ads stand a good chance of being effective.

Members of the advertising research community have been mindful of these problems and have sought a higher standard of performance from advertising researchers. A major document, called **Positioning Advertising Copytesting (PACT),** was formulated by leading U.S. advertising agencies to remedy the problem of mediocre or flawed advertising research. The document is directed primarily at television advertising but is relevant to the testing of advertising in all media.

The PACT document consists of nine message-testing principles.[5] More than mere pronouncements, these principles represent useful guides to how advertising research should be conducted. It is unnecessary that you attempt to commit these principles to memory; rather, your objective in reading the following principles should be to simply appreciate what constitutes good message research practice. (Please note that the developers of the PACT principles referred to copytest-

Sequence of Advertising Effects

Figure 11.1

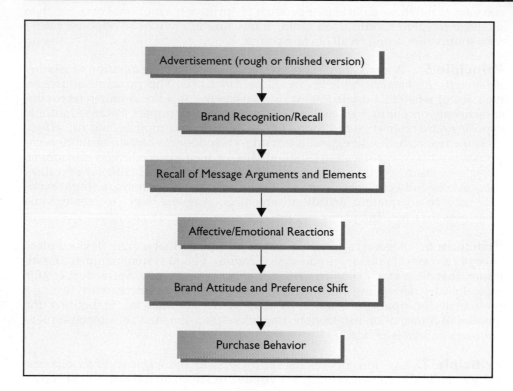

ing rather than message research. The descriptions that follow retain the use of copytesting, though as noted above, message research is a more apt label.)

Principle 1. A good copytesting system needs to provide measurements that are *relevant to the advertising objectives*. The specific objective(s) that an advertising campaign is intended to accomplish (such as creating brand awareness, influencing brand image, creating warmth) should be the first consideration in determining the methods to assess advertising effectiveness. For example, if the objective for a particular campaign is to evoke strong emotional reactions, a measure of recall would be patently inappropriate.

Principle 2. A good copytesting system is one that *requires agreement about how the results will be used in advance of each specific test*. Specifying the use of research results before data collection ensures that all parties involved (advertiser, agency, and research firm) agree on the research goals and reduces the chance of conflicting interpretations of test results. This principle's intent is to encourage the use of decision rules or action standards that, before actual testing, establish the test results that must be achieved for the test advertisement to receive full media distribution.

Principle 3. A good copytesting system provides *multiple measurements*, because single measurements are generally inadequate to assess the performance of an advertisement. The process by which advertisements influence customers is complex, so multiple measures are more likely than single measures to capture the various advertising effects.

Principle 4. A good copytesting system is based on *a model of human response to communications*—the reception of a stimulus, the comprehension of the stimulus, and the response to the stimulus. Because advertisements vary in the impact they are intended to achieve, a good copytesting system is capable of answering questions that are patterned to the underlying model of behavior. For example, if consumers purchase a particular product for primarily emotional reasons, then message research should use a suitable measure of emotional response rather than simply measuring recall of copy points.

Principle 5.   A good copytesting system allows for consideration of *whether the advertising stimulus should be exposed more than once*. This principle addresses the issue of whether a single test exposure (showing an ad or commercial to consumers only once) provides a sufficient test of potential impact. Because multiple exposures are often required for advertisements to accomplish their full effect, message research should expose a test ad to respondents on two or more occasions when the communication situation calls for such a procedure.[6] For example, a single-exposure test is probably insufficient to determine whether an advertisement successfully conveys a complex benefit. On the other hand, a single exposure may be adequate if an advertisement is designed solely to create name awareness for a new brand.

Principle 6.   A good copytesting system recognizes that a more finished piece of copy can be evaluated more soundly; therefore, a good system requires, at minimum, that *alternative executions be tested in the same degree of finish*. Test results typically vary depending on the degree of finish, as, for example, when testing a photomatic or ripamatic version of a television commercial. Sometimes the amount of information lost from testing a less-than-finished ad is inconsequential; sometimes it is critical.

Principle 7.   A good copytesting *system provides controls to avoid the bias normally found in the exposure context*. The context in which an advertisement is contained (e.g., the clutter or lack of clutter in a magazine) will have a substantial impact on how the ad is received, processed, and accepted. For this reason, copytesting procedures should attempt to duplicate the eventual context of an advertisement or commercial.

Principle 8.   A good copytesting system is one that takes into account *basic considerations of sample definition*. This typically requires that the sample be representative of the target audience to which test results are to be generalized and that the sample size be sufficiently large to permit reliable statistical conclusions.

Principle 9.   Finally, a good copytesting system is one that can *demonstrate reliability and validity*. Reliability and validity are basic requirements of any research endeavor. As applied to message research, a reliable test is one that yields consistent results each time an advertisement is tested, and a valid test is one that is predictive of marketplace performance.

The foregoing principles establish a high set of standards for the advertising research community. Yet they should not be regarded in the same sense as the earlier discussion of research ideals. Rather, these principles should be viewed as mandatory if advertising effectiveness is to be tested in a meaningful way.

What Do Brand Managers and Ad Agencies Want to Learn from Message Research?

As established back in Chapter 2, MarCom efforts are directed at enhancing brand equity with the expectation that enhanced equity will lead ultimately to increases in brand sales and market share. You will recall from the discussion in Chapter 2 that brand equity from the consumer's perspective consists of two elements: *brand awareness* and *brand image*. Advertising's role is thus to augment brand awareness, alter the brand-based attribute and benefit associations that constitute a brand's image, and ultimately effect increases in a brand's sales and market share. Hence, message research is needed to provide diagnostic information about an advertisement's prospective equity-enhancing and sales-expanding potential (pretesting research) and to determine whether finalized advertisements actually accomplished these goals (posttesting research).

Before proceeding, it is important to note that members of the advertising community have attempted for many years to ascertain which measures of advertising best predict advertising effectiveness. Particularly notable is a major study funded by the influential Advertising Research Foundation that assessed which of 35 different measures best predict the sales effectiveness of television commercials.[7] Although representing a heroic effort, results from the Copy Research Validity Project (CRVP) are both inconclusive and controversial.[8] Probably the only definitive conclusion that can be made is that *no one measure is always most appropriate or universally best*. Each brand advertising situation requires a careful assessment of the objectives that advertising is intended to accomplish and then the use of research methods that are appropriate for determining whether these objectives have been accomplished.

Given the scope of advertising research techniques in use, it would be impossible in this chapter to provide an exhaustive treatment. The intent, instead, is to provide a representative sampling of the primary procedures that are used by brand managers and their ad agencies for measuring advertising effectiveness. As summarized in Table 11.2, these methods examine four types of consumer responses to advertisements: (1) recognition and recall, (2) physiological arousal, (3) persuasive impact, and (4) sales response. Measures of recognition and recall assess whether advertising has successfully influenced brand awareness. Measures of physiological arousal provide unobtrusive indicators of whether advertisements have the potential to arouse consumers and enhance their receptiveness to advertising content. Measures of persuasive impact represent prebehavioral indicators of whether an advertisement is likely to influence purchase intentions and behavior. Finally, measures of sales response determine specifically whether an advertising campaign has affected a brand's sales activity.

MEASURES OF RECOGNITION AND RECALL

After exposure to an advertisement, consumers may experience varying degrees of awareness, the most basic of which is simply noticing an ad without processing specific elements. Advertisers intend, however, for consumers to heed specific parts, elements, or features of an ad and associate those with the advertised brand.[9] Recognition and recall both represent elements of consumers' memories for advertising information, but recognition measures, which can be equated with multiple-choice test questions, tap a more superficial level of memory compared with recall measures, which are similar to essay questions.[10] It will also be noted

Illustrative Message Research Methods   **Table 11.2**

Measures of Recognition and Recall
- **Starch Readership Service (magazines)**
- **Bruzzone tests (TV)**
- **Burke day-after recall (TV)**

Measures of Physiological Arousal
- **Psychogalvanometer**
- **Pupilometer**

Measures of Persuasion
- **Ipsos-ASI Next*TV method**
- **rsc's ARS Persuasion method**

Measures of Sales Response (single-source systems)
- **IRI's BehaviorScan**
- **Nielsen's SCANTRACK**

from the discussion of brand equity in Chapter 2 that recognition is a lower level of brand awareness than recall. In other words, brand managers want consumers not only to recognize a brand name and its attributes or benefits but also to freely recall this information from memory without any cues or reminders.

Several commercial research firms provide advertisers with information on how well their ads perform in terms of generating awareness, which typically is assessed with recognition or recall measures. Three services are described in the following sections: Starch Readership Service (magazine recognition); Bruzzone tests (television recognition); and Burke day-after recall rests (television recall).[11]

Starch Readership Service

Starch Readership Service measures the primary objective of a *magazine ad*—namely, to be seen and read. Starch examines reader awareness of advertisements in consumer magazines and business publications. Over 75,000 advertisements are studied annually based on interviews with more than 100,000 people involving more than 140 publications. Sample sizes range from 100 to 150 individuals per issue, with most interviews conducted in respondents' homes or, in the case of business publications, in offices or places of business. Interviews are conducted during the early life of a publication. Following a suitable waiting period after the appearance of a publication to give readers an opportunity to read or look through their issue, interviewing commences and continues a full week (for a weekly publication), two weeks (for a biweekly), or three weeks (for a monthly publication).

Starch interviewers locate eligible readers of each magazine issue studied. An eligible reader is one who has glanced through or read some part of the issue prior to the interviewer's visit and who meets the age, sex, and occupation requirements set for the particular magazine. Once eligibility is established, interviewers turn the pages of the magazine, inquiring about each advertisement being studied. Respondents are first asked, "Did you see or read any part of this advertisement?" If a respondent answers "Yes," a prescribed questioning procedure is followed to determine the respondent's awareness of various parts of the ad (illustrations, headline, etc.). Respondents are then classified as noted, associated, read-some, or read-most readers according to these specific definitions:[12]

- *Noted* is the percentage of people interviewed who remembered having previously seen the advertisement in the issue being studied.
- *Associated* is the percentage of people interviewed who not only noted the ad but also saw or read some part of it that clearly indicated the name of the brand or advertiser.
- *Read some* is the percentage of people interviewed who read any part of the ad's copy.
- *Read most* is the percentage of people interviewed who read half or more of the written material in the ad.

For each magazine advertisement that has undergone a Starch analysis, indices are developed for that ad's noted, associated, read-some, and read-most scores. Two sets of indices are established: One index compares an advertisement's scores against the average scores for *all ads* in the magazine issue, and the second (called the ADNORM index) compares an advertisement's scores against other ads in the *same product category* as well as the same size (e.g., full page) and color classifications (e.g., four-color). Hence, an advertisement that achieves an average value receives an index of 100. By comparison, a score of 130, for example, would mean that a particular ad scored 30 percent above comparable ads, whereas a score of 70 would indicate it scored 30 percent below comparable ads.

Figures 11.2 and 11.3 illustrate two Starch-rated advertisements from an issue of *Time* magazine. The first example (Figure 11.2) features actress and singer Vanessa Williams from the ongoing series of milk mustache advertisements. As can be seen, 73 percent of the respondents remembered having previously seen (or *noted*) the ad, 68 percent *associated* it, and 32 percent *read most* of it. The second illustration (Figure 11.3) is a "crash test" advertisement for the Toyota Sienna. This ad's noted, associated, and read-most scores are substantially lower at 49, 46, and 23 percent, respectively.

Starch-Rated Advertisement for Vanessa Williams and the Milk Mustache Campaign

Figure 11.2

© Courtesy of America's Dairy Farmers and Milk Processors

A basic assumption of the Starch procedure is that respondents in fact do remember whether they saw a particular ad in a specific magazine issue. The Starch technique has sometimes been criticized because in so-called *bogus ad studies* that use prepublication or altered issues, respondents report having seen ads that actually never ran. The Starch organization does not consider such studies valid because of the failure of researchers to follow proper procedures for qualifying issue readers and questioning respondents. Research by the Starch organization demonstrates that when properly interviewed, most respondents are able to identify the ads they have seen or read in a specific issue with a high degree of accuracy; according to this research, false reporting of ad noting is minimal.[13]

Due to the inherent frailties of people's memories, it is almost certain that Starch scores do *not* provide exact percentages but rather are biased to some degree by people reporting they have seen or read an ad when in fact they have not. Nonetheless, it is not exact scores that are critical but rather comparisons between scores for the same ad placed in different magazines or comparative scores among different ads placed in the same magazine issue. For example, the milk ad with Vanessa Williams in Figure 11.2 obtained readership index scores of 155 (noted), 162 (associated), and 188 (read most). These indices mean that the milk ad performed 55 percent better than the average noted score for all 31 one-half-page or larger ads tested in this particular issue of *Time,* 62 percent better than the median associated score, and 88 percent better than the median read-most score. ADNORM indices for the Toyota Sienna (Figure 11.3) are 102 (noted), 107 (associated), and 177 (read most). Compared to the other automobile and light truck advertisements in this particular issue of *Time*, the Toyota Sienna performed slightly

Figure 11.3   Starch-Rated Advertisement for the Toyota Sienna

above average in terms of noted and associated scores but dramatically above average with respect to its read-most score. Because Starch has been performing these studies since the 1920s and has compiled a wealth of baseline data, or norms, advertisers and media planners can make informed decisions concerning the relative merits of different magazines and informed judgments regarding the effectiveness of particular advertisements.

Bruzzone Tests

The Bruzzone Research Company (BRC) provides advertisers with a test of consumer recognition of television commercials. BRC mails a set of photoboard commercials to a random sample of households and encourages responses by providing a nominal monetary incentive. This token of appreciation along with individuals' inherent interest in the task typically yields a high response rate.[14] A Bruzzone test for a commercial is shown in Figure 11.4.[15] This is a standard, five-picture photoboard version of an American Express commercial (titled "Seinfeld/Superman") that was tested shortly after it was aired. Notice in the upper-left corner of Figure 11.4 that respondents are directed to "look over these pictures and words from a TV commercial and answer the questions on the right." At the top of the right side, the recognition question is asked immediately: "Do you remember seeing this commercial on TV?" Toward the bottom of the right side, respondents are asked to identify the name of the advertised brand (which is not included in the photoboard). Intervening questions ask respondents to indicate

Bruzzone-Tested Commercial
for American Express ("Seinfeld/Superman")

Figure 11.4

Please look over these pictures and words from a TV commercial and answer the questions on the right.

(Superman talking to Seinfeld) It's not like I asked to be famous.

(Seinfeld) Yeah, well, it's the price you pay.

(Superman) You sign a lot of autographs?

(Seinfeld) Oh yeah. You?

(Superman) Some. They ask me to bend stuff a lot.

(Seinfeld) I could see that. What?

(Superman) It's Lois. She's in trouble.

(Seinfeld) Did you look through that building?

(Superman) Well, kind of. It's glass.

(Lois) Superman I've forgotten my wallet.

(Superman) I can't carry any money in this. I'm powerless.

(Seinfeld) I'm not.

(Seinfeld spins around and produces the Name Brand * card.)

(Lois) My hero.

(Announcer) It's a huge comet hurdling toward earth. We're doomed.

(Seinfeld to Superman) I think you better get this one.
(Announcer) You can do more with the Name Brand * card.

© Courtesy of Bruzzone Research Company

Do you remember seeing this commercial on TV?

BRC

05-1 ☐ Yes   -2 ☐ No   -3 ☐ Not sure-I may have

(If no, skip the rest of these questions and go to the next page.)

How interested are you in what this commercial is trying to tell you or show you about the product?

06-1 ☐ Very   -2 ☐ Somewhat   -3 ☐ Not
        interested   interested   interested

How does it make you <u>feel</u> about the product?

07-1 ☐ Good   -2 ☐ OK   -3 ☐ Bad   -4 ☐ Not sure

Please check any of the following if you feel they describe this commercial.

08-1 ☐ Amusing	09-1 ☐ Familiar	10-1 ☐ Pointless
-2 ☐ Appealing	-2 ☐ Fast moving	-2 ☐ Seen a lot
-3 ☐ Believable	-3 ☐ Gentle	-3 ☐ Sensitive
-4 ☐ Clever	-4 ☐ Imaginative	-4 ☐ Silly
-5 ☐ Confusing	-5 ☐ Informative	-5 ☐ True to life
-6 ☐ Convincing	-6 ☐ Irritating	-6 ☐ Warm
-7 ☐ Dull	-7 ☐ Lively	-7 ☐ Well done
-8 ☐ Easy to forget	-8 ☐ Original	-8 ☐ Worn out
-9 ☐ Effective	-9 ☐ Phony	-9 ☐ Worth remembering

Thinking about the commercial as a whole would you say you:

11-1 ☐ Liked it a lot   -4 ☐ Disliked it somewhat
-2 ☐ Liked it somewhat   -5 ☐ Disliked it a lot
-3 ☐ Felt neutral

* We have blocked out the name.
Do you remember which credit card was being advertised?

12-1 ☐ MasterCard   -3 ☐ American Express
-2 ☐ Visa   -4 ☐ Don't know

Does anyone in your household use this type of product?

13-1 ☐ Regularly   -2 ☐ Occasionally   -3 ☐ Seldom or never

2-20

---

their reactions to and liking of the tested commercial. Respondents also describe their feelings toward the commercial by checking any of 27 adjectives that describe the commercial. (See items starting with "Amusing" in the middle of the page on the right side of Figure 11.4.)

Because BRC has performed hundreds of such tests, it has established norms for particular product categories against which a newly tested commercial can be compared. Moreover, BRC has developed an Advertising Response Model (ARM), which links responses to the 27 descriptive adjectives to consumers' attitudes toward both the advertisement and the advertised brand, and ultimately to interest in purchasing the brand. Figure 11.5 presents the ARM analysis for American Express' "Seinfeld/Superman" commercial. Notice first in the upper-right corner the color coding for this analysis. Specifically, adjectives coded in yellow indicate that the commercial performed better than average (compared to BRC norms), words coded in blue reveal average performance, and those adjectives coded in red indicate below-average performance. A review of Figure 11.5 shows that the American Express commercial scored above-average on indicators of humor, uniqueness, energy, and appeal, all of which generated an above-average "attitude toward the ad" for this commercial. At the same time, the "Seinfeld/Superman" execution performed below average in terms of perceived credibility and relevance. Along with just an average performance on

Figure 11.5

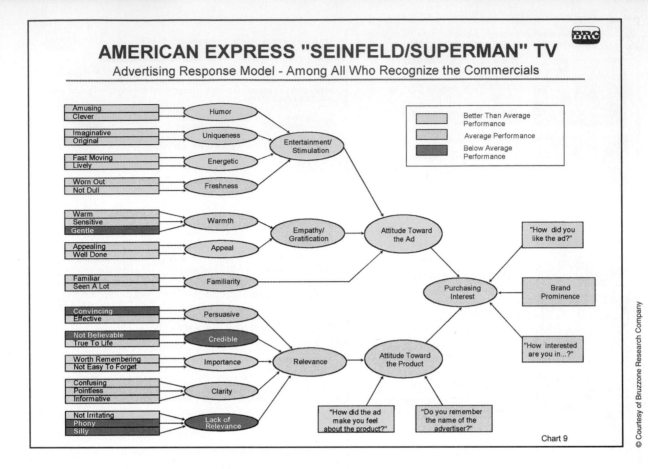

persuasiveness and clarity, the net result was only an average "attitude toward the product" and, in turn, only an average "purchasing interest." Thus, this American Express commercial was effective in terms of its entertainment and stimulation value, but it seems to have lacked the requisite persuasiveness, credibility, and relevance to create anything other than just an average interest in the American Express card.

Bruzzone testing provides a valid prediction of actual marketplace performance along with being relatively inexpensive compared with other copytesting methods. Because a Bruzzone test cannot be implemented until after a finished TV commercial has actually been aired, it does not provide a before-the-fact indication of whether a commercial should be aired in the first place. Nevertheless, these tests offer important information for evaluating a commercial's effectiveness and whether it should continue to run. As previously noted, the Bruzzone method has historically involved traditional surface *mailing* of photoboards to a sample of consumers. However, with the Internet's growth and widespread usage, Bruzzone now performs online testing. The *Online Focus* section describes how this is accomplished. Please review this section carefully because it provides additional insight about the Bruzzone testing method.

Burke Day-After Recall Testing

Various companies test advertisements to determine whether viewers have been sufficiently influenced to recall having seen the advertisement in a magazine or on television. For example, Gallup & Robinson and Mapes & Ross are two well-known research companies that provide recall testing of ads placed in print me-

Online Ad Tracking Using the Bruzzone Method

Whereas the Bruzzone method has historically involved the use of the U.S. Postal Service for mailing photoboards and corresponding questionnaires to households, in recent years it increasingly has moved its research to online testing. To justify using online testing rather than the standard mailed-questionnaire approach, it was necessary to validate the procedure—that is, to establish that the results produced by online testing were similar to those obtained from the mail procedure. Toward this end, Bruzzone performed a comparative test of six Super Bowl commercials. Photoboard versions of these commercials and accompanying questionnaires were mailed to a random sample of 1,000 households selected from all 50 states (the mail survey), whereas 1,700 members of an online group were encouraged to visit a Web site that housed the photoboards and questionnaires (the online survey). An illustrative five-picture photoboard for one of the six commercials is shown in Figure 11.6; excerpts from the remaining five commercials are presented in Figure 11.7.

Comparative test results appear in Figure 11.8 on page 338. The top panel of Figure 11.8 provides results from the online survey, and the bottom panel has the conclusions from the mail survey. Notice first that in each panel the bar chart contains three values for each commercial: (1) the percentage of respondents who recognize having seen a particular commercial during the 1999 Super Bowl (shown in orange); (2) the percentage of respondents who both recognized seeing the commercial and knew the name of the advertised brand (shown in red); and (3) the percentage of respondents who recognized the commercial, knew what brand it was for, and liked it (shown in blue). It obviously would be expected that the percentages would get progressively smaller moving from recognized to recognized and knew brand name to recognized, knew brand name, and liked the commercial.

Figure 11.8 shows that the online and mail test results are identical in their ability to spot the best- through worst-performing commercials. Although the percentage scores for the online test (top panel) are systematically higher than the scores for the mail test (bottom panel), the overall pattern is identical. For example, considering just the Bud Frogs "Yappin" commercial, the bar chart results show that the percentages of respondents who indicated that they had recognized seeing this commercial during the 1999 Super Bowl were approximately 87 percent for the online survey and 61 percent for the mail survey. The comparative percentages for the other two indicators of commercial effectiveness can be similarly read from the top and bottom panels of the charts in Figure 11.8.

These results thus provide tentative evidence that the online procedure replicates the pattern of results obtained from traditional mail testing. Needless to say, mail surveys still are needed to reach households that do not have Internet access, but online testing provides a viable option for reaching "wired" households. Online testing possesses two obvious advantages over mail surveys: It is much quicker and less expensive.

Source: Don Bruzzone, "Online Ad Tracking: Does It Work?" Report from the Bruzzone Research Company, November 1999. www.bruzzone-research.com. © 1999 and reprinted with permission.

dia. Ipsos-ASI and Burke are notable firms that test consumer recall of television commercials. The following discussion focuses on Burke's procedure. A later section describes the Ipsos-ASI method in the context of persuasion measurement.

Burke's day-after recall (DAR) procedure tests commercials that have been aired as part of normal television programming. The day following the first airing of a new commercial, Burke's telephone staff conducts interviews with a sample of consumers. The sample includes individuals who watched the program in which the test commercial was placed and who were physically present at the time the commercial was aired. These individuals receive a product or brand cue,

Figure 11.6   Bruzzone-Tested Commercial for MasterCard

Five Picture Photoboard for MasterCard

Please look over these pictures and words from a TV commercial and answer the questions on the right.

(Mr. Magoo) Elevator to lobby. Hmm..by George!

(Announcer) Contacts, $320

Treadmill, $800

Wonderbra, $26

Face lift, $3000

Being happy with who you are, priceless.

There are some things money can't buy. For everything else, there is [Name]*.

Happily accepted... (explosion) ...most everywhere.

Do you remember seeing this commercial on TV?

05 - 1 ☐ Yes   -2 ☐ No   -3 ☐ Not sure-I may have

(If no, skip to the last question on this page.)

How interested are you in what this TV commercial is trying to tell you or show you about the product?

06 - 1 ☐ Very interested   -2 ☐ Somewhat interested   -3 ☐ Not interested

How does it make you feel about the product?

07 - 1 ☐ Good   -2 ☐ OK   -3 ☐ Bad   -4 ☐ Not sure

Please check any of the following if you feel they describe this commercial.

08 - 1 ☐ Amusing	09 - 1 ☐ Familiar	10 - 1 ☐ Pointless
-2 ☐ Appealing	-2 ☐ Fast moving	-2 ☐ Seen a lot
-3 ☐ Believable	-3 ☐ Gentle	-3 ☐ Sensitive
-4 ☐ Clever	-4 ☐ Imaginative	-4 ☐ Silly
-5 ☐ Confusing	-5 ☐ Informative	-5 ☐ True to life
-6 ☐ Convincing	-6 ☐ Irritating	-6 ☐ Warm
-7 ☐ Dull	-7 ☐ Lively	-7 ☐ Well done
-8 ☐ Easy to forget	-8 ☐ Original	-8 ☐ Worn out
-9 ☐ Effective	-9 ☐ Phony	-9 ☐ Worth remembering

Thinking about the commercial as a whole would you say you:

11 - 1 ☐ Liked it a lot   -4 ☐ Disliked it somewhat
-2 ☐ Liked it somewhat   -5 ☐ Disliked it a lot
-3 ☐ Felt neutral

* We have blocked out the name.
Do you remember which credit card was being advertised?

12 - 1 ☐ American Express   -3 ☐ Visa USA
-2 ☐ MasterCard   -4 ☐ Don't Know

Do you use a credit card?

13 - 1 ☐ Regularly   -2 ☐ Occasionally   -3 ☐ Seldom or never

3-05

© Courtesy of Bruzzone Research Company

are asked whether they saw the test commercial in question, and then are asked to recall all they can about it.

For each tested commercial, Burke reports findings as (1) *claimed-recall scores*, which indicate the percentage of respondents who recall seeing the ad; and (2) *related-recall scores*, which indicate the percentage of respondents who accurately describe specific advertising elements.

Advertisers and agencies use this information, along with verbatim statements from respondents, to assess the effectiveness of test commercials and to identify a commercial's strengths and weaknesses. On the basis of this information, a decision is made to advertise the commercial nationally, to revise it first, or possibly even to drop it.

The Recall Controversy. Considerable controversy has surrounded the use of DAR testing.[16] For example, Coca-Cola executives reject recall as a valid measure of advertising effectiveness because, in their opinion, recall simply measures whether an ad is received but not whether the message is accepted.[17] It also is known that measures of recall are biased in favor of younger consumers. This is to say that recall scores deteriorate with age progression.[18] Third, there is mounting evidence that the recall scores generated by advertisements are not predictive of sales performance; that is, regardless of which measure of recall is used, the evidence suggests that sales levels do not increase with increasing levels of recallability.[19] Finally, it has been established that day-after recall testing is biased against certain types of advertising content, as next explained.

Foote, Cone & Belding (FCB), a major advertising agency, claims that DAR tests significantly *understate the memorability* of commercials that employ *emotional or feeling-oriented themes* and are biased in favor of rational or thought-oriented

Excerpts from Five Commercials Tested Online by Bruzzone　　　Figure 11.7

Excerpts from Budweiser Commercial:

(Frog #1) You know something, Lou. I know why we got fired. Too much of your yappin and not enough of this...
(Lou the Lizard) What's that?
(Frog #1) Tongue lashing lizard.
(Lou, the Lizard) Hey, that was uncalled for.

(Frog #2) And, electrocuting us last year was OK?
(Lou, the Lizard) That was a joke.
(Frog #1) You like jokes, huh. Here's one for you. Two frogs walk into a bar and do this.

Excerpts from Apple Commercial:

(Computer) Hello Dave, you're looking well today. Dave, do you remember the year 2,000 when computers began to misbehave?

When the new millennium arrived we had no choice but to cause a global, economic disruption. It was a bug Dave.

You like your Apple better than me, don't you Dave? Dave... Can you hear me Dave?

Excerpts from Blockbuster Video Commercial:

Blockbuster Video is giving away trips to glamarous events like film festivals, award shows, MGM movie premieres.

Excerpts from Blockbuster Video Comm'l (cont.):

So, play the trip a day give away every day. And get caught up in the bright lights of stardom.

Excerpts from Hotjobs Commercial:

(Announcer) Where can you find your dream job? Hotjobs.com. Thousands of hot jobs at top companies. Like YAHOO, ebaY and ORACLE. So you'll find your perfect job.

(Security guard) Bingo... Oh yeah.

Hotjobs.com

Excerpts from Siebel Commercial:

(Announcer) What does success mean to a sales professional? Everything!

(Announcer) Companies worldwide are providing their sales professionals with unprecedented power to succeed with enterprise relationship software from Siebel Systems.

Siebel Systems: Sales, marketing, service.

commercials.[20] To test the assertion that DAR testing is biased against emotionally oriented commercials, FCB conducted a study that compared three thinking and three feeling commercials. The six commercials were tested with two methods: the standard DAR measurement described previously and a *masked-recognition test*. The latter test involves showing a commercial to respondents on one day, telephoning them the next, requesting that they turn on their television sets to a given station where the commercial is shown once again (but this time *masked*, i.e., without any brand identification), and then asking them to identify the brand. FCB defines correct brand-name identification by this masked-recognition procedure as *proven recognition*, or *true remembering*.[21]

The results from FCB's research, shown in Table 11.3 on page 339, demonstrate clearly the bias in day-after recall procedures against emotional, feeling commercials. It can be seen that the thinking commercials (coded A, D, and E in Table 11.3) perform only slightly better under masked-recognition measurement than under the standard DAR test. For example, commercial A obtained a DAR score of 49 percent and a masked-recognition score of 56 percent, thereby yielding a ratio of 114 (i.e., 56/49). In fact, as shown in Table 11.3, the average ratio for the three thinking commercials is 119. This indicates that an average of only 19 percent more people recognized the advertised brand when prompted again by seeing the product advertised with the brand masked compared with recalling the brand entirely from memory.

Comparatively, Table 11.3 shows that the feeling commercials (B, C, and F) performed considerably better under masked-recognition than under day-after recall procedures. Overall, the masked-recognition method reveals that proven recognition for the three feeling commercials is 68 percent higher than the day-after recall scores (i.e., their average ratio of masked recognition to recall is 168).

These results clearly suggest that day-after recall tests may be biased against emotional, or feeling, commercials. A different research method, such as masked recognition, is needed when testing whether this type of commercial accomplishes suitable levels of awareness.[22]

Figure 11.8

**Comparative Results for Bruzzone-Tested Commercials
via Mail and Online Surveys**

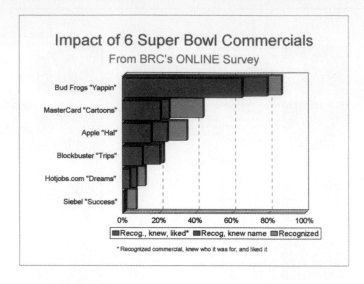

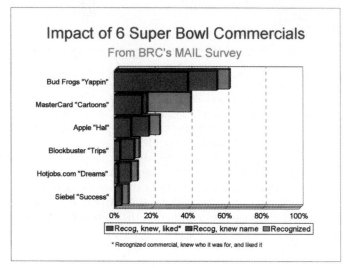

MEASURES OF PHYSIOLOGICAL AROUSAL

Researchers have increasingly recognized that advertisements that positively influence receivers' feelings and emotions can be extremely successful for certain products and situations. Research has shown that ads that are better liked—often because they elicit positive emotions—are more likely to be remembered and to persuade.[23] (Recall P&G's shift to more emotional advertising as described in the *Opening Vignette*.) Along with the trend toward more advertising directed at emotions, there has been a corresponding increase in efforts to measure consumers' affective and emotional reactions to advertisements.[24] Advertising researchers have used various physiological testing devices to measure these reactions. These include such techniques as the galvanometer (which measures minute levels of perspiration in response to emotional arousal) and pupillometric tests (which measure pupil dilation).

Psychologists have concluded that these physiological functions are indeed sensitive to psychological processes of concern in advertising.[25] Physiological

Day-After Recall Versus Masked-Recognition Research Findings			Table 11.3

	Day-After Recall	Masked Recognition	Ratio of Masked Recognition to Recall
Thinking Commercials			
A	49%	56%	114
D	24	32	133
E	21	24	114
Average	31	37	119
Feeling Commercials			
B	21%	37%	176
C	25	36	144
F	10	23	230
Average	19	32	168

functions such as galvanic skin response and pupil dilation can be measured unobtrusively and without conscious consumer reaction, because these functions are controlled by the *autonomic nervous system*. The autonomic nervous system consists of the nerves and ganglia that furnish blood vessels, the heart, smooth muscles, and glands. Because individuals have little voluntary control over the autonomic nervous system, advertising researchers use changes in physiological functions to indicate the actual, unbiased amount of arousal resulting from advertisements.

To appreciate the potential value of such physiological measurement, consider the case of an advertisement that promotes the advertised brand by associating it with an attractive model, such as illustrated in a Kellogg's ad featuring a well-muscled man, bursting out of the water with a refreshed smile. In pretesting this ad, some women, when asked what they think of it, may indicate that they dislike the ad because they consider the "buffed" model an unnecessary adjunct to a cereal ad. Others may respond that they really find it appealing. Still others may even feign aggravation to make (what they perceive to be) a favorable impression on the interviewer. That is, the latter group may actually enjoy the ad but say otherwise in response to an interviewer's query, thereby disguising their true evaluation. Here is where measures of physiological arousal have a potential role to play in advertising research—namely, to prevent self-monitoring of feelings and biased responses.

The Galvanometer

The **galvanometer** (also referred to as the psychogalvanometer) is a device for measuring *galvanic skin response*, or *GSR*. (*Galvanic* refers to electricity produced by a chemical reaction.) When the consumer's autonomic nervous system is activated by some element in an advertisement, a physical response occurs in the sweat glands located in the palms and fingers. These glands open in varying degrees depending on the intensity of the arousal, and skin resistance drops when the sweat glands open. By sending a very fine electric current through one finger and out the other and completing the circuit through an instrument called a *galvanometer*, testers are able to measure both the degree and frequency with which an advertisement activates emotional responses. Simply, the galvanometer indirectly assesses the degree of emotional response to an advertisement by measuring minute amounts of perspiration.

There is evidence to indicate that galvanic skin response is a valid indicator of the amount of warmth generated by an advertisement.[26] Many companies have found the galvanometer to be a useful tool for assessing the potential effectiveness of advertisements, direct-mail messages, package copy, and other MarCom messages. Advertising research practitioners who use the galvanometer claim that it is a *valid* predictor (see PACT principle 9) of an advertisement's ability to *motivate* consumer purchase behavior.[27] Indeed, in recognition of the galvanometer's ability to reveal an advertisement's motivational properties, practitioners refer to GSR research as the Motivational Response Method, or MRM.[28]

Pupillometer

Pupillometric tests in advertising are conducted by measuring respondents' pupil dilation as they view a television commercial or focus on a printed advertisement. Respondents' heads are in a fixed position to permit continuous electronic measurement of changes in pupillary responses. Responses to specific elements in an advertisement are used to indicate positive reaction (in the case of greater dilation) or negative reaction (smaller relative dilation). Although not unchallenged, there has been scientific evidence since the late 1960s to suggest that pupillary responses are correlated with people's arousal to stimuli and perhaps even with their likes and dislikes.[29]

MEASURES OF PERSUASION

Measures of persuasion are used when an advertiser's objective is to influence consumers' attitudes toward and preference for the advertised brand. Firms that perform this type of research include, among others, Ipsos-ASI and rsc. The following sections describe, first, the Ipsos-ASI Next*TV method, and then rsc's ARS Persuasion method is explained in detail. More discussion is devoted to the latter advertising research procedure because rsc has done a particularly outstanding job in documenting its commercial service. (Parenthetically, it may have occurred to you that companies in the advertising research business have strange names. Actually, these names are no stranger than are the names of well-known companies such as IBM or AT&T. The research companies' names just seem strange because you probably were unfamiliar them prior to reading this chapter.)

The Ipsos-ASI Next*TV Method

Ipsos is a French company that purchased ASI Market Research, an American company, in 1998. This international firm (which goes by Ipsos-ASI, the Advertising Research Company) performs various forms of advertising research in more than 50 countries. One of its most important advertising research services is the Next*TV method. This method tests television commercials in consumers' homes.[30] Here is how the procedure works:

1. The company recruits consumers by informing them that their purpose, if they agree to participate, is to evaluate a television program. This is actually a disguise because the real purpose of the research is to evaluate consumer responses to advertisements that are embedded in a TV program.
2. The company mails to a national sample of consumers a videotape that contains a 30-minute TV program (such as a situation comedy or soap opera) and in which are embedded television commercials. This procedure essentially replicates the actual prime time viewing context.
3. Consumers are instructed to view the program (and, implicitly, the embedded advertising) from the videotape. The viewing context is thus actual, in-home viewing, the same as when consumers view any television advertising under natural viewing conditions.
4. One day after viewing the videotaped TV program (and advertisements), Ipsos-ASI personnel contact sampled consumers and measure their reactions to the TV program (in concert with the original disguise) and to the advertisements, which, of course, is the primary objective.

5. Ipsos-ASI then measures message recall and persuasion. Persuasion is measured by assessing consumers' attitudes toward advertised brands, their shift in brand preferences, and their brand-related purchase intent and frequency.

Ipsos-ASI Next*TV employs the same basic methodology around the world. The in-home videotape methodology provides a number of advantages. First, the in-home exposure makes it possible to measure advertising effectiveness in a natural environment. Second, by embedding test advertisements in actual programming content along with other advertisements, it is possible to assess the ability of TV commercials to break through the clutter, gain the viewer's attention, and influence message recallability and persuadability. Third, by measuring recall one day after exposure, Ipsos-ASI can determine how well tested commercials are remembered after this delay period. Fourth, the videotape technology allows the use of representative national sampling. Finally, by providing several alternative measures of persuasion, the Next*TV method allows brand managers and their ad agencies to select the measures that best meet their specific needs.

The ARS Persuasion Method

Rsc, the Quality Measurement System, is one of the most active message-testing research suppliers. This company tests individual selling propositions as well as entire television commercials. Commercials are tested at varying stages of completion ranging from rough cut (e.g., animatics or photomatics) to finished form. rsc's testing procedure is called the ARS Persuasion® method, where ARS stands for Advertising Research System. The ARS testing procedure is as follows:

> *Commercials are exposed in regular ARS test sessions to [800 to 1,000] men and women (aged 16+) drawn randomly from [eight] metropolitan areas and invited to preview typical television material. Each test commercial and other unrelated commercials are inserted into the television programs. While at the central location, a measurement of ARS Persuasion is made by obtaining brand preferences before and after exposure to the programs. The ARS Persuasion measure is the percent of respondents choosing the test product over competition after exposure to the TV material minus the percent choosing the test product before exposure.*[31]

In other words, the ARS Persuasion method first has respondents indicate what brands they would prefer to receive among various product categories if their names were selected in a drawing to win a "basket" of free items (the *premeasure*). Among the list of products and brands is a "target brand" for which, unbeknownst to respondents, they subsequently will be exposed to a commercial that is being tested. After exposure to a television program, within which is embedded the test commercial, respondents again indicate what brands they would prefer to receive if their names were selected in a drawing (the *postmeasure*). The ARS Persuasion score simply represents the postmeasure percentage of respondents preferring the target brand minus the premeasure percentage who prefer that brand (see the following equation). A positive score indicates that the test commercial has shifted preference *toward* the target brand.

ARS Persuasion Score =
Post % for target brand – Pre % for target brand   **Equation. 11.1**

The average ARS Persuasion score in testing commercials in the United States is 5.8, which means that on average 5.8 percent more people exposed to test commercials prefer the brand after exposure to its advertising than before exposure.[32] This average score provides a benchmark against which ARS-tested commercials can be evaluated—the higher the score, the greater a commercial's potential persuasive power. rsc has tested over 30,000 commercials in its 25-year history, and from these tests it has been able to establish—albeit not without challenge[33]—that its ARS Persuasion scores predict actual sales performance when commercials are aired. That is, higher-scoring commercials generate greater sales volume and larger market share gains.

Predictive Validity of ARS Persuasion Scores.   Based on the results of 155 tested commercials from Belgium, Canada, Germany, Mexico, the United Kingdom, and the United States, principals at rsc have demonstrated how ARS Persuasion scores relate to market-share changes.[34] A total of 84 brands (some with multiple commercials tested) representing 54 product categories were involved in the analysis. All 155 commercials were tested under the procedures described above, and then market-share levels under actual in-market circumstances were compared during a period after advertising commenced for the brands versus a period prior to any advertising. Hence, the key issue is whether ARS Persuasion scores accurately predict the magnitude of market-share gain following advertising. In other words, are the scores that rsc generates from its laboratory testing predictive of actual marketplace performance? This obviously is a validity issue as described previously under PACT principle 9. Results from these 155 tests are presented in Table 11.4.

To understand what these results reveal, let us carefully examine the first row in Table 11.4. This row includes all commercials that received very low (less than 2.0) ARS Persuasion scores. rsc defines scores of 2.0 or lower as inelastic, implying that commercials scoring this poorly are probably incapable of driving market-share gains. Looking at the four columns of positive share-point differences reveals that for those commercials yielding inelastic ARS Persuasion scores, only 18 percent were able to maintain market share or yield some small incremental growth. Comparatively, 82 percent (i.e., 100 minus 18) of these low-scoring (inelastic) commercials actually suffered market share losses! None of the inelastic commercials generated gains exceeding a full share point.

At the other extreme, 100 percent of the highly elastic commercials (with Persuasion scores at least 12) yielded positive share gains. Indeed, all 100 percent of these high-performance commercials produced gains of 0.5 share points or better, with 92 percent yielding gains of at least 1 share point and 80 percent providing gains of at least 2 share points. Cell entries for the low elastic, moderately elastic, and elastic categories can be interpreted in a similar fashion.

It is apparent from these 155 test cases that ARS Persuasion scores are valid predictors of in-market performance. In sum, the higher the score (or, stated alternatively, the more elastic the score), the greater the likelihood that a tested commercial will produce positive sales gains when the focal brand is advertised under real-world, in-market conditions. This global study thus informs advertisers that they should not place advertising weight behind commercials that have tested poorly. Table 11.4 reveals, in fact, that commercials with a 2.0 or lower ARS Persuasion score most likely will not produce a positive share gain, and that a large percentage (i.e., 40 percent) of those scoring in the low elastic range (2.0 to 3.9) also suffer share losses. It is only when commercials test in the moderately elastic (4.0 to 6.9) or higher ranges that meaningful share gains can be anticipated.

This company, of course, has a vested interest in reporting that its testing system provides accurate predictions of marketplace performance; nonetheless,

Table 11.4

**rsc's Global Validation Study:
ARS Persuasion Scores and In-Market Results**

ARS Persuasion Score Range	Positive Share-Point Difference of at Least:			
	0.0+	0.5+	1.0+	2.0+
<2.0 ("Inelastic")	18%	9%	0%	0%
2.0–3.9 ("Low elastic")	60%	26%	11%	0%
4.0–6.9 ("Moderately elastic")	80%	55%	43%	20%
7.0–11.9 ("Elastic")	100%	97%	69%	43%
12.0+ ("Highly elastic")	100%	100%	92%	80%

the fact that articles authored by rsc principals have been published in peer-reviewed journals (e.g., the *Journal of Advertising Research*) authenticates their conclusions. Moreover, advertising scholars have provided independent endorsement of rsc's ARS Persuasion technique.[35]

Beyond providing evidence that the ARS Persuasion measure is a good predictor of a brand's sales performance, the extensive testing performed by rsc has played a significant role in enhancing our understanding of the strengths and limitations of television advertising. Indeed, three major conclusions can be drawn regarding what it takes for television advertising to successfully enhance a brand's equity and sales performance: (1) Ad copy must be distinctive, (2) ad weight without persuasiveness is insufficient, and (3) the selling power of advertising wears out over time.[36]

Conclusion 1: Ad Copy Must Be Distinctive ("All Ads Are Not Created Equal").

What is distinctive ad copy? Research by rsc has shown that commercials having *strong selling propositions* are distinctive and thereby tend to achieve higher ARS Persuasion scores. What determines whether a commercial has a strong selling proposition? Research indicates that any differentiating information concerning a new brand or new feature of an existing brand gives a selling proposition a significantly higher chance of a superior score.[37] Although commercials for new brands and those with new features are more persuasive on average, advertising for established brands also can be very persuasive via *brand differentiation* — that is, by distinguishing the advertised brand from competitive offerings and providing consumers with a distinctive reason to buy it.[38] The photoboard version of a Mentadent ProCare toothbrush television commercial (Figure 11.9) illustrates an advertisement that obtained a high ARS Persuasion score of 11.2 (thus falling in the elastic range) because the ad contained a strong selling proposition — namely, that this toothbrush has a flexible handle that allows gentle brushing.

The foregoing discussion has illustrated a key advertising principle: Effective advertising must be persuasive and distinctive; that is, it must possess a strong selling proposition. Appreciation of this point necessitates rigorous testing of proposed advertisements prior to committing any media dollars to their airing or printing. Reminiscent of the classic parental admonition to young children ("Look before you cross the street"), a similar exhortation can be made to advertisers when formulating advertising messages: "Test before you air or print!" To put it bluntly, it is foolhardy to invest money in a media campaign without first having ensured that the advertising message is fully capable of "moving the dial" — that is, shifting brand preference toward the advertised brand.

Conclusion 2: Weight Is Not Enough ("Who Needs an Overweight, Untalented Sumo Wrestler?").

Before presenting this second major conclusion about advertising effectiveness, we first need to introduce the concept of advertising weight. This concept will be covered more in the next several chapters, but for now, ad *weight* should be understood as meaning a combination of two factors: (1) the percentage of the target audience that has an opportunity to see a brand's advertising during a particular period (an issue of reach), and (2) the number of times the audience has an opportunity to see the ad (an issue of frequency). These two factors combine to form *gross rating points,* or *GRPs*. More GRPs equate to more advertising weight. Obviously, advertising weight and spending also correlate.

Given this background, we now consider a second important conclusion about advertising effectiveness — namely, that the amount of advertising weight invested in a brand does *not* by itself provide a good predictor of sales performance. In other words, merely increasing advertising weight (qua GRPs, qua spending) does not directly translate into better performance for a brand. Advertising copy *must also be distinctive and persuasive* (as previously established) for advertising to have a positive impact on a brand's sales and market share. An advertising practitioner perhaps said it best when stating that "Airing ineffective

Figure 11.9

Illustration of a Commercial with a Strong Selling Proposition

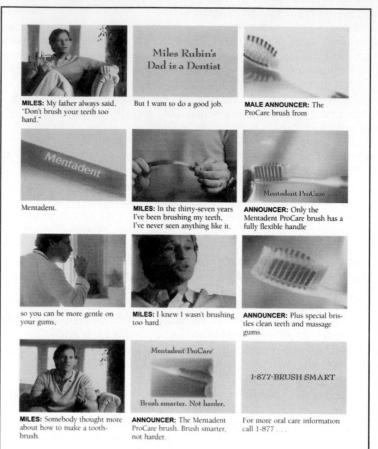

MILES: My father always said, "Don't brush your teeth too hard."

Miles Rubin's Dad is a Dentist

But I want to do a good job.

MALE ANNOUNCER: The ProCare brush from

Mentadent.

MILES: In the thirty-seven years I've been brushing my teeth, I've never seen anything like it.

Mentadent ProCare

ANNOUNCER: Only the Mentadent ProCare brush has a fully flexible handle

so you can be more gentle on your gums,

MILES: I knew I wasn't brushing too hard.

ANNOUNCER: Plus special bristles clean teeth and massage gums.

MILES: Somebody thought more about how to make a toothbrush.

Mentadent ProCare

Brush smarter. Not harder.

ANNOUNCER: The Mentadent ProCare brush. Brush smarter, not harder.

1-877-BRUSH SMART

For more oral care information call 1-877 . . .

© Courtesy of Unilever & Personal Care, USA

advertising is like being off-air; it just costs more."[39] It cannot be overemphasized that unpersuasive, nondistinctive advertising is not worth airing or printing.

This conclusion receives support from a landmark study that analyzed numerous tests based on BehaviorScan single-source data (a methodology that will be thoroughly described in the next section). A well-known advertising scholar and his colleagues determined from their research that when advertisements are unpersuasive, there is no more likelihood of achieving sales volume increases even with doubling and tripling TV advertising weight.[40]

The virtual independence between advertising weight and sales is clearly demonstrated in Table 11.5. The results presented in this table are based on studies using single-source data *and split-cable tests* for various brands of consumer packaged goods. As will be discussed more fully in a later section about BehaviorScan single-source data, split-cable testing involves either weight tests or copy tests. The data in Table 11.5 involve only weight tests whereby two panels of households have an opportunity to see the identical commercial for a particular brand, but the amount of spending, or weight, is varied between the two panels. These households' subsequent purchases of the advertised brand are later compared based on purchase data acquired via optical scanning devices in grocery stores. Split-cable tests generally run for a full year. (The following section on single-source data describes this methodology in detail.)

Table 11.5 presents data from 20 split-cable tests, each involving an actual marketplace examination of advertising's influence on the sales of a branded grocery product. In each test, there are two key features of the advertising effort.

Relations Among Advertising Weight, Persuasion Scores, and Sales   **Table 11.5**

Test Number	Weight Difference	ARS Persuasion Score	Sales Difference
1	334 GRPs	−1.3	NSD*
2	4,200	0.6	NSD
3	406	1.8	NSD
4	1,400	2.6	NSD
5	695	2.7	NSD
6	800	2.8	NSD
7	2,231	3.5	NSD
8	1,000	3.6	NSD
9	900	3.7	NSD
10	1,800	4.0	NSD
11	947	4.2	NSD
12	820	4.3	NSD
13	1,364	4.4	NSD
14	1,198	4.4	NSD
15	583	5.9	SD†
16	1,949	6.7	SD
17	580	7.0	SD
18	778	7.7	SD
19	1,400	9.0	SD
20	860	9.3	SD

*NSD: Purchases of the advertised brand were *not* significantly different between the two split-cable panels at a 90 percent confidence level.

†SD: Purchases of the advertised brand *were* significantly different between the two split-cable panels at a 90 percent confidence level.

Source: Margaret Henderson Blair, "An Empirical Investigation of Advertising, Wearin and Wearout," *Journal of Advertising Research* 27 (December 1987/January 1988), 45–50.

First is the number of GRPs, or weight, used to advertise the brand; in Table 11.5 this is expressed as the *weight difference* between the two panels of households. A difference of zero would mean that an identical amount of advertising (in terms of GRPs) was aired during the test period to both groups of households. The second key advertising feature is the ARS Persuasion score that the test commercial obtained. Recall that the average ARS Persuasion score is 5.8. Scores in Table 11.5 lower than 5.8 indicate a below-average commercial in terms of persuasiveness, whereas scores above 5.8 indicate above-average performers. Finally, for each test reported, the last column of the table indicates whether a statistically significant sales difference occurred between the two panels.

Thus, test 8, for example, shows a weight difference of 1,000 GRPs between the two panels. However, the tested commercial in this case received a below-average ARS Persuasion score of 3.6. Given this combination of a heavy weight difference between the two panels but a relatively unpersuasive commercial, the result was no significant difference (NSD) in sales between the two panels of households. In other words, heavy advertising weight was unable to compensate for an unpersuasive commercial.

Now let us examine test 15, in which the weight difference between the two panels of households amounts to 583 GRPs. However, the new commercial in this test received an above-average ARS Persuasion score of 5.9. The result: A significant difference (SD) in sales was recorded when the tested brand was advertised with a persuasive commercial.

Table 11.5 also demonstrates that no significant sales differences are obtained even in instances of huge weight differences such as in tests 2 (a 4,200 GRP difference) and 7 (a 2,231 GRP difference). These two tests correspond (at the time of the research) with annual ad expenditures of $21 million and $11 million, yet no differential sales response materialized after a full year. Comparatively, notice in tests 15 through 20 that significant sales differences are observed even when the weight differences are relatively small compared with the weight differences in tests 2 and 7. Also, the ARS Persuasion score is above average in every instance for tests 15 through 20. Hence, it can be concluded that the primary determinant of sales differences in these split-cable tests was the *persuasiveness* of the tested commercials. Whenever the ARS Persuasion score was above the average ARS score (i.e., greater than 5.8), significant sales differences were detected; in all instances in which the ARS Persuasion score was below average, no significant sales differences were obtained.

Provided these results generalize beyond the tested commercials, the implication is that a commercial's persuasiveness is absolutely critical: Persuasiveness, and not mere advertising weight, is the prime determinant of whether an advertising campaign will translate into improved sales performance. Indeed, investing advertising in nonpersuasive commercials is akin to throwing money away. Advertising weight is important, but only if a commercial presents a persuasive story.[41]

Research conducted by rsc for the Campbell's Soup Company provides additional evidence regarding the importance of commercial persuasiveness.[42] Figure 11.10 presents the results of rsc's testing of various commercials for an undisclosed Campbell's Soup Company brand, which we will assume to be V8 vegetable juice. Note that the horizontal axis is broken into 18 four-week periods, whereas the vertical axis of the graph depicts market shares for this brand. It can be seen that V8's market share during the first four-week period was 19.6. Notice next that a new commercial (titled "Tastes Great 30," with the 30 signifying a 30-second commercial) was aired during the second four-week period. This commercial, when tested by rsc, received an ARS Persuasion score of 5.8. Shortly after airing this new commercial, V8's market shared jumped from 19.6 to 21.4—an increase of nearly 2 share points. Thereafter, V8's market share varied from a low of 20.4 (period 5) to a high of 21.5 (period 4). Then in period 7, when a new commercial started airing ("Beauty Shot Revised 15"), V8's market share jumped by an incredible 4.5 share points. Notice how this result correlates to the strength of the new commercial, which obtained an ARS Persuasion score of 10. Over the next several months, the market share for V8 fell to 22 (period 14). At this point (period 15) another new commercial began airing ("Beauty Shot Poolout 2 15"). This commercial, which obtained an ARS Persuasion score of 10.9, immediately increased V8's sales to a 25.9 market share. By period 18 the share had declined to a 23.9, but compared with the initial share of 19.6 in period 1, this still represented a gain of 4.3 share points in slightly more than a year—a substantial market-share gain in an established product category by any standard. These results indicate that persuasive commercials can have a rather dramatic effect in increasing market share.

Conclusion 3: Advertising Eventually Wears Out ("All Good Things Must End").   Another important lesson from the Campbell's V8 case presentation, as well as support from abundant other evidence, is that advertising ultimately *wears out* and hence must be periodically refreshed to maintain or increase a brand's sales.[43] Research in the academic community as well as by practitioners has convincingly demonstrated that with the accumulation of GRPs for a brand, the persuasive power of that brand's advertising declines over time.[44] This is referred to as **wearout**, the result of which is diminished effectiveness of advertising as GRPs accumulate over time. The implication is that it is important to periodically retest commercials (using, for example, ARS Persuasion measurement) to determine how much persuasive power remains in a commercial. When the persuasive power falls into the low elastic or inelastic range (see Table 11.4), it probably is time to replace the commercial with a new or revised execution.

The Role of Persuasiveness for an Undisclosed Brand from the Campbell's Soup Company

Figure 11.10

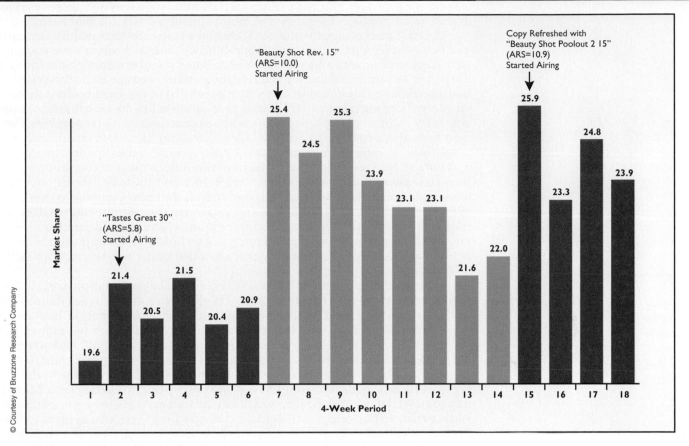

MEASURES OF SALES RESPONSE (SINGLE-SOURCE SYSTEMS)

Determining the sales impact of advertising is, as explained in Chapter 8, a most difficult task. However, substantial efforts have been made in recent years toward developing research procedures that are able to assess the sales-generating ability of advertising.

So-called **single-source systems (SSSs)** have evolved to measure the effects of advertising on sales. SSSs became possible with the advent of three technological developments: (1) *electronic television meters*, (2) *optical laser scanning* of universal product codes (UPC symbols) at retail checkouts, and (3) *split-cable* technology. Single-source systems gather purchase data from panels of households using optical scanning equipment and merge it with household demographic characteristics and, most important, with information about causal marketing variables that influence household purchases. The following sections describe two single-source systems: IRI's BehaviorScan (which was alluded to when discussing Table 11.5) and Nielsen's SCANTRACK.

IRI's BehaviorScan

Information Resources Inc. (IRI) pioneered single-source data collection when it introduced its BehaviorScan service nearly a generation ago. IRI operates BehaviorScan panel households in four markets around the United States: Pittsfield, Massachusetts; Eau Claire, Wisconsin; Cedar Rapids, Iowa; and Midland, Texas. These small cities were chosen because they are located far enough from television stations that residents must depend on *cable TV* to receive good reception. Moreover, grocery and drug stores in these cities are equipped with optical scanning devices that read UPC symbols from packages and thereby record exactly what product categories and brands panel households purchase.

In each market, approximately 3,000 households are recruited to participate in a BehaviorScan panel, and about one-third of these households are equipped with electronic meters attached to TV sets. Panel members are eligible for prize drawings as remuneration for their participation. Because each BehaviorScan household has an *identification card* that is presented at the grocery store checkout on every shopping occasion, IRI knows precisely what items each household purchases by merely linking up optically scanned purchases with ID numbers. Panel members also provide IRI with detailed demographic information, including family size, income level, number of televisions owned, the types of newspapers and magazines read, and who in the household does most of the shopping. IRI then combines all these data into a *single source* and thereby determines which households purchase what products and brands and how responsive they are to advertising and other purchase-causing variables. Thus, **single-source data** consists of (1) household demographic information, (2) household purchase behavior, and (3) household exposure to (or, more technically, the opportunity to see, or OTS) new television commercials that are tested under real-world, or *in-market*, test conditions.

The availability of cable TV enables IRI (with the cooperation of cable companies and advertisers) to intercept a cable signal before it reaches households, *split the signal*, and send different advertisements to two panels of households (test versus control). Hence, the split-cable feature and optically scanned purchase data enable IRI to know which commercial each household had an opportunity to see and how much of the advertised brand the household purchases.

IRI's BehaviorScan allows for the testing of television commercials. Two types of tests are offered: weight tests and copy tests. In both types of tests, a test commercial is aired in, say, two BehaviorScan markets for up to a full year. With *weight tests*, panel households are divided into test and control groups. The identical commercial is transmitted to both groups, but the number of GRPs, or weight, is varied between the groups during the course of the test period. Any difference between the groups' aggregate purchase behavior for the tested brand is obviously attributable to the advertising weight differential between the two groups—such as described above in the context of rsc's weight test results (Table 11.5).

The second form of testing, *copy tests*, holds the amount of weight constant but varies commercial content. That is, a test group is exposed during the course of the testing period to a new commercial, whereas a control group has an opportunity to see public service announcements (PSAs) inserted in place of the new commercial. Regardless of the type of test, aggregating purchase data across all households in each of the two groups simplifies determining whether differences in advertising copy or weight generate differences in purchase behavior.

To better understand how BehaviorScan's single-source data can be used to show the relationship between advertising and sales activity, consider a situation in which a manufacturer of a new snack food is interested in testing the effectiveness of a television commercial promoting this product. BehaviorScan would do the following: (1) select, say, two markets in which to conduct the test; (2) stock the manufacturer's brand in all grocery stores and perhaps drug stores located in these markets; (3) selectively broadcast a new commercial for the brand using special split-cable television so approximately one-half of the panel members in each market are exposed either to the new commercial or to PSAs; (4) record electronically (via optical scanners) grocery purchases made by all panel members; and (5) compare the purchase behavior of the two groups of panel members who were potentially exposed to the new commercial versus PSAs.

If the advertising is effective, a greater proportion of the panel members exposed to the test commercial should buy the promoted item than those only exposed to the PSAs. The percentage of panel members who undertake a trial purchase behavior would thereby indicate the effectiveness of the new television commercial, and the percentage that make a repeat purchase would indicate how much the brand is liked. The use of BehaviorScan testing of Frito-Lay brands is described next.

Frito-Lay's BehaviorScan Copy Tests.

To test the effectiveness of television advertising for its various brands of salted snack and cookie brands, marketing researchers and brand managers at Frito-Lay commissioned IRI to perform 23 split-panel experiments in BehaviorScan markets over a recent four-year period.[45] All 23 experiments were copy (versus weight) tests that involved comparing one group of households who were exposed to advertising for a Frito-Lay brand (advertising households) against another group who had no opportunity to see the advertising (control households). Each of the 23 tests was conducted in at least two BehaviorScan markets and lasted a full year. In addition to the advertising versus no-advertising condition, Frito-Lay's BehaviorScan tests also were classified in terms of (1) whether the tested brand was a new brand (e.g., SunChips) or an established brand (e.g., Ruffles); and (2) whether sales for the brand were relatively large (e.g., Doritos) or small (e.g., Rold Gold).

The objective in conducting these tests was to determine whether sales volume would be greater in households exposed to advertisements for Frito-Lay brands versus those households that had no opportunity to be exposed to commercials for these brands. Results from the 23 Frito-Lay BehaviorScan tests are summarized in Table 11.6.

The first notable observation from Table 11.6 is that advertising for 57 percent of the 23 tested brands generated significant increases in sales volume during the one-year test duration. (Though not shown in Table 11.6, the average gain in sales volume between the advertising versus no-advertising household panels was 15 percent across the 12 advertisements that yielded significant sales increases.) A second key finding shown in Table 11.6 is that advertising for the small sales-volume brands was much more effective in driving sales gains than was advertising for the large brands. In fact, of the 12 small brands tested, 83 percent, or 10 brands, experienced significant increases in sales as a result of their one-year advertising efforts. A third important finding is that advertising for 88 percent of the new brands generated significant sales gains, whereas only 40 percent of the established brands resulted in sales gains from advertising. A fourth notable finding, though not apparent in Table 11.6, is that in all 12 (of 23) cases where advertisements for Frito-Lay brands drove significant sales increases, the effects occurred within the first six months and in 11 of the 12 tests within the first three months. In other words, when advertising works, it works relatively quickly or not at all.

The 23 BehaviorScan tests of Frito-Lay brands reveal that advertising is not always effective; indeed, it was effective in slightly more than one-half of the tests. Moreover, as demonstrated earlier when discussing rsc's ARS Persuasion method, this research supports the finding that advertising generally is effective only when it provides distinctive, newsworthy information, such as when introducing new brands or line extensions. Finally advertising works relatively quickly if at all.

BehaviorScan Tests of Advertising Effectiveness for 23 Frito-Lay Brands			**Table 11.6**
	Established Brands	**New Brands**	**Total**
Large Brands	13% (n=8)*	67% (n=3)	27% (n=11)
Small Brands	71% (n=7)	100% (n=5)	83% (n=12)
Total	40% (n=15)	88% (n=8)	57% (n=23)

* Table entries are to be interpreted as follows: A total of eight (out of 23) tests involved large, established brands. Of the eight tests conducted with this particular combination of brands, only one test, or 13 percent, detected a statistically significant increase in sales volume in those households exposed to advertising compared to the no-advertising control households.

Nielsen's SCANTRACK

The A. C. Nielsen company entered into a joint venture with another research firm, the NPD Group, to form the SCANTRACK single-source system. SCAN-TRACK differs from BehaviorScan in a couple of interesting respects. First, and most important, whereas BehaviorScan collects purchase data via optical scanners located only in supermarkets, SCANTRACK collects purchase data by having its 15,000 panel households use *handheld scanners*. These scanners are located in panel members' homes, usually mounted to a kitchen or pantry wall. Hence, with SCANTRACK panelists record purchases of *every bar-coded product purchased* regardless of the store where purchased—a major grocery chain, independent supermarket, mass merchandiser, or wholesale club.[46]

A second distinguishing characteristic of SCANTRACK is that panel members also use their handheld scanners to enter any coupons used and to record all store deals and in-store features that influenced their purchasing decisions. Each panel member transmits purchases and other data to Nielsen every week by calling a toll-free number and holding up the scanner to a phone, which records the data via a series of electronic beeps. Nielsen's SCANTRACK has provided advertisers and their agencies with invaluable information about the short- and long-term effects of advertising.

SUMMARY

Though difficult and often expensive, measuring message effectiveness is essential for advertisers to better understand how well their ads are performing and what changes they need to make to improve performance. Message-based research evaluates the effectiveness of advertising messages. Dozens of techniques for measuring advertising effectiveness have evolved over the years. The reason for this diversity is that advertisements perform various functions and multiple methods are needed to test different indicators of advertising effectiveness.

Starch Readership Service, Bruzzone tests, and Burke day-after recall tests are techniques for measuring recognition and recall. Physiological measures such as galvanic skin response and pupil dilation are used to assess physiological arousal activated by advertisements. The Ipsos-ASI Next*TV method is a videotape, in-home system for measuring consumer reactions to television commercials. rsc's ARS Persuasion testing is used to measure preference shifts to advertising employing a pre- and postmeasurement of consumer preference for a brand before and after they have seen an advertisement for that brand. The impact of advertising on actual purchase behavior is assessed with single-source data collection systems (IRI's BehaviorScan and Nielsen's SCANTRACK) that obtain optical-scanned purchase data from household panels and then integrate this with television viewing behavior and other marketing variables.

No single technique for measuring advertising effectiveness is ideal, nor is any particular technique appropriate for all occasions. The choice of technique depends on the specific objective an advertising campaign is intended to accomplish. Moreover, multiple measurement methods are usually preferable to single techniques to answer the diversity of questions that are typically involved in attempts to assess advertising effectiveness.

Find more resources to help you study at http://shimp.swcollege.com!

DISCUSSION QUESTIONS

1. It is desirable that measurements of advertising effectiveness focus on sales response rather than on some precursor to sales, yet measuring sales response to advertising is typically difficult. What complicates the measurement of sales response to advertising?

2. PACT principle 2 states that a good copytesting system should establish how results will be used in advance of each copytest. Explain the specific meaning and importance of this copytesting principle. Construct an illustration of an anticipated result lacking a sufficient action standard and one with a suitable standard.

3. If you were an account executive in an advertising agency, what would you tell clients to convince them to use (or not to use) the Starch Readership Service?

4. A test of television advertising effectiveness performed by BehaviorScan will cost you, as brand manager of a new brand of cereal, over $250,000. Why might this be a prudent investment in comparison to spending $50,000 to perform an awareness study?

5. Assume that several years from now you are purchasing your own home. One day you open your mail and find a letter from Information Resources Inc. (IRI) that requests you to become a BehaviorScan panel member. Would you have any reservations about agreeing to do this? Assume that the letter is from A.C. Nielsen, instead of IRI, requesting your participation in SCANTRACK. What would be your reservations, if any, in this case?

6. Select three recent television commercials for well-known brands, identify the objective(s) each appears to be attempting to accomplish, and then propose a procedure for how you would go about testing the effectiveness of each commercial. Be specific.

7. Television commercials are tested in various stages of completion, including storyboards, animatics, photomatics, ripamatics, livamatics, and finished commercials. What reservations might you have concerning the ability to project results from testing prefinished commercials to actual marketplace results with real commercials? Be specific and refer to the PACT principles when appropriate.

8. What are your thoughts about the value (or lack of value) from using measures of physiological response such as the galvanometer?

9. Turn to Table 11.4 and inspect the row in that table having an ARS Persuasion score range of 4.0 to 6.9 (moderately elastic). With that particular row in mind, interpret the cell entries under each of the four columns of share-point differences. For example, what is the specific interpretation of 55 percent under the column headed 0.5+?

10. Compare and contrast the Ipsos-ASI Next*TV measure with rsc's Advertising Persuasion method.

11. In your own words, specifically explain the meaning of the statement that "ad weight without persuasiveness is insufficient."

12. In the context of the discussion of single-source data, explain the difference between weight tests and copy tests. Illustrate your understanding of the difference between these two types of tests by designing a hypothetical weight test and then a copy test for the same brand.

13. With reference to Frito-Lay's copy tests in Table 11.6, the results reveal that of the 23 commercials tested, only 57 percent of the tests generated significant differences in sales between the split panels tested. Assume that Frito-Lay's results are applicable to television advertising in general. What is your general conclusion from this key finding?

ENDNOTES

1. Karen Whitehill King, John D. Pehrson, and Leonard N. Reid, "Pretesting TV Commercials: Methods, Measures, and Changing Agency Roles," *Journal of Advertising* 22 (September 1993), 85–97.

2. Ibid.

3. William A. Cook and Theodore F. Dunn, " The Changing Face of Advertising Research in the Information Age: An ARF Copy Research Council Survey," *Journal of Advertising Research* 36 (January-February 1996), 55–71.

4. Leonard M. Lodish, *The Advertising and Promotion Challenge: Vaguely Right or Precisely Wrong?* (New York: Oxford University Press, 1986).

5. Material for this section is extracted from the PACT document, which is published in its entirety in the *Journal of Advertising* 11, no. 4 (1982), 4–29.

6. Herbert E. Krugman, "Why Three Exposures May Be Enough," *Journal of Advertising Research* 12 (December 1972), 11–14.

7. Russell I. Haley and Allan L. Baldinger, "The ARF Copy Research Validity Project," *Journal of Advertising Research* 31 (March/April 1991), 11–32.

8. John R. Rossiter and Geoff Eagleson, "Conclusions from the ARF's Copy Research Validity Project," *Journal of Advertising Research* 34 (May/June 1994), 19–32.

9. Ivan L. Preston, "The Association Model of the Advertising Communication Process," *Journal of Advertising* 11, no. 2 (1982), 3–15.

10. For an in-depth discussion of the differences between recognition and recall measures, see Erik du Plessis, "Recognition versus Recall," *Journal of Advertising Research* 34 (May/June 1994), 75–91.

11. For further details on other services, see David W. Stewart, David H. Furse, and Randall P. Kozak, "A Guide to Commercial Copytesting Services," in *Current Issues and Research in Advertising*, ed. James H. Leigh and Claude R. Martin, Jr. (Ann Arbor: Division of Research, Graduate School of Business, University of Michigan, 1983), 1–44; and Surendra N. Singh and Catherine A. Cole, "Advertising Copy Testing in Print Media," in *Current Issues and Research in Advertising*, ed. James H. Leigh and Claude R. Martin, Jr. (Ann Arbor: Division of Research, Graduate School of Business, University of Michigan, 1988), 215–284.

12. These definitions are derived from Roper Starch Worldwide, as available in any Starch Readership Report prepared by this research firm.

13. D. M. Neu, "Measuring Advertising Recognition," *Journal of Advertising Research* 1 (1961), 17–22. For an alternative view, see George M. Zinkhan and Betsy D. Gelb, "What Starch Scores Predict," *Journal of Advertising Research* 26 (August/September 1986), 45–50.

14. David A. Aaker and Donald E. Bruzzone, "Causes of Irritation in Advertising," *Journal of Marketing* 49 (spring 1985), 47.

15. Appreciation for this illustration is extended to Mr. R. Paul Shellenberg, director of sales, and Mr. Donald E. Bruzzone, president of Bruzzone Research Company, Alameda, Calif.

16. The value of commercial recall testing, and Burke's DAR in particular, have been questioned by Joel S. Dubow, "Point of View: Recall Revisited: Recall Redux," *Journal of Advertising Research* 34 (May/June 1994), 92–106.

17. "Recall Not Communication: Coke," *Advertising Age*, December 26, 1983, 6.

18. Joel S. Dubow, "Advertising Recognition and Recall by Age—Including Teens," *Journal of Advertising Research* 35 (September/October 1995), 55–60.

19. Leonard M. Lodish et al., "How T.V. Advertising Works: A Meta-Analysis of 389 Real World Split Cable T.V. Advertising Experiments," *Journal of Marketing Research* 32 (May 1995), 135. See also John Philip Jones and Margaret H. Blair, "Examining 'Conventional Wisdoms' about Advertising Effects with Evidence from Independent Sources," *Journal of Advertising Research* 36 (November/December 1996), 42.

20. Jack Honomichl, "FCB: Day-After-Recall Cheats Emotion," *Advertising Age*, May 11, 1981, 2; David Berger, "A Retrospective: FCB Recall Study," *Advertising Age*, October 26, 1981, S36, S38.

21. Honomichl, "FCB," 82.

22. Ibid.

23. Steven P. Brown and Douglas M. Stayman, "Antecedents and Consequences of Attitude toward the Ad: A Meta-Analysis," *Journal of Consumer Research* 19 (June 1992), 34–51; Haley and Baldinger, "The ARF Copy Research Validity Project"; David Walker and Tony M. Dubitsky, "Why Liking Matters," *Journal of Advertising Research* 34 (May/June 1994), 9–18.

24. Judie Lannon, "New Techniques for Understanding Consumer Reactions to Advertising," *Journal of Advertising Research* 26 (August/September 1986), RC6–RC9; Judith A. Wiles and T. Bettina Cornwell, "A Review of Methods Utilized in Measuring Affect, Feelings, and Emotion in Advertising," in *Current Issues and Research in Advertising*, ed. James H. Leigh and Claude R. Martin, Jr. (Ann Arbor: Division of Research, Graduate School of Business, University of Michigan, 1991), 241–275.

25. Paul J. Watson and Robert J. Gatchel, "Autonomic Measures of Advertising," *Journal of Advertising Research* 19 (June 1979), 15–26.

26. For an especially thorough and insightful report on the galvanometer, see Priscilla A. LaBarbera and Joel D. Tucciarone, "GSR Reconsidered: A Behavior-Based Approach to Evaluating and Improving the Sales Potency of Advertising," *Journal of Advertising Research* 35 (September/October 1995), 33–53.

27. Ibid.

28. Ibid., 40.

29. For detailed discussion of pupil dilation and other physiological measures, see Joanne M. Klebba, "Physiological Measures of Research: A Review of Brain Activity, Electrodermal Response, Pupil Dilation, and Voice Analysis Methods and Studies," in *Current Issues and Research in Advertising*, ed. James H. Leigh and Claude R. Martin, Jr. (Ann Arbor: Division of Research, Graduate School of Business, University of Michigan, 1985), 53–76. See also John T. Cacioppo and Richard E. Petty, *Social Psychophysiology* (New York: The Guilford Press, 1983).

30. This account is an adaptation of Ipsos-ASI's description on its Web page (http://www.ipsos-asi.com).

31. Anthony J. Adams and Margaret Henderson Blair, "Persuasive Advertising and Sales Accountability: Past Experience and Forward Validation," *Journal of Advertising Research* 32 (March/April 1992), 25. Note: This quotation actually indicated that 1,000 respondents are drawn from four metropolitan areas. However, subsequent company newsletters and reports indicate that 800 to 1,000 respondents are randomly selected from eight metropolitan areas.

32. This average *ARS Persuasion* score of 5.8 is an increase from rsc's previously published average of 5.7. This change was brought to the author's attention by correspondence dated November 24, 1998, with rsc's Karen M. Harvey, senior manager, Marketing Communications Team.

33. Leonard M. Lodish, "J. P. Jones and M. H. Blair on Measuring Advertising Effects—Another Point of View," *Journal of Advertising Research* 37 (September/October 1997), 75–79.

34. Margaret Henderson Blair and Michael J. Rabuck, "Advertising Wearin and Wearout: Ten Years Later: More Empirical Evidence and Successful Practice," *Journal of Advertising Research* 38 (September/October 1998), 1–13.

35. For example, John Philip Jones, "Quantitative Pretesting for Television Advertising," in John Philip Jones, ed., *How Advertising Works: The Role of Research* (Newbury Park, CA: Sage Publications 1998), 160–169.

36. These conclusions are based on Margaret Henderson Blair and Karl E. Rosenberg, "Convergent Findings Increase Our Understanding of How Advertising Works," *Journal of Advertising Research* 34 (May/June 1994), 35–45. Of course, other research by practitioners and academics converge on these same general conclusions.

37. Scott Hume, "Selling Proposition Proves Power Again," *Advertising Age*, March 8, 1993, 31.

38. Lee Byers and Mark Gleason, "Using Measurement for More Effective Advertising," *Admap*, May 1993, 31–35.

39. The quote is from Jim Donius as cited in Don Bruzzone, "The Top 10 Insights about Measuring the Effect of Advertising," Bruzzone Research Company Newsletter, October 28, 1998, principle 8.

40. Lodish et al., "How T.V. Advertising Works," 128.

41. Compared with the results presented in Table 11.5, research by Lodish et al. does not demonstrate a strong relationship between commercial persuasiveness and sales. See table 11 in "How T.V. Advertising Works," 137.

42. Adams and Blair, "Persuasive Advertising and Sales Accountability."

43. Lodish et al.'s findings also support this conclusion. See "How T.V. Advertising Works."

44. For review, see Connie Pechmann and David W. Stewart, "Advertising Repetition: A Critical Review of Wearin and Wearout," *Current Issues and Research in Advertising* 11 (1988), 285–330; David W. Stewart, "Advertising Wearout: What and How You Measure Matters," *Journal of Advertising Research* 39 (September/October 1999), 39–42; Blair and Rabuck, "Advertising Wearin and Wearout."

45. Dwight R. Riskey, "How T.V. Advertising Works: An Industry Response," *Journal of Marketing Research* 34 (May 1997), 292–293. For more complete reporting on the effectiveness of TV advertising, see Lodish et al., "How T.V. Advertising Works: A Meta-Analysis of 389 Real World Split Cable T.V. Advertising Experiments," 125–139; and Leonard M. Lodish et al., "A Summary of Fifty-Five In-Market Experimental Estimates of the Long-Term Effect of TV Advertising," *Marketing Science* 14, no. 3 (1995), G133–G140.

46. Information from this description is from Andrew M. Tarshis, "The Single Source Household: Delivering on the Dream," *AIM* (a Nielsen publication) 1, no. 1 (1989).

TRADITIONAL ADVERTISING MEDIA

Chapter Objectives

After studying this chapter, you should be able to:

1. Describe the five major traditional advertising media.
2. Discuss out-of-home advertising and its strengths and limitations.
3. Discuss newspaper advertising and its strengths and limitations.
4. Discuss magazine advertising and its strengths and limitations.
5. Discuss radio advertising and its strengths and limitations.
6. Discuss television advertising and its strengths and limitations.

Opening Vignette: General Motors and the Consolidation of Media Buying

As discussed in Chapter 9, traditional full-service advertising agencies have historically been responsible for both creating advertising messages for their clients' brands and planning and buying media space in which to place those messages. This *Opening Vignette* points out that a recent and dramatic change has occurred in the manner in which media planning is performed.

An event that rocked the advertising industry was General Motors' decision to consolidate in a single company its media planning and buying for its many automobile brands. Whereas in the past media planning and buying took place in each advertising agency that represented each GM brand, now *all* media planning is done in a single company under an organization referred to as GM Planworks. This single unit handles media planning amounting annually to approximately $3 billion. By consolidating all media planning, GM achieves significant cost savings for its various brands.

Other major corporations have followed GM's lead in "unbundling" media planning from creative services, which, it should be clear, have historically been bundled together in the services performed by traditional full-service advertising agencies. Unilever moved its $700 million U.S. media buying clout from its various ad agencies to a single media buyer. Likewise, Kraft Foods consolidated its $800 million North American media planning and buying account into a single media planner/buyer.

Needless to say, traditional full-service advertising agencies have criticized these moves. Their claim is that creative services and media planning go hand in hand, and that the symbiotic relation between these services is damaged when ad agencies are relegated to just creating ad messages while independent firms are fully responsible for planning media selection. A top official of a major ad agency has this to say:

> You can't keep compartmentalizing each aspect of an account. Many of the insights we get come from the media side, and that informs the creative side and vice versa. I have a hard time believing that [ad agencies]can be as effective without that kind of close relationship.

By comparison, the CEO of a media planning company presents a counterperspective:

> Separating media buying and planning [from creative]can be beneficial to clients who work in a multi-brand environment. Even though GM has different car lines, with different goals and strategies, there's something to be said for bringing all the planning operations together into one centralized location. It gives them an opportunity to apply learning and strategic thinking across the portfolio in a way that's faster and more efficient.

Source: Adapted from Laura Freeman, "Taking Apart Media," *Agency*, winter 2001, 20–25.

There obviously are arguments on both sides of this issue. Yet the proverbial genie is now out of the bottle. The historical role of the all-powerful full-service advertising agency has diminished; ad agencies of the future will be responsible primarily for creative services, whereas separate firms will take care of the media planning aspect of the advertising business. Perhaps of greatest significance is that this development accentuates the importance of the media planning aspect of the advertising process. Creating effective advertising messages is critical, but it is essential also that these messages be placed in the right media and vehicles.

The previous three chapters have examined the message component of advertising strategy. Though effective messages are essential for successful advertising, these messages are of little use unless advertising media effectively reach the intended target audience. This and the following three chapters are devoted to media considerations. The present chapter examines the traditional mass media. Chapter 13 will focus on online media (wired and wireless) and what might be referred to as alternative advertising media (e.g., product placements in movies). Chapter 14 will investigate direct advertising that is targeted to individual households and other "addressable" customers using traditional direct mail and increasingly more opt-in, or permission, e-mail advertising. Finally, Chapter 15 will explore the various factors and analytic methods that are used in making media selection decisions.

It is important to appreciate the fact that ad message and media considerations are inextricably related. Media and message represent a hand-in-glove relationship, where each must be compatible with and fit the other. It has been said that advertising creatives "can't move until they deal with a media strategist."[1] That is, creatives and media specialists must team up to design advertisements that effectively and efficiently deliver the right brand concept to the intended target audience. Indeed, advertising practitioners agree that reaching a specific audience effectively is the most important consideration in selecting advertising media.[2] Only time will tell whether the unbundling of advertising creative and media planning functions (see *Opening Vignette*) will enhance or diminish the ultimate delivery of brand concepts to targeted audiences.

Some Important Terminology: Media Versus Vehicles

Advertising industry terminology conventionally distinguishes between advertising media and vehicles. **Media** are the general communication methods that carry advertising messages—that is, television, magazines, newspapers, and so on. **Vehicles** are the specific broadcast programs or print choices in which advertisements are placed. Hence, for example, television is a specific medium, and *Friends, CBS Evening News,* and *Monday Night Football* are vehicles for carrying television advertisements. Magazines are another medium, and *Time, Business Week, Ebony*, and *Cosmopolitan* are vehicles in which magazine ads are placed. Each medium and each vehicle has a set of unique characteristics and virtues. Advertisers attempt to select those media and vehicles whose characteristics are most compatible with the advertised brand in reaching its target audience and conveying its intended message.

Some Cautionary Comments

Virtually any environment in which messages can be printed, sung, blared, or announced in any other fashion is a potential advertising medium. Ads appear on blimps, restroom walls, T-shirts, buses and bus stops, shopping carts, store floors, race cars, boats, athletes' apparel, and signs that trail behind small airplanes. And products that appear in movies and television programs constitute advertising as well. These "special purpose" media are minor, albeit growing, in relation to the traditional advertising media—television, radio, newspaper, magazines, and out-of-home advertising—also known as the *major* advertising media and the target of the majority of advertising expenditures.

The following sections are devoted to each of the five major advertising media, placing considerable emphasis on each medium's strengths and limitations. A few words of caution are in order before proceeding. In particular, it might be tempting to play a count-'em game when examining each medium's strengths and limitations. That is, the reader might erroneously conclude that one medium is superior to another simply because more advantages and fewer limitations are listed. But this assuredly is not the intent of the following discussions.

The overall value or worth of an advertising medium depends on the advertiser's specific needs in a particular situation and the overall budget available for advertising a brand. No advertising medium is always best. The value or worth of a medium depends on the circumstances confronting a brand at a particular time: its advertising objective, the target market toward which this objective is aimed, and the available budget. An analogy will clarify this point. Suppose someone asked you, "What type of restaurant is best?" An immediate single answer is difficult to offer because you undoubtedly would recognize that what is best in a restaurant depends on your particular needs on a specific dining occasion. In some circumstances price and speed of service are of the essence, and restaurants like McDonald's would win out by these criteria. On other occasions ambiance rules the day, and a classy French restaurant might be considered ideal. In yet another situation you may be looking for a balance between dining elegance and reasonable price and favor a middle-of-the-road eating establishment. In sum, there is no such thing as a universally "best" restaurant.

The same is true of advertising media. What medium is "best" depends entirely on the advertiser's objectives, the creative needs, the competitive challenge, and budget availability. The best medium, or combination of media, is determined not by counting advantages and limitations but by conducting a careful examination of the advertised brand's needs and resources.

The presentation of ad media progresses in the following order: First discussed is the smallest major ad medium, out-of-home advertising. Coverage turns next to the two print media, newspapers and magazines, and then to the two electronic media, radio and television.

OUT-OF-HOME ADVERTISING

Outdoor advertising is regarded as a supplementary, rather than primary, advertising medium. The Outdoor Advertising Association, the industry's trade association, claims that out-of-home advertising expenditures in the United States exceeded $5 billion in 2000.[3] Out-of-home, or *outdoor*, advertising is the oldest form of advertising with origins dating back literally thousands of years. Although billboard advertising is the major aspect of out-of-home advertising, outdoor encompasses a variety of other delivery modes: advertising on bus shelters, giant inflatables (blimps), various forms of transit advertising (including ads on buses, taxis, and trucks), shopping-mall displays, skywriting, and so on. The one commonality among these is that they are seen by consumers outside of their homes (hence the name) in contrast to television, magazines, newspapers, and radio, which are received in the home (or in other indoor locations).

Billboard Advertising

Billboard advertising is the major outdoor medium. There are approximately 400,000 billboards in the United States.[4] Advertising on billboards is designed with name recognition as the primary objective. The major forms of billboard advertising are poster panels and painted bulletins.

Poster Panels.   These billboards are what we regularly see alongside highways and in other heavily traveled locales. Posters are silk-screened or lithographed and then pasted in sheets to the billboard. Companies typically sell billboard space on a monthly basis. Posters can be either 8-sheet or 30-sheet, literally designating the number of sheets of paper required to fill the allotted billboard space. An *8-sheet poster* is 6 feet, 2 inches high by 12 feet, 2 inches wide, although the actual viewing area is a slightly smaller 5 feet by 11 feet (in other words, 55 square feet of viewing space). The much larger *30-sheet poster* is 12 feet, 3 inches high by 24 feet, 6 inches wide, with a viewing area of 9 feet, 7 inches by 21 feet, 7 inches (roughly 207 square feet).

Painted Bulletins.   Painted bulletins are hand painted directly on the billboard by artists hired by the billboard owner. Standard bulletins measure 14 feet high by 48 feet wide and represent a total viewing space of 672 square feet. These bulletins are generally repainted every several months to provide a fresh look. Advertisers typically purchase these large bulletins for a one- to three-year period with the objective of achieving a consistent and relatively permanent presence in heavily traveled locations.

Buying Out-of-Home Advertising

Outdoor advertising is purchased through companies that own billboards, called *plants*. Plants are located in all major markets throughout the nation. To simplify the national advertiser's task of buying outdoor space in multiple markets, buying organizations, or agents, facilitate the purchasing of outdoor space at locations throughout the country.

Plants have historically sold poster-advertising space in terms of so-called showings. A *showing* is the percentage of the population that is theoretically exposed to an advertiser's billboard message. Showings are quoted in increments of 25 and are designated as #25, #50, #75, and #100. The designation #50, for example, means that 50 percent of the population in a particular market is expected on any given workday to pass the billboards on which an advertiser's message is posted.

In recent years plants have converted to gross rating points (GRPs) as the metric for quoting poster prices. As will be discussed more thoroughly in Chapter 15, GRPs represent the percentage and frequency of an audience being reached by an advertising vehicle. Specifically, one outdoor GRP means reaching 1 percent of the population in a particular market a single time. Outdoor GRPs are based on the daily duplicated audience (meaning that some people may be exposed on multiple occasions each day) as a percentage of the total potential market. For example, if four billboards in a community of 200,000 people achieve a daily exposure to 80,000 persons, the result is 40 gross rating points. As with traditional showings, GRPs are sold in blocks of 25, with 100 and 50 being the two levels purchased most.[5]

Outdoor Advertising's Strengths and Limitations

Outdoor advertising in the form of posters and bulletins presents the advertiser with several unique strengths and problems, which are summarized in Table 12.1.

Outdoor Advertising's Strengths.   A major strength of outdoor advertising is its *broad reach and high frequency levels*. Outdoor advertising is effective in reaching virtually all segments of the population. The number of exposures is especially high when signs are strategically located in heavy traffic areas. Automobile advertisers are heavy users of outdoor media because they can reach huge numbers of potential purchasers with high frequency. The same can be said for fast-food advertisers.

Another advantage is *geographic flexibility*. Outdoor advertising can be strategically positioned to supplement other advertising efforts in select geographic areas where advertising support is most needed.

Outdoor Advertising Strengths and Limitations   **Table 12.1**

Strengths	Limitations
Broad reach and high frequency levels	Nonselectivity
Geographic flexibility	Short exposure time
Low cost per thousand	Difficult to measure audience size
Prominent brand identification	Environmental problems
Opportune purchase reminder	

Low cost per thousand is a third advantage. The cost-per-thousand metric (abbreviated as CPM, where *M* is the Roman numeral for 1,000) is literally the cost, on average, of exposing 1,000 people to an advertisement. It is estimated that the 8- and 30-sheet poster CPMs are $0.85 and $1.78, respectively. Comparatively, a full-page four-color magazine ad has an average CPM of $9.62, and a 30-second advertisement during prime time on network TV has an average CPM of $11.31.[6] It is obvious that outdoor advertising is the least expensive advertising medium on a cost-per-thousand basis.

Because outdoor advertising is literally bigger, than life, *brand identification is substantial.* The ability to use large representations offers marketers excellent opportunities for brand and package identification.

Outdoor advertising also provides an excellent opportunity to reach consumers as a *last reminder before purchasing.* This explains why products such as beer and restaurants are among the heaviest users of outdoor advertising. (Tobacco advertisers in the United States also used to be heavy outdoor advertisers, but as part of a legal settlement with the state attorneys general, tobacco brands stopped advertising in outdoor media in 1999.)

Outdoor Advertising's Limitations.   A significant problem with outdoor advertising is *nonselectivity.* Outdoor advertising can be geared to general groups of consumers (such as inner-city residents) but cannot pinpoint specific market segments (say, professional African American men between the ages of 25 and 39). Advertisers must turn to other advertising media (such as magazines) to better pinpoint audience selection.

Short exposure time is another drawback. "Now you see it, now you don't" appropriately characterizes the fashion in which outdoor advertising engages the consumer's attention. For this reason, outdoor messages that have to be read are less effective than predominantly visual ones.

It also is *difficult to measure outdoor advertising's audience.* The lack of verified audience measurement is regarded by some as a significant impediment that must be overcome if outdoor advertising is to become a more widely used advertising medium.

A final outdoor advertising problem involves *environmental concerns.* Billboards, the so-called litter on a stick, have been banned in some manner by several U.S. states and more than 1,000 local governments.[7] Although some would argue that attractive billboards can enliven and even beautify neighborhoods and highways with attractive messages, others consider this advertising medium to be ugly and intrusive. This largely is a matter of personal taste. The articles cited in the following endnote explore the issue in some depth, including a discussion of the value and potential hazards attendant to the growing use of *changeable message signs*—that is, billboards that vary the advertising message on a schedule of every 4 to 10 seconds.[8]

NEWSPAPERS

Newspapers in the United States reach approximately 60 million households during the week and over 62 million on Sundays.[9] Newspapers have historically been the leading advertising medium, but recently television surpassed newspapers as the medium that receives the greatest amount of advertising expenditures. This is partially attributable to the fact that newspaper readership has been on a constant cycle of decline for a number of years.

Local advertising is clearly the mainspring of newspapers. However, newspapers have become more active in their efforts to increase national advertising. These efforts have been facilitated by the Newspaper Advertising Bureau (NAB), a nonprofit sales and research organization. The NAB offers a variety of services that assist both newspapers and national advertisers by simplifying the task of buying newspaper space and by offering discounts that make newspapers a more attractive medium. Moreover, the trend toward regional marketing has led to greater use of newspaper advertising by major consumer-packaged-goods companies.

Buying Newspaper Space

A major problem in the past when buying newspaper space, especially for advertisers that purchased space from newspapers in many cities, was that newspaper page size and column space varied, thereby preventing an advertiser from preparing a single advertisement to fit every newspaper. Analogously, imagine what it would be like to advertise on television if, rather than having fixed 15-, 30-, or 60-second commercials for all networks and local stations, some local stations ran only 28-second commercials, while others preferred 23-second, 16-second, or 11-second commercials. Buying time on television would be nightmarish for advertisers. So it was in buying newspaper space until the 1980s, when the advertising industry adopted a standardized system known as the **Standardized Advertising Unit (SAU) system**. The implementation of the SAU system made it possible for advertisers to purchase any one of 56 standard ad sizes to fit the advertising publishing parameters of all newspapers in the United States.

Under this system, advertisers prepare advertisements and purchase space in terms of column widths and depth in inches. There are six column *widths*:

1 column: $2\frac{1}{16}$ inches
2 columns: $4\frac{1}{4}$ inches
3 columns: $6\frac{7}{16}$ inches
4 columns: $8\frac{5}{8}$ inches
5 columns: $10\frac{13}{16}$ inches
6 columns: 13 inches

Space *depth* varies in size from 1 inch to 21 inches. Thus, an advertiser can purchase an ad as small as 1 inch by $2\frac{1}{16}$ inches or as large as 13 inches by 21 inches with numerous in-between combinations of column widths and depths in inches. A chosen size for a particular advertisement can then be run in newspapers throughout the country. Space rates can be compared from newspaper to newspaper and adjusted for circulation differences. For example, the daily SAU column-inch rate for the *Chicago Tribune* (circulation: 665,000) is $476, whereas the same rate in the competitive *Chicago Sun Times* (circulation: 491,000) is $406.[10] On the surface, the *Sun Times* is cheaper than the *Tribune*, but when adjusted to a per-thousand-readers basis, the CPM of procuring a column inch in the *Tribune* is approximately $0.72 (i.e., $476 ÷ 665) compared with a cost of about $0.83 (i.e., $406 ÷ 491) to advertise in the *Sun Times*. Hence, it is actually cheaper to advertise in the *Tribune*. Of course, the advertiser must observe audience characteristics, newspaper image, and other factors when making an advertising decision rather than considering only cost.

The choice of an advertisement's position must also be considered when buying newspaper space. Space rates apply only to advertisements placed *ROP* (run of press), which means that the ad appears in any location, on any page, at the discretion of the newspaper. Premium charges may be assessed if an advertiser has a preferred space positioning, such as at the top of the page in the financial section. Whether premium charges are actually assessed is a matter of negotiation between the advertiser and the newspaper.

Newspaper Advertising's Strengths and Limitations

As with all advertising media, newspaper advertising has various strengths and limitations (see Table 12.2).

Newspaper Advertising's Strengths.   Because people read newspapers for news, they are in the right mental frame to process advertisements that present news of store openings, new products, sales, and so forth.

Mass audience coverage is a second strength of newspaper advertising. Coverage is not restricted to specific socioeconomic or demographic groups but rather extends across all strata. However, newspaper readers on average are more economically upscale than television viewers. College graduates are more likely to read a newspaper than the population at large. Because economically advantaged consumers are usually light TV viewers, newspaper advertising provides a relatively inexpensive medium for reaching these consumers. Special interest newspapers

Table 12.2   Newspaper Advertising's Strengths and Limitations

Strengths	Limitations
Audience in appropriate mental frame to process messages	Clutter
	Not a highly selective medium
Mass audience coverage	Higher rates for occasional advertisers
Flexibility	Mediocre reproduction quality
Ability to use detailed copy	Complicated buying for national advertisers
Timeliness	Changing composition of readers

also reach large numbers of potential consumers. For example, the vast majority of college students read a campus newspaper.

Flexibility is perhaps the greatest strength of newspapers. National advertisers can adjust copy to match the specific buying preferences and peculiarities of localized markets. Local advertisers can vary copy through in-paper inserts targeted to specific zip codes. In addition, advertising copy can be placed in a newspaper section that is compatible with the advertised product. Retailers of wedding accessories advertise in the bridal section, providers of financial services advertise in the business section, sporting goods stores advertise in the sports section, and so forth.

The *ability to use detailed copy* is another strength of newspaper advertising. Detailed product information and extensive editorial passages are used in newspaper advertising to an extent unparalleled by any other medium.

Timeliness is a final significant strength of newspaper advertising. Short lead times (the time between placing an ad and having it run) permit advertisers to tie in advertising copy with local market developments or newsworthy events. Advertisers can develop copy or make copy changes quickly and thereby take advantage of dynamic marketplace developments.

Newspaper Advertising's Limitations. *Clutter* is a problem in newspapers, as it is in all of the other major media. A reader perusing a newspaper is confronted with large numbers of ads, all of which compete for the reader's limited time and only a subset of which receive the reader's attention. It is noteworthy, however, that a national survey of consumers revealed that they perceived newspapers as being significantly less cluttered with advertisements than television, radio, and magazines.[11]

A second limitation of newspaper advertising is that newspapers are *not a highly selective medium.* Newspapers are able to reach broad cross sections of people but, with few exceptions (such as campus newspapers), are unable to reach specific groups of consumers effectively. Media specialists consider newspapers to fare poorly in comparison to network television in efficiently reaching specific audiences.[12]

Occasional users of newspaper space (such as national advertisers who infrequently advertise in newspapers) *pay higher rates* than do heavy users (such as local advertisers) and have difficulty in securing preferred, non-ROP positions. In fact, newspapers' price lists (called *rate cards*) show higher rates for national than local advertisers.

Newspapers generally offer a *mediocre reproduction quality*. For this and other reasons, newspapers are not generally known to enhance a product's perceived quality, elegance, or snob appeal, as do magazines and television.

Buying difficulty is a particularly acute problem in the case of the national advertiser who wishes to secure newspaper space in a variety of different markets. On top of the high rates charged to national advertisers is the fact that each newspaper must be contacted individually. Fortunately, as mentioned previously, the NAB has made great strides toward facilitating the purchase of newspaper space by national advertisers.

A final significant problem with newspaper advertising involves the *changing composition of newspaper readers*. While most everyone used to read a daily newspaper, readership has declined progressively over the past two decades. The most faithful newspaper readers are individuals aged 45 and older, but the large and attractive group of consumers aged 30 to 44 are reading daily newspapers less frequently than ever.[13] Daily newspaper readership in this age group has fallen dramatically in the last quarter century.

MAGAZINES

Although considered a mass medium, there are literally hundreds of special interest magazines, each appealing to audiences that manifest specific interests and lifestyles. In fact, Standard Rate and Data Services (SRDS), the technical information source for the magazine industry, identifies well over 1,000 consumer magazines in dozens of specific categories, such as automotive (e.g., *Motor Trend*); general editorial (e.g., the *New Yorker*); sports (e.g., *Sports Illustrated*); women's fashions, beauty, and grooming (e.g., *Glamour*); and many others. In addition to consumer magazines, hundreds of other publications are classified as farm magazines or business publications. Advertisers obviously have numerous options when selecting magazines to promote their products.

Buying Magazine Space

A number of factors influence the choice of magazine vehicles in which to advertise. Most important is selecting magazines that reach the type of people who constitute the advertiser's target market. However, because the advertiser typically can choose from several alternative vehicles to satisfy the target market objective, cost considerations also play an extremely important role.

Advertisers who are interested in using the magazine medium can acquire a wealth of data about the composition of a magazine's readership (in terms of demographic and lifestyle profiles). This information is provided in each magazine's *media kit* that is made available to ad agencies and prospective advertisers. For example, Figure 12.1 presents *Rolling Stone*'s adult demographic profile. The first column contains audience size expressed in thousands, column two then presents percentage breakdowns for each demographic subgroup, and the last column indexes each percentage against that group's proportionate population representation. Men, for example, are substantially more likely to read *Rolling Stone* than are women (63.4 percent vs. 36.6 percent). Also, the readership of this magazine is disproportionately drawn from young adults, especially those in the 18-to-24 (41.3 percent) and 25-to-35 (29.7 percent) age groups. Obviously, this magazine, with its more than 8.7 million readers, is a very appropriate vehicle for reaching college students and graduates. Another demographic profile (of *Cosmopolitan* readers) is provided in Figure 12.2.

Media kits also provide prospective advertisers with pertinent cost information in the form of a rate card. A partial rate card for *Rolling Stone* magazine is presented in Figure 12.3. This card includes advertising rates for different page sizes (e.g., full page, three-quarter page), and for black and white (B&W) and four-color (4C) ads. For example, an advertiser would pay $103,455 to place a full-page, four-color ad in *Rolling Stone* on a one-time (open) rate basis. However, by contracting to advertise 25 times (25×) in a single year, the per-page rate for the advertiser would drop to $91,050. As is typical in magazines' price policies, cumulative discounts are available based on the number of pages advertised in *Rolling Stone* during 12 consecutive months. Cumulative quantity discounts provide clear incentives for advertisers to maintain continuity with a particular magazine.

Although every magazine has its own media kit, advertisers and their agencies do not have to contact each magazine to obtain them. SRDS compiles media kits and then makes these available (of course, for a fee) to advertisers and their agencies. Also, rate cards can be obtained online. For example, the data in Figure 12.3 come from http://www.MediaStart.com. To search for a class of magazines, such as those targeted to people interested in music, all the media buyer need do is input a key word—in this case, *music*—and then browse for magazines that

Figure 12.1

Rolling Stone **Adult Demographic Profile**

Rolling Stone
ADULT DEMOGRAPHIC PROFILE

	Aud(000)	% Comp	Index
TOTAL ADULTS	8,757	100.0	100
Men	5,553	63.4	132
Women	3,204	36.6	70
AGE			
18-24	3,612	41.3	324
25-34	2,604	29.7	142
25-44	4,364	49.8	115
35-44	1,760	20.1	90
45+	781	8.9	20
18-34	6,216	71.0	211
18-39	7,146	82.2	180
Median Age		27.5 years	
EDUCATION			
Att/Graduated College+	5,343	61.0	127
Attending College	1,815	20.7	296
HOUSEHOLD INCOME			
HHI $75,000+	1,810	20.7	105
HHI $60,000+	2,911	33.2	109
HHI $50,000+	3,912	44.7	112
HHI $40,000+	4,918	56.2	109
HHI $30,000+	6,243	71.3	111
Median HHI		$45,213	
EMPLOYMENT STATUS			
Total Employed	7,035	80.3	123
White Collar	3,502	40.0	104
MARITAL STATUS			
Single	5,161	58.9	255
LOCALITY TYPE/COUNTY SIZE			
MSA Central City/Suburban	7,720	88.2	110
A/B County	6,793	77.6	109

Source: 1998 Spring MRI

appeal to music aficionados. Information for each magazine (or *book* as they are referred to by the advertising industry) includes editorial features, rates, readership profiles, circulation, and contact information for each magazine.

The CPM measure introduced earlier is used by advertisers to compare different magazine buys. CPM information for each magazine is available from two syndicated magazine services: Mediamark Research Inc. (MRI) and Simmons Market Research Bureau (SMRB). These services provide CPM figures for general reader categories (e.g., total men) and also break out CPMs for subgroups (e.g., men aged 18 to 49, male homeowners). These more specific subgroupings enable the advertiser to compare different magazine vehicles in terms of cost per thousand for reaching the target audience (or *CPM-TM*) rather than only in terms of gross CPMs. Cost-per-thousand data are useful in making magazine vehicle selection decisions, but many other factors must be taken into account.

COSMOPOLITAN
fun fearless female

COSMOPOLITAN
Demographic Profile

	Audience	Percent of Magazine Readership	Index*
Readers per Copy	5.82		
Age			
Total Women	13,970	84.8	163
18-24	4,298	30.8	252
25-34	4,011	28.7	142
18-34	8,309	59.5	183
35-49	3,824	27.4	88
Median	31.3		
HHI			
$30,000+	9,544	68.3	113
$40,000+	7,463	53.4	112
Median	$42,678		
Education			
Attended/Graduated College+	8,241	59.0	125
Employment			
Total Employed	9,682	69.3	120
Full-Time	7,577	54.2	121
Marital Status			
Single	5,601	40.1	202
Married	5,648	40.4	73
Div/Wid/Sep	2,720	19.5	79
Other			
Women w/children	6,497	46.5	106
Working Women w/children	4,506	32.3	112
County			
A/B	10,838	77.6	110
C/D	3,132	22.4	77

Source: 1998 Spring MRI; Women

*Computed as percent of group in population ÷ groups percentage of magazine readership × 100.
Source: 1998 Spring MRI. www.mediamark.com. © 1998 by Mediamark Research, Inc. a NOP World company, a subsidiary of United Business Media Company. All rights reserved.

Magazine Advertising's Strengths and Limitations

Magazine advertising too has both strengths and limitations, depending on the advertisers' needs and resources (see Table 12.3).

Magazine Advertising's Strengths.   Some magazines reach *very large audiences*. For example, magazines like *TV Guide, Reader's Digest, Sports Illustrated,* and *Time* have total audiences that exceed 20 million readers.

However, the ability to pinpoint specific audiences (termed *selectivity*) is the feature that most distinguishes magazine advertising from other media. If a potential market exists for a product, there most likely is at least one periodical that reaches that market. Selectivity enables an advertiser to achieve effective, rather

Figure 12.3   Partial Rate Card for *Rolling Stone*

B&W	Open (1X)	7X	13X	25X
Full page	$93,110	$90,320	$86,600	$81,940
¾ page	83,800	81,290	77,940	73,750
½ page	55,870	54,200	51,960	49,170
¼ page	27,940	27,110	25,990	24,590

4C	Open (1X)	7X	13X	25X
Full page	$103,455	$100,360	$96,220	$91,050
¾ page	93,110	90,320	86,600	81,940
½ page	62,080	60,220	57,740	54,640
¼ page	31,040	30,110	28,870	27,320

Source: *Rolling Stone* Rate Card #45, January 1, 2001 (http://www. MediaStart.com). © 2001 MediaStart.

than wasted, exposure. This translates into more efficient advertising and lower costs per thousand target customers.

Magazines are also noted for their *long life*. Unlike other media, magazines are often used for reference and kept around the home (and barber shops, beauty salons, and dentists' and doctors' offices) for weeks. Magazine subscribers often pass along their copies to other readers, further extending a magazine's life.

In terms of qualitative considerations, magazines as an advertising medium are exceptional with regard to elegance, quality, beauty, prestige, and snob appeal. These features result from the *high level of reproduction quality* and from the surrounding editorial content that often transfers to the advertised product. For example, food items advertised in *Bon Appetit* always look elegant, furniture items in *Better Homes and Gardens* look tasteful, and clothing items in *Cosmopolitan* and *Gentlemen's Quarterly (GQ)* appear especially fashionable.

Magazines are also a particularly good source for providing *detailed product information* and for conveying this information with a *sense of authority*. That is, because the editorial content of magazines often includes articles that themselves represent a sense of insight, expertise, and credibility, the advertisements carried in these magazines convey a similar sense of authority, or correctness. (See *Global Focus* for a discussion of differences in advertising content between U.S. magazines and those from Arab countries.)

Table 12.3   Magazine Advertising's Strengths and Limitations

Strengths	Limitations
Some magazines reach large audiences	Not intrusive
	Long lead times
Selectivity	Clutter
Long life	Somewhat limited geographic options
High reproduction quality	
Ability to present detailed information	Variability of circulation patterns by market
Ability to convey information authoritatively	
High involvement potential	

Differences in Advertising Content in Arab and U.S. Magazines

Bahrain, Egypt, Kuwait, Lebanon, Saudi Arabia, the United Arab Emirates, and other countries in the Arab world have a total population roughly the same size as that of the United States (approximately 275 million). The Arab world represents an attractive market for many luxury goods and other products. However, "outsiders" advertising in these countries must accommodate cultural and religious differences and adapt to the unique advertising practices in Arabic countries.

To better understand the differences in Arabic and American magazine advertising, researchers selected a sampling of advertisements from general interest, family, and women's magazines. Selected for analysis were 1,064 ads from a variety of magazines from Saudi Arabia (e.g., *Al Majalla*), Egypt (e.g., *Hawaa*), Lebanon (e.g., *Wafaa*) and the United Arab Emirates (e.g., *Kul Al Usra*). Three American magazines (*Time, Family Circle*, and *Vogue*) with common editorial profiles provided the comparative referents. A total of 540 full-page ads were extracted from these three magazines for comparison to the more than 1,000 magazine ads from the Arab world.

Key findings from this research follow:

1. Magazine ads from the United States are much more likely to depict people (75 percent) than are ads from the Arab world (45 percent).
2. In ads in which people are depicted, women appear in Arab ads as often (77 percent) as do women in American ads (81 percent).
3. Ads from the Arab world are substantially more likely to include products geared toward women (93 percent) than are American ads (39 percent).
4. Comparative advertising is prevalent in U.S. magazines (26 percent) but is rarely used in Arabic magazines (6 percent).
5. Ads in American magazines use price appeals to a far greater extent (20 percent) than is the case in the Arab world (8 percent).
6. Finally, the number of information cues in the 540 U.S. ads is significantly greater (3.67 cues on average) than is the case in the 1,064 Arabic ads (2.24 cues).

In sum, this study reveals that magazine advertising in the United States tends to focus more on presenting detailed brand information, including price details, and use comparative techniques than does magazine advertising in the culturally different Arab world. Advertisers from North America, South America, Europe, and Asia must be sensitive to these cultural differences when advertising their wares in Arabic magazines.

Source: Adapted from Fahad S. Al-Olayan and Kiran Karande, "A Content Analysis of Magazine Advertisements from the United States and the Arab World," *Journal of Advertising* 29 (fall 2000), 69–82.

A final and especially notable feature of magazine advertising is its creative ability to get consumers *involved in ads* or, in a sense, to attract readers' interest and to encourage them to think about the advertised brands. This ability is due to the self-selection and reader-controlled nature of magazines compared with more intrusive media such as radio and television. A cute, albeit unintentional, portrayal of this ability appeared in the *Family Circus* comic strip, which typically presents the thoughts of preschool-age children as they contemplate the world around them. This particular strip opens with Billy saying to his sister, Dolly, "I'll tell you the difference between TV, radio, and books. . . . TV puts stuff into your mind with pictures and sound. You don't even hafta think." In the next box he states, "Radio puts stuff into your mind with just sounds and words. You make up your own pictures." And in the final section, Billy proclaims: "Books are quiet friends! They let you make up your own pictures and sounds. They make you *think*."[14] Substitute the word *magazines* for *books*, and you have a pretty good characterization of the power of magazine advertising.

In addition to the standard magazine advertising practices that are appealing and attention gaining, magazine advertisers sometimes go to dramatic lengths to enhance reader involvement. For example, Revlon and Estee Lauder have offered eye-shadow and blusher samples on the pages of fashion magazines. Rolls-Royce included a scent strip in one of its ads that imitated the smell of the leather interior of its cars. Absolut vodka used an ad with microchips to play songs when the page opened.

Magazine Advertising's Limitations.   Several limitations are associated with magazine advertising. First, unlike TV and radio, which by their very nature infringe on the attention of the viewer/listener, magazine advertising is *not intrusive*; readers control whether to be exposed to a magazine ad.

A second limitation is *long lead times*. In newspapers and the broadcast media, it is relatively easy to change ad copy on fairly short notice and in specific markets. Magazines, by comparison, have long closing dates that require advertising materials to be on hand for weeks in advance of the actual publication date. For example, for four-color ads the closing dates for the following sampling of magazines are shown in parentheses: *Better Homes & Gardens* (12 weeks), *National Geographic* (8 weeks), *Sports Illustrated* (5 weeks), and *Time* (4 weeks).

As with other advertising media, *clutter* is a problem with magazine advertising. In certain respects clutter is a worse problem with magazines than, say, television, because readers can become engrossed in editorial content and skip over advertisements so as not to have their reading disrupted.

Magazine advertising also provides fewer *geographic options* than do other media. For example, *Cosmopolitan* offers advertisers the opportunity to place ads just in any of seven regions or any particular state. An advertiser that is interested only in select markets—say, Dallas/Fort Worth and Houston, Texas—would probably refrain from advertising in *Cosmopolitan* (or in other magazine vehicles) because much of the magazine circulation would be wasted on readers outside these two metropolitan areas. It is important to note, however, that greater selectivity is provided by some magazines. *Sports Illustrated*, for example, offers advertising rates for five key regions, all 50 states, and 50 metropolitan areas. An advertiser could choose to advertise in *Sports Illustrated* only in the Dallas/Fort Worth area, and in so doing pay $8,796 for a full-page, four-color ad.[15] As can be seen by these two illustrations, there is variance in magazine selectivity.

A final limitation of magazine advertising is variability in circulation patterns from market to market. *Rolling Stone*, for example, is read more in metropolitan than rural areas. Hence, advertisers who are interested, say, in reaching young males would not be very successful in reaching nonmetropolitan readers. This would necessitate placing ads in one or more magazines other than *Rolling Stone*, which would up the total cost of the media buy. Radio, TV, or both might better serve the advertiser's needs and provide more uniform market coverage.

Magazine Audience Measurement

It is critical for advertisers in selecting magazine vehicles to know the audience size reached by candidate magazines. Determining the size of a particular magazine's readership might seem an easy task. All one need do is tally the number of people who subscribe to a magazine, right? Unfortunately, it is not that simple; several complicating factors make subscription counting an inadequate way of determining a magazine's readership. First, magazine subscriptions are collected through a variety of intermediaries, making it difficult to obtain accurate lists of who subscribes to what magazines. Second, magazines often are purchased from newsstands, supermarkets, and other retail outlets rather than through subscriptions, thus completely eliminating knowledge of who purchases what magazines. Third, magazines that are available in public locations such as doctors' offices, barber shops, and beauty salons are read by numerous people and not just the subscriber. Finally, individual magazine subscribers often share issues with other people.

For all these reasons, the number of subscriptions to a magazine and the number of people who actually read the magazine are not equivalent. Fortunately, two previously mentioned services—MRI and SMRB—specialize in measuring magazine readership and determining audience size. These two companies offer very similar, yet competitive, services.

In brief, both services take national probability samples of 25,000 households and query respondents to identify their media consumption habits (e.g., what magazines they read) and determine their purchase behaviors for an extensive variety of products and brands. Statisticians then employ statistical inference procedures to generalize sample results to the total population. Advertisers and media planners use the readership information along with detailed demographic and product and brand usage data to evaluate the absolute and relative value of different magazines.

Advantages aside, not all is perfect in the world of magazine audience measurement. At least three notable problems are recognized: (1) Respondents to readership surveys are asked to rate numerous magazines, which can lead to fatigue and hasty or faulty responses; (2) sample sizes often are small, especially for small-circulation magazines, which leads to high margins of sampling error when generalizing to the total population; and (3) sample composition may be unrepresentative of audience readership.[16] Also, because these two readership services use different research methods, their results often are discrepant. Consider, for example, SMRB's estimates versus MRI's estimates for the following magazines: *Ebony* (12.44 million vs. 10.79 million), *Golf Digest* (7.16 million vs. 5.68 million), *Health* (7.80 million vs. 5.84 million), and *Modern Maturity* (20.94 million vs. 15.16 million).[17] In percentage terms and using the smaller estimate as the base, these differences are 15.3, 26.1, 33.6, and 38.1 percent, respectively. Media planners thus confront the challenge of determining which service is right or whether both are wrong in their estimates of audience size.[18]

Despite these problems, media planners must make the most of the audience estimates and readership profiles generated by Simmons Market Research Bureau and Mediamark Research Inc. Both SMRB and MRI produce annual multivolume reports of product and brand usage data and detailed media information. Using bottled water and seltzer as an illustration, Table 12.4 provides a pared-down report that will be useful for explaining the construction and interpretation of SMRB and MRI reports.[19] For ease of exposition, we will hereafter refer to the bottled-water and seltzer category simply as "bottled water."

MRI and SMRB reports are structurally equivalent to the data contained in Table 12.4. Each of the detailed tables in these reports present cross-tabulations of demographic segments or media by product or brand usage. Table 12.4 presents usage of bottled water delineated by gender, educational status, age groupings, geographic region, and radio vehicles. The table is to be interpreted as follows:

1. The first row (Total) shows the occurrence of bottled-water purchases in the total U.S. population. Thus, of the 197,462,000 adults living in the United States at the time of data collection (March 1999), 46,248,000 (see column A), or 23.4 percent (see column C, % Across), purchased bottled water at least once in recent months.
2. Each set of detailed entries shows the estimate in four different ways (denoted as columns A, B, C, and D) for the product category (bottled water in this case), and the specified population grouping.
    a. Column A presents the estimate of *total product users* (expressed in thousands). For example, of the 46,248,000 product users, 19,536,000 are men and 26,711,000 are women.
    b. Column B (% Down) represents the *composition of buyers* in each demographic group. For example, the 26,711,000 women users of bottled water represent 57.8 percent of all product users; that is, 26,711,000 ÷ 46,248,000 = 57.8 percent. Please note that each value in column B (% Down) is calculated by dividing the column A value for a particular row by the total value in column A (i.e., 46,248,000).
    c. Column C (% Across) reflects each demographic group's *coverage* with respect to the particular product category. For example, women purchasers of bottled water (26,711,000) represent 26.0 percent of the 102,635,000 women who live in the United States.
    d. Column D (Index) is a measure of the particular demographic group compared with the total population. For example, 26 percent of women are bottled water purchasers compared with 23.4 percent of all adults. (See the % Across figure in the top, or Total, row). The index is a

Table 12.4

Adults	Total '000	A '000	B % Down	C % Across	D Index
Total	197,462	46,248	100.0	23.4	100
Men	94,827	19,536	42.2	20.6	88
Women	102,635	26,711	57.8	26.0	111
Graduated College	43,406	11,933	25.8	27.5	117
Graduated High School	66,168	14,726	31.8	22.3	95
18-24	24,807	7,640	16.5	30.8	131
25-34	40,154	11,150	24.1	27.8	119
35-44	44,393	12,058	26.1	27.2	116
45-54	33,700	7,982	17.3	23.7	101
55-64	22,149	3,979	8.6	18.0	77
65 or over	32,260	3,438	7.4	10.7	46
Northeast	39,284	9,572	20.7	24.4	104
North Central	46,039	8,960	19.4	19.5	83
South	69,564	14,865	32.1	21.4	91
West	42,574	12,851	27.8	30.2	129
Radio: Classic Rock	21,275	5,699	12.3	26.8	114
Radio: Classical	3,128	919	2.0	29.4	125
Radio: Country	38,490	8,925	19.3	23.2	99
Radio: Adult Contemporary	41,362	11,674	25.2	28.2	121
Radio: Modern Rock	9,465	3,039	6.6	32.1	137

calculation of this relationship: (26 ÷ 23.4) × 100 = 111. This index indicates that women are 11 percent more likely than the general population to purchase bottled water. Men, with an index of 88, are disproportionately less likely (compared with women) to purchase bottled water.

The educational status, age, and radio listenership data can be interpreted in an analogous fashion. Regarding age, it can be seen that proportionately the greatest consumption of bottled water is by consumers in the 18-to-24 (index = 131), 25-to-34 (119), and 35-to-44 (116) age categories. Comparatively, consumers in the older age categories are less likely to purchase bottled water. Does this mean that bottled-water marketers should cater only to the younger age groups and neglect the others? Probably not. For example, although people aged 45 to 54 (index of 101) are proportionately less likely than the younger age groups to consume bottled water, there are, nonetheless, a total of nearly 8 million people in this age group who *do* consume bottled water. It thus would make little sense to disregard such a large number of consumers simply because the index number is barely greater than 100. Although prudent bottled-water marketers would not neglect these older consumers, the index numbers in Table 12.4 suggest that less media emphasis, or weight, should be directed at older consumers than the weight targeted at the younger consumers.

Turning to the radio data in Table 12.4, it can be seen that listeners of country radio stations have the lowest index number (99) compared with listeners of the other four types of radio programming, which range from 114 for classic rock to 137 for modern rock. How might an advertiser use these data? Looking just at index numbers, modern rock stations represent the best choice for bottled-water ads, but the index number conveys only part of the story.[20] Note carefully that a bottled-water advertisement placed on modern rock stations would potentially reach only a few more than 3 million bottled-water purchasers. There would be relatively little wasted coverage with this vehicle, but not many bottled-water purchasers would be reached. Comparatively, an advertisement placed on adult contemporary stations would have a chance of reaching nearly 11.7 million potential bottled-water consumers. Although a smaller percentage of the listeners of adult contemporary stations purchase bottled water compared with the percentage of modern rock listeners, advertisements placed on adult contemporary stations reach a far greater number of actual and potential bottled-water consumers.

In using media data supplied in MRI and SMRB reports, the advertiser must weigh various pieces of information to make intelligent media selection decisions. This includes (1) the size of the potential audience that a vehicle might reach, (2) the attractiveness of its coverage as revealed by the total product purchasers exposed to that vehicle (column A) and compared with other media (column D), (3) its cost compared with other vehicles; and (4) its appropriateness for the advertised brand. It thus should be apparent that making intelligent advertising-vehicle decisions cannot be reduced to simply comparing index numbers. These numbers are merely input into a judgment that a careful decision maker must make after considering all of the available information.

RADIO

Radio is a nearly ubiquitous medium: Almost 100 percent of all homes in the United States have radios; most homes have several; virtually all cars have a radio; more than 50 million radios are purchased in the United States each year; and radio in the U.S. reaches about 96 percent of all consumers every week.[21] These impressive figures indicate radio's strong potential as an advertising medium. Although radio has always been a favorite of local advertisers, regional and national advertisers have increasingly recognized radio's advantages as an advertising medium.

Buying Radio Time

Radio advertisers are interested in reaching target customers at a reasonable expense while ensuring that the station format is compatible with a brand's image and its creative message strategy. Several considerations influence the choice of radio vehicle. *Station format* (classical, progressive, country, top 40, talk, and so forth) is a major consideration. Certain formats are obviously most appropriate for particular products and brands.

A second consideration is the *choice of geographic areas to cover*. National advertisers buy time from stations whose audience coverage matches the advertiser's geographic areas of interest. This typically means locating stations in preferred metropolitan statistical areas (MSAs) or in so-called *areas of dominant influence* (ADIs), which number approximately 200 in the United States and correspond to the major television markets.

A third consideration in buying radio time is the *choice of daypart*. Radio dayparts include the following:

Morning drive:	6 a.m. to 10 a.m.
Midday:	10 a.m. to 3 p.m.
Afternoon drive:	3 p.m. to 7 p.m.
Evening:	7 p.m. to midnight
Late night:	Midnight to 7 a.m.

Rate structures vary depending on the attractiveness of the daypart; for example, morning and afternoon drive times are more expensive than midday and

commercials are aired, prompting one observer to comment (only partially with tongue in cheek) that the remote control "zapper" is the greatest threat to capitalism since Karl Marx.[38] Research reveals that perhaps as high as one-third of the potential audience for a TV commercial may be lost to zapping.[39] Although zapping is extensive, one intriguing study presented evidence suggesting that commercials that are zapped are actively processed prior to being zapped and may have a more positive effect on brand purchase behavior than commercials that are not zapped.[40]

In addition to zapping, television viewers also engage in zipping. *Zipping* takes place when ads that have been recorded with a VCR along with program material are fast-forwarded (zipped through) when the viewer watches the prerecorded material. Research has shown that zipping is extensive.[41] Personal video recorders (PVRs), which are essentially VCRs with the storage powers of personal computers, make zipping behavior easier than ever. PVRs from companies such as TiVo and ReplayTV allow viewers to fast-forward past commercials by simply pushing a skip button that fast-forwards in 30-second intervals, which, by no coincidence, is the standard length of a TV commercial.[42]

Clutter is a fifth serious problem with television advertising. Clutter refers to the growing amount of nonprogram material: commercials, public service messages, and promotional announcements for stations and programs. As noted earlier, consumers perceive television to be the most cluttered of all major advertising media.[43] Clutter has been created by the network's increased use of promotional announcements to stimulate audience viewing of heavily promoted programs and by advertisers' increased use of shorter commercials. Whereas 60-second commercials once were prevalent, the duration of the vast majority of commercials today is only 30, 20, or 15 seconds.[44] The effectiveness of television advertising has suffered from the clutter problem, which creates a negative impression among consumers about advertising in general, turns viewers away from the television set, and perhaps reduces brand name recall.[45]

Infomercials

Discussion of television advertising would not be complete without at least a brief mention of the *infomercial*. Introduced to television in the early 1980s, the long commercial, or **infomercial**, is an alternative to the conventional, short form of television commercial. By comparison, infomercials are full-length commercial segments run on cable television that typically last 28 to 30 minutes and combine product news and entertainment. Infomercials account for nearly one-fourth of the programming time for most cable stations.[46] The increased used of infomercials by legitimate (as well as illegitimate) marketers extends from two primary factors: First, technologically complicated products and those that require detailed explanations benefit from the long commercial format. Second, the infomercial format is in lockstep with increasing demands for marketing accountability insofar as the number of orders obtained from an infomercial occurs within 24 hours or so after an infomercial is aired.[47]

It is claimed that a successful infomercial uniquely blends both entertainment and selling. Here, according to an industry spokesperson, is what an infomercial must do to be successful:

> With an infomercial you're asking people to find you by accident. Once they find you, they must find the show so compelling, so entertaining, that they watch 'till the very end. By that time they've got to be so excited that they pick up the telephone and give the producers money.[48]

In the early years, infomercials were restricted primarily to unknown companies selling skin care products, balding treatments, exercise equipment, and other feel-good products. However, the growing respectability of this form of advertising has encouraged a number of consumer goods companies to promote their brands via infomercials. Well-known infomercial users include Avon, Braun, Clairol, Chrysler, Estee Lauder, Hoover, Pioneer, Procter & Gamble, and Sears. Manufacturers of consumer durables are increasingly using infomercials. For example, General Motors' Chevrolet division featured famous baseball star

Cal Ripken Jr. in an infomercial touting its Silverado pickup truck. Phillips Consumer Electronics used a 30-minute infomercial in marketing its digital videodisc player. Consider the following successful infomercial application by Kodak.

Kodak in the late 1990s introduced a 30-minute infomercial to promote its new DC210 Digital Zoom Camera. Up to this time Eastman Kodak had little sales and profit to show for the $500 million it had invested in digital imaging. The infomercial, which cost nearly $400,000 to produce, included a toll-free number that invited viewers to request a $175 coupon that was good toward the purchase of the camera and other Kodak products at retail locations. Follow-up research indicated that approximately one out of 12 callers who received the discount coupon ordered the camera at a retail outlet, an impressive statistic in view of the fact that the DC210's retail price was $899 at the time of the promotion. Retail sales in cities where the DC210 infomercials were aired exceeded by 80 percent sales of these digital cameras in cities without infomercials. Moreover, retail selling time was substantially reduced insofar as consumers already were presold by the infomercial. Kodak officials concluded that the infomercial was a cost-effective way to introduce consumers to the advantages of digital imaging.[49]

Cable programming obviously does not deliver the numbers of consumers that network programming generates, but numerous advertisers have found infomercials on cable television to be an extremely effective tool for moving merchandise. This long-form commercial is apparently here to stay. Although consumers have complaints with infomercials (e.g., that some make false claims and are deceptive),[50] this form of long commercial appears to be especially effective for consumers who are brand and price conscious, who are innovative and impulsive, and who place high importance on shopping convenience.[51]

Brand Placements in Television Programs

Returning to our earlier discussion of advertising clutter along with consumers' responses in the form of zipping and zapping behavior, many observers fear that television advertising is no longer as effective as it used to be. Brand managers and network television executives have reacted to consumers' zipping/zapping behavior by borrowing from the movie industry and finding a way to circumvent TV viewers' penchant for avoiding commercials. Have you noticed brands appearing more often in television programs? This is not by happenstance; rather, brand managers pay to get prominent placements for their brands—precisely as they have done to receive attractive brand positioning in movies. The widely viewed *Survivor* program has been described as "the poster child for this trend."[52] Advertisers purchasing commercial time in *Survivor* episodes also received prime brand placements in the program. Contestants on *Survivor* were shown consuming Doritos and Mountain Dew and wearing Reebok shoes.

Brand placements represent a growing form of marketing communications. Placements occur not just in TV programs and movies but also in music videos, video games, and even in novels.[53] Brand placements in prime-time TV programs appear most often in sporting competitions, news programs, and feature-magazine and game shows.[54] Compared with movie placements, brand appearances in TV programs have the advantages of (1) much larger audiences, (2) more frequent exposure, and (3) global reach, especially when programs are rerun around the world under syndication.[55] It perhaps goes without saying that brand placements on TV can be very effective provided the brand is displayed in a context that appropriately matches the brand's image. The downside with placements in TV programs is that brand managers relinquish the full control available to them by comparison when providing the final approval for TV commercials.

Television Audience Measurement

As noted earlier, a 30-second commercial on prime-time television can cost as much as $2,000,000 (for a Super Bowl spot) or less than $100,000. The reason for the disparity is ratings. Generally speaking, higher-rated programs command higher prices. Because prices and ratings go hand in hand, the accurate measurement of program audience size, or ratings, is a critically important, multimillion-dollar industry. Advertising researchers continuously seek ways to measure more accurately the size of program audiences.

Nielsen's People Meter Technology.   The People Meter, by Nielsen Media Research, represents perhaps the most important research innovation since the advent of television audience measurement.[56] The **People Meter** is a handheld device slightly larger than a typical television channel selector that has eight buttons for family members and two additional buttons for visitors. A family member (or visitor) must push his or her designated numerical button each time he or she selects a particular program. The meter automatically records what programs are being watched, how many households are watching, and which family members are in attendance. Information from each household's People Meter is fed daily into a central computer via telephone lines. This viewing information is then combined with each household's pertinent demographic profile to provide a single source of data about audience size and composition.

Considerable controversy has surrounded its implementation, however, as demonstrated in the following brief review of television audience measurement. Before the introduction of the People Meter system, Nielsen measured television program ratings by combining two data collection methods. One involved attaching electronic meters to the television sets of a national sample of households (the electronic meter panel). These electronic meters—called *black boxes*—determined the number of households attuned to particular programs. Statistical inference techniques were used to estimate program ratings on a national basis. A separate national panel of households—the diary panel—maintained diaries of their ongoing viewing habits and supplied pertinent demographic information on household size, income, education, race, and so on. When combined, the data from the two panels indicated the program ratings and demographic characteristics of each program's audience. This information was used by networks to set advertising rates and by advertisers to select programs on which to advertise their products.

This method worked well during a simpler time when fewer program options were available to television viewers. It became less suitable as independent stations, cable networks, and VCRs increased the number of choices available to viewers. Diary data diminished in accuracy because people became less willing or able to maintain precise accounts of their viewing behavior. In response, the People Meter was developed by a British research firm, Audits Great Britain (AGB Television Research). This firm introduced People Meters to the United States in 1984 but withdrew from the business several years later. Nielsen followed with its own People Meter system shortly after AGB entered the U.S. market.

The People Meter controversy ensued from the substantial decline—almost 10 percent—in network ratings as a result of the transition from diary panels to People Meters. The big three networks (ABC, CBS, and NBC) lost millions of dollars in advertising revenues because smaller-rated programs were unable to command higher prices. The networks placed much of the blame on People Meters, claiming that the meters have fundamental faults responsible for erroneous ratings data.

People Meters likely are here to stay in one form or another, and probably so is the controversy surrounding their use. The major networks, which pay Nielsen more than $10 million annually for its data, are growing increasingly critical of Nielsen's data. They claim that Nielsen undercounts major segments of the population, especially young people and viewers watching TV outside the home.[57]

SRI's SMART System: An Innovative but (Perhaps) Impractical Solution.   Statistical Research Inc. (SRI) has worked on developing its own TV measurement system called SMART, which stands for Systems for Measuring and Reporting Television.[58] The SMART system consists of meters that are attached with Velcro strips to television sets. The attached meters have sensors that pick up signals from the air. Television viewers log in and out before and after watching TV using a remote control device. The user-friendly device contains a dozen icons (telephone, flower, smiley face, apple, heart, etc.), one of which each family member selects as his or her unique log-in symbol. The SMART system was pilot-tested in Philadelphia in the late 1990s. Although SRI intended to roll out the SMART system throughout the United States by 2001, it appears doubtful that SMART will become a reality. Some advertising practitioners question the SMART system's practicality because they doubt that TV viewers will regularly log in with their unique symbols.

It is interesting to note that Arbitron, of radio-audience measurement fame, introduced a service in the early 1990s called ScanAmerica to compete with Nielsen's rating system. However, within two years Arbitron discontinued the service due to lack of industry support.[59] Nielsen remains the only major service involved with estimating national TV audiences. The challengers have come and gone. Nielsen's system certainly is not without problems, but it remains the sole surviving option for the measurement of audience size.

SUMMARY

Five major media are available to media planners: television, radio, magazines, newspapers, and outdoor advertising. Each medium has unique qualities with both strengths and weaknesses. The chapter provides a detailed analysis of each medium. Outdoor advertising is particularly notable for its broad reach, geographic flexibility, and low cost. At the same time, this medium suffers from nonselectivity and short exposure time. Newspapers provide mass audience coverage and reach readers who are in the appropriate mental frame to process messages. Newspapers suffer from high clutter and limited selectivity, among other limitations. Magazines enable advertisers to reach selective audiences and to present detailed information in an involving manner. This medium lacks intrusiveness, however, and also experiences considerable clutter. Radio also has the ability to reach segmented audiences and is economical. Clutter and the lack of visuals are notable weaknesses. Finally, television is an intrusive medium that is able to generate excitement, demonstrate brands in use, and achieve impact. Television advertising suffers from clutter, audience fractionalization, and high cost.

Find more resources to help you study at http://shimp.swcollege.com!

DISCUSSION QUESTIONS

1. What are the advantages and disadvantages of cable television advertising? Why are more national advertisers turning to cable television as a viable advertising medium?

2. Assume you are brand manager for a product line of thermos containers. Your products range from thermos bottles to small ice chests. You have $5 million to invest in a three-month magazine advertising campaign. What magazines would you choose for this campaign? Justify your choices.

3. Cigarettes and liquor products were responsible for a very large percentage of all billboard advertising. Why did these two product categories dominate the billboard medium?

4. Changeable message signs are billboards that vary the advertising message on a schedule of every 4 to 10 seconds. What, in your opinion, is the value of this technology to the advertiser, and what are the potential hazards to society?

5. Assume you are a manufacturer of various jewelry items. Graduation rings for high school and college students are among the most important items in your product line. You are in the process of developing a media strategy aimed specifically at high school students. With an annual budget of $5 million, what media and specific vehicles would you use? How would you schedule the advertising over time?

6. Examine a copy of the most recent Spot Radio Rates and Data available in your library and compare the advertising rates for three or four of the radio stations in your hometown or university community.

7. Pick your favorite clothing store in your university community (or hometown), and justify the choice of one radio station that the clothing store should select for its radio advertising. Do not feel constrained by what the clothing store may be doing already; focus instead on what you think is most important. Be certain to make explicit all criteria used in making your choice and all radio stations considered.

8. Magazine A is read by 20,450,000 people and costs $80,000 for a full-page, four-color advertisement. Magazine B reaches 15,700,000 readers and costs $65,000 for a full-page, four-color advertisement. Holding all other factors constant, in which magazine would you choose to advertise and why?

9. Radio is the only major medium that is nonvisual. Is this a major disadvantage? Thoroughly justify your response.

10. One advertiser declared: "Infomercials are junk. I wouldn't waste my money advertising on this medium." What is your response to this assertion?

11. Representatives of the major TV networks (e.g., ABC, CBS, Fox, and NBC) often claim that People Meters are flawed. What are some of the reasons why People Meters may not yield precise information about the number of households tuned into a specific television program or provide accurate demographic information of the people who actually do view a particular program?

12. Locate a recent SMRB or MRI publication in your library, and select a product used by large numbers of consumers (soft drinks, cereal, candy bars, etc.). Pick out the index numbers for the 18–24, 25–34, 35–44, 45–54, 55–64, and 65 and older age categories. Show how the index numbers were calculated. Also, identify some magazines that would be especially suitable for advertising to the *heavy users* of your selected product category.

13. With the following data, fill in the empty blanks.

Age Range	Total '000	A '000	B % Down	C % Across	D Index
All Adults	169,557	49,639	100.0	29.3	100
18–24	14,859	6,285	___	___	___
25–34	38,494	10,509	___	___	___

14. Based exclusively on the data in question 13, if you were an advertiser deciding whether to advertise your brand just to people aged 18 to 24, just to the 25-to-34 age group, or to both age groups, what would be your decision? Provide a detailed rationale for your decision.

ENDNOTES

1. Thom Forbes, "Consumer Central: The Media Focus Is Changing—And So Is the Process," *Agency*, winter 1998, 38.

2. Karen Whitehill King and Leonard N. Reid, "Selecting Media for National Accounts: Factors of Importance to Agency Media Specialists," *Journal of Current Issues and Research in Advertising* 19 (fall 1997), 55–64.

3. "The Great Outdoors," special advertising insert in *Agency* 11 (fall 2001).

4. Ibid.

5. Anthony F. McGann and J. Thomas Russell, *Advertising Media: A Managerial Approach* (Homewood, Ill.: Irwin, 1988), 272.

6. Estimates by the Media Edge as reprinted in "The Great Outdoors."

7. Adam Snyder, "Outdoor Forecast: Sunny, Some Clouds," *Adweek's Marketing Week*, July 8, 1991, 18–19.

8. Myron Laible, "Changeable Message Signs: A Technology Whose Time Has Come," *Journal of Public Policy & Marketing* 16 (spring 1997), 173–176; Frank Vespe, "High-Tech Billboards: The Same Old Litter on a Stick," *Journal of Public Policy & Marketing* 16 (spring 1997), 176–179; and Charles R. Taylor, "A Technology Whose Time Has Come or the Same Old Litter on a Stick? An Analysis of Changeable Message Boards," *Journal of Public Policy & Marketing* 16 (spring 1997), 179–186.

9. *Marketer's Guide to Media* 2000, vol. 23 (New York: BPI Communications), 189.

10. These figures are based on ibid., 190.

11. Michael T. Elliott and Paul Surgi Speck, "Consumer Perceptions of Advertising Clutter and Its Impact across Various Media," *Journal of Advertising Research* 38 (January/February 1998), 29–41.

12. Karen Whitehill King, Leonard N. Reid, and Margaret Morrison, "Large-Agency Media Specialists' Opinions on Newspaper Advertising for National Accounts," *Journal of Advertising* 26 (summer 1997), 1–18. This article indicates that ad agencies consider the newspaper to be less effective as an advertising medium in most all respects compared with network television.

13. Joe Schwartz and Thomas Exter, "The News from Here," *American Demographics*, June 1991, 50–53.

14. Bill Keane, "The Family Circus," ©1992, Bill Keane, Inc., August, 9, 1992.

15. Based on *Sports Illustrated's* rate card #56, January 12, 1998, 5.

16. Stephen M. Blacker, "Magazines Need Better Research," *Advertising Age*, June 10, 1996, 23; Erwin Ephron, "Magazines Stall At Research Crossroads," *Advertising Age*, October 19, 1998, 38.

17. *Marketer's Guide to Media 2000*, 164–171.

18. For additional information on magazine audience measurement, see Thomas C. Kinnear, David A. Horne, and Theresa A. Zingery, "Valid Magazine Audience Measurement: Issues and Perspectives," in *Current Issues and Research in Advertising*, ed. James H. Leigh and Claude R. Martin, Jr. (Ann Arbor: Division of Research, Graduate School of Business, University of Michigan, 1986), 251–270.

19. The following information is based on Mediamark Reporter (Mediamark Research Inc., March 2000).

20. For an interesting critique of making vehicle selection decisions based exclusively on index numbers, see Theodore F. D'Amico, "Magazines' Secret Weapon: Media Selection on the Basis of Behavior, as Opposed to Demography," *Journal of Advertising Research* 39 (November/December 1999), 53–60.

21. Special advertising section to *Adweek*, *Brandweek*, and *Mediaweek* by the Radio Advertising Bureau in 2000; also, Marc Beauchamp, "Radio Days," *Forbes*, November 30, 1987, 200, 204.

22. Burt Manning, "Friendly Persuasion," *Advertising Age*, September 13, 1982, M8.

23. Ibid.

24. Kerry J. Smith, "Cranking Up the Volume," *Promo*, October 1994, 106.

25. Rhody Bosley, "Radio Study Tells Imagery Potential," *Advertising Age* (advertising supplement), September 6, 1993, R3.

26. For further reading on the nature and value of imagery in advertising, see Paula Fitzgerald Bone and Pam Scholder Ellen, "The Generation and Consequences of Communication-Evoked Imagery," *Journal of Consumer Research* 19 (June 1992), 93–104; and Darryl W. Miller and Lawrence J. Marks, "Mental Imagery and Sound Effects in Radio Commercials," *Journal of Advertising* 21 (December 1992), 83–93.

27. "Radio's Personalities Help Find Snapple's Sales Targets," *Advertising Age* (special advertising section), October 18, 1993, R3.
28. A thorough study of this behavior was conducted by Avery M. Abernethy, "The Accuracy of Diary Measures of Car Radio Audiences: An Initial Assessment," *Journal of Advertising* 18, no. 3 (1989), 33–49.
29. For the summer 2001 ratings, go to http://www.arbitron.com/ newsroom/archive/09_24_01.htm.
30. "For Their Eyes Only," *Promo*, November 2001, 19.
31. Elliott and Speck, "Consumer Perceptions of Advertising Clutter and Its Impact across Various Media."
32. *Marketer's Guide to Media 2000*, "Average Cost Per 30–Second Commercial, 1999," 25.
33. Ibid., 51.
34. Based on famous advertising practitioner Raymond Rubicam as quoted in Richard C. Anderson, "Eight Ways to Make More Impact," *Advertising Age*, May 17, 1982, M23.
35. James B. Arndorfer and Chuck Ross, "A-B Shells Out Record Price for '99 Super Bowl," *Advertising Age*, April 13, 1998, 1.
36. Sally Beatty, "Cost of Making a TV Commercial Leaped 11% in 1997, Survey Shows," *The Wall Street Journal Interactive Edition*, August 19, 1998.
37. Nielsen Ratings published in Doug Nye, "NBC's 'Friends' Thumps 'Survivor,'" *The State*, Columbia, S.C., October 20, 2001.
38. "The Toughest Job in TV," *Newsweek*, October 3, 1988, 72; Dennis Kneale, "'Zapping' of TV Ads Appears Pervasive," *The Wall Street Journal*, April 25, 1988, 21.
39. John J. Cronin, "In-Home Observations of Commercial Zapping Behavior," *Journal of Current Issues and Research in Advertising* 17 (fall 1995), 69–76.
40. Fred S. Zufryden, James H. Pedrick, and Avu Sankaralingam, "Zapping and Its Impact on Brand Purchase Behavior," *Journal of Advertising Research* 33 (January/February 1993), 58–66.
41. John J. Cronin and Nancy E. Menelly, "Discrimination vs. 'Zipping' of Television Commercials," *Journal of Advertising* 21 (June 1992), 1–7.
42. Jeff Howe, "Ready for Prime Time," *IQ*, September 10, 2001, 10 (http://www.adweek.com).
43. Elliott and Speck, "Consumer Perceptions of Advertising Clutter and Its Impact across Various Media."
44. For an interesting article that compares the effectiveness of 15– and 30–second commercials, see Surendra N. Singh and Catherine A. Cole, "The Effects of Length, Content, and Repetition on Television Commercial Effectiveness," *Journal of Marketing Research* 30 (February 1993), 91–104.
45. Whether advertising clutter has adverse effects on brand name recall and message memorability is a matter of some dispute. For somewhat different accounts, see Tom J. Brown and Michael L. Rothschild, "Reassessing the Impact of Television Advertising Clutter," *Journal of Consumer Research* 20 (June 1993), 138–146; Robert J. Kent and Chris T. Allen, "Does Competitive Clutter in Television Advertising 'Interfere' with the Recall and Recognition of Brand Names and Ad Claims?" *Marketing Letters* 4, no. 2 (1993), 175–184; Robert J. Kent and Chris T. Allen, "Competitive Interference in Consumer Memory for Advertising: The Role of Brand Familiarity," *Journal of Marketing* 58 (July 1994), 97–105; and Robert J. Kent, "Competitive Clutter in Network Television Advertising: Current Levels and Advertiser Response," *Journal of Advertising Research* 35 (January/February 1995), 49–57.
46. Julie Steenhuysen, "Adland's New Billion-Dollar Baby," *Advertising Age*, April 11, 1994, S8.
47. Jim Edwards, "The Art of the Infomercial," *Brandweek*, September 3, 2001, 14–18.
48. Steve Dworman, "The Infomercial," special sourcebook issue to *Brandweek*, 1994, 5.
49. "Digital Profits: A Case Study of Kodak's Infomercial," *Infomercial and Direct Response Television Sourcebook '98*, a supplement to *Adweek Magazines*, 20–21.
50. Paul Surgi Speck, Michael T. Elliott, and Frank H. Alpert, "The Relationship of Beliefs and Exposure to General Perceptions of Infomercials," *Journal of Current Issues and Research in Advertising* 14 (spring 1997), 51–66; Edwards, "The Art of the Infomercial."
51. Naveen Donthu and David Gilliland, "Observations: The Infomercial Shopper," *Journal of Advertising Research* 36 (March/April 1996), 69–76.
52. Terry Lefton, "You Can't Zap These Ads," *The Industry Standard*, March 26, 2001, 54–55.
53. James A. Karrh, "Brand Placement: A Review," *Journal of Current Issues and Research in Advertising*, 20 (fall 1998), 31–50.
54. Rosellina Ferraro and Rosemary J. Avery, "Brand Appearance on Prime-Time Television," *Journal of Current Issues and Research in Advertising*, 22 (fall 2000), 1–16.
55. Ibid.

56. A sampling of the many articles written about people meters and the surrounding controversy includes Verne Gay, "Vindication?" *Advertising Age*, May 30, 1988, 66; Ira Teinowitz, "People Meters Miss Kids: JWT," *Advertising Age*, July 18, 1988, 35; and Joe Mandese, "Groups Propose TV Rating Changes," *Advertising Age*, September 9, 1991, 33. For a technical analysis, see Roland Soong, "The Statistical Reliability of People Meter Ratings," *Journal of Advertising Research* 28 (February/March 1988), 50–56.

57. Kyle Pope, "TV Networks Decide to Launch a Rival to Nielsen Media Research," *The Wall Street Journal Interactive Edition*, August 3, 1998 (http://interactive.wsj.com).

58. Michelle Wirth Fellman, "A SMART Move," *Marketing News*, September 14, 1998, 1, 7, 43.

59. Joe Mandese, "Nielsen Marketing May Bring Back TV Viewing Diaries," *Advertising Age*, October 19, 1992, 6.

Chapter Thirteen

ALTERNATIVE OFFLINE ADVERTISING MEDIA AND MASS ONLINE ADVERTISING

Chapter Objectives

After studying this chapter, you should be able to:

1. Describe the various alternative advertising media.
2. Realize that these media typically are complements to rather than substitutes for traditional mass media, such as television and magazines.
3. Understand the magnitude and value of yellow-pages advertising.
4. Appreciate the magnitude, nature, and potential for Internet advertising.
5. Understand how Internet advertising differs from advertising in conventional mass-oriented advertising media, as well as how the same fundamentals apply to both general categories of ad media.
6. Recognize the different forms of Internet advertising, such as banner ads, pop-ups, interstitials/superstitials, and sponsorships.
7. Appreciate the importance of measuring Internet advertising effectiveness and the various metrics used for this purpose.
8. Understand the value of targeting Internet ad recipients and the Web analytic procedures used for this purpose.

Opening Vignette: A Tale of Two Tails in Using the Internet

The Internet has become a staple medium in most firms' integrated marketing communication (IMC) programs. Though the dot-com crash of 1999–2000 represents dramatic testimony to the fact that the Internet is anything but magic in its ability to market products, the fact remains that it represents a valuable adjunct to most companies' IMC programs. Following are the tales of two companies and their use/nonuse of the Internet. The first account describes how one company depended almost exclusively on the Internet when introducing a new product, whereas the second report describes how another company virtually eschews the use of the Internet.

The title of this vignette uses the term *tails* in its statistical sense. In a bell-shaped normal distribution, for example, the tails of the distribution represent the two extremes—the areas of the distribution that are most unlike the distribution's average value. The following two tales capture the extremes, or tails, in Internet usage rather than the more typical use of this medium.

We Don't Need TV: The Volvo S60.   Automobile companies when introducing new models have relied heavily on TV for launching new models. Volvo recently broke the mold when introducing the S60 sedan exclusively via its Web site and without any television advertising. This was a calculated decision that was deemed appropriate for Volvo's target consumers, who research reveals are early adopters of new technology. Eschewing TV advertising, the S60 was launched with banner ads placed in prime locations on AOL. Volvo's manager of e-business said nearly 1 million people visited Volvo's Web site (revolvolution.com), and, of these visitors, more than 20 thousand configured customized S60s online while disclosing their names and addresses and requesting quotes from nearby dealers.

Unfortunately, the Web-only launch failed to bring shoppers to dealer showrooms in nearly the same numbers as did conventional launches using TV and print media. Volvo's marketing communications director commented in retrospect that he doubted Volvo would ever again do an Internet-only launch. Some of Volvo's dealers commented that the company did a disservice to the S60 by launching it exclusively online. Dealer sales were hurt by the lack of major television and magazine advertising support behind the S60's launch.

The moral is clear: Banner ads and Web pages have an important role to play in IMC programs for launching new automobiles as well as other products. The Internet cannot perform the entire communication function on its own, however. In retrospect, the marketing folks at Volvo probably made a costly mistake when experimenting with this alternative way of launching a new product. According to a spokesperson for J. D. Power and Associates, a global market research firm, it is extremely difficult to recover from a weak launch after squandering momentum from dealerships and their sales staffs.[a]

The Internet Is Not a Panacea: Drs. Foster & Smith Inc.
Virtually every imaginable product and service was marketed on the Internet during the heyday of the dot-coms in the late 1990s. Among the hundreds of product/service offerings, several pet supply companies gravitated toward the Net, most notably Pets.com (remember the advertisements with the sock dog?). After spending millions of dollars advertising on TV and other media, most of these pet supply companies went belly up in a matter of only a few short years. The Pets.com companies of the world are nowhere to be found. But have you ever heard of Drs. Foster & Smith Inc.? This company, founded by two veterinarians, sells high-quality medical supplies, mostly for dogs. The company has annual sales of $100 million that has been generated primarily through print catalogs and more recently with the addition of a Web site (http://www.drsfostersmith.com).

Whereas the now-vanquished pet supply companies considered the Internet a panacea that would propel them to huge profits, the managers of Drs. Foster & Smith recognize the Internet as merely another mechanism by which their customers can conveniently place orders. The company, unlike its now-fallen competitors, chose not to invest heavily in advertising merely as a means of hyping the operation and permitting taking the company public via an IPO offering. Instead, Drs. Foster & Smith Inc. stuck to its primary catalog business with focus on supplying high-quality products and providing impeccable customer service. Having a Web site provides a valuable promotional and order-taking device to supplement the conventional catalog business, but the company's managers have remained ever mindful that solid business practice (good products, good service, reasonable prices) represents the pathway to long-term success. In the meantime, the instant-riches, new-economy Pets.com companies of the world are nothing now but a memory. Depending exclusively on an attractive Web site and good advertising does not lead to success, as so many entrepreneurs and venture capitalists have sadly learned.[b]

The previous chapter explored five major mass (offline) media: television, radio, magazines, newspapers, and outdoor media. These media dominate ad spending and, though declining in importance, still represent the backbone of advertising efforts by most companies. However, given the disadvantages of these media (e.g., high cost, clutter, inability to target specific customer groups), advertisers continue to seek other media options that will effectively reach targeted customers and achieve communication objectives within budget constraints. This chapter examines two broad groupings of alternatives to the conventional mass media: alternative offline mass media and mass online ad media. Both sets of alternatives to the conventional mass media are themselves directed at masses of customers rather than pinpointed to more specific targets. The folllowing chapter focuses on both offline and online *direct* advertising options.

ALTERNATIVE OFFLINE ADVERTISING MEDIA

Virtually any space is a potential medium for a marketer's advertisement. This section focuses on the following alternative media: product placements in movies, videos for VCRs, virtual signage at sports stadiums and other venues, CD-ROM advertising, and a potpourri of additional alternative advertising media. A concluding section focuses on yellow-pages advertising.

Sources: [a]Karen Lundegaard, "Volvo's Web-Only Vehicle Launch Ends Amid Ford's Unit's Questioning of Tactic," *Wall Street Journal Online*, January 11, 2001 (http://interactive.wsj.com). [b]Lee Gomes, "Just Say No: A Pet-Supply Company Has Refused to Advertise on the Web. And It's Doing Just Fine, Thank You," *Wall Street Journal Online*, April 23, 2001 (http://interactive.wsj.com) Copyright 2001 by DOW JONES & CO INC. Reproduced with permission of DOW JONES & CO INC. in the format Textbook via Copyright Clearance Center.

Product Placements in Movies

Product placements in movies date back to the 1940s, yet the frequency of occurrence is greater now than ever. The typical price for a product placement ranges between $25,000 to $225,000 or even higher if the sponsoring brand demands a highly prominent placement.[1] Does it work? Public evidence of whether such "advertising" is effective is limited though growing. There is evidence that brand awareness and recall increase with more prominent placements.[2] Beyond building brand name awareness and enhancing recall, it can be expected that product placements serve further to enhance brand attitudes in a fashion akin to the *peripheral route* of persuasion discussed in Chapter 5.[3] It would seem that advertisers have little to lose and much to gain when using this form of relatively inexpensive advertising.[4]

Video Advertising

This form of advertising involves capturing key visual and audio information about a brand and distributing the information to business customers or final consumers in the form of videotapes. Because more than 90 percent of American households own at least one VCR, the video advertising medium is capable of reaching most everyone. One company, Technicolor Video Services, promotes itself as being able to deliver videotapes via the mail at a total cost of less than $1.50 per tape. Although there is limited research to verify the effectiveness of video advertising, firms in this industry maintain (albeit not without self-interest) that video advertising is both more effective and less expensive than comparable print advertising in the form of brochures. It is claimed that business customers and consumers are less likely to throw away an unsolicited video than they are a brochure and that videos are more persuasive.[5] Although unverified in a scientific sense, it stands to reason that video advertising is potentially more entertaining than comparable print advertising and thus more effective in gaining attention and influencing memorability of an advertising message.

Virtual Signage

Unbeknownst to television viewers, the brand logos sometimes seen on sports fields, tennis courts, and other venues actually are not there. That is, computer technology is used to "paint" advertisers' logos at these venues. Attendees at a sporting event cannot see the signs because they are not there, but television viewers have no idea that what they are viewing is merely a computer-generated image rather than a "real" sign. Virtual signs have been used in boxing, football, tennis, baseball, and basketball coverage. These signs enable advertisers to use state-of-the-art graphics to attract and hold viewer attention during the actual playing of a sporting event. Companies such as Imagine Video Systems and Princeton Video Image charge about $20,000 for a half-inning of national baseball coverage.[6] Advertisers in the United States have enthusiastically embraced virtual signage as a potentially promising advertising medium, but in Europe regulators such as the European Broadcasting Union have categorically banned virtual advertising from events in which it holds broadcasting rights.[7]

CD-ROM Advertising

Advertisers have not as yet used CD-ROM software as a significant advertising medium, but companies are increasingly using this medium to present consumers and business-to-business (B2B) customers with detailed product information. Consider, for example, the use of CD-ROMs in marketing new automobiles and vacation spots. When used for the introduction of new automobiles, the car company can provide detailed product information as well as show scenes of the product in use and illustrations of the "typical" purchaser of the new car.

Consider also how a tourist destination might effectively use CD-ROM advertising. When a prospective tourist requests information, a disc could be

Macy's Effort to Attract Teen Shoppers with CD-ROMs

Macy's, the famous New York City–based department store chain, is like every other apparel retailer in its desire to appeal to the teenage shopper, especially the heavy-spending and fashion-conscious female segment. Macy's interest in the teenage market is fired by teens' vast apparel expenditures, which annually exceed $50 billion! In the past Macy's attempted to reach teens through catalogs, TV, radio, and other media, but these efforts were expensive and failed to enhance Macy's image as a hip store or to significantly increase sales volume to this demographic.

In an appeal to back-to-school shoppers, Macy's mailed 500,000 CD-ROMs to teenagers in 15 states. Playing the disc was similar to an MTV experience combined with an interactive fashion show—teens wearing the hot fashions of the day shown strolling on a boardwalk or lounging on a beach—accompanied by pop music. Disc recipients clicked on pictures of fashion items and obtained information about clothing brands and prices. A wish-list feature enabled the CD-ROM "shopper" to add items to a list that could be printed and used for future reference when shopping at a Macy's store.

Will this CD-ROM promotion justify the $1 million investment and be more successful than, say, a conventional paper catalog? Needless to say, there is no assurance that a disc recipient will undertake the effort to load the disc on a computer just because it arrived in the mail. To overcome natural inertia and encourage teens to load the disc, Macy's enclosed an "instant $5" gift card. At the time of this writing, it is unknown whether Macy's CD-ROM succeeded in generating business from teenage back-to-school shoppers. However, competitor Nordstrom's had previously tried a similar CD-ROM promotion to teens and concluded that the effort was a flop.

Source: Adapted from Vanessa O'Connell, "Macy's Tries a CD-ROM to Draw Teen Shoppers," *Wall Street Journal Online*, August 2, 2001 (http://interactive.wsj.com/). Copyright 2001 by DOW JONES & CO INC. Reproduced with permission of DOW JONES & CO INC in the format Textbook via Copyright Clearance Center.

mailed out that would contain the sights (video as well as still pictures) and sounds (music, wildlife and outdoor sounds, etc.) of the area and would present this information in a newsworthy and entertaining fashion. CD-ROMs also have considerable potential in the area of B2B marketing. Audio/video CD presentations of new products can be mailed to prospective customers, who are encouraged to call for additional information or a personal sales visit. Even retailers are using CD-ROMs to advertise their products, as evidenced, for example, by the Macy's advertising described in the *IMC Focus*.

Some Additional Alternative Media

Creative advertisers have virtually unlimited sources to convey their messages. For example, some companies sell advertising space in restrooms. An enterprising firm called The Fruit Label Company has used apples and other fruit and vegetable items to carry mini-ads for movies such as *Liar, Liar* and *Jurassic Park*.[8] Levi's advertised 501 jeans on the back covers of *Marvel Comics* and *DC Comics*, an excellent medium because these two comic-book companies combined sell more than 10 million copies of their comic books every month. The comics provided Levi's with an outlet for reaching the notoriously difficult-to-reach segment of boys aged 12 to 17. The *Global Focus* section describes several interesting alternative advertising media that are in use around the world.

This brief discussion of alternative media has been intended merely to demonstrate that the imagination along with good taste are the only limits to the choice of advertising media. Creative advertisers find many ways to reach

Alternative Advertising Media Around the World

Car Advertising in Spain

Americans over the age of 30 might remember advertisers' using Volkswagen Beetles back in the late 1960s and early 1970s as advertising vehicles (in the most literal sense of the term) for their brands. The retro version of the Beetle is again being used for this purpose in different markets around North America and elsewhere. A company called Logocar has done the same thing in the Spanish capital of Madrid. Logocar recruited car owners who are willing to have their vehicles covered in a vinyl skin that bears an advertising message. Figure 13.1 shows an ad done by a similar company in the United States. Car owners who sign up with Logocar receive $230 per month for allowing their cars to serve as roving billboards. Advertisers are charged a basic cost of $29,000 per month for a 25-car advertising fleet.[a]

Sailboat Advertising in Egypt

An advertising axiom says advertise where the customers are. An advertiser in Egypt can find no better place to reach potential consumers than the Nile River, near which millions of Egyptians reside. The ancient sailboats that travel the Nile are called *feluccas*. These boats have huge white sails that represent an ideal location for advertising messages. Coca-Cola signed a two-year contract to have its logo displayed on the sails of boats owned by one of Cairo's popular *felucca* operators. The cost to Coke was around $8,000. Egyptian citizens have criticized the commercialization of the Nile, and some prospective advertisers doubt this form of advertising holds much promise of being effective due to the clutter from too many *feluccas* carrying ad messages. Their concern echoes critics of outdoor advertising in the United States, who refer to billboards as "litter on a stick." In Egypt, the potential counterpart to this criticism is "litter on a sail."[b]

Free Telephone Service in Sweden ... But at a Cost

An enterprising company in Sweden, Gratistelefon Svenska AB, came up with the creative idea of giving away local and long-distance telephone service to residential customers. To receive the free service, customers had to be willing to listen to 10-second advertising spots every three minutes during a phone conversation. In addition, customers provided Gratistelefon with detailed personal information (family size, hobbies, tastes, and demographics) when signing on for free service. Advertisements could then be customized based on a customer's market segmentation profile. The potential beauty of this advertising medium is that advertisers have the caller's undivided attention during the 10 seconds when an ad is transmitted. Gratistelefon has patented its process in dozens of other countries, and now this form of "gratis telephone" is available in countries such as Australia and the Philippines.[c]

Sources: [a]"Driver's Paid to Carry Ads." *Ad Age International,* April 1997, i18. ©1997 by Crain Communications, Inc. Reprinted by permission.

[b]Amy Dockser Marcus, "Latest Ad Trend in Cairo: Company Logos on Sailboats," *Wall Street Journal Online,* July 18, 1997 (http://interactive.wsj.com).

[c]Gautam Naik, "For Free Calls, Users Must Listen to Marketing Pitches," *Wall Street Journal Online,* September 29, 1997. Copyright 1997 by DOW JONES & CO INC. Reproduced with permission of DOW JONES & CO INC in the format Textbook via Copyright Clearance Center.

customers using alternative media that either substitute for or complement more conventional advertising media. For example, Figure 13.2 is an advertisement from the 3M Company that is directed at advertising agencies and their clients. On reading the advertisement you will see that 3M is suggesting that Post-it Notes can be used as a powerful advertising medium that will reach potential customers day after day, note after note. Figure 13.3 is a photo taken at a professional football stadium (the Carolina Panthers stadium in Charlotte, North Carolina), showing a cup holder emblazoned with an advertisement for Coca-Cola.[9]

Logo Cars in the United States

Figure 13.1

3M's Post-it Notes as an Advertising Medium

Figure 13.2

Figure 13.3

A Football Stadium's Cup Holders as an Advertising Medium

Photo by Terence A. Shimp

These examples illustrate rather vividly that virtually any blank surface can be converted into space for an advertisement. In the final analysis, we must be mindful of the advice about integrated marketing communications presented in Chapter 1: Effective communications require that all points of contact with customers speak with a single voice. Multiple media are to little avail if their messages are inconsistent or possibly even in conflict.

Yellow-Pages Advertising

Any discussion of alternative media would be incomplete without coverage of yellow-pages advertising. The yellow pages is an advertising medium that consumers turn to when they are seeking a product or service supplier and are prepared to make a purchase. The yellow pages represent a huge advertising medium with annual revenues exceeding $14 billion.[10] Over 6,000 localized yellow pages directories are distributed annually to hundreds of millions of consumers.[11] There are currently more than 4,000 headings for different product and service listings. Local businesses place the majority of yellow-pages ads, but national advertisers also are frequent users of the yellow pages. For example, U-Haul International, Ford Motor Company, Allstate Insurance, General Motors, State Farm Mutual Auto Insurance, and Sears, Roebuck & Company all invested more than $20 million in yellow-pages advertising in 2000.[12]

Research shows that users of yellow pages tend to be young (aged 25 to 49); are employed in professional, technical, clerical, or sales positions; have relatively high household incomes ($60,000 and up); and are better educated than the population at large.[13] Reasons for using yellow pages include (1) saving time spent shopping around for information, (2) saving energy and money, (3) finding information quickly, and (4) learning about products and services.[14] In a typical week, an estimated 60 percent of all American adults use the yellow pages at least once. Clearly, this is a valuable advertising medium.

The yellow pages differ from other ad media in several respects.[15] First, whereas consumers often avoid exposure to advertisements in other media, customers actively seek out ads in the yellow pages. Second, the advertiser largely determines the quality of ad placement in the yellow pages by the actions it takes. For example, by placing a large ad, the advertiser receives earlier placement than do purchasers of small ads; also, companies that are long-time yellow-pages advertisers receive the best ad placements.

A third distinguishing feature of yellow-pages advertising is that there are clear-cut limits on possible creative executions. In past years yellow-pages advertisements were almost exclusively black print against a yellow background with limited graphic options. Now, however, there is increased use of color and sophisticated graphics. Preliminary research indicates that the use of color and higher-quality graphics have positive effects in attracting attention, signaling product quality, and even increasing the likelihood that the advertised brand will be selected over competitive options.[16]

A fourth distinguishing characteristic of yellow-pages advertising is the method of purchase. Whereas advertising in other mass media such as TV, radio, magazines, and newspapers allows for frequent adjustments in the creative execution and budget allocations, yellow-pages advertisements are purchased for a full year and thus cannot be changed either in purchase amount or creative execution.

Advertising in the yellow pages is not a substitute for but a complement to other advertising media when used in an IMC program. This old advertising medium, with a past as a static form of communication in the pages of telephone directories, is seeing a new life with the creation of online yellow pages.

MASS ONLINE ADVERTISING

Conventional advertising media have served advertisers' needs for many years, but recently there have been increased efforts on the part of advertisers and their agencies to locate new advertising media that are less costly, less cluttered, and potentially more effective than the established media. Some observers have gone so far as to claim that traditional advertising is on its deathbed.[17] The contention is that online advertising via the Internet is superior to traditional media because it provides consumers with virtually full control over the commercial information they choose to receive or avoid. Various commentators have claimed that the Internet as a communications medium is more versatile than other media and superior at targeting customers.[18] Most agree, however, that the Internet is nothing more than a potentially key element of IMC programs and not a replacement for conventional media.[19]

Though dating back only to 1994, the Internet has potential to become an invaluable advertising medium. Nearly 60 percent of the U.S. population, or 165 million people, had Internet access at home as of July 2001. Other countries with high Internet usage include Germany (28 million), the United Kingdom (24 million), Italy (18 million), Taiwan (12 million), and Australia (10 million).[20] As shown in Table 13.1, online advertising spending amounted to only $3.5 billion in 1999, which represented 2 percent of all advertising spending in that year. But it is projected that by 2005 online spending will represent 8 percent of overall advertising and amount to $16.5 billion. In comparing the Internet to other ad media, here is what the CEO of the Internet Advertising Bureau (IAB), the trade association for Internet advertising, had to say:

> *The Internet is a medium that consumers spend more time with than either newspapers or magazines and is the only medium where consumers are one click from a purchase. It has all the capabilities of direct mail at a fraction of the cost, and reaches the most educated and affluent Americans where they live and work.*[21]

Table 13.1

Year	Online Ad Spending (in billions)	Percentage of Overall U.S. Advertising Spending
1999	$3.5	2%
2000	$5.3	3%
2001	$7.3	4%
2002	$9.5	5%
2003	$11.9	6%
2004	$14.3	7%
2005	$16.5	8%

Source: Jupiter Communications in Terry Lefton, "Online Advertising's Anxiety Attack," *The Industry Standard,* December 11, 2000, 102. www.thestandard.com. © 2000 and reprinted with permission from International Data Group.

The Two I's of the Internet: Individualization and Interactivity

Individualization and interactivity (the Internet's two I's) are key features of the Internet and of advertising in that medium.[22] *Individualization* refers to the fact that the Internet user has control over the flow of information. This feature leads, in turn, to the ability to target advertisements and promotions that are relevant to the consumer. *Interactivity,* which is intertwined with individualization, allows for users to select the information they perceive as relevant and for brand managers to build relationships with customers via two-way communication.[23] We now elaborate on the importance of the Internet's interactivity feature.

Traditional advertising media (magazines, TV, etc.) vary in the degree to which they are able to generate mental activity from consumers. Nonetheless, all these media engage the consumer in a relatively passive fashion: The consumer listens to and/or sees information about the advertised brand, but he or she has limited control over the amount or rate of information received. What you see (or hear) is what you get. There is action but no interaction. Whereas action involves a flow in one direction, interaction entails reciprocal behavior. This idea of *reciprocity* generally defines the nature of the new interactive media.

Interactive advertising is defined here as encompassing all media that enable the *user* (who no longer is a "receiver" in the traditional, passive model of communication) to *control the amount or rate of information* that she or he wishes to acquire from a commercial message. The user can choose to devote one second or 15 minutes to a message. He or she is, for all intents and purposes, involved in a "conversation" with the commercial message at a subvocal level. A request for additional information occurs with the push of a button, the touch of a screen, or the click of a mouse. In all instances, the user and source of commercial information are engaged in a give-and-take exchange of information—intercourse rather than mere transmission and reception. By analogy, a North American football quarterback and receivers are somewhat equivalent to the traditional media: The quarterback throws the ball, and the receivers attempt to catch it. Comparatively, in British rugby, players toss the ball back and forth as they advance the ball downfield—each player both passes and receives; their relation is analogous to the give-and-take reciprocity that defines interactive media.

The Internet is, of course, the major interactive medium. This huge worldwide network of interconnected computers permits the electronic transfer of information, including advertising messages. Millions of people around the world have access to the Internet and to the World Wide Web (the Web, or WWW).

Thousands of marketers have turned to the Internet as a prospective medium for promoting their brands and transacting sales. The Internet and its World Wide Web shell provide a medium for the consumer both to interact with the marketer and to transact commercial exchanges. Internet advertisers face a challenge in making their messages acceptable and enjoyable while simultaneously conveying information about brand virtues without being perceived as hucksters.

The Internet Compared with Other Ad Media

In the early days of the Internet (roughly from 1994 to 1999), many businesspeople thought this new medium would be an advertising panacea—a means of reaching millions of customers worldwide with ad messages in a way that would allow for greater accountability than would traditional media. The assumption was that people would be interested in receiving Internet ads and that the advertising would be effective in creating brand awareness, influencing attitudes and purchase intentions, and driving sales. The notion that the Internet was somehow different from conventional ad media (TV, magazines, etc.) was as simplistic as the corresponding idea of a "new economy" that assumed that dot-com companies played under rules different from the conventional microeconomic principles that for generations have explained the requirements for success in the "old economy."

As covered in detail in the previous chapter, each of the major advertising media has its unique set of advantages and disadvantages. Each ad medium is capable of achieving particular advertising objectives (creating brand awareness, influencing a brand's image, etc.) at a cost to the advertiser. In planning for and selecting a single advertising medium or, more likely, a portfolio of integrated media, the advertiser's objective is to achieve against the target market necessary objectives for the brand as inexpensively as possible. (Recall our mantra presented initially in Chapter 2 and then again in Chapter 8: All marketing communications should be (1) clearly *positioned*, (2) directed to a particular *target market*, (3) created to achieve a *specific objective*, and (4) undertaken to accomplish the objective *within budget constraint*.)

From the discussion in the previous chapter, it should be obvious that no advertising medium is perfect for all purposes. The Internet is no exception, contrary to the early hype. In fact, it can be argued that the Internet's interactivity feature may represent a disadvantage rather than an advantage. According to this argument, the Internet user is in a "leaning forward" mind-set compared with, say, the TV viewer who is "leaning back." In other words, whereas the TV viewer is casually watching TV programs and advertisements in a relaxed mood (leaning back, so to speak), the Internet user is goal driven and on a mission to obtain information (leaning forward). In this mind-set banner ads and pop-ups simply represent an interruption, an obstacle to the users primary mission for connecting to the Internet.[24] Advertisements seen while in a leaning-forward mission mind-set are actively avoided and thus can have little possible effect, beyond perhaps mere brand identification. Of course, Internet advertising comes in several forms and generalizations such as these are not necessarily appropriate to all. We direct our attention now to the various forms of Internet ads and examine the role each performs and the accompanying advantages and disadvantages.

Internet Advertising Formats

Internet advertisers use several formats: Web sites, banner ads, pop-ups, interstitials/superstitials, and site sponsorships.[25] An additional major form of Internet advertising is the widespread use of e-mail, or what in an advertising context is referred to as opt-in, or permission, e-mailing. Discussion of this particular practice will be delayed until the following chapter, which focuses on direct advertising. The remaining practices are more mass oriented and thus are appropriately covered in the present chapter.

In preparation for the discussion of each online ad format, it is useful to make a sobering comment about how much is known about online advertising. A *Wall Street Journal* editor perhaps said it best:

> *Here's what we know so far [as of 2001] when it comes to online advertising: Most banner ads aren't all that effective. Here's what we don't know: just about everything else. . . . Yes, we don't know an awful lot. But remember this: We know more than we did a couple of years ago — when we thought we knew everything.*[26]

The following presentation provides what is hoped to be a current, accurate treatment of online advertising formats. But, as the previous quote so accurately described, we really don't know a lot. Any sweeping and definitive claims would simply be misleading, because Internet advertising is so new, with a history dating back less than one decade. Imagine, by comparison, the futility in the mid-1950s of providing a definitive treatment about the nature and effectiveness of TV advertising. Only with time have we come to know how TV advertising performs and what its strengths and limitations are. Similarly, more time is needed before conclusive statements are possible about online advertising.

Web Sites.   Thousands of corporations have Web sites, and many companies have brand-specific Web sites that often, though not always, are linked to their companies' homepages. Only recently, however, has the company/brand Web site been considered a specific form of online advertising.[27] Surely the Web site is a qualitative different form of advertising from, say, a banner or pop-up ad. The Web site for a brand is an invaluable advertising medium for conveying much more information about the brand, its character, and its promotional offerings than can be provided by any of the online advertising formats described later in this chapter. Perhaps the major difference between Web sites and these alternative online ad formats is that users seek out Web sites in a goal-oriented fashion (e.g., to learn more about a company or brand, to play a game, to register for a contest), whereas the other online formats are "stumbled upon accidentally."[28]

The advertising value of a Web site is well documented in a recent study that found that Web site visits for newly released movies play a prominent role in predicting box office performance. Specifically, the greater the number of unique (not repeat) visits to a new movie's Web site, the more people who actually see the movie in a cinema.[29]

A small-town retailer was fond of saying that "merchandise well displayed is half sold," implying, of course, that attractively displayed items capture the shopper's attention and invite purchase.[30] The same advice applies to Web site construction: Attractive and user-friendly sites invite usage and revisits. Research on the "look" of Web pages is in its infancy, but there is some tentative evidence that Web pages designed with relatively simple backgrounds (i.e., without a lot of color and animation) might be better liked than more complex pages. In a study using a state lottery as the focal Web site, it was learned that the most complex background produced the least favorable attitudes toward the site and toward the advertised service and the weakest purchase intentions.[31] It would be foolhardy to generalize this finding to other products, but it does suggest that too many bells and whistles in a Web site may serve to distract attention away from the key message arguments on which involved consumers form their attitudes toward advertised products and services. Because consumers visit Web sites with the objective of obtaining useful information, it follows that Web sites are of most value when they fulfill consumers' goal-seeking needs by providing useful information rather than attempting to dazzle with excessive graphic cleverness. The architect's advice that "form follows function" certainly applies to the Web site as a form of online advertising.

Banner Ads.   Banner ads are the most common form of Internet advertising. They are the staple of Internet advertising and play a role equivalent to that of 30-second commercials on television.[32] These are typically small, static ads placed in frequently visited Web sites. The cost range for banner ads is from $5 to $50 per 1,000 ad impressions.[33] Higher-costing ads are more targeted and appear in more attractive Web sites. Banner ads on the Internet are ubiquitous. Ads, ads, and more ads. But who pays attention?

Jupiter Media Metrix, a firm that tracks the Internet advertising industry, estimates that the average Internet user was exposed to over 700 banner ads per day in 2002 and that this will increase to 950 banner ads daily by 2005. The vast majority of these ads never received user attention, however. According to Nielsen/NetRatings, the average click-through rate in 2001 was a paltry 0.49 percent, and some sources even claim that the average rate is only around 0.2 percent.[34] In other words, online users pay attention and solicit information from only a small percentage of all the Internet banner ads to which they are exposed. (Remember: Exposure is necessary for but not equivalent to attention. Exposure merely indicates that the consumer has a chance to see an advertisement.)

There is evidence that click-through rates are a function of brand familiarity, with brands that consumers know best receiving a substantially higher click-through rate than unfamiliar brands.[35] Importantly, but not particularly surprisingly, this same research revealed that click-through rates decrease with multiple exposures to banner ads for familiar brands, whereas the rates increase with more exposures to ads for unfamiliar brands. New and relatively unknown brands thus need to produce a banner-ad media schedule that allows for multiple exposures. Established brands, on the other hand, may not experience increased click-through rates with multiple exposures. This, however, does not necessarily imply that established brands do not benefit from banner advertising. On the contrary, such brands may achieve increasing levels of brand awareness—culminating in top-of-mind awareness, or TOMA, even though consumers choose not to click through to the brand's Web site. (The student may recall the discussion of brand awareness back in Chapter 2, where a brand awareness pyramid was shown in Figure 2.9. This pyramid portrayed a progression from brand unawareness, to brand recognition, to brand recall, and, ideally, ultimately to TOMA.) Banner advertising, along with other communication elements in an IMC program, can serve to facilitate increasing levels of brand awareness and thus enhance brand equity.

Because click-through rates are trivially small, online advertisers have turned to new technology and larger ad sizes to grab the online surfer's attention. Many of these changes and the standardization of banner sizes have been facilitated by the efforts of the Internet Advertising Bureau (IAB), a trade association that is a leader in the Internet advertising industry. In early 2001 the IAB endorsed seven new Internet ad formats, labeled Internet marketing units (IMUs).[36] These seven new IMUs compare with the earlier full banner, the size of which was 468 x 60 pixels (28,080 square pixels).

Table 13.2 contrasts the new IMUs against this original full banner. This table makes it clear that the new (as of 2001) IMUs are generally considerably

Types and Sizes of Internet Marketing Units (IMUs)   Table 13.2

Type and Size of IMU (pixel size)	Square Pixels	Percentage Change Compared with 468 x 60 Full Banner
Skyscraper (120 x 600)	72,000	156%
Wide Skyscraper (160 x 600)	96,000	242%
Rectangle (180 x 150)	27,000	– 4%
Medium Rectangle (300 x 250)	75,000	167%
Large Rectangle (336 x 280)	94,080	235%
Vertical Rectangle (240 x 400)	96,000	242%
Square Pop-up (250 x 250)	62,500	123%

larger than the original full banner ad. It is likely that the larger ad sizes increase attention and thus click-through rates. A study conducted by a research firm for the IAB determined that the skyscraper and large rectangle IMUs were more than three to six times as effective in increasing brand awareness and favorable message associations as was the 468 x 60 standard banner IMU.[37]

In addition to increasing the size and differentiating the shapes of banner ads, Internet advertisers, like the savvy conventional advertisers who preceded them, have turned increasingly to *customer targeting* as a means of increasing click-through rates and achieving their objectives for brand equity enhancement.[38] With improved tracking technology, it has become possible to determine more about Internet surfers' consumer behavior and then to tailor the specific banner ads that surfers are exposed to. This is accomplished with electronic files (called cookies) that track users' online behavior. The following quote illustrates how cookies enable Internet advertisers to direct ads that are compatible with Internet users' product usage interests:

> If a golfer clicks on an ad for a golf magazine, that click is recorded. The next time our golf-loving Web surfer goes online, an ad server detects him or her, finds a golf banner and serves it up. By isolating that user, Internet ad companies can sell targeted golf-related advertising. The user doesn't have to go back to the same site to get the targeted ad, either. The ad-server companies [e.g., DoubleClick, 24/7 Media, Engage Technologies] sign up hundreds of client Web sites onto their ad networks, which enables the ad servers to follow users from Web site to Web site.[39]

DoubleClick, perhaps the most prominent Internet ad server company, claims it has 100 million user profiles that advertisers can use for targeting their ads.[40] These profiles are created when users register for something online or make online purchases. Often a profile contains detailed demographic information, including the profiled user's age, gender, and income. Needless to say, these user profiles represent a marvelous advertising tool, and, at the same time, create the potential for invasion of users' privacy.[41] In an Internet advertising variation on the well-known principle of physics that for every action there is an equally strong and opposing reaction, many consumers have begun to avoid Web ads by downloading ad-blocking software that is marketed under names such as AdKiller, AdSubtract, and WebWasher. Of course, nothing in life comes for free. Consumers receive free television programming because advertisers subsidize this freedom. Likewise, if ad-killing software becomes widely used, Internet users may have to pay for the Web content that we presently enjoy at no cost.[42]

Pop-Up Ads, Interstitials, and Superstitials.

In view of the low click-through rates for banner ads, Internet advertisers have turned increasingly to using aggressive forms of Web ads that virtually demand the user's attention. These obtrusive ads—pop-ups, interstitials, and superstitials—might even be compared to the low-budget ads on cable TV with obnoxious car salesmen and other fast-talking hucksters. Let us briefly distinguish these ad formats. **Pop-ups** are ads that appear in a separate window that materializes on the screen seemingly out of nowhere while a selected Web page is loading. **Interstitials**—based on the word *interstitial*, which describes the space that intervenes between things—are, by comparison, ads that appear between (rather than within, as is the case with pop-ups) two content Web pages.[43] The difference between pop-ups and interstitials is more than trite, as described compellingly in this quote:

> First, unlike pop-ups, interstitials do not interrupt the user's interactive experience because they tend to run while the user waits for a page to download. Users, however, have less control over interstitials because there is no "exit" option to stop or delete an interstitial, which is common among pop-ups. In other words, with interstitials, users have to wait until the entire ad has run.[44]

In short, both pop-up ads and interstitials are obtrusive, but in different ways. **Superstitials**, an even newer entry to Internet advertising intrusion, are short, animated ads that play over or on top of a Web page.[45]

Pop-up ads, interstitials, and superstitials, though often a source of irritation, are effective attention-getters. Internet advertisers, like advertisers in all other media, have to fight through the clutter to find ways to attract and hold the online user's attention. Bigger ads, ads popping up, and ads that offer sound and visuals are just some of the ways that have been devised to accomplish these objectives. All these ad formats are more eye-catching and memorable than are standard (i.e., static) banner ads. Whereas banner ads typically cost in the $5 to $15 range per 1,000 impressions, superstitials are more likely to cost between $40 and $50 per 1,000 ad impressions.[46] However, the click-through rates for superstitials are substantially higher than banners, perhaps between 3 percent and 7 percent for superstitials compared with less than 0.4 percent for banners.[47] However, the substantially higher click-through rate for superstitials is likely to abate as the novelty of this technology wears off.

Sponsorships. Another form of Internet advertising is *sponsorship advertising*, whereby an advertiser is a partial or exclusive sponsor of a Web site and benefits from the many visitations to that site. For example, IBM paid $1 million to be sole sponsor of the National Football League's Superbowl.com Web site. The site generated more than 8 million hits.[48] As another example, pharmaceutical companies are increasingly sponsoring medical Web sites such as WebMD.com and DrKoop.com. The pharmaceutical companies supply these sites with information content about various ailments and in return receive prominent links to their products on the site—and, most importantly, appear to the Internet user as unbiased purveyors of information rather than mere advertisers.[49] In general, the cost of sponsorships range from $30 to $75 per 1,000 viewers, depending on the exclusivity of the sponsorship, with more exclusive sponsorships costing more.[50]

Measuring Internet Ad Effectiveness

A major concern for Internet advertisers is *measuring* the effectiveness of their advertising placements. This is, of course, precisely the same concern that brand managers have when advertising in conventional media, as was mentioned in the previous chapter when discussing audience measurement in the context of each of the major conventional media. You will recall, for example, the services available for magazine audience measurement (Mediamark Research and Simmons Market Research Bureau), radio audience measurement (Arbitron's RADAR service), and television audience measurement (Nielsen's People Meters). In every instance, these audience measurement services have been developed to determine as precisely as possible the numbers of readers/listeners/viewers of particular advertising vehicles and to identify their demographic characteristics. With the conventional media as a benchmark, the student can easily appreciate that Internet advertisers have precisely the same measurement concerns—questions such as, How many people clicked through a particular Web ad? What are the demographic characteristics of these people? How many visited a particular Web site? What actions were taken following click-throughs or site visits.

The Tools of Internet Audience Measurement. Three primary methods of Internet audience measurement are in use: (1) analysis of server log files, (2) surveys of sample users using recall measurement, and (3) electronic measurement of a sample of Internet users.[51] Each of these measurement methods is briefly discussed.

Log file analysis involves examining server log files. When a file is requested from a particular Web site, its computer server records the request in a so-called log file along with any subsequent actions taken by the Web user. Hence, the primary advantage of log file analysis is that it effectively provides a census of all user activity at a particular Web site. The downside of this analysis, however, is that it tracks machines and provides no information about the people who request particular files. Another drawback from this type of analysis is the difficulty of distinguishing individual users from the computer programs, called robots and spiders, that companies create to automatically surf the Internet and covertly gather competitive information.

The second tool, *surveys of sample users using recall measures*, involves the use of survey methods (telephone interviews, mail questionnaires, or in-person interviews) to obtain information about consumers' Web site use along with their demographic and perhaps psychographic characteristics. The objective is, of course, to relate Web site use as recalled from memory by interviewees to their demographic/psychographic characteristics. The problems with this method include the fact that (1) memories are fallible, (2) people overstate their use of popular Web sites and understate their use of less popular sites, and (3) people often provide responses that involve putting themselves in a positive light rather than necessarily revealing their true Internet use (socially desirable responding). These limitations are not unique to Internet usage measurement. You will recall from the previous chapter that radio and magazine audience measurements also use survey techniques and thus suffer from the same deficiencies.

Electronic measurement of a sample of users is possibly the most valuable tool for assessing Internet usage activity. Software meters are installed in the computers of a large sample of Internet users, and this software records electronically precisely how each sampled user actually uses the Internet. Statistical procedures are used to draw inferences from the electronically metered sample to the population of Internet users. Companies such as Media Metrix and Nielsen Media Research are among the best-known researchers using electronic measurement. Nielsen, for example, attaches software tracking meters to the computers of a panel of 30,000 randomly selected Internet users.[52] These meters allow Nielsen to record everything the sampled users do online—what sites are visited, how long they stay at each site, which ad banners they click on, and so on. This information is sent instantly to a central database, which enables Nielsen to prepare periodic reports on Internet traffic and usage. Because each panel member provides Nielsen with information about gender, educational level, income, household size, geographic location, and other pertinent data, it subsequently is possible for Nielsen to link this demographic information with use of particular Web sites. The characteristics of users of particular Web sites thus are acquired from this electronic metering, and brand managers can then target ads to Web sites that best match the demographic characteristics of the brand's target market.

The Metrics of Internet Advertising.

The word *metric* refers, in general, to meters and measures. A metric is, in other words, a unit of measurement. As applied in the present context, the issue is one of what particular indicators of Internet advertising usage are most appropriate for assessing the effectiveness of banner ads and other forms of Internet advertising. What usage metrics, in other words, provide useful information about Internet advertising? Click-through rates, cost per thousand impressions (CPM), and cost per actions (CPA) are the metrics most widely used.

Click-through rates, as alluded to several times already, simply represent the percentage of people who are exposed to, say, a banner ad that actually clicked their mouse on. The click-through percentage has continued to decline, and many in the advertising community (brand managers, Internet advertising providers, and ad agencies) have become disenchanted with this metric. It is claimed that banner ads can have positive effect on brand awareness even if Internet users do not click through to learn more about the advertised brand. This argument is not without merit, yet it begs the question of what alternative metric can be used to assess ad effectiveness.

Cost per thousand impressions (CPM) is a simple alternative to click-through rates that assesses how much (on a per-thousand-impressions basis) it costs to place an ad on a particular Web site. The only information revealed by the CPM metric is what it costs (again, on a per-thousand-impressions basis) to have an ad come into potential contact with the eyeballs of Internet users. This measure captures Internet users' "opportunity to see" an ad but provides no information about the actual effect of an advertisement.

Use of the CPM metric is beginning to give way to the cost-per-action, or CPA, metric. The *action* in CPA refers to determining the number of users who actually click on a banner ad, visit a brand's Web site, register their names on the brand's site, or actually purchase (electronically) the advertised brand.[53] Many advertisers prefer to pay for Internet advertising on a CPA rather than a CPM basis. The terms of purchasing Internet advertising on a CPA basis vary greatly, with higher prices paid for actions involving actual purchases or actions closer to purchase (such as registering for free samples of a brand) compared with merely clicking on a banner ad.

In the final analysis it should be apparent that there is no such thing as perfect measurability—for the Internet or for that matter any other advertising medium. The difficulty of determining how effective is an ad medium is illustrated, in the extreme, by the following set of questions: "Consider the Nike logo on Tiger Woods's baseball cap: Does it make you more likely to buy a pair of the company's shoes? If so, would you admit it to a surveyor? Would you admit it to yourself? Would you even know it?"[54]

Profiling and Targeting Internet Ad Recipients

The Internet's real potential as an advertising medium will be realized when brand managers can turn to particular Web sites and know with some degree of certainty who the users of these sites are and when they are willing to look at advertisements. Armed with this information, brand managers and their ad agencies will be in a position to systematically plan Internet advertising rather than "take a shot in the dark," which has, to this point, been the less-than-acceptable default option. Changes are occurring quickly, however, as sophisticated Web analytics companies are providing the methods and data to profile consumers and their Internet usage preferences.[55] The term *profiling* is an apt descriptor for this activity, though unfortunately the term might be associated with the unsavory practice of racial profiling. This concern aside, let's briefly examine the tools and practice of profiling Internet customers.

Companies involved in the Web analytics business construct detailed portraits of consumers by collecting and analyzing huge quantities of information from log files about what people do online.[56] Advertisers use these profiles to identify the best Web sites for their brands, track individual consumers' habits and preferences, target ads to consumers most likely to buy the advertiser's brand, and thus, ultimately, achieve a better return on their advertising investments.[57] It is estimated that the market for Web analytics services will grow from a modest $425 million in 2000 to $4 billion by 2004.[58]

Targeting based on consumers' psychographic profiles or, especially, on past purchase behavior are much more valued than profiles based exclusively on demographic data.[59] Some of the major players in the Web analytics business include companies such as IBM Global Services, DoubleClick, Epiphany, Accrue Software, and Primary Knowledge. Because the ability to accurately target customers is a prime condition for successful advertising, it would seem that the services of these companies will be highly demanded and that their offerings will substantially improve the effectiveness and accountability of Internet advertising.

SUMMARY

This chapter has combined the coverage of two quite disparate forms of advertising: offline mass advertising through alternatives to the conventional mass media, and online mass advertising. Alternative mass-oriented advertising media covered in this chapter included product placements in movies, videotape advertising, virtual signage in sports stadiums, CD-ROM advertising, and a potpourri of other alternative forms of advertising (e.g., automobiles as carriers of ads). A concluding section devoted coverage to the significant yellow-pages advertising medium.

The second major section was devoted to online advertising. Interactive advertising on the Internet will not supplant traditional advertising media, but advertisers and their agencies now have a revolutionary new medium for reaching present users of their brands and prospective customers. Just as advertising was altered forever with the introduction of television in the late 1940s, another seismic shift has occurred with the opportunity to advertise on the Net. In the spirit of the IMC mind-set that pervades this text, Internet advertising should provide brand marketers with another medium that complements more traditional media. The Internet enables the brand marketer to extend and deepen relationships with consumers that have been initially established via traditional media.

Find more resources to help you study at http://shimp.swcollege.com!

DISCUSSION QUESTIONS

1. Early in the chapter it was claimed that virtually any space is a potential medium for a marketer's advertisement. Please identify several novel forms of advertising media that go beyond the alternative mass-oriented media described in this chapter. Describe the target for each of these novel media, and offer an explanation as to why in your opinion each novel medium is effective or ineffective.

2. Can you recall any prominent brand placements in movies you have seen lately? What were these placements? Were the products "positioned" in positive or negative contexts? How successful, in your opinion, were these placements?

3. Have you ever viewed a videotape advertisement? If so, what are your views on why the tape was or was not effective?

4. Have you ever viewed a CD-ROM advertisement? If so, what are your views on why the disc was or was not effective?

5. What are your views on the Macy's CD-ROM advertising effort as described in the *IMC Focus*? Using the CPM framework covered in Chapter 4 (i.e., exposure, selective attention, comprehension, agreement, etc.), conceptualize why CD-ROM advertising of the Macy's variety may be problematic.

6. How responsive do you think most North American consumers would be to a gratis telephone service such as the one described in the *Global Focus*?

7. Describe your use, if any, of yellow-pages advertising in recent months.

8. Assume you are the proprietor of a sports bar–type of restaurant in a community of, say, 250,000 people. Can you offer any good reasons for *not* advertising your restaurant in the yellow pages?

9. As noted in the text, some observers have gone so far as to claim that traditional advertising is on its deathbed and will eventually be supplanted by Internet advertising. What are your views on this?

10. Provide an interpretation of the meaning and importance of the Internet's Two I's, individualization and interactivity, for advertisers. Use your own words and ideas rather than merely feeding back what is described in the text.

11. The text described the Internet user as being in a "leaning forward" mindset compared with, say, the TV viewer who is "leaning back." Explain what this means and why the distinction is advantageous or problematic for Internet advertisers.

12. Describe your typical response behavior to Internet ads. That is, do you often click on banner ads? What's your reaction to pop-ups and interstitials/superstitials?

13. Can banner ads be effective if less than 0.5 percent of all people click through these ads? Use the CPM model from Chapter 4 (as in question 5) to frame your response.

14. Do you believe that Internet companies' use of cookies invades your privacy? Would you favor legislation that prevents the use of this technology? If such a law were passed, what would be the downside from the consumer's perspective?

15. Have you personally downloaded ad-blocking software onto your computer? What are the implications of this practice of millions of consumers had ad-blocking software loaded on their PCs and other Internet appliances?

16. The following set of questions were quoted in the chapter in reference to the Nike logo on Tiger Woods's baseball cap: Does it make you more likely to buy a pair of the company's shoes? If so, would you admit it to a surveyor? Would you admit it to yourself? Would you even know it? What implications do these questions (and their answers) hold for measuring Internet advertising effectiveness?

17. Does Web analytics technology and its ability to better profile Internet users represent a positive or a negative for consumers?

18. Identify three homepages on the Web that you consider particularly effective. What, in your opinion, contributes to their effectiveness?

19. Based on your reading in Chapter 12, would you say that banner advertising is more similar to outdoor or magazine advertising? Support your

answer with specific comparisons of the advertising implications associated with each medium.

20. Describe how the following aspects of Web sites could allow for "premium" banner ad pricing: (a) Web site sponsorship; (b) special Web "events" such as online concerts, interviews, or broadcasts; and (c) time of day.

ENDNOTES

1. Pola B. Gupta and Kenneth R. Lord, "Product Placement in Movies: The Effect of Prominence and Mode on Audience Recall," *Journal of Current Issues and Research in Advertising* 20 (spring 1998), 47–60.

2. Ibid. See also, Emma Johnstone and Christopher A. Dodd, "Placements As Mediators of Brand Salience within a UK Cinema Audience," *Journal of Marketing Communications* 6 (September 2000), 141–158; Alain d'Astous and Francis Chartier, "A Study of Factors Affecting Consumer Evaluations and Memory of Product Placements in Movies," *Journal of Current Issues and Research in Advertising* 22 (fall 2000), 31–40.

3. Pola B. Gupta, Siva K. Balasubramanian, and Michael L. Klassen, "Viewers' Evaluations of Product Placements in Movies: Public Policy Issues and Managerial Implications," *Journal of Current Issues and Research in Advertising* 22 (fall 2000), 41–52.

4. For additional reading on this topic, *see Proceedings of the 1994 Conference of the American Academy of Advertising*, ed. Karen Whitehall King (Athens, Ga.: The American Academy of Advertising, 1994): Barry Sapolsky and Lance Kinney, "You Oughta Be in Pictures: Product Placements in the Top-Grossing Films of 1991," 89; James A. Karrh, "Effects of Brand Placements in Motion Pictures," 90–96; and Stacy Vollmers and Richard Mizerski, "A Review and Investigation into the Effectiveness of Product Placements in Films, 97–102.

5. Based on promotional literature received from Technicolor Video Services. Interested readers can contact this firm at (800) 732-4555.

6. Terry Lefton, "The New Signage," *Brandweek*, January 27, 1997, 35; William Porter, "The Virtual Ad: On TV You See It, But at Baseball Games You Don't," *The Wall Street Journal Interactive Edition*, July 30, 1998.

7. Kimberley A. Strassel, "Virtual Ads Vie for Field Position, But Regulators Move to Stop Them," *The Wall Street Journal Interactive Edition*, October 17, 1997.

8. Lisa Bannon, "Jim Carrey Is Coming Soon to a Fruit Bin Near You," *The Wall Street Journal Interactive Edition*, August 21, 1997.

9. Appreciation is extended to my great friend, John Kuhayda, for loaning his leg and foot for this photograph. (Thanks also to Judy and Patty for being there with us!)

10. "U.S. Ad Expenditures by Type of Media, 1997–2001," *Marketing News*, July 2, 2001, 11.

11. Joel J. Davis, *Understanding Yellow Pages* (Troy, Mich.: Yellow Pages Publishers Association, 1995).

12. "Top 10 Advertisers in 13 Measured Media," *Advertising Age*, September 24, 2001, s16.

13. Davis, *Understanding Yellow Pages*, 18.

14. Ibid., 19.

15. Avery M. Abernethy and David N. Laband, "The Customer Pulling Power of Different Sized Yellow Page Ads," Auburn University working paper, April 2001.

16. For details see Karen V. Fernandez and Dennis L. Rosen, "The Effectiveness of Information and Color in Yellow Page Advertising," *Journal of Advertising* 29 (summer 2000), 61–73; Gerald L. Lohse and Dennis L. Rosen, "Signaling Quality and Credibility in Yellow Pages Advertising: The Influence of Color and Graphics on Choice, *Journal of Advertising* 30 (summer 2001), 73–85.

17. Roland T. Rust and Richard W. Oliver, "Notes and Comments: The Death of Advertising," *Journal of Advertising* 23 (December 1994), 71–77. See also Roland T. Rust and Sajeev Varki, "Rising from the Ashes of Advertising," *Journal of Business Research* 37 (November 1996), 173–181.

18. For example, Rafi A. Mohammed, Robert J. Fisher, Bernard J. Jaworski, and Aileen M. Cahill, *Internet Marketing: Building Advantage in a Networked Economy* (New York: McGraw-Hill, 2002), 370.

19. Ibid., 375.

20. http://www.nielsen-netratings.com.

21. Robin Webster, "IAB Aim Is to Lower Interactive Ad Hurdles," *Advertising Age*, March 19, 2001, 28.

22. Mohammed, et al., *Internet Marketing: Building Advantage in a Networked Economy*, 371.

23. Ibid.

24. The ideas in this paragraph are adapted from Terry Lefton, "The Great Flameout," *The Industry Standard*, March 19, 2001, 75–78.

25. Based on Shelly Rodgers and Esther Thorson, "The Interactive Advertising Model: How Users Perceive and Process

Online Ads," *Journal of Interactive Advertising* 1 (fall 2000; http://jiad.org/vol1/no1/Rodgers/index.html).

26. Lawrence Rout, "Editor's Note to E-Commerce Special Report," *Wall Street Journal Interactive Edition*, April 23, 2001 (http://interactive.wsj.com).

27. For further discussion, see Rodgers and Thorson, "The Interactive Advertising Model: How Users Perceive and Process Online Ads."

28. Ibid.

29. Fred Zufryden, "New Film Website Promotion and Box-Office Performance," *Journal of Advertising Research* 40 (January/April 2000), 55–64.

30. I learned this advice from my dear late father, who worked in retailing for many years. I'm not sure whether this was his own wisdom or whether it can be attributed to another source.

31. Julie S. Stevenson, Gordon C. Bruner II, and Anand Kumar, "Webpage Background and Viewer Attitudes," *Journal of Advertising Research* 40 (January/April 2000), 29–34. See also Gordon C. Bruner II, and Anand Kumar, "Web Commercials and Advertising Hierarchy-of-Effects," *Journal of Advertising Research* 40 (January/April 2000), 35–42. The latter article involves research using a non-student sample and provides interesting refinement concerning the role of Web page complexity.

32. Jennifer Rewick, "Choices, Choices: A Look At the Pros and Cons of Various Types of Web Advertising," *Wall Street Journal Interactive Edition*, April 23, 2001 (http://interactive.wsj.com).

33. Ibid.

34. Carolyn Goldhush, "A Banner Move," *Agency*, summer 2001, 21–22.

35. Micael Dahlen, "Banner Advertisements through a New Lens," *Journal of Advertising Research* 41 (July/August 2001), 23–30.

36. Dana Blankenhorn, "Bigger, Richer Ads Go Online," *Advertising Age*, June 18, 2001, T10; Sarah J. Heim, "IAB Establishes New Guidelines for Banners," *Brandweek*, February 26, 2001, 48. Go to the IAB's Web site to see illustrations of the various IMUs (http://www.iab.net).

37. "Interactive Advertising Bureau/Dynamic Logic Ad Unit Effectiveness Study," March/June 2001. (http://www.iab.net).

38. For an interesting application, see Lee Sherman and John Deighton, "Banner Advertising: Measuring Effectiveness and Optimizing Placement," *Journal of Interactive Marketing* 15 (spring 2001), 60–64.

39. Alex Frangos, "How It Works: The Technology Behind Web Ads," *Wall Street Journal Interactive Edition*, April 23, 2001 (http://interactive.wsj.com).

40. Ibid.

41. For reading on privacy and ethical issues in interactive marketing, see the special issue of *Journal of Public Policy & Marketing* 19 (spring 2000), 1–73.

42. Terry Lefton, "Disappearing Act," *The Industry Standard*, April 23, 2001, 49.

43. Dan Steinbock, *The Birth of Internet Marketing Communications* (Westport, Conn.: Quorum Books, 2000), 204.

44. Rodgers and Thorson, "The Interactive Advertising Model: How Users Perceive and Process Online Ads."

45. Frank Abate and Fred Shapiro, "With Interstitials, Superstitials, Ads Pop Up All Over the Place," *Wall Street Journal Interactive Edition*, November 6, 2001 (http://interactive.wsj.com).

46. Rewick, "Choices, Choices: A Look at the Pros and Cons of Various Types of Web Advertising."

47. Patricia Riedman, "Poor Rich Media," *Advertising Age*, February 5, 2001, 26.

48. Terry Lefton, "IBM's $1M Super Buy Is Web-Topper; Phoenix Close on $9M NCAA Pact," *Brandweek*, November 24, 1997, 8.

49. Alex Frangos, "Prescription for Change: Drug Companies Are Slowly Starting to Warm Up to the Web as a Place to Advertise," *Wall Street Journal Interactive Edition*, April 23, 2001 (http://interactive.wsj.com).

50. Rewick, "Choices, Choices: A Look At the Pros and Cons of Various Types of Web Advertising."

51. Steve Coffey, "Internet Audience Measurement: A Practitioner's View," *Journal of Interactive Advertising* 1 (spring 2001; http://jiad.org/vol1/no2/coffey/index.html). Much of the following discussion is based on this article.

52. This discussion is based on Chris Warren, "Tools of the Trade," *Critical Mass*, fall 1999, 22–27.

53. Nick Wingfield, "Calling the Shots: Web Advertisers Are in the Driver's Seat These Days. Just Ask Half.com," *Wall Street Journal Interactive Edition*, April 23, 2001 (http://interactive.wsj.com).

54. Rob Walker, "The Holy Grail of Internet Advertising, the Ability to Measure Who Is Clicking on the Message, Is Under Assault," *The New York Times*, August 27, 2001, C4.

55. Tim Devaney, "Advertising: Marketers Try Yet Again to Get Personal," *Red Herring*, March 20, 2001, 64.

56. Ibid.

57. Jennifer Lewis, "Customers in the Crosshairs: Web Analytics Promises to Get Advertisers Closer to Consumers," *Red Herring*, March 20, 2001, 66–68.

58. Devaney, "Advertising: Marketers Try Yet Again to Get Personal"; Lewis, "Customers in the Crosshairs," 66.

59. Lewis, ibid.

Chapter Fourteen

OFFLINE AND ONLINE DIRECT ADVERTISING

Chapter Objectives

After studying this chapter, you should be able to:

1. Explain direct advertising and the reasons underlying its growth.
2. Describe the characteristics of direct-response advertising.
3. Discuss the distinctive features of p-mail advertising.
4. Explain the role of databases and data mining.
5. Perform lifetime value analyses of database entries.
6. Discuss the distinctive features and advantages of opt-in e-mail advertising.
7. Evaluate the role and future prospects of wireless advertising.

Opening Vignette: Effective E-Mail Advertising for SmarterKids.com

SmarterKids.com is a company that has survived the great dot-com collapse that destroyed so many other companies. SmarterKids.com has endured because it offers a product line—educational toys, books, and games—that meets the needs of parents interested in their children's educational achievements. The company also has become an effective e-mail advertiser. This success has been accomplished by conveying appealing advertising messages to finely targeted lists of parents who are Internet users.

How does a company like SmarterKids.com acquire a list of prospective customers? As described later in the chapter, companies sometimes put together their own mailing lists from consumers who have previously purchased their products or have indicated interest in their products. Alternatively, companies can purchase mailing lists from other companies that specialize in the marketing of up-to-date lists. SmarterKids.com pursued this latter tact by securing the services of PostMasterDirect.com (PMD), an opt-in e-mail marketing company.

PMD has accumulated a database of nearly 10 million consumers. Database "members" have provided PMD with their names and e-mail addresses and, more importantly, have granted permission to receive e-mail advertisements in designated areas of personal interest. From a list of 3,000 lifestyle categories, members select precisely those areas for which they are willing to receive commercial e-mail messages.

PostMasterDirect.com groups its millions of members into a subset of customer categories based on a combination of their demographic characteristics (age, gender, income, household size, children's ages, etc.) and lifestyle interests. Companies such as SmarterKids.com then send mailings to PMD's members who satisfy desired characteristics. For example, SmarterKids.com might specify that it is interested in e-mailing messages through PMD only to Internet users who are parents of children aged 5 through 12, who have incomes in excess of $40,000, and who live in certain zip code areas. SmarterKids.com pays PMD a fee ranging from 10 to 35 cents for mailing SmarterKids.com's e-mail advertisement to each name and address that satisfies the specified criteria.

By working through PMD, SmarterKids.com is able to target its message to desired households without having to put together its own list of prospects. This makes business sense because SmarterKids.com has expertise in marketing educational products, not in compiling mailing lists. PostMasterDirect.com regularly updates its list by constantly purging outdated and changed e-mail listings and removing members who have opted-out of receiving additional commercial messages. SmarterKids.com is thus able to contact prospective customers at a cost-per-thousand ranging between $10 and $35.

Source: Adapted from Heidi Anderson, "SmarterKids.com: List Rental Done Right," Special Advertising Section on E-Mail Marketing to *Adweek*, *Brandweek*, and *Mediaweek*, 2001.

By mailing messages to PMD's list of people who specify SmarterKids.com's prospect-profile characteristics, SmarterKids.com has achieved *click-through rates* to its e-mail advertisements that over time have averaged 5 percent. In other words, 50 out of every 1,000 people receiving SmarterKids.com's messages click through to http://www.SmarterKids.com, where they can learn more about its products and place orders. Of the 50 out of 1,000 people who, on average, click through, the percentage ultimately making a purchase ranges between 5 to 20 percent. This percentage range is referred to as the *conversion rate*. Thus, a click-through rate of 5 percent and a conversion rate of, say, 10 percent, indicates that 5 out of 1,000 recipients to a SmarterKids.com e-mail message actually purchase something from the company—that is, 50 out of 1,000 click through and 10 percent of these, or 5, actually make a purchase. If each of these consumers purchases, on average, $100 worth of merchandise, this means that SmarterKids.com generates $500 revenue for a direct advertising investment as little as $10 and at most $35.

It should be obvious from this illustration that e-mail advertising can be a very profitable business model. Achieving success requires that the right message be sent to a well-targeted list of prospective customers, and that the message accomplish high click-through and conversion rates. SmarterKids.com in conjunction with PostMasterDirect.com has developed a winning formula for success.

The previous two chapters emphasized first, in Chapter 12, the major advertising media (television, magazines, newspapers, radio, and outdoor advertising), and then, in Chapter 13, alternative offline media and mass-oriented online advertising. These media have been used to reach *mass audiences* for purposes of creating brand awareness, conveying product information, and building or reinforcing brand images. Marketers, however, are turning increasingly to direct advertising and database marketing, the topics of the present chapter, to fine-tune their customer selection, better serve customer needs, and fulfill their own needs by achieving advertising results that can be measured by actual sales response.

This chapter covers the related topics of direct advertising and database marketing. **Direct advertising** involves the use of any of several media to transmit messages that encourage purchases of the advertiser's brands. Land-surface mail (postal mail) and electronic mail (e-mail) are the most important direct advertising media. Direct advertising is facilitated by the increasingly sophisticated practice of database marketing. **Database marketing** involves collecting and electronically storing (in a database) information about present, past, and prospective customers. Typical databases include customers' past purchase details (buyographic data), and other types of relevant information (demographic, geographic, and psychographic data). The information is used to profile customers and to develop effective and efficient marketing programs by communicating with individual customers and by establishing long-term communication relationships.[1]

By targeting advertisements to a company's best prospects—who can be identified by buyographic, geographic, demographic, and perhaps psychographic characteristics—direct advertising enables pinpointed communications, or what is also referred to as *niche marketing*. More powerful and faster computers have increasingly enabled "marketers to zero in on ever smaller niches of the population, ultimately aiming for the smallest consumer segment of all: the individual."[2]

In addition to the growth of consumer-oriented direct advertising, business-to-business (B2B) marketers have expanded their use of direct advertising. This is largely accounted for by the rising cost of personal sales calls, which on average exceed $250 per call. As a result, postal mail and electronic mail marketing (along with telemarketing) have actually replaced the sales force in some B2B companies, whereas in others, direct advertising is used to supplement the sales force's efforts by building goodwill, generating leads, and opening doors for salespeople.

This chapter covers three major, interrelated topics: Database marketing and data mining, postal mail advertising, and electronic mail advertising. However, before proceeding, some shorthand language needs to be introduced. The term *electronic mail advertising* may have surprised readers who have learned to automatically truncate *electronic mail* into its shorthand, *e-mail.* By contrast, marketing academics and practitioners continue to call postal mail by its original but now cumbersome name, direct mail. Because e-mail advertising also represents a form of direct mail, use of the term *direct mail* is misleading because it is unclear as to whether it refers to just the postal variety of direct mail or postal mail and electronic mail. To both clarify and simplify matters in this chapter, the postal mail version of direct mail is referred to as *p-mail* so that it is structurally equivalent to its much younger but already truncated *e-mail* cousin.

DATABASE MARKETING AND DATA MINING

Successful direct mailing of both the *p* and *e* varieties necessitates the availability of computer databases and the *addressability* inherent in the databases.[3] That is, databases enable contacts with present or prospective customers who can be accessed by companies whose databases contain postal and electronic addresses along with the buyographic, geographic, demographic, and, perhaps, psychographic data of the nature previously described. In general, an *address* is "anything that locates the customer uniquely in time and space in a database, so that responses, marketing actions, and respondents can be matched."[4] Direct advertising, in comparison to broadcast advertising, does not deal with customers as a mass but rather creates individual relationships with each customer or prospective customer. The following analogy aptly pits addressable media, such as p-mail and e-mail, against broadcast media: "Broadcast media send communications; addressable media send and receive. Broadcasting targets its audience much as a battleship shells a distant island into submission; addressable media initiate conversations."[5]

Database Assets

An up-to-date database provides firms with a number of assets, including the ability to do the following:

1. Direct advertising efforts to those people who represent the best prospects for the company's products or services.
2. Offer varied messages to different groups of customers.
3. Create long-term relationships with customers.
4. Enhance advertising productivity.
5. Calculate the lifetime value of a customer or prospect.[6]

Due to the importance of customer lifetime value, the following section focuses exclusively on the fifth database asset.

Lifetime Value Analysis

A key feature of database marketing is the need to consider each address contained in a database from a lifetime value perspective. That is, each present or prospective customer is viewed as not just an address but rather as a *long-term asset*. **Customer lifetime value** is the *net present value (NPV)* of the profit that a company stands to realize on the average new customer during a given number of years.[7] This concept is best illustrated using the data in Table 14.1.[8]

Assume, for illustration purposes, that a retailer has a database of 1,000 customers (the intersection of row A and Year 1 column in Table 14.1). The analysis examines the net present value of each customer over a five-year period. Row B, the *retention rate*, indicates the likelihood that people will remain customers of this particular retailer during a five-year period. Hence, 40 percent of 1,000 customers in Year 1 will continue to be customers in Year 2, or, in other words, 400 of the initial 1,000 customers will be remaining in Year 2 (see intersection of row A and the Year 2 column). Forty-five percent of these 400 customers, or 180 customers, will remain into Year 3, and so on.

Row C indicates that the *average yearly sales* in Years 1 through 5 are constant at $150. That is, customers on average spend $150 at this particular retail establishment. Thus, the *total revenue*, row D, in each of the five years is simply the

Customer Lifetime Value

Table 14.1

	Year 1	Year 2	Year 3	Year 4	Year 5
Revenue					
A Customers	1,000	400	180	90	50
B Retention rate	40%	45%	50%	55%	60%
C Average yearly sales	$150	$150	$150	$150	$150
D Total revenue	$150,000	$60,000	$27,000	$13,500	$7,500
Costs					
E Cost %	50%	50%	50%	50%	50%
F Total costs	$75,000	$30,000	$13,500	$6,750	$3,750
Profits					
G Gross profit	$75,000	$30,000	$13,500	$6,750	$3,750
H Discount rate	1	1.2	1.44	1.73	2.07
I NPV profit	$75,000	$25,000	$9,375	$3,902	$1,812
J Cumulative NPV profit	$75,000	$100,000	$109,375	$113,277	$115,088
K Lifetime value (NPV) per customer	$75.00	$100.00	$109.38	$113.28	$115.09

product of rows A and C. For example, the 1,000 customers in Year 1 who spend on average $150 produce $150,000 of total revenue.

Row E reflects the cost of selling merchandise to the store's customers. For simplification it is assumed that the cost is 50 percent of revenue. Total costs in each year, row F, are thus calculated by simply multiplying the values in rows D and E.

Gross profit, row G, is calculated by subtracting total costs (row F) from total revenue (row D). The *discount rate*, row H, is a critical component of net present value analysis and requires some discussion. This rate reflects the idea that money received in future years is not equivalent in value to money received today. This is because money received today, say $100, can be immediately invested and begin earning interest. Over time, the $100 grows more valuable as interest accumulates and compounds. Delaying the receipt of money thus means giving up the opportunity to earn interest. This being the case, $100 received in the future, say in three years, is worth less than the same amount received today. Some adjustment is needed to equate the value of money received at different times. This adjustment is called the *discount rate* and can be expressed as

$$D = (1 + i)^n$$

where D is the discount rate, i is the interest rate, and n is the number of years before the money will be received. The discount rate given in row H of Table 14.1 assumes an interest rate of 20 percent. Thus, the discount rate in Year 3 is 1.44, because the retailer will have to wait two years (from Year 1) to receive the profit that will be earned in Year 3. That is,

$$(1 + 0.2)^2 = 1.44$$

The *net present value (NPV) profit*, row I, is determined by simply taking the reciprocal of the discount rate (i.e., $1 \div D$) and multiplying the gross profit, row G, by that reciprocal. For example, in Year 3, the reciprocal of 1.44 is 0.694, which implies that the present value of $1 received two years later is only about $0.69 at an interest rate of 20 percent. Thus, the NPV of the $13,500 gross profit to be earned in Year 3 is $9,375. (You should perform the calculation for Years 4 and 5 to ensure that you understand the derivation of NPV. Recall that the reciprocal of a particular value, such as 1.44, is calculated by dividing that value into 1.)

The *cumulative NPV profit*, row J, simply sums the NPV profits across the years. This summation reveals that the cumulative NPV profit to our hypothetical retailer, who had 1,000 customers in Year 1, of whom 50 remain after five years, is $115,088. Finally, row K, the *lifetime value (NPV) per customer*, shows the average worth of each of the 1,000 people who were customers of our hypothetical retailer in Year 1. The average lifetime value of each of these customers, expressed as NPV over a five-year period, is thus $115.09.

Now that you understand the concept of lifetime value analysis, we can turn to more strategic concerns. The key issue is this: What can a database marketer do to enhance the average customer's lifetime value? There are five ways to augment lifetime value:[9]

1. Increase the *retention rate*. The greater the number of customers and the longer they are retained, the greater the lifetime value. It therefore behooves marketers and advertisers to focus on retention rather than just acquisition. Database marketing is ideally suited for this purpose, because it enables regular communication with customers (through newsletters, frequency programs, and so on) and relationship building. Customer relationship management (CRM) is a widespread marketing practice—a practice justified by the ability to enhance the lifetime value of the average customer.

2. Increase the *referral rate*. Positive relations created with existing customers can influence others to become customers through the positive word of mouth expressed by a company's satisfied product/service users.

3. Enhance the average *purchase volume per customer*. Existing customers can be encouraged to purchase more of a brand by augmenting their brand loyalty. The greater customer loyalty, the more often they will buy that brand rather than competitive offerings. Product satisfaction and capable management of customer relations are means to building the base of loyal customers.

4. Cut *direct costs*. By altering the channel of distribution via direct marketing efforts, a firm may be able to cut costs and hence increase profit margins.

5. Reduce *marketing communication costs*. Effective database marketing can lead to meaningful reductions in marketing communication expenses because direct advertising often is more productive than mass media advertising.

Mailing Lists

Achieving p- and e-mail success depends greatly on the quality of mailing lists contained in a company's database. Mailing lists of past or prospective customers enable direct marketers to pinpoint the best candidates for future purchases. One observer has aptly dubbed mailing lists "windows to our pocketbooks."[10]

There are two broad categories of mailing lists, as summarized in Table 14.2: internal (house lists) and external (public lists). **House lists** are based on a company's internal list of present or prospective customers. For example, Disney has a list consisting of 31 million households. This list was compiled from various sources, including the Walt Disney Internet Group and customers of Disney's various products: Walt Disney World, Disneyland, the Disney stores, and miscellaneous other Disney offerings.[11] Because house lists contain the names of cus-

Table 14.2	Types of Mailing Lists

1. **A Company's Internal, or House, List**
2. **External Lists**
   a. **House lists purchased from other companies**
   b. **Compiled lists**
      i. **Compiled by a company for its own purposes**
      ii. **Purchased from a list compiler**

IMC focus

Golfers and Database Marketing at Taylor Made-Addidas Golf

Taylor Made-Addidas Golf (TMAG) is a company that manufactures and markets golf clubs and footwear. Both product lines are well known and widely used by millions of golfers in countries around the world. The golfing industry is highly competitive, with many prominent and heavily advertised brands competing for the golfer's dollars (or Euros, pesos, yen, etc.). However, TMAG's leadership in database marketing efforts has given it a significant advantage over its competitors.

TMAG's database consists of more than 1.4 million names and addresses compiled from a variety of sources. The list includes, among other information, golfers' birthdays and other demographic data, the type of courses—public or private—they regularly play, and whether they play golf while on vacations. The database enables TMAG to maintain contact and enhance relations with the users of its products. For example, individuals on the list who have Internet access receive a weekly online magazine that provides information about golfing destinations and offers playing tips from professionals. In each mailing of the online magazine, readers are asked questions about what they are looking for in golf balls, what types of clubs they play with, what prices they prefer to pay for balls and clubs, and so on. This information is shared with product managers as one source of input into product design and pricing decisions. TMAG also merges its list with the lists of subscribers to golf magazines and then tailors e-mail ads to specific categories of subscribers. It estimates having an ongoing dialogue via e-mail with about 100,000 customers.

Source: Adapted from Chuck Stogel, "Driving to Break Par," *Brandweek*, February 28, 2000, p. 46. © 2000 VNU Business Media, Inc.

tomers who previously responded to a company's offering, they are generally more valuable than external lists. (See the *IMC Focus* for another example.)

There are various means by which companies acquire names and addresses for compiling their house lists. For a retailer or direct marketer, it is a matter of saving the names of past customers or those who have interacted with the company's Web site and provided address information. The situation is more complicated, however, for manufacturers who market their products through retail outlets. With creativity, they too can generate databases. Following are some methods used by marketers that lack direct contact with consumers—such as manufacturers using indirect channels of distribution—to obtain database information:[12]

- *Feedback from promotions.* When a company includes a promotional offer in or on a package (such as a game or contest), customers must identify their names and addresses to participate in the promotional offer. These names are entered into the marketer's database for future contact. For example, Black & Decker built an impressive database by offering free vacuum cleaner bags to its Dust Buster purchasers. Lea & Perrin built a list of its sauce buyers by offering free recipe books.[13] Online promotions are another source for collecting names and addresses. Thousands of names can be acquired in the first month of a sweepstake, contest, game, or other type of brand promotion. However, a potential drawback with using online promotional offers for capturing data is that some of the addressees will be people who are interested in the promotional offer alone but not the brand.[14] Any additional efforts directed at marketing products at such consumers will likely be ineffective.
- *Information from warranty cards.* When a customer mails a completed warranty card for, say, a new television, the manufacturer has another address for its database.
- *Data from registration programs.* Manufacturers often have consumers complete registration cards that reveal the date of product purchase and provide classification information about the purchaser. At one time Levi

Strauss placed registration cards in every pair of jeans it sold in the United States.[15]

- *Participation in rebate programs.* To receive rebates, customers supply information that the database builder enters for future contact.
- *Telemarketing efforts.* Names and addresses can be requested from toll-free callers and entered into the database. In-bound customer service calls represent a good opportunity to collect p- and e-mail addresses.

The other type of mailing list is the **external list,** which comes in two forms. The first, *another company's house list,* is bought by a firm to promote its own products. This type of list is effective because it comprises the names of people who have responded to another company's direct-response offer. The greater the similarity of the products offered by both the buyer and the seller of the list, the greater the likelihood that the purchased list will be effective.

For example, imagine a company that markets coverings that protect automobile exteriors from exposure to the elements. New automobile purchasers who do not have a garage are the best market for this company's products. The coverings marketer could purchase and merge mailing lists from automobile manufacturers and rental companies and specify names of buyers who have purchased an automobile within, say, the past six months and who rent apartments rather than own homes. Additionally, this marketer, using geodemographic segmentation (as discussed in Chapter 3), could identify zip code areas that are known to consist of high proportions of smaller homes without garages and send blanket mailings to all households in those areas.

Compiled lists, the second type of external list, include lists compiled by a company for its own purposes or lists purchased from another company that specializes in list compilation. The first type of compiled list is illustrated by a direct marketing effort at Kimberly-Clark, makers of Huggies disposable diapers. Each year, Kimberly-Clark's database developers identify by name 75 percent of the approximately 3 million to 4 million new mothers in the United States. (The names are obtained from hospitals and doctors.) Kimberly-Clark sends the new mothers personalized letters, educational literature about caring for a new baby, and cents-off coupons for Huggies.[16] Huggies' database program has been extremely effective, resulting in market share growth and an accompanying decrease in media expenses.[17]

The other type of compiled list comes from businesses that specialize in compiling lists and selling them to other companies. List compilers are typically involved in businesses that give them access to millions of consumer names and vital statistics. For example, the Lifestyle Selector File, a service of R. L. Polk & Co. (see http://www.polk.com/products/lifestyle_data.asp), is a database that contains more than 35 million names as well as demographic characteristics (age, sex, education, etc.) and lifestyle characteristics (sports participation, travel activities, etc.). The list is updated every six weeks.

The Lifestyle Selector enables a direct advertiser to order a list containing names and addresses that have been identified based on any combination of lifestyle and demographic characteristics. A manufacturer of men's sporting goods, for example, would be able to request a list matching its desired target market—for example, people between the ages of 35 and 54 who are outdoor enthusiasts; who are business executives, professionals, or technicians earning $75,000 or more annually; and who possess an American Express credit card.

Other companies compile lists and make them available (for a fee) on CD-ROM and DVD. Figure 14.1 shows, for example, several types of compiled lists marketed by a company called infoUSA (http://www.directoriesUSA.com). For example, the list of 120 million U.S. households (see Figure 14.1) contains names, addresses, and telephone numbers as well as age, income, and other demographic data. Purchasers of this CD-ROM, which costs $795, can use this information for targeting prospective customers, designing p-mail campaigns, undertaking telemarketing efforts, and other purposes. The physicians and surgeons directory is a database containing 575,000 medical professionals, including their names, mailing addresses, telephone numbers, areas of specialization, office size, age, gender, and even psychographic details. This CD-ROM, costing $695, would be invaluable for companies marketing their products and services to medical specialists.

Illustration of Compiled Lists Available on CD-ROM   **Figure 14.1**

Courtesy of infoUSA

Compiled lists are not as desirable as a company's house list because they do not contain information about the willingness of a person to purchase the marketer's products. The characteristics of the members of compiled lists may also be too diversified to serve the purposes of the p-mailer. However, some compiled lists are put together with considerable care and may well serve the p-mailer's specific needs.

The Practice of Data Mining

Databases can be massive in size with millions of addresses and hundreds of variables for each database entrant. The availability of high-speed computers and inexpensive computer software has made it possible for companies to literally mine their data warehouses for the purpose of learning more about customers' buying behavior. The process of **data mining** has been defined as an "information extraction activity whose goal is to discover hidden facts contained in databases."[18] Sophisticated data miners look for revealing relations that can be used to better target prospective customers, develop cooperative marketing relations with other companies, and otherwise better understand who buys what, when, how often, and along with what other products and brands.

Consider, for example, a credit card company that mines its huge data warehouse and learns that its most frequent and largest-purchase users are disproportionately more likely than the average credit card user to vacation in exotic locations. The company could use this information to design a promotional offering that has an exotic vacation site as the grand prize. A furniture store chain mining its database learns that families with two or more children rarely make major furniture purchases within three years of buying a new automobile. Armed with this information, the chain could acquire automobile purchase lists and then direct advertisements to households that have *not* purchased a new automobile for three or more years. These examples are purely illustrative, but they provide a sense of how databases can be mined and used for making strategic advertising and promotion decisions.

Another use of data warehouses is to segregate a company's customer list by the *recency (R)* of a customer's purchase, the *frequency (F)* of purchases, and the *monetary value (M)* of each purchase. Companies typically assign point values to accounts based on these classifications. Each company has its own customized procedure for point assignment (i.e., its own R-F-M formula), but in every case more points are assigned to more recent, more frequent, and more expensive purchases. The R-F-M system offers tremendous opportunities for database manipulation and mail targeting. For example, a company might choose to send out free catalogs only to accounts whose point totals exceed a certain amount.

Another application of the R-F-M categories is for a company to divide customers into equal-sized groupings such as quartiles (four equal-sized groups) or quintiles (five equal-sized groups) for each of the R, F, and M categories. Hence, with respect to recency of purchase, the first quintile would consist of the top one-fifth of the customer database who have most recently purchased from the company, and the last quintile would include the bottom one-fifth of customers who have least recently purchased the company's products. Likewise, customers' purchase frequencies also would be delineated into five equal quintiles, ranging from the top (most frequent purchasers) to bottom quintiles (least frequent purchasers). Finally, customers' amount of purchases of the company's products would also be delineated into five equal-sized quintiles. These quintile delineations of the R-F-M categories would thus lead to 125 total combinations of customer groupings, or cells—that is, 5 recency quintiles × 5 frequency quintiles × 5 monetary value quintiles. Cell 1 (cell 125) would include customers who have purchased the company's products most (least) recently, have purchased most (least) frequently, and have spent the most (least) amount in purchasing from the company. Customers in the 123 intermediate cells would fall between these two extremes.

Having delineated all customers into one of 125 cells, a company can then test the effectiveness of a proposed p-mailing or catalog distribution using the following procedure:

1. Take a representative random sample of customers from each of the 125 cells.
2. Distribute a catalog, brochure, or other p-mailing to the sampled customers from each of the 125 cells. This mailing would encourage recipients to purchase the company's advertised product(s).
3. Provide sufficient time for sampled customers to respond to the mail offering.
4. After sufficient time has elapsed (based on past mailing experience), determine the response rate and average expenditure for each of the 125 R-F-M cells.
5. Project these statistics to the full membership of each of the 125 groupings.
6. Based on these response rate and average expenditure projections, and with knowledge of the cost of distributing the mailing to all customers in each group, it is easy to calculate whether distributing the mailing to *all* customers in a particular cell would be a profitable proposition.
7. The decision rule is simple: Based on the sample results, mail the catalog, brochure, or other piece only to those cells whose revenue potential outstrips the mailing expense.

It should be clear from this description that testing of the sort just described can be performed to determine which customers in a company's database represent the best prospects for future mailings. Based on these results, a decision is made to mail, say, a catalog just to a portion of database entrants who occupy only a subset of the R-F-M cells. In the absence of testing a proposed new mailing, a company would be taking a "shot in the dark" if it were to mail its catalog to all customers in its database. The testing procedure represents a systematic approach that likely will produce a more profitable outcome compared with blanketing a mailing to all database occupants.

P-MAIL ADVERTISING

P-mail advertising refers to any advertising matter delivered by the postal service to the person whom the marketer wishes to influence. These advertisements can take the form of letters, postcards, programs, calendars, folders, catalogs, videocassettes, blotters, order blanks, price lists, menus, and so on. A direct-mail campaign for the Saab 9-5 typifies effective p-mailing.[19] In the late 1990s, Saab, the Swedish automobile maker, introduced a new luxury sedan named the Saab 9-5. This model represented Saab's first entry in the luxury category and was designed to compete against well-known high-equity brands, including Mercedes, BMW, Volvo, Lexus, and Infiniti. A total of 200,000 consumers, including 65,000 current Saab owners and 135,000 prospects, were targeted with the objective of encouraging them to test-drive the 9-5. The Martin Agency of Richmond, Virginia, developed an IMC strategy, prominent among which were multiple p-mailings and outbound telemarketing. The effort was designed to engage prospects in a dialogue about the new 9-5 and to learn more about their automobile purchase interests. Mailings provided prospects with brand details, made an appealing offer for them to test-drive the 9-5. Names of the most qualified prospects were then fed to dealers for follow-up.

The Martin Agency designed four mailings: (1) a countdown mailing announced the new Saab 9-5, provided a "teaser" photo of the car, and requested recipients to complete a survey of their automobile purchase interests and needs; (2) a subsequent qualification mailing provided respondents to the countdown mailing with product information addressing their specific purchase interests (performance, safety, versatility, etc.) and offered a test-drive kit as an incentive for returning an additional survey; (3) a third mailing included a special issue from *Road & Track* magazine that was devoted to the Saab 9-5's product development process; and (4) a final test-drive kit mailing extended an offer to test-drive the 9-5 for three hours and also provided an opportunity for prospects to win an all-expenses-paid European driving adventure (through Germany, Italy, and Sweden) as incentive for test-driving the 9-5.

An outbound telemarketing campaign was conducted as a follow-up to the p-mailings. Telephone calls were made to all people who responded to the "countdown" and "qualification" mailings as well as to all prospects who had automobile leases or loans that were expiring prior to mailing of the test-drive kit. These callings reinforced the European test-drive offer and set up times for local dealers to call back to schedule a test-drive.

The direct marketing effort for the 9-5 was fabulously successful. Of the 200,000 initial prospects who were contacted by the introductory mailing, 16,000 indicated interest in test-driving the 9-5 (an 8 percent response rate), and more than 2,200 test-drives were scheduled.

In general, distinctive features of p-mailing (shared also by e-mailing efforts) include targetability, measurability, accountability, flexibility, and efficiency.

- *Targetability*. P-mail is capable of targeting a precisely defined group of people. For example, The Martin Agency selected just 200,000 consumers to receive mailings for the Saab 9-5. These included 65,000 current Saab owners and 135,000 prospects who satisfied income, car ownership, and other hurdles.
- *Measurability*. With p-mail it is possible to determine exactly how effective the effort was because the marketer knows how many mailings were sent and how many people responded. This enables ready calculations of cost-per-inquiry and cost-per-order. As previously noted, more than 2,200 consumers signed up for test-drives of the Saab 9-5. Proprietary dealer

sales data reveal how many of the initial 200,000 mailings resulted in purchases.

- *Accountability.* Every business decision must be held accountable for results. Marketing communicators increasingly are being required to justify the results of their communication efforts. P-mailing simplifies this task. Because results can be readily demonstrated (as in the case of the Saab 9-5), brand managers can justify budgets allocated to p-mail.
- *Flexibility.* Effective p-mail can be produced relatively quickly (compared with, say, producing a TV commercial), so it is possible for a company to launch a p-mail campaign that meets changing circumstances. For example, if inventory levels are excessive, a quick postcard or letter may serve to reduce the inventory. P-mail also offers the advantage of permitting the marketer to test communication ideas on a small-scale basis quickly and out of the view of competitors. Comparatively, a mass media effort cannot avoid the competition's eyes. P-mail also is flexible in the sense that it has no constraints in terms of form, color, or size (other than those imposed by cost and practical considerations). It also is relatively simple and inexpensive to change p-mail ads. Compare this with the cost of changing a television commercial.
- *Efficiency.* P-mail makes it possible to direct communication efforts only to a highly targeted group, such as the 200,000 consumers who received mailings for the Saab 9-5. The cost-efficiency resulting from such targeting is considerable compared with mass advertising efforts.

An alleged disadvantage of p-mail is its *expense.* On a cost-per-thousand (CPM) basis, p-mail typically is more expensive than other media. For example, the CPM for a particular mailing may be as high as $200 to $300, whereas a magazine's CPM might be as low as $4. However, compared with other media, p-mail is much less wasteful and will usually produce the highest percentage of responses. Thus, on a *cost-per-order basis*, p-mail is often *less expensive* and a better bargain.

Perhaps the major problem with p-mail is that many people consider it excessively *intrusive and invasive of privacy.* Americans are accustomed to receiving massive quantities of mail (on average, American households receive 12.5 pieces of p-mail each week, a third of which is trashed without being read)[20] and so have been "trained" to accept the voluminous amount of p-mail received. It is not the amount of mail that concerns most people but the fact that virtually any business or other organization that has a product, service, or idea to promote can readily obtain their names and addresses.

What Can P-Mail Accomplish?

Research and practical experience indicate that p-mail campaigns achieve the following objectives. This list is straightforward and requires no explanation.[21]

1. Increase sales and usage from current customers.
2. Sell products and services to new customers.
3. Build traffic at a specific retailer or Web site.
4. Stimulate product trial with promotional offers and incentives.
5. Generate leads for a sales force.
6. Deliver product-relevant information and news.
7. Gather customer information that can be used in building a database.
8. Communicate with individuals in a relatively private matter and thereby minimize the likelihood of competitive detection; in other words, p-mail advertising, unlike mass advertising, reaches the customer and prospects "under the radar" of your competitors.

Who Uses P-Mail Advertising?

All types of marketers use p-mail as a strategically important advertising medium. Seventy-seven percent of U.S. companies reported using p-mail in a survey conducted by the Gallup Organization.[22] *Business Week* magazine claimed (albeit with some hyperbole) that marketers of all types of consumer goods "are turning from the TV box to the mailbox."[23] Some automobile manufacturers, for example, budget as much as 10 percent of their advertising expenditures to p-mail, with mailing expenditures in the U.S. alone having exceeded $70 million in 2000.[24]

Both B2B companies and marketers of consumer goods have turned increasingly to database marketing and p-mailing as advertising options. Packaged goods companies such as Philip Morris, RJR Nabisco, Ralston Purina, Adolph Coors, Kraft, Gerber Products, Sara Lee, Quaker Oats, Sandoz Consumer, and Procter & Gamble are some of the primary users of p-mailings.[25] P-mailing by firms such as these is especially valuable for introducing new brands. Packaged goods companies increasingly use the mail for distributing product samples. A typical mailing includes (1) a product sample, (2) attractive coupons to encourage consumers to make a brand purchase following sample usage, and (3) detailed consumer surveys that provide the brand marketer with names and addresses for its database along with valuable information regarding respondents' purchases of other product categories and brands marketed by the company.

Why the Trend Toward P-Mailing?

At least four factors account for the widespread use of p-mail by all types of marketers. First, the *rising expense of television advertising* along with increased audience fragmentation have led many advertisers to reduce investments in television advertising. Second, as noted earlier, p-mailing enables *unparalleled targeting* of messages to desired prospects. Why? Because, according to one expert, it is "a lot better to talk to 20,000 prospects than 2 million suspects."[26] Third, increased emphasis on *measurable advertising results* has encouraged advertisers to use the medium—namely, p-mail—that most clearly identifies how many prospects purchased the advertised product. Fourth, consumers are responsive—surveys indicate that Americans like mail advertisements. For example, Louis Harris & Associates learned that 40 percent of consumers would be "very or somewhat upset" if they could not get mail offers or catalogs.[27]

In addition to the above reasons for p-mail's surge, this medium also provides marketers with a valuable means for *offsetting competitors' marketing efforts*. For example, the USA Carnation division of Nestlé was faced with a competitive challenge from Heinz, which was introducing its brand of Reward dog food and spending $10 million in introductory advertising and promotions. To blunt this brand introduction, which assuredly would have stolen share from Carnation's own brand, Mighty Dog, Carnation delivered coupons via p-mail for Mighty Dog to user households two weeks before Reward's launch. The coupons were of high value and also included a proof-of-purchase premium offer to create purchase continuity. The coupons were mailed to more than 525,000 households. The coupon redemption rate was an extremely high 6.7 percent, and the premium offer obtained a 13 percent redemption rate, both of which are far above typical redemption rates. This effort resulted in a minimal loss of Mighty Dog's market share to Reward. Carnation was able to blunt Heinz's brand introduction for a total expenditure of only $400,000.[28]

The Special Case of Catalog Marketing

No treatment of p-mailing would be complete without at least a brief discussion of catalog marketing, which, though a form of direct mail, deserves a separate discussion due to its distinctiveness and importance. Catalog marketing is a huge enterprise, with more than 16 billion catalogs distributed in 2000.[29] Name a product, and at least one company is probably marketing that item by catalog—food items (cheese, candy, pastry, steaks), clothing, furniture—the list goes on and on. New catalogs appear regularly. Levi Strauss recently introduced a catalog aimed at teenagers. Limited Too, a division of giant retailer Limited Inc., came out with a clothing catalog targeted to preteen girls.

The growth rate for catalog sales in the United States has exceeded that enjoyed by fixed-site retailers. Various factors account for this. From the *marketer's perspective*, catalog selling provides an efficient and effective way to reach prime prospects. From the *consumer's perspective*, shopping by catalog offers several advantages: (1) It saves time because people do not have to find parking spaces and deal with in-store crowds; (2) catalog buying appeals to consumers who are fearful of shopping due to concerns about crime; (3) catalogs allow people the convenience of making purchase decisions at their leisure and away from the pressure of a retail store; (4) the availability of toll-free 800 numbers and online Web sites, credit card purchasing, and liberal return policies make it easy for people to order from catalogs; (5) consumers are confident in purchasing from catalogs because merchandise quality and prices often are comparable, or even superior, to what is available in stores; and (6) guarantees are attractive.

Illustrative of this last point, consider the policy of L. L. Bean, the famous retailer from Maine:

> *All of our products are guaranteed to give 100 percent satisfaction in every way. Return anything purchased from us at any time if it proves otherwise. We will replace it, refund your purchase price or credit your credit card, as you wish. We do not want you to have anything from L. L. Bean that is not completely satisfactory.*

Although catalog marketing is pervasive, signs indicate it has reached the mature stage in its life cycle. First, industry observers note that the novelty of catalog scanning has worn off for many consumers. Second, as typically is the case when a product or service reaches maturity, the costs of catalog marketing have increased dramatically. A primary reason is that firms have incurred the expenses of developing more attractive catalogs and compiling better mailing lists in an effort to outperform their competitors. Costs have been further strained by third-class postal rate increases in recent years and sharp increases in paper prices.

Some catalog companies have responded to the slowdown by sending out even more catalogs than they mailed in the past. Other companies have scaled back their efforts. Marginal companies have dropped out, which invariably is the case when an industry reaches maturity. Many catalog companies have found it unprofitable to remain in the catalog business, but the best companies continue to flourish. In their efforts to achieve steady growth, some U.S. catalogers have expanded to markets overseas, and European catalogers have made inroads into the U.S. market. For example, Lands' End has opened a distribution center in Japan and mass mails catalogs to consumers in that country. Lands' End also is actively pursuing German consumers, which is understandable in view of the fact that mail order accounts for nearly 6 percent of overall retail sales in Germany compared with 3 percent in the United States. L. L. Bean mails catalogs to more than 100 countries, although nearly 70 percent of its international sales comes from Japan alone. Achieving success in global markets requires that U.S. catalog companies undertake aggressive marketing communications backed up with high-quality offerings, provide reliable and dependable delivery, and achieve high customer service levels. Catalog companies, just like marketers in every other endeavor, are challenged by the need to enhance brand equity by creating name awareness in countries where they are just beginning to establish an identity and building strong and favorable brand associations among consumers in these countries.

European catalogers have also intensified their marketing efforts in the attractive U.S. market. The strongest European catalogers are huge concerns that offer a vast array of merchandise—everything from clothing and furniture to consumer electronics and appliances. U.S. catalogers, by comparison, tend to concentrate on specialty lines of merchandise. European catalogs are massive, ranging in size from 700 to 1,300 pages. Most European catalog companies are experienced international marketers. For instance, the French cataloger La Redoute earns about one-third of its sales in 12 other countries. Otton Versand, a German cataloger, earns almost one-half of its sales outside Germany.[30]

E-MAIL ADVERTISING

Internet users love the ability to send and receive e-mail; indeed, a study by a major consulting firm determined that 83 percent of Internet users regarded e-mailing as their primary reason for using the Internet.[31] With millions of people presently online and the numbers substantially increasing each year, it is little wonder that marketing communicators have turned to e-mail advertising as a viable alternative or complement to their p-mail programs.

What is e-mail advertising? **E-mail advertising** is simply the use of the Internet for sending commercial messages in the form of e-mail messages as an alternative to banner ads, pop-ups, or other forms of rich-media presentations. As with any other advertising medium, there is no such thing as a single type of e-mail message; rather, e-mail messages appear in many forms, ranging from pure-text documents to more sophisticated versions that use all the audio-video powers of the Internet. E-mail now is the most heavily used form of Internet advertising and far exceeds the amount invested in alternative advertising forms such as banners, pop-ups, and interstitials.

It has been estimated that over 20 percent of the e-mail that users receive is marketing related.[32] Expenditures on e-mail advertising in 2000 were less than $500 million but are expected to exceed $2 billion by 2003 and exceed $9 billion by 2006.[33] Roughly half of the marketing-related e-mail is opt-in, or permission-granted, e-mail, whereas the remainder is unsolicited, or so-called "spam."

Opt-In E-Mailing Versus Spam

Opt-in e-mailing is the practice of marketers asking for and receiving consumers' permission to send them messages on particular topics. The consumer has agreed, or opted-in, to receive messages on topics of interest rather than receiving messages that are unsolicited. Imagine, for example, that a hypothetical consumer is interested in purchasing a digital camera and visits a Web site that came up when she conducted a Google.com search for "digital cameras." While logged into this Web site, which was quite informative, she received a query that asked whether she would be interested in receiving more information about photographic equipment. She replied "yes" and provided her e-mail address as well as other information. The Web site electronically recorded her "permission granted" and, unknown to the unsuspecting shopper, sold her name and address to a broker that specializes in compiling lists. This list broker, in turn, sold her name and e-mail address to companies that market photographic equipment and supplies. Our hypothetical Internet user's name and e-mail address would eventually appear on a variety of lists, and she would receive regular e-mail messages for photographic equipment and supplies.

In theory, opt-in e-mailing serves both the marketer's and the consumer's interests. However, frequency and quantity of e-mail messages can become intrusive as more and more companies have access to your name and areas of interest. Consumers feel especially violated when the e-mail messages deal with topics that are tangential to their primary interests. For example, when granting the original Web site permission to send photography-related messages, our unsuspecting consumer may have been interested only in information about digital cameras, when in fact she subsequently was bombarded with messages involving more aspects of photography and more photography products than she ever could have imagined. She knew not what she had opted for—some of the information received was relevant, most was not.

Although this example may appear to cast a negative evaluation of opt-in e-mail, the fact remains that advertisers who send messages to individuals whose interests are known, if only somewhat broadly, increase their odds of providing consumers with relevant information. Moreover, sophisticated marketers are using a more detailed opt-in procedure so they can better serve both their own needs for accurate targeting and consumers' needs for relevant information. For example, a consumer might say "Send me information about men's clothes; but I don't have any kids, so don't send me anything about kids' clothiers. And I want to hear from you only once a month."[34]

Compare this with the practice of sending unsolicited e-mail messages, a practice pejoratively referred to as spam. As you may know, Spam is a brand of canned, processed meat that people love to joke about. For whatever reason, Internet users and pundits began using the word **spam** in reference to unsolicited and unwanted commercial e-mail messages. Such messages offer little prospect that recipients will do much more than click on and then rapidly click off. It could be argued that spam at least has a chance of influencing brand awareness, perhaps much

E-mail Advertising Is Highly Regulated in Europe

Much of the e-mail received by North American consumers is spam. Moreover, when consumers provide companies and other organizations with their e-mail addresses and supply personal information about themselves, there is a high likelihood that this information will be sold to a list broker, who in turn will sell the information to other companies and organizations. In short, once given, your address and other marketing-pertinent information virtually becomes part of the public domain.

Regulation is more stringent in Europe. In 1999 the European Commission of European Union (EU) countries issued a directive designed to create An EU-wide standard to regulate the way marketers are permitted to collect, retain, and disseminate consumers' private data. Marketers, in keeping with this directive, must inform consumers about what data is being collected and retained, instruct them as to how the data will be used in the future, and then provide consumers with the opportunity to opt in or out of the process. The European Commission's directive also prevents any company with European operations from sending data on European consumers or B2B customers to any country whose consumer protection laws do not equal those of the European Commission.

Beyond this EU-wide directive, individual countries have developed laws that are stricter than the European Commission's direction. Germany has the strictest consumer-protection laws in the EU. German courts are in the process of stopping unsolicited e-mail all together. The United Kingdom also has strict protection laws, including, for example, the limit against transferring consumer data to other countries unless these countries have regulations that are as strict as the U.K.'s. Moreover, every Web site in the U.K. must register two people who will be held responsible, and thus accountable, for upholding data protection laws for that site.

Marketers must be careful to abide by these regulations. The regulations are not insurmountable, however, and e-mail advertising in Europe is attractive because response rates in Europe are much higher than in North America.

Source: Adapted from Lisa Bertagnoli, "E-Marketing Tricky in Europe," *Marketing News*, July 16, 2001, p. 19. Reprinted with permission from Marketing News, Published by the American Marketing Association.

---

like may happen when the consumer is perusing a magazine and unintentionally comes across an ad for a product in which she or he has little interest. However, whereas the consumer expects to see ads in magazines and realizes that this is part of the "cost of entry," the consumer does not, at least at the present time, expect to receive unsolicited e-mail messages. Hence, any brand awareness gain a marketer might obtain from e-mailing unsolicited messages is likely to be offset by the negative reaction consumers have to this form of advertising. At the present time (as of early 2002), regulations against unsolicited e-mail are much more stringent in Europe than in North America. (See the *Global Focus* for elaboration.)

The Virtues of E-Mail Advertising

E-mail advertising is no different than p-mail in the sense that both forms of direct advertising have the objective of putting "an actionable message in front of a predisposed buyer."[35] The following discussion focuses on e-mail advertising's merits, yet it should be realized that many of these qualities apply as well to the older form of p-mail direct advertising. Points of distinction between e- and p-mail will be noted where appropriate. Table 14.3 lists seven virtues of e-mail advertising, each of which is now described.

Targeting. As described earlier when discussing databases and mining of data warehouses, e- as well as p-mailers can target specific messages to well-

Virtues of E-Mail Advertising

Table 14.3

- **Targeting**
- **Personalization**
- **Efficiency**
- **Effectiveness**
- **Measurability/Accountability**
- **Speed**
- **Safety**

defined groups of present customers or prospects by selecting just those who have particular "graphic" characteristics (buyographic, demographic, geographic, psychographic, or some combination of these). When discussing the role and importance of targeting back in Chapter 3, the point was made that marketing communicators, like golfers, should take dead aim on their target. No advertising medium provides this capability better than the Internet. By gaining detailed opt-in data, advertisers know precisely which prospects or past customers are likely to respond favorably to e-mail messages.

Personalization.   In addition to targeting, e-mail messages can be personalized to individuals' unique information needs. J. C. Penney, for example, has a database containing nearly 5 million e-mail addresses from customers who have opted to receive e-mail messages from the retailer. J. C. Penney tailors messages to the individual customer's interest and needs. Digital Impact, a California-based company that makes its services available to brand marketers, created a 100,000-recipient e-mailing for one client in which there were 35,000 variations of the same message![36] Digital Impact and other specialists in the e-mail business personalize messages based on where people live, what products and brands they have purchased in the recent past, and, based on a predictive model of past behavior, what people in their demographic/psychographic category generally look for and want in products. Barnes & Noble, the well-known book retailer, personalizes messages in a variety of ways. For example, if an author were at a particular store signing his or her latest book for interested purchasers, Barnes & Noble would send e-mail messages just to customers in zip codes located within the store's trading area.[37] Because e-mail advertising is so inexpensive, it is possible (and desirable) to test various versions of e-mail ads against samples drawn from different customer/prospect groups and then, based on results from this testing, to customize messages based on which worked best with each customer group.

Cost-Efficiency.   E-mail advertising is a relative bargain compared with p-mail. Whereas (as of 2001) it cost about 18 cents to send a letter at the bulk postage rate, e-mail messages cost as little as half a cent to deliver.[38] The price of e-mail varies as a function of volume, but a typical rate is around 5 cents per message.[39] (Only when millions of e-mail messages are sent does the rate fall as low as a penny or less per mailing.)

Effectiveness.   Response rates to p-mail messages often are less than 2 percent. Comparatively, response rates to e-mail messages sometimes exceed 20 percent. However, an important cautionary note is needed in this regard. E-mail advertising is a relatively novel practice at the time of this writing (early 2002). As the practice increases in magnitude and as consumers are increasingly bombarded, it can be expected that response rates to e-mail messages will fall considerably to a level only slightly higher than that achieved with p-mail messages. Beyond the comparison with p-mail, the evidence at this point indicates that e-mail advertising is substantially more effective than banners, pop-ups, and interstitials in generating click throughs and in terms of other performance metrics such as return on investment.

E-mail advertising is effective in one other sense. In particular, it has been demonstrated to be a very effective means of generating word-of-mouth buzz (of the type discussed in detail in Chapter 6) among Internet users. Buzz generation, also referred to as viral marketing, perhaps works even better online than offline because it is so easy to forward e-mail messages. This is why so many e-mail advertisements encourage the recipient to forward the message to a friend.

Measurability/Accountability.   A feature common to p- and e-mail messages is that both call for a *specific action* from message recipients — place an order, request a visit from a salesperson (in the case of B2B advertising), participate in a game, and so on. The comparative beauty of e-mail advertising, however, is that because the response medium is the same as the advertising medium (the Internet in both instances) it is possible to directly calibrate the percentage of message recipients that undertakes the requested action. It is in this sense, then, that e-mail is a highly measurable and thus accountable advertising medium, because response rates can readily be translated into return-on-investment terms.

Speed.   E-mail messages to millions of people can be transmitted rapidly and received as quickly as recipients read their e-mail. The two-to-three day period required for domestic p-mail deliveries (and up to a week or more for international deliveries) is not a problem from which e-mail suffers. Messages can be delivered throughout the world within a day of each other (due to time zone differences), and prospective customers can respond quickly via the same Internet medium from which they received the message. E-mail messages also can be changed relatively quickly, if conditions demand adjustments, inasmuch as printing time is eliminated.

Safety.   Sad to say, but in a world where terrorists and crazy people mail letters laced with anthrax and other dangerous items or hazardous substances, e-mail avoids the hazards of p-mail. A balanced perspective must recognize, on the other hand, that electronic viruses are problematic when opening e-mail messages. Many Internet users immediately delete messages from senders whose identities are unknown, especially after news of a recent electronic virus. P-mail has historically been a very safe medium, and absent additional anthrax-type scares of the sort following the World Trade Center and Pentagon bombings on September 11, 2001, it may be that e-mail is no more safe (and even less safe due to electronic viruses) than its p-mail cousin.

Acquiring Opt-In Lists

As with p-mail, e-mail advertising is only as effective as the list of customers and prospects to whom the message is sent. Although e-mail advertisers, like their p-mail counterparts, often purchase external lists from list brokers, it is generally considered that a house list is considerably better in generating high response rates to the action requested. The *Opening Vignette* described the practice of list rental in some detail in the context of the SmarterKids.com discussion. Now that you have a better understanding of the issues, it would be worthwhile to return to that story for a more complete reading.

The Special Case of Wireless E-mail Advertising

Laptops with wireless modems, handheld computers — so called personal digital assistants, or PDAs (see Figure 14.2) — cell phones, and pagers are invaluable tools for millions of businesspeople and consumers around the globe. These mobile appliances enable people to remain connected to the Web without being tethered to a wired laptop or desktop PC. Needless to say, advertisers would like to reach businesspeople and consumers on their wireless devices just as much as they covet contacting them when they are electronically wired into the Internet. This section offers a brief discussion of the nature and future of wireless advertising. Because wireless advertising is in its infancy, the following comments are necessarily somewhat speculative.

   Wireless devices are widespread. It is estimated that by 2005 more than 60 million North Americans will be using Internet access devices such as cell phones

The Palm Handheld Device for Internet Access   **Figure 14.2**

equipped with wireless access protocol (WAP), PDAs, and two-way messaging devices.[40] Vodafone estimates that about 70 percent of wireless users also use the Internet, and Motorola speculates that by 2004 more people will access the Internet via a wireless than wired device.[41]

These statistics clearly indicate considerable potential for advertisers to reach people through their wireless devices. Perhaps the more important issue, however, is whether people want to be accessed via their wireless items. Because mobile phones, PDAs, and pagers are highly personal items (i.e., they go with us everywhere and often are in constant contact with our bodies), many critics of wireless advertising (as well as advertisers themselves) are concerned that unwanted messages represent an invasion of privacy. Feeling invaded, recipients of undesired advertisements may immediately zap the intruding item and hold negative feelings toward the offending advertiser—"How dare you send me a message for a product or service about which I have absolutely no interest!"

In addition to privacy invasion, others are skeptical about wireless advertising's future on grounds that advertising is antithetical to the reasons why people own wireless devices in the first place.[42] The argument, in other words, is that people own wireless devices for reasons of enhancing time utilization and increasing work-related productivity while away from the workplace or home, and the last thing they want to happen while using these devices is to receive unwanted, interrupting advertising messages. Another potential limit on the immediate future of effective wireless advertising is that the small screens on cell phones and handheld devices (see Figure 14.2) limit the space for presenting a creative advertising message.

It would seem, based on the downside arguments just noted, that wireless advertising is not a viable prospect. Only the future will tell for sure. It is certain at the present time, however, that many advertisers much desire the opportunity to reach prospective customers via their wireless appliances. Another certainty is that successful e-mail advertising on wireless devices must be based on an opt-in model, where message recipients have absolutely indicated their interest in receiving certain types of messages via their wireless devices. Wireless ad recipients must, in other words, have complete *control* over the advertising content they are willing to receive as well as when and where they receive ad messages.[43] Advertisers must secure the wireless device user's permission to send him or her ad messages and make the user a quid pro quo: If you grant me (the advertiser) permission to send messages to you regularly, say once a week, I will provide you with useful information on topics of interest to you.[44] Such an arrangement benefits the interests of both advertiser and consumer and thus provides an opportunity for the advertising community to profit from ads placed on wireless devices.

Many who are skeptical of a successful future for wireless advertising nonetheless believe this ad medium may have value for local retailers such as restaurants, entertainment complexes, and various service operations.[45] Retail outlets can send promotional offers, price discounts, and other pertinent information to consumers who are in the vicinity of the retailer's store. This is made possible by positioning systems (similar to the Global Positioning Satellite) available on all wireless devices that pinpoint a wireless user's location to a particular retail outlet within 100 or less feet (30.5 meters or less). For example, Jiffy Lube, the retail chain offering quick oil changes, tested the use of wireless advertisements in San Francisco. Recipients received oil change reminders on their pagers or cell phones whenever they passed a Jiffy Lube franchise and were promised an attractive discount if they came in for an oil change during nonpeak times.[46]

In the final analysis, wireless advertising offers a potentially attractive advertising medium, but there are notable problems that may or may not be overcome. It is clear that spamming wireless device users is totally ineffective and that successful advertising must gain the user's permission and allow him or her control over message content and how often, when, and where message receipt is acceptable. The next several years will provide us with a rearview mirror perspective on whether wireless advertising is merely a passing fad or a long-term, viable advertising medium.

SUMMARY

Direct advertising is an important and rapidly growing aspect of marketing communications activity. Direct advertising, in comparison to broadcast advertising, does not deal with customers as a mass but rather creates individual relationships with each customer or prospective customer. Historically, most organizations regarded direct advertising as a minor supplement to their mass advertising efforts. Today, however, direct advertising is increasingly being viewed as a critical component of successful IMC programs. Indeed, rather than treating direct advertising as an afterthought, or little more than a practice that completes a mass-oriented advertising program, many firms are handling direct advertising as the cornerstone of their communication efforts. The increased sophistication of database marketing has been largely responsible for the growing use and effectiveness of direct advertising. Major advances in computer technology and database marketing have made it possible for companies to maintain huge databases containing millions of prospects and customers.

Successful direct advertising, of both the postal (p-mail) and electronic (e-mail) varieties, necessitates the availability of computer databases and their inherent addressability. Direct advertising's notable advantages vis-à-vis mass advertising are that marketers can target messages to specific market segments and determine success (or failure) virtually immediately. P- and e-mail also permit greater personalization than mass media advertising and are not subject to the same degree of clutter as with print and broadcast media. On a cost-per-order basis, direct advertising is often less expensive and more efficient than alternative media.

Direct advertising requires the advertiser to maintain a current database of present and prospective customers or to acquire a list of prospects from a company that specializes in list construction. An up-to-date database allows targeting of messages to prime prospects, provides for an ability to vary message content to different groups, enhances advertising productivity, enables the determination of a customer's lifetime value, and affords an opportunity to build long-term relations with customers. Databases can be massive in size with millions of addresses and hundreds of variables for each database entrant. The availability of high-speed computers and inexpensive computer software has made it possible for companies to literally mine their data warehouses for the purpose of learning more about customers' buying behavior. Sophisticated data miners look for revealing relations that can be used to target prospective customers, develop cooperative marketing relations, and otherwise better understand who buys what, when, how often, and along with what other products and brands.

In addition to the widespread use of p-mailing by all types of marketing communicators, e-mail advertising represents a potentially huge growth area. E-mail now is the most heavily used form of Internet advertising, far exceeding the amount invested in alternative advertising forms such as banners, pop-ups, and interstitials. Estimates peg the percentage of marketing-related e-mail received by Internet users as over 20 percent of all the e-mail transmitted. Roughly half the marketing-related e-mail is opt in, or permission granted, whereas the remainder is unsolicited, or so-called spam. European countries are more rigorous in their regulation of unsolicited e-mail than are regulators in North America. Virtues of e-mail advertising include (1) the ability to target messages to well-defined customer/prospect groups, (2) the opportunity to personalize messages to fit each group's unique information needs, (3) the relative inexpensiveness of e-mail versus p-mail, (4) the effectiveness in obtaining high response rates, (5) the ability to measure effectiveness and thus accomplish financial accountability, (6) the speed of transmission, and (7) the relative safety in comparison to p-mail, where anthrax-type scares are a fact of life in the post–September 11 world.

Wireless e-mail advertising (to handheld computers, cell phones, and pagers) provides another horizon for direct advertisers. Although there is considerable potential for advertisers to reach people via their wireless appliances, there is much concern that people do not want to be bothered. Only time will tell whether wireless advertising achieves the prominence that some optimists forecast it will.

Find more resources to help you study at http://shimp.swcollege.com!

DISCUSSION QUESTIONS

1. Four types of "graphics" are used in compiling databases: buyographics, demographics, geographics, and psychographics. Provide one illustrative variable that a catalog marketer of women's clothing might include in its database for each of these "graphics."

2. Explain the meaning and importance of database "addressability."

3. The section describing database assets included the claim that an up-to-date database allows a marketing organization to create long-term relationships with customers. Offer an explanation of what this means to you.

4. Assume you are a direct marketer for a line of merchandise imprinted with the logos of major universities. These items are targeted to the fans and supporters of university athletic programs. Detail how you would compile a mailing list. Use your college or university for illustration.

5. Following is a lifetime value analysis framework similar to that presented in the chapter. Perform the calculations necessary to complete row K.

	Year 1	Year 2	Year 3	Year 4	Year 5
Revenue					
A Customers	2,000	_____	_____	_____	_____
B Retention rate	30%	40%	55%	65%	70%
C Average yearly sales	$250	$250	$250	$250	$250
D Total revenue	_____	_____	_____	_____	_____
Costs					
E Cost percentage	50%	50%	50%	50%	50%
F Total costs	_____	_____	_____	_____	_____
Profits					
G Gross profit	_____	_____	_____	_____	_____
H Discount rate	1	1.15	_____	_____	_____
I NPV profit	_____	_____	_____	_____	_____
J Cumulative NPV profit	_____	_____	_____	_____	_____
K Lifetime value (NPV)	_____	_____	_____	_____	_____

6. You may have noticed that Web sites seem to know more and more about you each time you visit. For instance, you may bookmark a popular site such as http://www.cdnow.com or http://home.microsoft.com and find that the computer on the other end knows not only that you've been there before but exactly when you last visited, what you were looking at the last time you visited, and so forth. Most Web sites accomplish this with HTTP cookies. A cookie is a small piece of information that's sent to your browser along with an HTML page when you access a particular site. When a cookie arrives, your browser saves this information to your hard drive; when you return to that site, some of the stored information is sent back to the Web server, along with your new request. The Web site http://www.cookiecentral.com is dedicated to explaining ex-

actly what cookies are and what they can do. Visit this site and present a discussion on how cookies can be and are used to compile direct marketing lists. Additionally, comment on the ethical debate surrounding the use of cookies.

7. Your college or university no doubt has an organizational unit that is responsible for marketing merchandise to alumni and other customers—items such as sweatshirts, T-shirts, caps, cups emblazoned with your school's logo, and so on. Assume that this unit in your school does *not* have an up-to-date computerized database. Explain how you would go about putting together such a database. What specific information would you maintain in your computerized database for each customer? How would you use this information?

8. As a consumer who probably has spent considerable time perusing the pages of different catalogs, provide your perspective on the value of catalogs to you. Why (or why not) would you purchase from a catalog company?

9. What has been your personal experience with e-mail advertising? Are you part of any opt-in lists whereby you receive regular (say once a week) e-mail messages? Can you recall having been spammed?

10. One virtue of e-mail advertising is that different messages for the same product or service can be mailed to various customer groups who differ with respect to pertinent buyographic, demographic, or other characteristics. This ability to "mass customize" messages should increase MarCom effectiveness, yet a cynic might look at this practice as a bit deceptive—somehow saying different things about your product to different audiences seems misleading. What is your view on this?

11. During the relatively few years in which e-mail advertising has been practiced, it has been able to achieve considerably higher response rates in comparison to its older and more established p-mail cousin. Do you think this response-rate differential between p- and e-mail will remain by, say, 2010, or will the two forms of direct mailing ultimately be equally effective after the novelty of e-mail wears off?

12. E-mail advertising is claimed to be very effective for viral marketing purposes—that is, buzz generation. This is accomplished by requesting an e-mail recipient to forward the message to a friend. Return to the discussion of buzz generation in Chapter 6, and then present your views on the effectiveness of the e-mail viral marketing practice. In other words, explain what makes e-mail buzz generation effective or not.

13. Present your views on the future of wireless advertising. That is, do you expect wireless devices such as handheld computers, cell phones, and pagers to be effective ad media. Offer your specific views on the effectiveness of each of these mobile devices rather than lumping them together as if they are identical.

ENDNOTES

1. This description is adapted from Don E. Schultz, "The Direct/DataBase Marketing Challenge to Fixed-Location Retailing," in *The Future of U.S. Retailing: An Agenda for the 21st Century*, ed. Robert A. Peterson (New York: Quorum Books, 1992), 165–184.

2. Jonathan Berry, John Verity, Kathleen Kerwin, and Gail DeGeorge, "A Potent New Tool for Selling: Database Marketing," *Business Week*, September 5, 1994, 56–57.

3. An excellent review of the history of database marketing is provided in Lisa

A. Petrison, Robert C. Blattberg, and Paul Wang, "Database Marketing: Past, Present, and Future," *Journal of Direct Marketing* 7 (summer 1993), 27–43.

4. Robert C. Blattberg and John Deighton, "Interactive Marketing: Exploiting the Age of Addressability," *Sloan Management Review* (fall 1991), 5.

5. Ibid.

6. The list of database assets is adapted from the following sources: Blattberg and Deighton, "Interactive Marketing: Exploiting the Age of Addressability," 14; Rob Jackson and Paul Wang,

Strategic Database Marketing (Lincoln-wood, Ill.: NTC Business Books, 1994), 14–15; Stan Rapp and Thomas L. Collins, *MaxiMarketing: The New Direction in Advertising, Promotion, and Marketing Strategy* (New York: McGraw-Hill, 1987), 216–231; Terry G. Vavra, *Aftermarketing* (Homewood, Ill.: Business One Irwin, 1992).

7. Arthur M. Hughes, *Strategic Database Marketing* (Chicago: Probus, 1994), 17.

8. This table and the following discussion are based on ibid., 47–50. There are more sophisticated approaches to lifetime value analysis, but this example contains all the elements essential to understanding the fundamentals of the approach.

9. Op. cit., 17.

10. Robert J. Samuelson, "Computer Communities," *Newsweek*, December 15, 1986, 66.

11. Lorraine Calvacca, "Mouse Trapping," *Promo*, May 2001, 47–50.

12. Edward L. Nash, *Database Marketing: The Ultimate Marketing Tool* (New York: McGraw-Hill, 1993), 15–20.

13. Ibid., 18.

14. Matthew Kinsman, "Netting Consumers," *Promo*, October 2000, 55–60.

15. Jane Hodges and Alic Z. Cuneo, "Levi's Registration Program Will Seek to Build Database," *Advertising Age*, February 24, 1997, 86.

16. Rapp and Collins, *MaxiMarketing*, 50.

17. Lynn G. Coleman, "Data-Base Masters Become King of the Marketplace," *Marketing News*, February 18, 1991, 13.

18. Todd Wasserman, Gerry Khermouch, and Jeff Green, "Mining Everyone's Business," *Brandweek*, February 28, 2000, 36.

19. Information provided by The Martin Agency, Richmond, VA, 1998.

20. George E. Bardenheier, Jr., "More to Database Brand Building than Filling Up a Lot of Mail Boxes," *Brandweek*, May 2, 1994, 20.

21. This list is slightly adapted from that provided by the United States Postal Service in a CD-ROM titled "How to Develop and Execute a Winning Direct Mail Campaign," circa 2001 (http://www.usps.com).

22. "P-B Survey: Direct Mail Is First Among Marketers," *Promo*, June 1996, 106.

23. "What Happened to Advertising," *Business Week*, September 23, 1991, 69.

24. Jean Halliday, "Driving Sales Directly," *Advertising Age*, October 22, 2001, 22.

25. Laura Loro, "Package Goods Expands Database," *Advertising Age*, August 14, 1995, 29.

26. Don Schultz as quoted in Gary Levin, "Going Direct Route," *Advertising Age*, November 18, 1991, 37.

27. Annetta Miller, "My Postman Has a Hernia!" *Newsweek*, June 10, 1991, 41.

28. Glenn Heitsmith, "Database Promotions: Marketers Move Carefully, but Some Are Still Faking It," *Promo*, October 1994, 39, 46.

29. Eric Yoder, "Driving Value from the Catalogue Customer," *1to1 Magazine*, November/December 2001, 31–35.

30. Gregory A. Patterson, "U.S. Catalogers Test International Waters," *The Wall Street Journal*, April 19, 1994, B1; Cacilie Rohwedder, "U.S. Catalog Firms Target Avid Consumers Overseas," *The Wall Street Journal Interactive Edition*, January 6, 1998 (http://interactive.wsj.com).

31. Jim Sterne and Anthony Priore, *Email Marketing* (New York: John Wiley & Sons, Inc., 2000), 1.

32. Jodi Mardesigh, "Too Much of a Good Thing," *The Industry Standard*, March 19, 2001, 84–85.

33. The 2003 estimate is from ibid., and the 2006 estimate is from Jupiter Media Metrix as cited in Suzanne Vranica, "Marketers Face Problem as Consumers Gripe About Receiving E-Mail Pitches," *Wall Street Journal Interactive Edition*, November 2, 2001 (http://interactive.wsj.com).

34. Jane E. Zarem, "Predicting the Next Email Business Model," *1to1 Magazine*, May/June 2001, 23.

35. Internet Business Center, "Why Does E-mail Work?" (http://www.ibizcenter.com/why_does_email_work.htm).

36. Eileen McCooey, "Making an Impact," *Brandweek*, April 17, 2000, 72–74.

37. Zarem, "Predicting the Next Email Business Model."

38. Vranica, "Marketers Face Problem as Consumers Gripe About Receiving E-Mail Pitches."

39. Thomas E. Weber, "Why Companies Are So Eager to Get Your E-Mail Address," *Wall Street Journal Interactive Edition*, February 12, 2001 (http://interactive.wsj.com).

40. Dana James, "It'll Be a Wireless, Wireless, Wireless, Wireless, World," *Marketing News*, July 17, 2000, 25–29.

41. Karl Greenberg, "Golden Age of Wireless," *Brandweek*, May 15, 2000, 104–110.

42. Stacy Lawrence, "Getting Ads on the Go," *The Industry Standard*, November 20, 2000, 289. This article cites a Forrester Research analyst who presented this position.

43. Ibid. Also, James, "It'll Be a Wireless, Wireless, . . . World"; Craig Krueger,

"A Medium That's Well Done," *Promo*, November 2001, 33.

44. This description is adapted from a statement made by Internet practitioner Seth Godin as cited in Bridget Eklund, "Ad Infinitum," *Red Herring*, March 20, 2001, 70.

45. Pui-Wing Tam, "Ads on Wireless Devices Are Seen As the Next Frontier. Or Is It Just Wishful Thinking?" *Wall Street Journal Interactive Edition*, April 23, 2001 (http://interactive.wsj.com)

46. Jeff Green, "Leveraging the Lube Job," *Brandweek*, July 17, 2000, 48–50.

Chapter Fifteen

MEDIA PLANNING AND ANALYSIS

Chapter Objectives

After studying this chapter, you should be able to:

1. Describe the major factors used in segmenting target audiences for media planning purposes.
2. Explain the meaning of reach, frequency, gross rating points, target rating points, effective rating points, and other media concepts.
3. Discuss the logic of the three-exposure hypothesis and its role in media and vehicle selection.
4. Describe the use of the efficiency index procedure for media selection.
5. Distinguish the differences among three forms of advertising allocation: continuous, pulsed, and flighted schedules.
6. Explain the principle of the recency, or shelf-space model, and its implications for allocating advertising expenditures over time.
7. Perform cost-per-thousand calculations.
8. Interpret the output from a computerized media model.

Opening Vignette: The Introductory Media Campaign for the Saab 9-5

The previous chapter included a discussion of Saab and noted that in the late 1990s, the Swedish automobile maker introduced a new luxury sedan named the Saab 9-5. This model represented Saab's first entry in the luxury category and was designed to compete against well-known high-equity brands including Mercedes, BMW, Volvo, Lexus, and Infiniti. Despite being a unique automobile company—with a respected background in airplane manufacturing—Saab had done relatively little to enhance its brand image in the United States. Saab suffered both from a low level of consumer awareness and a poorly defined brand image. Particularly troubling for Saab was the fact that its product mix had historically attracted younger consumers, but achieving success for its new luxury sedan would require that the 9-5 appeal to upscale families and relatively affluent older consumers.

In addition to an aggressive direct-mail campaign, as described in the previous chapter, Saab undertook a mass advertising campaign to achieve the following objectives: (1) generate excitement for the new 9-5 model line, (2) increase overall awareness for the Saab name, (3) encourage consumers to visit dealers and test-drive the 9-5, and (4) retail 11,000 units of the 9-5 during the introductory year.

The Saab 9-5 was positioned as a luxury automobile capable of delivering an ideal synthesis of performance and safety. Creative advertising executions portrayed Saab as a premium European luxury manufacturer and were designed to have a hint of mystery and wit. An intensive media campaign was needed to deliver the creative executions and achieve the company's three advertising objectives.

Television commercials for the Saab 9-5 were run throughout May on network TV and network cable, generating a total of 620 gross rating points (a concept discussed later in the chapter). A national newspaper campaign began even earlier, in early March, and ran regular advertisements throughout the remainder of the year in *USA Today* and the *Wall Street Journal*. An aggressive magazine campaign also ran throughout the year with insertions in automobile magazines (*Car & Driver*, *Road & Track*, etc.), sports publications (e.g., *Ski* and *Tennis*), home magazines (*Martha Stewart Living, Southern Living, Architectural Digest*), business and personal finance publications (*Money, Forbes, Fortune, Working Women*, etc.), and general interest magazines (*Time, New York Magazine*, and *Vanity Fair*). The ad campaign also included Internet banner ads throughout the year.

This integrated advertising campaign was designed to generate high levels of reach and frequency (concepts introduced later in this chapter) among the tar-

Source: Information provided by The Martin Agency, Richmond, VA.

get group of older and financially well-off consumers and ultimately to sell at retail 11,000 Saab 9-5 vehicles. The extensive mass-media advertising campaign in conjunction with the intensive direct-mailing effort (Chapter 14) provided every opportunity for the Saab 9-5 to achieve its ambitious introductory sales goals and enjoy success in future years.

The present chapter builds on the foundation established in the three previous chapters, which overviewed the major offline and online *mass media* (Chapters 12 and 13) and explored the role of offline and online *direct advertising media* (Chapter 14). These prior chapters examined the process by which advertisers select media categories and vehicles from the vast array of available alternatives. (You will recall from Chapter 12 that **media** are the *general* communication carriers of advertising messages—that is, television, magazines, newspapers, and so on— whereas **vehicles** are the *specific* broadcast programs or print choices in which advertisements are placed.)

Advertisers are placing more emphasis than ever on media planning, and media planners have achieved a level of unparalleled stature.[1] This is because an advertising message can be effective only when placed in the media and vehicles that best reach the target audience at a justifiable expense. The choice of media and vehicles is, in many respects, the most complicated of all marketing communications decisions due to the variety of decisions that must be made. In addition to determining which general media categories to use (television, radio, magazines, newspapers, outdoor, Internet, or alternative media), the media planner must also pick specific vehicles within each medium and decide how to allocate the available budget among the various media and vehicle alternatives. Additional decisions involve choosing geographical advertising locations and determining how to distribute the budget over time. The complexity of media selection is made clear in the following commentary:

> An advertiser considering a simple monthly magazine schedule, out of a pool of 30 feasible publications meeting editorial environment and targeting requirements, must essentially consider over one billion schedules when narrowing the possibilities down to the few feasible alternatives that maximize campaign goals within budget constraints. Why over one billion possible schedules? There are two outcomes for each monthly schedule, either to use a particular publication or not to do so. Therefore, the total number of possible schedules equals two raised to the 30th power (i.e., $2^{30} = 1,073,741,800$). . . . Now imagine how the options explode when one is also considering 60 prime time and 25 daytime broadcast television network programs, 12 cable television networks, 16 radio networks, 4 national newspapers, and 3 newspaper supplements, with each vehicle having between 4.3 [i.e., the average number of weeks in a month] and perhaps as many as 20 or more possible insertions per month.[2]

THE MEDIA-PLANNING PROCESS

Media planning is the design of a strategy that shows how investments in advertising time and space will contribute to the achievement of marketing objectives. The challenge in media planning is determining how best to *allocate* the fixed advertising budget for a particular planning period (say, a fiscal year) among ad media, across vehicles within media, and over time. As shown in Figure 15.1, media planning involves coordination of three levels of strategy formulations: marketing strategy, advertising strategy, and media strategy. The overall *marketing strategy* (consisting of target market identification and marketing mix selection) provides the impetus and direction for the choice of both advertising and media strategies. The *advertising strategy*—involving advertising objectives, budget, and message and media strategies—thus extends naturally from the overall marketing strategy.

Consider, for example, a *hypothetical* new sport utility vehicle (SUV) named the Dodge Rambler.[3] Assume that this name was selected as an extension of the

Figure 15.1

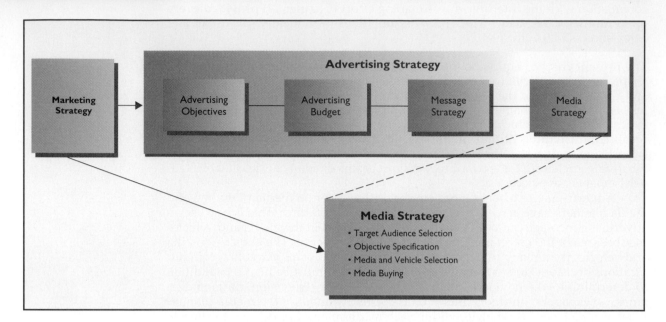

Ram name that Dodge carries on its truck line and also because the name Rambler appropriately connotes a rather carefree and leisurely lifestyle. Assume further that outdoor-oriented men represent the Rambler's primary target market and that prospective owners desire practicality along with a carefree, adventuresome image in a sport utility vehicle. The media strategy for the Rambler naturally must extend from Dodge's 2002 strategy to sell approximately 20,000 Ramblers at retail.

Media strategy necessarily evolves from the more general advertising strategy (see Figure 15.1). Let us assume that the Dodge Rambler had a $20 million advertising budget in 2002. Suppose further that Dodge's objective was to create brand awareness for the Rambler among targeted consumers and convey the desired image. Advertising strategy decisions simultaneously impose constraints on media strategy ($20 million is the maximum amount that could be spent on the 2002 Rambler campaign) and provide direction for media selection.

The media strategy itself consists of four sets of interrelated activities (see Figure 15.1):

1. Selecting the target audience.
2. Specifying media objectives.
3. Selecting media categories and vehicles.
4. Buying media.

The following sections discuss the first three activities in detail. Media buying is discussed only in passing because it is a specialized topic better suited for an elective course one might take as part of a communications or journalism major.

SELECTING THE TARGET AUDIENCE

Effective media strategy requires, first, that the target audience be pinpointed. Failure to precisely define the audience results in wasted exposures; that is, some nonpurchase candidates are exposed to advertisements while prime candidates are missed. Saab, for example, selected families and older "empty nesters" (i.e.,

[handwritten margin notes: Def. / Calc. p 435 / p 44a cost/thousand / Objectives in front of chapter / Chart. p 432]

couples without children living at home) as its primary target for the 9-5's advertising and direct mailing efforts.

Four major types of information are used in segmenting target audiences for media strategy purposes: (1) buyographics, (2) geographics, (3) demographics, and (4) lifestyle/psychographics. Product usage information (buyographics), when available, generally provides the most meaningful basis for determining which target audience(s) should be pinpointed for receiving an advertising message.[4] Geographic, demographic, and psychographic considerations are typically combined to define the target audience. Dodge, for example, might define the target audience for the Rambler in terms such as the following: men between the ages of 18 and 49 (a demographic variable), who have incomes exceeding $50,000 (also demographic), who enjoy the outdoors (psychographic), and are carefree and adventurous (psychographic). A target audience defined in such specific terms has obvious implications for both message and media strategy. For example, magazines and TV programs that appeal to outdoor enthusiasts who are adventurous and carefree ("ramblers") would effectively reach the Rambler's target audience.

SPECIFYING MEDIA OBJECTIVES

Having pinpointed the audience to whom advertising messages will be directed, the next media-planning consideration involves specifying the *objectives* that an advertising schedule is designed to accomplish during an advertising period. Media planners, in setting objectives, confront issues such as the following: (1) What proportion of the population (or of a target audience) do we want to reach with our advertising message during a specified period? (2) How frequently do we need to expose the audience to our message during this period? (3) How much total advertising is necessary to accomplish the reach and frequency objectives? (4) How should we allocate the advertising budget over time? (5) How close to the time of purchase should the target audience be exposed to our advertising message? (6) What is the most economically justifiable way to accomplish the other objectives?

Advertisers practitioners have technical terms they associate with each of these six objectives, namely (1) reach, (2) frequency, (3) weight, (4) continuity, (5) recency, and (6) cost. The following sections treat each objective as a separate matter. A later section addresses their interdependence.

Reach   *[handwritten: Test 3 is n1619 Wednesday]*

Reach represents the *percentage of the target audience* that is exposed, *at least once*, during a specified time frame to the vehicles in which our advertising message is inserted. The time frame used by the majority of media planners is a *four-week period*. (Thus, there are 13 four-week media-planning periods during a full year.) Some media specialists also use the single week as the planning period.

Regardless of the length of the planning period—whether one week, four weeks, or some other length of time—reach represents the percentage of all target customers who have an *opportunity to see or hear* the advertiser's message one or more times during this time period. (Advertising people use the expression *opportunity to see*, or *OTS*, to refer to all advertising media, whether visual or auditory.) Advertisers never know for sure whether members of their target audiences actually see or hear an advertising message (How possibly could that be known?). Advertisers only know what media vehicles the target audience is exposed to. From this vehicle exposure data (such as the Nielsen TV data described in Chapter 12), it then can be inferred that people have had an opportunity to see the advertising message carried in the vehicles.

Other terms used by media planners for describing reach are *1+* (read "one-plus"), *net coverage, unduplicated audience*, and *cumulative audience* (or *"cume"*). Later it will become clear why these terms are interchangeable with reach.

Determinants of Reach.

Several factors determine the reach achieved by an advertised brand's media schedule during, say, a four-week planning period. Generally speaking, more prospective customers are reached when a media schedule uses *multiple media* rather than a single medium. For example, if the Saab 9-5 were advertised only on network television, its advertisements would reach fewer people than if it were also advertised on cable TV, in magazines, and in national newspapers. In general, the more media used, the greater the chances that an advertising message will come into contact with people whose media habits differ. If an advertiser were to advertise a brand only in, say, newspapers, it would miss one-third of the adult population in the United States that does not regularly read a daily newspaper. Likewise, advertising only on select TV programs would miss people who do not view those particular programs. Hence, using multiple media increases the odds of reaching a greater proportion of the target audience.

A second factor influencing reach is the *number and diversity of media vehicles used*. For example, if Saab's media planners had chosen to advertise the 9-5 regularly in just a couple of magazines rather than the wide variety of magazines listed in the *Opening Vignette*, far fewer consumers would have been reached by the magazine advertising effort.

Third, reach can be increased by *diversifying the dayparts* used to advertise a brand. For example, network television advertising during prime time and cable television advertising during fringe times would reach more potential automobile purchasers than advertising exclusively during prime time.

In sum, reach is an important consideration when developing a media schedule for a brand. However, reach by itself is an inadequate objective for media planning because it tells nothing about *how often* target customers need to be exposed to the brand's advertising message for it to accomplish its goals. Therefore, frequency of advertising exposures must also be considered.

Frequency

Frequency signifies the number of times, on average, during the media-planning period (say four weeks) that members of the target audience are exposed to the media *vehicles* that carry a brand's advertising message. Frequency actually represents a media schedule's *average frequency*, but media people use the term *frequency* as a shorthand way of referring to average frequency.

To better understand the concept of frequency and how it relates to reach, consider the simplified example in Table 15.1. This example provides information about 10 hypothetical members of the target audience for the Dodge Rambler and their exposure to *Rolling Stone* magazine over four consecutive weeks. (We are assuming for purposes of this simplified example that *Rolling Stone* is the sole vehicle used for advertising the Rambler.) Member A, for example, is exposed to *Rolling Stone* on two occasions, namely, weeks two and three. Member B is exposed to *Rolling Stone* all four weeks. Member C is never exposed to the magazine during this four-week period. Member D is exposed three times, in weeks 1, 3, and 4; and so on for the remaining six members of Rambler's target audience. Notice in the last column of Table 15.1 that for each week, only 5 of 10 households (50 percent) are exposed to *Rolling Stone* and thus have an opportunity to see an advertisement for Rambler placed in this vehicle. This reflects the fact that a single vehicle (in this case, *Rolling Stone*) rarely reaches the full target audience, and exposure to an advertising vehicle does not guarantee that consumers will see a particular advertisement placed in that vehicle.

The Concept of Frequency Distribution. At the bottom of Table 15.1 are presented the frequency distribution and summary reach and frequency statistics for the Rambler's media schedule. A *frequency distribution* represents the percentage of audience members (labeled in Table 15.1 as "Percentage f") who are exposed f times (where $f = 0, 1, 2, 3$, or 4) to the *Rolling Stone* magazine and thus who had an opportunity to see ads for Rambler carried in this magazine. The cumulative frequency column (labeled "Percentage $f+$") indicates the percentage of the 10-member audience that has been exposed f times or more to *Rolling Stone* magazine during this four-week period (again, $f = 0, 1, 2, 3$, or 4). For example, the percentage exposed at least two times is 70 percent. Note carefully that for any value of f, the percentage in the Percentage $f+$ column simply represents the sum-

**Hypothetical Frequency Distribution for
Dodge Rambler Advertised in *Rolling Stone* Magazine**

Table 15.1

Target Audience Member

Week	A	B	C	D	E	F	G	H	I	J	Total Exposures
1		x		x	x		x		x		5
2	x	x			x		x		x		5
3	x	x		x				x		x	5
4		x		x		x	x			x	5
Total exposure	2	4	0	3	2	1	3	1	2	2	

Summary Statistics

Frequency Distribution (f)	Percentage f	Percentage f+	Audience Members
0	10%	100%	C
1	20	90	F, H
2	40	70	A, E, I, J
3	20	30	D, G
4	10	10	B

```
Reach (1+ exposures) = 90
Frequency = 2.2
GRPs = 200
```

mation from the Percentage *f* column of that value plus all values greater than
that value. Reading from the Percentage *f* column in Table 15.1, you will see that
the percentage of target audience members exposed exactly two times is 40 percent (i.e., audience members A, E, I, and J). The percentage exposed exactly three
times is 20 percent (members D and G). And the percentage exposed four times is
10 percent (member B). Hence, the cumulative percentage of audience members
exposed two or more times (i.e., the percentage *f*+ when *f* = 2) is 70 percent (40 +
20 + 10 = 70).

With this background, we now are in a position to illustrate how both frequency and reach are calculated. It can be seen in Table 15.1 that 90 percent of the
hypothetical audience for the Rambler advertisement have been exposed to one
or more ads during the four-week advertising period. (Reading from the Percentage *f* + column, with *f* = 1, it can be seen that the 1+ cumulative percentage is 90.)
This figure, 90 percent, represents the reach for this advertising effort. Please note
that advertising practitioners drop the percent sign when referring to reach and
simply refer to the number. In this case, reach is expressed simply as 90.

Frequency is the average of the frequency distribution. In this situation, frequency equals 2.2. That is, 90 percent of the target audience are reached one or
more times, 20 percent are reached one time, 40 percent are reached two times, 20
percent are reached three times, and 10 percent four times. Or, arithmetically,

$$\frac{(1 \times 20) + (2 \times 40) + (3 \times 20) + (4 \times 10)}{90} = \frac{200}{90} = 2.2$$

This hypothetical situation thus indicates that 90 percent of the Rambler's target
audience is reached by the advertising schedule and that they are exposed an average of 2.2 times during the four-week advertising schedule in *Rolling Stone*.
This value, 2.2, represents this simplified media schedule's frequency. (The exact

frequency actually is 2.22; however, media practitioners round frequency figures to a single decimal place.)

Weight

A third objective involved in formulating media plans is determining how much advertising volume (termed *weight* by practitioners) is required to accomplish advertising objectives. Different metrics are used in determining an advertising schedule's weight during a specific advertising period. This section describes three weight metrics: gross ratings, target ratings, and effective ratings.

Gross Rating Points (GRPs).   Notice at the bottom of Table 15.1 that Rambler's ad schedule in *Rolling Stone* yields 200 GRPs. **Gross rating points, or GRPs, reflect the gross weight that a particular advertising schedule** has delivered. The term *gross* is the key. GRPs indicate the gross coverage, or *duplicated audience*, exposed to a particular advertising schedule. Compare these terms with the alternative terms given earlier for reach—that is, *net coverage* and *unduplicated audience*.

Returning to our hypothetical example, the reach (net coverage, unduplicated audience) is 90. The gross rating points (gross coverage, duplicated audience) amount to 200 because audience members are exposed multiple times (2.2 times on average) to the vehicles that carry the Rambler advertisement during the four-week ad schedule.

It should be apparent from this discussion that GRPs represent the arithmetic product of reach times frequency.

$$\text{GRPs} = \text{Reach (R)} \times \text{Frequency (F)}$$
$$= 90 \times 2.22$$
$$= 200$$

By simple algebraic manipulation the following additional relations are obtained:

$$R = \text{GRPs} \div F$$
$$F = \text{GRPs} \div R$$

Determining GRPs in Practice.   In advertising practice, media planners make media purchases by deciding how many GRPs are needed to accomplish established objectives. However, because the frequency distribution and reach and frequency statistics are unknown before the fact (i.e., at the time when the media schedule is determined), media planners need some other way to determine how many GRPs will result from a particular schedule.

There is, in fact, a simple way to make this determination. GRPs are ascertained by simply summing the ratings obtained from the individual vehicles included in a prospective media schedule. Remember: Gross rating points are nothing more than *the sum of all vehicle ratings in a media schedule.*

But what are ratings? Let us illustrate the meaning of ratings using television as an example. In 2001 there were approximately 102.2 million households in the United States. A single **rating point** represents 1 percent, or 1,022,000 households. Table 15.2 presents the top 10 TV programs and their ratings for a single week in early February 2001. *ER*, the top-rated program during this particular week, had a rating of 17.9, which means that 17.9 percent, or approximately 18.3 million households (i.e., $1{,}022{,}000 \times .179$), were tuned in to this program on Thursday, February 2, 2001.

If during this particular week in 2001 an advertiser had placed one ad each on all 10 of the programs listed in Table 15.2, that advertiser would have accumulated 140.2 GRPs. You can prove this for yourself by summing the rating entries in the last column of Table 15.2.

Target Rating Points (TRPs).   A slight but important variant of GRPs is the notion of target rating points. **Target rating points, or TRPs, adjust a vehicle's rating to reflect just those individuals** *who match the advertiser's target audience*. Returning to the Rambler example, let us assume that the target for this rugged SUV

Gross Ratings for Top 10 TV Programs for One Week in 2001

Table 15.2

Program	Network	Night	Gross Rating
ER	NBC	Thursday	17.9
Survivor	CBS	Thursday	17.3
Friends	NBC	Thursday	14.2
CSI	CBS	Thursday	14.0
Everybody Loves Raymond	CBS	Monday	13.9
Millionaire	ABC	Wednesday	13.4
Will & Grace	NBC	Thursday	12.6
Millionaire	ABC	Sunday	12.4
Saturday Night Live Primetime	NBC	Thursday	12.4
The Practice	ABC	Sunday	12.1

Source: Nielsen Media Research. © 2001 Nielsen Media Research, a subsidiary of VNU Business Media, Inc. www.vnu.com

Target Ratings for the Top 10 TV Programs for One Week in 2001

Table 15.3

Program	Gross Rating	Target Rating
ER	17.9	5.9
Survivor	17.3	8.7
Friends	14.2	5.7
CSI	14.0	6.3
Everybody Loves Raymond	13.9	6.5
Millionaire	13.4	4.6
Will & Grace	12.6	3.1
Millionaire	12.4	4.1
Saturday Night Live Primetime	12.4	5.6
The Practice	12.1	3.2

Source: Gross Ratings from Nielsen Media Research. Target Ratings are hypothetical. © 2001 Nielsen Media Research, a subsidiary of VNU Business Media, Inc. www.vnu.com

is primarily men between the ages of 18 and 49 who have incomes of $50,000 or more. Considering the TV programs listed in Table 15.2, it is obvious that not all viewers of these programs match the profile of Rambler's target market. Table 15.3 adjusts the gross ratings presented in Table 15.2 to reflect the percentage of each program that matches Rambler's target market. Summing the ratings in the target ratings column reveals that one advertisement aired on each of these 10 TV programs would yield a total of 53.7 target rating points. *ER's* target rating of 5.9, for example, indicates that only one-third of this program's total viewership (from Table 15.2) matches Rambler's target market with respect to gender (male), age (18 to 49), and income ($50,000 or more).

Effective Rating Points (ERPs).   Alternative media schedules are usually compared in terms of the number of GRPs (or TRPs) that each generates. It is important to realize, however, that a greater number of GRPs (TRPs) does not necessarily indicate superiority. Consider, for example, two alternative media plans, X and Z, both of which require the same budget. Plan X generates 90 percent reach and an average frequency of 2.0, thereby yielding 180 GRPs. (Note again that reach is defined as the proportion of the audience exposed one or more times to an advertising vehicle during the course of a four-week campaign.) Plan Z provides for 166 GRPs from a reach of 52 percent and a frequency of 3.2. Which plan is better? Plan X is clearly superior in terms of total GRPs and reach, but Plan Z has a higher frequency level. If the brand in question requires a greater number of exposures for the advertising to achieve effectiveness, then Plan Z may be superior even though it yields fewer GRPs.

It is for the reason suggested in the preceding comparison that many advertisers and media planners have become critical of the GRP concept, contending that "it rests on the very dubious assumption that every exposure is of equal value, that the 50th exposure is the same as the tenth or the first."[5] Although the GRP concept remains very much a part of media planning, the advertising industry has turned away from the exclusive use of "raw" advertising weight (i.e., GRPs) toward a concept of media *effectiveness*.[6] The determination of media effectiveness takes into consideration *how often* members of the target audience have an opportunity to be exposed to advertising messages for the focal brand. The terms *effective reach* and *effective frequency* often are used interchangeably by media practitioners to capture the idea that an effective media schedule delivers a sufficient but not excessive number of ads to the target audience. Because the term *effective reach* creates less confusion when discussing the meaning and calculation of effective rating points (ERPs), that term is preferred in this text over effective frequency.

Effective reach is based on the idea that an advertising schedule is effective only if it does not reach members of the target audience *too few or too many times*. In other words, there is a theoretical optimum range of exposures to an advertisement with minimum and maximum limits. But what constitutes too few or too many exposures? This, unfortunately, is one of the most complicated issues in all of advertising. The only statement that can be made with certainty is, "It depends!"

It depends, in particular, on considerations such as the level of consumer awareness of the advertised brand, its competitive position, the audience's degree of loyalty to the brand, message creativity and novelty, and the objectives that advertising is intended to accomplish for the brand. In fact, high levels of weekly exposure to a brand's advertising may be unproductive for loyal consumers because of a leveling off of ad effectiveness.[7] Specifically, brands with higher market shares and greater customer loyalty typically require fewer advertising exposures to achieve minimal levels of effectiveness. Likewise, it would be expected that distinctive advertising requires fewer exposures. The higher up the hierarchy of effects the advertising is attempting to move the consumer, the greater the number of exposures needed to achieve minimal effectiveness. For example, more exposures probably are needed to convince consumers that the Rambler provides the dual advantages of practicality and excitement than merely to make them aware that there is a brand named Rambler.

How Many Exposures Are Needed?   It follows from the foregoing discussion that the minimum and maximum numbers of effective exposures can be determined only by conducting sophisticated research. Because research of this nature is time-consuming and expensive, advertisers and media planners generally have used rules of thumb in place of research in determining exposure effectiveness. Advertising industry thinking on this matter has been heavily influenced by the so-called **three-exposure hypothesis**, which addresses the *minimum* number of exposures needed for advertising to be effective. Its originator, an advertising practitioner named Herbert Krugman, argued that a consumer's initial exposure to a brand's advertising initiates a response of "What is it?" The second exposure triggers a response of "What of it?" And the third exposure and those thereafter are merely reminders of the information that the consumer already has learned from the first two exposures.[8] This hypothesis, which was based on little empirical data and a lot of intuition, has virtually become gospel in the advertising industry. Many advertising practitioners have interpreted the three-exposure hypothesis to mean that media schedules are ineffective when they deliver average frequencies of fewer than three exposures to the vehicle in which a brand's advertisement is placed.

Although there is some intuitive appeal to the notion that average frequencies of fewer than three are insufficient, this interpretation of the three-exposure hypothesis is too literal and also fails to recognize that Krugman's hypothesis had in mind three exposures to an advertising *message* and not three exposures to an advertising *vehicle*.[9] The difference is that vehicle exposure, or what we previously referred to as *opportunity to see* an ad *(OTS)*, is not tantamount to advertising exposure. A reader of a magazine issue certainly will be exposed to some advertisements in that issue, but the odds are that he or she will not be exposed to all, or even most, of them. Likewise, a viewer of a TV program will probably miss some of the commercials placed during a 30- or 60-minute program. Hence, the number of consumers who are actually exposed to any particular advertising message carried in a vehicle—what Krugman had in mind—is less than the number of people who are exposed to the vehicle that carries the message.[10]

Aside from this general misunderstanding of the three-exposure hypothesis, it must also be recognized that no specific number of minimum exposures—whether 3+, 5+, or x+—is absolutely correct for all advertising situations. It cannot be overemphasized that what is effective (or ineffective) for one product or brand may not necessarily be so for another. "There is no magic number, no comfortable '3+' level of advertising exposures that works, even if we refer to advertising exposure rather than OTS."[11]

An Alternative Approach: The Efficiency Index Procedure. Advertising scholars have proposed an alternative approach to the three-exposure doctrine.[12] The objective of the *efficiency index procedure* (as it will be referred to here) is to select that media schedule (from a set of alternative schedules) that generates the most exposure value per GRP—or, stated differently, provides a "bigger bang for the buck." This approach entails the following straightforward steps:

1. Estimate the *exposure utility* for each level of vehicle exposure, or OTS, that a schedule would produce.[13] Exposure utility represents the worth, or value, of each additional opportunity for audience members to see an ad for a brand during an advertising period such as four weeks. Table 15.4 lists OTSs (from 0 to 10+) and their corresponding exposure utilities. (Please note that these utilities are not invariant across all situations but have to be determined uniquely for each brand-advertising situation.) It can be seen that 0 vehicle exposures has, of course, an exposure utility of 0. One exposure adds the greatest amount of utility, assumed here to be 0.50 units; a second OTS contributes 0.13 additional units of utility (for an overall utility of 0.63); a third exposure contributes 0.09 more units to the second exposure (for an overall utility of 0.72 units); and so on. One can readily see that this utility function reflects decreasing marginal utility with each additional OTS. At an OTS of 10, the maximum utility of 1.00 is achieved. Hence, this illustration proposes that OTSs in excess of 10 offer

Exposure Utilities for Different OTS Levels — Table 15.4

OTS	Exposure Utility
0	0.00
1	0.50
2	0.63
3	0.72
4	0.79
5	0.85
6	0.90
7	0.94
8	0.97
9	0.99
10+	1.00

no additional utility. By graphing the utilities in Table 15.4, one can readily see that the function is nonlinear and concave to the origin. In other words, each additional exposure contributes decreasing utility.

2. Estimate the *exposure distribution* of the various media schedules that are under consideration. Computer programs, such as the ADplus program discussed later, are available for this purpose. Table 15.5 shows the distributions for two schedules. It can be seen that schedule 1 will reach 85 percent of the target. That is, if 15 percent of the target are exposed zero times (i.e., OTS = 0 = 15 percent), the remaining 85 percent are exposed one or more times (1+). Reading from columns B (schedule 1) and D (schedule 2) in Table 15.5, it can be seen that 11.1 percent of the target audience is estimated to be exposed exactly one time to schedule 1 (21.0 percent are exposed one time to schedule 2); 12.5 percent of the audience exposed exactly two times to schedule 1 (17.6 percent to schedule 2); 13.2 percent three times to schedule 1 (13.6 percent to schedule 2); and so on.

3. Estimate the *value at each OTS level* and then the *total value across all OTS levels*. Entries in the *OTS value* columns in Table 15.5 (column C for schedule 1 and column E for schedule 2) are calculated at each OTS level (OTS = 1, 2, 3, . . . , 10+) by taking the arithmetic product of the Percentage of Target column times the exposure utility at each OTS level. Hence, at an OTS of one exposure, the exposure value is $0.5 \times 11.1 = 5.55$ for schedule 1 and 10.5 for schedule 2 (0.5×21.0). At an OTS of two exposures, the exposure value is $0.63 \times 12.5 = 7.875$ (schedule 1) and $0.63 \times 17.6 = 11.088$ (schedule 2); and so on. After the value at each OTS level is determined, the *total value* is obtained by simply summing the individual exposure values ($5.55 + 7.875 + 9.504 + . . . + 10.5 = 66.481$ for schedule 1). The total value for schedule 2 is similar at 66.482.

4. Develop an *index of exposure efficiency* by dividing the *total value* for each schedule by the number of *GRPs* produced by that schedule. Total GRPs are determined from the data in Table 15.5 in the same way they were

Table 15.5 — Frequency Distributions and Valuations of Two Schedules

OTS	(A) Exposure Utility	Schedule 1 (B) Percentage of Target	Schedule 1 (C) OTS Value (A × B)	Schedule 2 (D) Percentage of Target	Schedule 2 (E) OTS Value (A × D)
0	0.00	15.0%	0.000	8.0%	0.000
1	0.50	11.1	5.550	21.0	10.500
2	0.63	12.5	7.875	17.6	11.088
3	0.72	13.2	9.504	13.6	9.792
4	0.79	11.0	8.690	10.9	8.611
5	0.85	8.4	7.140	8.6	7.310
6	0.90	6.3	5.670	6.6	5.940
7	0.94	5.0	4.700	5.2	4.888
8	0.97	3.9	3.783	3.9	3.783
9	0.99	3.1	3.069	3.0	2.970
10+	1.00	10.5	10.500	1.6	1.600
Total Value:			66.481		66.482
GRPs:			398.6		333.8
Index of Exposure Efficiency (Value/GRPs):			0.167		0.199
3+ Reach:			61.4%		53.4%

identified earlier from Table 15.1 data. Specifically, schedule 1's total of 398.6 GRPs (see bottom of Table 15.5) is calculated as $(1 \times 11.1) + (2 \times 12.5) + (3 \times 13.2) + \ldots + (10 \times 10.5)$. You should ensure that you understand this by calculating the GRPs for schedule 2. The index of exposure efficiency for schedule 1 is 0.167 (i.e., $66.481 \div 398.6$), whereas the index value for schedule 2 is 0.199 (i.e., $66.482 \div 333.8$).

With higher index values representing greater exposure efficiency, it should be clear that the second media schedule in Table 15.5 is more efficient. That is, schedule 2 has a higher efficiency index than schedule 1 because schedule 2 accomplishes an equivalent exposure value (66.482 versus 66.481) but with fewer GRPs and hence less expense. Moreover, whereas schedule 1 reaches a high percentage of the target audience 10 or more times (i.e., OTS = 10+ = 10.5 percent), schedule 2 focuses more on reaching the audience at least one time (OTS = 1 = 21 percent) rather than wasting expenditures on reaching the audience 10 or more times.

In concluding this section, it should be further noted from the bottom of Table 15.5 that schedule 1 is superior to schedule 2 in terms of its 3+ reach (61.4 percent versus 53.4 percent). However, when using the systematic and logical procedure described here, schedule 2 is superior to schedule 1 when applying the criterion of efficiency. In other words, schedule 2 reaches proportionately fewer audience members three or more times, but it produces an exposure value comparable to that produced by schedule 1 at a lower expense and with fewer GRPs.

Although this index of exposure efficiency is theoretically more sound than the three-exposure heuristic, the latter is embedded in advertising practice whereas the former has just recently been introduced. We therefore return to standard advertising practice and discuss the heuristics used by advertising practitioners in determining the effective number of exposures. The implication is not that this new procedure should be dismissed out of hand; the point, instead, is that advertising practice has not as yet had time to widely adopt the approach.

Effective Reach in Advertising Practice.   Although effective reach planning is widely practiced by large consumer-product advertisers, media planners remain divided on the matter of what constitutes effective reach.[14] Nevertheless, the mostly widely accepted view is that *fewer than three exposures* during a four-week media schedule is generally considered ineffective, while *more than 10 exposures* during this period is considered excessive. The range of effective reach, then, can be thought of as *three to 10 exposures* during a designated media-planning period, which, as previously noted, typically is four weeks.

The use of effective reach rather than gross rating points as the basis for media planning can have a major effect on overall media strategies. In particular, effective reach planning generally leads to using *multiple media* rather than depending exclusively on television, which is often the strategy when using the GRP criterion. Prime-time television is especially effective in terms of generating high levels of reach (1+ exposures) but may be deficient in terms of achieving effective reach (3+ exposures). Thus, the use of effective reach as the decision criterion often involves giving up some of prime-time television's reach to obtain greater frequency (at the same cost) from other media.

This is illustrated in Table 15.6, which compares four media plans involving different combinations of media expenditures from an annual advertising budget of $12 million.[15] Plan A allocates 100 percent of the budget to network television advertising; plan B allocates 67 percent to television and 33 percent to network radio; plan C splits the budget between network television and magazines; and plan D allocates 67 percent to television and 33 percent to outdoor advertising.

Notice first that plan A (the use of network television only) leads to the lowest levels of reach, effective reach, frequency, and GRPs. An even split of network television and magazines (plan C) generates an especially high level of reach (91 percent), while combinations of network television with network radio (plan B) and network television with outdoor advertising (plan D) are especially impressive in terms of frequency, GRPs, and the percentage of consumers exposed three or more times.

More to the point, notice that the network-television-only plan compared with the remaining plans yields far fewer GRPs and considerably fewer ERPs.

Table 15.6	Alternative Media Plans Based on a $12 Million Annual Budget and Four-Week Media Analysis			
	Plan A: TV (100%)	Plan B: TV (67%), Radio (33%)	Plan C: TV (50%), Magazines (50%)	Plan D: TV (67%), Outdoor (33%)
Reach (1+ exposures)	69%	79%	91%	87%
Effective reach (3+ exposures)	29%	48%	53%	61%
Frequency	2.8	5.5	3.2	6.7
GRPs	193	435	291	583
ERPs	81	264	170	409
Cost per GRP	$62,176	$27,586	$41,237	$20,583
Cost per ERP	$148,148	$45,455	$70,588	$29,340

Adapted from, "The Muscle in Multiple Media," Marketing Communications, December 1983, p. 25. Reprinted by permission.

(Please note that in Table 15.6 that ERPs equal the product of effective reach, or 3+ exposures, times frequency; plan A, for example, yields 81 ERPs, i.e., 29 × 2.8 = 81.) Plan D, which combines 67 percent network television and 33 percent outdoor advertising, is especially outstanding in terms of the numbers of GRPs and ERPs generated. This is because outdoor advertising is seen frequently as people travel to and from work and engage in other activities.

Should we conclude from this discussion that plan D is the best and plan A is the worst? Not necessarily! Clearly, the impact from seeing one billboard advertisement is probably far less than being exposed to a captivating television commercial. This points out a fundamental aspect of media planning: *Subjective factors* also must be considered when allocating advertising dollars. Superficially, the numbers do favor plan D. However, judgment and past experience may favor plan A on the grounds that the only way to effectively advertise this particular product is by presenting dynamic action shots of people consuming and enjoying the product. Only television could satisfy this requirement. Other media (radio, magazines, and outdoor advertising) may be used to complement the key message driven home by TV ads.

It is useful to return again to a point established in Chapter 9: *It is better to be vaguely right than precisely wrong.*[16] Reach, frequency, effective reach, GRPs, TRPs, and ERPs are precise in their appearance but, in application, if used blindly, may be precisely wrong. Discerning decision makers never rely on numbers to make decisions for them. Rather, the numbers should be used solely as additional inputs into a decision that ultimately involves insight, wisdom, and judgment. For further discussion of the role of subjectivity in media buying, see the *IMC Focus* discussion of Super Bowl advertising.

Continuity

A fourth general concern of the media planner is the timing of advertising. Continuity involves the matter of how advertising is allocated during the course of an advertising campaign. The fundamental issue is this: Should the media budget be distributed uniformly throughout the period of the advertising campaign; should it be spent in a concentrated period to achieve the most impact; or should some other schedule between these two extremes be used? As always, the determination of what is best depends on the specifics of the situation. In general, however, a uniform advertising schedule suffers from too little advertising weight at any one time. A heavily concentrated schedule, on the other hand, suffers from excessive exposures during the advertising period and a complete absence of advertising at all other times.

IMC
focus

Is Super Bowl Advertising Worth the Expense?

Nielsen Media Research determined that the 2001 National Football League Super Bowl televised on CBS had a 41.1 rating. Advertisers paid $2.05 million for placing a 30-second commercial on this program. Just three years earlier, in 1998, the cost of a 30-second advertisement during the Super Bowl was $1.3 million. Now, at the time of this writing, just about two weeks before the 2002 Super Bowl, the Fox network had failed to sell about 20 percent of the total advertising time available during the Super Bowl. Early buyers paid $2 million for 30-second spots, but buyers of the remaining inventory (available mostly for the game's least attractive fourth quarter) can purchase 30-second spots for as "little" as $1.5 million. Considering that 30-second spots on the top-rated prime-time television programs sell for less than $450,000 (see Table 12.7), one may wonder whether the investment in Super Bowl advertising can be justified.

Media planners at a company called Media Edge questioned whether the Super Bowl represents a prudent media buy and proposed another way to spend the amount of money equivalent to purchasing a 30-second Super Bowl spot. They developed an alternative media plan that consisted of (1) buying advertising time on all network programs aired at the same time on Tuesday night; (2) securing advertising time on all network programs aired at the same time on Sunday night (e.g., Sunday night movies); and (3) purchasing a final single spot from the Fox network's Saturday night programming. (The Tuesday and Sunday night buys are called *roadblocks* because advertising purchased on all network programs aired simultaneously acts, metaphorically, as a roadblock to ensure that all consumers viewing TV at this time will be exposed to the brand's advertising.) This alternative media plan was able to secure 13 prime-time advertising spots, or a to-

tal time of 6.5 minutes, compared with purchasing a single 30-second ad on the Super Bowl. Comparative GRPs for the Super Bowl media buy and the alternative plan appears below.

Whereas a single 30-second ad on the Super Bowl provided 40 GRPs based on the 18-to-49 age group, 42 GRPs based on the 25-to-54 group, and so on, the equivalently priced 13 spots yielded considerably more GRPs. For example, for all adults aged 25 to 54, the 78 GRPs from the 13 prime-time spots were 86 percent greater than the 42 GRPs generated by the Super Bowl advertisement.

Hence, one can conclude that advertisers should not have advertised on the Super Bowl but rather would have been better served by investing their advertising money elsewhere. Correct? Not necessarily, especially considering advertising *impact*. People react with a relatively unenthusiastic response to advertisements placed on the programs contained in the alternative media buy. Comparatively, advertisements placed on the Super Bowl are, like the program itself, a special event. Consumers look forward to new, dramatic advertisements and often talk about the advertisements well after the Super Bowl is completed. Journalists write about these advertisements in magazines, newspapers and on the Internet, so that advertisers receive a secondary form of brand contact. In short, all advertising does not have equivalent impact. When planners are buying advertising media, considerations, often subjective, other than mere comparisons of cost and rating points have to be factored into the decision.

Source: The 2002 cost data are from Wayne Friedman and Alice Z. Cuneo, "Safety Bowl," *Advertising Age*, January 14, 2002, 3. The 2001 rating and cost data are from Richard Linnett and Wayne Friedman, "No Gain," *Advertising Age*, January 15, 2001, 43. The 1998 ratings and cost data are from Kyle Pope, "NBC Scores Big With the Super Bowl; Game Is Among Most-Watched Ever," *The Wall Street Journal Interactive Edition*, January 27, 1998 (http://interactive.wsj.com). The information about the Media Edge's test is from Rob Frydlewicz, "Missed Super Bowl? Put Your Bucks Here," *Advertising Age*, January 30, 1995, 18.

Group	Super Bowl GRPs	Alternative 13-Spot GRPs	13-Spot Advantage Over Super Bowl
Adults, 18–49	40	65	+62%
Adults, 25–54	42	78	+86%
Men, 18–49	46	63	+37%
Men, 25–54	48	68	+42%

Advertisers have three general alternatives related to allocating the budget over the course of the campaign: *continuous*, *pulsing*, and *flighting* schedules. To understand the differences among these three scheduling options, consider the advertising decision faced by a dairy company that markets ice cream and other dairy-based dessert items. Figure 15.2 shows how advertising allocations might differ from month to month depending on the use of continuous, pulsing, or flighting schedules. Assume the annual advertising budget available to this marketer is $3 million.

Continuous Schedule.   In a **continuous advertising schedule**, an equal or relatively equal amount of ad dollars is invested throughout the campaign. The illustration in panel A of Figure 15.2 shows an extreme case of continuous adver-

Figure 15.2

Continuous, Pulsing, and Flighting Advertising Schedules for a Brand of Ice Cream

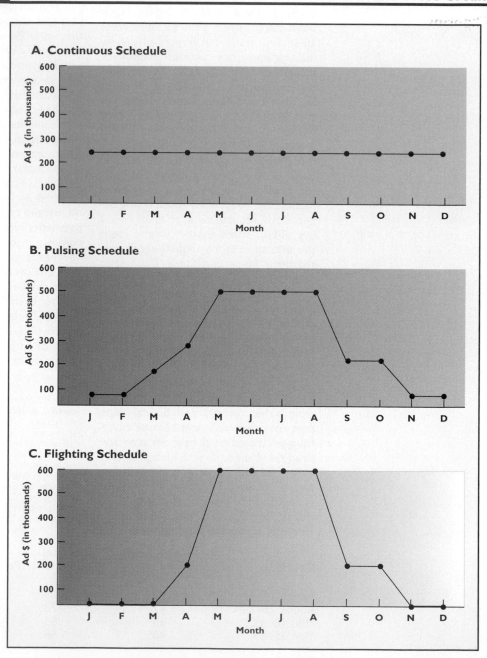

tising in which the advertiser allocates the $3 million advertising budget in equal amounts of exactly $250,000 for all 12 months throughout the year.

Such an advertising allocation would make sense only if ice cream were consumed in essentially equal quantities throughout the year. However, though ice cream is consumed year-round, consumption is particularly high during May, June, July, and August. This calls for a *discontinuous* allocation of advertising dollars throughout the year.

Pulsing. In a pulsing advertising schedule, some advertising is used during every period of the campaign, but the amount of advertising varies considerably from period to period. In panel B of Figure 15.2, a pulsing schedule for the hypothetical ice cream marketer shows that the company advertising is especially heavy during the high-consumption months of May through August (spending $500,000 each month) but continuing to advertise in every month throughout the year. The minimum advertising expenditure is $50,000 even in the slow sales months of January, February, November, and December.

Flighting. In a flighting schedule, the advertiser varies expenditures throughout the campaign and allocates *zero* expenditures in some months. As demonstrated in panel C of Figure 15.2, the ice cream advertiser allocates $600,000 to each of the four high-consumption months (May through August), $200,000 each to moderate-consumption months (April, September, and October), but zero dollars to five low-consumption months (January, February, March, November, and December).

Thus, pulsing and flighting are similar in that they both involve *differential levels of advertising expenditures* throughout the year, but the schedules differ in that some advertising takes place during every period with pulsing but not with flighting. The following analogies may help to eliminate any confusion between pulsing and flighting. Pulsing in advertising is similar to an individual's heartbeat or pulse. One's *pulse* changes continuously between some lower and upper bounds but is always present in a living person. Comparatively, a flighting schedule is like an airplane, which at times is at ground zero but at different altitudes when in flight. Thus, a pulsed advertising schedule is always beating (some advertising is placed in every ad period), whereas a flighted schedule soars at times to very high levels but is nonexistent on other occasions.

Recency Planning

Some advertising practitioners argue that flighted and pulsed advertising schedules are necessitated by the tremendous increases in media costs, especially the cost of network television advertising. Few advertisers, according to the logic of discontinuous ad scheduling (i.e., flighted or pulsed schedules), can afford to advertise consistently heavily throughout the year. According to this argument, advertisers are forced to advertise only at select times—namely, during periods when there is the greatest chance of accomplishing communication and sales objectives. This argument holds further that during periods when advertising is undertaken, there should be *sufficient frequency* to justify the advertising effort. In other words, the argument favoring discontinuous advertising (pulsing or flighting) goes hand in hand with the goal of achieving effective reach (3+) during any advertising period in which a brand manager chooses to have an advertising presence.

At first blush, the logic of discontinuous scheduling appears unassailable. However, the prudence of this argument has been challenged in recent years, most forcefully by Erwin Ephron, a New York media specialist. Ephron and his supporters assert that the advertising industry has failed to prove the value of the effective reach (3+) criterion for allocating advertising budgets and that this dubious criterion leads inappropriately to flighted allocations. Ephron has formulated an argument favoring continuous advertising that he terms the principle of recency, also called the shelf-space model or the theory of effective weekly planning.[17]

Because flighting is an on-and-off advertising proposition, consider by analogy what would happen to a brand's sales if retail shelves were out of stock for that brand during various times throughout the year. The brand obviously would experience zero sales during those periods of stock-outs when the shelves were empty. Sales would be obtained only during those times when the shelves held some amount of the brand. This, in a sense, is the way it is with flighted advertising schedules: The "shelves" are empty during certain periods (when no advertising is being run) and full during others.

The **recency principle**, or *shelf-space model*, is built on three interrelated ideas: (1) that consumers' *first exposure* to an advertisement for a brand is the most powerful; (2) that advertising's primary role is to influence brand choice, and that advertising does indeed influence choice for the *subset of consumers who are in the market* for the product category at the time a brand in that category advertises; and (3) that achieving a *high level of weekly reach* for a brand should be emphasized over acquiring heavy frequency. Let's examine all three ideas.

The Powerful First Exposure.   Empirical evidence (albeit somewhat tentative) has demonstrated that the first exposure to advertising has a greater effect on sales than do additional exposures.[18] (The utility function given previously in Table 15.4 was based on the logic that the first exposure has the greatest impact.) Using single-source data, which was covered in Chapter 12, an advertising researcher produced provocative findings based on an extensive study of 142 brands representing 12 product categories (detergents, bar soaps, shampoos, ice cream, peanut butter, ground coffee, etc.). The researcher demonstrated that the first advertising exposure for these brands generated the highest proportion of sales and that additional exposures added very little to the first.[19]

Influencing Brand Choice.   The concept of recency planning is based on the idea that consumer needs determine advertising effects. Advertising is especially effective when it occurs close to the time when consumers are in the market for a particular product. There is, in other words, a "window of advertising opportunity" for capturing the consumer's selection of the advertised brand versus other brands in the product category. "Advertising's job is to influence the purchase. Recency planning's job is to place the message in that window."[20]

Though recency planning is based on the idea that the first advertising exposure is the most powerful, this does not mean that a single exposure is sufficient. The point instead is that in the short-term additional exposures are likely to be wasted on consumers who are not in the market for the product. The logic, in other words, is that a brand can achieve greater sales volume by reaching more consumers a single time during an advertising period (a reach objective) rather than reaching fewer consumers more often (a frequency objective).[21] The advertising budget is not necessarily lower with recency planning; rather, the budget is allocated differently than is a flighted advertising budget. In particular, recency planning allocates the budget over more weeks throughout the year and invests less weight (fewer GRPs or TRPs) during the weeks in which advertising is undertaken. Recency planning uses one week, rather than four weeks, as the planning period and attempts to reach as many target consumers as possible in as many weeks as the budget will permit.[22]

Optimizing Weekly Reach.   Accordingly, it can be argued that media planners should devise schedules that are geared toward providing a continuous (or near continuous) presence for a brand with the objective of optimizing *weekly reach* rather than effective reach as embodied in the three-exposure hypothesis. Erwin Ephron's argument can be summarized as follows:

1. Contrary to the three-exposure hypothesis, which has been interpreted to mean that advertising must *teach* consumers about brands (therefore requiring multiple exposures), the recency principle, or shelf-space model, assumes that the role of advertising is *not* to teach but to influence consumers' *brand selection*. "Unless it's a new brand, a new benefit, or a new use, there is not much learning involved."[23] Hence, the purpose of most

advertising is to remind, reinforce, or evoke earlier messages rather than to teach consumers about product benefits or uses.

2. With the objective of influencing brand selection, advertising must therefore reach consumers when they are ready to buy a brand. The purpose of advertising by this logic is to "rent the shelf" so as to ensure a brand presence close to the time when consumers make purchase decisions. *Out of sight, out of mind* is the first principle of advertising according to Ephron.

3. Advertising messages are most effective when they are *close to the time of purchase*, and a single advertising exposure is effective if it reaches consumers close to the time when they are making brand-selection decisions.

4. The cost effectiveness of a single exposure is approximately *three times greater* than the value of subsequent exposures.[24]

5. Hence, rather than concentrating the advertising budget to achieve multiple exposures only at select times throughout the year, planners should allocate the budget to *reach more consumers more often*.

6. In a world without budget constraints, the ideal advertising approach would be to achieve a weekly reach of 100 (i.e., to reach 100 percent of the target audience at least one time) and to sustain this level of reach for all 52 weeks of the year. Such a schedule would yield 5,200 weekly reach points. Because most advertisers cannot afford to sustain such a constant level of advertising, the next best approach is to *reach as high a percentage of the target audience as possible for as many weeks as possible*. This goal can be accomplished by using: (1) 15-second TV commercials as well as more expensive 30-second spots; (2) spreading the budget among cheaper media rather than spending exclusively on television advertising; and (3) buying cheaper TV programs (cable, syndicated) rather than exclusively prime-time network programs. All of these strategies free up advertising dollars and permit an advertising schedule that will reach a high percentage of the target audience continuously rather than sporadically.

Toward Reconciliation.   The concept of scheduling media to achieve a continuous rather than sporadic presence has considerable appeal. However, no single approach is equally effective for all brands. Ephron has recognized as much when suggesting (in the first point above) that for new brands, benefits, or uses, the advertising objective may indeed be to teach rather than merely to remind. Another advertising executive summarizes the issue well:

> *We've always believed that the first exposure is the most powerful, yet we don't want to have hard and fast rules. Every brand is a different situation. The leader in a category has different frequency needs than a competitor with less market share. It's not fair to say every brand has the same need for frequency.*[25]

As a student it may be somewhat disconcerting to receive "mixed signals" such as these. Assuredly, it would be easier if there were hard-and-fast rules or straightforward principles that said, "Here is how you should do it." Advertising practice, unfortunately, is not as simple as this. We repeat a theme that has been emphasized at different points throughout the text: What works best depends on the specific circumstances facing a brand. If the brand is mature and well established, then effective weekly reach (the shelf-space model) is probably an appropriate way to allocate the advertising budget. On the other hand, if the brand is new, or if new benefits or uses for the brand have been developed, or if the advertising message is complex, then the budget should be allocated in a manner that achieves the frequency necessary to teach consumers about brand benefits and uses.

These opposing viewpoints about how advertising works can be distinguished as the "strong" and "weak" models of advertising.[26] The *strong model* takes the position that advertising is important because it teaches consumers about brands and encourages trial purchases leading to the prospect of repeat buying. The *weak model* contends that most advertising messages are not important to consumers and that consumers do not learn much from advertising. This is because advertising usually is for brands that consumers already know about.

In this case, advertising merely serves to remind consumers about brands they already know.

A reconciliation between these opposing viewpoints comes from appreciating the fact that advertising at any time *does* have influence on a relatively small percentage of consumers, and these are the consumers who happen to be in the market for the product at the time of the advertising. For example, a newspaper advertisement announcing a retailer's special sale for a particular brand of television may encourage store traffic and purchases from the relatively small subset of consumers who, at this time, need a new television set. Most consumers, however, do not need a new television set at this particular time. It thus may be said that advertising achieves its effectiveness "through a chance encounter with a ready consumer."[27] The advertisement for *Parade* magazine (Figure 15.3), which is directed at the advertising community and not consumers, illustrates this "chance encounter" idea and the importance of reaching consumers at a time when they are prepared to make a buying decision.

Should it be concluded from this discussion that a single advertising exposure is all that is necessary and that advertising time and space should be scheduled so that recency is optimized and frequency is neglected? Absolutely not. Rather, what you should understand is that the specific advertising situation dictates whether emphasis on reach or frequency is more important. Brands familiar to consumers require less frequency, whereas new or relatively unfamiliar brands require higher levels of frequency. Brands that employ complex messages (e.g., containing technical details or subtle claims) also generally require more frequency.[28]

Figure 15.3   Illustration of Advertising's "Chance Encounter"

When you're putting together a media plan, shouldn't this be the moment you plan for?

It's the moment of truth. The moment when someone is ready to buy. The challenge is to reach

as many people as possible at that moment, increasing the chances that the product they buy will be yours.

Parade does that better than any magazine in America. 82 million readers. In just 24 hours. Every week.

Call Jennifer Gallo at 212-450-7093.

NOTHING MOVES AMERICA LIKE PARADE

Cost Considerations

Media planners attempt to allocate the advertising budget in a cost-efficient manner subject to satisfying other objectives. One of the most important and universally used indicators of media efficiency is the cost-per-thousand criterion. Cost per thousand (abbreviated **CPM**, with the M representing the Roman numeral for 1,000) is the cost of reaching 1,000 people. The measure can be refined to mean the cost of reaching 1,000 members of the target audience, excluding those people who fall outside the target market. This refined measure is designated **CPM-TM**.[29]

CPM and CPM-TM are calculated by dividing the cost of an advertising insertion by a vehicle's circulation within the total market (CPM) or in just the target market (CPM-TM):

CPM = Cost of ad ÷ Number of total contacts (expressed in thousands)
CPM-TM = Cost of ad ÷ Number of target market (TM) contacts
(expressed in thousands)

The term *contacts* is used here in a general sense to include any type of advertising audience (television viewers, magazine readers, radio listeners, etc.).

Illustrative Calculations. To illustrate how CPM and CPM-TM are calculated, consider the following unconventional advertising situation. During Saturday football games at a major university, a local airplane advertising service flies messages on a trailing device that extends behind the plane. The cost is $300 per message. The football stadium holds 80,000 fans and is filled to capacity every Saturday. Hence, the CPM in this situation is $3.75, which is the cost per message ($300) divided by the number of thousands of people (80) who potentially are exposed to (i.e., have an opportunity to see, or OTS) an advertising message trailing from the plane.

Now assume that a new student bookstore uses the airplane advertising service to announce its opening to the 20,000 students who are in attendance at the game. Because the target market in this instance is only a fraction of the total audience, CPM-TM is a more appropriate cost-per-thousand statistic. CPM-TM in this instance is $15 ($300 ÷ 20)—which of course is four times higher than the CPM statistic because the target audience is one-fourth the size of the total audience.

To further illustrate how CPM and CPM-TM are calculated, consider a more conventional advertising situation on television. Suppose an advertiser promoted its brand on the hospital drama *ER*. Using the ratings data from Table 15.3, which were based on a single week in February 2001, *ER* on that particular Thursday evening had a gross rating of 17.9, meaning that viewers in approximately 18.3 million households had an OTS for any commercial aired on that program. At a cost of $425,400 for a 30-second commercial on this program during the 2001–2002 season, the CPM is as follows:

Total viewership = 18,293,800 Households
Cost of 30-second commercial = $425,400
CPM = $425,400 ÷ 18,293.8
= $23.25

If we assume that the target market consists only of women between the ages of 18 and 49 and that this submarket represents 63 percent of the total audience—or 11,525,094 women—then the CPM-TM is

CPM-TM = $425,400 ÷ 11,525.1
= $36.91

Use with Caution! The CPM and CPM-TM statistics are useful for comparing the *cost-efficiency* of different advertising vehicles. They must be used cautiously, however, for several reasons. First, these are measures of cost-efficiency—not of effectiveness. A particular vehicle may be extremely efficient but totally ineffective because it (1) reaches the wrong audience (if CPM is used rather than CPM-TM) or (2) is inappropriate for the product category and brand advertised. By analogy, a Volkswagen Beetle may be more efficient in terms of miles-per-gallon than a BMW but less effective for one's purposes.[30]

A second limitation of CPM and CPM-TM measures is their lack of comparability across media. As emphasized in Chapter 12, the various media perform unique roles and are therefore priced differently. A lower CPM for radio does not mean that buying radio time is better than buying a more expensive (CPM-wise) television schedule.

Finally, CPM statistics can be misused unless vehicles within a particular medium are compared on the same basis. For example, the CPM for an advertisement placed on daytime television is lower than that for a prime-time program, but this represents a case of comparing apples with oranges. The proper comparison would be between two daytime programs or between two prime-time programs rather than across dayparts. Similarly, it would be inappropriate to compare the CPM for a black-and-white magazine ad against a four-color magazine ad unless the two ads are considered equal in terms of their ability to present the brand effectively.

TRADE-OFFS, TRADE-OFFS, TRADE-OFFS

The various media-planning objectives (reach, frequency, weight, continuity, recency, and cost) have now been discussed in some detail. Each was introduced without direct reference to the other objectives. It is important to recognize, however, that these objectives are actually somewhat at odds with one another. That is, given a fixed advertising budget (e.g., $20 million for the Dodge Rambler), the media planner cannot simultaneously optimize reach, frequency, and continuity objectives. Trade-offs must be made because media planners operate under the constraint of fixed advertising budgets. Hence, optimizing one objective (e.g., minimizing CPM or maximizing GRPs) requires the sacrifice of other objectives. This simply is due to the mathematics of constrained optimization: Multiple objectives cannot simultaneously be optimized when constraints (like limited budgets) exist.

For example, with a fixed advertising budget, the media planner can choose to maximize reach or frequency but not both. With increases in reach, frequency is sacrificed and vice versa—if you want to reach more people, you cannot reach them as often with a fixed advertising budget; if you want to reach them more often, you cannot reach as many. Similarly, with a fixed advertising budget, an advertiser cannot simultaneously increase advertising recency and also frequency. This discussion may remind you of the lesson in basic statistics about the trade-off between committing Type I (alpha) and Type II (beta) errors while holding sample size constant. That is, with a fixed sample size, decisions to decrease a Type I error (say, from .05 to .01) must inevitably result in an increase in the Type II error and vice versa.

As an advertising practitioner "you can't have your cake and eat it too." The brand manager faced with an advertising budget constraint, which always is the case, must decide whether frequency is more important (the three-exposure hypothesis) or reach is more imperative (the recency principle).

Thus, each media planner must decide what is best given the particular circumstances surrounding the advertising decision facing his or her brand. As previously discussed, achieving *effective reach* (3+ exposures) is particularly important when brands are new or when established brands have new benefits or uses. In these circumstances, the task of advertising is to teach consumers, and part of teaching is repetition. The more complex the message, the greater the need for repetition to convey the message effectively. However, for established brands that already are well known by consumers, the advertising task is more one of reminding consumers about the brand. The ad budget in this situation is best allocated to achieve the maximum level of *reach*.

Media-Planning Software

On top of the difficult task of making intelligent trade-offs among sometimes opposing objectives (reach, frequency, etc.), there literally are thousands, if not millions, of possible advertising schedules that could be selected depending on how the various media and media vehicles are combined. Fortunately, this daunting task is facilitated by the availability of computerized models to assist media planners in selecting media and vehicles. These models essentially attempt to optimize an objective function (e.g., selecting a schedule that yields the greatest level of reach), subject to satisfying constraints such as not exceeding the upper limit on the advertising budget. A computer algorithm searches through the possible solutions and selects the specific media schedule that optimizes the objective function and satisfies all specified constraints.

The functioning of computerized media models will be illustrated with the ADplus software. ADplus is a comprehensive personal computer program that allows the user to evaluate all major advertising media categories and subcategories and to find optimum schedules based on selecting multiple vehicles from within a single advertising medium.[31]

Using for illustration purposes a hypothetical magazine campaign for the Dodge Rambler during its introductory month of March 2002, the following steps are involved in using ADplus to develop a media schedule:

1. The user develops a *media database*. This strategic aspect of media planning involves selecting prospective advertising vehicles and specifying their ratings and cost. Table 15.7 illustrates the essential information contained in the media database for the Rambler.
2. The user selects the *criterion for schedule optimization*. The available optimization alternatives include maximizing reach (1+), effective reach (3+), frequency, and GRPs. In the illustration to follow, maximizing reach (1+) has been selected as the optimizing criterion for Rambler's March 2002 campaign.

Media Database for the Dodge Rambler, March 2002   Table 15.7

Magazine	Rating	4C/Open Cost*	Maximum Insertions**
Sports Illustrated	30.5	$203,000	4
Field & Stream	15.1	101,750	1
Popular Mechanics	14.2	84,330	1
Playboy	12.7	116,740	1
Outdoor Life	9.2	69,830	1
Men's Health	9.1	104,900	1
Hot Rod	8.6	58,020	1
Golf Digest	8.1	126,930	1
Rolling Stone	8.0	103,455	2
Guns & Ammo	7.7	36,345	1
Muscle & Fitness	7.6	31,933	1
GQ	7.5	68,760	1
Road & Track	7.4	77,770	1
Ebony	7.1	54,609	1
Golf Magazine	6.7	98,950	1
American Rifleman	5.7	41,315	1
Sports Afield	4.7	43,300	1
Sporting News	4.2	31,256	4

* 4C/open stands for a full-page, four-color ad purchased without a quantity discount. Cost information is from http://www.MediaStart.com/INDEX.htm (January 2002). © 2002 MediaStart
** Maximum insertions are based on how frequently a magazine is published. *Sports Illustrated* and *Sporting News* are published weekly, which thus would allow four ads in each of the weeks during the four-week planning period. With the exception of *Rolling Stone*, which is published every other week, all other magazines under consideration are published monthly.

3. The user *specifies constraints*. These include (1) specifying a *budget constraint* for the media planning period, and (2) identifying *the maximum number of ad insertions for each vehicle*. The magazine budget constraint for March 2002 is $1 million. Magazine insertion constraints are identified in Table 15.7.

4. The ADplus algorithm seeks out the optimum media schedule according to the specified objective function and subject to satisfying the budget and number-of-insertion constraints. The following illustration reveals how this is accomplished.

Hypothetical Illustration

Let's assume that a media planner for the Dodge Rambler is in the process of choosing the optimal four-week schedule — during the March 2002 introduction of the Rambler — from among 18 magazines considered appropriate for reaching outdoor-oriented males, aged 18 to 49, who have incomes of $50,000 or greater. We also assume that as of 2002 there were approximately 64 million American males aged 18 to 49, and that only 50 percent of this group satisfy the Rambler's income target of $50,000 or greater. Thus, the target market is reduced to 32 million customers. All subsequent planning is based on this estimate.

The Dodge Rambler Database.   The media planner has prepared a database consisting of 18 magazines considered suitable for reaching the target audience (see Table 15.7). These magazines were selected on the grounds that they have predominantly male readers who engage in outdoor activities such as hunting, fishing, and golfing. The second key input was magazine ratings. Ratings (see the second column in Table 15.7) were determined by dividing each magazine's audience size by the size of Rambler's target market, which was estimated as 32 million potential customers.[32] Next, costs (the third column) were designated according to the price charged by each magazine for a one-time placement of a full-page, four-color advertisement.[33] Finally, maximum insertions (the last column) were based on each magazine's publication cycle. Fifteen of the 18 magazines are published once per month, whereas *Rolling Stone* is published bimonthly and *Sporting News* and *Sports Illustrated* are published weekly. Hence, only one ad each can be placed during the four-week period in 15 of the magazines, whereas it is possible to place up to two ads in *Rolling Stone* and up to four ads each in *Sporting News* and *Sports Illustrated*.

The Objective Function and Constraints.   The information in Table 15.7 was input into the ADplus program.[34] With this information, the ADplus program was instructed to maximize reach without exceeding a budget of $1 million for this four-week introductory campaign. Earlier it was indicated that the first-year advertising budget for the Rambler totaled $20 million. The media planner has decided to invest $1 million in magazine advertising in the introductory month and another $4 million on TV advertising during this month. The remainder of the budget, $15 million, will be allocated during the remainder of 2002. (To simplify the discussion, only the magazine component of the media schedule is described here.)

The Optimal Schedule.   Had advertisements been placed in all 18 magazines listed in Table 15.7 (including multiple insertions in the three magazines — *Sports Illustrated*, *Rolling Stone*, and *Sporting News* — where multiple insertions were permissible), the total advertising cost would have amounted to $2,259,416. This amount would have been unacceptable, however, because a $1 million budget constraint was imposed on magazine advertising in March 2002. It thus was necessary to make a selection from these magazines such that the budget constraint was met and the goal to maximize reach was satisfied. This is precisely what a media algorithm accomplishes. Given 18 magazines with different numbers of maximum insertions in each, there are numerous combinations of magazines that could be selected. However, in a matter of seconds, the ADplus algorithm identified the single combination of magazines that would maximize reach for an expenditure of $1 million or less. The solution is displayed in Table 15.8.

ADplus Optimum Reach Schedule for the Dodge Rambler— Magazine Campaign for March 2002

Table 15.8

Client:	Dodge Rambler
Planning period:	March 2002
Target size:	32,000,000
Target description:	Males 18–49, Incomes $\geq$ $50,000
Message/vehicle ratio:	52.5%

Frequency (f) Distributions

	Vehicle		Message	
f	Percentage f	Percentage f+	Percentage f	Percentage f+
0	34.7	100.0	62.1	100.0
1	22.2	65.3	11.7	37.9
2	22.3	43.0	13.1	26.2
3	13.3	20.7	8.3	13.1
4	5.4	7.4	3.5	4.9
5	1.6	2.0	1.1	1.4
6	0.4	0.4	0.2	0.3
7	0.1	0.1	0.0	0.1
8	0.0	0.0	0.0	0.0
9	0.0	0.0	0.0	0.0
10+	0.0	0.0	0.0	0.0

Summary Evaluation	Vehicle	Message
Reach (1+)	65.3%	37.9%
Effective reach (3+)	20.7%	13.1%
Gross rating points (GRPs)	139.0	83.8
Average frequency (F)	2.1	2.2
Gross impressions (000s)	44,480.0	26,830.7
Cost per thousand (CPM)	$21.86	$36.24
Cost per rating point (CPP)	$6,996	$11,598

Vehicle List	Rating	Ad Cost	CPM-MSG	Ads	Total Cost	Mix
Muscle & Fitness	7.60	$ 31,933	$25.01	1	$31,933	3.3%
Guns & Ammo	7.70	36,345	28.10	1	36,345	3.7
Popular Mechanics	14.20	84,330	35.35	1	84,330	8.7
Sports Illustrated	30.50	203,000	39.62	1	203,000	20.9
Field & Stream	15.10	101,750	40.11	1	101,750	10.5
Hot Rod	8.60	58,020	40.16	1	58,020	6.0
American Rifleman	5.70	41,315	43.14	1	41,315	4.2
Sporting News	4.20	31,256	44.30	2	62,512	6.4
Outdoor Life	9.20	69,830	45.18	1	69,830	7.2
Ebony	7.10	54,609	45.78	1	54,609	5.6
GQ	7.50	68,760	54.57	1	68,760	7.1
Playboy	12.70	116,740	54.72	1	116,740	12.0
Sports Afield	4.70	43,300	54.84	1	43,300	4.5
Totals:			$36.24	14	$972,444	100.0%

Table 15.8 shows that the optimal schedule consists of two ads in *Sporting News* along with one ad each in *Muscle & Fitness*, *Guns & Ammo*, *Popular Mechanics*, *Sports Illustrated*, *Field & Stream*, *Hot Rod*, *American Riflemen*, *Outdoor Life*, *Ebony*, *GQ*, *Playboy*, and *Sports Afield*. (Five magazines—*Men's Health*, *Golf Digest*, *Rolling Stone*, *Road & Track*, and *Golf Magazine* were not included in the final solution. Perusal of Table 15.7 reveals that these magazines are relatively expensive in view of the ratings delivered.) The total cost is $972,444, just under the specified upper limit of $1 million by $27,556. Note that the inclusion of any single additional advertisement would have exceeded the imposed budget limit. (The least expensive magazine in Table 15.7 is *Muscle & Fitness* at $31,933.)

Interpretation of the Solution.   Let us carefully examine the data in Table 15.8. Notice first that the shaded section at the top provides pertinent details about the media schedule (client name, planning period, target size, target description, and message/vehicle ratio). The only explanation needed is in regard to the message/vehicle ratio, which equals 52.5 percent. This value represents the likelihood that consumers who are exposed to the magazine vehicle *also* will be exposed to the advertising message within it. In other words, the expectation is that only slightly more than 50 percent of consumers exposed to any particular magazine in the Rambler's schedule will actually be exposed to a Rambler ad inserted in these magazines. This ratio, although a rough estimate, was obtained from a survey of media directors who were asked to identify the message/vehicle ratios they employ for different media categories.[35] The corresponding ratios for television, radio, and newspapers have been estimated at 32 percent, 16 percent, and 16 percent, respectively.[36] These ratios mean that roughly one of three TV viewers and one of six radio listeners and newspaper readers are expected to be exposed to any particular advertisement contained in each medium. These ratios are, of course, imperfect estimates that are not applicable to every advertising situation. For example, people watching the NFL Super Bowl are probably much more likely to view advertisements than normally is the case.

The next pertinent information to observe in Table 15.8 is the vehicle and message *frequency distributions*. Conceptually these are identical, but the percentages in the message distribution are lower for the reasons described in the previous paragraph. To interpret the *vehicle distribution*, recall the earlier discussion (Table 15.1) of the 10-household market for the Dodge Rambler advertised in *Rolling Stone* magazine. It will be helpful to review the concepts of (1) exposure level (f); (2) frequency distribution, or percent of audience exposed at each level of f (Percentage f), and (3) cumulative frequency distribution (Percentage $f+$). When f equals zero, the Percentage f and Percentage $f+$ values in Table 15.8 are 34.7 and 100, respectively. This is to say that the 34.7 percent of the 32 million audience members will not be exposed to any of the 13 magazines that made it into the optimal solution and that are listed at the bottom of Table 15.8. The cumulative frequency when f equals zero is of course 100—that is, 100 percent of the audience members will be exposed zero or more times to magazine vehicles in Rambler's four-week advertising schedule. Note further that Percentage f and Percentage $f+$ are 22.2 and 65.3 when f equals 1. That is, the media algorithm estimates that 22.2 percent of the target audience will be exposed to *exactly* one of the 13 magazines, and 65.3 percent of the audience will be exposed to one or more of the magazines during this four-week period in March 2002. Note carefully under the summary evaluation in the middle of Table 15.8 that vehicle reach equals 65.3 percent. With reach defined as the percentage of the target audience exposed one or more times (i.e., 1+), the level of reach is determined merely by identifying the corresponding value in the Percentage $f+$ column, which, when f equals 1, is 65.3 percent. It should also be clear that because 34.7 percent of the audience is exposed zero times, the complement of this value (100 percent − 34.7 percent = 65.3 percent) is the percentage of the audience exposed one or more times—that is, the percentage of the audience reached.

Hence, this optimum schedule yields a *vehicle reach* of 65.3, which is the maximum level of reach that any combination of the selected magazines could achieve within a budget constraint of $1 million.

This optimal vehicle schedule produces 139 *GRPs*. These GRPs, by the way, are calculated simply by multiplying the ratings for each magazine by the number of ads placed in that magazine [(*Muscle & Fitness* = 7.6 × 1) + (*Guns & Ammo* = 7.7 × 1) + . . . + (*Sports Afield* = 4.7 × 1) = 139 GRPs].

Further, this magazine schedule during March 2002 is estimated to reach the audience an average of 2.1 times (see *average frequency* under the summary evaluation in Table 15.8). Having defined earlier that frequency = GRPs ÷ reach, you can readily calculate that frequency = 139 ÷ 65.3 = 2.13 (rounded in Table 15.8 to 2.1).

Effective reach (i.e., 3+) is 20.7 percent. That is, only about 21 percent of the total audience are exposed to three or more vehicles. This value is obtained, of course, by reading across from $f = 3$ to the corresponding *percentage f+* column.

The *cost per thousand (CPM)* is $21.86. This value is calculated as follows: (1) Audience size is 32,000,000; (2) 65.3 percent, or 20,896,000 of the people are reached by the schedule of magazines shown in Table 15.8; (3) each person reached is done so on average 2.13 times (in Table 15.8, frequency is presented only to a single decimal point); (4) the number of gross impressions, which is the number of people reached multiplied by the average number of times they are reached, is thus 44,508,480 (slightly off due to rounding error); (5) the *total cost* of this media schedule is $972,444 (see the bottom of the Total Cost column in Table 15.8); and (6) hence, the CPM is $972,444 ÷ 44,480 = $21.86.

Finally, the *cost per rating point (CPP)* is $6,996. This is calculated simply by dividing total cost by the number of GRPs produced (i.e., $972,444 ÷ 139 GRPs).

Does Table 15.8 present a good media schedule? In terms of reach, the schedule is the best of all possible schedules that could have been produced from the various combinations of 18 magazines that were input into the ADplus algorithm. No other combination from among these magazines could have exceeded this schedule's vehicle reach of 65.3 percent. Note carefully, however, that this *opportunity to see* (OTS) the advertisement for Dodge Rambler is not tantamount to having actually seen the advertisement. Indeed, it can be seen under the *message* frequency distribution that the advertising message for Dodge Rambler is estimated to reach only 37.9 percent of the audience one or more times. (By contrast, the vehicle reach is 65.3 percent.) Such an achievement would be inadequate were it not for the fact, as earlier noted, that television advertising is to be run simultaneously with the magazine schedule. The combination of these media can be expected to produce much more impressive numbers and to achieve Rambler's introductory advertising objectives.

There's No Substitute for Judgment and Experience.   It is critical to emphasize that media models such as ADplus do not make the ultimate scheduling decision. All they can do is efficiently perform the calculations needed to determine which single media schedule will optimize some objective function such as maximizing reach or GRPs. Armed with the answer, it is up to the media planner to determine whether the media schedule satisfies other, nonquantitative objectives such as those described in Chapter 12.

Now that fundamental issues in media scheduling have been identified, it is useful to consider two actual media campaigns. First discussed is the introductory campaign for the Saab 9-5 luxury automobile, which was previously discussed in Chapter 14 and was the subject of this chapter's *Opening Vignette*. Then an award-winning campaign for Diet Dr Pepper is presented.

THE SAAB 9-5 MEDIA CAMPAIGN

As described in Chapter 14, Saab, the Swedish automobile maker, introduced a new luxury sedan named the Saab 9-5. This model represented Saab's first entry in the luxury category and was designed to compete against well-known high-equity brands including Mercedes, BMW, Volvo, Lexus, and Infiniti. In addition to innovative and aggressive direct-mail and outbound telemarketing campaigns (the subject of Chapter 14), The Martin Agency representing Saab also developed a thoroughly integrative media schedule. The media schedule is presented in Table 15.9.

It first will be noted from Table 15.9 that TV advertising started in January, which was before the 9-5's introduction in April. Network and cable TV advertis-

Table 15.9   Media Plan for the Saab 9-5

	JAN				FEB				MAR					APR				MAY					JUN			
	29	5	12	19	26	2	9	16	23	2	9	16	23	30	6	13	20	27	4	11	18	25	1	8	15	22
Network TV				74 wk	→	→												95 wk	→	→						
Network Cable				40 wk	→	→												60 wk	→	→						
Magazines					◀━━━━━━━━━━━━━━━━━━ continuous ━━━━━━━━━━━━━━━━━━━▶																					
Newspapers																										
USA Today																										
3 PBW (2X)														1X		1X										
SPBW (1X)															1X											
PBW (12X)																										
T Page (58X)		1X		1X	1X	1X		1X		2X	2X	2X	2X	2X	2X	2X	2X	2X	1X	1X		1X		1X		1X
1/4 PBW (8X)												4X	2X	2X												
Wall Street Jrnl																										
3 PBW (2X)														1X		1X										
SPBW (1X)															1X											
PBW (12X)																										
4 col x 14" (63X)	1X	1X		1X	1X	1X			1X	2X	2X	2X	2X	2X	2X	2X	2X	2X	1X	1X	1X	1X	1X	1X	1X	1X
4 col x 8" (8X)													2X	4X	2X											
Interactive	◀━━━━━━━━━━━━━━━━━━━━━━━━ continuous ━━━━━━━━━━━━━━━━━━━━━━━━▶																									

Legend:
1X, 2X, etc. = Number of insertions per week placed in *USA Today* or *WSJ* (1X = one insertion, 2X = two insertions, etc.)
3 PBW = 3 pages black & white magazine ad
SPBW = Spread page B&W (ad runs across 2 pages like a centerfold)
PBW = 1-page black & white
T Page = An odd shaped add placement
¼ PBW = ¼ page B&W
Interactive = Internet banner ad placed on *The Wall Street Journal Interactive Edition*

ing ran in late January and into February and then again throughout May following the 9-5's introduction. Notice that the initial network TV campaign accumulated 74 GRPs for each of three weeks (the weeks beginning January 19, January 26, and February 2) and that accompanying advertising on cable TV amassed 40 GRPs for each of these same three weeks. Following the 9-5's introduction, the May television schedule accumulated 95 and 60 GRPs, respectively, on network and cable TV. Or, in other words, a total of 620 television GRPs [(95 × 4) + (60 × 4)] were purchased in May.

Table 15.9 further reveals that magazine advertising for the Saab 9-5 started in late January and continued for the remainder of the year without interruption. A wide variety of magazines was used to reach Saab's designated market for the 9-5. These included such outlets as automotive magazines (e.g., *Car & Driver, Road & Track*), sports publications (e.g., *Ski, Tennis*), home magazines (e.g., *Martha Stewart Living, Architectural Digest*), business magazines (e.g., *Money, Forbes, Working Women*), and general interest publications (e.g., *Time, New York Magazine*). National newspaper advertising in *USA Today* and the *Wall Street Journal* also ran throughout the year. And finally, Internet banner advertising ran

Continued **Table 15.9**

Media	29	6	13	20	27	3	10	17	24	31	7	14	21	28	5	12	19	26	2	9	16	23	30	7	14	21
	JUL				AUG					SEP				OCT				NOV					DEC			
Network TV																										
Network Cable																										
Magazines	■	■	■	■	■	■	■	■	■	■	■	■	■	■	■	■	■	■	■	■	■	■	■	■	■	■
Newspapers																										
USA Today																										
3 PBW (2X)																										
SPBW (1X)																										
PBW (12X)														1X	3X	2X					3X	1X	2X			
T Page (58X)		1X	1X	1X	1X	1X	1X	1X	1X	1X	1X	1X	2X	1X		1X	2X	2X	2X	2X		1X	1X	2X	2X	1X
1/4 PBW (8X)																										
Wall Street Jrnl																										
3 PBW (2X)																										
SPBW (1X)																										
PBW (12X)														1X	2X	2X	1X				2X	1X	2X	1X		
4 col x 14" (63X)	1X	2X	1X	1X	1X	1X	1X	1X	1X	1X		1X	2X	1X	1X	1X	1X	2X	2X	2X	1X	1X	1X	1X	2X	1X
4 col x 8" (8X)																										
Interactive	■	■	■	■	■	■	■	■	■	■	■	■	■	■	■	■	■	■	■	■	■	■	■	■	■	■

continuously throughout the introductory year on the *Wall Street Journal's Interactive Edition*.

THE DIET DR PEPPER CAMPAIGN

An award-winning advertising campaign for Diet Dr Pepper developed by the Young & Rubicam advertising agency provides an exemplary application of media scheduling and the advertising creative process around which scheduling takes place. This campaign received a major award from the advertising community in tribute to its accomplishment.[37]

Marketing Situation and Campaign Objectives

Diet Dr Pepper competes in a dynamic and constantly changing category that makes it difficult to increase market share and sustain long-term brand growth. Major factors that challenge the brand's growth include the following:

- *Sluggish category growth.* The diet, carbonated soft-drink category was growing at an average annual rate of only 1.4 percent.
- *Growth of new-age beverages.* The new-age segment—consisting of sparkling juices, natural sodas, flavored sodas, and other items—was growing at a

rapid rate (10 percent annual growth), posing a strong challenge to Diet Dr Pepper and other diet soft drinks.

- *Price sensitivity of soft-drink category.* Price is a major brand choice determinant in this category, but Diet Dr Pepper is at a competitive disadvantage because it is priced higher on a cents-per-ounce basis than Coca-Cola and Pepsi-Cola brands.
- *Lack of bottler attention and focus.* Approximately three-fourths of Diet Dr Pepper's volume is distributed via the Coke and Pepsi bottler distribution network, which in many instances causes Diet Dr Pepper to be a low-priority item with insufficient retailer support.
- *Inadequate distribution.* Relative to its larger competitors, Diet Dr Pepper's distribution is insufficient in trial-inducing outlets such as fountain/food service and vending machines.
- *Greater spending by major competitors.* Diet Dr Pepper's share of voice (SOV) at the onset of the advertising campaign was only 4.8 percent in this highly competitive and advertising-sensitive category.

Campaign Target and Objectives.   The target audience for Diet Dr Pepper consists primarily of adults aged 18 to 49 who are present or prospective diet soft-drink consumers. In view of its marketing challenges, the objectives for the Diet Dr Pepper advertising campaign (titled "The Taste You've Been Looking For") were as follows:

1. To increase Diet Dr Pepper sales by 4 percent and improve its growth rate to at least 1.5 times that of the diet soft-drink category.
2. To heighten consumers' evaluations of the key product benefit and image factors that influence brand choice in this category: It is refreshing, tastes as good as regular Dr Pepper, is a good product to drink at any time, and is a fun brand to drink.
3. To enhance those key brand-personality dimensions that differentiate Diet Dr Pepper from other diet drinks—particularly that Diet Dr Pepper is a unique, clever, fun, entertaining, and interesting brand to drink.

Creative Strategy and Supportive Promotions

The creative strategy for Diet Dr Pepper positioned the brand as "tasting more like regular Dr Pepper." This was a key claim based on research revealing that nearly 60 percent of initial trial users of Diet Dr Pepper were motivated by the desire to have a diet soft drink that tasted like regular Dr Pepper. The cornerstone of the campaign entailed the heavy use of 15-second commercials, which historically had not been used by Coca-Cola and Pepsi-Cola, which instead preferred the entertainment value of longer commercials. The aggressive use of 15-second commercials enabled Diet Dr Pepper to simply convey its key taste claim ("tastes more like regular Dr Pepper") and differentiate the brand from competitive diet drinks. Moreover, by employing cheaper 15-second commercials, it was possible to buy many more commercial spots and hence achieve greater reach, frequency, and GRPs for the same advertising budget. Diet Dr Pepper's advertising expenditures for the year totaled $20.3 million.

In addition to the advertising campaign, the brand marketers for Diet Dr Pepper implemented several sales promotion programs to achieve their lofty goals. From January through April, a trade promotion called "The Pepper Advantage" provided bottlers with $30 gift certificates (for use at apparel retailer Eddie Bauer) that they could distribute to retailers to encourage greater display space for Diet Dr Pepper. In addition, attractive coupons were placed on 2- and 3-liter bottles of Diet Dr Pepper to encourage repeat purchasing by consumers.

From April to September, during baseball season, the "Pepper Pastime" promotion was run to enhance sales of Diet Dr Pepper to consumers in convenience stores. Promotions included free bottles of Diet Dr Pepper and premium objects, including autographed baseballs and baseball jerseys emblazoned with the Diet Dr Pepper brand name. During May through August, a promotional tie-in with the Foot Locker chain of athletic stores was undertaken. Purchasers of 12- and 24-packs of Diet Dr Pepper received Foot Locker gift certificates if their pack contained a winning game card inside. Collectively, these sales promotion programs were designed to complement the advertising campaign and substantially boost immediate sales of Diet Dr Pepper products.

Media Strategy

The advertising schedule for Diet Dr Pepper generated a total of 1,858 GRPs, with a cumulative annual reach of 95 and frequency of 19.6. These media-weight values were accomplished with the national media plan summarized as a flowchart in Table 15.10.

The 12 months and the week-beginning dates (Mondays) throughout the year are listed across the top of the chart. Table entries reflect the target rating points achieved by each advertised event for each weekly period. The first entry, a 41 for the *NFL Championship Games*, indicates that 41 gross rating points were produced by placing advertisements for Diet Dr Pepper during these televised football games.

It can be seen that the Diet Dr Pepper media plan consisted of (1) placing advertisements during professional and college football games (the SEC stands for Southeastern Conference); (2) sponsoring various special events (e.g., the *Country Music Awards*, the *Garth Brooks Special*, and golfing events); and (3) continuously advertising during prime time, on late-night television (e.g., *David Letterman*), on syndicated programs, and on cable stations.

At the bottom of Table 15.10 is a summary of GRPs broken down by week (e.g., 86 GRPs during the week beginning January 10), month (e.g., 227 GRPs during January), and quarter (e.g., 632 GRPs produced during the first quarter, January through March). It can be seen that the media schedule was *flighted* insofar as advertisements were placed during approximately two-thirds of the 52 weeks with no advertising during the remaining weeks. In sum, the media schedule was designed to highlight Diet Dr Pepper during a variety of special events and to maintain continuity throughout the year with prime-time network advertising and less expensive support on syndicated and cable programming.

Results

The advertising campaign for Diet Dr Pepper was extremely successful, even surpassing the ambitious goals established for the brand. Sales of Diet Dr Pepper increased by 6.6 percent compared with the increase of only 1.4 percent for other diet soft-drink brands during the same year.[38] Research also revealed that consumer brand ratings of Diet Dr Pepper improved over the previous year and surpassed ratings achieved by Diet Coke and Diet Pepsi on several important dimensions: refreshing, tastes as good as regular, good anytime, fun to drink, and unique.

All in all, "The Taste You've Been Looking For" campaign was extremely successful and served well to enhance Diet Dr Pepper's image and sales volume. The bold and innovative use of 15-second commercials allowed the brand to advertise aggressively, to maintain an almost continuous presence on television, and to differentiate Diet Dr Pepper successfully from competitive diet soft drinks. This is what good advertising is all about. Creative advertising and proper media selection can yield dramatic increases in sales volume and enhance a brand's equity.

SUMMARY

Selection of advertising media and vehicles is one of the most important and complicated of all marketing communications decisions. Media planning must be coordinated with marketing strategy and with other aspects of advertising strategy. The strategic aspects of media planning involve four steps: (1) selecting the target

Table 15.10

Media Plan for Diet Dr Pepper

	JAN					FEB				MAR				APR				MAY					JUN			
ADULTS 18–49 GRPs	27	3	10	17	24	31	7	14	21	28	7	14	21	28	4	11	18	25	2	9	16	23	30	6	13	20
SPORTS																										
NFL Championship Games				41																						
Road to the Superbowl					10																					
FOX "Game of the Month"																										
NBC "Game of the Month"																										
NBC Thanksgiving Game																										
ABC Monday Night Football																										
4Q Sports Total				41	10																					
SEC Championship Game																										
SEC-CFA Regular Game																										
SEC Thanksgiving Game																										
SEC Local/Conference Fee																										
SEC Sponsorship Total																										
TOTAL SPORTS				41	10																					
EVENTS																										
McDonald's Golf Classic																					1					
Daytime Emmy Awards																						23				
Country Music Awards																			32							
Garth Brooks Special																			12							
Michael Bolton Sponsorship																										
May Event Print																				17	18					
JC Penney LPGA Golf																										
Harvey Penick Special																							1			
Diners Club Golf																										
TOTAL EVENTS																			61	18	17	41	1			
CONTINUITY																										
Prime			53					53				53	54	34	35			35			35				35	
May Event Prime Scatter																				29	28					
Late Night		6	5								5			3				3			4					
Syndication		14					14				13			8				8			8			8		
Cable		13					14				14			11				11			11					
TOTAL CONTINUITY		86	126	15		86	81			85		68		56		57		54	86	28	86	58			43	
Integration-to-date																										
Total Diet Plan		86	126	15		86	81			85		68		56		57		54	147	46	103	127	59		43	
A18-49 GRPs/Week																										
Amount Over Budget																										

A18-49 GRPs/Month	JAN 227	FEB 167	MAR 238	APR 167	MAY 477	JUN 102
A18-49 GRPs/Quarter	632			746		

Continued

Table 15.10

ADULTS 18–49 GRPs	JUL					AUG				SEP				OCT					NOV					DEC		
	27	4	11	18	25	1	8	15	22	29	5	12	19	26	3	10	17	24	31	7	14	21	28	5	12	19
SPORTS																										
NFL Championship Games																										
Road to the Superbowl																										
FOX "Game of the Month"														28							24			25		
NBC "Game of the Month"																13				22				20		
NBC Thanksgiving Game																						22				
ABC Monday Night Football																22	20	10		24						25
4Q Sports Total														28		35	20	10		46	24	22		45		25
SEC Championship Game																								33		
SEC-CFA Regular Game															8											
SEC Thanksgiving Game																						6				
SEC Local/Conference Fee																										
SEC Sponsorship Total															8							6		33		
TOTAL SPORTS														28	8	35	20	10		46	24	28		78		25
EVENTS																										
McDonald's Golf Classic																										
Daytime Emmy Awards																										
Country Music Awards																										
Garth Brooks Special																										
Michael Bolton Sponsorship																										
May Event Print																										
JC Penney LPGA Golf																										
Harvey Penick Special																										
Diners Club Golf																										
TOTAL EVENTS																										
CONTINUITY																										
Prime		25				25				26																
May Event Prime Scatter																										
Late Night																										
Syndication																										
Cable																										
TOTAL CONTINUITY		25				25				26																
Integration-to-date																										
Total Diet Plan		25				25				26				28	8	35	20	10		46	24	28		78		15
A18-49 GRPs/Week																										
Amount Over Budget																										

	JUL	AUG	SEP	OCT	NOV	DEC
A18-49 GRPs/Month	75	51	52	91	108	103
A18-49 GRPs/Quarter	178			302		

audience toward which all subsequent efforts will be directed; (2) specifying media objectives, which typically are stated in terms of reach, frequency, gross rating points (GRPs), or effective rating points (ERPs); (3) selecting general media categories and specific vehicles within each medium; and (4) buying media.

Media and vehicle selection are influenced by a variety of factors; most important are target audience, cost, and creative considerations. Media planners select media vehicles by identifying those that will reach the designated target audience, satisfy budgetary constraints, and be compatible with and enhance the advertiser's creative message. There are numerous ways to schedule media insertions over time, but media planners have typically used some form of pulsed or flighted schedule whereby advertising is on at times, off at others, but never continuous. The principle of recency, also referred to as the shelf-space model of advertising, challenges the use of flighted advertising schedules and purports that weekly efficient reach should be the decision criterion of choice because this approach ensures that advertising will be run at the time when consumers are making brand selection decisions.

The chapter provided detailed explanations of the various considerations used by media planners in making advertising media decisions. These included the concepts of reach, frequency, gross rating points (GRPs), effective rating points (ERPs), and cost and continuity considerations. Media vehicles within the same medium are compared in terms of cost using the cost-per-thousand criterion.

The chapter included a detailed discussion of a computerized media-selection model called ADplus. This model requires information about vehicle cost, ratings, maximum number of insertions, and a budget constraint and then maximizes an objective function subject to that budget. Optimization criteria include maximizing reach (1+), effective reach (3+), frequency, or GRPs.

The chapter concluded with descriptions of media plans for the Saab 9-5 and Diet Dr Pepper.

Find more resources to help you study at http://shimp.swcollege.com!

DISCUSSION QUESTIONS

1. Why is target audience selection the critical first step in formulating a media strategy?
2. Explain the problems associated with using GRPs as a media selection criterion. In what sense is the concept of ERPs superior?
3. Why is reach also called net coverage or unduplicated audience?
4. A television advertising schedule produced the following vehicle frequency distribution:

f	Percentage f	Percentage f+
0	31.4	100.0
1	9.3	68.6
2	7.1	59.4
3	6.0	52.2
4	5.2	46.2
5	4.6	41.0
6	4.1	36.4
7	3.7	32.3
8	3.4	28.5
9	3.1	25.1
10+	22.0	22.0

(a) What is the reach for this advertising schedule?
(b) What is the effective reach?
(c) How many GRPs does this schedule generate?

5. Assume that the TV advertising schedule in question 4 cost $2 million and generated 240 million gross impressions. What are the CPM and CPP for this schedule?
6. *Golf Digest* and *Golf Magazine* were two of six advertising vehicles not included in the optimal media schedule for the Dodge *Rambler*. Why do you think that they were excluded?
7. A publication called the *$ Ad Summary* (also generally known as *Leading National Advertisers,* or *LNA*) is an invaluable source for determining how much money brands invest in advertising. Go to your library and find the most recent version of *LNA*. Identify the advertising expenditures and the media used in advertising the following brands: Diet Coke, Tide detergent, and the Jeep Cherokee.
8. With reference to the three-exposure hypothesis, explain the difference between three exposures to an advertising message versus three exposures to an advertising vehicle.
9. When an advertiser uses the latter, what implicit assumption is that advertiser making?
10. Describe in your own words the fundamental logic underlying the principle of recency, or the shelf-space model of advertising. Is this model always the best model to apply in setting media allocations over time?
11. A TV program has a rating of 17.6. With approximately 104 million television households in the United States as of 2002, what is that program's CPM if a 30-second commercial costs $550,000? Now assume that an advertiser's target audience consists only of people aged 25 to 54, which constitutes 62 percent of the program's total audience. What is the CPM-TM in this case?
12. Which is more important for an advertiser: maximizing reach or maximizing frequency? Explain in detail.

It also is important to note at this point that although consumer packaged goods (CPG) companies are the biggest users of promotions, all types of companies and other organizations use promotional incentives. For example, automobile companies regularly offer rebates and cheap financing to attract purchasers. Retailers woo consumers with special offers, discounts, and incentives to attract immediate purchasing. A Nordstrom store in California, for example, gave shoppers the opportunity to have their name drawn from a raffle and win a $500 shopping spree. Following a strike by its pilots, American Airlines offered attractive discounts and double frequent-flier miles to lure back customers who boarded other airlines during the strike.

In an unconventional yet increasingly practiced form of promotion by not-for-profit organizations, a major state university wrote letters to hundreds of high school students who had been named National Merit Semifinalists and offered the following:

> *If you attain **finalist** status in the National Merit competition, we will offer you, upon admission to the university, a Presidential Scholarship that will pay the value of tuition for four years as well as on-campus housing during your freshman year. You will also receive a University National Merit Scholarship of at least $1,000 . . . if, as a finalist, you do not receive another National Merit sponsored scholarship. In addition, you will receive $2,000 for use in summer research or study abroad. If you list [name of university] as your college of choice with the National Merit Scholarship Corporation, you also will receive a free laptop computer when you enroll.*

Though not your typical $1.00 coupon, free sample, or mail-in premium, this offer attempts to induce an action (enroll at this particular university) that is no different than efforts brand managers employ to encourage purchases of their brands. The point is clear: Promotions are used universally.

Promotion Targets

To appreciate more fully the role of promotion, consider the following promotion from Schering-Plough, a leader in the foot care category. Schering-Plough markets two well-known foot care brands: Lotrimin AF and Tinactin. To gain greater trade support for these brands and to generate excitement and enthusiasm among its own sales force of 152 people, Schering-Plough introduced the "Howwe Gosell" promotion. (This promotional label plays on the name of the famous sportscaster, the late Howard Cosell, who gained celebrity for his outspoken personality and quirky mannerisms while announcing major sporting events, especially boxing matches featuring Muhammad Ali, and football games on *Monday Night Football*.) The promotion appealed to Schering-Plough's sales force to be part of the "team" coached by Howwe Gosell, who encouraged his "players" (the sales force) on to a victory ending in higher sales of Lotrimin AF and Tinactin. In keeping with the football motif, salespeople received "playbooks" and had a chance to score points that would earn them NFL merchandise or expense-paid trips to the Super Bowl. The result: Tinactin and Lotrimin AF gained 19 percent and 14 percent, respectively, in sales volume during the promotional period. Howwe Gosell was a topic of much discussion among the sales force, and the trade devoted more display space to these brands than they had ever previously enjoyed.[5]

For Schering-Plough's foot care brands to achieve their marketing objectives (sales volume, market share), several things had to happen: First, Schering-Plough's *sales force* had to enthusiastically and aggressively sell these brands to the trade. Second, *retailers* had to be encouraged to allocate sufficient store space to the brands and provide merchandising support to enable them to stand out, if only temporarily, from competitive brands. Third, consumers needed reasons for selecting Lotrimin AF and Tinactin over competitive foot care brands. Similarly, increased sales of the Fiat Marea (*Opening Vignette*) required dealership support, salesperson involvement, and consumer interest in test-driving this redesigned automobile. The promotion was extremely effective in appealing to all three groups.

All three groups—the sales force, retailers, and consumers—are targets of sales promotional efforts (see Figure 16.1). Allowances, discounts, contests, and

Brand-Level Promotional Imperatives   **Figure 16.1**

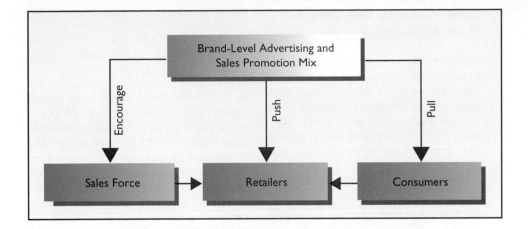

advertising support programs encourage retailers to stock and promote particular brands. Coupons, samples, premiums, cents-off deals, sweepstakes, and other incentives encourage consumers to purchase a brand on a trial or repeat basis. Trade- and consumer-oriented sales promotions also provide the manufacturer's sales force with the necessary tools for aggressively and enthusiastically selling to wholesale and retail buyers and for encouraging retail salespeople to emphasize the manufacturer's brand. The *IMC Focus* examines a brilliant effort from Packard Bell to get retail salespeople to better understand and more aggressively sell its computer products.

INCREASED BUDGETARY ALLOCATIONS TO PROMOTIONS

Advertising spending as a percentage of total marketing communications expenditures has declined in recent years, while promotion spending has steadily increased. Media advertising expenditures as a proportion of total marketing communications expenditures averaged *more than 40 percent* of companies' budgets until the early 1980s, but now media advertising's portion of the total budget has fallen to around just one quarter.[6]

Table 16.1 shows how CPG marketers from 1990 through 2001 have allocated expenditures among media advertising, trade promotions, and consumer promotions. Looking at the anchor years, 1990 and 2001, media advertising constituted 28 percent of total expenditures in 1990 but fell to 24 percent by 2001.

Average Allocations to Media Advertising, Trade, and Consumer Promotions, 1990–2001   **Table 16.1**

	Percentage of Expenditures											
	1990	1991	1992	1993	1994	1995	1996	1997	1998	1999	2000	2001
Media Advertising	28	25	25	24	25	24	24	26	25	23	24	24
Trade Promotions	47	48	48	49	49	51	50	50	56	60	60	61
Consumer Promotions	25	27	27	27	26	25	26	24	19	17	16	15

Source: 1990–1997 data are from Chart 25 in *Cox Direct 20th Survey of Promotional Practices* (Largo, FL: Cox Direct, 1998), 40. 1998–2001 data are from Cannondale Associates (Wilton, CT) as reproduced in Jack Neff, "Coupons Get Clipped," *Advertising Age*, November 5, 2001, 1.

Encouraging Retail Salespeople to Sell Packard Bell Computers More Aggressively

Packard Bell at one time was the top brand in home PC sales, only to lose its commanding presence to Compaq, Dell, Gateway, and Hewlett-Packard. In an effort to regain some of its lost market share, Packard Bell designed an innovative program to influence the retail salespeople in electronic and computer stores, who play a major role in directing PC purchases. In conjunction with its promotion agency, Packard Bell developed a "Home Delivery" program that was designed to enhance Packard Bell's equity in the minds of retail salespeople, who are predominantly young males.

After acquiring a mailing list of names and home addresses, Packard Bell mailed retail salespeople a series of three interactive CD-ROMs that were packaged as take-out food items (a pizza box, Chinese food container, and a chicken bucket). These food items were appropriately themed to the take-out eating habits of the targeted group of youthful male salespeople. Each CD-ROM contained information about the latest features of Packard Bell computers along with interesting supplemental segments, including movie trailers, classic TV advertising spots, and music videos. The "Home Delivery" program was a major success. Follow-up research determined that 95 percent of the targeted salespeople wanted to receive more CD-ROMs; 64 percent reported having viewed the CD-ROMs on multiple occasions; and, of greatest significance, 70 percent of the salespeople acknowledged that their perceptions of Packard Bell had improved after viewing the CD-ROMs and that they recommended Packard Bell PCs more often than before.

Source: Adapted from Tobi Elkin, "Packard Bell Delivers," *Brandweek*, March 2, 1998, R3-R6. © 1998 VNU Business Media, Inc.

On the other hand, trade promotions represented 47 percent of total expenditures in 1990 but 61 percent by 2001. Consumer promotions fell from a high of 27 percent in the early 1990s to just 15 percent in 2001. The trend, in short, is that advertising expenditures and consumer promotions have declined at the expense of greater trade promotions.[7] We now will examine the major reasons underlying this shift.

Factors Accounting for the Shift

Several factors account for why CPG brand managers have shifted budgetary allocations increasingly toward a greater proportion of trade promotions. However, before we describe the reasons for this shift, it first will be beneficial to briefly review the concepts of push and pull marketing strategies.

Push and pull are physical metaphors characterizing the promotional activities manufacturers undertake to encourage channel members (the trade) to handle products. **Push** involves a *forward thrust* of effort, metaphorically speaking, whereby a manufacturer directs personal selling, trade advertising, and trade-oriented sales promotion to wholesalers and retailers. Through this combination of sales influence, advertising, and, perhaps especially, promotions in the form of allowances and other deals, manufacturers "push" channel members to increase their inventories of the manufacturer's brand versus competitive brands. **Pull**, on the other hand, entails a *backward tug*, again speaking metaphorically, from consumers to retailers. This tug, or pull, is the result of a manufacturer's successful advertising and consumer promotion efforts that encourage consumers to prefer, at least in the short term, the manufacturer's brand versus competitive offerings.

Table 16.2 illustrates the differences between push- and pull-oriented promotional strategies based on two companies' allocations of $20 million among different promotional activities. Company A emphasizes a *push strategy* by allocating most of its promotional budget to personal selling and trade pro-

Push Versus Pull Strategies

Table 16.2

	Company A (Push)	Company B (Pull)
Advertising to consumers	$ 1,200,000	$13,700,000
Advertising to retailers	1,600,000	200,000
Personal Selling to retailers	9,000,000	4,000,000
Sales Promotion to consumers	200,000	2,000,000
Sales Promotion to retailers	8,000,000	100,000
TOTAL	$20,000,000	$20,000,000

Source: Arnold M. Barban, Steven M. Cristol, and Frank J. Kopec. *Essentials of Media Planing: A Marketing Viewpoint* (Lincolnwood, Ill.: NTC Books, 1987). p. 15. © 1987 NTC/Contemporary Publishing Group.

motions aimed at retail customers. Company B, on the other hand, uses a *pull strategy* by investing the vast majority of its budget in consumer advertising.

It is important to recognize that pushing and pulling are *not* mutually exclusive activities. Both efforts occur simultaneously. Manufacturers promote to consumers (creating pull) *and* to trade members (accomplishing push). *The issue is not which strategy to use but rather which to emphasize.* Effective marketing communication involves a *combination of forces*: exerting push to the trade and creating pull from consumers.

Historically, at least through the mid-1970s, the emphasis in CPG marketing was on promotional pull (such as company B's budget in Table 16.2). Manufacturers advertised heavily, especially on network television, and literally forced retailers to handle their brands by creating consumer demand for those heavily advertised items. However, over the past generation, pull-oriented marketing has become less effective due in large part to the splintering of the mass media and audience fractionalization as discussed in Chapter 12. Along with this reduced effectiveness has come an increase in the use of push-oriented sales promotion practices (such as company A's budget in Table 16.2).[8]

Increased investment in sales promotion, especially trade-oriented promotions, has gone hand in hand with the growth in push marketing. Major developments that have given rise to sales promotion are summarized in Table 16.3 and discussed hereafter.[9] It is important to emphasize at this point that these developments are interdependent rather than separate and distinct. Hence, there is no particular order of importance implied by the listing in Table 16.3.

Balance-of-Power Shift.
Until roughly the early 1980s, national manufacturers of CPG products generally were more powerful and influential than the supermarkets, drugstores, and mass merchandisers that carried the manufacturers' brands. The reason was twofold. First, manufacturers were able to create consumer *pull* by virtue of heavy network television advertising, thus effectively requiring retailers to handle their brands whether retailers wanted to or not. Second, retailers did little research of their own and, accordingly, were dependent on

Developments Underlying the Growth in Promotions

Table 16.3

- Shift in manufacturer versus retailer balance of power
- Increased brand parity and price sensitivity
- Reduced brand loyalty
- Splintered mass market and reduced media effectiveness
- Emphasis on short-term results in corporate reward structures
- Responsive consumers

manufacturers for information such as whether a new product would be successful. A manufacturer's sales representative could convince a buyer to carry a new product using test-market results suggesting a successful product introduction.

The balance of power began shifting when network television dipped in effectiveness as an advertising medium and, especially, with the advent of optical scanning equipment. Armed with a steady flow of data from optical scanners, retailers now know virtually on a real-time basis what products are selling and which advertising and promotion programs are working. Retailers no longer need to depend on manufacturers for data. Instead, retailers use the facts they now possess to demand terms of sale rather than merely accepting manufacturers' terms. The consequence for manufacturers is that for every promotional dollar used to support retailers' advertising or merchandising programs, one less dollar is available for the manufacturer's own advertising.

Increased Brand Parity and Price Sensitivity.

In earlier years when truly new products were being offered to the marketplace, manufacturers could effectively advertise unique advantages over competitive offerings. As product categories have matured, however, most new offerings represent only slight changes from existing products, thus resulting, more often than not, in greater similarities between competitive brands. With fewer distinct product differences, consumers have grown more reliant on price and price incentives (coupons, cents-off deals, refunds, etc.) as ways of differentiating parity brands. Because concrete advantages are often difficult to obtain, firms have turned increasingly to promotion as a means of achieving temporary advantages over competitors.

Reduced Brand Loyalty.

Consumers probably are less loyal than they once were. This is partly due to the fact that brands have grown increasingly similar, thereby making it easier for consumers to switch among brands. Also, marketers have effectively trained consumers to expect that at least one brand in a product category will always be on deal with a coupon, cents-off offer, or refund; hence, many consumers rarely purchase brands other than those on deal. (The term **deal** refers to any form of sales promotion that delivers a *price reduction* to consumers. Retailer discounts, manufacturer cents-off offers, and the ubiquitous coupon are the most common forms of deals.)

One team of researchers investigated the impact that deal promotions have on consumers' price sensitivity using eight years of scanner panel data for a nonfood packaged good product. These researchers determined that price promotions make consumers more price sensitive in the long run. Moreover, increased use of price promotions serves, for all intents and purposes, to "train" consumers to search for deals. Nonloyal consumers are especially likely to be conditioned by marketers' use of price deals.[10] Another study discovered that the use of coupons by brands in the liquid detergent category (brands such as Wisk, Era, and Bold) resulted in increased consumer price sensitivity and reduced brand loyalty.[11]

The upshot of heightened dealing activity is that marketers have created a "monster" in the form of consumers' desire for deals. Reduced loyalty and increased brand-switching behavior have resulted, requiring more dealing activity to feed the monster's insatiable appetite. A major international study of sales promotion activities in Germany, Japan, the United Kingdom, and the United States investigated the effects of price-related promotions (such as cents-off deals and coupons) on a brand's sales *after* a promotional period is over. The dramatic finding from this research, which examined dozens of brands in 25 consumer goods categories, is that these promotions have virtually *no impact* on a brand's long-term sales or on consumers' repeat buying loyalty. No strong aftereffects occurred because extra sales for the promoted brands came almost exclusively from a brand's long-term customer base. In other words, the people who normally buy a brand are the ones who are most responsive to the brand's price promotion. Hence, price promotions effectively serve to induce consumers to buy on deal what they would have bought at regular prices anyway. In sum, although price-related promotions typically result in immediate and huge sales spikes, these short-term gains do not positively influence long-term brand growth.[12]

Splintering of the Mass Market and Reduced Media Effectiveness.

Advertising *efficiency* is directly related to the degree of homogeneity in consumers' consumption needs and media habits. The greater their homogeneity, the less costly it is for mass advertising to reach target audiences. However, as consumer lifestyles have diversified and advertising media have narrowed in their appeal, mass media advertising's efficiency has weakened. On top of this, advertising effectiveness has declined with simultaneous increases in ad clutter and escalating media costs. These combined forces have influenced many brand managers to devote proportionately larger budgets to sales promotion.

Short-Term Orientation and Corporate Reward Structures.

Sales promotions go hand in hand with the brand management system, which is the dominant organizational structure in CPG firms. The reward structure in firms organized along brand manager lines emphasizes *short-term sales response* rather than slow, long-term growth. And sales promotion is incomparable when it comes to generating quick sales response. In fact, the majority of packaged-good brand sales are associated with some kind of promotional deal.[13]

Consumer Responsiveness.

A final force that explains the shift toward sales promotion at the expense of advertising is that consumers respond favorably to money-saving opportunities and other value-adding promotions. Coupons in particular have nearly universal acceptance, with over 80 percent of consumers using coupons.[14]

Consumers would not be responsive to promotions unless there was something in it for them—and, in fact, there is. All promotion techniques provide consumers with *rewards* (benefits, incentives, or inducements) that encourage certain forms of behavior desired by brand managers. These rewards, or benefits, are both utilitarian and hedonic.[15] Consumers using sales promotions receive *utilitarian*, or functional, benefits of (1) monetary savings (e.g., when using coupons); (2) reduced search and decision costs (e.g., by simply availing themselves of a promotional offer and not thinking about other alternatives); and (3) improved product quality, because price reductions allow consumers to buy superior brands they might not otherwise purchase.

Consumers also obtain *hedonic*, nonfunctional benefits when taking advantage of sales promotion offers, including (1) a sense of being a wise shopper when taking advantage of sales promotions,[16] (2) a need for stimulation and variety when, say, trying brands they otherwise might not purchase if it were not for attractive promotions, and (3) entertainment value when, for example, consumers compete in promotional contests or participate in sweepstakes.

SALES PROMOTION CAPABILITIES AND LIMITATIONS

Trade and consumer promotions are capable of accomplishing certain objectives and not others. Table 16.4 summarizes these "can" and "cannot" capabilities, which now are discussed.[17]

What Promotions *Can* Accomplish

Promotions cannot work wonders but are well-suited to accomplishing the following tasks.

Stimulate Sales Force Enthusiasm for a New, Improved, or Mature Product.

There are many exciting and challenging aspects of personal selling; there also are times when the job can become dull, monotonous, and unrewarding. For example, imagine what it would be like to repeatedly call on a customer if you never had anything new or different to say about your brands or the marketing efforts that support them. Maintaining enthusiasm would be difficult, to say the least. Exciting sales promotions give salespeople persuasive

Table 16.4 — Tasks That Promotions Can and Cannot Accomplish

Sales Promotions *Can*

- **Stimulate sales force enthusiasm for a new, improved, or mature product**
- **Invigorate sales of a mature brand**
- **Facilitate the introduction of new products to the trade**
- **Increase on- and off-shelf merchandising space**
- **Neutralize competitive advertising and sales promotions**
- **Obtain trial purchases from consumers**
- **Hold current users by encouraging repeat purchases**
- **Increase product usage by loading consumers**
- **Preempt competition by loading consumers**
- **Reinforce advertising**

Sales Promotions *Cannot*

- **Compensate for a poorly trained sales force or for a lack of advertising**
- **Give the trade or consumers any compelling long-term reason to continue purchasing a brand**
- **Permanently stop an established brand's declining sales trend or change the basic nonacceptance of an undesired product**

ammunition when interacting with buyers; they revive enthusiasm and make the salesperson's job easier and more enjoyable. A case in point is the previously described Howwe Gosell promotion for Schering-Plough's two foot care brands, Lotrimin AF and Tinactin.

Invigorate Sales of a Mature Brand. Promotions cannot reverse the sales decline for an undesirable product or brand. Promotions can, however, invigorate sales of a mature product that requires a shot in the arm. A working example is the Quaker Oats Cap'n Crunch efforts. After nearly one-quarter of a century on the market, Cap'n Crunch dropped from a 3.2 percent market share to a 2.8 percent share in less than two years. This may appear to be a minuscule drop but actually amounted to a $16 million loss in annual sales in the huge ready-to-eat-cereal business, in which annual sales in the United States exceed $4 billion.

A major promotional effort was needed to invigorate Cap'n Crunch sales. Accordingly, promotional planners at Quaker Oats developed the "Find the Cap'n" sales promotion game to increase brand interest among children between the ages of 6 and 12 and to encourage repeat purchasing. Cap'n Horatio Crunch's picture was temporarily dropped from the cereal package; in his place appeared the question "Where's the Cap'n?" Package directions informed children that they could share in a $1 million reward for finding the Cap'n. Consumers had to buy three boxes of Cap'n Crunch to get clues to Horatio Crunch's whereabouts. At the game's end, 10,000 children's names were drawn from the pool of thousands of correct answers, and each child received $100.

The "Find the Cap'n" promotion involved heavy television and magazine advertising along with the promotion effort. In addition to the cash giveaway, coupons and cents-off deals were used to stimulate consumer purchasing. An incredible 50 percent increase in sales resulted during the promotion.[18]

A similarly successful promotion took place for Bazooka bubble gum in Latin America, where, as in the United States, Bazooka bubble gum comes wrapped with a Bazooka Kid comic strip. The character in this comic strip is known to children in Argentina, Paraguay, and Uruguay as *El Pibe Bazooka*. Bazooka commanded over 40 percent of the gum market in these countries, but its share had fallen by more than 10 points due to an onslaught of competitors. The maker of Bazooka gum, Cadbury, turned to its promotion agency for ideas to offset competitive inroads. The agency devised a promotion that led to temporarily replacing *El Pibe Bazooka* with Secret Clues that, when placed under a decoder screen, would reveal keys to "Bazooka Super Treasure." Over 150 million Secret Clues hit the market, and 3 million decoder screens were made available to kids through magazine and newspaper inserts and at candy stands and schools. After buying Bazooka and placing a Secret Clue under a decoder screen, kids learned immediately whether they would receive instant-win prizes such as T-shirts, soccer balls, and school bags. Kids could also enter a super treasure sweepstakes by mailing in 10 proofs of purchase. Top prizes included multimedia computers for winners and their schools along with stereo systems, TVs, bicycles, and other attractive items.

Consumer response was so overwhelming that Bazooka experienced distribution problems within several weeks of initiating the promotion. Bazooka sales increased by 28 percent and gained back about 7 share points. This successful promotion demonstrates the power of sales incentives that catch the imagination of a receptive target market. Kids were encouraged to buy Bazooka gum to win instant prizes and to purchase the brand on repeated occasions to become eligible for very attractive sweepstake awards.[19]

Facilitate the Introduction of New Products to the Trade.

To achieve sales and profit objectives, marketers continuously introduce new products and add new brands to existing categories. Promotions to wholesalers and retailers are typically necessary to encourage the trade to handle new offerings, which practitioners refer to as stock keeping units, or SKUs. In fact, many retailers refuse to carry additional SKUs unless they receive extra compensation in the form of off-invoice allowances, display allowances, and slotting allowances. (The following chapter discusses each of these various forms of allowances.)

Increase On- and Off-Shelf Merchandising Space.

Trade-oriented promotions, often in conjunction with consumer promotions, enable a manufacturer to obtain extra shelf space or more desirable space for a temporary period. This space may be in the form of extra facings on the shelf or off-shelf space in a gondola or end-of-aisle display.[20] As established in Chapter 7 in the discussion of point-of-purchase materials, preferred shelf space plays an important role in lifting a brand's sales volume.

Neutralize Competitive Advertising and Sales Promotions.

Sales promotions can effectively offset competitors' advertising and promotion efforts. For example, one company's 50-cent coupon loses much of its appeal when a competitor simultaneously comes out with a $1 coupon. As previously described, Bazooka's promotion in Argentina, Paraguay, and Uruguay offset competitors' promotions and won back lost market share.

Obtain Trial Purchases from Consumers.

Marketers depend on free samples, coupons, and other sales promotions to encourage trial purchases of new brands. Many consumers would never try new products or previously untried brands without these promotional inducements. Please read the *Global Focus* for a fascinating promotion that was extraordinarily successful in introducing a new line of light bulbs in England.

Hold Current Users by Encouraging Repeat Purchases.

Brand switching is a fact of life faced by all brand managers. The strategic use of certain forms of promotion can encourage at least short-run repetitive purchasing. Premium programs, refunds, sweepstakes, and various continuity programs (all described in Chapter 18) are useful promotions for encouraging repeat purchasing.

A promotion for the Butterfinger brand of candy illustrates a promotional event that encouraged repeat purchasing. Butterfinger, a popular brand of candy

How Do You Get Consumers to Try an Ordinary Light Bulb?

Consumers worldwide use massive quantities of light bulbs. It seems that bulbs constantly burn out and have to be replaced. Many people consider the brand name not all that important when selecting light bulbs, because they assume that light bulbs are essentially commodities—one bulb is as good (or bad) as the next. Against this perception Phillips Lighting attempted to create a differential advantage for its brand when introducing the Softone line of colored bulbs back in 1988. But after more than a decade of marketing the brand, it had achieved a loyal following only among a small and predominantly older group of consumers. With a surge in home improvement activity in England in the late nineties, Phillips attempted one more time to build demand for its Softone line—especially among younger families, who might become loyal product users for years.

This was quite a challenge considering that TV advertising was unable to adequately convey the subtle colors of Softone bulbs. It therefore was necessary to use some form of promotion to build brand awareness among the target segment and encourage trial purchase behavior—leading, hopefully, to repeat purchasing among loyal brand users. Phillips hired a promotion agency to create a campaign that would achieve the dual awareness-building and trial-generating objectives. And, the available budget was approximately only $2 million.

The agency developed a program based on what it described as a "ludicrously simple idea." Certain households were selected to receive bags, each of which contained an information brochure, a coupon, and a brief questionnaire. The attractive brochure described the product's benefits and emphasized the mood-generating ability of colored light bulbs. The coupon was for 50 pence (approximately 75 cents) off the purchase of a bulb. A five-question survey queried recipients on their household's lighting needs—in the quest by Phillips to build its database (as described in Chapter 14). Bags were distributed just to households targeted based on a combination of their demographic and psychographic characteristics that made them prime prospects for purchasing the product. The distribution crews placed the bags in mailboxes. (Parenthetically, this would be illegal in the United States, which permits only the Postal Service to use mailboxes, but such a restriction does not exist in England.)

You will note that the bags did *not* contain light bulbs. Rather, a response sheet inside the bags asked recipients if they were interested in receiving a free bulb and, if so, which of seven colors they wanted. Interested households were instructed to hang the bag with the completed questionnaire on their outside doorknob. Then, that same evening distribution crews inspected each household's response sheet and slipped the preferred color into the bag.

A total of 2 million bags were distributed. Of these, 700,000 households requested a free bulb—for a response rate of 35 percent. Follow-up surveys revealed that more than 50 percent of bulb recipients actually used the bulbs. A total of 160,000 coupons were redeemed, which at 8 percent is an incredibly high redemption level—as you will see later in Chapter 18. Sales in the six-month period following this special promotion doubled the prior average. Moreover, after analyzing the completed surveys that were received from over 500,000 consumers, the promotion agency learned how to better target its sample distribution. A subsequent bag distribution campaign was three times more efficient than the inaugural effort by focusing on neighborhoods near key retail accounts. This simple program illustrates how creative and strategically sound promotions can be highly successful.

Source: Adapted from "Adventures in Light Bulbs," *PROMO*, December 2000, p. 89. Used with permission from PROMO.

bar with annual sales exceeding $30 million, is a favorite of predominantly male consumers in the 12-to-24 age range. Nestlé, the marketer of Butterfinger, wanted to introduce a promotional event that would reinforce the brand's identification with fun and increase purchase frequency. Toward this end, a tie-in arrangement with Bart Simpson and *The Simpsons* television show was established. A mystery program was created featuring Bart on 65 million Butterfinger bars. Consumers participated by collecting "alibis" from candy wrappers to identify the mystery culprit. The grand prize for identifying the culprit was a $50,000 cash award. Ten thousand additional winners received "Most Wanted" T-shirts emblazoned with Bart Simpson in his detective outfit. The result was increased purchase frequency and a 51 percent sales gain during the promotion period.[21]

Increase Product Usage by Loading Consumers.
The effect of many deal-oriented promotions is to encourage consumer *stockpiling* — that is, to influence consumers to purchase more of a particular brand than they normally would to take advantage of the deal. Research has found that when readily stockpiled items are promoted with a deal (e.g., canned goods, paper products, and soap), purchase quantity increases by a substantial magnitude.[22]

This practice prompts a critical question: Do these short-term increases resulting from consumer stockpiling actually lead to *long-term* consumption increases of the promoted product category or do they merely represent *borrowed future sales*? One study has found that price promotions do not increase category profitability but simply serve to shift short-term sales revenue from one brand to another. That is, sales gains in the short term induced by consumer stockpiling are offset by reduced demand in the long term.[23] This finding thus suggests that price-oriented promotions may encourage consumers to load up in the short term, but that this short-term *loading* simply steals purchases that otherwise would have been made during subsequent periods.

Please note that the foregoing finding is based on research involving a single product—namely, a nonfood item (probably a brand from the household cleaning category) that could not be disclosed by the researchers due to the manufacturer's proprietary concerns. Is this finding generalizable or is the result idiosyncratic to this particular product category? No simple answer is possible, and, as usual, it depends on the circumstances surrounding a particular brand and promotional event. Other researchers, however, have provided tentative evidence that establishes when the practice of loading might have positive long-term effects. These researchers have determined that loading does increase consumers' product usage, especially when usage-related thoughts about a product are vivid in the consumer's memory. For example, people will not necessarily consume more soup just because they have stockpiled above-average quantities. However, if soup is on their minds (due to the presence of an advertising campaign touting soup's versatility), consumption is likely to increase. Also, products that are regularly visible (such as perishable items placed in the front of the refrigerator) are likely to receive greater use when consumers have stockpiled quantities of such products.[24]

This finding receives more recent support from research that has examined the impact of consumer inventory levels on the amount of usage for two product categories, ketchup and yogurt. Researchers predicted that consumption of yogurt would be more sensitive to inventory level because unlike ketchup, yogurt can be consumed at different times of day and under a variety of circumstances (with meals, as a snack, etc.). Their results supported this expectation as the amount of yogurt consumption, but not ketchup, was influenced by the quantity of yogurt available in consumer refrigerators—more yogurt, more (than normal) consumption; more ketchup, no more (than normal) consumption.[25]

Although no simple conclusion is available at this stage of research, the empirical evidence suggests that marketer's price-oriented deals that encourage stockpiling promote increased long-term consumption for some product categories but not others. The evidence suggests two conditions when increased consumption occurs from stockpiling. First, when consumers stockpile products that are *physically visible* to consumers as well as perishable, the effect may be to encourage increased short-term consumption without stealing sales from future periods. Second, consumers seem to increase their consumption rate of stockpiled products when the product is *convenient to consume* compared with when it requires preparation. Hence, it would be expected that snack foods would be consumed more rapidly when larger quantities are available in the household than would, say, a product such as pasta that has to be prepared.[26]

On the other hand, the use of price deals that lead consumers to stockpile products like ketchup and household cleaning products may simply serve to increase product purchasing in the short term without increasing long-term consumption. Consumers, in effect, stockpile these items when they go on deal but do not increase normal product usage. Thus, we would tentatively conclude that price dealing is a useful offensive weapon (that is, for purposes of increasing total consumption) only for items such as yogurt, cookies, and salty snacks, whereas products such as ketchup should be price promoted only for defensive reasons such as offsetting competitive efforts that attempt to steal market share.

Preempt Competition by Loading Consumers.

When consumers are loaded with one company's brand, they are temporarily out of the marketplace for competitive brands. Hence, one brand's promotion serves to preempt sales of competitive brands.

Reinforce Advertising.

A final can-do capability of sales promotion is to reinforce advertising. An advertising campaign can be strengthened greatly by a well-coordinated sales promotion effort.

The relationship between advertising and promotion is two way. On the one hand, an exciting promotion can reinforce advertising's impact. On the other, advertising is increasingly being used as a communication mechanism for delivering promotional offerings. It is estimated, in fact, that upwards of one-third of all media advertisements (TV, print, Internet, etc.) carry a promotional message.[27] The growing importance of promotion-oriented advertising is evidenced by the fact that promotion agencies are increasingly responsible for creating advertisements—a role historically of the traditional full-service advertising agency.

What Promotions *Cannot* Accomplish

As with other marketing communications elements, there are limits to what sales promotions are incapable of accomplishing. Particularly notable are the following three limitations.

Inability to Compensate for a Poorly Trained Sales Force or for a Lack of Advertising.

When suffering from poor sales performance or inadequate growth, some companies consider promotion to be the solution. However, promotions will provide at best a *temporary fix* if the underlying problem is due to a poor sales force, a lack of brand awareness, a weak brand image, or other maladies that only proper sales management and advertising efforts can overcome.

Inability to Give the Trade or Consumers Any Compelling Long-Term Reason to Continue Purchasing a Brand.

The trade's decision to continue stocking a brand and consumers' repeat purchasing are based on continued satisfaction with the brand. Satisfaction results from the brand's meeting profit objectives (for the trade) and providing benefits (for consumers). Promotions cannot compensate for a fundamentally flawed or mediocre brand unless the promotions offset the flaws by offering superior value to the trade and consumers.

Inability to Permanently Stop an Established Brand's Declining Sales Trend or Change the Basic Nonacceptance of an Undesired Product.

Declining sales of a brand over an extended period indicate poor product performance or the availability of a superior alternative. Promotions cannot reverse the basic nonacceptance of an undesired brand. A declining sales trend can be reversed only through product improvements or perhaps an advertising campaign that breathes new life into an aging brand. Promotions used in combination with advertising effort or product improvements may reverse the trend, but sales promotion by itself would be a waste of time and money when a brand is in a state of permanent decline.

WHAT GENERALIZATIONS CAN BE MADE ABOUT PROMOTIONS?

The foregoing discussion has referred to research evidence regarding how promotions work and the objectives accomplished. Researchers—especially during the past two decades—have vigorously studied the functioning and effectiveness of sales promotions. Empirical efforts have enabled researchers to draw some tentative conclusions. These conclusions, more formally termed *empirical generalizations*, represent consistent evidence regarding different facets of promotion performance. Nine empirical generalizations are noteworthy (see Table 16.5).[28]

Generalization 1: Temporary retail price reductions substantially increase sales. The evidence is clear that temporary retail price reductions generally result in substantial increases in short-term sales. These short-term sales increases are termed *sales spikes*. These spikes in the short term generally occur, however, at the expense of some reduction in consumer purchases of the promoted brand either preceding or following the promotional period.[29]

Generalization 2: The greater the frequency of deals, the lower the height of the deal spike. When manufacturers (and thus retailers) offer frequent deals, consumers learn to anticipate the likelihood of future deals, and thus their responsiveness to any particular deal is diminished. In short, infrequent deals generate greater spikes, whereas frequent deals generate less dramatic sales increases. The psychology of deal responsiveness also entails an issue of *reference prices*. When deals are frequently offered, the consumer's internal reference price (i.e., the price the consumer expects to pay for a particular brand) is lowered, thus making the deal price less attractive and generating less responsiveness than would be the case if the deal were offered less frequently.

Nine Generalizations About Promotions	Table 16.5

1. Temporary retail price reductions substantially increase sales.
2. The greater the frequency of deals, the lower the height of the deal spike.
3. The frequency of deals changes the consumer's reference price.
4. Retailers pass through less than 100% of trade deals.
5. Higher market share brands are less deal elastic.
6. Advertised promotions can result in increased store traffic.
7. Feature advertising and displays operate synergistically to influence sales of discounted brands.
8. Promotions in one product category affect sales of brands in complementary and competitive categories.
9. The effects of promoting higher- and lower-quality brands are asymmetric.

Adapted from Robert C. Blattberg, Richard Briesch, and Edward J. Fox, "How Promotions Work," *Marketing Science* 14 (No. 3, 1995), G122–G132.

Generalization 3: The frequency of deals changes the consumer's reference price. A corollary to the above generalization is that frequent deals on a brand tend to reduce consumers' price expectation, or reference price, for that brand. This lowering of a brand's reference price has the undesirable consequence of lowering the brand's equity and thus the seller's ability to charge premium prices. Taken together, generalizations 2 and 3 indicate that excessive dealing has the undesirable effects of both reducing a brand's reference price and diminishing consumer responsiveness to any particular deal.

Generalization 4: Retailers pass through less than 100 percent of trade deals. The simple reality is that manufacturers' trade deals, which typically are offered to retailers in the form of off-invoice discounts, are not always passed on to consumers. Though a manufacturer offers, say, a 15 percent off-invoice allowance, perhaps only 60 percent of retailers will extend this allowance to consumers as lower retail prices. There is no legal obligation for retailer's to pass through trade discounts. Retailers choose to pass along discounts only if their profit calculus leads them to the conclusion that greater profits can be earned from passing discounts to consumers rather than directly "pocketing" the discounts. This issue will be discussed further in the following chapter.

Generalization 5: Higher market share brands are less deal elastic. Suppose that a certain brand's price is reduced at retail by 20 percent and that sales volume increases by 30 percent. This would represent an elasticity coefficient of 1.5 ($30 \div 20$), a value indicating that the increase in demand is proportionally one and one-half times greater than the reduction in price. Generalization 5 suggests that for brands holding larger market shares, the deal elasticity coefficient generally is smaller than is the case for smaller-share brands. The reason is straightforward: Smaller-share brands have proportionately more customers to gain when they are placed on deal, whereas larger-share brands have fewer remaining customers. In short, a larger-share brand when placed on deal gains "less bang for the promotional buck" compared with a smaller-share brand.

Generalization 6: Advertised promotions can result in increased store traffic. On balance the research suggests that store traffic benefits from brand-dealing activity. When exposed to a retailer's advertising featuring brands on deal, some consumers will switch stores, if only temporarily, so as to take advantage of attractive deals from stores other than those in which they most regularly shop. Retailers refer to this temporary store-switching behavior as consumer "cherry picking," an apt metaphor.

Generalization 7: Feature advertising and displays operate synergistically to influence sales of discounted brands. When brands are placed on price deal, sales generally increase (see generalization 1). When brands are placed on price deal and are advertised in the retailers' advertised features, sales increase even more (see generalization 6). When brands are placed on price deal, are feature advertised, and receive special display attention, sales increase by substantially more. In other words, the combined effects of advertising and display positively interact to boost a dealt brand's retail sales. (This point was made previously in Chapter 7 in a slightly different manner when discussing point-of-purchase advertising.)

Generalization 8: Promotions in one product category affect sales of brands in complementary and competitive categories.
An interesting thing often happens when a brand in a particular product category is promoted—namely, sales for brands in complementary and competitive categories are affected. For example, when Tostitos nacho chips are promoted, sales of complementary salsa brands likely increase. On the other hand, sales of brands in the competitive potato chip category could be expected to decrease as nacho purchases by consumers reduces their selection of potato chips.

Generalization 9: The effects of promoting higher- and lower-quality brands are asymmetric. When a higher-quality brand is promoted, say, via a substantial price reduction, there is a tendency for that brand to attract switchers and thus steal sales from lower-quality brands. However, a lower-quality brand on promotion is proportionately less likely to attract switchers from higher-quality brands. In other words, switching behavior is *asymmetric*—the proportion of switchers drifting from low- to high-quality brands, when the latter is on deal, is higher than the proportion moving in the other direction when a low-quality brand is on deal.[30]

PROMOTION DEALING IS NOT ALWAYS PROFITABLE

Almost always during the period of a coupon offering or price-off deal, a brand experiences increased sales. This is because consumers are highly responsive to deals, especially when they are advertised.[31] However, increases in sales volume do not necessarily lead to increased profits. Indeed, many promotion deals spur sales but not profits. (For accounting-challenged students, it is noteworthy that profit equals revenue (sales) minus expenses. Increased revenues do not equate with increased profits if the expenses needed to generate revenues are greater than the revenue gains that result.)

As we will see, whether or not a promotion is profitable *depends on consumers' deal responsiveness*. For example, if consumers are relatively insensitive to deals, sales promotions are necessarily *unprofitable*. This is because the per-unit profit margin is reduced during a promotion and the additional sales volume is insufficient to offset the reduction in profit margin. Essential to this process is the basic accounting concept of contribution margin. **Contribution margin**, or simply *margin*, is a brand's selling price minus its per-unit variable cost. When a brand is on deal, its variable cost increases due to the expense of offering, say, a coupon worth 50 cents. This results in reduced margin. When a brand's margin is reduced, profit will increase only if the incremental sales volume is proportionately greater than the percentage reduction in margin.

Consumer Responsiveness to Promotional Deals

The market for any product category is made up of consumers who differ in their responsiveness to deals. Some consumers are loyal to a single brand in a category and buy only that brand. Other consumers have absolutely no brand loyalty and will purchase only those brands that are on deal.[32] Most consumers fall somewhere between these extremes. Figure 16.2 presents a framework showing various segments of consumers in terms of their *deal proneness*.[33] (Remember, a deal represents a reduction in a brand's normal price at the retail level. Price reductions result from retailers passing to consumers allowances provided by manufacturers. Coupon offers and cents-off deals that are offered by manufacturers directly to consumers represent other common forms of dealing activity.)

As shown in Figure 16.2, a market can be segmented into eight groups based on the pattern of consumers' deal responsiveness. There are two critical points about these groupings and the purchase patterns on which they are based: First, the patterns are obtained from optically scanned purchase data obtained from consumers who are members of household panels such as IRI's BehaviorScan or Nielsen's SCANTRACK (as described in Chapter 11). Second, the eight segments are based on consumers' purchase patterns within a *single product category*. The segmentation of consumers into deal responsiveness segments is meaningful only on a product-by-product basis inasmuch as consumers exhibit different deal responsiveness patterns across product categories.

Returning to the eight segments in Figure 16.2, the most general distinction is between consumers who purchase *only when a brand is on deal* (segment 8, or S8) and all remaining consumers who do not restrict their purchasing to such times.

Figure 16.2

A Segmentation Model of Consumer Responsiveness to Promotion Deals

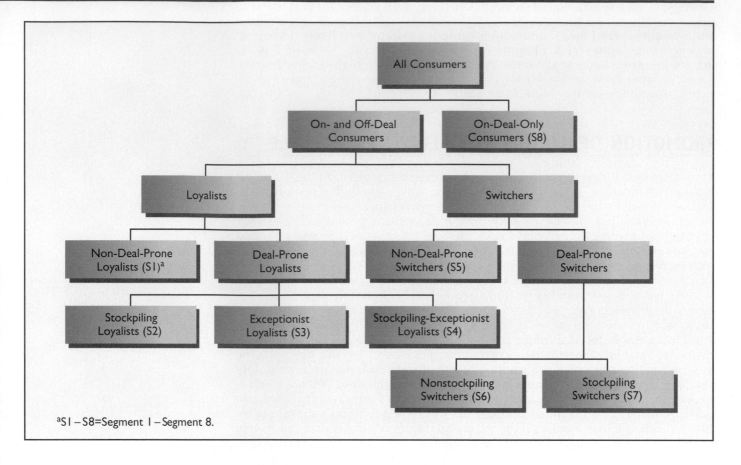

ªS1–S8=Segment 1–Segment 8.

Source: Adapted from Leigh McAlister, "Continued Research into Sales Promotion: Product Line Management Issues" (Research report and proposal prepared for the Marketing Science Institute and other sponsors, circa 1986). Adapted with permission.

These *on- and off-deal consumers* fall into two general categories, *loyalists* and *switchers*.

The distinction between loyalists and switchers is based on purchase behavior *when no brands in a product category are on deal*. **Loyalists** are consumers whose purchase patterns reflect that they buy the same brand over and over when no brands are on deal—that is, when the category is *off deal*. Looking again at Figure 16.2, you can see that some loyalists are deal prone and some are not. **Switchers**, on the other hand, are consumers who, even when all brands in a category are off deal, switch among different brands. Like loyalists, switchers may or may not be deal prone. Now let's track the various types of loyalist and switcher consumers.

Non-deal-prone loyalists (S1) are consumers who invariably buy a single brand in a product category and are not influenced by that brand's deals or the deals from competitive brands. Segment 1 represents consumers who are truly brand loyal. Most brands today have relatively few consumers who are non-deal-prone loyalists. **Non-deal-prone switchers** (S5) are like their loyalist counterparts insofar as they are not responsive to deals. They switch among brands, but this is due to a need for novelty rather than to avail themselves of deals.

Deal-prone loyalists come in three varieties: (1) **Stockpiling loyalists** (S2) purchase only the single brand to which they are loyal but take advantage of savings by stockpiling when that brand is on deal (e.g., buying three instead of the customary one box of their favored cereal when a 75-cents-off deal is offered); (2) **exceptionist loyalists** (S3), though loyal to a single brand when all brands in the category are off deal, will make an exception and purchase another, nonpreferred brand when it, but not their preferred brand, is on deal; (3) **stockpiling-exceptionist loyalists** (S4) not only make exceptions by choosing nonpreferred brands but also stockpile quantities of other brands when they are on deal.

Deal-prone switchers break into two groups: **Nonstockpiling switchers** (S6) are responsive to deals but do not purchase extra quantities when any of their acceptable brands are on deal; **stockpiling switchers** (S7) exploit deal opportunities by purchasing multiple units when any acceptable brand is on deal.

Because several of the loyalist and switcher segments are conceptually overlapping, we can eliminate any further need to distinguish between segments 1 and 5, segments 3 and 6, and segments 4 and 7. All subsequent discussion is based on the following five categories of purchase patterns:

1. Promotion insensitives (S1 and S5)
2. Stockpiling loyalists (S2)
3. Nonstockpiling promotion sensitives (S3 and S6)
4. Stockpiling promotion sensitives (S4 and S7)
5. On-deal-only consumers (S8)

Profit Implications for Each Consumer Segment

The profit implications of dealing can be illustrated using shampoo as the product category. Shampoo is an appropriate choice because it is a product category in which many consumers frequently switch among brands, whereas other consumers are highly loyal to a single brand.[34] For illustration we have chosen a hypothetical brand named SynActive—a brand name that suggests that this shampoo fits with active lifestyles. (Before proceeding, please return to Figure 16.2 and identify which segment of shampoo purchase behavior you belong to on the basis of your responsiveness, or lack of responsiveness, to shampoo deals.)

Promotion Insensitives (S1 and S5).   Assume that the market for shampoo consists entirely of consumers who are *insensitive* to promotional deals. Would it be profitable in such a situation to place SynActive on deal? Your answer should be a resounding NO! The reason is depicted in Figure 16.3, which portrays the sales pattern that would result from a market made up entirely of consumers whose purchase patterns indicate that they are insensitive to deals in the shampoo category.

Notice first in Figure 16.3 the labels for the horizontal and vertical axes. The horizontal axis is a *time dimension*, which indicates that SynActive, like most real brands, is off deal for a period of time, then on deal, then off, and so on. (Actually, most brands of packaged goods are on deal for approximately 4 weeks out of 13 weeks in a business quarter, or about 30 percent of the time.) The vertical axis graphs SynActive's *sales volume*. The line indicating SynActive's *market share* represents the amount of sales volume that this brand normally would be expected to garner in the shampoo category when it is *not* on deal.

The reason it would be unprofitable to place SynActive on deal is because promotion insensitives will *not,* by definition, alter their purchase behavior in response to this brand's dealing activity. Hence, when SynActive is placed on deal, the same number of units will be sold that would have been sold without the promotion—except now these units are being sold *at a lower margin*. The total amount of loss from the sales promotion would thus equal the number of units sold when SynActive is on deal times the cost per unit of running the deal.

Stockpiling Loyalists (S2).   These shampoo purchasers are loyal to SynActive and will stockpile quantities of that brand when it is on deal. Should

Figure 16.3   Promotion Insensitives' Deal Responsiveness

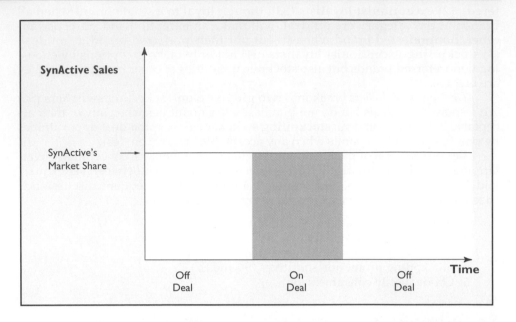

Source: Adapted from Leigh McAlister, "Continued Research into Sales Promotion: Product Line Management Issues" (research report and proposal prepared for the Marketing Science Institute and other sponsors, circa 1986), p. 7. Adapted with permission.

SynActive be placed on deal if all consumers are stockpiling loyalists? The answer again is no. It would be *unprofitable* for a brand manager to deal this brand if the shampoo market consisted entirely or predominantly of stockpiling loyalists.

The reason is shown in Figure 16.4. Note first from the vertical axis that Syn-Active would experience a *sales depression* when it is off deal due to its dealing activity in prior weeks and perhaps also its upcoming promotions that consumers anticipate. In other words, sales during off-deal periods are below SynActive's regular sales volume because consumers who stockpiled in response to past promotions have no need to now purchase SynActive at its regular, nondeal price. When the brand is on deal, sales bump up considerably because stockpiling loyalists take advantage of the deal (see the massive sales increase in Figure 16.4 when SynActive is on deal). However, this sales increase when the brand is on deal is simply *borrowed from future sales* that would have occurred if it had not been placed on deal. Hence, the deal results in an increase in short-term sales volume, but it is unprofitable because (1) sales when SynActive is on deal are made at a lower margin, and (2) when the brand is off deal, fewer sales are made at the full margin.

Nonstockpiling Promotion Sensitives (S3 and S6).

This group consists of loyalists (S3) and switchers (S6), who *take advantage of promotional deals but do* not *stockpile*. In terms of shampoo purchasing, these consumers will switch among several brands of acceptable shampoos depending on which brand is on deal on any particular shopping occasion. They choose not to stockpile, however, perhaps because they have insufficient storage space at home. This segment represents a large percentage of consumers in many product categories. For example, one study determined that increases in coffee sales from promotions were due almost entirely to brand switching (84 percent) rather than from accelerated purchasing (14 percent) or stockpiling (2 percent).[35]

Stockpiling Loyalists' Deal Responsiveness   Figure 16.4

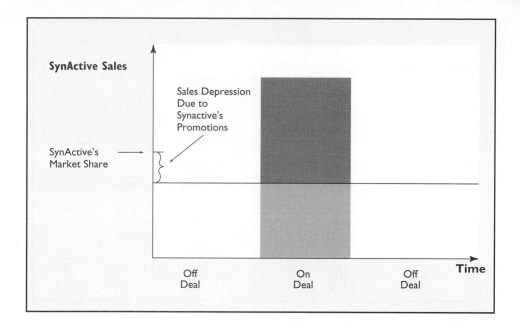

How profitable would a promotional offering by SynActive be if the market for shampoo consisted entirely, or predominantly, of consumers who switch among shampoo brands but do not stockpile? Figure 16.5 displays this situation. As in the case of stockpiling loyalists, *a sales depression* exists between SynActive's market share and its nondeal, or theoretical baseline, sales level. However, in the present case the depression is due entirely to *competitive promotions*. That is, when SynActive is off deal, its sales level is below its theoretical market share level (see the depression in Figure 16.5) because consumers who might normally purchase this brand have switched to competitive brands that are on deal. (Of course, when SynActive is on deal, its sales are bumped up measurably over the baseline level due to capturing purchases from consumers who have switched from competitive shampoo brands that now are off deal.)

SynActive's sales during the promotional period are made at a margin, M_D, which stands for the per-unit margin, M, during the period when SynActive is on deal, D. If SynActive did not deal, its sales volume would remain at a level equal to the blue-colored portion in Figure 16.5 (labeled S_N, or the sales volume when SynActive is *not* on deal). These sales would have been made at a margin, M_N. (SynActive's profit margin is, of course, greater when it is *not* on deal compared to when it is; i.e., $M_N > M_D$.) Total sales due to the deal are shown in Figure 16.5 by S_D, which includes incremental sales from the promotion (maroon-colored area) plus regular nonpromotional sales, S_N.

Let us define R as the ratio of sales volume when SynActive is on deal to when it is not on deal (i.e., R equals the ratio of S_D to S_N). We conclude that it will be *profitable* to put SynActive on deal only if $(R \times M_D) > M_N$.

An example will clarify the point. Assume that SynActive's sales volume, S_N, is 2,000,000 units when it is *off deal* with a margin, M_N, of 25 cents, and that *on deal* its sales volume, S_D, increases to 4,200,000 units but its margin, M_D, falls, due to the deal, to 15 cents. Hence, in this case R equals 2.1 (4,200,000 ÷ 2,000,000). It thus would be profitable to promote SynActive because R times M_D is greater than M_N (that is, $2.1 \times 15 = 31.5 > 25$).

Stockpiling Promotion Sensitives (S4 and S7). This segment switches among brands, depending on which is on deal, and stockpiles extra

Figure 16.5

Nonstockpiling Promotion Insensitives' Deal Responsiveness

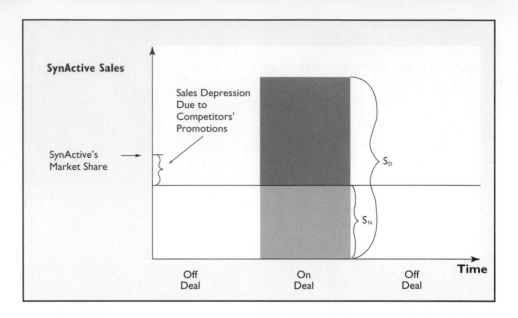

Source: Adapted from Leigh McAlister, "Continued Research into Sales Promotion: Product Line Management Issues" (research report and proposal prepared for the Marketing Science Institute and other sponsors, circa 1986), p. 7. Adapted with Permission.

quantities when an attractive deal is located. In this case, SynActive's baseline sales are depressed both by its own dealing activity and by competitive dealing. If SynActive's dealing activity *is* profitable when consumers do *not* stockpile (the situation in the previous case), then stockpiling behavior will lead to even greater profitability. This is because SynActive will profit both by taking consumers away from competitors during the period the brand is on deal and by preempting competitors' sales in subsequent off-deal periods when consumers are "working off" their stockpiles of SynActive.

On-Deal-Only Consumers (S8). Because, by definition, SynActive makes no sales to these consumers *unless it is on deal*, it follows that promotions to a market made up exclusively of on-deal-only consumers will be *profitable*. The total amount of profit will equal the number of units sold, Q, times the profit margin when the brand is on deal, M_D.

In Conclusion

The discussion to this point has provided several guidelines regarding the profitability of dealing:

1. Putting a brand on deal is *unprofitable* if the market is composed of either promotion-insensitive consumers or stockpiling loyalists.
2. Putting a brand on deal is *profitable* if the market contains on-deal-only consumers.
3. Putting a brand on deal may or may not be profitable if the market consists of nonstockpiling or stockpiling promotion-sensitive consumers.

The preceding statements are based on the assumption that a brand's market consists exclusively of one or another type of consumer—for example, promotion insensitives or stockpiling loyalists. This obviously is a simplifying assumption. The market for any product (such as our illustrative shampoo brand, SynActive) contains consumers from all segments. The matter of whether promotion is profitable thus depends on the relative composition of customer types.

Fortunately, the availability of scanner data makes it possible for marketing researchers to identify the percentage of consumers who fall into each of these dealing categories. Armed with this information, brand managers can determine whether dealing activity is profitable or whether it merely results in a revenue-increasing but profit-losing endeavor.

THE ROLE OF PROMOTION AGENCIES

As discussed in Chapter 8, brand managers typically employ the services of advertising agencies to create advertising messages, buy advertising media, and perform other services related to a brand's advertising function. Though less well known than their ad agency counterparts, brand managers also hire specialized promotion agencies to perform sales promotion functions. These agencies—again like their advertising agency counterparts—work with brand managers in formulating promotion strategies and implementing tactical programs.

Assume, for example, that the brand manager of our hypothetical SynActive brand of shampoo believes that this new brand needs to be sampled in trial-sized bottles to facilitate high levels of trial purchase behavior. The promotion also will include coupons in the box containing the trial-size sample. Further, an introductory advertising campaign in magazines will include an attractive sweepstakes offer to draw attention to the ad and enhance consumer involvement with the brand. The brand manager determines that it will be best to use the services of a promotion agency that can expertly design a sampling program that efficiently targets sample distribution to young consumers and a sweepstakes program that would appeal to this age group. Table 16.6 lists the top 25 promotion agencies as identified in a recent year and provides pertinent information about each.

In addition to traditional promotion agencies, which traditionally have emphasized programs using offline media and in-store distribution, there is a new generation of promotion agencies that emphasize online promotions. See the *Online Focus* for a brief description.

SUMMARY

Sales promotion was introduced in this first of three chapters devoted to the topic. The precise nature of sales promotion was described, and specific forms of trade- and consumer-oriented promotions were discussed. Promotion was explained as having three targets: the trade (wholesalers and retailers), consumers, and a company's own sales force.

The chapter proceeded to discuss the reasons for a significant trend toward increased investment in promotions vis-à-vis advertising. This shift is part of the movement from pull- to push-oriented marketing, particularly in the case of CPG goods. Underlying factors include a balance-of-power transfer from manufacturers to retailers, increased brand parity and growing price sensitivity, reduced brand loyalty, splintering of the mass market and reduced media effectiveness, a growing short-term orientation, and favorable consumer responsiveness to sales promotions.

The chapter also detailed the specific tasks that promotions can and cannot accomplish. For example, promotions cannot give the trade or consumers compelling long-term reasons to purchase. However, promotions are ideally suited for generating trial-purchase behavior, facilitating the introduction of new products, gaining shelf space for a brand, encouraging repeat purchasing, and performing a variety of other tasks. Also discussed were nine empirical generalizations about sales promotions.

Table 16.6   Top 25 Promotion Agencies in 2001

Agency Name	Revenues (in millions $)	Location	URL
1. Draftworldwide	$324.33	Chicago, IL	http://www.draftworldwide.com
2. GMR Marketing	44.40	New Berlin, WI	http://www.gmrmarketing.com
3. Marketing Drive Worldwide	84.00	South Norwalk, CT	http://www.marketingdrive.com
4. Flair Communications Agency	86.17	Chicago, IL	http://www.flairpromo.com
5. Momentum	115.77	St. Louis, MO	http://www.momentum-na.com
6. 141 Communicator	22.38	Chicago, IL	http://www.communicatorww.com
7. Einson Freeman, Inc.	37.10	Paramus, NJ	http://www.einsonfreeman.com
8. U.S. Marketing & Promotions	79.70	Los Angeles, CA	http://www.usmpagency.com
9. Aspen Marketing Group	79.02	Los Angeles, CA	http://www.aspen-marketing.com
10. Wunderman	197.00	New York, NY	http://www.wunderman.com
11. Noble & Associates	8.14	Springfield, MO	http://www.noble.net
12. CMI	20.53	East Rutherford, NJ	Not available
13. Promotions.com	26.63	New York, NY	http://www.promotions.com
14. Frankel	99.65	Chicago, IL	http://www.frankel.com
15. Upshot	32.89	Chicago, IL	http://www.upshot.net
16. Ryan Partnership	47.88	Westport, CT	http://www.ryanpartnership.com
17. Colangelo Synergy Marketing	13.25	Darien, CT	http://www.colangelo-sm.coms
18. Equity Marketing	52.27	Los Angeles, CA	http://www.equity-marketing.com
19. Integer Group	88.49	Denver, CO	http://www.integer.com
20. Jack Nadel, Inc.	26.11	Culver City, CA	http://www.jacknadelinc.com
21. Hawkeye Communications	93.60	New York, NY	http://www.hawkeyeww.com
22. Promotion Group Central	2.99	Chicago, IL	http://www.promogroup.com
23. Zipatoni	27.25	St. Louis, MO	http://www.zipatoni.com
24. Bounty SCA Worldwide	183.76	Chicago, IL	http://www.bountysca.com
25. Marden-Kane	19.83	Manhasset, NY	http://www.mardenkane.com

Source: "The PROMO 100: Top 25 Agencies 2001," *PROMO*, June 2001, pp. 72–79. Used with permission from PROMO.

The Rise of the Online Promotion Agency

In the early years of the Internet, many marketing people claimed that the Web would become the perfect medium for mass advertising. Well, the fact of the matter is that online advertising has not lived up to its early hype. On the other hand, the Internet has become an increasingly important venue for conducting promotions. Coupons, sweepstakes offers, online promotional games, free sample offerings, and online continuity programs are just some of the promotions that are virtually ubiquitous on the Web. These programs are effective because they allow marketers to target promotions to preferred consumers, to deliver the programs relatively inexpensively, and to measure results with greater precision than what is possible with other marketing programs. Chapter 18 will provide more detail about online consumer promotions. For the present suffice it to say that online promotions are here to stay. Promotion agencies such as 24/7 iPromotions (Figure 16.6) are an invaluable resource for brand managers both in planning strategically sound promotions and carrying through their implementation.

Illustration of an Online Promotion Agency

Figure 16.6

Detailed discussion was devoted to the conditions under which the use of price-deal promotions are profitable. Various segments of consumers based on their responsiveness to promotional deals are described. It was concluded that promotional deals are unprofitable if a brand's market is composed of promotion-insensitive or brand-loyal stockpilers; sales promotion is always profitable if the market contains consumers who buy only on deal; and deals may be profitable if the market consists primarily of consumers who switch from brand to brand depending on which brand is on deal.

The following chapter will continue with a detailed treatment of sales promotion's role in influencing trade behavior, and Chapter 18 will examine its role in influencing the behavior of ultimate consumers.

Find more resources to help you study at http://shimp.swcollege.com!

DISCUSSION QUESTIONS

1. The term *promotional inducement* has been suggested as an alternative to *sales promotion.* Explain why this term is more descriptive than the established one.

2. Describe the factors that have accounted for sales promotion's rapid growth. Do you expect a continued increased in the use of promotion throughout the following decade?

3. Why, in your opinion, is the Internet a good medium for offering sales promotions to consumers?

4. Explain in your own words the meaning of push- versus pull-oriented promotional strategies. Using for illustration a well-known supermarket brand of your choice, explain which elements of this brand's marketing communications mix embody push and which embody pull.

5. Assume you are the vice president of marketing of a large, well-known CPG company (e.g., Procter & Gamble, Lever Brothers, Johnson & Johnson). What steps might you take to restore a balance of power favoring your company in its relations with retailers?

6. Are promotions able to reverse a brand's temporary sales decline and/or a permanent sales decline? Be specific.

7. The allocation of marketing communications dollars to advertising and promotions is influenced by a variety of factors, including life-cycle stage, the degree of brand differentiation, and the degree of brand dominance. Explain how these factors might influence the allocation decision.

8. How can a manufacturer's use of trade- and consumer-oriented promotions generate enthusiasm and stimulate improved performance from the sales force?

9. Offer a specific explanation of why you think the "Find the Cap'n" promotional campaign for Cap'n Crunch cereal was so successful.

10. If a market for a brand were composed entirely of brand-loyal stockpilers, why would promotional deals for this brand necessarily be unprofitable? Why are promotional deals profitable when a market consists of on-deal-only consumers?

11. Why is it critical that objectives be clearly specified when formulating a promotional program?

12. Assume you are brand manager of Mountain State Bottled Water. This new brand competes in a product category with several well-known brands. Your marketing communications objective is to generate trial purchases among predominantly younger and better-educated consumers. Propose a promotion that would accomplish this objective. Assume that your promotion is purely experimental and that it will be undertaken in a small city of only 250,000 people. Also assume that (1) you cannot afford product sampling, (2) you will not advertise the promotion, and (3) your budget for this experimental promotion is $5,000. What would you do?

13. Generalization 5 in the chapter claimed that higher market share brands are less deal elastic. Construct a realistic example to illustrate your understanding of this empirical generalization.

14. Generalization 8 asserted that promotions in one product category affect sales of brands in complementary and competitive categories. Tostitos tortilla chips was used as an example of this generalization. Provide examples of two additional brands and the complementary and competitive product categories that likely would be affected by promotions for your two illustrative brands.

15. A concluding section of the chapter indicated that promotion agencies have become an increasingly important resource for brand managers in planning and executing promotional programs. One could argue that the fees brand managers pay for the services of promotion agencies might better be spent elsewhere—for example, on increased advertising levels. Present arguments both in favor of and in opposition to hiring promotion agencies.

ENDNOTES

1. This definition combines the author's thoughts with those from two sources: Roger A. Strang, "Sales Promotion Research: Contributions and Issues" (unpublished paper presented at the AMA/MSI/PMAA Sales Promotion Workshop, Babson College, May 1983); and James H. Naber, James Webb Young address (University of Illinois, Urbana-Champaign, October 21, 1986).

2. Jacques Chevron, "Branding and Promotion: Uneasy Cohabitation," *Brandweek*, September 14, 1998, 24.

3. Don E. Schultz, William A. Robinson, and Lisa A. Petrison, *Sales Promotion Essentials: The 10 Basic Sales Promotion Techniques and How to Use Them,* 3rd. ed. (Chicago: NTC Business Books, 1998), 6.

4. Pierre Chandon, Brian Wansink, and Gilles Laurent, "A Benefit Congruency Framework of Sales Promotion Effectiveness," *Journal of Marketing* 64 (October 2000), 65–81. Robert M. Schindler, "Consequences of Perceiving Oneself as Responsible for Obtaining a Discount: Evidence for Smart-Shopper Feelings," *Journal of Consumer Psychology* 7, no. 4 (1998), 371–392.

5. Kellie Krumplitsch, "Promotion Explosion: The Reggie Awards," *Brandweek*, April 4, 1994, 29, 32.

6. These figures are based on annual surveys conducted by Donnelly Marketing and now Cox Direct that since 1979 have queried executives from packaged goods, health and beauty aids, and household products companies about their marketing communications expenditures. Trend data are from Cox Direct *20ᵗʰ Annual Survey of Promotional Practices* (Largo, FL: Cox Direct, 1998), Chart 63, 74. Cox Direct discontinued its annual survey after the 20th survey.

7. The source note to Table 16.1 indicates that these estimates are based on two different sources. Cox Direct provided the data for 1990–1997 in its *20ᵗʰ Survey of Promotional Practices* but subsequently discontinued performing the annual survey. The data from 1998–2001 are from Cannondale Associates. Hence, one cannot be certain whether the changes revealed, especially the increase in trade promotions vis-à-vis the decrease in consumer promotions is due to real changes or variations in measurement procedures. I suspect more of the latter than the former.

8. Alvin A. Achenbaum and F. Kent Mitchel, "Pulling Away from Push Marketing," *Harvard Business Review* 65 (May/June 1987), 38–40; Robert J. Kopp and Stephen A. Greyser, "Packaged Goods Marketing 'Pull' Companies Look to Improved 'Push,'" *The Journal of Consumer Marketing* 4 (spring 1987), 13–22.

9. For an excellent review of sales promotion trends in the U.K., see Ken Peattie and Sue Peattie, "Sales Promotion— Playing to Win?" *Journal of Marketing Management* 9 (1993), 255–269.

10. Carl F. Mela, Sunil Gupta, and Donald R. Lehmann, "The Long-Term Impact of Promotion and Advertising on Consumer Brand Choice," *Journal of Marketing Research* 34 (May 1997), 248–261.

11. Purushottam Papatla and Lakshman Krishnamurthi, "Measuring the Dynamic Effects of Promotions on Brand Choice," *Journal of Marketing Research* 33 (February 1996), 20–35.

12. A. S. C. Ehrenberg, Kathy Hammond, and G. J. Goodhardt, "The After-Effects of Price-Related Consumer Promotions," *Journal of Advertising Research* 34 (July/August 1994), 11–21.

13. Robert C. Blattberg and Scott A. Neslin, "Sales Promotion: The Long and the Short of It," *Marketing Letters* 1, no. 1 (1989), 81–97.

14. *20ᵗʰ Annual Survey of Promotional Practices* (Largo, FL: Cox Direct, 1998), 22.

15. Chandon, Wansink, and Laurent, "A Benefit Congruency Framework of Sales Promotion Effectiveness," 65–81. The following discussion of benefits is based on a typology provided by these offers. See Table 1 on pages 68–69. Another insightful perspective along similar lines is provided in Figure 2 of Kusum L. Ailawadi, Scott A. Neslin, and Karen Gedenk, "Pursuing the Value-Conscious Consumer: Store Brands Versus National Brand Promotions," *Journal of Marketing* (January 2001), 71–89.

16. Research indicates that consumers who take advantage of promotional deals feel good about themselves for being "smart shoppers" and that these feelings are particularly strong when consumers have a sense of being personally responsible for availing themselves of a deal. See Robert M. Schindler, "Consequences of Perceiving Oneself as Responsible for Obtaining a Discount," 371–392.

17. This discussion is guided by Charles Fredericks, Jr., "What Ogilvy & Mather Has Learned about Sales Promotion," *The Tools of Promotion* (New York: Association of National Advertisers, 1975); and Don E. Schultz and William A. Robinson, *Sales Promotion Management*

(Lincolnwood, Ill.: NTC Business Books, 1986), chap. 3.

18. "Quaker Oats Finds Cap'n Crunch Loot with Hide-and-Seek," *Advertising Age*, May 26, 1986, 53.

19. Amie Smith and Al Urbanski, "Excellence x 16," *Promo*, December 1998, 136.

20. A facing is a row of shelf space. Brands typically are allocated facings proportionate to their profit potential to the retailer. Manufacturers must pay for extra facings by offering display allowances or providing other inducements that increase the retailer's profit.

21. Krumplitsch, "Promotion Explosion: The Reggie Awards."

22. Chakravarthi Narasimhan, Scott A. Neslin, and Subrata K. Sen, "Promotional Elasticities and Category Characteristics," *Journal of Marketing* 60 (April 1996), 17–30.

23. Carl F. Mela, Kamel Jedidi, and Douglas Bowman, "The Long-Term Impact of Promotions on Consumer Stockpiling Behavior," *Journal of Marketing Research* 35 (May 1998), 250–262.

24. Brian Wansink and Rohit Deshpande, "'Out of Sight, Out of Mind': Pantry Stockpiling and Brand-Usage Frequency," *Marketing Letters* 5, no. 1 (1994), 91–100.

25. Kusum L. Ailawadi and Scott A. Neslin, "The Effect of Promotion on Consumption: Buying More and Consuming It Faster," *Journal of Marketing Research* 35 (August 1998), 390–398.

26. Pierre Chandon and Brian Wansink, "A Convenience-Salience Framework of Stockpiling-Induced Consumption," working paper (May 18, 2001).

27. Betsy Spethmann, "Value Ads," *Promo*, March 2001, 74–79.

28. The following discussion is based on the outstanding synthesis of the literature provided by Robert C. Blattberg, Richard Briesch, and Edward J. Fox, "How Promotions Work," *Marketing Science* 14, no. 3 (1995), G122–G132. The order of generalizations presented here is adapted from Blattberg et al.'s presentation. Please refer to this article for coverage of the specific studies on which the generalizations are based.

29. Harald J. van Heerde, Peter S. H. Leeflang, and Dick R. Wittink, "The Estimation of Pre- and Postpromotion Dips with Store-Level Scanner Data," *Journal of Marketing Research* 37 (August 2000), 383–395.

30. For a review of interesting experimental research on this issue, see Stephen M. Nowlis and Itamar Simonson, "Sales Promotions and the Choice Context as Competing Influences on Decision Making," *Journal of Consumer Psychology* 9, no. 1 (2000), 1–16.

31. Albert C. Bemmaor and Dominique Mouchoux, "Measuring the Short-Term Effect of In-Store Promotion and Retail Advertising on Brand Sales: A Factorial Experiment," *Journal of Marketing Research* 28 (May 1991), 202–214.

32. Research has shown that consumers possess a good understanding of when deals are offered by manufacturers as well as how much savings they can enjoy by purchasing on deal. See Aradhna Krishna, Imran S. Currim, and Robert W. Shoemaker, "Consumer Perceptions of Promotional Activity," *Journal of Marketing* 55 (April 1991), 4–16; and Aradhna Krishna, "The Effect of Deal Knowledge on Consumer Purchase Behavior," *Journal of Marketing Research* 31 (February 1994), 76–91.

33. The following discussion is based on the work of Leigh McAlister, "Continued Research into Sales Promotion: Product Line Management Issues" (research report and proposal prepared for the Marketing Science Institute and other sponsors, circa 1986); also, Leigh McAlister, "A Model of Consumer Behavior," *Marketing Communications*, April 1987, 27–30.

34. For a fascinating set of experiments using shampoo as the experimental product, see Barbara E. Kahn and Therese A. Louie, "Effects of Retraction of Price Promotions on Brand Choice Behavior for Variety-Seeking and Last-Purchase-Loyal Consumers," *Journal of Marketing Research* 27 (August 1990), 279–289.

35. Sunil Gupta, "Impact of Sales Promotion on When, What, and How Much to Buy," *Journal of Marketing Research* 25 (November 1988), 342–355.

Chapter Seventeen

TRADE-ORIENTED SALES PROMOTION

Chapter Objectives

After studying this chapter, you should be able to:

1. Discuss the objectives of trade-oriented promotions and the factors critical to building a successful trade promotion program.
2. Explain the various forms of trade allowances and the reasons for their use.
3. Understand forward buying and diverting and how these practices emerge from manufacturers' use of off-invoice allowances.
4. Explain the role of everyday low pricing (EDLP) and pay-for-performance programs as means of reducing forward buying and diverting.
5. Describe the concept and practice known as efficient consumer response (ECR).
6. Understand the practice of category management.
7. Describe the role of cooperative advertising and vendor support programs.
8. Appreciate the role of trade shows.

Opening Vignette: Is Clorox Glad It Bought Glad?

In the late 1990s Clorox Company acquired a firm named First Brands. One of First Brands' most important products was the line of plastic items (wraps and bags) under the Glad brand name. Clorox thought it could quickly boost sales of Glad products insofar as First Brands had previously invested virtually nothing in media advertising behind the brand and had instead relied almost exclusively on consumer promotions (primarily coupons) and heavy trade promotion spending.

Clorox's strategy was to cut Glad's consumer and trade price promotions and to invest heavily in mass media advertising. Clorox cut trade promotion spending on Glad both in 1999 and then again in 2000. Much to Clorox's surprise and frustration, competitors did not follow suit by also cutting trade promotions on their own brands. How did retailers react? They withdrew merchandise support, and Glad sales fell dramatically—as did Clorox's stock price, which dropped by about 20 percent in the two years after acquiring First Brands.

With declining market share and a sagging stock price, Clorox responded in the only way it could: It returned to couponing and trade promotion spending. Though Clorox's long-term strategy is to build Glad's brand equity via increased advertising spending and new product introductions, the fact remains that its effort to cut trade promotion spending was rebuffed by large, powerful retailers. As described in the previous chapter, the power of retailers continues to grow relative to that of manufacturers. As one observer noted, "Without unique products and strong advertising, package-goods brands have little choice but to pay up to maintain shelf space, especially as consolidation makes retailers more powerful."

With the shift in power from manufacturers to retailers, and with brands from competitive manufacturers becoming increasingly indistinct, retailers have pressured the manufacturers that supply them to also provide attractive price discounts and other forms of promotional dollars. Just as Clorox was effectively forced to spend more on trade promotions than it desired, so too are the manufacturers of numerous other products whose brands either are not leaders in particular product categories or are not much differentiated compared with competitive brands.

Source: Adapted from Jack Neff, "Clorox Gives in on Glad, Hikes Trade Promotion," *Advertising Age*, November 27, 2000, p. 22. © 2000 by Crain Communications, Inc. Reprinted by permission.

INTRODUCTION TO TRADE PROMOTION

As indicated in the previous chapter, trade promotions represent more than half of every manufacturer dollar invested in advertising and promoting new and existing products. Though there is some variance in estimates, surveys indicate that trade promotions average anywhere from 13 percent to 16 percent of manufacturers' sales.[1] Manufacturers direct trade promotions at wholesalers, retailers, and other marketing intermediaries (rather than at consumers). A manufacturer's consumer-oriented advertising and promotions are likely to fail unless trade promotions have succeeded in persuading channel intermediaries to stock adequate quantities. The special incentives offered by manufacturers to their distribution channel members are then expected to be passed through to consumers in the form of price discounts offered by retailers, often stimulated by advertising support and special displays.[2] As we will see later, however, this does not always occur.

Even though trade promotions do not always work the way they are designed to, manufacturers have various legitimate objectives for using trade-oriented promotions:[3]

1. Introduce new or revised products.
2. Increase distribution of new packages or sizes.
3. Build retail inventories.
4. Maintain or increase the manufacturer's share of shelf space.
5. Obtain displays outside normal shelf locations.
6. Reduce excess inventories and increase turnover.
7. Achieve product features in retailers' advertisements.
8. Counter competitive activity, and, ultimately.
9. Sell as much as possible to final consumers.

To accomplish these myriad objectives, several ingredients are critical to building a successful trade promotion program.[4]

Financial Incentive.   A manufacturer's trade promotion must offer wholesalers, retailers, and other channel intermediaries increased profit margins and/or increased sales volume.

Correct Timing.   Trade promotions are appropriately timed when they are (1) tied in with a seasonal event during a time of growing sales (such as candy sales during Valentine's Day, Halloween, and Christmas), (2) paired with a consumer-oriented sales promotion, or (3) used strategically to offset competitive promotional activity.

Minimize the Retailer's Effort and Cost.   The more effort and expense required, the less likely it is that retailers will cooperate in a program they see as benefiting the manufacturer but not themselves.

Quick Results.   The most effective trade promotions are those that generate immediate sales or increases in store traffic. (As you will see in the next chapter, *instant gratification* is an important motivator of consumers' response to consumer-oriented promotions. This same motive applies to retailers as well.)

Improve Retailer Performance.   Promotions are effective when they help the retailer do a better selling job or improve merchandising methods as, for example, by providing retailers with improved displays.[5]

Types of Trade Promotions

Manufacturers in dealing with their channel intermediaries use a variety of practices intended to encourage certain behaviors on the part of their customers and ultimately to boost the sales and profitability of the manufacturer's brands. These practices can be lumped under the general label "trade promotions," although, as will become apparent, these practices vary greatly in terms of their objectives, implementations, and effectiveness. Common to all, however, is the general objective to induce channel intermediaries (the trade) to devote greater attention to products of the manufacturer that is offering the promotion rather than to competitive offerings. Following sections discuss four forms of trade promotions:

1. Trade allowances
2. Cooperative advertising and vendor support programs
3. Trade contests and incentives
4. Trade shows

TRADE ALLOWANCES

Trade allowances are used by manufacturers to reward wholesalers and retailers for performing activities in support of the manufacturer's brand. These allowances, also called *trade deals*, encourage retailers to stock the manufacturer's brand, discount the brand's price to consumers, feature it in advertising, or provide special display or other point-of-purchase support.[6]

By using trade allowances, manufacturers hope to accomplish two interrelated objectives: (1) increase purchases of the manufacturer's brand by wholesalers and/or retailers, and (2) increase consumers' purchases of the manufacturer's brand from retailers. This latter objective is based on the expectations that consumers are receptive to price reductions and that retailers will in fact *pass along to consumers* the discounts they receive from manufacturers.

These expectations do not always become reality. Retailers often take advantage of allowances without performing the services for which they receive credit. In fact, a study of trade promotion spending by A. C. Nielsen revealed that 70 percent of surveyed manufacturers rated the value they receive from trade promotion spending as fair or poor—only 30 percent responded that the value was good or excellent.[7] Moreover, the vast majority of retailers think that trade promotions should serve to increase sales and profits of entire product categories without concern for whether a manufacturer's specific brand benefits from the trade promotion.[8]

There is, in short, a substantial rift between manufacturers and retailers over the matter of which party trade promotions are intended to benefit. Manufacturers use trade promotions, of course, to advance their brands' sales and profit performance. Retailers, on the other hand, tend to regard trade dollars as an opportunity for increasing their profit margins and thus boosting bottom lines. This schism is easy to understand because parties to economic transactions often have conflicting objectives yet depend on each other for success.

Major Forms of Trade Allowances

Three major forms of trade allowances are (1) off-invoice allowances, (2) bill-back allowances, and (3) slotting allowances.

Off-Invoice Allowances. The most frequently used form of trade allowance is an off-invoice allowance, which represents a manufacturer's *temporary price reduction* to the trade on a particular brand. **Off-invoice allowances** are, as the name suggests, deals offered periodically to the trade that permit retailers to deduct a fixed amount from the invoice—*merely by placing an order* during the period which the manufacturer is "dealing" a brand. (A slight variant is a deal that provides the trade with free goods for orders meeting or exceeding required quantities.) In offering an off-invoice allowance, the manufacturer's sales force informs retail buyers that a discount of, say, 15 percent can be deducted from the invoice amount for all quantities purchased during the specified deal period. Many manufacturers of consumer packaged goods (CPGs) provide off-invoice allowances at regularly scheduled intervals, which for many brands is one four-week period during every 13-week business quarter. This means that many brands are on off-invoice deals approximately 30 percent of the year. (The implications of this dealing frequency will be discussed later when describing the retailer practices of *forward buying* and *diverting*.)

A manufacturer in using an off-invoice allowance does so with the expectation that retailers will purchase more of the manufacturer's brand during the deal period than they normally would and, to rapidly sell off excess inventories, will pass the deals on to consumers in the form of reduced prices—which thus should spur consumers' purchasing of the manufacturer's price-reduced brand. However, as previously stated, retailers do not always comply with this expectation and, in fact, are typically not contractually bound to pass along discounted prices to consumers. Rather, retailers receive an off-invoice allowance (of, say, 15 percent) when purchasing the manufacturer's brand but often do not discount their selling prices to consumers or reduce prices by substantially less than the full 15 percent.[9] Manufacturers estimate that retailers pass through to consumers only about one-half of trade funds that they provide to retailers.[10]

Bill-Back Allowances.

Another form of trade allowance is the so-called bill-back allowance. Retailers receive allowances for featuring the manufacturer's brand in advertisements (**bill-back *ad* allowances**) or for providing special displays (**bill-back *display* allowances**). As the expression indicates, retailers do *not* deduct bill-back allowances directly from the invoice by virtue of ordering products (as is the case with off-invoice allowances) but rather *must earn the allowances* by performing designated advertising or display services in behalf of the manufacturer's brand. The retailer effectively bills (i.e., charges) the manufacturer for the services rendered, and the manufacturer pays an allowance to the retailer for the services received.

To illustrate, assume that the sales force for the Campbell Soup Company informs its many retailers that during October they will receive a 5 percent discount on all cases of V8 juice purchased during this period provided that they run newspaper advertisements in which V8 juice is prominently featured. With proof of having run feature ads in newspapers, retailers then would bill Campbell Soup for a 5 percent advertising allowance. Similarly, Campbell Soup's sales force could offer a 2 percent display allowance whereby retailers could receive an additional 2 percent discount on all purchases of V8 juice during the deal period for displaying V8 juice in a prime display location.

Slotting Allowances.

This form of trade allowance applies specifically to the situation where a manufacturer attempts to get one of its brands—typically a new brand—accepted by retailers. Also called a *stocking allowance* or *street money*, a slotting allowance is *not* something manufactures of branded products choose to offer retailers. To the contrary, retailers impose slotting allowances on manufacturers. Retailers demand this fee of manufacturers supposedly to compensate them for added costs incurred when taking a new brand into distribution and placing it on the shelf. **Slotting allowances** are the fees manufacturers pay retailers for access to the slot, or location, that the retailer must make available in its distribution center to accommodate the manufacturer's new brand. It should be obvious that manufacturers and retailers hold somewhat differing views regarding the appropriateness and value of the slotting-allowance practice. The following discussion examines many of the key issues.[11]

When first used back in the 1960s, slotting allowances compensated retailers for the *real costs* of taking on a new stock-keeping unit, or SKU. The cost at that time averaged $50 per SKU per *account*. However, by the mid-1990s slotting allowances had increased to an average charge of $42 per SKU per *store*, or a total cost to the manufacturer of approximately $1.2 million to introduce one SKU nationally.[12] You probably are thinking, "This sounds like bribery." You also may be wondering, "Why do manufacturers tolerate slotting allowances?" Let's examine each issue.[13]

First, slotting allowances are indeed a form of bribery. The retailer that demands slotting allowances denies the manufacturer shelf space unless the manufacturer is willing to pay the up-front fee—the slotting allowance—to acquire that space for its new brand. Second, manufacturers tolerate slotting allowances because they are confronted with a classic dilemma: Either they pay the fee and eventually recoup the cost through profitable sales volume, or they refuse to pay the fee and in so doing accept a fate of not being able to successfully introduce new brands.

The expression "between a rock and a hard place" appropriately describes the reality of slotting allowances from the manufacturer's perspective. Consider, for example, Eastman Kodak's introduction of Supralife alkaline batteries to compete against the likes of Duracell, Eveready, and Ray-O-Vac. After being on the market for only a few years, Supralife's performance was so weak that Kodak decided to discontinue all advertising and, in effect, to accept its destiny as a minor player in the alkaline battery business. Analysts estimate Kodak's battery business losses at somewhere between $100 million and $200 million. Among other reasons for Supralife's losses is the fact that Kodak in the first year had to pay millions of dollars in slotting allowances to gain distribution for this new battery brand.[14]

In certain respects, slotting allowances are a *legitimate cost* of doing business. When, for example, a large, multistore supermarket chain takes on a new brand, it does incur several added expenses. These expenses arise because the chain must make space for that new brand in its distribution center, create a new entry in its computerized inventory system, possibly redesign store shelves, and notify individual stores about the new SKU. In addition to these expenses, the chain takes the risk that the new brand will fail. This is a likely result in the grocery industry, where at least half of all new brands are failures. Hence, the slotting allowance provides the retailer with what effectively amounts to an insurance policy against the prospects that a brand will fail.

It is questionable, however, whether the actual expenses incurred by retailers are anywhere near the slotting allowances they charge. Actual charges are highly variable. Some supermarkets charge as little as $5 per store to stock a new item, while others charge as much as $100 per store. Large companies can afford to pay slotting allowances, because their volume is sufficient to recoup the expense. However, brands with small consumer franchises are frequently unable to afford these fees. Smaller manufacturers thus are placed at a competitive disadvantage when attempting to gain distribution for their new products.

How, you might be wondering, are retailers able to impose expensive slotting fees on manufacturers? The reason is straightforward: As noted in the previous chapter, the balance of power has shifted away from manufacturers and toward retailers. Power means being able to call the shots, and increasing numbers of retailers are doing this. Also, CPG manufacturers have hurt their own cause by introducing thousands of new brands each year, most of which are trivial variants of existing products rather than distinct new offerings with meaningful profit opportunities for retailers. As such, every manufacturer competes against every other manufacturer for limited shelf space, and slotting allowances are simply a mechanism used by retailers to exploit the competition among manufacturers. Furthermore, many grocery retailers find it easy to rationalize slotting allowances on the grounds that their net profit margins in selling groceries are minuscule (typically 1 percent to 1.5 percent) and that slotting allowances enable them to earn returns comparable to those earned by manufacturers.

Further understanding of the rationale and dynamics underlying slotting allowances is possible by comparing them to apartment prices in any college community. When units are abundant, different apartment complexes compete aggressively with one another and rental prices are forced downward to the benefit of students. On the other hand, when apartments are scarce (which typically is the case on most college campuses), prices often are inflated. The result: You may be forced to pay exhorbitant rent to live in a second-rate, albeit conveniently located, apartment.

This is also the case in today's marketing environment. Each year retailers are confronted with requests to stock thousands of new brands (consider these new brands equivalent to potential tenants). The amount of shelf space (the number of apartments) is limited because relatively few new stores are being built. Hence, retailers are able to command slotting allowances (charge higher rent), and manufacturers are willing to pay the higher rent to "live" in desirable locations.

What can a manufacturer do to avoid paying slotting allowances? Sometimes nothing. But powerful manufacturers such as Procter & Gamble and Kraft, for example, are less likely to pay slotting fees than are weaker national and particularly regional manufacturers. Retailers know that P&G's and Kraft's new brands probably will be successful. This is because P&G and Kraft invest heavily in research to develop meaningful new products; they spend heavily on advertising to create consumer demand for these products; and they use extensive consumer promotions (e.g., sampling and couponing) to create strong consumer pull for their brands. Another way to avoid paying slotting allowances is simply to refuse to pay them and, if need be, to accept the consequence of being refused shelf space by some, if not most, retail chains.

Whereas slotting allowances represent a form of *entry fee* for getting a new brand into a grocery chain's distribution center, some retail chains charge manufacturers a fee for having unsuccessful brands removed from their distribution centers. These **exit fees** could just as well be called *deslotting allowances*. Here is how they operate: When introducing a new brand to a retail chain, the manufacturer and chain enter into a contractual arrangement. This arrangement stipulates the average volume of weekly product movement during a specified period that must be achieved for the manufacturer's brand to be permitted to remain in the chain's distribution center. Then, if the brand has not met the stipulated average weekly movement, the chain will issue a deslotting charge. This charge, or exit fee, is intended to cover the handling costs for the chain to remove the item from its distribution center.

This practice may seem to be a marketplace application of the old saying about having salt rubbed into a wound. However, it really represents the fact that retailers, especially in the supermarket industry, no longer are willing to pay for manufacturers' new-product mistakes. There clearly is some economic logic to deslotting charges. Indeed, these charges are another form of insurance policy to protect retail chains from slow-moving and unprofitable brands. To continue the apartment rental analogy, a deslotting charge operates in much the same fashion as the stipulation between apartment owner and tenant regarding property damage. If as a tenant you damage an apartment, the apartment owner is fully justified in forfeiting all or part of your rental deposit. As such, your deposit provides the apartment owner with an insurance policy against your potential negligence. This is precisely how an exit fee, or deslotting charge, operates.

In the final analysis, the issue of slotting allowances is extremely complicated. Manufacturers have legitimate reasons for not wanting to pay slotting allowances, but retailers have justification for charging them. Can both sides be right? Is the practice of slotting allowances a case of free-market competition working at its best, or at its worst? Simple answers are unavailable because as the "correct" answer depends largely on which perspective—manufacturer's or retailer's—one takes on the matter.

And in the middle of this battle are government regulators, who have the responsibility of ensuring that the practice of slotting allowances does not reduce competition or harm consumers by forcing them to pay higher prices or limiting their options because smaller manufacturers are unable to gain shelf space for their new products. One regulatory agency, the Bureau of Alcohol, Tobacco, and Firearms, passed a ruling that prohibits the use of slotting fees in the marketing of alcohol products.[15] However, no prohibitions exist for the many other product categories where slotting allowances are charged. Although the Federal Trade Commission continues to investigate whether slotting allowances need to be regulated, it has not as of early 2002 issued any regulation against retailers charging these fees.[16] In the meantime, slotting allowances remain for manufacturers an additional cost of introducing new products and an additional source of revenue for retailers. The power struggle goes on!

Forward Buying and Diverting

Manufacturers' off-invoice allowances make considerable sense in theory, but in practice many retailers do not perform the services necessary to earn the allowances they receive from manufacturers. Large retail chains are particularly likely to take advantage of manufacturers' allowances without passing the savings along to consumers. A major reason is that large chains, unlike smaller chains, are able to promote and sell their own *private brands*. Because private brands can be sold at lower prices than manufacturers' comparable brands, large chains are able to use private brands to satisfy the needs of price-sensitive consumers while selling manufacturers' brands at their normal prices and pocketing the trade allowance as extra profit.

A second major problem with manufacturers' off-invoice allowances is that they often induce retailers to *stockpile* products to take advantage of the temporary price reductions. Forward buying and diverting are two interrelated practices used by retailers, especially those in the grocery trade, to capitalize on manufacturers' trade allowances. Table 17.1 illustrates these practices.[17]

Forward Buying.   As earlier noted, manufacturers' trade allowances are typically available every four weeks of each business quarter (which translates to about 30 percent of the year). During these deal periods, retailers buy larger quantities than needed for normal inventory and warehouse the excess volume, thereby avoiding purchasing the brand at its full price during the remaining 70 percent of the time when a deal is not offered. Retailers often purchase enough products on one deal to carry them over until the manufacturer's next regularly scheduled deal. This is the practice of **forward buying**, which, for obvious reasons, is also called *bridge buying*—the amount of inventory purchased during one deal period bridges all the way to the next deal period. Approximately 75 percent of all leading grocer retailers practice forward buying.[18]

When a manufacturer marks down a product's price by, say, 15 percent, retail chains commonly stock up with a 10- to 12-week supply.[19] A number of manufacturers sell 80 percent to 90 percent of their volume on deal. It is estimated that forward buying costs manufacturers between 0.5 percent to 1.1 percent of retail prices, which translates into hundreds of millions of dollars annually.[20]

The practice of forward buying has given rise to computer models that enable retail buyers to estimate the profit potential from a forward buy and the optimum weeks of inventory to purchase. The models take into consideration the amount of savings from a deal and then incorporate into their calculations the

---

Table 17.1   Illustration of Forward Buying and Diverting

1. **In preparation for a huge promotional event surrounding the Cinco de Mayo celebration of Mexican independence on May 5, 2002, Beauty Products Inc.—a hypothetical manufacturer of personal care products—extends an off-invoice offer to grocery chains in the Los Angeles area. This promotion is a 15 percent off-invoice allowance on all orders placed for SynActive shampoo during the week beginning April 1, 2002 and extending through April 26, 2002. (Recall that SynActive is the hypothetical brand introduced in Chapter 16.)**

2. **Assume that FB&D Supermarkets of Los Angeles orders 15,000 cases of SynActive shampoo—many more cases than it typically would sell in its own stores during any four-week period. Beauty Produts Inc. has offered the 15 percent off-invoice allowance to FB&D Supermarkets with the expectation that FB&D will reduce SynActive's retail price to consumers by as much as 15 percent during the week of Cinco de Mayo festivities.**

3. **FB&D sells at the discounted price only 3,000 of the 15,000 cases purchased. (The remaining cases include some that are forward bought and some that will be diverted.)**

4. **FB&D resells 5,000 cases of SynActive at a small profit margin to Opportunistic Food Brokers—a company that services grocery retailers throughout the West. (This is the practice of diverting.)**

5. **FB&D later sells the remaining 7,000 cases of SynActive to shoppers in its own stores but at the regular, full price. (These 7,000 cases represent forward buys.)**

various added costs from forward buying. These added costs include warehouse storage expenses, shipping costs, and the cost of tying up money in inventory when that money could be used to earn a better return in some other manner. When forward buying, retailers trade off savings from reduced purchasing expenses against the added expenses of the form just noted.

It may appear that forward buying benefits all parties to the marketing process, but this is not the case. First, as previously mentioned, a substantial portion of retailers' *savings from forward buying often are not passed on to consumers*. Second, forward buying leads to *increased distribution* costs because wholesalers and retailers pay greater carrying charges in holding inventories of large quantities of forward-bought items. In fact, the average grocery product takes up to 12 weeks from the time it is shipped by a manufacturer until it reaches retail store shelves. This delay obviously is not due to transit time but rather reflects storage time in wholesalers' and retailers' warehouses from stockpiling surplus quantities of forward-bought items.[21] Third, manufacturers experience *reduced margins* due to the price discounts they offer as well as the increased costs they incur.

A notable case in point is the situation that confronted the Campbell Soup Company with massive forward buying of its chicken noodle soup when that product was placed on trade deal. As much as 40 percent of its annual chicken noodle soup production was sold to wholesalers and retailers in just six weeks when this product was on deal. Because wholesalers and retailers forward-bought chicken noodle soup in large quantities, Campbell had to schedule extra work shifts and pay overtime to keep up with the accelerated production and shipping schedules. After years of falling prey to forward buying, Campbell implemented a *bill-and-hold program* whereby it invoices (bills) the retailer as soon as the retailer places a forward-bought order but delays shipping (holds) the order until desired quantities are requested by the retailer. This program smoothed out Campbell's production and shipping schedules by allowing retailers to purchase large amounts at deal prices while delaying shipments until inventory was needed. The bill-and-hold program has not eliminated forward buying, but the negative consequences for the Campbell Soup Company have been reduced.

Diverting.   Diverting occurs when a manufacturer *restricts a deal to a limited geographical area* rather than making it available nationally. In Table 17.1, Syn-Active shampoo is available only in Los Angeles as part of Beauty Products Inc.'s participation in the Cinco de Mayo festivities. The manufacturer intends for only retailers in that area (such as FB&D Supermarkets) to benefit from the deal. However, what happens with diverting is that retailers take advantage of the opportunity by buying abnormally large quantities at the deal price and then selling off, at a small profit margin, the excess quantities through food brokers in other geographical areas. (Finance people would label diverting as an application of *arbitrage* behavior.) It is estimated that 5 to 10 percent of grocery products sold on trade allowance are diverted.[22] Over 50 percent of retailers acknowledge engaging in the practice of diverting.[23]

Retailers blame manufacturers for offering irresistible deals and argue that they must take advantage of the deals in any way legally possible to remain competitive with other retailers. Manufacturers could avoid the diverting problem by placing brands on national deal only. This solution is more ideal than practical, however, since regional marketing efforts are expanding, and local deals and regional marketing go hand in hand. Further complicating the problem is that products intended for foreign markets sometimes are diverted back into a domestic market. The *Global Focus* describes one instance of this practice.

There are other negative consequences of diverting. First, product quality potentially suffers due to delays in getting products from manufacturers to retail shelves. For example, Tropicana requires its chilled juices to be stored at between 32 and 36 degrees. If unrefrigerated for a few hours because of careless diverting practices, the product can go bad, and consumers may form negative impressions of the brand.[24] A second and potentially more serious problem could result from product tampering—such as the infamous Tylenol incident in the early 1980s, when seven Chicago residents died from this brand being laced with cyanide by a lunatic. In the event of product tampering, it would be difficult, if not impossible, to identify exactly where a diverted brand may have been shipped.

Diverting Cigarettes

Cigarette prices increased in the United States by as much as 50 percent during the late 1990s. With price increases of this magnitude, it was only a matter of time before enterprising businesses found a way to beat the system. Diverting was the answer. Here is how it works. Large cigarette manufacturers such as Philip Morris and RJR ship their brands to foreign markets at prices below those charged in the United States. Diverters in foreign markets then resell these cigarettes to retailers back in the United States. Until 1999 it was perfectly legal to reimport cigarettes to the United States, but a federal statute went into effect in 2000 that made it illegal to divert tobacco products. Nonetheless, enforcement of this statute is extremely difficult and costly.

Cigarette diverting has taken a heavy toll on established tobacco dis-tributors and retailers that refuse to divert and thus lose business to their competitors that buy and sell diverted cigarettes. There is skepticism as to whether tobacco manufacturers are actually committed to stopping diverting. Indeed, the skeptics contend that diverting enables manufacturers to maintain the brand loyalty of price-sensitive consumers that otherwise would switch to cheaper brands if their preferred brands were not available at the lower diverted prices. Manufacturers deny that they encourage diverting and contend that the practice threatens the equity of their brands.

Source: Adapted from Suein L. Hwang, "'Diverted' Cigarettes are for Sale, Sparking Inquiries and a Backlash," The Wall Street Journal Online, January 28, 1999. Copyright 1999 by DOW JONES & CO INC. Reproduced with permission of DOW JONES & CO INC in the format Textbook via Copyright Clearance Center.

Don't Blame Retailers. The preceding discussion has perhaps made it seem that retailers are villains when engaging in the practice of forward buying and diverting. This would be an unfair representation of retail buyers who are simply taking advantage of an opportunity that is provided by manufacturers offering attractive trade deals. One retail executive explains his company's forward buying and diverting actions in this fashion: "We are very aggressive when it comes to buying at the best price. We have to be. If we don't, somebody else will."[25] In other words, retailers are simply exhibiting rational behavior when they forward buy and divert. The opportunity to increase profits is provided retailers by manufacturers' indiscriminate off-invoice allowances, and smart retailers take advantage of the break.

If Nobody Is at Fault, Then What's the Problem? In brief, the problem is that the present system is wasteful and inefficient. The overall level of costs throughout the distribution system is higher than it could be in a more "ideal" world where costs are better managed and inefficiencies are removed. What the ideal world might look like is the topic to which we now turn. It needs to be stated in advance that the "ideal" world may be just that, as business reality involves inherent conflicts between trading partners such as manufacturers and retailers. The concept of win-win situations is great in theory but not easy to implement in practice. Zero-sum thinking often rules ("What you gain is what I lose"), and it is for this reason that concessions and compromises give way to "get yours" type behavior.

EFFORTS TO RECTIFY TRADE ALLOWANCE PROBLEMS

Because trade allowances spawn inefficiencies, create billions of added dollars in distribution costs, are economically unprofitable for manufacturers, and perhaps inflate prices to consumers, a variety of efforts have been undertaken to fundamentally alter the way business is conducted, especially in the grocery industry.[26]

The following sections are devoted to five notable developments that hold important implications for trade allowances. Two of these represent major changes in the interrelations between manufacturers and retailers (namely, the efficient consumer response and category management movements), whereas the final three reflect more specific practices on the part of manufacturers (everyday low pricing, pay-for-performance programs, and account-specific marketing).

Efficient Consumer Response (ECR)

Efficient consumer response (ECR) is a broad-based concept of business management that is oriented toward enhancing efficiencies and reducing costs in the grocery industry. Kurt Salmon Associates, a consulting firm, issued a report that estimated that some $30 billion, or 10 percent of total grocery sales, is wasted. This waste, according to the Salmon report, is due to inefficient ordering procedures, maintenance of excessive inventories, and inefficient promotional practices. The report argued that billions of dollars could be saved if ECR were fully implemented throughout the distribution chain. The objective of ECR is to improve efficiencies in the grocery industry between all parties (manufacturers, wholesalers, brokers, and retailers) and reduce costs for everyone, especially the final consumer. ECR also includes the objective of reducing the huge expenditures on trade promotion. Although many of the ECR initiatives go beyond the scope of this chapter, several features are noteworthy:

1. *Improved product replenishment practices.* The objective is to move products more efficiently from manufacturers' production facilities to retailers' shelves. *Electronic data interchange (EDI)* between manufacturers and retailers is a major means of reducing the time and cost of order fulfillment. EDI essentially entails constant electronic exchanges between trading partners: Retailers are able to maintain minimal inventory levels because manufacturers ship required product quantities just in time to replenish depleting inventories. For example, the fully coordinated EDI system between Procter & Gamble and Wal-Mart allows Wal-Mart to carry minimal levels of P&G brands with the assurance that additional quantities of brands like Tide detergent and Pringles chips will be replenished as needed. Another example is the relation between Costco stores and Kimberly-Clark Corporation, which manufacturers Huggies disposable diapers. A contractual relationship between these two entities turns responsibility for stock replenishment over to Kimberly-Clark. Costco shares detailed data about individual store sales of diapers, and Kimberly-Clark uses this information to determine precisely when new inventories should be shipped.[27]

2. *Reduced trade promotions.* The objective is to minimize inventory costs in the system, and this necessitates reducing drastically the practices of forward buying and diverting. Everyday low pricing and pay-for-performance programs, as discussed later, represent major steps in this direction.

3. *Improved product introductions.* The objective is for manufacturers to bring to market new products meeting consumer needs rather than simply introduce slight variations on existing offerings. Fewer, more meaningful product introductions likely would cut substantially slotting allowances and exit fees.

In sum, the ultimate objective of ECR is to reduce wasteful practices that lead to excessive prices for consumers and diminished profits for manufacturers, wholesalers, and retailers. As with all revolutions, it will be a matter of years before the benefits of ECR are anywhere close to being fully realized.[28]

Category Management

Manufacturers produce different product lines of which the individual brands in each line constitute a group, or category. Likewise, retailers merchandise multiple brands that compete in each of many categories. A grocery store, for example,

Figure 17.1

The Five Stages of Category Management

Reviewing the product category → Targeting consumers → Planning merchandising → Implementing strategy → Evaluating results

has categories of detergents, breakfast cereals, and pain relievers; an appliance dealer has kitchen appliances, video devices, computer equipment, and audio equipment. Although manufacturers and retailers both work with categories, their interests are not necessarily equivalent. Whereas manufacturers are concerned with the profitability of their individual brands, retailers are more interested in the overall profitability of a product category. With growing retailer power, as discussed in the previous chapter, manufacturers have been forced to market their brands with greater concern for the retailer's broader category interests rather than focusing exclusively on the profitability of their own brands.

Category management involves the working relationship between manufacturers and retailers and attempts to find ways whereby both parties can be more profitable. The implementation of category management means that retailers and manufacturers must work together, share market intelligence, and develop strategies that are mutually beneficial.[29] Category managers from both the manufacturer and retailer sides of business jointly plan and execute merchandising programs, promotion deals, and advertising executions that are agreeable to both parties and improve the performance for both.

Figure 17.1 presents five interrelated stages involved in the actual process of implementing category management. Although both manufacturers and retailers must individually conduct these same five activities, the following discussion presents the manufacturer's perspective.[30]

1. *Reviewing the category:* A manufacturer would initiate a category management program by conducting a thorough study of the product category. After carefully defining the category (e.g., soft drinks) and its subcategories (colas, noncolas, regular, diet), the manufacturer must gather information pertaining to category sales volume and growth rate, sales by type of retail outlet, household purchasing patterns, and comparisons of the performances of the manufacturer's brands and its competitors'. By acquiring these data, the manufacturer can identify growth opportunities and develop new or modified marketing strategies that capitalize on the opportunities.

2. *Targeting consumers:* This stage requires the manufacturer to acquire an in-depth understanding of the typical consumer in the product category. The consumer is profiled with respect to relevant demographic characteristics (income level, age) and examined with respect to their product-purchase and usage patterns (Where do they shop? How much do they typically purchase?), lifestyles (What activities do they participate in?), and media preferences. Armed with this information, a manufacturer is prepared to know a brand's potential in specific stores and to make intelligent decisions about the choice of advertising media, promotions, and product offerings.

3. *Merchandise planning:* This stage entails developing a detailed strategy for the best mix of brands for each retail account within a particular category. The manufacturer recommends to the retailer an optimum mix of brands, prices, and shelf-space allocation that will enable the retailer to achieve desired volume and profit goals within the category. Sophisticated software applications enable manufacturers to assist retailers in developing product-stocking programs, called *planograms*, that designate the specific products and brands that the store should stock to best appeal to the consumers in its trade area.

4. *Implementing the strategy:* Results from the first three stages provide the content for an ongoing interaction between the manufacturer's sales team and a retail chain's category buyer. Merchandising plans are the foundation for the sales team's recommendations to the retailer concerning appropriate product mix, pricing, promotions, and shelf-space allocations for the category. The sales team also explains how the manufacturer's advertising program will target the retailer's consumers and thus generate business for the retailer.

5. *Evaluating results:* Effective implementation of category management programs requires that manufacturers answer this key question: Did the strategies proposed for the retail account achieve their objectives? If the program has not achieved these objectives, answering this question will direct manufacturers and retailers to alter their strategies; if objectives have been achieved, the prudence of continuing with the previously proposed strategy will be reinforced.

In sum, manufacturers are able to undertake category management programs that are mutually beneficial to themselves and their retail accounts. Sophisticated software applications backed by careful study of consumer behavior, competitor actions, and market developments enable manufacturers and retailers to formulate merchandising programs that suit the needs of all parties: retailers, manufacturers, and consumers.

Everyday Low Pricing (EDLP)

Manufacturers lose billions of dollars every year to inefficient and ineffective trade deals stemming from the trade's practice of forward buying and diverting. It is for this reason that the powerful Procter & Gamble Corporation, under the leadership of then CEO Edwin Artzt, undertook a bold move in the 1990s to bust the practice of forward buying and diverting. P&G introduced a new form of pricing called everyday low pricing, or EDLP, which the company also refers to as *value pricing* — signifying its desire to compete on the basis of providing product values and not mere price savings. Because some retailers also practice everyday low prices, we will distinguish between "back-door" EDLP as used by manufacturers from the "front-door" variety practiced by retailers.[31] Our interest is with the back-door variety of EDLP, which for clarity's sake we label EDLP(M) to stand for manufacturers' use of EDLP.

EDLP(M) is a form of pricing whereby a manufacturer charges the same price for a particular brand day in and day out. In other words, rather than charging *high-low prices* — that is, regular, or "high," prices for a period followed by off-invoice, or "low," prices for a shorter period — EDLP(M) involves charging the same price over an extended period. Because no off-invoice allowances are offered the trade under this pricing strategy, wholesalers and retailers have no reason to engage in forward buying or diverting. Hence, their profit is made from selling merchandise rather than from buying it.

How Has P&G Fared?
Researchers examined the effects of P&G's value pricing initiative over the first six years of its implementation.[32] The analysis encompassed a total of 24 product categories and 118 brands in these categories. From the year prior to P&G's implementation of value pricing and through the first six years of the practice, P&G's advertising expenditures and net prices both increased by approximately 20 percent. During this same period, its expenditures on trade deals decreased by nearly 16 percent, and coupon spending was reduced by about 54 percent.

What was the effect of these changes? P&G *lost* about 18 percent market share on average across the 24 product categories analyzed. Value pricing clearly has been a disaster for P&G, right? In actuality, it has not. Although P&G suffered a significant decline in market share (due largely to competitors' retaliatory increases in promotional deals while P&G was cutting its own dealing activity), at the same time its overall profits *increased* by virtue of cutting trade deals and coupon activity and increasing net prices.[33] It could be argued that it is unwise ever to relinquish market share; however, in the final analysis, giving up market share can be justified if the share that remains generates greater profitability than what was obtained with a larger but less profitable share. Over the long haul, the bottom line (profits) is a more telling indicator of firm success than is the top line (sales).

What Have Other Manufacturers Done?   Manufacturers less powerful than Procter & Gamble have found it difficult to convert to a pure system of everyday low pricing. Even P&G has experienced resistance and has deviated from a pure EDLP pricing with some brands such as laundry detergents.[34] Three major reasons account for why many retailers resist manufacturers' EDLP pricing initiatives. First, those retailers that established distribution infrastructures necessary to practice forward buying have resisted EDLP(M) pricing.[35] Second, there is some evidence that EDLP(M) pricing benefits the manufacturers that price their products in this fashion more than it does the retailers that pay EDLP(M) rather than high-low prices.[36] Finally, it also has been argued that EDLP(M) pricing takes some of the excitement out of retailing. With EDLP(M) pricing, the retailer charges the same price to consumers day after day. Comparatively, with high-low pricing, there are periods when retailers are able to advertise attractive price savings, which breaks the monotony of never varying the retail price. Although in the long term the consumer realizes no savings from high-low pricing, in the short term it may be exciting to receive an appealing discount.

Although pricing practices by manufacturers remain somewhat in a state of flux, it appears that a pure EDLP(M) pricing system will not dominate. Some combination of EDLP(M) pricing along with periodic promotional funds provided to the trade by manufacturers is the pricing system most likely to endure.

Pay-for-Performance Programs

As noted earlier, many trade promotions, especially in the grocery industry, are unprofitable for manufacturers because they merely shift future buying to the present when the trade engages in forward buying and diverting. Manufacturers, accordingly, have a strong incentive to devise an alternative system to the traditional off-invoice allowance. One such system is the pay-for-performance program.

Rewarding Selling Rather Than Buying.   As the name suggests, **pay-for-performance** is a form of trade allowance that rewards retailers for performing the primary function that justifies a manufacturer's offering a trade allowance—namely, *selling increased quantities of the manufacturer's brand to consumers*. In other words, pay-for-performance programs are designed to reward retailers for *selling* the manufacturer's brand supported with a trade allowance rather than for merely buying the brand at an off-invoice price.

Pay-for-performance programs also are called *scanner-verified trade promotions* or *scan-downs* because the retail sales volume for a trade-supported brand is recorded via optical scanning devices at the point of sale. Scan-downs entail three key facets:[37]

1. A manufacturer agrees with a retailer on a period during which the retailer receives an allowance for all quantities of a promoted brand that are *sold to consumers* at the designated deal price (e.g., an item that regularly sells to consumers at $1.99 per unit is to be reduced to $1.79).
2. The retailer's own scanning data *verify the exact amount* of the promoted brand that has been sold during this period at the deal price (e.g., 5,680 units at $1.79 each).
3. The *manufacturer pays the retailer quickly*, say within five days, at the designated allowance for the quantity sold. The manufacturer would reimburse the retailer for the reduced margin in selling a certain number of units (e.g., 5,680 units at a reduced margin of $0.20, or $1,136) and compensate the retailer for the amount of the trade allowance (e.g., 5,680 units

at $0.05 each, or $284; thus, the manufacturer would mail a check to the retailer totaling $1,420).

A Win-Win-Win Situation.   Scanner-verified, or pay-for-performance, programs provide an incentive to the retailer only for the items sold at discount to consumers during the agreed-on time period. Thus unlike off-invoice allowances, a manufacturer using scan-downs does *not* pay for allowances where no benefit is received. Rather, retailers get compensated only for items sold to consumers. Hence, this form of pay-for-performance program benefits all parties: consumers, retailers, and manufacturers. Consumers win by receiving reduced prices; retailers win by obtaining allowances for moving increased quantities of manufacturers' promoted brands; and manufacturers win by increasing sales of their brands, if only temporarily, by reducing prices to consumers. By comparison, when using off-invoice allowances, manufacturers have no assurance that the off-invoice allowances given to retailers will be passed on to consumers.

In theory, then, with pay-for-performance programs, everyone wins. The rub, however, is that retailers do not win as much as they do with "gain without pain" off-invoice programs that offer rewards and require no effort other than placing an order. It is for this reason that pay-for-performance programs are embraced more heartily by manufacturers than by retailers.

Pay-for-performance programs are a natural correlate to the efficient consumer response (ECR) initiative that was previously discussed. Only time will tell whether these programs become widely implemented. However, the technological infrastructure is available in the United States to support this new form of trade promotion. Moreover, well-known companies such as A. C. Nielsen and Information Resources have moved into this emerging business in the role of *scanning agents*. Scanning agents profit from performing the following functions: (1) *collecting* scanner data from retailers, (2) *verifying* the amount of product movement that meets the manufacturer's promotional requirements and warrants compensation, (3) *paying* the retailer, and (4) *collecting* funds from the manufacturer along with a commission for services rendered.

Account-Specific Marketing

Account-specific marketing, also called *co-marketing*, is a descriptive term that characterizes promotional and advertising activity that a manufacturer *customizes* to specific retail accounts. To appreciate this practice fully, it is necessary to place it in the context of the off-invoice allowance promotion, which is a temporary price reduction that is offered to *all* accounts. With off-invoice programs, a manufacturer's promotion dollars are anything but customized to the needs of specific retail accounts. On the other hand, account-specific marketing, or co-marketing, directs promotion dollars to specific retail customers and develops in concert with the retailer an advertising or promotion program that simultaneously serves the manufacturer's brand, the retailer's volume and profit requirements, and the consumer's needs. Local radio tie-in advertising and loyalty programs using retailers' shopper databases are especially popular account-specific practices.[38]

Some Examples.   When introducing its expensive PhotoSmart photography system—a photo-scanning and printing system for home computers—Hewlett-Packard (HP) developed co-marketing arrangements with a small number of retailers. HP selected prime consumer prospects in each retailer's trade area and mailed invitations customized to appear as if they were from the retailer, not HP. Prospective purchasers were invited to see an in-store demonstration and receive a chance to win a free PhotoSmart system.

An illustration from the CPG category is Hormel's account-specific effort with Spam (the canned-meat product). To boost sales and to lure new consumers to the brand, Hormel introduced the "Spam Stuff" continuity program. Following in the footsteps of Marlboro, Kool-Aid, and Pepsi, all of which had previously launched "stuff" programs, Hormel offered consumers points toward the acquisition of free items (such as bean bag characters, boxer shorts, mouse pads, mugs, and T-shirts) with each purchase of Spam products. In addition to offering "freebies" to encourage consumers to try Spam products, Hormel developed some account-specific programs to draw the trade's attention to the brand. Retailers were provided with Spam advertising materials (called ad slicks) for their advertising flyers. They also received local advertising support for promoting Spam on the radio and in newspapers. To further excite retailer participation, Hormel offered one supermarket per region with a "Spam Day" promotion for the best in-store display. Winning stores received Spam-wear for employees and customers, free Spam burgers grilled in the store's parking lot, and a personal appearance by Spam Cans characters.

It would also be understandable if the student were to consider this promotional program somewhat goofy. This surely is a lighthearted attempt on the part of Hormel to increase interest in Spam both from consumers and retailers. Silly as it may seem, programs like this often are effective in encouraging retailers to devote greater attention to a brand (e.g., providing increased display space) and to entice consumers to purchase the brand more regularly.[39]

What Does the Future Hold?   Account-specific marketing is a relatively recent innovation. First introduced by marketers in the packaged goods field, the practice has spread to companies that manufacture and market soft goods (e.g., apparel items) and durable items such as the HP PhotoSmart system. Because account-specific marketing requires a lot of effort both in development and implementation and is costly, the future of this practice is uncertain at the time of this writing. It appears that interest among packaged goods companies has peaked already.[40] The future will depend on results. As always, the proof is in the pudding. Account-specific marketing will increase in those industries and for those companies where programs yield increased results but decrease where the returns fail to justify the efforts. Because powerful retailers benefit from well-designed account-specific programs (oftentimes programs that they develop and then sell to manufacturers, who pay for the programs' implementation), it is likely that co-marketing is here to stay.

COOPERATIVE ADVERTISING AND VENDOR SUPPORT PROGRAMS

Another form of trade promotion occurs when manufacturers of branded merchandise pay for part of the expense that retailers incur when advertising manufacturers' brands. Both cooperative advertising and vendor support programs deal with the *advertising relation* between manufacturers and resellers. A fundamental distinction between the two is that manufacturers initiate cooperative advertising programs, whereas retailers instigate vendor support programs. The significance of this distinction will become clear in the following discussion.

Cooperative Advertising

Cooperative (co-op) advertising is an arrangement between a manufacturer and reseller (either a retailer or an industrial distributor) whereby the manufacturer pays for all or some of the advertising costs undertaken by the reseller in behalf of the manufacturer's products.[41] Co-op programs permit resellers to place ads promoting the manufacturers' products and their availability. The cost of a co-op ad placement is divided between the manufacturer and reseller according to the terms specified in the cooperative contract.

Though cooperative advertising programs vary, five elements are common to all. These elements are illustrated with the co-op advertising program from Lane Furniture, a manufacturer of reclining chairs, sofas, and other furniture items.

1. *Specified time period*: Co-op funds typically apply to a specified time period. Lane's program applies to funds accrued between January 1 and De-

cember 31. These funds can be applied only to advertising that is run during the same period.

2. *Accrual*: The retailer receives from the manufacturer an advertising fund, called an *accrual account*, against which advertising costs are charged. The accrual typically is based either on a fixed amount or a percentage of a retailer's net purchases from the manufacturer during the term of the co-op contract. In the case of Lane, which applies a *fixed accrual*, the retailer is credited with $4 on each Lane chair and $8 on each Lane sofa.

   To illustrate a *percentage accrual*, suppose a certain appliance retailer purchases $200,000 in products from a manufacturer in one year. Suppose further that the manufacturer's cooperative program allows 5 percent of purchases to accrue to the retailer's cooperative advertising account. Thus, the retailer would have built up $10,000 worth of cooperative advertising dollars. (The most frequently used rates of accrual are 2, 3, and 5 percent, with consumer goods companies offering slightly higher accrual rates than industrial goods companies.)[42]

3. *Payment share*: The payment share, also called the *participation rate*, is the amount the manufacturer reimburses the retailer for advertising. Manufacturers generally agree to pay a set percentage ranging from 25 to 100 percent of the cost for each advertisement placed by the retailer. Lane pays 50 percent of each advertisement. (The average payment share, or participation rate, is approximately 74 percent for consumer goods companies and 69 percent for industrial goods companies.)[43]

   For example, suppose that a retailer places a $1,000 newspaper ad featuring Lane recliners and sofas. Lane would pay $500, and the retailer would pay the remaining $500.

4. *Performance guidelines*: These are the manufacturer's requirements that the retailer must satisfy to qualify for advertising reimbursement. Guidelines typically deal with suitable media, size and type of logos, the use of trademarks, copy and art directions, and product content.

5. *Billing for reimbursement*: This prescribes how the retailer is to be reimbursed. To receive reimbursement from Lane Furniture, the retailer must present a copy of the invoice from the newspaper or other medium where the ad was placed, along with evidence of the actual advertising copy in the form of so-called tearsheets.

Why Is Cooperative Advertising Used?   There are several reasons.[44] First, consumers of infrequently purchased goods (appliances, apparel, furniture, etc.) are responsive to retailer advertisements, especially preceding a major buying decision. In the absence of co-op dollars, however, most retailers would not emphasize a specific manufacturer's products/brands in their advertisements but would rather simply mention the variety of products/brands that the retailer handles. Hence, co-op advertising enables manufacturers to achieve advertising support on a local-market basis and provides them with a way to *associate their products in the consumer's mind with specific retail outlets*.

Second, manufacturers have found that cooperative advertising *stimulates greater retailer buying and merchandising support*. Retailers, knowing they have accrued co-op dollars, are more likely to aggressively promote and merchandise a specific manufacturer's products. From the manufacturer's perspective, this amounts to greater stocking and more display space for its brands as well as more retail advertising support.

A third advantage of co-op advertising is that it *enables manufacturers to have access to local media at an advertising rate lower than would be paid if the manufacturer advertised directly rather than through retailers*. This cost savings reflects the fact that local media, particularly newspapers, charge lower advertising rates to local advertisers than to national advertisers. For example, average national rates for advertising in major U.S. newspapers were found to be over 66 percent higher than the average local rates.[45] By using cooperative advertising, a manufacturer thus gets exposure in local markets at a reduced rate.

From the retailer's perspective, cooperative advertising is a relatively inexpensive form of advertising. The advertising is not truly free, however, because the manufacturer's cooperative advertising costs are built into the price of the merchandise. Failure to take advantage of accrued co-op dollars means that the retailer is effectively paying more for the same merchandise than retailers that do use co-op funds.

Yet many retailers never spend the cooperative advertising dollars they have accumulated. Over $10 billion is available annually in co-op funds, and fully one-third of that amount goes unspent, due in large part to the fact that fewer than one-half of the retailers eligible for co-op funds actually spend these accruals.

Some manufacturers have implemented cooperative advertising programs that make it easier and more lucrative for retailers to use co-op funds. The objective is to make the program instructions simpler to read and easier to implement. Advertising media also offer programs to attract more co-op dollars. For example, the Newspaper Advertising Bureau has a program whereby salespeople of newspaper space are able to identify all the products in a retailer's store that carry co-op advertising, determine how much the retailer has accrued for each product, and then run an ad for the retailer that will use the accrued co-op funds.

Open-Ended Co-op Advertising.   The cooperative advertising programs discussed to this point relate the amount of co-op funds to the amount of products purchased by a retailer from a particular manufacturer. The more products purchased, the more co-op funds accrue to the retailer. **Open-ended co-op advertising** involves paying for part of the retailer's advertising cost without relating the reimbursement to the amount of products purchased from the manufacturer.

Open-ended programs make considerable sense when the manufacturer: (1) wants to encourage the use of co-op funds by smaller retailers or (2) when the manufacturer sells through intermediaries and does not have access to retailers' purchase figures. Major advantages of open-ended programs involve simplifying record-keeping tasks and, more important, making it possible to use advertising for generating sales rather than relying on sales to generate advertising.

Vendor Support Programs

In contrast to cooperative advertising, **vendor support programs (VSPs)** are *instigated by retailers*. A retailer, such as a supermarket chain, develops an advertising program in consultation with local advertising media and then invites its vendors (i.e., manufacturers) to pay for a specific percentage of the media cost for the proposed campaign. In other words, the retailer creates advertising dollars by exerting its power over a manufacturer, or vendor, which depends on the retailer for its marketplace success.

To illustrate, consider a hypothetical 250-store retail chain called BuyRight. BuyRight's advertising agency recommends that the chain undertake a major advertising campaign in April. The campaign will cost BuyRight $300,000. Where is the money to come from? Solution: Get 10 manufacturers to contribute $30,000 each to BuyRight's April campaign. In return for their participation, manufacturers will receive *feature time and space* in BuyRight's advertisements as well as *extra shelf space*. Extra sales volume, BuyRight assures the manufacturers, will more than compensate for their advertising support funds.

VSPs have clear advantages for the retailer. Indeed, these programs seem to benefit everyone (retailers, ad agencies, media), except perhaps the manufacturers that provide the financial support. Often a manufacturer pays a large sum to support a retailer's advertising efforts but receives very little actual promotion of its own brands to end users. The manufacturer's products may be lost amid the clutter of the other brands featured in, say, a supermarket chain's newspaper advertisement.

Why Do Manufacturers Participate in VSPs?   Vendor support programs are most likely used when the retailer's channel power is greater than that of manufacturers that compete against one another for the retailer's limited shelf space. This is particularly true in the case of smaller, regional manufacturers that have not created strong consumer franchises for their brands. These weaker manufacturers cannot afford to invest in consumer-pull programs, because their promotion funds are almost fully consumed by retailers' vendor support programs. As such, it becomes an irrevocable cycle: The less powerful a manufacturer, the more susceptible it is to retailers' demands for advertising support funds. In turn, the more the manufacturer invests in the retailers' advertising programs, the less funds it has available to build demand for its own brands.

TRADE CONTESTS AND INCENTIVES

Contests and incentive programs are developed by manufacturers to encourage better performance from retail managers and their salespeople. A trade contest typically is directed at store-level or department managers and generally is based on managers *meeting a sales goal* established by the manufacturer. For example, Almay, a division of Revlon, Inc., is a maker of hypoallergenic cosmetics that until the 1990s appealed mostly to middle-aged and medically minded consumers. One of Almay's products, waterproof mascara, reached a point where sales volume leveled off, thereby forcing the marketing staff to consider ways to invigorate the product. Almay's marketers made the resourceful move to introduce a new mascara brand, named Wetproof, to teens and women in their early 20s, consumers with whom Almay had not had much previous success. Some substantial marketing changes were needed to attract this market. Because mass merchandise cosmetics are typically purchased on impulse, Almay came up with a bold color combination, neon yellow and black, to use in both product packages and merchandise displays. This combination appealed to the youthful market and also differentiated Wetproof from competitive mascaras.

To encourage retailers to handle Wetproof and to support the brand's sales performance, a free gift of a floating air mattress—a product that tied into Wetproof's waterproof feature—was offered to the head buyer on all accounts. To further encourage retail support, a trade contest offered store managers the opportunity to win 35-millimeter cameras, cordless telephones, and other attractive items based on meeting specified sales goals. In a matter of months Wetproof found its way into 16,000 retail outlets, and sales to consumers were vigorous.[46]

Whereas contests are typically related to meeting sales goals, **trade incentives** are given to retail managers and salespeople for performing certain tasks. For example, when running sweepstakes or contests directed to final consumers (discussed fully in the following chapter), manufacturers often encourage retailers to display the object of merchandise that is being offered to consumers. As an incentive to encourage retailer participation, the manufacturer then gives the item to the store or departmental manager when the sales promotion is completed. Bigger prizes in the form of vacations and other high-ticket items are used sometimes as incentives.

Manufacturers employ another form of incentive when they provide financial incentives to retail salespeople to aggressively sell to consumers a select item in the manufacturer's product line. This practice is called **push money**, or spiffs. For example, Uniroyal offered a $4 spiff to retail salespeople for every NailGard tire sold during a two-month promotional period. Of course, the purpose of push money is to encourage salespeople to favor the manufacturer's model over competitors' offerings and thus to literally push the product on consumers.

When structured properly, trade contests and incentives can serve the manufacturer's interests very well. These programs may not serve the retailer's or the consumer's interests, however. For example, push money can cause retail salespeople to be overly aggressive in attempting to persuade consumers to purchase a particular brand. For this reason, many stores have policies that prevent their managers and salespeople from accepting any form of incentive from manufacturers.

An Online Trade Show for Craft Enthusiasts

The publisher of two well-known consumer magazines, *Better Homes & Gardens* and *Ladies Home Journal*, designed an online trade show to reach craft enthusiasts who participate in activities such as stitchery, quilting, sewing, painting, and decorating. These enthusiasts are not inspired to visit a physical show at a distant location, but are eager to learn about new products, innovative methods, and the companies who supply crafting materials. Upon entering the website (http://www.craftfest.com), the visitor sees a list of dozens of companies exhibiting their wares. The visitor can click on a specific "booth" to learn about products, projects, and even opportunities to receive free gifts. With another click the visitor enters the exhibitor's homepage and has the opportunity to place an order and enter it into a "shopping cart."

Source: Adapted from Eileen McCooey, "Crafting a Niche," *Brandweek*, January 24, 2000, pp. 64–68. © 2000 VNU Business Media, Inc.

TRADE SHOWS

A trade show is a temporary forum (typically lasting several days) for sellers of a product category (such as small appliances, toys, clothing, furniture, industrial tools, food products, or sporting goods) to exhibit and demonstrate their wares to present and prospective buyers. The trade show is not strictly a form of sales promotion. It nonetheless is appropriate to discuss trade shows in context of trade promotions because trade shows, like certain forms of sales promotions, provide an extremely effective mechanism for assisting customers in learning about and trying new products. Thousands of trade shows are conducted annually in the United States and Canada, and these shows attract millions of attendees to the booths of the more than 1 million companies that exhibit their products at these shows. Trade show activity is even greater in Europe, representing approximately one-fourth of the total marketing communications budgets for European business-to-business firms (compared to the one-fifth representation among North American companies).[47] Approximately 13 percent of the marketing communications budgets for business-to-business firms are allocated to trade shows.[48]

Trade show attendees include most of an industry's important manufacturers and major customers. This encapsulated marketplace enables the trade show exhibitor to accomplish both selling and nonselling functions. Specific functions include (1) servicing present customers, (2) identifying prospects, (3) introducing new or modified products, (4) gathering information about competitors' new products, (5) taking product orders, and (6) enhancing the company's image.[49]

Trade shows are an excellent forum for introducing new products. Products can be demonstrated and customer inquiries can be addressed at a time when customers are actively soliciting information. This allows companies to gather useful feedback. Positive information can be used in subsequent sales presentations and advertising efforts, while negative information can guide product improvements or changes in the marketing program. Trade shows also provide an ideal occasion to recruit dealers, distributors, and sales personnel. Although there is virtually no published research on the topic, one recent study provided evidence, albeit limited, that trade shows can enhance a company's sales and profits.[50]

A recent innovation is the conduct of trade shows online (*digital trade shows*). The traditional trade show is typically conducted at a convention center in a major city. Representatives for the numerous exhibitors along with hundreds, if not thousands, of potential customers travel to the trade show site to participate in a two-day or longer event. Needless to say, millions of dollars are invested in renting space, setting up exhibits, traveling, lodging, dining, and so on. The online trade show eliminates most of these expenses, and, of course, also lacks the opportunity for physically inspecting products and interacting with trade-show exhibitors on a personal, one-to-one basis. Online trade shows will not eliminate their traditional counterparts, but this would appear to be a growth area.[51] Prospective customers can click on displayed products and receive product descriptions and contact information for exhibitors. The *Online Focus* describes an online trade show directed at consumers rather than B2B customers.

SUMMARY

This chapter presents the topic of trade-oriented sales promotions and describes its various forms. Trade-oriented promotions represent on average over 50 percent of consumer packaged good companies' promotional budgets. These programs perform a variety of objectives.

Trade allowances, or trade deals, are offered to retailers for performing activities that support the manufacturer's brand. Manufacturers find allowance promotions attractive for several reasons: They are easy to implement, can successfully stimulate initial distribution, are well accepted by the trade, and can increase trade purchases during the allowance period. However, two major disadvantages of trade allowances, especially of the off-invoice variety, are that they often are not passed along by retailers to consumers and may induce the trade to stockpile a product in order to take advantage of the temporary price reduction. This merely shifts business from the future to the present. Two prevalent practices in current business are forward buying and diverting. Another form of trade deal, called a slotting allowance, applies to new-product introductions. Manufacturers of grocery products typically are required to pay retailers a slotting fee for the right to have their product carried by the retailer. Exit fees, or deslotting charges, are assessed to manufacturers whose products do not achieve prearranged levels of sales volume.

To reduce forward buying and diverting, some manufacturers have revised their method of pricing products. Procter & Gamble is most notable in this regard for introducing what it calls value pricing, or what others refer to as everyday low pricing by a manufacturer, or EDLP(M). This method of pricing eliminates the historical practice of periodically offering attractive trade deals and instead charges the same low price at all times. Another major development in the grocery industry that is aimed at curtailing forward buying and diverting is the implementation of pay-for-performance programs, which also are called scanner-verified systems, or scan-downs. With this method of trade allowance, retailers are compensated for the amount of a manufacturer's brand that they sell to consumers, rather than according to how much they purchase from the manufacturer (as is the case with off-invoice allowances). Pay-for-performance programs and everyday low pricing are both part of the paradigm shift in the grocery industry known as efficient consumer response (ECR). Category management is another development that is designed to create better working relations between manufacturers and retailers and to increase efficiency in their relations.

Cooperative advertising and vendor support programs are trade promotions in which manufacturers and retailers jointly pay for the retailer's advertising that features the manufacturer's product. Co-op advertising is initiated by the manufacturer, whereas vendor support programs are initiated by retailers.

Trade contests and incentives encourage retailer performance by offering gifts for meeting sales goals or for performing certain tasks deemed important for the success of the sponsoring manufacturer's products. Push money is one form of trade incentive used to encourage special selling efforts from retail salespeople.

Trade shows are a final type of trade-oriented sales promotion. Thousands of companies in North America and Europe participate in trade shows each year. Specific functions of trade shows include (1) servicing present customers, (2) identifying prospects, (3) introducing new or modified products, (4) gathering information about competitors' new products, (5) taking product orders, and (6) enhancing the company's image.

Find more resources to help you study at http://shimp.swcollege.com!

DISCUSSION QUESTIONS

1. A number of retailers have explicit policies that prevent their managers or salespeople from receiving any form of incentives from manufacturers. Are these policies wise? Under what conditions might manufacturer-sponsored incentives benefit the retail firm above and beyond their obvious material benefits for individual managers or salespeople?

2. Assume you are the marketing manager of a company that manufactures a line of paper products (tissues, napkins, etc.). Your current market share is 7 percent, and you are considering offering retailers an attractive bill-back allowance for giving your brand special display space. Comment on this promotion's chances for success.

3. Identify concepts in Chapter 10 that would be relevant to a furniture company's efforts to develop an effective exhibition at a trade show attended by major furniture retailers from around the country.

4. In your own words, explain the practices of forward buying and diverting. Also, describe the advantages and disadvantages of bill-and-hold programs.

5. Assume you are a buyer for a large supermarket chain and that you have been asked to speak to a group of marketing students at a nearby university. During the question-and-answer session following your comments, a student offers the following comment: "My father works for a grocery product manufacturer, and he says that slotting allowances are nothing more than a form of larceny!" How would you defend your company's practice to this student?

6. Explain why selling private brands often enables large retail chains to pocket trade deals instead of passing their reduced costs along to consumers in the form of lower product prices.

7. In your own words, explain why EDLP(M) pricing diminishes forward buying and diverting.

8. In your own words, discuss how pay-for-performance programs, or scandowns, would, if widely implemented, virtually eliminate forward buying and diverting.

9. It is estimated that at least one-third of the billions of co-op advertising dollars offered by manufacturers go unspent. Why? What could a manufacturer do to encourage greater numbers of retailers to spend co-op dollars? Do you think some manufacturers may not want their retail customers to spend co-op funds?

10. In discussing open-ended co-op programs, the text stated that this type of cooperative advertising makes it possible to use advertising for generating sales rather than relying on sales to generate advertising. Explain precisely what this means.

11. You are the Midwest sales manager for a product line marketed by a large, highly respected national manufacturer. Most of your products hold market shares of 30 percent or higher. The promotion manager for a big grocery chain approaches you about a vendor support program his company is in the process of putting together. It will cost you $50,000 to participate. What would be the reasons for and against your participation? On balance, would it be in your company's long-term interest to participate in this or other VSPs?

ENDNOTES

1. The lower-end estimate is based on research conducted by the consulting firm Accenture and published in *The Daunting Dilemma of Trade Promotion II* (Grocery Manufacturers of America), October 23, 2001. The upper-end estimated is from Cannondale Associates in its *2001 Trade Promotion Spending and Merchandising Study* as quoted in Betsy Spethmann, "Going for Broke," *Promo*, August 2001, 27–31.

2. Robert C. Blattberg and Alan Levin, "Modeling the Effectiveness and Profitablily of Trade Promotions," *Marketing Science* 6 (spring 1987), 125.

3. These objectives are adapted from a consumer promotion seminar conducted by Ennis Associates and sponsored by the Association of National Advertisers (New York, undated). See also Chakravarthi Narasimhan, "Managerial Perspectives on Trade and Consumer Promotions," *Marketing Letters* 1, no. 3 (1989), 239–251.

4. Don E. Schultz and William A. Robinson, *Sales Promotion Management* (Lincolnwood, Ill.: NTC Business Books, 1986), 265–266.

5. For further reading, see Kenneth G. Hardy, "Key Success Factors for Manufacturers' Sales Promotions in Package Goods," *Journal of Marketing* 50 (July 1986), 13–23.

6. Rajiv Lal, "Manufacturer Trade Deals and Retail Price Promotions," *Journal of Marketing Research* 27 (November 1990), 428–444. Ronald C. Curhan and Robert J. Kopp, "Obtaining Retailer Support for Trade Deals: Key Success Factors," *Journal of Advertising Research* 27 (December 1987/January 1988), 51–60.

7. "ACNielsen Study Finds Trade Promotion Disconnect Between Manufacturers and Retailers" (http://www.acnielsen.com/news/american/us/2000/20001221.htm).

8. This study is by Cannondale Associates as reported in Christopher W. Hoyt, "You Cheated, You Lied," *Promo*, July 1997, 64.

9. For a technical treatment regarding the profit implications of a retailer's decision to pass through a manufacturer's allowance, see Rajeev K. Tyagi, "A Characterization of Retailer Response to Manufacturer Trade Deals," *Journal of Marketing Research* 36 (November 1999), 510–516.

10. Spethmann, "Going for Broke."

11. For a more complete treatment of the issue, including the presentation of survey results from both manufacturers and retailers, see Paul N. Bloom, Gregory T. Gundlach, and Joseph P. Cannon, "Slotting Allowances and Fees: Schools of Thought and the Views of Practicing Managers," *Journal of Marketing* 64 (April 2000), 92–108.

12. Christopher W. Hoyt, "The Slotting Weevil," *Promo*, February 1997, 68.

13. For discussion of the legal issues surrounding the use of slotting allowances, see Joseph P. Cannon and Paul N. Bloom, "Are Slotting Allowances Legal under the Antitrust Laws?" *Journal of Public Policy and Marketing* 10, no. 1 (1991).

14. Julie Liesse, "Kodak Brand Calls Retreat in the Battery War," *Advertising Age*, October 15, 1990, 3, 69.

15. For an insightful discussion, see Gregory T. Gundlach and Paul N. Bloom, "Slotting Allowances and the Retail Sale of Alcohol Beverages," *Journal of Public Policy & Marketing* 17 (fall 1998), 173–184.

16. See http://www.ftc.gov/opa/2001/02/slotting.htm.

17. This illustration is adapted from Zachary Schiller, "Not Everyone Loves a Supermarket Special," *Business Week*, February 17, 1992, 64.

18. Christopher W. Hoyt, "Retailers and Suppliers Are Still Miles Apart," *Promo*, February 1996, 49.

19. Ronald Alsop, "Retailers Buy Far in Advance to Exploit Trade Promotions," *The Wall Street Journal*, October 9, 1986, 37.

20. Robert D. Buzzell, John A. Quelch, and Walter J. Salmon, "The Costly Bargain of Trade Promotion," *Harvard Business Review* 68 (March/April 1990), 145.

21. Patricia Sellers, "The Dumbest Marketing Ploy," Fortune, October 5, 1992, 88.

22. Jon Berry, "Diverting," *Adweek's Marketing Week*, May 18, 1992, 20.

23. Hoyt, "Retailers and Suppliers Are Still Miles Apart."

24. Berry, "Diverting," 22.

25. Ibid.

26. An insightful demonstration of why trade allowances are unprofitable is provided in Magid M. Abraham and Leonard M. Lodish, "Getting the Most out of Advertising and Promotion," *Harvard Business Review* 68 (May/June 1990), 50–60.

27. Emily Nelson and Ann Zimmerman, "How Kimberly-Clark Keeps Client Costco in Diapers," *Wall Street Journal Online*, September 7, 2000 (http://online.wsj.com).

28. For a fuller account of the ECR "movement," see Barbara E. Kahn and Leigh McAlister, *Grocery Revolution: The New Focus on the Consumer* (Reading, MA: Addison-Wesley, 1997), ch. 6.

29. *Category Management* (Northbrook, IL: Nielsen Marketing Research, 1992), 10.

30. The discussion is adapted from ibid., especially 112–121.

31. For discussion of everyday low pricing by retailers, see Stephen J. Hoch, Xavier Dreze, and Mary E. Purk, "EDLP, Hi-Lo, and Margin Arithmetic," *Journal of Marketing* 58 (October 1994), 16–27.

32. Kusum L. Ailawadi, Donald R. Lehmann, and Scott A. Neslin, "Market Response to a Major Policy Change in the Marketing Mix: Learning from Procter & Gamble's Value Pricing Strategy," *Journal of Marketing* 65 (January 2001), 44–61.

33. This conclusion is based on profit estimations made in ibid., 57.

34. Jack Neff, "Trade Promotion Rises," *Advertising Age*, April 3, 2000, 24.

35. Kenneth Craig Manning, "Development of a Theory of Retailer Response to Manufacturers' Everyday Low Cost Programs" (Ph.D. dissertation, University of South Carolina, 1994).

36. Christopher W. Hoyt, "More Cracks in the EDLP-ECR Marble," *Promo*, December 1993, 57. See also Hoch, Dreze, and Purk, "EDLP, Hi-Lo, and Margin Arithmetic."

37. Kerry E. Smith, "Scan Down, Pay Fast," *Promo*, January 1994, 58–59; "The Proof Is in the Scanning," *Promo*, February 1995, 15.

38. *20th Annual Survey of Promotional Practices* (Largo, FL: Cox Direct, 1998), 50, 65.

39. Adapted from Stephanie Thompson, "Hormel Seeks Frequent Spam-sters," *Brandweek*, May 18, 1998, 6.

40. Betsy Spethmann, "Wake Up and Smell the Co-Marketing," *Promo*, August 1998, 43–47.

41. Shantanu Dutta, Mark Bergen, George John, and Akshay Rao, "Variations in the Contractual Terms of Cooperative Advertising Contracts: An Empirical Investigation," *Marketing Letters* 6 (January 1995), 15.

42. Ibid., 16–17.

43. Ibid.

44. Stephen A. Greyser and Robert F. Young, "Follow 11 Guidelines to Strategically Manage Co-op Advertising Program," *Marketing News*, September 16, 1983, 5.

45. Newspaper Rate Differentials 1987 (New York: American Association of Advertising Agencies, 1988).

46. "Almay Catches the Wave with Wet-proof Mascara," *Adweek's Marketing Week*, March 25, 1991, 26, 28.

47. Srinath Gopalakrishna, Gary L. Lilien, Jerome D. Williams, and Ian K. Sequeira, "Do Trade Shows Pay Off?" *Journal of Marketing* 59 (July 1995), 75. For discussion of trade shows in the U.K., see Jim Blythe, "Does Size Matter?—Objectives and Measures at UK Trade Exhibitions," *Journal of Marketing Communications* 3 (March 1997), 51–59. For comparison between trade shows in the U.K. and U.S., see Marnik G. Dekimpe, Pierre Francois, Srinath Gopalakrishna, Gary L. Lilien, and Christophe Van den Bulte, "Generalizing About Trade Show Effectiveness: A Cross-National Comparison," *Journal of Marketing* 61 (October 1997), 65–73.

48. Cyndee Miller, "Marketing Industry Report: Who's Spending What on Biz-to-Biz Marketing," *Marketing News*, January 1, 1996, 1.

49. Roger A. Kerin and William L. Cron, "Assessing Trade Show Functions and Performance," *Journal of Marketing* 51 (July 1987), 88.

50. Gopalakrishna et al., "Do Trade Shows Pay Off?" 75–83.

51. Alan Cohen, "The Cyber-Show Must Go On," *Trade Media*, May 7, 2001, SR3–SR4.

Chapter Eighteen

CONSUMER-ORIENTED PROMOTIONS

Chapter Objectives

After studying this chapter, you should be able to:

1. Describe the objectives of consumer-oriented sales promotions.
2. Recognize that many forms of promotions perform different objectives for marketers.
3. Explain the role of sampling, the forms of sampling, and the trends in sampling practice.
4. Explain the role of couponing, the types of coupons, and the developments in couponing practice.
5. Understand the coupon redemption process and misredemption.
6. Explain the role of premiums, the types of premiums, and the developments in premium practice.
7. Describe the role of price-off promotions and bonus packages.
8. Discuss the role of rebates and refund offers.
9. Explain the differences among sweepstakes, contests, and games, and the reasons for using each form of promotion.
10. Understand the role of continuity programs.
11. Appreciate the growth of Internet promotions.
12. Evaluate the potential effectiveness of sales promotion ideas, and appraise the effectiveness of completed promotional programs.

Opening Vignette: "I Scream, You Scream, We All Scream for [Free] Ice Cream"

A detailed section on sampling later in the chapter describes conditions when a brand manager might consider providing consumers with free samples. A fundamental dictum among promotion managers is that a brand should not be sampled unless it has demonstrable advantages over competitive brands and when those advantages cannot be adequately communicated by advertising alone. It is in this light that you may appreciate the following description of how Ben & Jerry's ice cream was sampled.

Ben & Jerry's Homemade ice cream is a famous brand that many people associate almost as much with the social mission and philanthropic activities of its cofounders (Ben Cohen and Jerry Greenfield) as they do with the brand's scrumptious taste and clever names for different flavors (e.g., Cherry Garcia, named after the late Jerry Garcia of the Grateful Dead band). After Ben & Jerry's was purchased by Unilever in 2000, the brand managers decided to sample the product to increase its market penetration and to convert new users from competitive brands. But how do you sample ice cream? It could be done in supermarkets, but that venue somehow doesn't quite fit with Ben & Jerry's image. Obviously, unlike most other products, sampling through the mail also is out of the question. Given these product-sampling limitations, Ben & Jerry's marketing team decided to sample Ben & Jerry's ice cream at a special event titled "Urban Pasture," which was designed specifically for that purpose, and invited ice cream fans to "Stop and taste the ice cream."

Requiring the event to match Ben & Jerry's upscale, pastoral image, the promotion planners created an "Urban Pastures" motif complete with cow manikins, banners, lounge chairs, live bands, and, of course, free ice cream. The event toured 13 major U.S. cities, including Boston, Chicago, Los Angeles, and New York. The "Urban Pasture" set up in each city included a main stage from which music was played, and ice-cream-scooping matches were hosted by sports and entertainment celebrities, with the winner at each tour stop receiving the oppor-

Source: Adapted from Betsy Spethmann, "Branded Moments," *PROMO*, September 2000, pp. 83–98. Used with permission from PROMO.

tunity to select a charity to receive an attractive donation–clearly in line with the brand's philanthropic image. Each pasture was up for a single day, but sampling crews remained in each city for at least an additional week during which they sampled Ben & Jerry's ice cream from cow-bedecked buses.

In addition to giving away more than one million samples of the ice cream during the entire tour, a sweepstakes also was run at each tour stop, whereby winners received a month-long lease on a large recreational vehicle along with spending money and a year's supply of Ben & Jerry's ice cream. Also at each site, coupons were distributed and participants had an opportunity to receive T-shirts, ball caps, travel mugs, and other premium items. All in all, the promotional events in 13 cities for Ben & Jerry's Homemade ice cream increased consumer interest in the brand, encouraged subsequent trial purchasing, and undoubtedly influenced some consumers to become loyal repeat purchasers.

INTRODUCTION

This chapter discusses the many consumer-oriented sales promotions that are part of the brand manager's arsenal when attempting to influence desired behaviors from present and prospective customers. Building on the base developed in Chapters 16 and 17, the chapter focuses exclusively on *consumer-oriented promotions*. It describes the unique character of each promotion technique and explains the objectives each is intended to accomplish.

Before proceeding, it is appropriate to reiterate some advice that was provided in Chapter 2 and repeated in Chapters 8 and 13. That guidance involved the relations among brand positioning, target markets, objectives, and budgets and was summarized in the form of the following mantra:

> *All marketing communications should be (1) clearly **positioned,** (2) directed to a particular **target market,** (2) created to achieve a specific **objective,** and (3) undertaken to accomplish the objective **within the budget constraint.***

This counsel, when considered in the context of strategy formulation about consumer promotions, simply advises that brand positioning and target marketing are the starting points for all decisions. With a clear positioning and precise target, the brand manager is in a position to specify the objective(s) a particular promotion program is designed to accomplish. The manager also must work diligently to ensure that promotion spending does not exceed the budget constraint. This is the challenge that brand managers face when using consumer-oriented promotions to achieve strategic objectives.

Brand Management Objectives and Consumer Rewards

What objectives do brand managers hope to accomplish by using consumer-oriented promotions? Why are consumers receptive to samples, coupons, contests, sweepstakes, cents-off offers, and other promotional efforts? Answers to these interrelated questions constitute the core of this chapter. Before discussing brand management objectives and consumer rewards, we first need to set the stage for understanding why consumer promotions are used extensively.

Why Use Consumer Promotions?   In most every product category, whether durable products or consumer packaged goods (CPGs), there are several brands available to wholesalers and retailers (the trade) to choose among and for consumers ultimately to select or reject for personal or family consumption. As a brand manager, your objective is to get your brand adequately placed in as many retail outlets as possible and to ensure that the brand moves off the shelves with frequency sufficient to keep retailers satisfied with its performance and to achieve your own profit objectives. This requires that you get consumers to try your brand and purchase it regularly.

Your competitors, on the other hand, have identical goals. They are attempting to garner the support of the same wholesalers and retailers that you desire

Immediate vs. Delayed Response

and achieve purchase loyalty from the consumers you also covet. Their gain is your loss. It is a vicious zero-sum game in the battle for trade customers and final consumers. You are unwilling to make it easy for your competitors to succeed, and they are not inclined to make your life the proverbial bed of roses.

Though the stakes pale in comparison, brand managers—like their counterparts in the military—are constantly attacking, counterattacking, and defending their turf against competitive inroads. Advertising plays a major role in this battle, flying above the day-to-day action, in a manner of speaking, and dropping persuasive bombs. Sales promotion, on the other hand, is analogous to an army's ground troops who are engaged in the "dirty work" of fighting off the competition and engaging in hand-to-hand battle. Advertising alone is insufficient; promotion by itself is inadequate. Together they can make a formidable opponent.

Now, in answer to the question opening this section, consumer promotions are used because they accomplish goals that advertising by itself cannot achieve. Consumers oftentimes need to be induced to buy now rather than later, to buy your brand rather than a competitor's, and to buy more rather than less. Sales promotions are uniquely suited to achieving these imperatives. Whereas advertising makes consumers aware of your brand and promotes a positive image, promotions serve to consummate the transaction.

Before proceeding, I wish to make one final preliminary point. This actually is a personal request regarding your study of this chapter. In particular, as a consumer living in a market-oriented society who is exposed daily to the commonplace practice of marketers inundating us with promotions such as coupons, samples, and sweepstakes, you may think you already understand everything you need to know about these ordinary topics. I have no doubt that you do know a lot. Yet, just as you know of Einstein's theory of relativity ($E = MC^2$), you probably do not actually understand the theory any more than does the author of this text. Though promotions are trivial in comparison to Einstein's theory, the point I am attempting to make is that you probably also do not understand sales promotions beyond a relatively superficial level. It is my wish that you study the following material with the goal of *really* understanding why the various types of promotions are used and what unique objectives each is designed to accomplish. Sophisticated brand managers do not simply reach into a "bag" and pick out any promotional tool as if the multiple forms of promotions are completely interchangeable. Rather, each is chosen to accomplish strategic objectives to a degree better than alternative options.

Brand Management Objectives.

The overarching objective of consumer-oriented promotions is to promote increased sales. (Sales promotion = promoting sales.) Subsidiary to this overarching goal and in concert with trade-oriented promotions (the subject of the prior chapter), consumer promotions are capable of achieving various sales-influencing objectives for "our" brand:[1]

- Gaining trade support for inventorying increased quantities of our brand during a limited period and providing superior display space for our brand during this period.
- Reducing brand inventory for a limited period when inventories have grown to an excessive level due to slow sales caused by economic conditions or effective competitive actions.
- Providing the sales force with increased motivation during a promotional period to gain more distribution for our brand, better display space, or other preferential treatment vis-à-vis competitive brands.
- Protecting our customer base against competitors' efforts to steal them away.
- Introducing new brands to the trade and to consumers.
- Entering new markets with established brands.
- Promoting trial purchases among consumers who have never tried our brand or achieving retrial from those who have not purchased our brand for an extended period.

- Rewarding present customers for continuing to purchase our brand.
- Encouraging repeat purchasing of our brand and reinforcing brand loyalty.
- Enhancing our brand's image.
- Increasing advertising readership.
- Facilitating the process of continuously expanding the list of names and addresses in our database.

As can be seen, consumer promotions are used to accomplish a variety of objectives, with the ultimate goal of driving increased sales of our brand. Consumer promotions, when done effectively, can serve to gain the trade's support, inspire the sales force to improved performance, and, most important for present purposes, motivate consumers to commit a trial purchase of our brand and, ideally, to purchase it with greater frequency and perhaps even in larger quantities.

To simplify matters some, the following discussions of specific forms of consumer-oriented promotions (samples, coupons, etc.) focus primarily on objectives directed at influencing consumer behavior rather than initiating trade or sales force action. We will focus on three general categories of objectives: (1) generating trial purchases, (2) encouraging repeat purchases, and (3) reinforcing brand images.

Some sales promotions (such as samples and coupons) are used primarily for *trial impact*. A brand manager employs these promotional tools to prompt nonusers to try a brand for the first time or to encourage retrial from prior users who have not purchased the brand for perhaps extended periods. At other times, managers use promotions to hold onto their current customer base by rewarding them for continuing to purchase the promoted brand or loading them with a stockpile of the manufacturer's brand so they have no need, at least in the short run, to switch to another brand. This is sales promotions' *repeat-purchase objective*. Sales promotions also can be used for *image reinforcement* purposes. For example, the careful selection of the right premium object or appropriate sweepstakes prize can serve to bolster a brand's image.

Consumer Rewards.   Consumers would not be responsive to sales promotions unless there was something in it for them—and, in fact, there is All promotion techniques provide consumers with *rewards* (benefits, incentives, or inducements) that encourage certain forms of behavior desired by brand managers. These rewards, or benefits, are both utilitarian and hedonic.[2] Consumers who use sales promotions receive *utilitarian*, or functional, benefits of (1) obtaining monetary savings (e.g., when using coupons), (2) reducing search and decision costs (e.g., by simply availing themselves of a promotional offer and not thinking about other alternatives), and (3) obtaining improved product quality made possible by a price reduction that allows consumers to buy superior brands they might not otherwise purchase. Consumers also obtain *hedonic* benefits when taking advantage of sales promotion offers. These nonfunctional benefits include (1) accomplishing a sense of being a wise shopper when taking advantage of sales promotions, (2) achieving a need for stimulation and variety when, say, trying a brand one otherwise might not purchase if it were not for an attractive promotion, and (3) obtaining entertainment value when, for example, the consumer competes in a promotional contest or participates in a sweepstakes.

The rewards consumers receive from sales promotions sometimes are immediate, while at other times they are delayed. An *immediate reward* is one that delivers monetary savings or some other form of benefit as soon as the consumer performs a marketer-specified behavior. For example, you receive cash savings at the time you redeem a coupon, and you obtain pleasure immediately when you try a free food item or beverage. *Delayed rewards* are those that follow the behavior by a period of days, weeks, or even longer. For example, you may have to wait six or eight weeks before a mail-in premium item can be enjoyed.

Generally speaking, consumers are more responsive to immediate rewards than they are to delayed rewards. Of course, this is in line with the natural human preference for *immediate gratification*.

Classification of Promotion Methods

It is insightful to consider each consumer-oriented promotion technique in terms of its brand management objective simultaneously with its consumer reward. Table 18.1 presents a six-cell typology that was constructed by cross-classifying the two forms of consumer rewards (immediate versus delayed) with the three objectives for using promotions (generating trial, encouraging repeat purchases, and reinforcing brand image).

Cell 1 includes three promotion techniques—samples, instant coupons, and shelf-delivered coupons—that encourage *trial purchase* behavior by providing consumers with an immediate reward. The reward is either monetary savings, in the case of instant coupons, or a free product, in the case of samples. Media- and mail-delivered coupons, free-with-purchase premiums, and scanner-delivered coupons—all found in **cell 2**—are some of the techniques that generate consumer trial yet delay the reward.

Cells 3 and 4 contain promotional tools that are intended to encourage *repeat purchases* from consumers. Marketing communicators design these techniques to reward a brand's existing customers and to keep them from switching to competitive brands—in other words, to encourage repeat purchasing. Immediate reward tools, in **cell 3,** include price-offs; bonus packs; in-, on-, and near-pack premiums; and games. Delayed reward techniques, listed in **cell 4,** include in- and on-pack coupons, refund and rebate offers, phone cards, and continuity programs.

Building a brand's image is primarily the task of advertising; however, sales promotion tools may support advertising efforts by *reinforcing a brand's image.* By nature, these techniques are incapable of providing consumers with an immediate reward; therefore, **cell 5** is empty. **Cell 6** contains self-liquidating premiums and two promotional tools, contests and sweepstakes, that, if designed appropriately, can reinforce or even strengthen a brand's image in addition to performing other tasks.

Caution Is in Order!   Before proceeding, it is important to reemphasize that the classification of promotional tools in Table 18.1 is necessarily simplified. First, the table classifies each technique with respect to the *primary* objective it is designed to accomplish. It is important to recognize, however, that promotions

Table 18.1   Major Consumer-Oriented Promotions

Brand Manager's Objective

Consumer Reward	Generating Trial Purchases	Encouraging Repeat Purchases	Reinforcing Brand Image
Immediate	**Cell 1** • Samples • Instant coupons • Shelf-delivered coupons	**Cell 3** • Price-offs • Bonus packs • In-, on-, and near-pack premiums • Games	**Cell 5**
Delayed	**Cell 2** • Scanner-delivered coupons • Media- and mail-delivered coupons • Online coupons • Mail-in premiums • Free-with-purchase premiums	**Cell 4** • In- and on-pack coupons • Rebates/refunds • Phone cards • Continuity programs	**Cell 6** • Self-liquidating premiums • Sweepstakes and contests

are capable of accomplishing more than a single objective. For example, bonus packs (cell 3) are classified as encouraging repeat purchasing, but first-time triers also occasionally purchase brands that offer extra volume. The various forms of coupons located in cells 1 and 2 are designed primarily to encourage triers and to attract switchers from other brands. In actuality, however, most coupons are redeemed by current purchasers rather than by new buyers. In other words, though intended to encourage trial purchasing and switching, coupons also invite repeat purchasing by rewarding present customers for continuing to purchase "our" brand.

Second, the tools in Table 18.1 are categorized under the primary objective each is designed to accomplish *toward consumers*. It is important to recognize, however, that manufacturers use consumer-oriented sales promotions also to *leverage trade support*. For example, when a manufacturer informs retailers that a certain brand will be sampled during a designated period, the manufacturer is virtually assured that retailers will purchase extra quantities of that brand and possibly provide additional display space. In other words, consumer-oriented promotions can influence trade behavior as well as consumer action.

Finally, note that two techniques, coupons and premiums, are found in more than one cell. This is because these techniques achieve different objectives depending on the specific form of delivery vehicle. Coupons delivered through the media (newspapers and magazines) or in the mail offer a form of delayed reward, whereas instant coupons that are peeled from a package at the point of purchase offer an immediate reward. Similarly, premium objects that are delivered in, on, or near a product's package provide an immediate reward, while those requiring mail delivery yield a reward only after some delay.

SAMPLING

The baby-food division of H. J. Heinz Company developed a rather revolutionary product idea: a powdered, instant baby food. Although Heinz's management was optimistic about instant baby food, they knew consumers would resist trying the product because of a natural inertia regarding dramatic product shifts and the fear of treating their babies as guinea pigs. A further complication was the difficulty of communicating the product's benefits by advertising alone. Heinz needed a way to persuade mothers to try instant baby food. The solution was to employ the services of a company that specializes in delivering samples to mothers of newborn infants. This form of sampling avoided waste distribution and gave mothers firsthand experience with preparing and feeding their babies instant food. Many sample recipients became loyal users.[3]

This case illustrates the power of sampling as a promotional technique. Most practitioners agree that sampling is the *premier sales promotion device for generating trial usage*. In fact, some observers believe that sample distribution is almost a necessity when introducing *truly* new products. Sampling is effective because it provides consumers with an opportunity to personally experience a new brand. It allows an active, hands-on interaction with the sampled brand rather than a passive encounter, as is the case with the receipt of promotional techniques such as coupons.[4]

By definition, **sampling** includes any method used to deliver an actual- or trial-sized product to consumers. Over 80 percent of manufacturers use sampling as part of their consumer promotion mix for purposes of generating trial or retrial and to leverage trade support.[5] Brand managers in the United States invest over $1.2 billion annually on product sampling.[6]

Various distribution methods are used to deliver samples either alone (*solo sampling*) or in cooperation with other brands (*co-op* sampling):

- *Direct mail:* Samples are mailed to households targeted by demographic characteristics or in terms of geodemographics (as discussed in Chapter 3). Figure 18.1 (for Pert Plus shampoo plus conditioner) illustrates how direct mail was used effectively by Procter & Gamble to introduce consumers to this brand. The two foil packets allow two consumers in the

Sampling Problems

There are several problems with the use of sampling. First, sampling is expensive. Second, mass mailings of samples can be mishandled by the postal service or other distributors. Third, samples distributed door to door or in high-traffic locations may suffer from wasted distribution and not reach the hands of the best potential customers. Fourth, in- or on-package sampling excludes consumers who do not buy the carrying brand. Fifth, in-store sampling often fails to reach sufficient numbers of consumers to justify its expense.

A sixth problem with samples is that consumers may misuse them. Consider the case of Sun Light dishwashing liquid, a product of Lever Brothers. This product, which smells like lemons, was extensively sampled some years ago to more than 50 million households. Unfortunately, nearly 80 adults and children claimed that they became ill after consuming the product, having mistaken the dishwashing liquid for lemon juice! According to a Lever Brothers' marketing research director at the time of the sampling, there is always a potential problem of misuse when a product is sent to homes rather than purchased with prior product knowledge at a supermarket.[21]

A final sampling problem, pilferage, can result when samples are distributed through the mail. A case in point occurred in Poland shortly after the Iron Curtain separating eastern from western Europe was literally and symbolically demolished with the fall of communist dominion in the east. Procter & Gamble mailed 580,000 samples of Vidal Sassoon Wash & Go shampoo to consumers in Poland, the first ever mass mailing of free samples in that country. The mailing was a big hit—so big, in fact, that about 2,000 mailboxes were broken into. The shampoo samples, although labeled "Not for sale," turned up on open markets and were in high demand at a price of 60 cents each. P&G paid nearly $40,000 to the Polish Post, Poland's mail service, to deliver the samples. In addition to the cost of distribution, P&G paid thousands more to have mailboxes repaired.[22]

Due to its expense and because of waste and other problems, the use of sampling fell out of favor for a period of time as many marketers turned to less expensive promotions, especially couponing. However, with the development of creative solutions and innovations, promotion managers have again become enthusiastic about sampling. Sampling has become more efficient in reaching specific target groups, its results are readily measurable, and the rising costs of media advertising have increased its relative attractiveness.

COUPONING

A **coupon** is a promotional device that rewards consumers for purchasing the coupon-offering brand by providing either *cents-off savings* or *free merchandise*. Cents-off savings often are as high as 75 cents or more. Free-merchandise offers typically come in the form of "buy 2, get 1 free" in which the free item is either another unit of the same brand or a different brand as in the Special K offer for a 2-liter bottle of Diet Pepsi along with two packages of Special K cereal (see Figure 18.7).

Coupons are delivered through newspapers, magazines, freestanding inserts, direct mail, in or on packages, online, and, increasingly, at the point of purchase by package, shelf, and electronic delivery devices. It is important to appreciate the fact that not all delivery methods have the same objective. *Instant coupons* (that is, those that can be peeled from packages at the point of purchase) provide immediate rewards to consumers and encourage trial purchases as well as repeat buying from loyal consumers. *Mail- and media-delivered coupons* delay the reward, although they also generate trial purchase behavior. Before discussing these specific coupon delivery modes in detail, it first will be instructive to examine pertinent developments in coupon use.

Couponing Background

Couponing in the United States reached its peak with 327 billion coupons distributed in 1994.[23] Since then there has been a reduction in coupon distribution, with

A Buy Two, Get One Free Coupon Offer for a Different Brand

Figure 18.7

approximately 250 billion coupons distributed in 2000.[24] The decrease in couponing resulted not from diminished marketer interest in this promotional tool but rather is attributable to the fact that marketers have become more adept at targeting coupons to specific consumer groups. Because the use of coupons tends to decline during periods of economic upsurge and increase during recessions, it is expected that coupon usage will have increased during the recession of 2001–2002.

Virtually all CPG marketers issue coupons. The use of coupons is not, however, restricted to packaged goods. For example, General Motors Corporation mailed coupons valued as high as $1,000 to its past customers in hopes of encouraging them to purchase new cars. The Ford Motor Company quickly retaliated by offering to honor GM coupons.

Surveys indicate that virtually all American consumers (99 percent) use coupons at least on occasion and that almost all (93 percent) say that they like coupons "somewhat" or "very much."[25] However, research has established that consumers vary greatly in terms of their psychological inclination to use coupons and that this coupon proneness is predictive of actual coupon redemption behavior.[26]

The appeal of coupons is not limited to American consumers. A major international study found that consumers in every country included in the survey valued coupons. Although vastly more coupons are distributed in the United States than elsewhere, redemption rates (the percentage of all distributed coupons that are taken to stores for price discounts) are higher in most other countries.[27] However, couponing in some countries is virtually nonexistent or in the fledgling stage. For example, in Germany the government limits the face value of coupons to 1 percent of a product's value, which effectively eliminates this form of promotion in that country for consumer packaged goods. Only a small amount of couponing occurs in France because the few chains that control the retail grocery market in that country generally oppose the use of coupons. Couponing activity in Japan is in the early stages following the lifting of government restrictions.

Coupon Distribution Methods.   The method of coupon distribution preferred by brand managers is the *freestanding insert (FSI)*. FSIs, which are inserts appearing in Sunday newspapers, accounted for approximately 82 percent of all coupons distributed in the United States in 2000. The other media for coupon distribution are handouts at stores or other locations (7.7 percent), magazine and newspaper distribution (4.4 percent), inside or on product packages (2.9 percent), direct mail (2 percent), and in store or via the Internet (1 percent).[28] The dominance of FSIs is a dramatic change from just a quarter-century ago, when only 15 percent of coupons were distributed by FSI, and nearly 75 percent were distributed via newspapers and magazines.[29] The reason for these changes should be obvious: Freestanding inserts capture the consumer's attention more readily and therefore are superior in overcoming competitive clutter.

Another major trend in coupon distribution has been the establishment of *cooperative coupon programs*. These are programs in which a service distributes coupons for a single company's multiple brands or brands from multiple companies. Two such service companies—Valassis Inserts and News America Marketing—are responsible for distributing the billions of FSI coupons. Val-Pak Direct Marketing Systems is a cooperative program for distributing coupons by direct mail.

Economic Impact.   The extensive use of couponing has not occurred without criticism. Some critics contend that coupons are wasteful and may actually increase prices of consumer goods. Whether coupons are wasteful and inefficient remains problematic. However, it is undeniable that coupons are an expensive proposition. For a better understanding of coupon costs, consider the case of ConAgra's brand of Marie Callender's frozen entrees and its coupon with a face value of $1.00. The coupon's actual cost to ConAgra, as shown in Table 18.3, is substantially more at $1.59. As can be seen from the table, the major cost element is the face value of $1.00 that is deducted from the purchase price of a Marie Callender's frozen entree on redemption of the coupon. But the makers of this brand also incur (1) a hefty distribution and postage cost (40 cents), (2) a handling charge that is paid to retailers for their troubles (8 cents), (3) a misredemption charge resulting from fraudulent redemptions (estimated at 7 cents), (4) internal preparation and processing cost (2 cents), and (5) a redemption cost (2 cents). The actual cost of $1.59 per redeemed coupon is 59 percent greater than the face value of $1.00. Assume that ConAgra distributed 40 million of these FSI coupons and that 2 percent, or 800,000, were redeemed. The total cost to ConAgra of this coupon "drop" would thus amount to $1.272 million. It should be apparent that coupon activity requires substantial investment to accomplish desired objectives.

Table 18.3

	Full Coupon Cost
1. Face value	$1.00
2. Distribution and postage cost	.40
3. Handling charge	.08
4. Consumer misredemption cost	.07
5. Internal preparation and processing cost	.02
6. Redemption cost	.02
Total Cost	$1.59

Source: Adapted from an analysis performed by the McKinsey & Co. consulting firm.

Obviously, programs that aid in reducing costs, such as cooperative delivery programs, are eagerly sought. Creative and innovative couponing programs are constantly being developed. Coupons are indeed costly, some are clearly wasteful, and other promotional devices may be better. However, the extensive use of coupons either suggests that there are a large number of incompetent brand managers or that better promotional tools are not available or are economically infeasible. The latter explanation is the more reasonable when considering how the marketplace operates. If a business practice is uneconomical, it will not continue to be used for long. When a better business practice is available, it will replace the previous solution. Conclusion: It appears that coupons are used extensively because marketers have been unable to devise more effective and economical methods for accomplishing the objectives achieved with couponing.

Is Couponing Profitable?   Recall the discussion in Chapter 16 that examined when promotional dealing is and is not profitable. Among other conclusions, it was determined that putting a brand on deal is unprofitable if the market is composed entirely of promotion-insensitive consumers or entirely of stockpiling loyalists. On the other hand, dealing a brand is profitable if the market consists of on-deal-only consumers.

Of course, markets never consist entirely of just one type of consumer. However, there is evidence showing that those households most likely to redeem coupons are also the most likely to buy the brand in the first place. It has been estimated that as much as 70 to 80 percent of coupons are redeemed by a brand's current users.[30] Moreover, most consumers revert to their pre-coupon brand choice immediately after redeeming a competitive brand's coupon.[31]

Hence, when consumers who redeem would have bought the brand anyway, the effect of couponing, at least on the surface, is merely to increase costs and reduce the per-unit profit margin. However, the issue is more involved than this. Although it is undeniable that most coupons are redeemed by current brand users, competitive dynamics force companies to continue offering coupons to prevent losing consumers to other brands that do offer coupons, other promotional deals, or temporary price reductions.

Couponing is a fact of life that will continue to remain an important part of marketing in North America and elsewhere. The real challenge for promotion managers is to continuously seek ways to increase couponing profitability and to target coupons to consumers who may not otherwise purchase their brands.

The following sections describe the major forms of couponing activity, the objectives each is intended to accomplish, and the innovations designed to increase couponing profitability. The presentation of couponing delivery methods follows the framework presented earlier in Table 18.1.

Point-of-Purchase Couponing

As discussed in Chapter 7, approximately 70 percent of purchase decisions are made in the store. It thus makes sense to deliver coupons at the point where decisions are made. Point-of-purchase coupons come in three forms: instant, shelf delivered, and electronically delivered by optical scanner.

Instantly Redeemable Coupons.   Most coupon distribution methods have delayed impact on consumers because the coupon is received in the consumer's home and held for a period of time before it is redeemed. **Instantly redeemable coupons** (IRCs) are peelable from the package and are designed to be removed by the consumer and redeemed at checkout along with purchase of the couponing brand. This form of coupon represents an *immediate reward* that can spur the consumer to undertake a trial purchase of the promoted brand. Instant coupons provide a significant price reduction and an immediate point-of-purchase incentive for consumers.

Although the instant coupon is a minor form of couponing, it has emerged in recent years as an alternative to price-off deals (in which every package must be reduced in price). The redemption level for instant coupons is considerably higher than the level for other couponing techniques. Whereas the dominant couponing method, FSIs, generates an average redemption level of approximately 1.5 percent (i.e., on average about 15 out of every 1,000 households that receive FSIs actually redeem them at stores), the average redemption rate for instant coupons is about 30 percent.[32] One would think that most all purchasers would remove instant coupons at the time of making a purchase so as to receive the savings immediately, but obviously the majority do not take advantage of these instant coupons.

A study compared the effectiveness of instant redeemable coupons against freestanding inserts in generating sales for a brand of body wash.[33] The FSI and IRC coupons had face values of either 50 cents or $1. Each coupon type and value combination (that is, 50-cent FSI, $1 FSI, 50-cent IRC, $1 IRC) was placed on the body wash brand in each of two markets for a two-month period. Recorded sales data revealed that the IRCs out-performed FSIs of equal value. Moreover, the 50-cent IRC increased sales volume by 23 percent more than the $1 FSI! This obviously is a counterintuitive finding that requires some explanation.

A spokesperson for the company that conducted this research said that his company had no idea why the 50-cent IRC out-performed the $1 FSI. However, research from the academic front offers an answer. One study found that a 75-cent coupon was not considered any more attractive than a 40-cent coupon.[34] A more directly relevant study determined that higher-value coupons *signal* higher prices to consumers.[35] This is especially true when consumers are unfamiliar with a brand. In this situation, high coupon values may "scare them off" by suggesting, or signaling, that these brands are high priced.

Perhaps the $1 FSI for the body wash implied to prospective customers that the brand must be high priced or it could not justify offering such an attractive coupon offer. This being the case, they would not have removed the FSI coupon for later redemption. Comparatively, the 50-cent IRC was available to consumers at the point of purchase where the brand's actual price was available to them. They had no reason to expect a high price; rather, they saw an opportunity to receive an attractive discount by simply peeling the coupon and presenting it to the clerk when checking out. Ironically, higher-valued coupons may attract primarily current brand users who know the brand's actual price and realize the deal offered by the attractive coupon, whereas potential switchers from other brands may be discouraged by a higher-valued coupon if to them it signals a high price. This, of course, is particularly problematic in the use of FSIs, a form of coupon received away from the point of purchase and that, as a matter of practicality, include only the coupon value but not the brand's regular price. Such is not the case, however, with IRCs.

It would be unwise to draw sweeping generalizations from this single study based on only one product category (body wash), but the intriguing finding suggests that IRCs are capable of outperforming FSIs. Only with additional research will we know whether this finding holds up for other products.

Shelf-Delivered Coupons. Shelf-delivered coupon devices are attached to the shelf alongside coupon-sponsoring brands. A red device (referred to as the instant coupon machine from a company named SmartSource) is the best known among several shelf-delivered couponing services offered by other companies. Consumers interested in purchasing a particular brand can pull a coupon from the device and then redeem it when checking out. The average redemption rate for shelf-delivered coupons is approximately 9 percent to 10 percent.[36]

Scanner-Delivered Coupons. Several electronic systems for dispensing coupons at the point of purchase have been introduced in recent years. Although many of these systems have failed, one system that appears to be a success is from Catalina Marketing Corporation and is available in thousands of stores nationwide. Catalina offers two programs, one called Checkout Coupon and the other Checkout Direct. The Checkout Coupon program delivers coupons based on the particular brands a shopper has purchased. Once the optical scanner records that the shopper has purchased a *competitor's brand*, a coupon from the participating manufacturer is dispensed. By targeting competitors' customers, Catalina's Checkout Coupon program ensures that the manufacturer will reach people who buy the product category but are not currently purchasing the manufacturer's brand. The redemption rate is approximately 8 percent.[37]

The other couponing program from Catalina, called Checkout Direct, enables marketers to deliver coupons only to consumers who satisfy the coupon-sponsoring manufacturer's specific targeting requirements. The Checkout Direct program allows the coupon user to target consumers in various ways: (1) in terms of a purchase-relevant demographic variable (e.g., distribute coupons only to households with incomes greater than $50,000), (2) with respect to their purchase pattern for a particular product (e.g., direct coupons only to consumers who purchase toothpaste at least once every six weeks), and (3) based on the amount of product usage (e.g., deliver coupons only to heavy users of the product). Once the couponing requirements are established, Catalina's computer operators can identify coupon-target households by analyzing two databases: (1) optical-scanned purchase data and (2) household demographic variables acquired by supermarkets when requiring shoppers to complete a form to receive check-cashing privileges. When shoppers who satisfy the coupon-sponsoring manufacturer's requirement make a purchase (as indicated by their check-cashing ID number), a coupon for the sponsoring manufacturer's brand is automatically dispensed for use on the shopper's next purchase occasion.

Frito-Lay used the Checkout Direct system to increase trial purchases of its new Baked Lays brand. Marketers at Frito-Lay targeted super-heavy users of healthier snack foods such as its own Baked Tostitos. Based on optical scanner data that records and stores consumers' past purchase data, the Checkout Direct system was programmed to issue coupons for Baked Lays only to those consumers who purchased "better-for-you" snacks at least eight times during the past 12 months. When these consumers checked out, the scanner triggered a coupon for Baked Lays. In excess of 40 percent of the coupons were redeemed, and the repeat purchase rate was a very impressive 25 percent.[38]

Both Catalina programs are used to encourage trial purchasing. However, because coupons are distributed to consumers when they are checking out of a store and cannot be used until their next visit, the reward is *delayed*—unlike the instant or shelf-delivered coupons. Nevertheless, these scanner-delivered couponing methods are effective and cost-efficient because they provide a way to carefully target coupon distribution. Targeting, in the case of Checkout Coupon, is directed at competitive-brand users and, in the case of Checkout Direct, is aimed at users who satisfy a manufacturer's prescribed demographic or product usage requirements.

Mail- and Media-Delivered Coupons

These coupon delivery modes initiate trial purchase behavior by offering consumers *delayed* rewards. Mail-delivered coupons represent about 2 percent of all manufacturer-distributed coupons. Mass media modes (newspapers and magazines) are clearly dominant, carrying well over 85 percent of all coupons (the bulk of which is in the form of freestanding inserts).

Mail-Delivered Coupons. Marketers typically use mail-delivered coupons to introduce new or improved products. Mailings can be directed either at a broad cross section of the market or targeted to specific geodemographic segments. Mailed coupons achieve the *highest household penetration*. Coupon distribution via magazines and newspapers reaches fewer than 70 percent of all homes, whereas mail can reach as high as 95 percent. Moreover, direct mail achieves the *highest redemption rate* (3.5 percent) of all mass-delivered coupon techniques.[39] There also is empirical evidence to suggest that direct-mail coupons *increase the amount of product purchases*, particularly when coupons with higher face values are used by households that own their homes, have larger families, and are more educated.[40]

The major disadvantage of direct-mailed coupons is that they are *relatively expensive* compared with other coupon distribution methods. Another disadvantage is that direct mailing is especially inefficient and expensive for brands enjoying a high market share. This is because a large proportion of the coupon recipients may already be regular users of the coupon brand, thereby defeating the primary purpose of generating trial purchasing. The inefficiencies of mass mailing account for the rapid growth of efforts to target coupons to narrowly defined audiences such as users of competitive brands.

FSIs and Other Media-Delivered Coupons. As earlier noted, approximately 82 percent of all coupons distributed in the United States are freestanding inserts in Sunday newspapers. The cost per thousand for freestanding inserts is only about 50 percent to 60 percent of that for direct-mail coupons, which largely explains why FSIs are the dominant coupon delivery mode. Another advantage of FSIs is that they perform an extremely important reminder function for the consumer who peruses the Sunday inserts, clips coupons for brands she or he intends to buy in the coming weeks, and then redeems these at a later date.[41] Finally, there is some evidence that FSIs also perform an advertising function. That is, when perusing the Sunday inserts, consumers are exposed to FSI "advertisements" and are somewhat more likely to purchase promoted brands even without redeeming coupons.[42] This comes as no great surprise because FSI coupons often are extremely attractive, eye-catching "advertisements."

Research has shown that attractive pictures in FSIs function as peripheral cues (as discussed in Chapter 5) and are particularly effective when viewers of the FSI are loyal to a brand other than the one featured in the FSI. In this situation, consumers, loyal as they are to another brand, are not motivated to process arguments about a nonpreferred brand featured in the FSI. Hence, the use of attractive pictures (versus message arguments) is necessary to enhance consumer attitudes, if only temporarily, and increase the odds that consumers will clip the FSI coupon.[43]

In addition to FSIs, coupons also are distributed in magazines and as part of the regular (noninsert) newspaper page. Though relatively inexpensive distribution media, redemption rates for coupons distributed in magazines and newspapers average less than 1 percent.[44] A second problem with magazine- and newspaper-delivered coupons is that they do not generate much trade interest. Finally, coupons delivered via magazines and newspapers are particularly susceptible to misredemption. The latter issue is so significant to all parties involved in couponing that it deserves a separate discussion later.

In- and On-Pack Coupons

In- and on-pack coupons are included either inside a product's package or as a part of a package's exterior. This form of couponing should not be confused with the previously discussed instant, or peelable, coupon. Whereas IRCs are removable at the point of purchase and redeemable for that particular item while the shopper is in the store, an in- or on-pack coupon cannot be removed until it is in the shopper's home to be redeemed on a subsequent purchase occasion. This form of couponing thus affords consumers with a *delayed* reward.

A coupon for one brand often is promoted by another brand. For example, General Mills promoted its brand of granola bars by placing cents-off coupons in cereal boxes. Practitioners call this practice *crossruffing*, a term borrowed from bridge and bridge-type card games where partners alternate trumping one another when they are unable to follow suit.

Though marketers use crossruffing to create trial purchases or to stimulate purchase of products such as granola bars that are not staple items, in- and on-pack coupons carried by the same brand are generally intended to stimulate *repeat purchasing*. That is, once consumers have exhausted the contents of a particular package, they are more likely to repurchase that brand if an attractive inducement, such as a cents-off coupon, is available immediately. A package coupon has *bounce-back value*, so to speak. An initial purchase, the bounce, may stimulate another purchase, the bounce back, when a hard-to-avoid inducement such as an in-package coupon is made available.[45]

A major advantage of in- and on-pack coupons is that there are virtually no distribution costs. Moreover, redemption rates are much higher because most of the package-delivered coupons are received by brand users. The average re-demption rate for in-pack coupons is around 6 percent to 7 percent, whereas the redemption rate for on-pack coupons is slightly less than 5 percent.[46] Limitations of package-delivered coupons are that they offer delayed value to consumers, do not reach nonusers of the carrying brand, and do not leverage trade interest due to the delayed nature of the offer.

Online Couponing

A number of Internet sites now distribute coupons. Consumers print the coupons on their home (or work) printers, and then as with other modes of coupon delivery, redeem the printed coupon along with the purchased item at checkout. Allowing consumers to print their own coupons creates considerable potential for fraud because it leaves open the possibility that consumers will manipulate the face value and print multiple copies.[47] To avoid this problem, online couponing services allow the consumer to select the brands for which she or he would like to receive coupons, and then actual coupons are mailed. It is too early to know at the time of this writing whether online couponing will be a frequently used, effective, and efficient mode of coupon distribution. By offer-ing a *delayed reward*, it is likely that redemption rates for online coupons will be relatively low.

The Coupon Redemption Process and Misredemption

As alluded to earlier, misredemption is a problem, especially in the use of media-delivered coupons. The best way to understand how misredemption oc-curs is to examine the redemption process. A graphic of the process is provided in Figure 18.8.

The process begins with a manufacturer distributing coupons to consumers via FSIs, direct mail, or any of the other distribution modes previously described (see path A in Figure 18.8). Consumers collect coupons, take them to the store,

Coupon Redemption and Misredemption   **Figure 18.8**

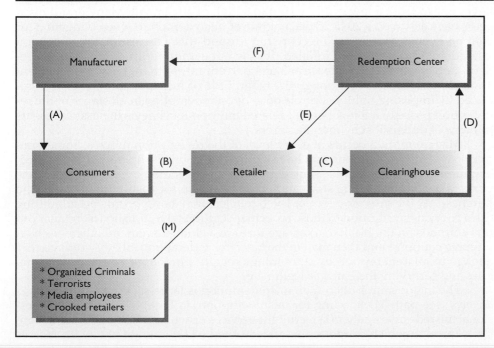

and present them to a checkout clerk, who subtracts each coupon's face value from the shopper's total purchase cost (path B). For the shopper to be entitled to the coupon discount, certain conditions and restrictions must be met: (1) she or he must buy the merchandise specified on the coupon in the size, brand, and quantity directed; (2) only one coupon can be redeemed per item; (3) cash may not be given for the coupon; and (4) the coupon must be redeemed before the expiration date. (Some coupon misredemption occurs because consumers present coupons that do not meet these requirements.)

Retailers, in turn, redeem the coupons they have received to obtain reimbursement from the manufacturers that sponsored the coupons. Retailers typically hire another company, called a *clearinghouse*, to sort and redeem the coupons in return for a fee (path C). The two major clearinghouses in the United States are Carolina Manufacturer's Service (CMS) and Nielsen Clearing House (NCH). Clearinghouses, acting on behalf of a number of retail clients, consolidate coupons before forwarding them. Clearinghouses maintain controls by ensuring that their clients sold products legitimately in the amounts they submitted for redemption.

Clearinghouses forward the coupons to *redemption centers* (path D), which serve as agents of coupon-issuing manufacturers. A redemption center pays off on all properly redeemed coupons (path E) and then is compensated for its services by the manufacturer (path F). If a center questions the validity of certain coupons, it may go to its client, a manufacturer, for approval on redeeming suspected coupons.[48]

The system is not quite as clear-cut as it may appear from this description. Some large retailers act as their own clearinghouses, some manufacturers serve as their own redemption centers, and some independent firms, such as NCH, offer both clearinghouse and redemption-center services.

However, regardless of the specific mechanism by which a coupon is ultimately redeemed (or misredeemed), the retailer is reimbursed for the amount of the *face value* paid to the consumer and for payment of a handling charge, which currently is 8 cents per coupon. Herein rests the potential for misredemption: An unscrupulous person could thus make a profit of $1.08 from a coupon with a face value of $1. One thousand such misredeemed coupons are worth $1,080! Exacerbating the potential for misredemption is the fact that many coupons now have face values worth as much as $1 or more.

Now with an understanding of the redemption process, how does misredemption occur and who participates in it? Estimates of the misredemption rate have ranged from a low of 15 percent to a high of 40 percent. Many brand managers have assumed a 20 to 25 percent rate of misredemption when budgeting for coupon events. However, a recent study found that past estimates of coupon misredemption have been inflated. It now appears that fraudulent coupon redemption is, on average, closer to 3 or 4 percent rather than the 20 to 25 percent assumed previously.[49] Although the magnitude of misredemption has been reduced by imposing tighter controls on coupon redemption at all stages of the redemption process, a 3 to 4 percent misredemption level nevertheless represents millions of dollars lost by manufacturers.

Misredemption occurs at every level of the redemption process. Sometimes *consumers* present coupons that have expired, coupons for items not purchased, or coupons for a smaller-sized product than that specified by the coupon. Some *clerks* take coupons to the store and exchange them for cash without making a purchase. At the *store management* level, retailers may boost profits by submitting extra coupons in addition to those redeemed legitimately. A dishonest retailer can buy coupons on the black market, age them in a clothes dryer, mix them with legitimate coupons, and then mail in the batch for redemption. Shady *clearinghouses* engage in misredemption by combining illegally purchased coupons with real ones and certifying the batch as legitimate.

The major source of coupon misredemption is large-scale *professional misredeemers* (see path M, standing for misredemption, in Figure 18.8). These professional misredeemers either (1) recruit the services of actual retailers to serve as conduits through which coupons are misredeemed or (2) operate phony businesses

sumers immediate value
from consumers who like

This form of premiu
rina offered tiny sports-c
Ten of these boxes contai
in the models for real Co

Near-pack premiur
mium pieces that retaile
product. Near-pack prem
not required. Furthermor
that put up displays and

Self-Liquidating C

The **self-liquidating offe**
fact that the consumer m
with sufficient money to
mailing costs of the prem
is paid for by consumers
free, or, in other words,
serve to enhance a brand'
ued premium item—and
tiple proofs of purchase
ingly being used by brar
The combination of these
teraction with the brand.

The Gerber Keepsa
liquidating offer. With 1
sumers received a cup en
at retail likely would hav
to have purchased Gerbe
purchase.

However, very few
only 0.1 percent of self-liq
example, would be expec
specialists generally conc
a self-liquidating offer is
and represent a meaning
for a savings of at least 50

Phone Cards

Phone cards, also called p
mium offer. Introduced i
Table 18.1 as performing
with a *delayed* reward. Th
are capable of generating
age. Although a variety o
fers a preset amount of lo
and easy to mail, provid
useful by consumers.[57] M
sumers, who typically are
are activated.[58] Phone care

> *Using a Touch-Tone p*
> *the card. The call is rot*
> *ory that stores all infor*
> *sonalized greeting from*
> *number imprinted on t*
> *amount of time remain*

that exist solely for the purpose of redeeming huge quantities of illegal coupons. Illegal coupons typically are obtained by removing FSIs from Sunday newspapers.

The following examples illustrate organized misredemption efforts. The proprietor of Wadsworth Thriftway store in Philadelphia illegally submitted in excess of 1.5 million coupons valued at over $800,000.[50] The top three executives of the Sloans Supermarket in New York were indicted for their role in a 20-year operation that led to $3.5 million in coupon misredemption.[51] Another Philadelphian acted as a middleman between charities, from which he purchased coupons in bulk, and a supermarket employee, who submitted them for repayment by manufacturers or their redemption centers. The middleman earned $200,000 from the couponing scam before he was arrested.[52] Five operators of Shop n' Bag supermarkets in Philadelphia (is there a pattern here?) bought nearly 12 million coupons for only 20 percent to 30 percent of their face value and then redeemed them prior to being arrested.[53] And finally, according to the *New York Post*, Mideast terrorists misredeemed perhaps up to $100 million by funneling illegally redeemed coupons through Arab mini-marts and Hispanic bodegas.[54]

PREMIUMS

Many business-to-business firms as well as consumer-oriented companies use premiums. Total expenditures on premiums in the United States amounted to nearly $27 billion in one recent year, though only about 20 percent of this was allocated toward consumer-oriented premiums.[55] Broadly defined, **premiums** are articles of merchandise or services (e.g., travel) offered by manufacturers to induce action on the part of the sales force, trade representatives, or consumers. Our focus in this chapter is on consumer-oriented promotions.

Consumer-oriented premiums are a versatile promotional tool, possessing the ability to generate trial, encourage repeat purchasing, and reinforce brand images. Brand managers use several forms of premium offers to motivate desired consumer behaviors: (1) free-with-purchase premiums; (2) mail-in offers; (3) in-, on-, and near-pack premiums; and (4) self-liquidating offers. These forms of premiums perform somewhat different objectives. Free-with-purchase and mail-in offers are useful primarily for generating brand *trial or retrial*. In-, on-, and near-pack premiums serve *customer-holding purposes* by rewarding present consumers for continuing to purchase a liked or preferred brand. And self liquidators perform a combination of *customer-holding* and *image-reinforcement* functions. A relatively new form of premium, phone cards, is discussed in a final section.

Free-with-Purchase Premiums

Whereas the subsequent types of premiums typically are offered by packaged-goods brands, **free-with-purchase premiums** more often are provided by durable goods brands. Examples of this type of free-with-purchase premium include an offer from Michelin to receive a $100 retail value emergency roadside kit with the purchase of four Michelin tires. Compaq offered a free Rio 600 MP3 digital audio player with the purchase of select computer models. Attractive premiums such as these might provide indecisive consumers with added reason to purchase the premium-offering brand rather than a competitive option.

Mail-in Offers

By definition, a **mail-in offer** is a premium in which consumers receive a free item from the sponsoring manufacturer in return for submitting a required number of proofs of purchase. For example, Vaseline Intensive Care lotion offered a free watch (see Figure 18.9) when purchasing one bottle of this brand and submitting a proof of purchase and $2 for shipping and handling. Although children and

Figure 18.9

Gaming in Canada for Dunkin' Donuts

Coffee has become a major profit producer for the retail chain known for its expansive assortment of donuts. After a major reformulation, Dunkin' Donuts' coffee is generally regarded as top of the line. A promotional game was designed to promote the chain's coffee, the first time the company ever promoted coffee without donuts. Dunkin' Donuts' Canadian stores ran The Magic Coffee Ring game by offering consumers a variety of prizes, including 17 grand-prize trips valued at $10,000 each, to any of the 40 countries in which Dunkin' Donuts has stores. Other prizes included Compaq computers, mountain bikes, and a half million Dunkin' Donuts food giveaways.

The game worked as follows: On purchasing a 10-ounce cup of coffee, customers received a cardboard ring that they slipped around the cup. The heat from the coffee activated a chemical in the ring and produced a message in a matter of seconds that announced if the customer had won a prize. In addition to the instant-win opportunity provided by this game, Dunkin' Donuts' brand management sought to build repeat purchasing with a continuity program whereby each cardboard ring included a letter. Consumers collecting all six letters spelling DUNKIN accumulated travel award points. The travel theme was employed in both the game and continuity program in hopes of enhancing Dunkin' Donuts global image among Canadian consumers. Game planners declared the promotion a huge success.

Source: Adapted from Amie Smith, "Heating Up," *PROMO*, July 2000, p. 95. Used with permission from PROMO.

The Beatrice Company's Monday Night Football promotion illustrates another failed game. Contestants scratched silver-coated footballs off cards to reveal numbers, hoping to win the prize offered if the numbers on the cards matched the number of touchdowns and field goals scored in the weekly Monday night NFL game. Game planners intended the chances of getting a match to be infinitesimal. However, to Beatrice's great surprise, a salesman for rival Procter & Gamble put in a claim for a great deal more money than Beatrice had planned on paying out. A computer buff, the salesman cracked the game code and determined that 320 patterns showed up repeatedly in the cards. By scratching off just one line, he could determine which numbers were underneath the rest. With knowledge of the actual numbers of touchdowns and field goals scored on a particular Monday night, he would start scratching cards until winning numbers were located. He enlisted friends to assist in collecting and scratching the cards. Thousands of cards were collected, mostly from Beatrice salespeople. The P&G salesman and friends identified 4,000 winning cards worth $21 million in prize money! Beatrice discontinued the game and refused to pay up.[77]

This section would be incomplete without discussing a major scandal that rocked the promotions industry in 2001. Brand managers for McDonald's restaurants and Simon Marketing, a company hired to run a summer promotion for McDonald's, created a Monopoly-type game that was to provide customers with millions in promotional prizes. Unfortunately, there was a major problem in the game's execution. An employee in charge of game security at Simon Marketing allegedly stole winning tickets and distributed them to various friends and accomplices, who obtained approximately $13 million in prize money. After learning of the theft and informing the Federal Bureau of Investigation, McDonald's immediately introduced a different promotional game run by another promotional agency so as to make good its promise to customers and restore its credibility. Apparently, the Simon Marketing employee who ripped off McDonald's had for several years been stealing winning game tickets from other games. A spokesperson for the Promotion Marketing Association, the trade association for the industry, characterized this debacle as a "black eye" for the promotion marketing industry. The moral is clear: Promotional games can go awry, and brand managers must go to extreme lengths to protect the integrity of the games that are designed to build, not bust, relationships with customers.[78]

Online Sweeps, Contests, and Games. Online promotional events are growing in importance. Increasing numbers of companies are encouraging participants to register online. For example, the retail chain Best Buy, which merchandises a wide assortment of electronic products, conducted its Go Mobile promotion that required entrants to log onto a Web site to determine if a unique code obtained on making a purchase at a retail site was an instant winner. Pepsi-Cola North America ran its annual Pepsi Stuff competition online in conjunction with Yahoo. Pepsi's sales increased 5 percent during the promotional period, and, as a bonus, brand managers amassed an e-mail database of 3.5 million names and addresses of mostly younger consumers.[79] (See the *Online Focus* for further reading about the Pepsi-Yahoo connection.)

Forrester Research, a company that tracks Internet developments, has estimated that online promotions will become a $6 billion business by 2005 and that 50 percent to 70 percent of Internet marketing budgets will be allocated to promotions rather than advertisements.[80] Online sweeps, contests, and games appeal to consumers and also further the interest of brands by creating awareness, building consumer interaction with the brand, and enabling the expansion of a brand's opt-in e-mail database (as discussed in the prior chapter).

A variety of companies have started businesses to assist brand planners in planning and executing online promotions. These include companies such as 24/7 iPromotions, ePrize, and DoubleClick. This latter Internet marketing communications company ran a sweepstakes for PlanetHollywood.com. The objective was to drive people to PlanetHollywood's Web site and to supplement its opt-in list. During the course of a 10-week period, over 31,000 people entered the sweep. Seventy-three percent gave PlanetHollywood.com permission to send them e-mail messages regarding future promotions and events.

CONTINUITY PROMOTIONS

Promotions sometimes reward consumers' repeat purchasing of a particular brand by awarding points leading to reduced prices or free merchandise. It is obvious from this description why continuity promotions also are referred to as loyalty programs or point programs. Frequent-flyer programs by airlines and frequent-guest programs by hotels represent one form of loyalty program. Fliers and hotel guests accumulate points that can be redeemed eventually for free flights and lodging. These programs encourage consumers to stick with a particular airline or hotel to accumulate requisite numbers of points as quickly as possible. Renaissance Hotels, for example, provided 1,000 bonus miles per stay plus three extra miles for every U.S. dollar spent. These points were added to hotel guests frequent-flyer point totals with designated airlines.

In general, continuity programs reward consumers for purchasing a particular brand repeatedly. The program need not be based on point accumulation and instead may simply require a certain number of purchases to be eligible for prizes. For example, Budget Rent a Car Corporation ran a continuity promotion whereby renters received free Bollé ski goggles with five car rentals from Budget.

Consumers who are already loyal to a brand that offers a point program or other continuity plan are rewarded for what they would have done anyway—namely, buying a preferred brand on a regular basis. In such a case, a point program does not encourage repeat purchasing; it does, however, serve to cement a relation with the consumer that is strong already. On the other hand, point programs can encourage consumers whose loyalty is divided among several

More Stuff from Pepsi-Cola

During a two-year period (1996 and 1997) Pepsi-Cola undertook a Pepsi Stuff giveaway event at a variety of sites around the United States. Each week a number of two-person crews would travel in vans to a particular city from which they would set up operations for the remainder of the week. A crew would go to two or three supermarkets each day, and outside the store set up a promotional stand from which they gave free samples of Pepsi and invited sample recipients to participate in games to win free Pepsi Stuff (i.e., merchandise such as caps, sunglasses, T-shirts, balls, etc.). These events operated in concert with advertising to inform consumers that they could collect points for purchasing Pepsi products and eventually redeem the points for attractive merchandise items, such as those items given away at the events. The events were very successful and increased Pepsi-Cola sales significantly; however, as might be expected, they also were extremely expensive. To maintain the Pepsi Stuff program but reduce the skyrocketing cost, planners at Pepsi-Cola decided to take the event online.

To run its program online, Pepsi decided to partner with the familiar Yahoo search engine. Millions of people search the Web using Yahoo, and its hip image is appropriate for Pepsi's core consumers aged 13 to 34. The first Pepsi-Stuff.com program ran in the summer of 2000, and, as noted in the text, resulted in a sales spike of 5 percent during the promotional period. The event was so successful that Pepsi decided to partner again with Yahoo in a promotion that urged consumers to vote for their favorite Pepsi commercial among the many classic commercials in Pepsi's illustrative advertising history, including spots with stars such as Michael J. Fox and Cindy Crawford. Pepsi sent 3 million e-mails to its database of consumers and encouraged them to select a favorite commercial. (Needless to say, this is a great way to get consumers to view Pepsi commercials—at virtually zero advertising cost—and to further interact with the brand!) A total of 165,000 votes were cast, exceeding Pepsi's goal by 65 percent, and most of the voters also entered a sweepstakes that gave away 100 prizes worth $2,001 each.

Later in 2001 Pepsi used its Yahoo partnership to drive consumers to a special Web site to review a new Pepsi commercial featuring Britney Spears. Site visitors could see the new commercial two hours before its debut on the Academy Awards show. Driving consumers to the Britney Web site was accomplished by sending 1 million opt-in e-mail messages to appropriately aged consumers from Pepsi's larger database. These e-mail recipients viewed more than 1 million video streams of the commercial, and over 50,000 entered a sweepstakes competition for Britney-related items. Pepsi continues its relation with Yahoo, having just several months before the time of this writing launched PepsiStuff 2 with new incentives. Consumers logging onto the PepsiStuff.com were selected daily as instant winners, much in the spirit of offline games.

The partnership between Pepsi-Cola and Yahoo demonstrates how online sales promotions can be extremely successful. In addition to being able to target consumers who have opted in to receive e-mail messages and who obviously are core consumers, Pepsi is able to continuously introduce new promotions that offer appealing incentives and strengthen consumers' relationship with the brand—in the very best spirit of the integrated marketing communications' principle of building relationships.

Source: Adapted from Kenneth Hein, "Stuff Expander," *Brandweek*, October 22, 2001, pp. 19–20. © 2001 VNU Business Media, Inc.

brands to purchase more frequently the brand that awards promotion points or rewards repeat purchases in some other fashion. This is perhaps where continuity programs have the greatest value.

OVERLAY AND TIE-IN PROMOTIONS

Discussion to this point has concentrated on individual sales promotions. In practice, promotions often are used in combination to accomplish objectives that could not be achieved by using a single promotional tool. Furthermore, these techniques, individually or in conjunction with one another, are used oftentimes to promote simultaneously two or more brands either from the same company or from different firms.

The use of *two or more sales promotion techniques in combination* with one another is called an **overlay,** or *combination,* **program.** The *simultaneous promotion of multiple brands in a single promotional effort* is called a **tie-in,** or *group,* **promotion.** In other words, *overlay* refers to the use of multiple promotional tools, whereas *tie-in* refers to the promotion of multiple brands from the same or different companies. Overlay and tie-ins often are used together, as the following sections illustrate.

Overlay Programs

Media clutter, as noted repeatedly in past chapters, is an ever present problem facing marketers. When used individually, promotion tools (particularly coupons) may never be noticed by consumers. A combination of tools, such as the use of a coupon offer with another promotional device, increases the likelihood that consumers will attend a promotional message and process the promotion offer. In addition, the joint use of several techniques in a well-coordinated promotional program equips the sales force with a strong sales program and provides the trade with an attractive incentive to purchase in larger quantities (in anticipation of enhanced consumer response) and to increase display activity. Nearly all the illustrative figures used previously in the chapter have overlayed a coupon with a refund, sweepstakes, contest, or other promotional offer.

Tie-In Promotions

Growing numbers of companies use tie-ins (group promotions) to generate increased sales, to stimulate trade and consumer interest, and to gain optimal use of their promotional budgets. Tie-in promotions are cost-effective because the cost is shared among multiple brands. Two or more brands, either from the same company (intracompany tie-ins) or from different companies (intercompany tie-ins) are involved in a tie-in. For example, Figure 18.15 illustrates a tie-in promotion for a variety of candy brands marketed by the Hershey Foods Corporation. Notice also that this tie-in offer overlays a coupon (buy two, get one free), a sweepstakes, and a game. Tie-in relationships between complementary brands from different companies are being used with increasing regularity. For example, a freestanding insert showed a breakfast plate of Black Label bacon (from Hormel) and Grands! buttermilk biscuits (from Pillsbury). The FSI included coupons for each brand. These companies shared the cost of producing and distributing this FSI offer.

Implementation Problems.   Tie-in promotions are capable of accomplishing useful objectives, but not without potential problems.[81] Promotion lead time — the amount of time required to plan and execute a promotion — is lengthened because two or more entities have to coordinate their separate promotional schedules. Creative conflicts and convoluted messages may result from each partner trying to receive primary attention for its product or service.

To reduce problems as much as possible and to accomplish objectives, it is important that (1) the profiles of each partner's customers be similar with regard to pertinent demographic or other consumption-influencing characteristics; (2) the partners' images should reinforce each other (e.g., Hormel and Pillsbury both are well-known brands with images of consistently high quality); and (3) the partners must be willing to cooperate rather than imposing their own interests to the detriment of the other partner's welfare.[82]

Figure 18.15

An Intracompany Tie-in Promotion

RETAILER PROMOTIONS

Discussion to this point has focused on manufacturer promotions that are directed at consumers. Retailers also design promotions for their present and prospective customers. These retailer-inspired promotions are created for purposes of increasing store traffic and offering shoppers attractive price discounts or other deals. Couponing is a favorite promotion among many retailers in the grocery, drug, and mass merchandise areas of business. Some grocery retailers hold special "coupon days" when they redeem manufacturer coupons at double or even triple their face value. For example, a grocery store on a "triple-coupon day" would deduct $1.50 from the consumer's bill when she or he submits a manufacturer's coupon with a face value of 50 cents. Retailers typically limit their double- or triple-discount offers to manufacturer coupons having face values of 50 cents or less.

A number of retailers offer their customers frequent-shopper cards that entitle shoppers to discounts on select items purchased on any particular shopping occasion. For example, in a Wednesday advertising flyer, one grocery retailer offered its cardholders savings such as $2.99 on the purchase of two Mrs. Paul's fish filets, $1.25 when buying two cans of Minute Maid juice, and $1.70 with the purchase of Freschetta pizza. Customers receive these savings on submitting their frequent-shopper cards to clerks at checkout, who scan the card number and deduct savings from the shopper's bill when discounted items are scanned. These frequent-shopper cards encourage repeat purchasing from a particular retail chain. Because they are designated with labels such as VIC (very important customer), they also serve to elevate the shopper's sense of importance to a store. Finally, frequent-shopper card programs provide retailers with valuable databases containing information on shopper demographics and purchase habits.

Sampling is another form of retailer-based sales promotion that is in wide use. Although many instances of store sampling represent joint programs between stores and manufacturers, retailers are sampling their own store/private label products increasingly.

Stores also offer premiums to encourage purchases of select items. Figure 18.16 illustrates this in the case of Lowe's Companies, a major retail chain in the home improvement industry. This figure actually is an advertisement from Omaha Steaks in its effort to recruit promotional partners. The advertisement notes that Lowe's partnered with Omaha Steaks with the objective of increasing sales of gas grills priced at more than $150. The giveaway of steaks and burgers increased Lowe's grill sales by 35 percent in participating stores.

EVALUATING SALES PROMOTION IDEAS

It should be apparent by this point that numerous alternatives are available to manufacturers and retailers when planning sales promotions. There also are a variety of objectives that effective promotion programs are able to achieve. The combination of numerous alternatives and diverse objectives leads to a staggering array of possibilities. A systematic procedure for selecting the type of sales promotion is therefore essential. The following sections outline procedures for appraising potential promotions during the idea stage and then, after they have run, for evaluating their effectiveness.

A Procedure for Evaluating Promotion Ideas

The following straightforward, three-step procedure directs a brand manager in determining which promotion ideas and approaches have the best chance of succeeding.[83]

Step 1: Identify the Objectives.　The most basic yet important step toward successful consumer-oriented promotions is the clear identification of the specific objective(s) that is (are) to be accomplished. Objectives should be specified as they relate both to the trade and to ultimate consumers; for example, objectives may be to generate trial, to load consumers, to preempt competition, to increase display space, and so on.

In this first step, the promotional planner must commit the objectives to writing and state them specifically and in measurable terms. For example, "to increase sales" is too general. In comparison, the objective "to increase display space by 25 percent over the comparable period last year" is specific and measurable.

Step 2: Achieve Agreement.　Everyone involved in a brand's marketing must agree with the objectives developed. Failure to achieve agreement on objectives results in various decision makers (such as the advertising, sales, and brand managers) pushing for different programs because they have different goals in mind. Also, a promotion program can more easily be evaluated in terms of a specific objective than can a vague generalization.

Step 3: Evaluation System.　With specific objectives established and agreement achieved, the following five-point evaluation system can be used to rate alternative sales promotion ideas:

Figure 18.16

1. *Is the idea a good one?* Every idea should be evaluated against the promotion's objectives. For example, if increasing product trial is the objective, a sample or a coupon would be rated favorably, whereas a sweepstakes would flunk this initial evaluation.

2. *Will the promotion idea appeal to the target market?* A contest, for example, might have great appeal to children but for certain adult groups have disastrous results. In general, remember that the target market represents the benchmark against which all proposals should be judged.

3. *Is the idea unique, or is the competition doing something similar?* The prospects of receiving interest from both the trade and consumers depend on developing promotions that are not ordinary. Creativity is every bit as important to the success of promotions as it is with advertising.

4. *Is the promotion presented clearly so that the intended market will notice, comprehend, and respond positively to the promotion?* Sales promotion planners should start with one fundamental premise: Most consumers are unwilling to spend much time and effort figuring how a promotion works. It is critical to a promotion's success that instructions be user friendly. Let consumers know quickly and clearly what the offer is and how to respond to it.

5. *Is the proposed idea cost-effective?* This requires an evaluation of whether or not the proposed promotion will achieve the intended objectives at an

affordable cost. Sophisticated promotion planners cost-out alternative programs and know in advance the likely bottom-line payoff from a promotion.

Post Mortem Analysis

The previous section described a general procedure for evaluating proposed promotion ideas while they are in the planning stage, before actual implementation. It would be useful to also have a way of evaluating a promotional program after it has been implemented. Such evaluation would be useful for future planning purposes, especially if the evaluation becomes part of brand management's "institutional memory" rather than discarded shortly after the evaluation is completed. A seasoned practitioner in the promotion industry has proposed judging completed promotion programs in terms of five characteristics: efficiency, execution ease, expense, equity enhancement, and effectiveness.[84]

Efficiency.   Efficiency represents a promotion's *cost-per-unit moved*. The efficiency metric is calculated simply by dividing the total cost of the completed promotion by the total units sold during the promotional period.

Execution Ease.   This represents the total time and effort that went into the planning and execution of a promotion. Obviously, everything else held constant, promotions that require less time and effort are preferred.

Expense.   A promotion program's expense is the sum of the direct outlays invested in the promotion. Typical cost elements include the expense to create the promotion, costs to advertise it, and payouts for coupons redeemed, refunds paid, game prizes awarded, and so on.

Equity Enhancement.   This criterion cannot be measured objectively but involves a subjective assessment of whether a promotion has enhanced a brand's image or possibly even detracted from it. A sweepstakes offer, for example, may serve to enhance a brand's equity by associating it with, say, a prestigious grand prize. A self-liquidating premium may accomplish the same goal. Comparatively, a game may be inappropriate for some brands by virtue of appearing tacky. As always, the evaluation depends on the brand positioning and target market situation.

Effectiveness.   A promotion's effectiveness can best be assessed by determining the total units of the promoted item that were sold during the promotional period.

Combining the Individual Factors.   Having evaluated a completed promotion program along the "E" dimensions just noted, it would be helpful if the five individual evaluations could be combined into a single score. This can be done simply enough by using a straightforward model that weights each of the five factors in importance and then summates the products of each factor's score by its weight. A model such as the following could be used:

$$\text{Program } j\text{'s Score} = \sum_{i=1}^{5} (E_{ij} \times W_i)$$

where,

Program j =   A just completed promotional program (one of many potential promotional programs that have been run and subsequently evaluated).

E_{ij} =   Evaluation of the jth promotional program on the ith evaluation factor (i.e., the efficicency factor, the executional ease factor, etc.).

W_i =   Weight, or relative importance, of the ith factor in determining promotion success. (Note that the weight

Table 18.4

Evaluation of Three Completed Promotional Programs

Program j	Efficiency Weight $= .1$	Execution Ease Weight $= .1$	Expense Weight $= .2$	Equity Enhancement Weight $= .3$	Effectiveness Weight $= .3$	Total Score
Program 1	6	7	7	5	9	6.9
Program 2	8	8	9	7	8	7.9
Program 3	9	8	8	10	9	9.0

component is subscripted just with an i, and not also a j, because the weights are constant across program evaluations. Comparatively, evaluations of the individual factors, E_{ij}, require a j subscript to reflect the likelihood of varying evaluations across different promotional programs.)

Table 18.4 illustrates this straightforward model.[85] Consider a company that has run three promotional programs during a particular year. On completion, each program was evaluated with respect to the five evaluative criteria (efficiency, etc.) on 10-point scales, with 1 indicating poor performance and 10 reflecting an excellent execution on each evaluative criterion. Notice also in Table 18.4 that the five criteria have been weighted as follows: efficiency = .1, execution ease = .1, expense = .2, equity enhancement = .3, and effectiveness = .3. These weights sum to 1 and reflect the relative importance *to this particular brand manager* of the five factors. (Relative importance of these factors will obviously vary across different brands, depending on each brand's image, the company's financial standing, and so on.)

Given this particular set of weights and evaluations, it can be concluded that program 1 was the least successful of the three promotions, whereas program 3 was the most successful. These evaluations can thus be archived for reference by future brand managers. Eventually, norms can be established for specifying the average effectiveness level achieved by different types of promotions (samples, coupon programs, rebates, etc.).

Of course, Table 18.4 is purely illustrative. However, in actual promotion situations it is possible for brand managers to formally evaluate promotions, provided that the procedure for evaluating each criterion is clearly articulated, systematically implemented, and consistently applied (as best as possible) to all promotions that are appraised. The point to be appreciated is that the model on which Table 18.4 is based is suggestive of how promotional programs can be evaluated.

Intelligent brand managers must develop their own models to accommodate their brand's specific needs, but the point to be emphasized is that this can be accomplished with application of thought and effort. The alternative to having a formalized evaluation system, such as proposed here, is simply to run promotion events and then never to evaluate their success. Can you imagine as a student what it would be like to take courses but never to receive grades, never to be evaluated? How would you know how well you have done? How would your institution know whether grading standards have changed over the years? Like it or not, evaluation is essential. Good business practice requires it. The issue is not whether to evaluate promotions but how to do it in a valid and reliable manner.

SUMMARY

This chapter focused on consumer-oriented promotions. The various sales promotion tools available to marketers were classified in terms of whether the reward offered consumers is immediate or delayed and whether the manufacturer's objective is to achieve trial impact, customer holding/loading, or image reinforcement. Specific sales promotion techniques fall into one of six general categories (see Table 18.1).

Specific topics addressed in the chapter included sampling effectiveness; conditions when sampling should be used; coupon usage and growth; couponing costs; coupon misredemption; reasons for using in- and on-pack premiums, self-liquidators, and other types of premiums; FTC price-off regulations; differences between refunds and rebates and when each is used; phantom rebates and rebate fraud; the roles of sweepstakes, contests, and games; the innovation of phone cards as promotional incentives; Internet promotions; the nature of overlay and tie-in promotions; retailer promotions; and promotional program evaluation.

The first and most critical requirement for a successful sales promotion is that it be based on clearly defined objectives. Second, the program must be designed with a specific target market in mind. It should also be realized that many consumers, perhaps most, desire to maximize the rewards gained from participating in a promotion while minimizing the amount of time and effort invested. Consequently, an effective promotion, from a consumer-response perspective, must make it relatively easy for consumers to obtain their rewards, and the size of the reward must be sufficient to justify the consumers' efforts. A third essential ingredient for effective sales promotions is that programs must be developed with the interests of retailers in mind—not just those of the manufacturer.

Find more resources to help you study at http://shimp.swcollege.com!

DISCUSSION QUESTIONS

1. Why are immediate (versus delayed) rewards more effective in inducing consumer behaviors desired by a brand marketer? Use a specific, concrete illustration from your own experience to support your answer.

2. In view of the promotional disasters described at points throughout the chapter, what specific moral would you suggest should be taken from these examples? Be specific.

3. One of the major trends in product sampling is selective sampling of targeted groups. Assume you work for a company that has just developed a candy bar that tastes almost as good as other candy bars but has far fewer calories. Marketing research has identified the target market as economically upscale consumers, aged primarily 25 to 54, who reside in suburban and urban areas. Explain specifically how you might selectively sample your new product to approximately 2 million such consumers.

4. Compare and contrast sampling and media-delivered coupons in terms of objectives, consumer impact, and overall roles in marketing communication strategies.

5. A packaged-goods company plans to introduce a new bath soap that differs from competitive soaps by virtue of a distinct new fragrance. Should sampling be used to introduce the product?

6. A manufacturer of golf balls introduced a new brand that supposedly delivered greater distance than competitively priced balls. However, in accordance with restrictions established by the governing body that regulates balls and other golfing equipment and accessories, this new ball when struck by a driver travels on average only a couple of yards farther than competitive brands. The manufacturer identified a list of 2 million golfers and mailed a single golf ball to each. In view of what you have learned about sampling in this chapter, comment on the advisability of this sampling program.

7. Present your personal views concerning the number of coupons distributed annually in the United States. Is widespread couponing in the best interests of consumers? Could marketers use other promotional methods more effectively and economically to achieve the objectives accomplished with coupons?

8. Present a position on the following statement (voiced by a student who read a previous edition of this textbook): "I can't understand why in Table 18.1 mail-in premiums are positioned as accomplishing just a trial-impact function. It would seem that this form of promotion also accomplishes repeat-purchasing objectives."

9. Using Table 18.3 as a rough guide, calculate the full cost *per redeemed coupon* given the following facts: (1) face value = 75 cents; (2) 20 million coupons distributed at $7 per thousand; (3) redemption rate = 3 percent; (4) handling cost = 8 cents; and (5) misredemption rate = 7 percent.

10. Your company markets hot dogs, bologna, and other processed meats. You wish to offer a self-liquidating premium that would cost consumers approximately $25, would require five proofs of purchase, and would be appropriately themed to your product category during the summer months. Your primary market segment consists of families with school-age children crossing all socioeconomic strata. Suggest two premium items and justify your choice.

11. What is the purpose of the FTC price-off regulations?

12. Compare bonus packs and price-off deals in terms of consumer impact.

13. What is sales promotion crossruffing, and why is it used?

14. How can sales promotion reinforce a brand's image? Is this a major objective of sales promotion?

15. Compare sweepstakes, contests, and games in terms of how they function and their relative effectiveness.

16. Your company markets antifreeze. Sales to consumers take place in a very short period, primarily September through December. You want to tie in

a promotion between your brand and the brand of another company that would bring more visibility to your brand and encourage retailers to provide more shelf space. Recommend a partner for this tie-in promotion and justify the choice.

17. Go through a Sunday newspaper and select five FSIs. Analyze each in terms of what you think are the marketer's objectives in using this particular promotion.

18. What are your thoughts regarding the future of online promotions?

19. Have you participated in online promotions, and if so, what has been your experience? Considering just a single online promotion that you participated in and considering yourself representative of the brand's target market, do you think the promotion accomplished its objective.

ENDNOTES

1. Though the following discussion is based mostly on the author's prior writing and thinking on the topic, these points are influenced by descriptions obtained from various practitioners, especially the following at pages 35 and 36: http://www.santella.com/marketing.htm.

2. Pierre Chandon, Brian Wansink, and Gilles Laurent, "A Benefit Congruency Framework of Sales Promotion Effectiveness," *Journal of Marketing* 64 (October 2000), 65–81. The following discussion of benefits is based on a typology provided by these authors. See their Table 1 on pages 68–69.

3. "Products on Trial," *Marketing Communications*, October 1987, 73–74.

4. Eric A. Johnson, "Consumers Still Trying It and Liking It," *Promotion Marketing*, October 2000, 53–57.

5. *20th Annual Survey of Promotional Practices* (Largo, FL: Cox Direct, 1998), 47.

6. "Give and Take," *Promo's 8th Annual Sourcebook 2001*, 41.

7. *20th Annual Survey of Promotional Practices*, 48.

8. Scott Hume, "Prom Night: Free Samples with Tux," *Advertising Age*, March 13, 1989, 53.

9. "Sampling Wins Over More Marketers," *Advertising Age*, July 27, 1992, 12.

10. Terry Lefton, "Try It, You'll Like It," *Brandweek*, May 24, 1993, 32.

11. Lafayette Jones, "A Case for Ethnic Sampling," *Promo*, October 2000, 41–42.

12. David Vaczek, "Points of Switch," *Promo*, September 1998, 39–40.

13. Kate Fitzgerald, "Targeted Sampling Fits in Integrated Mix," *Advertising Age*, July 5, 1993, 22.

14. Kate Fitzgerald, "Sampling & Singing," *Advertising Age*, June 8, 1998, 32.

15. Stephanie Thompson, "Mobile Marie," *Brandweek*, March 2, 1998, R11.

16. Dan Hanover, "We Deliver," *Promo*, March 2001, 43–45.

17. Adapted from Glenn Heitsmith, "Gaining Trial," *Promo*, September 1994, 108; and "Spend a Little, Get a Lot," Trial and Conversion III: Harnessing the Power of Sampling Special Advertising Supplement (New York: Promotional Marketing Association, Inc., 1996–1997), 18.

18. *Insights: Issues 1-13*, 1979–1982 (New York: NPD Research, 1983), 6–7. These results are particularly interesting because they run somewhat contrary to experimental research, which has detected a tendency for sampling to diminish repeat purchasing. See Carol Scott, "Effects of Trial and Incentives on Repeat Purchase Behavior," *Journal of Marketing Research* 13 (August 1976), 263–269. See also Joe A. Dodson, Alice M. Tybout, and Brian Sternthal, "Impact of Deals and Deal Retraction on Brand Switching," *Journal of Marketing Research* 15 (February 1978), 72–81.

19. "Sampling Wins Over More Marketers."

20. Charles Fredericks, Jr., "What Ogilvy & Mather Has Learned about Sales Promotion," *The Tools of Promotion* (New York: Association of National Advertisers, 1975). Although this is an old source, the wisdom still holds true today.

21. Lynn G. Reiling, "Consumers Misuse Mass Sampling for Sun Light Dishwashing Liquid," *Marketing News*, September 3, 1982, 1, 2.

22. Maciek Gajewski, "Samples: A Steal in Poland," *Advertising Age*, November 4, 1991, 54.

23. Daniel Shannon, "Couponing into the Millennium," *Promo*, April 1995, 75.

24. Based on Nielsen Clearing House estimates as published in *Promo's 9th Annual SourceBook 2002*, 22.

25. Kerry J. Smith, "Shoppers Get Promotion Active," *Promo*, July 1995, 70.

26. Donald R. Lichtenstein, Richard G. Netemeyer, and Scot Burton,

"Distinguishing Coupon Proneness from Value Consciousness: An Acquisition-Transaction Utility Theory Perspective," *Journal of Marketing* 54 (July 1990), 54–67. For a detailed treatment of factors that influence consumers' coupon redemption behavior, see also Banwari Mittal, "An Integrated Framework for Relating Diverse Consumer Characteristics to Supermarket Coupon Redemption," *Journal of Marketing Research* 31 (November 1994), 533–544.

27. Betsy Spethmann, "Countries Crave Coupons," *Advertising Age,* July 15, 1991, 26.

28. Based on Nielsen Clearing House estimates as published in *Promo's 9th Annual SourceBook 2002,* 23.

29. "Couponing Distribution Trends and Patterns," *PMAA Promotion Update '82* (New York: Promotion Management Association of America, Inc., 1983).

30. Nathaniel Frey, "Targeted Couponing: New Wrinkles Cut Waste," *Marketing Communications,* January 1988, 40.

31. Kapil Bawa and Robert W. Shoemaker, "The Effects of a Direct Mail Coupon on Brand Choice Behavior," *Journal of Marketing Research* 24 (November 1987), 370–376.

32. Daniel Shannon, "Still a Mighty Marketing Mechanism," *Promo,* April 1996, 86.

33. "Checkout: Instant Results," *Promo,* October 1998, 75.

34. Kapil Bawa, Srini S. Srinivasan, and Rajendra K. Srivastava, "Coupon Attractiveness and Coupon Proneness: A Framework for Modeling Coupon Redemption," *Journal of Marketing Research* 34 (November 1997), 517–525.

35. Priya Raghubir, "Coupon Value: A Signal for Price?" *Journal of Marketing Research* 35 (August 1998), 316–324.

36. Russ Bowman and Paul Theroux, *Promotion Marketing* (Stamford, CT: Intertec Publishing Corporation, 2000), 24.

37. Ibid.

38. "When the Chips Are Down," *Promo Magazine Special Report,* April 1998, S7.

39. Bowman and Theroux, *Promotion Marketing,* 24.

40. Kapil Bawa and Robert W. Shoemaker, "Analyzing Incremental Sales from a Direct Mail Coupon Promotion," *Journal of Marketing Research* 53 (July 1989), 66–78.

41. Erwin Ephron, "More Weeks, Less Weight: The Shelf-Space Model of Advertising," *Journal of Advertising Research* 35 (May/June 1995), 18–23.

42. Srini S. Srinivasan, Robert P. Leone, and Francis J. Mulhern, "The Advertising Exposure Effect of Free Standing Inserts," *Journal of Advertising* 24 (spring 1995), 29–40.

43. France Leclerc and John D. C. Little, "Can Advertising Copy Make FSI Coupons More Effective?" *Journal of Marketing Research* 34 (November 1997), 473–484.

44. Bowman and Theroux, *Promotion Marketing,* 24.

45. For a technical analysis of the role of crossruffing, see Sanjay K. Dhar and Jagmohan S. Raju, "The Effects of Cross-Ruff Coupons on Sales and Profits," *Marketing Science* 44 (November 1998), 1501–1516.

46. Bowman and Theroux, *Promotion Marketing,* 24. It is noteworthy that one clearinghouse, CMS, estimates the on-pack redemption rate at 4.7 percent, whereas the other, NCH, estimates it at 11.5 percent. This latter figure seems out of line and perhaps is a misprint.

47. Michael Scroggie, "Online Coupon Debate," *Promo,* April 2000, 53–55.

48. "The Route to Redemption," *Advertising Age,* May 30, 1983, 57.

49. "A Drop in the Crime Rate," *Promo,* December 1997, 12.

50. Cecelia Blalock, "Another Retailer Nabbed in Coupon Misredemption Plot," *Promo,* December 1993, 38.

51. Ibid.

52. Cecelia Blalock, "Tough Sentence for Coupon Middle Man," *Promo,* June 1993, 87.

53. "Clipped, Supermarket Owners Charged with Coupon Fraud," *Promo,* May 1997, 14.

54. "Report: Coupon Scams Are Funding Terrorism," *Promo,* August 1996, 50.

55. "Motivational Skills," *Promo's 9th Annual SourceBook 2002,* 16–18.

56. Dan Hanover, "Not Just for Breakfast Anymore," *Promo,* September 2001, S13–S17.

57. John Palmer, "Still on the Line," *Promo,* December 2000, 73–76.

58. Ibid.

59. Carolyn Shea, "Calling All Cards: Prepaid Phone Cards Are Ringing Up Sales," *Promo,* March 1995, 42.

60. The Clamato case is from ibid. and the others are extracted from Shea, "Calling All Cards: Prepaid Phone Cards Are Ringing Up Sales," 37–46.

61. Fredericks, "What Ogilvy & Mather Has Learned about Sales Promotion."

62. *Consumer Promotion Seminar Fact Book* (New York: Association of National Advertisers, undated), 7.

63. Ronnie Telzer, "Rebates Challenge Coupons' Redeeming Values," *Advertising Age,* March 23, 1987, S18.

64. "With Rebates Aplenty, Car Buyers Are in the Driver's Seat," *U.S. News and World Report,* March 12, 2001, 12.

65. Sholnn Freeman and Joseph B. White, "Auto Price War Persists with GM Expected to Introduce $2002 Cash-Rebate Campaign," *Wall Street Journal Online*, January 3, 2002 (http://online.wsj.com).

66. "Walking the Tightrope," *Promo*, March 2001, 48–51.

67. William M. Bulkeley, "Rebates' Appeal to Manufacturers: Few Consumers Redeem Them," *The Wall Street Journal Interactive Edition*, February 10, 1998.

68. Dilip Soman, "The Illusion of Delayed Incentives: Evaluating Future Effort-Money Transactions," *Journal of Marketing Research* 35 (November 1998), 427–437.

69. Ira Teinowitz and Tobi Elkin, "FTC Cracks Down on Rebate Offers," *Advertising Age*, July 3, 2000, 29.

70. Kerry J. Smith, "Postal Inspectors Target Rebate Fraud," *Promo*, April 1994, 13; Kerry J. Smith, "Marketers Huddle on Rebate Fraud," *Promo*, June 1994, 39.

71. Smith, "Postal Inspectors Target Rebate Fraud."

72. The following examples are from Kerry J. Smith, "The Promotion Gravy Train," *Promo*, August 1995, 51.

73. "Back to Work," *Promo's 9th Annual SourceBook 2002*, 31.

74. "Healthy, Wealthy, and Wiser, *Promo's 8th Annual SourceBook 2001*, 38–39.

75. Glenn Heitsmith, "Botched Pepsi Promotion Prompts Terrorist Attacks," *Promo*, September 1993, 10.

76. Laurie Baum, "How Beatrice Lost at Its Own Game," *Business Week*, March 2, 1987, 66.

77. Ibid.

78. For further reading, see Bob Sperber and Karen Benezra, "A Scam to Go?" *Brandweek*, August 27, 2001, 4, 10; Kat MacArthur, "McSwindle," *Advertising Age*, August 27, 2001, 1, 22, 23; Donald Silberstein, "Managing Promotional Risk," *Promo*, October 2001, 57; "Arch Enemies," *Promo*, December 2001, 17.

79. Kenneth Hein, "Stuff Expander" *Brandweek*, October 22, 2001, 19–20.

80. Bob Hamman, "Forget the Web Ads: Online Promos Capture Attention," *Marketing News*, November 6, 2000, 28–29.

81. Melvin Scales, "What Tie-in Promotions Can Do for You," *Outlook* (a publication of the Promotion Marketing Association of America) 12 (fall 1988), 10–11.

82. "Creating Synergy through Tie-in Promotions," *Marketing Communications*, April 1988, 45.

83. Adapted from Don E. Schultz and William A. Robinson, *Sales Promotion Management* (Lincolnwood, Ill.: NTC Business Books, 1986), 436–445.

84. Sara Owens, "A Different Kind of E-marketing," *Promo*, May 2001, 53–54.

85. This table is an adaptation of ibid., 53.

Chapter Nineteen

MARKETING PUBLIC RELATIONS AND SPONSORSHIP MARKETING

Chapter Objectives

After studying this chapter, you should be able to:

1. Explain the nature and role of marketing public relations (MPR).
2. Distinguish between proactive and reactive MPR.
3. Understand the types of commercial rumors and how to control them.
4. Explain event sponsorships and how to select appropriate events.
5. Explain the nature and role of cause-oriented marketing.

Opening Vignette: A Slam Dunk Choice to Sponsor the Globetrotters

Denny's is a 3,000-plus chain of family restaurants with franchises and company-owned stores located throughout the United States. Denny's restaurants are notable for their brightly hued exteriors, children's menus, and generous portions. Regrettably, Denny's also is known for past incidents of racial discrimination against African American consumers, who in the mid-1990s filed a large class-action suit against the company. Denny's paid millions of dollars in reparations and since then has embarked on a company-wide racial sensitivity program that is a model for other corporations. Though having made amends, Advantica Restaurant Group, the corporate owner of Denny's restaurants, was harmed seriously by past insensitivities committed by a handful of employees.

   In addition to implementing a corporate-wide racial sensitivity program, Denny's made another effort to connect with the African American community as well as nonblack consumers who are equally offended by racial discrimination. Denny's became a sponsor of the Harlem Globetrotters. This famous basketball team was formed in the 1920s and since that time has toured literally around the globe bringing its unique brand of dazzling basketball skills to people worldwide. Bedecked in red and white striped pants and blue jerseys, the Globetrotter players are renowned for their fancy passing, great shooting skills, and an exciting warm-up routine played to the music of "Sweet Georgia Brown." (Forgive me for this personal note, but this old author remembers attending his first Globetrotters game in the mid-1950s along with brother Mac and enjoying the incredible talents of legends Marques Haynes and Meadowlark Lemon.)

   Denny's could not have aligned itself with a better-known and more respected entity. The Globetrotters stand for wholesomeness. Globetrotter players continuously reinforce the message to youth that they must stay in school and avoid drugs. As the sponsor of the team's national tour, which includes hundreds of annual events, Denny's has managed to closely link its name to that of the Globetrotters. In addition to the positive publicity received from constant association with the Globetrotters, Denny's also has leveraged the sponsorship into its advertising and sales promotion efforts—including Globetrotters premium items and sweepstakes that provide children with chances to attend summer basketball camps. Denny's has made an earnest effort to improve its image, and indeed it has.

The *Opening Vignette* illustrates some of the major topics that will be covered in this chapter, which explores the multiple roles performed by the public relations aspect of an integrated marketing communications program. Also examined are the related topics of event and cause marketing as part of the more general practice known as sponsorship marketing. These growing aspects of IMC are concep-

Sources: Adapted from Theresa Howard, "Jumping Through Hoops," *Brandweek*, January 31, 2000; "Diversity at Denny's Restaurant," http://www.pbs.org/als/race/media/dennys.htm.

tually aligned with public relations and in some organizations are administratively part of the public relations department.

THE MPR ASPECT OF GENERAL PUBLIC RELATIONS

Public relations, or PR, is an organizational activity involved with fostering *goodwill* between a company and its various publics. PR efforts are aimed at various corporate constituencies, including employees, suppliers, stockholders, governments, the public, labor groups, citizen action groups, and consumers. As just described, PR involves relations with *all* of an organization's relevant publics. In other words, most PR activities do *not* involve marketing per se but rather deal with general management concerns. This more encompassing aspect of public relations can be called *general PR*.

Our concern in this chapter is only with the narrow aspect of public relations involving an organization's interactions with *consumers*. The marketing-oriented aspect of public relations is called *marketing public relations*, or *MPR* for short.[1]

Though general PR historically played a relatively minor MarCom role, today MPR plays an increasingly important part in organizations' IMC efforts. Whereas advertising messages are paid for by identified sponsor and are regarded by consumers as direct attempts to influence their attitudes and behaviors, MPR messages come across not as advertisements but as unbiased reports from journalists. An MPR message in comparison with an advertisement assumes a mantle of credibility. MPR messages also are considerably less expensive than advertisements because the airtime or newspaper space is provided free of charge by the newspaper, magazine, radio, or television station that prints or airs the message. Hence, for the dual reasons of *high credibility* and *low expense*, MPR messages (and thus the PR departments that produce them) have achieved a more prominent position in firms' IMC efforts. MPR performs a particularly important role in new-product introductions and in overall brand-building efforts.[2]

MPR can be further delineated as involving either proactive or reactive public relations.[3] **Proactive MPR** is dictated by a company's marketing objectives. It is offensively rather than defensively oriented and opportunity seeking rather than problem solving. Proactive MPR is a tool for communicating a brand's merits and is used typically in conjunction with advertising, promotions, and personal selling.

Reactive MPR, by comparison, describes the conduct of public relations in response to outside influences. It is undertaken as a result of external pressures and challenges brought by competitive actions, shifts in consumer attitudes, changes in government policy, or other external influences. Reactive MPR deals typically with changes that have *negative consequences* for an organization. Reactive MPR attempts to repair a company's reputation, prevent market erosion, and regain lost sales.

Proactive MPR

The major role of proactive MPR is in the area of product introductions or product revisions. Proactive MPR is integrated with other IMC tools to give a product additional exposure, newsworthiness, and credibility. This last factor, *credibility*, largely accounts for the effectiveness of proactive MPR. Whereas advertising is sometimes suspect—because we question advertisers' motives, knowing they have a personal stake in persuading us—product announcements by a newspaper editor or television broadcaster are notably more believable. Consumers are less likely to question the motivation underlying an editorial-type endorsement.

Publicity is the major tool of proactive MPR. Like advertising, the fundamental purposes of marketing-oriented publicity are to enhance a brand's equity in a twofold manner: (1) by facilitating brand awareness and (2) by augmenting brand image via forging strong and favorable associations with the brand in the minds of consumers.

Companies obtain publicity using various forms of news releases, press conferences, and other types of information dissemination. News releases concerning new products, modifications in old products, and other newsworthy topics are

RR

Proactive vs Reactive

Differences & tools for each

Sponsorship, Markets

Events & causes-defin

examples of both

delivered to editors of newspapers, magazines, and other media. Press conferences announce major news events of interest to the public. Photographs, tapes, and films are useful for illustrating product improvements, new-product introductions, advanced production techniques, and so forth. Of course, all forms of publicity are subject to the control and whims of the media. However, by disseminating a large volume of publicity materials and by preparing materials that fit the media's needs, a company increases its chances of obtaining beneficial publicity.[4]

Three widely used forms of publicity in MPR are product releases, executive-statement releases, and feature articles.

Product releases announce new products, provide relevant information about product features and benefits, and inform interested listeners/readers how additional information can be obtained. A product release is typically aired on television networks or published in a product section of trade magazines or business publications (such as *Business Week*, *Forbes*, *Fortune*, and the *Wall Street Journal*), in the business or consumer news section of consumer magazines (such as *Time* or *Newsweek*), or in local, national (e.g., *USA Today*), or international papers (e.g., the *International Herald Tribune*).

Audiovisual product releases (called video news releases, or VNRs) have gained wide usage in recent years. For example, Hershey introduced its new Hershey Kisses with almonds by showing a 6-foot, 500-pound replica of a Hershey Kiss covered in gold sequins and foil being dropped from a Times Square building in New York City, reminiscent of New Year's Eve. Hershey's PR agency videotaped the event, distributed tapes to New York networks, and the same evening the event was seen on TV by millions of Americans. For less than $100,000, Hershey's new product received tremendous exposure.

Executive-statement releases are news releases quoting CEOs and other corporate executives. Unlike a product release, which is restricted to describing a new or modified product, an executive-statement release may address a wide variety of issues relevant to a corporation's publics, such as the following:

- Statements about industry developments and trends
- Forecasts of future sales
- Views on the economy
- Comments on R&D developments or market research findings
- Announcements of new marketing programs launched by the company
- Views on foreign competition or global developments
- Comments on environmental issues

Whereas product releases are typically published in the business or product section of a publication, executive-statement releases are published in the *news section*. This location carries with it a significant degree of credibility. Note that any product release can be converted into an executive-statement release by changing the way it is written.

Feature articles are detailed descriptions of products or other newsworthy programs that are written by a PR firm for immediate publication or airing by print or broadcast media or distribution via appropriate Internet sites. Materials such as this are inexpensive to prepare, yet they can provide companies with tremendous access to many potential customers as well as prospective investors.

Reactive MPR

Unanticipated marketplace developments can place an organization in a vulnerable position that demands reactive MPR. Firestone tires—made by Firestone, a U.S. subsidiary of Japan's Bridgestone Corporation—was the focus of negative publicity when Ford Explorer sport utility vehicles fitted with Firestone tires experienced numerous rollover accidents. The particular tire in question was eventually recalled, but both Firestone and the Explorer were subjected to intense public scrutiny and even scorn. Product defects and failures are the most dramatic factors underlying the need for reactive MPR. Following are some illustrations of product crises that have received widespread media attention. The ordering is chronological and ranges from an event occurring back in the early 1980s until a crisis happening some two decades later.

Product Tamperings: Tylenol and Sudafed.

In 1982, seven people in the Chicago area died from cyanide poisoning after ingesting Tylenol capsules. Many analysts predicted that Tylenol would never regain its previously sizable market share. Some observers even questioned whether Johnson & Johnson ever would be able to market anything under the Tylenol name.

Johnson & Johnson's handling of the Tylenol tragedy was nearly brilliant. Rather than denying a problem existed, J&J acted swiftly by removing Tylenol from retail shelves. Spokespersons appeared on television and cautioned consumers not to ingest Tylenol capsules. A tamper-proof package was designed, setting a standard for other companies. As a final good-faith gesture, J&J offered consumers free replacements for products they had disposed of in the aftermath of the Chicago tragedy. Tylenol regained its market share shortly after this campaign began.

In a tragic replay of the Tylenol case, two people in the state of Washington died in 1991 after ingesting cyanide-laced Sudafed capsules. Following Tylenol's lead, Burroughs Wellcome Company, Sudafed's maker, immediately withdrew the product from store shelves, suspended advertising, established an 800-number phone line for consumer inquiries, and offered a $100,000 reward for information leading to the arrest of the product tamperer. Burrough's quick and effective response resulted in only a brief sales slump for Sudafed.[5]

The Perrier Case.

Perrier was the leading brand of bottled water in the United States until 1990 when Source Perrier, the manufacturer, announced that traces of a toxic chemical, benzene, had been found in some of its products. Perrier recalled 72 million bottles from U.S. supermarkets and restaurants and subsequently withdrew the product from distribution elsewhere in the world. The total cost of the global recall was about $166 million. Perrier's sales in the United States declined by 40 percent, and Evian replaced it as the leading imported bottled water.[6] Perrier's business has never fully recovered.

The Pepsi Hoax.

PepsiCo was the target of a hoax when a New Orleans man contacted the Cable News Network and alleged that he had found a syringe in a can of Diet Pepsi. This was only the first of several reported contaminations from different geographical areas. PepsiCo officials, knowing the reports were false and that the Diet Pepsi bottling process was completely safe, reacted to the negative publicity by using the media. A video showing the bottling process of PepsiCo products was released shortly after the initial news broke and was seen by an estimated 187 million viewers. It demonstrated the remote possibility that a foreign object, especially something as large as a syringe, could be inserted in cans in the less than one second they are open for filling and capping. That same day, PepsiCo's president and CEO appeared on ABC's *Nightline* along with the commissioner of the Food and Drug Administration (FDA), Dr. David Kessler. PepsiCo's CEO assured viewers that the Diet Pepsi can was 99.9 percent safe, and the FDA commissioner warned consumers of the penalties for making false claims.

Two days later, Dr. Kessler noted at a news conference that "It is simply not logical to conclude that a nationwide tampering has occurred" and that the FDA was "unable to confirm even one case of tampering." These statements were later broadcast over national TV along with a video news release showing a consumer inserting a syringe into a Diet Pepsi can. She had been caught by the store's surveillance camera. With this exposure, the crisis was essentially over.

PepsiCo ran nationwide newspaper advertisements to assuage any residual consumer fears. The headlines to these full-page ads read: "Pepsi is pleased to announce . . . nothing." The ads proceeded to inform readers that "those stories about Diet Pepsi were simply a hoax. Plain and simple, not true." Although volume case sales dropped 2 percent during the period following the hoax, sales returned to normal in a matter of weeks.[7]

Coke in Europe.

An accident in a Coca-Cola bottling plant in Belgium in 1999 introduced some tainted carbon dioxide into bottles of Coke, and European consumers, mostly in Belgium, reported becoming ill after drinking the product. Coca-Cola's initial response was to deny that its product was at fault, which prompted a public outcry in reaction to this corporate denial and created feelings among consumers that Coca-Cola officials did not care about their health and safety. Media throughout Europe wrote articles asserting that Coca-Cola products had poisoned consumers. Senior officers at Coca-Cola eventually got the message, and its PR people were put to work to offset the considerable damage to Coke's brand equity and profitability. Among other initiatives, the company hired thousands of Belgians to distribute coupons to grocery store shoppers for free 1.5-liter bottles. TV and newspaper ads proclaimed that "Your Coca-Cola is Back." And beach parties (with live music, dance acts, tropical beaches with sand, palm trees, and free Coke) were staged to reach out to thousands of teenage attendees. This incident resulted in millions of dollars of lost revenue, much more than likely would have been lost had the company responded more quickly and apologetically.[8]

Corporate Response and Crisis Management.   As these above examples illustrate, product crises and negative publicity can hit a company at any time. The lesson to be learned is that quick and positive responses to negative publicity are imperative. Negative publicity is something to be dealt with head-on, not denied. When done effectively, reactive MPR can virtually save a brand or a company. A corporate response immediately following negative publicity can lessen the damage that will result, damage such as a diminution in the public's confidence in a company and its products or a major loss in sales and profits. And in the era of the Internet, a company's brand image can be tarnished as the result of a product failure at a rate unprecedented in the pre-Internet age. For further commentary on this point, please see the *Online Focus* as it relates to the Firestone/Ford Explorer debacle.

Just as Ford used the Internet to its advantage in offsetting bad publicity about Firestone tires and the Explorer's rollover accidents (see *Online Focus*), other company's faced with negative publicity must also avail themselves of the power of this medium. One observer has compared the spread of negative product news via the Internet as equivalent to "reverse viral marketing."[9] To offset this "virus," company's can use the Internet to convey their own news in hopes of partially offsetting the negative information about their brands. This is especially important in the present era of great skepticism where consumers have grown increasingly cynical of corporations as result of the shenanigans of companies such as Enron and its auditing firm, Arthur Andersen.

It is important to note, however, that not all consumers are equally swayed by negative publicity about a brand or company. In particular, consumers who hold more positive evaluations of a company are more likely to challenge negative publicity about that company and thus are less likely to experience diminished evaluations following negative publicity. On the other hand, those who are less loyal are especially susceptible to the adverse effects of negative publicity.[10]

The Special Case of Rumors and Urban Legends

You have heard them and probably helped spread them since you were a child in elementary school. They are often vicious and malicious. Sometimes they are just comical. Most always they are false. We are talking about rumors and urban legends. As a technical aside, urban legends and rumors capture slightly different phenomena. Whereas *urban legends* are a form of rumor, they go beyond rumor by transmitting a story involving the use of irony; that is, urban legends convey subtle messages that are in contradiction of what is literally expressed in the story context.[11] As a case in point, consider the following "Gucci Kangaroo" legend:

> *Have you heard about the American tourists who were driving in the outback of Australia? They had been drinking, and it seems that their car hit a kangaroo. Thinking the kangaroo to be dead, the tourists decided to take a gag photograph. They hastily propped the kangaroo up against a fence and dressed it in the driver's Gucci jacket. They proceeded to take photographs of the well-dressed marsupial. Well, it seems that the kangaroo had merely been stunned rather than dead. All of a sudden he revived and jumped away wearing the*

Bad Publicity Spread at the Speed of Fire(stone)

In the wake of news that its 15-inch tires fitted on Ford Explorer SUVs were responsible, at least in part, for hundreds of rollovers and nearly 100 deaths, Bridgestone/Firestone issued a massive recall. This was *not* the first major recall of Firestone tires; in fact, nearly a quarter of century earlier (in 1978) Firestone recalled hundreds of thousands of faulty tires. The damage was relatively minimal in that earlier time, however, perhaps because consumers were unaware of the severity of the problem and due to the hiring of highly respected actor Jimmy Stewart, who appeared in multiple TV commercials publicizing the brand's long history as a successful and trusted company.

Let's now move the calendar forward to August 2000 and Bridgestone/Firestone's recall of 6.5 million Firestone tires in that year. Newspapers, television, and other media constantly reported one rollover accident after another. Officials at Ford denied that that company was at fault and placed the blame squarely on the shoulders of Bridgestone/Firestone. Consumer groups such as the Tire Action Group immediately had a presence on the Internet, and people in chat rooms routinely discussed the Ford Explorer's rollover accidents and the potential fault of Firestone's tires.

With the near-viral proliferation of information made possible via the Internet, it is difficult for companies to control the spread of negative information. According to some observers, the Internet magnifies consumer concerns, thus making it especially difficult to manage bad publicity in the Internet age.

Although Bridgestone/Firestone was incredibly slow to respond to the negative publicity being disseminated, Ford realized the power of the Internet and created a banner ad that it placed on about 200 Web sites with the potential of reaching millions of people. The ad invited viewers to click through to Ford's recall site, which included information about the specific tire models included in the recall, the tire models that were appropriate for replacement, and locations of authorized replacement dealers. The site also provided press releases from Ford and a statement from the company's CEO claiming that Ford does not take lightly its customers' safety and trust.

Whereas Bridgestone/Firestone was slow to react to the negative publicity, Ford adroitly took advantage of the speed and impact of the Internet to offset negative publicity directed toward it. Perhaps the Ford Explorer was itself not free of blame for the numerous rollover accidents, but due in large part to Ford's PR efforts, the general public placed the blame almost exclusively on Firestone. A consultancy firm reported that Firestone's score on a reputation index had plummeted by an amount never before registered in its research on company and brand reputations.

Sources: Adapted from Jean Halliday, "Firestone's Dilemma: Can This Brand Be Saved?" *Advertising Age*, September 4, 2000, I, 54; William H. Holstein, "Guarding the Brand Is Job I," *U.S. News & World Report*, September 11, 2000; Karen Lundegaard, "The Web @ Work? / Ford Motor Company," *Wall Street Journal Online*, October 16, 2000 (http://online.wsj.com).

---

man's jacket, which also contained the driver's license, money, and airline ticket.[12]

Technical distinction noted, we need not get hung up in differentiating between the more general case of rumors and the specific instance of urban legends. Hereafter we will refer simply to rumors in a sense that encompasses urban legends. It further is noteworthy that our interest involves only those rumors that involve products, brands, stores, or other objects of marketing practice. A variety of Internet Web sites focus on rumors and urban legends, and many of these refer to products, technological developments, and even specific brands.[13]

Commercial rumors are widely circulated but unverified propositions about a product, brand, company, store, or other commercial target.[14] Rumors are probably the most difficult problem faced by public relations personnel. What makes rumors so troublesome is that they spread like wildfire and most always state or imply something very undesirable, and possibly repulsive, about the target of the rumor.[15] For example, the rumor spread quickly around the United States that because Mountain Dew is colored with a dye (Yellow 5), drinking the product lowers a man's sperm count. Though untrue, this urban legend influenced teenager's soft drink consumption behavior, with some actually consuming *more* Mountain Dew than normal as a means of birth control and others consuming less for fear that later in life they would not be able to have children.[16]

Consider also the case of the persistent rumor/urban legend that surrounded Procter & Gamble for years. The rumor involved P&G's famous man-in-the-moon logo, which was claimed to be a symbol of the devil. According to the rumormongers, when the stars in the old logo were connected, the number 666 (a symbol of the Antichrist) was formed. Also, the curls in the man-in-the-moon's beard also supposedly formed 666 when held up to a mirror.

Although nonsensical, this rumor spread for years throughout the Midwest and South. P&G eventually decided to drop the old logo and change to a new logo. The new logo retains the 13 stars, which represent the original United States colonies, but eliminates the curly hairs in the beard that appeared to form the number 666.

Following are some other rumors/urban legends you may have heard at one time or another. (Some of these are pretty old, so you might want to ask someone else about them.) None are true, but all have been widely circulated.

- The McDonald's Corporation makes sizable donations to the Church of Satan.
- Wendy's hamburgers contain something other than beef, namely red worms. (Other versions of this rumor have substituted McDonald's or Burger King as the target.)
- Pop Rocks (a carbonated, candy-type product made by General Foods) explode in your stomach when mixed with soda.
- Bubble Yum chewing gum contains spider eggs.
- A woman while shopping in a Kmart store was bitten by a poisonous snake when trying on a coat imported from Taiwan.
- A boy and his date stopped at a Kentucky Fried Chicken (Figure 19.1) restaurant on their way to a movie. Later the girl became violently ill, and the boy rushed her to the hospital. The examining physician said the girl appeared to have been poisoned. The boy went to the car and retrieved an oddly shaped half-eaten piece from the KFC bucket. The physician recognized it to be the remains of a rat. It was determined that the girl died from consuming a fatal amount of strychnine from the rat's body.[17]

Figure 19.1

Kentucky Fried Chicken

© Terri Miller/e-visual Communications

- In what is referred to as the Gerber Myth, thousands of consumers sent letters to a post office box in Minneapolis following a rumor circulating on the Internet (as well as in church bulletins and day-care centers) that Gerber, a baby-food company, was giving away $500 savings bonds as part of a lawsuit settlement. Complying with the rumor's advice, parents mailed copies of their child's birth certificate and Social Security card to the Minneapolis address. For a period of time, the post office box received daily between 10,000 to 12,000 pieces of Gerber Myth mail.[18]

The preceding examples illustrate two basic types of commercial rumors: conspiracy and contamination.[19] **Conspiracy rumors** involve supposed company policies or practices that are threatening or ideologically undesirable to consumers. For example, a conspiracy rumor circulated in New Orleans claiming that the founder of the Popeyes restaurant chain, Al Copeland, supported a reprehensible politician known to have Ku Klux Klan and Nazi connections. Copeland immediately called a press conference, vehemently denied any connections with the politician, and offered a $25,000 reward for information leading to the source of the rumor. This swift response squashed the rumor before it gained momentum.[20]

Another example of a conspiracy rumor involved the little known Brooklyn Bottling Corporation. This company introduced an inexpensive line of soft drinks under the name Tropical Fantasy. Tropical Fantasy quickly gained sales momentum and was heading toward becoming the top-selling brand in small grocery stores in many northeastern markets. But then rumor peddlers went to work. Leaflets started appearing in low-income neighborhoods warning consumers away from Tropical Fantasy and claiming that the brand was manufactured by the Ku Klux Klan and contained stimulants that would sterilize African American men. Angry Tropical Fantasy drinkers threatened distributors with baseball bats and threw bottles at delivery trucks. Some stores stopped accepting shipments. Sales of Tropical Fantasy plummeted.[21]

Contamination rumors deal with undesirable or harmful product or store features. For example, a rumor started in Reno, Nevada, that the Mexican-imported beer Corona was contaminated with urine. A beer distributor in Reno who handled Heineken, a competitive brand, actually had initiated the rumor. Corona sales fell by 80 percent in some markets. The rumor was hushed when an out-of-court settlement against the Reno distributor required a public statement declaring that Corona was not contaminated.

What Is the Best Way to Handle a Rumor? When confronted with a rumor, some companies believe that doing nothing is the best way to handle it. This cautious approach is apparently based on the fear that an antirumor campaign will call attention to the rumor itself.[22]

An expert on rumors claims that rumors are like fires, and, like fires, time is the worst enemy. His advice is to not merely hope that a rumor will simmer down but to combat it swiftly and decisively to *put it out!*[23] Table 19.1 recommends steps for rumor control. It will be worth your time to review these recommendations, though assuredly there is no need to attempt to commit these points to memory.

SPONSORSHIP MARKETING

Sponsorships represent a rapidly growing aspect of marketing communications. Sponsorships involve investments in *events* or *causes* for the purpose of achieving various corporate objectives, especially ones involving increased brand awareness, enhanced brand image, and heightened sales volume.[24] The following definition captures the practice of sponsorship marketing:

> [S]ponsorship involves two main activities: (1) an exchange between a sponsor [such as a brand] and a sponsee [such as a sporting event] whereby the latter receives a fee and the former obtains the right to associate itself with the activity sponsored and (2) the marketing of the association by the sponsor. Both activities are necessary if the sponsorship fee is to be a meaningful investment.[25]

Table 19.1   Recommended Steps for Rumor Control

A. Alert Procedure

1. On first hearing a rumor, note the location and wording of the allegation and target.
2. Keep alert for any other rumors to see if the original report was spurious.
3. more, send requests to distributors, franchise managers, and whoever else meets the public to find out who told the rumor to the person reporting it. It is important to specify the regional boundaries of the problem and the characteristics of the participating population. Distribute forms that can be filled out for the above information, as well as fact sheets rebutting the rumor.
4. Check with competitors to see if they share the problem. Try to find out if the target has moved from your company to them or from them to yours, or if it has spread throughout the industry.

B. Evaluation

1. Check for a drop in sales or a slowdown in sales increase.
2. Monitor person-hours required to answer phone calls and mail.
3. Keep tabs on the morale of the company personnel meeting people in the corporation. Do they feel harassed? Do they feel that management is doing enough to help them?
4. Design a marketing survey to find out what percentage of the public believes any part of the rumor.
5. Make an assessment of the threat or potential threat the rumor poses to profits. Is the corporation in danger of appearing to be an inept, impotent, and passive victim of the rumor problem? How much is management's image affected by the way things are going? The next move is a judgment call. If it seems that something more should be done, then it is time to move to the next phase.

C. Launch a Media Campaign

1. Assemble all facts about the extent of the problem to present to co-workers and superiors. Be prepared for resistance from people who support the myth that "pussyfooting is the best policy."
2. Based on information gathered in the previous phases, decide on the geographical regions for implementing the campaign. If it is a local rumor, treat it locally; if it is a national rumor, treat it nationally.
3. Based on information gathered in the previous phases, decide on the demographic features of the carrying population.
4. Select appropriate media outlets and construct appropriate messages.
5. Decide on what points to refute. (Don't deny *more* than is in the allegation.) If the allegation is of the contamination variety, be careful not to bring up any offensive association or to trigger potential "residuals" in the refutation.
6. Two important points to make in any campaign are that the allegations are *untrue* and *unjust*. It should be implied that the company's business is not suffering, but that "what's right is right" and that people who pass on the rumor are "going against the American sense of fair play!"
7. Line up spokespeople such as scientists, civic and/or religious leaders, rumor experts—whomever you think appropriate—to make statements on the company's behalf.

If all of the above is done properly, the problem is well on the way to being solved.

Source: Fredrick Koenig, *Rumor in the Marketplace: The Social Psychology of Commercial Hearsay* (Dover, MA: Auburn House, 1985), pp. 171–173. © 1985 Auburn House. Reproduced with permission of GREENWOOD PUBLISHING GROUP, INC., Westport, CT.

IMC
focus

Even You Can Be a Sponsee

As previously defined, sponsorship relations involve an exchange between a sponsor and a sponsee whereby the latter receives a fee and the former obtains the right to associate itself with the activity sponsored. Sponsors in the ordinary course of business are companies and their brands, whereas sponsees are athletic, entertainment, festivals, fairs, arts, and other types of events. However, of late there have been cases of enterprising individuals who have placed themselves in the role of sponsee and who have sought and obtained sponsorship funds from businesses. Here are two such examples.

Chris and Luke Go to College
Getting a college education is an expensive proposition. Sometimes parents pay all expenses, but in many other instances students have to work to pay at least part of their educational fees. Two New Jersey high school students (Chris and Luke) decided to attend universities in Southern California. Taking the lead from corporate sponsorships of athletic events, these enterprising guys solicited corporations to foot the bill for their university educations. After approaching a number of companies, First USA—a credit-card division of Bank One Corporation—decided to sponsor Chris's and Luke's educations to the tune of approximately $40,000 each per year! The one-year contractual arrangement gave First USA right of first refusal on subsequent years.

What, as sponsees, did Chris and Luke have to do to earn these sponsorship fees? They first made public appearances wearing First USA–logoed clothing on campus. They also were expected to talk informally with other students throughout the year about financial planning and saving. By contract, each student was required to maintain at least a C grade point average and to adhere to high moral standards. Not a bad deal, for Chris and Luke. You might be thinking, why didn't I come up with this idea?

Sabrina and Tom Tie the Knot
Okay, things really get bizarre now. A Philadelphia couple, Sabrina and Tom, wanted an elegant wedding. But neither they nor their parents could afford the fancy wedding they had in mind—with an expensive wedding dinner, exotic floral arrangements, a luxurious honeymoon, a $1,600 wedding dress, and so on. So they did what any inventive couple would do—they solicited local businesses to pay the price! Their obligation in turn was to thank each of 24 sponsors prior to the first wedding toast and provide publicity for the businesses on the wedding invitations, on cards at the buffet, and on notices on the dinner tables. Does the word *gauche* come to mind?

Event sponsorships range from supporting athletic events (such as golf and tennis tournaments, college football bowl games, and the Olympics) to underwriting rock concerts and supporting festivals and fairs. *Cause-oriented sponsorships* typically involve supporting causes deemed to be of interest to some facet of society, such as environmental protection, wildlife preservation, and raising funds for charities.

At least five factors account for the growth in sponsorships.[26] First, by attaching their names to special events and causes, companies are able to avoid the clutter inherent in advertising media. For example, Visa USA sponsors the Triple Crown of horse racing consisting of the Kentucky Derby, the Preakness, and the Belmont Stakes. Visa's VP of marketing justified this choice on grounds that horse racing is an uncluttered area, thus allowing Visa to receive primary attention from consumers.[27]

Second, sponsorships help companies respond to consumers' changing media habits. For example, with the decline in network television viewing, sponsorships offer a potentially effective and cost-efficient way to reach customers. Third, sponsorships help companies gain the approval of various constituencies, including stockholders, employees, and society at large. Fourth, sponsorship relationships between a brand and an event can serve to enhance a brand's equity.[28]

Finally, the sponsorship of special events and causes enables marketers to target their communication and promotional efforts to specific geographic regions and/or to specific demographic and lifestyle groups. For example, Kodak has been an annual sponsor of the Kodak Albuquerque International Balloon Fiesta. This event attracts thousands of amateur and professional photographers and is thus an ideal venue for creating a strong, positive link with the Kodak name.[29] Similarly, Denny's restaurants' sponsorship of the Harlem Globetrotters (*Opening Vignette*) enables this company to appeal to children of all ages who love the unique style of basketball played by the Globetrotters.

Now that we have overviewed the general features of sponsorship marketing, the following sections detail the practice of event and cause-oriented sponsorships, respectively. First, however, you might want to quickly review the *IMC Focus* for a brief discussion of a couple of bizarre sponsorship relations.

Event Sponsorships

Though relatively small compared to the two major components of the MarCom mix—that is, advertising and promotions—expenditures on event sponsorship are increasing. As shown in Table 19.2, North American marketers in 2001 invested an estimated $9.55 billion in various forms of sponsorship. Roughly two-thirds of this amount ($6.51 billion) went to various sporting events such as motor sports (e.g., NASCAR), golf and tennis, professional sports leagues and teams, and the Olympics. Companies also sponsor entertainment events and tours, festivals and fairs, and the arts. Event sponsorship is practiced worldwide, with total expenditures easily doubling North American spending.[30]

Thousands of companies invest in some form of **event sponsorship,** which is defined as a form of brand promotion that ties a brand to a meaningful athletic, entertainment, cultural, social, or other type of high-interest public activity. Event marketing is distinct from advertising, promotion, point-of-purchase merchandising, or public relations, but it generally incorporates elements from all these communication tools.

Selecting Sponsorship Events.   Marketers sponsor events for purposes of developing relationships with consumers, enhancing brand equity, and strengthening ties with the trade. Successful event sponsorships require a meaningful fit among the brand, the event, and the target market. Budget Rent a Car Corporation, for example, oriented much of its marketing communications efforts toward women—the key decision makers on business car rentals, both as business and leisure travelers and as coordinators of company travel. Accordingly, Budget

Table 19.2   Estimated Sponsorship Spending in North America for 2001

Sponsorship Event/Cause	Amount
Sports	$6.51 billion
Entertainment, tours, and attractions	$893 million
Festivals, fairs, and annual events	$777 million
Causes	$769 million
Arts	$599 million
TOTAL	$9.55 billion

Source: IEG, Inc. in "Getting in on the Action," *PROMO's 9th Annual SourceBook 2002*, 25. Used with permission from PROMO.

became a major sponsor of women's sporting events—the Ladies Professional Golf Association, the Women's Tennis Association, and the Women's Sports Foundation.[31]

What specific factors should a company consider when selecting an event? The following questions represent a good starting point when evaluating whether an event represents a suitable association for a brand:[32]

1. *Is the event consistent with the brand image, and will it benefit the image?* Coleman Company, a maker of grills and other outdoor equipment, sponsors NASCAR races, fishing tournaments, and country music festivals. All these events match Coleman's image. Its sales have increased 50 percent since adopting an event-marketing strategy.[33] Unionbay, a jeans and sportswear brand, along with soft drink brand Mountain Dew and snowboard maker Burton, sponsored the U.S. Open Snowboarding Championships. It would seem that this event matches perfectly the images of all three brands.

2. *Does the event offer a strong likelihood of reaching the desired target audience?* The Old Navy chain of retail clothing stores has sponsored Major League Soccer. The demographics of Old Navy's typical customer match well the characteristics of consumers who both participate in soccer and view it live or on television.[34] H.J. Heinz Company's frozen pizza-flavored snack, Bagel Bites, has sponsored the Winter and Summer X games (X stands for extreme sports) in an appeal to teenagers. This event is just behind the Olympic Games in its appeal to 6- to 17-year-olds.[35] Professional bull riding (yes, there is such a sport) holds a tour that visits more than 70 cities annually. Cowboys from Australia, Brazil, Canada, and the United States compete on the bull-riding tour, and millions of TV viewers and event attendees are loyal followers. Sponsoring companies whose products match well with the demographic and lifestyle profiles of bull-riding enthusiasts include Anheuser-Busch's Bud Light, Carhart work clothing, DeWalt tools, Jack Daniels whiskey, and Wrangler jeans.

3. *Is this event one that the competition has previously sponsored, and is there a risk in sponsoring the event of being perceived as "me-tooistic" and confusing the target audience as to the sponsor's identity?* Sponsor misidentification is not a trivial issue. For example, Coca-Cola paid $250 million to be the official soft drink of the National Football League (NFL) for a five-year period. After sponsoring the NFL for several years, a general survey (not about Coca-Cola per se) asked football fans to name brands that sponsor the NFL. Thirty-five percent of the respondents named Coke as an NFL sponsor. Unfortunately (for Coca-Cola), another 34 percent falsely identified Pepsi-Cola as a sponsor![36]

4. *Is the event cluttered?* Like every "advertising" medium, an event sponsor typically competes for signage and attention from every other company that sponsors the event. It obviously makes little sense to sponsor an event unless live participants and television viewers are likely to notice your brand and associate it with the event that it is paying to sponsor. NASCAR, for example, attracts a large number of sponsors due to the extraordinary growth rate in fan interest. However, recognizing the problem with sponsorship clutter, one observer noted that a brand "can get lost on the bumper" unless it is a prime NASCAR sponsor.[37]

5. *Does the event complement existing sponsorships and fit with other MarCom programs for the brand?* Many brands sponsor multiple events. In the spirit of integrated marketing communications, it is important that these events "speak with a single voice." (If the notion of speaking with a single voice is unclear, please refer back to the IMC discussion in Chapter 1.)

6. *Is the event economically viable?* This last point raises the all-important issue about budget constraints. Companies that sponsor events must support the sponsorships with adequate advertising, point-of-purchase, and publicity.[38] One professional in the sponsorship arena uses the rule of thumb that two to three times the cost of a sponsorship must be spent in properly supporting it and offers the following advice:

A sponsorship is an opportunity to spend money. But like a car without gasoline, sponsorship without sufficient funds to maximize it goes nowhere. Therein lies the biggest secret to successfully leveraging sponsorship: It's not worth spending money for rights fees unless you are prepared to properly support it.[39]

Creating Customized Events.   Firms are increasingly developing their own events rather than sponsoring existing events. For example, managers of the Kibbles and Bits brand of dog food developed the "Do Your Bit for Kibbles and Bits" tour that covered 33 U.S. cities during a three-month period. The event involved having consumers in each of these cities enter their dogs into a competition to determine which dog would be picked for the brand's next TV commercial based on the quality of tricks the dog would perform to receive Kibbles and Bits food. Over 11,000 people attended the event, and 2,500 dogs were entered into the competition. The Kibbles and Bits brand gained anywhere from one to four share points in key markets during this event.[40]

In general, brands are increasingly customizing their own events for at least two major reasons. First, having a customized event provides a brand total control over the event. This eliminates externally imposed timing demands or other constraints and also removes the problem with clutter from too many other sponsors. Also, the customized event is developed to match perfectly the brand's target audience and to maximize the opportunity to enhance the brand's image and sales.

A second reason for the customization trend is that there is a good chance that a specially designed event is more effective but less costly than a preexisting event. For example, being a sponsor of the International Olympic Games cost $40 million in one recent Olympics competition. Many brand managers simply refuse to pay such staggering fees.

It would be simplistic to conclude that brand managers or higher-level marketing executives should eschew sponsoring well-known and prestigious events. Sponsoring the Olympics or another major sporting or entertainment event can greatly enhance a brand's image and boost sales volume. Indeed, successfully achieving a strong link with an event that is highly valued means that the event's stature may transfer at least in some small part to the sponsoring brand. However, achieving such an outcome requires that a strong, durable, and positive link be established between the sponsoring brand and the event.[41] All too often individual brands are swamped by larger and better-known sponsoring brands and no solid or durable link is formed. This being the case, it is doubtful that the sponsorship represents a good return on investment.[42]

Ambushing Events.   In addition to increased customization, a number of companies engage in what is called ambush marketing, or simply ambushing. **Ambushing** takes place when companies that are not official sponsors of an event undertake marketing efforts to convey the impression that they are.[43] For example, research following the Summer Olympics in Atlanta determined that 72 percent of respondents to a survey identified Visa as an official sponsor of the Olympic Games and that 54 percent named American Express as a sponsor. As a matter of fact, Visa paid $40 million to sponsor the Olympics, whereas American Express simply advertised heavily during the telecast of the Olympics.[44] One may question whether it is ethical to ambush a competitor's sponsorship of an event, but a counterargument can easily be made that ambushing is simply a financially prudent way of offsetting a competitor's effort to obtain an advantage over your company or brand. (The ethical aspects of ambushing would make for interesting class discussion.)

Measuring Success.   Whether participating as an official sponsor of an event, customizing your own event, or ambushing a competitor's sponsorship, the results from all these efforts must be measured to determine effectiveness. As always, *accountability* is the key. Sponsorships cannot be justified unless there is proof that brand equity and financial objectives are being achieved. It has been asserted that many sponsorship arrangements involve little more than managerial ego trips—that is, key executives sponsor high-profile events as a means of meeting famous athletes or entertainers and gaining great tickets and luxurious accommodations.[45] Whether this cynical perspective is correct is beyond this text to resolve, but the point to be emphasized is that a brand's welfare cannot be compromised by executive caprice.

As always, measuring whether an event has been successful requires, first, that the brand marketer specify the *objective(s)* that the sponsorship is intended to accomplish. Second, to measure results, there has to be a *baseline* against which to compare some outcome measure. This baseline is typically a premeasure of brand awareness, brand associations, or attitudes prior to sponsoring an event. Third, it is necessary to measure the same variable (awareness, associations, etc.) after the event to determine whether there has been a positive change from the baseline premeasure.

Cause-Related Marketing

A relatively minor but important aspect of overall sponsorships (representing about 8 percent of total sponsorships; see Table 19.2), cause-related marketing involves an amalgam of public relations, sales promotion, and corporate philanthropy. More specifically, **cause-related marketing (CRM)** refers to alliances that companies form with nonprofit organizations to promote their mutual interests. Companies wish to enhance their brands' images and sales, whereas nonprofit partners obtain additional funding by aligning their causes with corporate sponsors. Though CRM was initiated in the United States in the early 1980s, companies throughout the world have become active participants in supporting causes.

Although there are several varieties of cause-related practices, the most common form of CRM arrangement involves a company contributing to a designated cause every time the customer undertakes some action that supports the company and its brands.[46] The company's contribution is, in other words, contingent on the customer performing a behavior (such as buying a product or redeeming a coupon) that benefits the firm. Obviously, firms aligning themselves with particular causes do so partially with philanthropic intentions but also with interest in enhancing their brands' images and, frankly, selling more products, preferably at higher prices. As always, whether cause-related alignments accomplish these goals depends very much on the specifics of the situation—in this case, the nature of the product involved and the magnitude of the contribution offered.[47]

The following examples illustrate how cause-related marketing operates.

- Whirlpool Corporation's KitchenAid division has been a supporter of the Susan G. Komen Breast Cancer Foundation. In a unique program, Whirlpool donated $50 to the Foundation for every purchase of a pink mixer (pink being the symbol for breast cancer awareness) that was purchased via the company's Web site or a toll-free telephone number.[48] The $50 donation represented a generous 17 percent of the revenue Whirlpool obtained for this special-colored mixer priced at $289.99.
- General Mills' Yoplait brand yogurt also supports the Susan G. Komen Breast Cancer Foundation. In its Save Lids to Save Lives promotion, Yoplait made a 10-cent contribution to the Komen Foundation for every lid that consumers mailed back to the company. Millions of lids were redeemed, and Yoplait contributed $1 million to the foundation. Although it is impossible to attribute Yoplait's sales growth exclusively to this CRM effort, the brand has experienced an average 16 percent sales growth for several years, which is spectacular for an established brand.[49]
- In another breast cancer CRM program, Lee Jeans conducted Lee National Denim Day®. Individuals were urged to wear jeans to work on one particular day in October and to donate $5 to the Susan G. Komen Breast Cancer Foundation. Figure 19.2 shows an ad paid for by Lee Jeans. This CRM program is somewhat unconventional in that Lee does not benefit financially; rather, Lee funds a multilayered advertising/marketing/public relations campaign to encourage individuals and their companies to participate. The Komen Foundation receives 100 percent of the donations.

Figure 19.2   Lee Jean's National Denim Day CRM Program

wear jeans *for* life

a life **free** of breast cancer

Lee **National Denim Day** october 5, 2001

© Courtesy of Lee Jeans

- The Campbell Soup Company has for over a quarter century sponsored the Labels for Education program (see Figure 19.3), which helps schools obtain classroom supplies by asking families to collect labels from various Campbell's brands. Since the program began, Campbell has contributed items worth nearly $100 million to schools and organizations in exchange for the millions of labels submitted.[50]
- CRM programs are being offered online as well as promoted through conventional media. One particularly interesting offering is by a new dotcom company named Dan's Chocolates (http://www.dans.com). For every purchase of its chocolate products made online, Dan's donates a percentage (amount unspecified) to a nonprofit organization that the purchaser chooses from a list of organizations partnering with Dan's, including ACCION International, American Forests, America's Second Harvest, CARE, Citizen Schools, Jane Doe, New Orleans Musicians Clinic, and Teach America.
- For each Heinz baby-food label mailed in by consumers, H. J. Heinz Company contributed 6 cents to a hospital near the consumer's home.
- Nabisco Brands donated $1 to the Juvenile Diabetes Foundation for each certificate that was redeemed with a Ritz brand proof of purchase.
- Hershey donated 25 cents to local children hospitals for each Hershey coupon redeemed.

Campbell's Labels for Education CRM Program   **Figure 19.3**

- Reynolds Metals Company, a maker of aluminum foil and other products, contributed 5 cents to local Meals on Wheels programs every time any of three Reynolds brands was purchased.
- Domino's Pizza teamed with Easter Seals in an ambitious CRM effort. Twenty-eight million Domino's Pizza box tops offered customers a coupon worth up to $10 toward the purchase of the electronic game called SimCity 3000. When redeeming coupons, consumers were required to send in $5 donations to Easter Seals.[51]

Though these illustrations are drawn exclusively from the United States, cause-related marketing has spread throughout the world. A survey of 12,000 consumers drawn from 12 European countries revealed that approximately 40 percent of respondents indicated having bought a product because of its links with a worthy cause. In fact, nearly 20 percent of the respondents indicated a willingness to pay a higher price for a product aligned with a good cause.[52] The *Global Focus* describes an interesting CRM program implemented in the United Kingdom.

The Benefits of CRM.   Cause-related marketing is corporate philanthropy based on profit-motivated giving.[53] In addition to helping worthy causes, corporations satisfy their own tactical and strategic objectives when undertaking cause-related efforts. By supporting a deserving cause, a company can (1) enhance its

The Trees for Life CRM

Yorkshire Tea is the best-selling product of a British company named Bettys and Taylors of Harrogate. This company has funded a massive tree-planting program as a means of dealing with soil erosion and forest degradation. It has been responsible for planting more than 1 million trees around the world, with special emphasis on placing trees in developing countries in which its teas are grown. Yorkshire Tea, in a millennium celebration, ran an on-package promotion that had consumers collect tokens from the packages. The company donated £1 to the tree-planting project for every six tokens returned by consumers.

Promotional tokens were placed on 8 million packs of Yorkshire Tea, and nearly 60,000 consumers returned tokens. The funds generated enabled Oxfam—the tree-planting nonprofit organization with which Yorkshire Tea was aligned in the CRM effort—to plant 1.2 million trees in developing countries. The donated funds amounted to a generous 2 percent of Bettys and Taylors after-tax profits. The company's sales and marketing director commented that the program has enhanced Yorkshire Tea's reputation and has enabled it to build long-term relationships with its environmentally conscious customer base, adding that "We know [our customers] see 'good value' in [our company's] 'good values.'"

Source: Adapted from http//www.crm.org.uk/case7.html.

corporate or brand image, (2) thwart negative publicity, (3) generate incremental sales, (4) increase brand awareness, (5) broaden its customer base, (6) reach new market segments, and (7) increase a brand's retail merchandising activity.[54]

Research reveals that consumers have favorable attitudes toward cause-related marketing efforts. According to a Cone/Roper Cause-Related Marketing Report, 83 percent of Americans feel more positive about a company that supports a cause they care about. Moreover, 77 percent of consumers want companies to commit to a cause for a long time rather than conducting short-term promotions with several causes.[55] On the downside, about one-half of the sample in another study expressed negative attitudes toward CRM; this negativity is due in large part to consumers' cynicism about the sponsoring firm's self-serving motive.[56]

The September 11, 2001 terrorist attack on the World Trade Center and Pentagon had a dramatic effect on Americans' expectations about companies' support of causes. The 2001 Cone/Roper Corporate Citizenship Study reported that since the terrorist attacks, more Americans than ever (about 80 percent) believe that companies have a responsibility to support causes. Whereas preceding the attacks, 54 percent of respondents to a March 2001 survey indicated that they would switch brands to support a cause when price and quality were equal, following the attacks, 81 percent of respondents to an October 2001 survey indicated that they would switch brands to support a cause.[57] A spokesperson for the Cone/Roper organization believes that the elevated cause mindedness among both consumers and corporations represents a significant trend rather than a "tragedy-inspired fad."[58] As such, it is obvious that companies will continue to support causes and consumers are likely to be responsive to these CRM efforts, provided, of course, that the sponsoring company and the supported cause fit together in a manner that justifies to consumers the reason for their alignment.

It's a Matter of Fit. How should a company decide what cause to support? Although there are many worthy causes, only a subset is relevant to the interests of any brand and its target audience. Selecting an appropriate cause is a matter of fitting the brand to a cause that is naturally related to the brand's attributes, benefits, or image and also relates closely to the target market's interests.[59] For example, Campbell Soup Company's Labels for Education program beautifully matches the target audience of children and their parents who consume Campbell's branded products displayed in the lower-right corner of Figure 19.3.

Accountability. In the final analysis, brand marketers are obligated to show that their CRM efforts yield sufficient return on investment or achieve other important, nonfinancial objectives. Corporate philanthropy is wonderful, but cause-related marketing is not needed for this purpose—companies can contribute to worthy causes without tying the contribution to consumers' buying a particular brand. However, when employing a cause-related marketing effort, a company intends to accomplish marketing goals (such as improved sales or enhanced image) rather than merely exercising its philanthropic aspirations. Hence, a CRM effort should be founded on specific objectives—just the same as any advertising campaign. Research—such as a pre- and posttest, as described for event sponsorships—is absolutely essential to determine whether a CRM effort has achieved its objective and is thereby strategically and financially accountable.

Colgate-Palmolive has applied a straightforward formula in measuring the effectiveness of one of its sponsorships in which the CRM program is based on consumers redeeming freestanding inserts. Using scanner data, Colgate compares product sales in the three weeks following a coupon drop with the average sales for the preceding six months. The difference between these two sales figures is multiplied by the brand's net profit margin, and the event's cost on a per-unit basis is subtracted to determine the incremental profit.[60]

SUMMARY

This chapter covered two major topics: marketing public relations and sponsorship marketing. Public relations (PR) entails a variety of functions and activities that are directed at fostering harmonious interactions with an organization's public (customers, employees, stockholders, governments, and so forth). An important distinction was made between general public relations (general PR), which deals with overall managerial issues and problems (such as relations with stockholders and employees), and marketing public relations (MPR). The chapter focused on MPR.

Marketing PR consists of proactive MPR and reactive MPR. Proactive MPR is an increasingly important tool in addition to advertising and promotions for enhancing a brand's equity and market share. Proactive MPR is dictated by a company's marketing objectives. It seeks opportunities rather than solves problems. Reactive MPR responds to external pressures and typically deals with changes that have negative consequences for an organization. Handling negative publicity and rumors are two areas in which reactive PR is most needed.

The other major topic covered in this chapter was sponsorship marketing. Sponsorships involve investments in events and causes to achieve various corporate objectives. Event marketing is a rapidly growing facet of marketing communications. Though small in comparison with advertising and other major promotional elements, expenditures on event promotions exceeded $9 billion in 2001. Event marketing is a form of brand promotion that ties a brand to a meaningful athletic, entertainment, cultural, social, or other type of high-interest public activity. Event marketing is growing because it provides companies with alternatives to the cluttered mass media, an ability to segment on a local or regional basis, and opportunities for reaching narrow lifestyle groups whose consumption behavior can be tied to the local event.

Cause-related marketing (CRM) is a relatively minor aspect of overall sponsorship but a practice that is perhaps more important than ever, especially in the wake of the terrorist attacks on September 11, 2001. Although there are several varieties of CRM programs, the distinctive feature of the most common form of CRM is that a company's contribution to a designated cause is linked to customers engaging in revenue-producing exchanges with the firm. Cause-related marketing serves corporate interests while helping worthy causes.

Find more resources to help you study at http://shimp.swcollege.com!

Chapter Twenty

REGULATORY, ETHICAL, AND "GREEN" ISSUES IN MARKETING COMMUNICATIONS

Chapter Objectives

After studying this chapter, you should be able to:

1. Explain the role and importance of governmental efforts to regulate marketing communications.
2. Understand deceptive advertising and the three elements that guide the determination of whether a particular advertisement is potentially deceptive.
3. Explain the regulation of unfair business practices and the three major areas where the unfairness doctrine is applied.
4. Understand the role of the states in regulating unfair or deceptive marketing communications practices.
5. Understand the process of advertising self-regulation.
6. Appreciate the ethical issues in marketing communications.
7. Explain why the targeting of products and marketing communications is a heatedly debated practice.
8. Appreciate the role of marketing communications in green marketing.
9. Understand the principles that apply to all environmental (green) marketing efforts.

Opening Vignette: The American Association of Advertising Agencies' Code of Ethical Standards

The American Association of Advertising Agencies (AAAA, or 4A's), which was founded in 1917, is the national trade association representing the advertising agency business in the United States. AAAA member organizations are responsible for creating approximately three-quarters of the total advertising volume placed nationwide by ad agencies. The mission of the AAAA organization is to improve and strengthen the ad agency business, to advocate advertising, to influence public policy, to resist advertising-related legislation that it regards as unwise or unfair, and to work with governmental regulators with the goal of achieving desirable social and civic goals.

The AAAA promulgated a code of high ethical standards in 1924, which was revised in 1990. It is presented here in verbatim form because it represents, on the one hand, a set of lofty goals for the advertising industry and, on the other, a framework that relates to many of the issues discussed in this chapter.

> *We, the members of the American Association of Advertising Agencies, in addition to supporting and obeying the laws and legal regulations pertaining to advertising, undertake to extend and broaden the application of high ethical standards. Specifically, we will not knowingly create advertising that contains:*
>
> a. *False, or misleading statements or exaggerations, visual or verbal*
> b. *Testimonials that do not reflect the real opinion of the individual(s) involved*
> c. *Price claims that are misleading*
> d. *Claims insufficiently supported or that distort the true meaning or practicable application of statements made by professional or scientific authority*
> e. *Statements, suggestions, or pictures offensive to public decency or minority segments of the population.*
>
> *We recognize that there are areas that are subject to honestly different interpretations and judgement [sic]. Nevertheless, we agree not to recommend to*

an advertiser, and to discourage the use of, advertising that is in poor or questionable taste or that is deliberately irritating through aural or visual content or presentation.

Comparative advertising shall be governed by the same standards of truthfulness, claim substantiation, tastefulness, etc., as apply to other types of advertising.

These Standards of Practice of the American Association of Advertising Agencies come from the belief that sound and ethical practice is good business. Confidence and respect are indispensable to success in a business embracing the many intangibles of agency service and involving relationships so dependent upon good faith.

Clear and willful violations of these Standards of Practice may be referred to the Board of Directors of the American Association of Advertising Agencies for appropriate action, including possible annulment of membership as provided by Article IV, Section 5, of the Constitution and By-Laws.

This chapter examines three interrelated issues: the regulation of MarCom activities, ethics in marketing communications, and environmentally oriented, or "green," MarCom practices. To appreciate the importance of these topics and their interrelatedness, consider the following scenario. Though this set of circumstances pales in comparison to the Enron scandal that has received widespread journalistic coverage and close governmental scrutiny, it nonetheless is a situation that is not unlike the decisions many businesspeople make on a regular basis.

Imagine you are the vice president of marketing and sales for the consumer products division of a large chemical company. One of your products, plastic trash bags, is likely to experience lost sales because your competitors are promoting their brands as degradable. To nontechnical consumers, the word *degradable* implies that these trash bags literally disintegrate within a relatively short period after they leave the consumer's curbside and are buried in a landfill. Although these bags *are* photodegradable (they will degrade if left out in the sun and rain for an extended period), you know they are *not* biodegradable. That is, they will not disintegrate when placed in landfills, rather, like most everything else that is buried in landfills, these so-called degradable bags will remain intact for decades.

You know your own yet-to-be introduced degradable brand is not biodegradable either. However, your regular brand of nondegradable trash bags may lose shelf space to competitive brands and sales to environmentally concerned consumers who think they are serving the environment by using your competitors' degradable bags. You could introduce a photodegradable bag, but you know that it, like the competitors' bags, is not truly degradable and will not solve the solid waste problem. Hence, if you introduce a new bag labeled degradable, you can prevent potential lost sales to competitors, but at the same time you will be misleading consumers into thinking that they are purchasing a truly degradable bag.

What would you do if you were placed in this position? Would you introduce your own brand of degradable trash bag, or would you be willing to suffer the consequences of lost sales to unethical competitors? Perhaps available to you are alternatives other than the choice between merely introducing versus not introducing a degradable bag. Before reading on, think about what you would have done if you had been the key decision maker in this situation. Think about the consequences of your decision for your company, its employees, and for your career. Attempt, as best you can, to balance idealistic and practical considerations. Write down what you would do, and justify your choice.

The situation just described is not hypothetical. Something very similar to this confronted the Mobil Chemical Company at a time when American consumers' concerns about environmental protection were elevated over their prior take-the-environment-for-granted mind-set. Concurrently, many marketers were beginning to respond to consumers' concerns, sometimes in exploitative ways. Mobil's brand of regular Hefty trash bags was, in fact, losing shelf space in supermarkets and experiencing lost sales to brands such as First Brands' degradable Glad bags. Nonetheless, Mobil fully recognized that degradable bags were no panacea. Mobil's general manager of solid waste management solutions stated, "Mobil has concluded that biodegradable plastics will *not* [emphasis added] help solve the solid waste problem."[1]

This acknowledgment notwithstanding, Mobil introduced its own line of degradable trash bags. No advertising was undertaken; rather, the promotional burden fell entirely on the Hefty package itself. The package was labeled Hefty® Degradable*, with the asterisk qualifying the degradable property as photodegradable ("*Activated by Exposure to the Elements"). The package front included a scene of a pine tree with bright sunlight shining through and an osprey preparing to land on the tree—all presumably chosen as emblematic of the implied claim that Hefty bags are themselves compatible with the environment. The back of the package made additional claims about the degradability of Hefty trash bags.

Shortly after Mobil introduced Hefty® Degradable, the Federal Trade Commission requested both Mobil and First Brands (Glad bags) to provide substantiation for the degradability claims. Within a year Mobil voluntarily decided to discontinue using degradability claims on its trash bag packages. Nonetheless, several months later the attorneys general of seven states (California, Massachusetts, Minnesota, New York, Texas, Washington, and Wisconsin) brought suits against Mobil on grounds that it had engaged in deceptive communications and consumer fraud by falsely claiming that trash bags degrade in landfills. Although refusing to admit wrongdoing, Mobil settled the suits out of court and arranged to pay the states an agreed-on sum to fund environmental educational programs.[2]

This case encapsulates much of the material covered in this chapter. In particular, the chapter addresses three major topics: (1) the *regulation* of marketing communications practices, (2) *ethical issues* in marketing communications, and (3) *environmental matters* and their implications for marketing communications. All three topics are interrelated: Ethical issues confronting contemporary marketing communicators sometimes occur over environmental marketing efforts, and regulation (from federal and state governmental bodies and by industry self-regulators) is needed due in large part to unethical marketing communications practices.[3]

REGULATION OF MARKETING COMMUNICATIONS

Advertisers, sales promotion managers, and other MarCom practitioners are faced with a variety of regulations and restrictions that influence their decision-making latitude. The history of the past century has shown that regulation is necessary to protect consumers and competitors from fraudulent, deceptive, and unfair practices that some businesses choose to perpetrate. In market economies there is an inevitable tension between the interests of business organizations and the rights of consumers. Regulators attempt to balance the interests of both parties while ensuring that an adequate level of competition is maintained.

When Is Regulation Justified?

Strict adherents to the ideals of free enterprise would argue that government should rarely if ever intervene in the activities of business. However, more moderate observers believe that regulation is justified in certain circumstances. Regulation is perhaps needed most *when consumer decisions are based on false or limited information.*[4] Under such circumstances, consumers are likely to make decisions they would not otherwise make and, as a result, incur economic, physical, or psychological injury. Competitors also are harmed because they lose business they might have otherwise enjoyed.

In theory, regulation is justified if the *benefits realized exceed the costs*. What are the benefits and costs of regulation?[5] Regulation offers three major benefits: First, *consumer choice* among alternatives is improved when consumers are better informed in the marketplace. For example, consider the Alcoholic Beverage Labeling Act, which requires manufacturers to place the following warning on all containers of alcoholic beverages:

GOVERNMENT WARNING: (1) According to the Surgeon General, women should not drink alcoholic beverages during pregnancy, due to the risk of birth defects. (2) Consumption of alcoholic beverages impairs your ability to drive a car or operate machinery, and may cause health problems.[6]

This regulation serves to inform consumers that drinking has negative consequences. Pregnant women can help themselves and especially their unborn children by heeding this warning to refrain from drinking alcoholic beverages.[7] It is unlikely, however, that warning labels alone have a major impact in curbing drinking among pregnant women.[8]

A second benefit of regulation is that when consumers become better informed, *product quality tends to improve* in response to consumers' changing needs and preferences. For example, when consumers began learning about the dangers of fat and cholesterol, manufacturers started marketing healthier food products. When regulators prevented makers of aspirin and analgesic products from making outrageously false and misleading claims, companies introduced new alternatives such as Tylenol, Advil, Motrin, and Aleve as a means of taking market share away from entrenched aspirin brands.[9]

A third regulatory benefit is *reduced prices* resulting from a reduction in a seller's "informational market power." For example, prices of used cars undoubtedly would fall if dealers were required to inform prospective purchasers about a car's defects, because consumers would not be willing to pay as much for automobiles with known problems.

Regulation is not costless. Companies often must incur the *cost of complying* with a regulatory remedy. For example, U.S. cigarette manufacturers are required to rotate over the course of a year four different warning messages for three months each. Obviously, this is more costly than the previously required single warning message. *Enforcement costs* incurred by regulatory agencies and paid for by taxpayers represent a second cost category. The *unintended side effects* that might result from regulations represent a third cost to both buyers and sellers.

There are a variety of potential side effects from regulatory efforts that are unforeseen at the time legislation is written. For example, a regulation may unintentionally harm sellers if buyers switch to other products or reduce their level of consumption after regulation is imposed. The cost to buyers may increase if sellers pass along, in the form of higher prices, the costs of complying with a regulation.

In sum, regulation is theoretically justified only if the benefits exceed the costs. The following sections examine the two forms of regulation that affect many aspects of marketing communications: governmental regulation and industry self-regulation.

Regulation of Marketing Communications by Federal Agencies

Governmental regulation takes place at both the federal and state levels. All facets of marketing communications are subject to regulation, but advertising is the one area in which regulators have been most active. This is because advertising is the most conspicuous aspect of marketing communications. The discussion that follows examines federal governmental regulation of advertising in the United States. Readers who wish to know more about advertising regulation in European Union countries are directed to the source cited in the following endnote.[10]

The Federal Trade Commission (FTC) is the U.S. government agency with primary responsibility for regulating advertising at the federal level. The FTC was created in 1914 principally to prevent anticompetitive practices — that is, it functioned to protect businesses rather than consumers. By 1938, Congress realized that the FTC's mandate should be expanded to offer more assistance to consumers as well as businesses, especially in the area of false and misleading advertising. The Wheeler-Lea Amendment of 1938 accomplished this objective by changing a principal section of the original FTC Act of 1914 from "unfair methods of competition" to "unfair methods of competition and unfair or deceptive acts or practices in commerce." This seemingly minor change enhanced the FTC's regulatory powers appreciably and provided a legal mandate for the FTC to protect consumers against fraudulent business practices. The FTC's regulatory authority cuts across three broad areas that directly affect marketing communicators: deceptive advertising, unfair practices, and information regulation.

Regulation of Deceptive Advertising.

In a general sense, consumers are deceived by an advertising claim or campaign when (1) the impression left by the claim or campaign is false — that is, there is a *claim-fact discrepancy*, and (2) the false claim or campaign is *believed* by consumers. The important point is that a false claim is not necessarily deceptive by itself. Rather, consumers must believe a claim to be deceived by it: "A false claim does not harm consumers unless it is believed, and a true claim can generate harm if it generates a false belief."[11]

Although the FTC makes deception rulings case by case, it does employ some general guidelines in deciding whether deceptive advertising has occurred. Deception policy at the FTC is not inscribed in granite but rather is subject to shifts, depending on the regulatory philosophy of different FTC chairpersons and the prevailing political climate. The current deception policy declares that the FTC will find a business practice deceptive "if there is a representation, omission or practice that is likely to mislead the consumer acting reasonably in the circumstances, to the consumer's detriment."[12] The three elements that follow provide the essence of this policy.[13]

1. *Misleading:* There must be a representation, omission, or a practice that is likely to mislead the consumer. A *misrepresentation* is defined by the FTC as an express or implied statement contrary to fact, whereas a *misleading omission* is said to occur when qualifying information necessary to prevent a practice, claim, representation, or reasonable expectation or belief from being misleading is *not* disclosed.

2. *Reasonable consumer:* The act or practice must be considered from the perspective of the reasonable consumer. The FTC's test of reasonableness is based on the consumer's interpretation or reaction to an advertisement — that is, the commission determines the effect of the advertising practice on a reasonable member of the group to which the advertising is targeted. The following quote indicates that the FTC evaluates advertising claims case by case in view of the target audience's unique position — its education level, intellectual capacity, mental frame, and so on.

   > For instance, if a company markets a cure to the terminally ill, the practice will be evaluated from the perspective of how it affects the ordinary member of that group. Thus, terminally ill consumers might be particularly susceptible to exaggerated cure claims. By the same token, a practice or representation directed to a well-educated group, such as a prescription drug advertisement to doctors, would be judged in light of the knowledge and sophistication of that group.[14]

3. *Material:* The representation, omission, or practice must be material. A *material representation* involves information that is important to consumers and that is likely to influence their *choice* or *conduct* regarding a product. In general, the FTC considers information to be material when it pertains to the central characteristics of a product or service (including performance features, size, and price). Hence, if an athletic-shoe company falsely claimed that its brand possesses the best shock absorption feature on the market, this would be a material misrepresentation to the many runners who make purchase choices based on this factor. On the other hand, for this same company to falsely claim that it has been in business for 25 years — when in fact it has been in business for only 22 years — likely would not be regarded as material because most consumers would not make a purchase choice based on this claim.

An important case involving the issue of materiality was brought by the FTC against Kraft Foods and its advertising of Kraft Single American cheese slices.[15] The FTC challenged Kraft on grounds that advertisements for Kraft Singles falsely claimed that each slice contains the same amount of calcium as *five* ounces of milk. In fact, each slice of Kraft Singles begins with five ounces of whole milk, but during processing 30 percent, or 1.5 ounces of milk, is lost. In other words, each slice contains only 70 percent of the amount of calcium claimed in Kraft's advertisements.[16] Kraft responded that its $11 million advertising campaign did not influence consumer purchases. Kraft's legal counsel argued that the advertisements (1) did not convey the misleading representation claimed by the FTC, but (2) even if this representation had been conveyed, it would not have mattered because calcium is a relatively unimportant factor in consumers' decision to purchase Kraft Singles. (Out of nine factors rated by consumers in a copy test, calcium was rated no higher than seventh.)

Whereas the FTC's position was that Kraft's advertising was likely to mislead consumers, Kraft's defense was that its calcium claim, whether false or not, is nondeceptive because the difference between 5 ounces of milk and 3.5 ounces is an immaterial difference to consumers. Or, in other words, Kraft's defense amounted to the following: Yes, we (Kraft) made claims about the calcium benefits of Kraft Singles, but the issue of deceptiveness is moot because the difference in calcium content between what we claimed (a single slice contains the calcium equivalency of 5 ounces of milk) and what is reality (a single slice contains the calcium equivalency of 3.5 ounces of milk) is immaterial to consumers and hence not deceptive.

After hearing detailed testimony on the matter and following an appeal process, the five commissioners of the FTC determined that Kraft's advertising claim was indeed material.[17] Accordingly, the FTC ordered Kraft to cease and desist (literally, "stop and go no more," or discontinue) further misrepresentations of Kraft Singles' calcium content. The Kraft case has generated much discussion and controversy. The articles cited in the following endnote are worthwhile reading for this particular case as well as its broader significance for advertising practice and public policy involving deceptive advertising.[18] The *Online Focus* describes efforts to prevent deceptive e-mailing.

Regulation of Unfair Practices. As noted at the beginning of this section, the Wheeler-Lea Amendment of 1938 gave the Federal Trade Commission authority to regulate unfair as well as deceptive acts or practices in commerce. Unfairness is necessarily a somewhat vague concept. For this reason, the unfairness doctrine received limited use by the FTC until 1972, when in a famous judicial decision (*FTC v. Sperry & Hutchinson Co.*) the Supreme Court noted that consumers as well as businesses must be protected from unfair trade practices.[19] Unlike deception, a finding of unfairness to consumers may go beyond questions of fact and relate merely to public values.[20] The criteria used to evaluate whether a business act is unfair involve such considerations as whether the act (1) offends public policy as it has been established by statutes, (2) is immoral, unethical, oppressive, or unscrupulous, and (3) causes substantial injury to consumers, competitors, or other businesses.[21]

The Federal Trade Commission's right to regulate unfair advertising was a matter of considerable dispute for years, because the precise meaning of "unfair" was not clear.[22] The dispute was ended in 1994 when Congress devised a definition of unfairness that is satisfactory to all parties. **Unfair advertising** is defined as "acts or practices that cause or are likely to cause *substantial injury to consumers*, which is *not reasonably avoidable* by consumers themselves and *not outweighed by countervailing benefits to consumers or competition*" (emphasis added).[23] The italicized features of the definition point out Congress's intention to balance the interests of advertisers with those of consumers and to prevent capricious applications of the unfairness doctrine by the FTC.

The FTC has applied the unfairness doctrine in three major areas: (1) advertising substantiation, (2) promotional practices directed to children, and (3) trade regulation rules.

1. *Advertising substantiation:* The ad substantiation program is based on a simple premise: It is unfair for advertisers to make claims about their products without having a *reasonable basis* for those claims. According to the FTC, unfairness results from imposing on the consumer the unavoidable economic risk that a product may not perform as advertised. The ad substantiation program thus requires advertisers to have documentation in the form of test results or other data that verifies that the advertised claim is based on fact rather than supposition.[24]

Be Gone Junk E-mail

In Chapter 14 we discussed the practice of opt-in, or permission, e-mailing and also the unacceptable form of e-mail known as spam. Spam represents a blight on the Internet medium and a major source of irritation to millions of people who are subjected to unwanted, and sometimes deceptive messages. The Federal Trade Commission recently undertook aggressive action against deceptive spam. This action resulted from a so-called sting operation by the FTC that detected widespread spam scams. One spam scam was a chain-letter e-mail message sent to thousands of people promising the message recipients they could earn thousands of dollars simply by mailing $5 to each of the four or five people named at the top of the list. They were informed that their names would eventually reach the top of the chain-letter list and that people then would mail batches of $5 to them.

The FTC sent letters to 1,000 spam scammers that informed them that these chain letters were illegal and they must discontinue the practice. A year later the FTC's online search revealed that the practice remained prevalent. At this point the FTC set up undercover post office boxes and e-mail accounts in a sting operation. FTC investigators mailed $5 to individuals who had been warned the previous year to discontinue the practice. Those eventually caught participating in the spam scam were charged and required to return money received from people who had participated in the chain-letter activity. The FTC chairman commented that e-mail spam is "intrusive, unwelcome, annoying, [and illegal]. We want to send a message [that the FTC] is going after deceptive spam and the people who send it. We want if off the Net." Stamping out false e-mail advertising has become one of the FTC's major programs.

In addition to the FTC's proactive efforts to rid the Internet of deceptive spam messages, individual states are becoming vigilant in policing the practice. For example, a state law in California requires spammers to identify their e-mail messages as advertisements and to provide recipients ways to get off mailing lists.

Sources: Jeff Bater, "U.S. Regulators Crack Down on E-Mail Chain-Letter Scam," *Wall Street Journal Interactive Edition*, February 12, 2002 (http://online.wsj.com); Christopher Saunders, "FTC to Pursue Deceptive E-mail Advertisers," February 1, 2002 (http:///www.internetnews.com/IAR/article/0,,12_967151,00.html); "California Appeals Court Upholds Law Regulating Unsolicited E-Mail," January 4, 2002 (http://online.wsj.com).

The FTC charged Walgreen, a large retail drugstore chain, with making unsubstantiated claims for Advil pain reliever. Walgreen had advertised Advil as a "prescription pain reliever . . ." and "an anti-inflammatory . . . source of comfort for people who experience arthritis pain." The FTC ruled that Walgreen did not have a reasonable basis for this claim. The case was dropped when Walgreen consented not to make unsubstantiated claims for Advil or other analgesic drug products.[25]

2. *Unfairness involving children:* Because children are more credulous and less well-equipped than adults to protect themselves, public-policy officials are especially concerned with protecting youngsters. When applied to cases involving children, the unfairness doctrine is especially useful because many advertising claims are not deceptive per se but are nonetheless potentially unethical, unscrupulous, or inherently dangerous to children. For example, the FTC considered one company's use of Spider-Man vitamin advertising unfair because such advertising was judged capable of inducing children to take excessive and dangerous amounts of vitamins.[26]

3. *Trade regulation rules:* Whereas most Federal Trade Commission actions are taken on a case-by-case basis, the use of trade regulation rules (TRRs) enables the FTC to issue a regulation that restricts an *entire industry* from some unfair and objectionable practice. For example, the FTC issued a TRR to vocational schools requiring the schools to disclose enrollment and job placement statistics in their promotional materials.[27]

The FTC has used industry-wide trade regulation rules sparingly. However, some government officials, perhaps especially Senator Hillary Clinton, want new legislation passed that would empower the FTC to prepare industry-wide rules against unfair marketing and advertising practices directed at children. Senator Clinton and other critics are concerned that young children, including preschoolers, are inundated with advertising and promotions that unfairly influence their behavior and complicate parent-child relations by encouraging children to nag their parents into buying items. Clinton's proposal would give the FTC authority to ban all ad messages aimed at preschoolers and all marketing in elementary schools.[28]

Information Regulation.   Although the primary purpose of advertising regulation is the prohibition of deceptive and unfair practices, regulation also is needed at times to provide consumers with information they might not otherwise receive.[29] The corrective advertising program is the most important of the FTC's information provision programs.[30]

Corrective advertising is based on the premise that a firm that misleads consumers should have to use future advertisements to rectify the deceptive impressions it has created in consumers' minds. Corrective advertising is designed to prevent a firm from continuing to deceive consumers rather than to punish the firm.

The most prominent corrective advertising order issued by the FTC involved Warner-Lambert's Listerine mouthwash. According to the FTC, Warner-Lambert had misled consumers for a number of years and required them to run this corrective statement: "Listerine will not help prevent colds or sore throats or lessen their severity." The corrective campaign ran for 16 months at a cost of $10.3 million to Warner-Lambert, most of which was spent on television commercials.

Several studies evaluated the effectiveness of the Listerine corrective advertising order.[31] The FTC's own study revealed only partial success for the Listerine corrective campaign. On the positive side, there was a 40 percent drop in the amount of mouthwash used for the misconceived purpose of preventing colds and sore throats; on the negative side, 57 percent of Listerine users continued to rate cold and sore throat prevention as a key factor in their purchasing decision (only 15 percent of Scope users reported a similar goal), and 39 percent of Listerine users reported continued use of the mouthwash to relieve or prevent a cold or sore throat.

In the first case of corrective advertising in 25 years since Listerine mouthwash, the FTC issued a corrective order against the Novartis Corporation and its Doan's Pills. Doan's advertisements referred to the brand's special or unique ingredients, called itself the "back specialist," and in a comparative format (as discussed in Chapter 10) depicted the brand against packages of competitors Advil, Bayer, and Tylenol. The FTC concluded that the advertising campaign created the false impression that Doan's was more effective than other over-the-counter drugs for combating back pain. The FTC ordered Novartis to undertake an $8 million advertising campaign to correct the misimpression among consumers that Doan's Pills outperform other over-the-counter analgesics in treating back pain. This order required Doan's packaging and advertising to carry the message, "Although Doan's is an effective pain reliever, there is no evidence that Doan's is more effective than other pain relievers for back pain." Novartis' legal counsel claimed the order was excessive, whereas others have appraised the order as an inadequate remedy in the face of compelling evidence that Doan's advertising was deceptive.[32]

The FTC walks a fine line when issuing a corrective advertising order and specifying the remedial action a deceptive advertiser must take. The objective is to restore the marketplace to its original position prior to the deceptive advertising so that a firm does not continue to reap the rewards from its past deception. However, there is always the possibility that the corrective advertising effort may go too far and severely damage the firm and perhaps, unintentionally, hurt other companies in the industry.[33]

Regulation of Product Labeling.   The Food and Drug Administration (FDA) is the federal body responsible for regulating information on the packages of food and drug products. The FDA was inactive for many years until a new director of the agency in the early 1990s took action against Procter & Gamble's Citrus Hill brand of concentrated orange juice. Citrus Hill's package falsely represented the brand as being fresh orange juice when in fact the product is concentrated. The FDA made a point of showing its revived regulatory vigilance by literally seizing 2,000 cases of Citrus Hill orange juice from a Minnesota warehouse. Just two days after the FDA action, P&G agreed to remove all references to "fresh" from its packaging.[34] The action against P&G's Citrus Hill had strong symbolic impact and notified other marketers that the FDA was prepared to vigorously regulate deceptive and misleading package labeling.

Regulation of Prescription Drug Advertising.   Whereas the Federal Trade Commission is responsible for regulating deceptive and unfair advertising for all products (including over-the-counter drugs), the Food and Drug Administration is charged with regulating advertisements for *prescription drugs*. This has been a major challenge in recent years with the onset of direct-to-consumer (DTC) advertising, which began in the United States in 1997. As the name suggests, this form of advertising involves messages for prescription drugs that are directed to consumers. Pharmaceutical companies expect DTC ads to motivate consumers to urge their physicians to prescribe advertised drug brands. The FDA's role is, in this regard, to police the truthfulness of DTC ads and to ensure that any claims made by prescription drug advertisers are supported by science.

The FDA requires prescription drug advertisers to present a *balanced perspective* when advertising drugs. That is, in addition to touting product benefits, they must also identify the side effects and risks of using particular drugs. You may have noticed that TV commercials for DTC drugs show how wonderful a drug is in treating arthritis, weight problems, or other health issues only at the end of the commercial to note that in using the drug one may experience nausea, diarrhea, reduced sexual functioning, or any of a number of other undesirable side effects. Drug companies would prefer not to mention these effects, but doing so is required—for the protection of consumers in the best spirit of regulation.

In the case of TV advertising, pharmaceutical companies are required to mention side effects only in full-length commercials. Hoffman-LaRoche Inc., the makers of weight-loss drug Xenical, came up with a strategy for avoiding the regulation by putting together two shorter commercials separated by an unrelated commercial for another product. The first commercial showed an image of a baby morphing into a heavyset woman without mentioning the name Xenical—thus avoiding the full-length commercial status. The second ad, which appeared after an unrelated product, used the same images and music and mentioned the drug's name, but this ad stated nothing about losing weight, thus again avoiding being considered a full-length commercial. Taken together, these ads lasted 45 seconds, which is as long as many full-length prescription drug ads; however, side effects were never mentioned. Xenical thus avoided the letter of the law, but the FDA has looked unkindly on this maneuver.[35] This case illustrates the constant tension between regulator and "regulatee." The makers of Xenical do not want to mention the unpleasant side effects from using this product, whereas the FDA regards this information as critically important to consumers in making rational judgments as to whether to request their physicians to prescribe the drug.

Regulation of Marketing Communications by State Agencies

Individual states have their own statutes and regulatory agencies to police the marketplace from fraudulent business practices. Most, if not all, states have departments of consumer affairs or consumer protection. During the sweeping deregulation climate in Washington under the Reagan administration, states became more vigorous in their own regulatory activities. The **National Association of Attorneys General (NAAG),** which includes attorneys general from all 50 states, has played a particularly active role. For example, the NAAG issued guidelines directed at advertising practices in the airline and car rental industries. In another instance, attorneys general from 22 states filed a complaint against

Honda of America, alleging that Honda's three-wheel, all-terrain vehicles are "rolling death traps."[36]

A particularly interesting case involved a lawsuit filed by the Texas attorney general against Volvo North America. Volvo had produced a television commercial showing Bear Foot, a monster truck with huge wheels, running over a string of automobiles. All the automobiles collapsed except the Volvo station wagon. An investigation revealed, however, that the Volvo had been reinforced with steel and wood, while the other cars had their roof supports severed.[37]

There is every indication that states will remain active in their efforts to regulate advertising deception and other business practices.[38] This poses a potentially significant problem for many national advertisers who might find themselves subject to multiple, and perhaps inconsistent, state regulations. It is somewhat ironic that many national companies would prefer to see a stronger Federal Trade Commission. In other words, these firms are better off with a single regulatory agency that institutes uniform national guidelines and keeps the marketplace as free as possible from the fly-by-night operators that tarnish the image of all businesses.

Advertising Self-Regulation

Self-regulation, as the name suggests, is undertaken by advertisers themselves rather than by governmental bodies. Self-regulation is a form of *private government* whereby peers establish and enforce voluntary rules of behavior.[39] Advertising self-regulation has flourished in countries such as Canada, France, the United Kingdom, and the United States.[40] Self-regulation programs are undertaken by industry groups such as the Council of Better Business Bureaus, the media, and trade associations such as the American Association of Advertising Agencies.[41]

Media Self-Regulation: The Advertising Clearance Process. The advertising clearance process is a form of self-regulation that takes place behind the scenes before a commercial or other advertisement reaches consumers. Before its media appearance, a magazine advertisement or television commercial undergoes a variety of clearance steps, including (1) advertising agency clearance, (2) approval from the advertiser's legal department and perhaps also from an independent law firm, and (3) media approval (such as television networks' guidelines regarding standards of taste).[42] A finished ad that makes it through the clearance process and appears in advertising media is then subject to the possibility of post hoc regulation from federal (e.g., the FTC), state (e.g., NAAG), and self-regulators (e.g., the National Advertising Review Council).

The National Advertising Review Council. Self-regulation by the National Advertising Review Council (NARC) has been the most publicized and perhaps most effective form of self-regulation. NARC is an organization formed via a partnership among the Association of National Advertisers, the American Association of Advertising Agencies, the American Advertising Federation, and the Council of Better Business Bureaus National Advertising Division (NAD).

NARC consists of three review units: the Children's Advertising Review Unit (CARU), NAD, and the National Advertising Review Board (NARB). CARU monitors children's television programming and commercials, whereas the NAD and NARB were established to sustain standards of truth and accuracy in national advertising to adults. NARB is the umbrella-like term applied to the combined NAD/NARB self-regulatory mechanism; however, by strict definition, NARB is a court consisting of 50 representatives who are formed into five-member panels to hear appeals of NAD cases when an involved party is dissatisfied with the initial verdict.[43] NAD is the investigative arm of NARB and is responsible for evaluating, investigating, and holding initial negotiations with an advertiser on complaints involving truth or accuracy of national advertising.[44]

The number of cases investigated and resolved varies, but NAD/NARB often becomes involved in as many as 150 cases a year. Cases are brought to the NAD by competing advertisers, initiated by the NAD staff itself, or originate from local Better Business Bureaus, consumer groups, and individual consumers.

NAD/NARB Complaint Resolution Process.   This section details the specific activities that are involved from the time a complaint alleging false and misleading advertising is initiated until it is resolved.[45]

> *Step 1: Complaint screening and case selection:* The self-regulatory process begins with the NAD screening complaints against allegedly deceptive or misleading advertising. The NAD pursues only those complaints that it regards meritorious.
>
> *Step 2: Initial NAD evaluation:* Some cases are administratively closed because they fall outside NAD's jurisdiction, but in most cases NAD contacts the advertiser to open a dialogue. There are three possible outcomes from this dialogue: (1) The disputed advertisement is found acceptable; (2) the advertisement is considered questionable; or (3) the advertisement is deemed unacceptable because NAD feels it violates a precedent or may be misinterpreted by consumers.
>
> *Step 3: Advertiser's initial response:* Advertisers can respond to NAD by providing sufficient substantiation to show that the disputed advertising claim is justified or by discontinuing or modifying the claim.
>
> *Step 4: NAD's final evaluation:* The NAD publicly reports all ads that have been discontinued or modified in outlets that reach the advertising community. In the case of ads for which advertisers have provided substantiation, NAD reviews these to assess the adequacy of the provided evidence. In most instances NAD rules that the disputed claims have been adequately substantiated. Claims that NAD considers insufficiently substantiated are subject to appeal to NARB, though this rarely happens.[46]
>
> *Step 5: Advertiser's final response:* The NAD's ruling may be upheld, reversed, or dismissed by NARB. However, because NAD/NARB is merely a self-regulatory body without legal jurisdiction or power, the ultimate resolution of disputed cases depends on voluntary cooperation between advertisers and NAD/NARB.

In conclusion, self-regulation has a variety of potential benefits to consumers and businesses. Self-regulation reduces the need for government regulation. Furthermore, because advertisers are strongly motivated to point out competitor's deceptive advertising practices, their efforts to protect themselves help to maintain the general integrity of advertising and, in so doing, to protect consumers. The president of NARC has succinctly captured the value of self-regulation:

> *Self-regulation is smart business. It provides a level playing field. Continuing NAD improvements provide the quickest, least expensive and most effective way for advertisers to challenge one another's claims. A court case can take over a year (vs. NAD's 60 business days) and cost 10 times as much as a NAD case.*[47]

ETHICAL ISSUES IN MARKETING COMMUNICATIONS

Advertisers, sales promoters, package designers, public relations representatives, and point-of-purchase designers regularly make decisions that have ethical implications. This section examines many of the ethical issues involved with all elements of marketing communications.

Ethics in our context involves matters of right and wrong, or *moral*, conduct pertaining to any aspect of marketing communications. Hence, for our purposes, ethics and morality will be used interchangeably and considered synonymous with societal notions of *honesty, honor, virtue,* and *integrity* in matters of marketing communications conduct. It is relatively easy to define ethics, but it is difficult to identify what is or is not ethical conduct in marketing communications. Indeed, throughout the field of marketing (as well as elsewhere in society) there is a lack of consensus about what is ethical conduct.[48] Consensus notwithstanding, we nevertheless can identify marketing communications practices that are especially susceptible to ethical challenges. The following sections examine, in order, ethical issues in (1) targeting marketing communications efforts, (2) advertising, (3) public relations, (4) packaging communications, (5) sales promotions, and (6) online marketing communications.

The Ethics of Targeting

According to widely accepted dictates of the marketing concept and sound marketing strategy (as described in Chapters 2 and 3), firms should direct their offerings at specific segments of customers rather than use a scatter or shotgun approach. Nonetheless, ethical dilemmas are sometimes involved when special products and corresponding marketing communications efforts are directed at particular segments.[49] Especially open to ethical debate is the practice of targeting products and communications efforts to segments that, for various psychosocial and economic reasons, are vulnerable to marketing communications—such as children and economically disadvantaged groups.[50]

Targeting to Children and Teens. Advertising and in-school marketing programs continuously urge kids to desire various products and brands. Critics such as Senator Hillary Clinton, as previously discussed, contend that many of the products targeted to children are unnecessary and that the communications are exploitative. Because it would involve debating personal values to discuss what kids do or do not need, the following presentation merely presents the critics' position and allows you to draw your own conclusions.

Consider the advertising of Gatorade to kids. Advertisements claimed that Gatorade is the "healthy alternative for thirsty kids." Nutritionists and other critics charged that Gatorade is unnecessary for kids and no better than water—no harm or benefit arises from its consumption.[51] If indeed Gatorade does not benefit kids, is it ethical to urge them to encourage their gatekeeping parents to purchase this product?

Another criticized aspect of children-directed marketing communications is the practice of using posters, book covers, free magazines, advertising, and other so-called learning tools. Disguised as educational materials, these communications often are little more than attempts to persuade schoolchildren to want the promoted products and brands. Critics contend these methods are unethical because they use children's trust in educational materials as a deceptive means of hawking merchandise.[52]

In addition to classroom tactics, critics also question the ethics of practices such as placing products in movies and supporting the product-movie connection with tie-in merchandise programs. Another criticized practice is the use of magazine *advertorials*—that is, advertisements disguised as editorial opinions. For example, *Seventeen* magazine runs a personal-advice column providing answers to makeup and wardrobe questions. Sometimes, however, the editorial-seeming advice is little more than a product plug.[53]

Marketers also have been criticized for targeting adult products to preadults. The Miller Brewing Company, for example, was challenged for using a television commercial for its Molson Ice brand that focuses on a label displaying 5.6 percent alcoholic content at the same time that an off-camera announcer utters that Molson Ice is a "bolder" drink. A spokesperson for the Center for Science in the Public Interest asserted that the Molson Ice commercial appeals to kids because they "drink to get drunk" and higher alcohol content is "what they want in a beer."[54] The beer industry itself would be opposed to this advertising inasmuch as one of the brewing industry's advertising guidelines explicitly states that beer advertisements "should neither state nor carry any implication of alcohol strength."[55]

More recently, the Distilled Spirits Council of the United States voted in 1996 to lift its voluntary ban on advertising "hard" liquor on television and radio. This self-imposed ban had been in effect for nearly a half-century, and during this period no liquor ads were aired in the United States. NBC is the only television network at the time of this writing that accepts liquor ads. NBC does not accept just any liquor ad but requires a prospective liquor advertiser to run four months of responsible-drinking advertisements before NBC will broadcast a single brand advertisement from that company.[56] Critics' primary concern is that liquor advertising will encourage young consumers to hold more favorable views toward hard liquor and to increase consumption. Only time will tell whether these concerns are justified.[57]

Critics also are up in arms over the marketing of adult-oriented entertainment products to children and teens. The Federal Trade Commission issued a report, *Marketing Violent Entertainment to Children*, criticizing the entertainment industry for targeting kids with advertisements for violent films, video games, and music. However, the FTC believes that its authority in regulating such advertising is limited in that it would have difficulty proving that such ads are deceptive or unfair.[58] The FTC has called for the entertainment industry to self-regulate and rigorously apply its own codes of conduct, though there are serious concerns that the industry is much motivated or even capable of cleaning its own house.[59] An editor of *Advertising Age*, a publication widely read by advertising practitioners and a voice of reason in the ad industry, offers the following appropriate conclusion to this discussion:

> *This publication's editors — myself included — almost always side with the advertising industry in preferring self-regulation to government intervention. But self-regulation is a privilege earned with responsible behavior and voluntary restraint. In the marketing of entertainment products to children, marketers have shown little restraint. If they continue to act irresponsibly, they will have invited the regulation they so desperately want to avoid.*[60]

By far the greatest controversy to erupt in many years involving claims of unfair targeting to children was the advertising campaign for Camel cigarettes using the anthropomorphized camel character known as Joe Camel — a man-like camel that was portrayed in advertisements as the embodiment of hipness. This campaign, which was introduced in 1987 by R. J. Reynolds, the makers of Camel cigarettes, was widely criticized as responsible for increased smoking among teenagers.[61] The campaign consistently portrayed Joe Camel as a swank character in various social settings, aided perhaps by the ubiquitous cigarette hanging in his lips or dangling from his fingertips.

With cigarette smoking among teenagers on the rise, many parties urged a ban be imposed on Joe Camel advertisements. Responsible commentators argued that such a ban would be unfair to advertisers and in violation of their First Amendment rights.[62] Under pressure from antismoking activists, the U.S. Congress, and the Federal Trade Commission, R. J. Reynolds discontinued its use of the Joe Camel advertising campaign in 1998, although the character will still appear in advertising outside the United States.[63]

Research has been conducted to determine whether the Joe Camel advertising campaign was indeed responsible for more positive smoking attitudes and increased smoking among youth. The research is itself highly controversial and has been both celebrated and pilloried.[64] Has the Joe Camel campaign targeted nonadults? Is it responsible for increased smoking? Is it unethical? These are complicated questions and simple answers are not possible. The issues need to be debated both in and outside the classroom. The following *IMC Focus* includes a provocative position on the topic. It is presented here *not* as the final statement on the issue but rather as an intelligent and sobering statement that should serve to spark further discussion.

Targeting Economically Disadvantaged Consumers. Makers of alcohol and tobacco products frequently employ billboards and other advertising media to target brands to economically disadvantaged consumers. Although billboard advertising of tobacco products is restricted under the Master Settlement Agreement between the federal government and firms in the tobacco industry, in the past billboards advertising tobacco (and alcohol) were disproportionately more likely to appear in inner-city areas.[65]

Two celebrated cases illustrate the concerns.[66] A national uproar ensued when R. J. Reynolds (RJR) was preparing to introduce Uptown, a brand of menthol cigarette aimed at African Americans, and planned for test marketing in

IMC
f o c u s

An Adman's Struggle with Joe Camel and Free Speech

Last week, just over the Howard Street Bridge, I crossed a camel's path. Stopped at a traffic light on my way to a business meeting, I glanced up and saw the camel rising above the brick building tops in vibrant, unnatural hues, stretching, it seemed, far into the sky.

I thought he saw me, too; he winked at me with a grin. And there was an understanding between us—camel and man, man and camel.

But his wink and grin were not meant for me alone.

I am a local advertising professional, and the camel is the symbol for Camel cigarettes. He speaks to the city from high atop Howard Street and North Avenue on his billboard perch. As an "adman," I am impressed by the camel. The cartoonish, humanistic depiction of the desert beast in a jazz jam session with his camel buddies is intriguing. It doesn't ask for your attention, it grabs it. And once you are hooked, as it were, on the visual, the message is clear: Camels are cool; they're fun; they make you part of the desirable crowd. All of this, conveyed in just a glance.

More than that, the cartoons speak most persuasively to the "target market" the company wishes to reach. All in all, it is an expert use of the medium and an excellent piece of advertising.

As a man, as a father, I am appalled by the camel. To me, he is perverse, a distortion. Strip away his sleek, tan exterior and what is left? Not a camel, but a purplish, black-plumed raven forlornly whispering to the children of the streets when their parents and teachers are not looking. He beckons the poor, preying upon their weaknesses and panhandling their few coins.

The spectacle leaves me between a rock and a camel's hump—and not only for selfish reasons. Of course, being a glad participant in the free-enterprise system, I am all for the aggressive manufacturing and marketing of any legal product. Beyond that, I believe that free speech, even for ignoble, detestable causes, should be protected without reservation.

But is it free speech to lure children with images they've been taught to trust, cartoon images, to a product the surgeon general has called an addiction that can lead to death? In fact, *The New York Times Magazine* recently reported that "the product kills more than 420,000 Americans a year—surpassing the combined deaths from homicide, suicide, AIDS, automobile accidents, alcohol and drug abuse."

I came to the conclusion that, yes, it is free speech. People are, and should be, allowed to convey whatever message they choose. That is the American way.

But freedom of expression also includes the freedom not to express one's self. No one forces an advertising agency to devise strategies and create images for a tobacco company targeting an inappropriate market. No one forces the media outlets to provide them a forum. And finally, no one should overlook them when it comes time to pass out blame.

But it is not enough, either, to merely ignore the camel. Those of us in the marketing business know exactly what he's up to; we should be the first to denounce him. Even in public and professional life, there is a place for personal morality and common decency.

These meager thoughts passed through my head as I sat at that light just over the Howard Street Bridge. When the signal turned green, I waited for a group of school kids to cross the street, then I gently pulled away. A couple of blocks later, I was stopped again at a light. This time, under a billboard for malt liquor.

Source: *Advertising Age*, September 26, 1994, p. 23. © 1994 by Crain Communications, Inc. Reprinted by permission.

Philadelphia, where African Americans make up 40 percent of the population. Because African Americans have more than a 50 percent higher rate of lung cancer than whites, many critics, including the U.S. government's secretary for Health and Human Services, were incensed by the product launch. In response to the public outcry, RJR canceled test marketing, and the brand died.[67]

Following in the wake of Uptown's demise, critics challenged another firm, the Heileman Brewing Company, for introducing its PowerMaster brand of high-alcohol malt liquor targeted to inner-city residents—a brand containing 5.9 percent alcohol compared with the 4.5 percent content of other malt liquors.[68] Brewing-industry supporters claimed that rather than being exploitative, PowerMaster and other malt liquors merely meet the demand among African Americans and Hispanics, who buy the vast majority of malt liquor.[69] Nonetheless, the U.S. Treasury Department's Bureau of Alcohol, Tobacco, and Firearms (ATF), which regulates the brewing and liquor industries, would not permit the Heileman Brewing Company to market malt liquor under the name PowerMaster. The ATF arrived at this decision because it considered the name PowerMaster as promoting the brand's alcoholic content in violation of federal regulations.

The R. J. Reynolds tobacco company was again widely criticized when preparing to introduce its Dakota brand of cigarettes to young, economically downscale women. RJR's plans to test market Dakota in Houston were squashed when critics created an outcry in response to what was considered to be exploitative marketing.[70]

Is Targeting Unethical or Just Good Marketing?   The foregoing discussion points out instances where advertising and other forms of marketing communications are criticized because they are directed at specific target markets. Proponents of targeting respond to such criticisms by arguing that targeting benefits rather than harms consumers. Targeting, according to the proponents, provides consumers with products best suited to their particular needs and wants. Not to be targeted, according to the advocates' position, is to have to choose a product that better accommodates someone else's needs.[71]

The issue is, of course, more complicated than whether targeting is good or bad. Sophisticated marketing practitioners and students fully accept the strategic justification for target marketing. There is the possibility, however, that some instances of targeting are concerned not with fulfilling consumers' needs and wants but rather with exploiting consumer vulnerabilities—so that the target marketer gains while society loses. Herein rests the ethical issue that cannot be dismissed with a mere claim that targeting is sound marketing. You should discuss the ethical ramifications of targeting in class and benefit from the views of your fellow students and professor.[72]

Ethical Issues in Advertising

The role of advertising in society has been debated for centuries. Advertising ethics has been a topic that has commanded the attention of philosophers, practitioners, scholars, and the church. For example, the Vatican recently prepared a report on advertising ethics.[73] The *Opening Vignette* presented the AAAA's ethical code of conduct. This code indicates that practitioners are themselves greatly concerned with ethical advertising practice. Opponents of advertising contend that it is the cause of much of what is bad in society. The following is a succinct yet eloquent account of why advertising is so fiercely criticized:

> As the voice of technology, [advertising] is associated with many dissatisfactions of the industrial state. As the voice of mass culture it invites intellectuals' attack. And as the most visible form of capitalism it has served as nothing less than a lightning-rod for social criticism.[74]

A variety of ethical criticisms have been leveled against advertising. Because the issues are complex, it is impossible in this chapter to treat each criticism in great detail. The purpose of this discussion is merely to introduce the basic issues.[75] The criticisms that follow are illustrative rather than exhaustive.

Advertising Is Untruthful and Deceptive.   The majority (roughly two-thirds) of American consumers think that advertising often is untruthful.[76] As mentioned previously when discussing advertising regulation, deception occurs when an advertisement falsely represents a product and consumers believe the false representation to be true. Is advertising deceptive according to this general definition? Some advertising *is* deceptive—the existence of governmental regulation and industry self-regulation attests to this fact. It would be naïve, however, to assume that most advertising is deceptive. The advertising industry is not much different than other institutions in a pluralistic society. Lying, cheating, and outright fraud are universal, occurring at the highest levels of government and in the most basic human relationships (for example, unfaithful husbands and wives). Advertising is not without sin, but neither does it hold a monopoly on it.

Advertising Is Manipulative.   The criticism of manipulation asserts that advertising has the power to influence people to behave atypically, or do things they would not do if they were not exposed to advertising. Taken to the extreme, this suggests that advertising is capable of moving people against their free wills. What psychological principles would account for such power to manipulate? As was discussed in detail in Chapter 10, the evidence certainly does *not* support subliminal advertising, which has provided advertising critics with the most provocative explanation underlying the claim of manipulation.

In general, the contention that advertising manipulates is without substance. Undeniably, advertisements can influence consumers to purchase particular products and brands. But persuasion and manipulation are not tantamount. Persuasion is a legitimate form of human interaction undertaken by all individuals and institutions.

Advertising Is Offensive and in Bad Taste.   Advertising critics contend that many advertisements are insulting to human intelligence, vulgar, and generally offensive to the tastes of many consumers. Several grounds exist for this criticism: (1) inane commercials; (2) sexual explicitness or innuendo in all forms of advertisements; (3) television commercials that advertise unpleasant products (hemorrhoid treatments, diarrhea products, etc.); and (4) repetitious use of the same advertisements ad infinitum, ad nauseam.

Undeniably, much advertising is disgusting and offensive. Yet the same can be said for all forms of mass media presentations. For example, many network television programs verge on the idiotic, and movies are often filled with inordinate amounts of sex and violence. This certainly is not to excuse advertising for its excesses, but a balanced view demands that critical evaluations of advertising be conducted in a broader context of popular culture and other forms of mass media presentations.

Advertising Creates and Perpetuates Stereotypes.   The contention at the root of this criticism is that advertising tends to portray certain groups in a very narrow and predictable fashion: minorities were historically portrayed disproportionately in working-class roles rather than in the full range of positions they actually occupy; women were stereotyped as homemakers or as sex objects; and senior citizens sometimes were, and still are, characterized as feeble and forgetful people. Advertising has been guilty of perpetuating stereotypes. However, it would be unfair to blame advertising for creating these stereotypes, which, in fact, are perpetuated by all elements in society. Spreading the blame does not make advertising any better, but it does show that advertising is probably not any worse than the rest of society.

People Buy Things They Do Not Really Need.   A frequently cited criticism suggests that advertising causes people to buy items or services that they do not need. This criticism is a value-laden judgment. Do you need another pair of shoes? Do you need a college education? Who is to say what you or anyone else needs? Advertising most assuredly influences consumer tastes and encourages people to undertake purchases they may not otherwise make, but is this unethical?

Advertising Plays on People's Fears and Insecurities.   Some advertisements appeal to the negative consequences of not buying a product—rejection by members of the opposite sex, bad breath, failure to have provided for the family if one should die without proper insurance coverage, and so on. (Recall the discussion of appeals to fear and guilt back in Chapter 10.) Some advertisers must certainly plead guilty to this charge. However, once again, advertising possesses no monopoly on this transgression.

In sum, the institution of advertising is certainly not free of criticism. What should be clear, however, is that advertising reflects the rest of society, and any indictment of advertising probably applies to society at large. It is doubtful that advertisers and other marketing practitioners are any less ethical in their practices than are other elements of society.[77] Responsible advertising practitioners, knowing that their practice is particularly susceptible to criticism, have a vested interest in producing legitimate advertisements.

Ethical Issues in Public Relations

Publicity, the one aspect of public relations that relates primarily to marketing communications, involves disseminating positive information about a company and its products and handling negative publicity. Because publicity is like advertising in that both are forms of mass communications, many of the same ethical issues apply and need not be repeated. The one distinct aspect worthy of separate discussion is the matter of *negative publicity*.

There have been a number of celebrated cases in recent years in which companies have been widely criticized for marketing unsafe products—such as Firestone tires as discussed in the previous chapter in the context of the raft of Ford Explorer rollover accidents. The way firms confront negative publicity has important strategic as well as ethical ramifications. The primary ethical issue concerns whether firms confess to product shortcomings and acknowledge problems or, instead, attempt to cover up the problems.

Consider, for example, the case of Tylenol capsules, which was described in the previous chapter. Seven people in the Chicago area died in 1982 after ingesting cyanide-poisoned capsules. The publicity people at Johnson & Johnson (J&J), the makers of Tylenol, could have claimed that the problem was not of their making but rather was the fault of an isolated lunatic in Chicago. Such a position would have led J&J to continue selling Tylenol in all markets except Chicago. However, because it was unknown at the time whether the capsules had been poisoned at the factory or by a deranged person in retail outlets, the cautionary and ethical response was to remove Tylenol from store shelves throughout the country. This is precisely what J&J chose to do in taking the moral high road. It turned out that the problem was restricted to Chicago, but the ethics of the situation required caution to prevent the possibility of widespread deaths around the country.

Ethical Issues in Packaging

Four aspects of packaging involve ethical issues: (1) label information, (2) packaging graphics, (3) packaging safety, and (4) environmental implications of packaging.[78] *Label information* on packages can mislead consumers by providing exaggerated information or by unethically suggesting that a product contains more of desired attributes (for instance, nutrition) or less of undesired attributes (such as cholesterol or fat) than is actually the case. *Packaging graphics* are unethical when the picture on a package is not a true representation of product contents (as when a children's toy is made to appear much bigger on the package than it actually is). Another case of unethical behavior is when a store brand is packaged so that it looks virtually identical to a well-known national brand. *Unsafe packaging* problems are particularly acute with dangerous products that are unsafe for children and the package is not tamper-proof. *Environmental issues* in packaging are typified by the discussion of Hefty trash bags earlier in the chapter. Packaging information is misleading and unethical when it suggests environmental benefits that cannot be delivered.[79]

A packaging decision for Excedrin by Bristol-Myers Squibb exemplifies both smart marketing and *ethical* packaging. Excedrin is the fourth-highest selling analgesic brand in the United States. Consumers have for decades used this brand to fight headaches and muscle pains. In the late 1990s a brand extension, Excedrin Extra Strength, was approved by the Food and Drug Administration (FDA) as the first over-the-counter treatment for mild to moderate migraine relief. This decision by the FDA posed a wonderful opportunity for Bristol-Myers Squibb, but it also created a major marketing and packaging challenge. The FDA required Bristol-Myers to develop a new package that would alert migraine sufferers to the distinct warnings about the use of Excedrin, warnings different than those already on the packaging and designed primarily for users suffering regular headaches and muscle pains.

Working with officials at the FDA, the marketing people at Bristol-Myers decided to develop two packages, one for the "regular" Excedrin and the other for the new "Excedrin Migraine." But in fact, Excedrin and Excedrin Migraine are the *identical product*. It may have been possible to mislead consumers into thinking that Excedrin Migraine was a dramatic new product formulation, but Bristol-Myers decided to be up-front with consumers and take a responsible course of action. Advertising messages for the "new" Excedrin Migraine were straightforward in stating, "Next to Excedrin, there's a new package—same medicine—called Excedrin Migraine." You might wonder why a company would want two separate packages for the identical product. The reason is straightforward: Having separate packages enables more overall shelf space, and sales revenue is correlated with the amount of retail space that a brand is able to garner.[80]

Ethical Issues in Sales Promotions

Ethical considerations are involved with all facets of sales promotions, including manufacturer promotions directed at the trade (wholesalers and retailers) and to consumers. As detailed in Chapter 16, retailers have gained considerable bargaining power vis-à-vis manufacturers. One outcome of this power shift has been retailers' increased demands for deals by manufacturers. *Slotting allowances* illustrate the power shift. This practice (thoroughly discussed in Chapter 17) requires manufacturers to pay retailers a per-store fee for their willingness to handle a new stock unit from the manufacturer. Critics of slotting allowances contend this practice represents a form of bribery and is therefore unethical.

Consumer-oriented sales promotions (including practices such as coupons, premium offers, rebates, sweepstakes, and contests) are unethical when the sales promoter offers consumers a reward for their behavior that is never delivered—for example, failing to mail a free premium object or to provide a rebate check. Sweepstakes and contests are potentially unethical when consumers think their odds of winning are much greater than they actually are.[81]

As a matter of balance, it is important to note that marketers are not the only ones guilty of unethical behavior in the area of sales promotions. Consumers also engage in untoward activities such as submitting coupons at the point of checkout for items not purchased or submitting phony rebate claims. One woman, who eventually was sentenced to 20 years in prison and $1 million in fines, obtained in excess of $700,000 from manufacturers by submitting thousands of rebate claims using fictitious names and addresses. She paid people to steal proofs-of-purchase from products in stores or from discarded packages in trash receptacles and then mailed these in for rebates.[82]

Ethical Issues in Online Marketing

As detailed in Chapters 13 and 14, online advertising and promotions are pervasive and growing. Ethical issues abound in the use of this medium, many of which overlap with the prior, general discussions involving the ethics of advertising and promotions. Aside from the general ethical issues already discussed, all of which are applicable to online as well as offline MarCom efforts, *privacy* is probably the most important ethical issue that is somewhat unique to the online medium.

Because online marketers are able to collect voluminous information about people's personal characteristics, online shopping behavior, and use of information, it is easy to invade individuals' privacy rights by selling information to other sources and divulging information that should be confidential—all without the individual's consent. It would take us too far afield to get into a detailed discussion of all the issues surrounding the matter of privacy invasion, but interested readers are directed to the articles listed in the following endnote.[83] Also worth reviewing are the self-regulatory principles espoused by the Network Advertising Initiative (http://www.networkadvertising.org), a trade association of online media companies.

Fostering Ethical Marketing Communications

Primary responsibility for ethical behavior resides within each of us when placed in any of the various marketing communicator roles. We can take the easy route and do those things that are most expedient, or we can pursue the moral high road and treat customers in the same honest fashion that we expect to be treated. In large part it is a matter of our own personal integrity. *Integrity* is perhaps the pivotal concept of human nature.[84] Although difficult to precisely define, integrity involves avoiding deceiving others or behaving purely in an expedient fashion.[85] Hence, marketing communications itself is not ethical or unethical—it is the degree of integrity exhibited by communications practitioners that determines whether their behavior is ethical or unethical.

Placing the entire burden on individuals is perhaps unfair, because how we behave as individuals is largely a function of the organizational culture in which we operate. Businesses can foster ethical or unethical cultures by establishing *ethical core values* to guide marketing communications behavior. Two core values that would go a long way toward enhancing ethical behavior are (1) treating customers with respect, concern, and honesty—the way you would want to be treated or the way you would want your family treated—and (2) acting toward the environment as though it were your own property.[86]

Firms can foster ethical marketing communications behavior by encouraging their employees to apply each of the following tests when faced with an ethical predicament: (1) Act in a way that you would want others to act toward you (the *Golden Rule test*); (2) take only actions that would be viewed as proper by an objective panel of your professional colleagues (the *professional ethic test*); and (3) always ask, "Would I feel comfortable explaining this action on television to the general public?" (the *TV test*).[87]

We conclude this section by presenting the mission statements of two companies that exemplify ethical advertising and marketing communications. First is an extract from Caterpillar Corporation's code of worldwide business conduct, and the second is from Dayton Hudson Corporation's general policy on advertising.[88]

> *[Caterpillar's] most valuable asset is a reputation for integrity. If that becomes tarnished, customers, investors, suppliers, employees, and those who sell our products and services will seek affiliation with other, more attractive companies. We intend to hold to a single high standard of integrity everywhere. We will keep our word. We won't promise more than we can reasonably expect to deliver; nor will we make commitments we don't intend to keep. In our advertising and other public communications, we will avoid not only untruths, but also exaggeration and overstatement.*

> *We [at Dayton Hudson] are an honest-dealing business. No deceptions. No shortcuts. No gray areas. Being honest is not only right, it's good business. The trust of our customers is one of our greatest assets. That trust must be reinforced and preserved by our advertising practices. The basis of our advertising is providing clear and accurate information that our customers need to make their buying decisions.*

GREEN MARKETING COMMUNICATIONS

Many Europeans, Canadians, Americans, Asians, and other people around the world are concerned with the depletion of natural resources and the degradation of the physical environment. These concerns have led to demands for companies to do something to ensure a cleaner and safer environment. Many companies have responded to environmental concerns by introducing environmentally oriented products and undertaking aggressive marketing communications programs to promote these products. These actions are referred to as *green marketing*.[89] Unfortunately, for every truly green product there are probably an equal number of bogus entries. This is why green marketing has been referred to in such unflattering terms as *greenscam, greenwashing,* and *big green lies*.[90] Companies have jumped on the green bandwagon and sometimes exploited consumers' sensitivity to products claiming to be recyclable, degradable, safe for the ozone layer, and so on. As one journalist put it: "Declarations of environmental sensitivity cannot be taken at face value. Everybody wears green on St. Patrick's Day, too—but it doesn't make them Irish."[91]

I wish in writing this section that I could be more positive about consumers' interest in environmental issues and marketers' actions to redress past practices that insulted the environment. Indeed, during a period in the 1990s it appeared that both consumers and marketers were very serious about environmentalism as a key consideration in both marketing and consumption decisions. A Harvard Business School professor asserted that green products are to the 1990s what "lite" products (i.e., low-calorie versions of regular food items) were to the 1980s.[92] In retrospect, it would seem that this claim was premature and excessively enthusiastic. There now is little evidence that many brands are being promoted on the basis of their environmental efficacy. It appears that the optimism over green marketing and green consumer behavior was overstated. For example, in multiple concept tests of new product ideas in recent years, American consumers have rated environmental issues as no more important than about a 6 on a 10-point scale. Ratings as low as these simply do not motivate purchase decisions.[93] One journalist concluded that green marketing "is fading faster than the ozone over Antarctica."[94]

Environmental concerns remain in parts of Europe, Canada, select areas of the United States (such as college campuses), and elsewhere, but in large part consumers are more interested in acquiring products that are convenient, priced right, high performing, and symbolically appealing than they are in acquiring biodegradable items for which they might have to pay a price premium. Nonetheless, it is clear that the green movement is here to stay to one degree or another. Because many countries outside North America and Western Europe have far greater environmental problems, it may be that the opportunity for responsive green marketing is stronger in these countries than in highly advanced economies.

Green Marketing Initiatives

Pessimism aside, companies have made a number of legitimate responses to environmental problems. They have been motivated for reasons such as achieving regulatory compliance, gaining competitive advantage, and being socially responsible.[95] Some of these responses have been in the form of *new* or *revised products*. Illustrative green products include the following:

- Personal computers are now equipped with energy-efficient features and are made with some recycled materials.
- Furniture manufacturers make environmentally friendly furniture from recycled wood, plastic, and even paper.
- Volvo recently advertised a pollution-fighting radiator in its S80 sedan.
- Now available are cordless lawn mowers powered by rechargeable batteries. In addition to being noiseless and easy to start and maintain, battery-charged mowers reduce pollution significantly.
- Perhaps the major recent product initiative is the electric-gas hybrid automobile marketed under brand names such as the Honda Insight and the

Figure 20.1   Green Advertising Addressing the Biophysical Environment

Toyota Prius (see two advertisements in Figure 20.1). These hybrids use gasoline for fuel, and the gas engine then serves to recharge the batteries. Combined sales of these two models will roughly represent only 0.1 percent of the 17 million vehicles purchased annually in the United States.[96]

Although these product innovations are important, of greater direct relevance to this text are the MarCom efforts that appeal to environmental sensitivities. The major green communications efforts involve advertisements that promote green products, environmentally friendly packaging, seal-of-approval programs that promote green products, cause-oriented communication efforts that support green products, and point-of-purchase display materials that are environmentally efficient.

Green Advertising.   Environmental appeals in advertising were commonplace in American advertising for a short period in the early to mid-1990s, but the initial enthusiastic response to the deteriorating physical environment has waned. In fact, in writing the sixth edition of this text, I was hard pressed to locate many examples of environmentally oriented advertising.

There are three types of green advertising appeals when this form of advertising occasionally surfaces: (1) ads that address a relationship between a product/service and the biophysical environment (such as those for the Prius in Figure 20.1); (2) those that promote a green lifestyle without highlighting a product or service; and (3) ads that present a corporate image of environmental responsibility (see Fig-

Green Advertising Promoting an Image of Environmental Responsibility

Figure 20.2

ure 20.2 for Honda automobiles).[97] In addition to the latter advertisement—which, as you might notice, indicates that the Union of Concerned Scientists recently named Honda Motor Company the cleanest car company in the world—Honda has undertaken other advertising initiatives to promote its green and clean image.

In one particularly clever project, managers of Honda Motor Company decided to develop a corporate campaign that would solidify Honda's reputation as an environmentally friendly car company. They faced the challenge of somehow developing an icon that could be associated with the Honda Accord and thus serve to entrench in consumers' minds a strong, favorable, and somewhat unique image of the Honda Accord as a "clean" automobile. Who of all marketplace icons better represents the quality of cleanliness than Mr. Clean himself? In case you don't know, Mr. Clean is a bald, muscled, and earring-wearing cartoon-like character that Procter & Gamble has used for decades on its famous old brand of household cleaner named, of course, Mr. Clean.

Although realizing that environmental concerns are not a high priority for most consumers, Honda managers nonetheless were eager to bolster the Accord's reputation for fuel efficiency and cleanliness. After undertaking negotiations with P&G officials, both companies agreed that partnering these two brands (recall the discussion of co-branding in Chapter 2) would be mutually advantageous. Honda would benefit by enhancing its environmental image, and P&G's Mr. Clean brand would get a lot of free publicity from Honda's advertising. Honda invested approximately $25 million in an ad campaign that presented the Mr. Clean character strutting around Honda Accords in TV commercials as well as displayed in dealer showrooms throughout America, with six-foot-high cutouts of Mr. Clean placed next to four-cylinder LEV (low-emission vehicle) Honda Accord automobiles.[98]

Packaging Responses.   A number of efforts have been initiated to improve the environmental effectiveness of packaging materials. Illustrative programs include packaging soft drinks and many other products in recyclable plastic bottles; switching from polystyrene clamshell containers to paperboard packages for burgers and other sandwiches; changing from plastic containers for the L'eggs brand of pantyhose to a cardboard container that maintained the famous silhouette of the plastic egg (what may appear to be a trivial packaging changeover actually cost Hanes, the maker of L'eggs, millions of dollars in packaging materials and displays);[99] and introducing concentrated laundry detergents as a way of achieving smaller packages and thus less waste disposal to be placed in already crowded landfills.

As counter to these positive packaging developments, there is evidence that package materials often are wasted due to a practice called *short filling*. For example, over 40 percent of juice containers, milk cartons, and other dairy products contain a smaller amount of product—from 1 to 6 percent less—than what the package labels promise.[100] This short-filling problem is partially due to profit skimming and also results, more innocently, from poorly calibrated packing machines. Whatever the reason, the fact remains that short filling results annually in thousands of tons of wasted packaging materials.[101]

Seal-of-Approval Programs.   Many countries around the world have programs designed to assist consumers in identifying environmentally friendly products and brands.[102] In Germany, for example, the Blue Angel seal represents a promise to consumers that a product carrying an environmental claim is in fact legitimate. Green Seal, a Washington, D.C., nonprofit organization, has developed standards and awarded seals to companies that meet environmental standards, which fewer than 20 percent of all products in the category are able to satisfy. General Electric, for example, received a seal for developing compact fluorescent light bulbs. In addition to Green Seal, there are various product-category-specific seal programs such as the "chasing arrows logo" that specifies recycled paperboard content. It is interesting to note, however, that the 100% Recycled Paperboard Alliance—the group that came up with the symbol in 1970—claims that the symbol has lost its meaning because it was used illegitimately by too many firms. The Alliance is attempting to supplant the chasing arrows symbol with a new logo, namely a semicircle of 10 small arrows pointing to the words *100% Recycled Paperboard*.[103] Programs such as these provide consumers with assurance that the products carrying these seals legitimately are environmentally friendly, though the chasing arrows logo failed because some firms used it inappropriately.

Cause-Oriented Programs.   As described in the prior chapter, cause-oriented marketing is practiced when companies sponsor or support worthy causes. In doing so, the marketing communicator anticipates that associating the company and its brands with a worthy cause will generate goodwill. It is for this reason that companies sponsor various environmental causes. At one time General Motors planted a tree for every Chevrolet Geo car sold. Evian, a company that markets mineral water, had representatives visit college campuses to raise environmental awareness and recruit new members for the World Wildlife Fund. Cause-oriented programs can be effective if they are not overused and if consumers perceive a company's involvement in an environmental cause as sincere and not just naked commercialism.

Point-of-Purchase Programs.   A major area for savings is in conserving materials that go into point-of-purchase displays. Billions of dollars are invested in plastic, wood, metal, paper, and other materials used in constructing displays. However, many of the displays sent by manufacturers to retailers are never used and simply end up in landfills. Closer consultations with retailers regarding their point-of-purchase needs would lead to fewer unused and summarily discarded displays, and increased use of permanent displays (those engineered to last at least six months) would substantially reduce the number of temporary displays that are quickly discarded.

Guidelines for Green Marketing

The significance of the environmental problem demands that marketing communicators do everything possible to ensure that green claims are credible, realistic, and believable. To assist companies in knowing what environmental claims can and cannot be communicated in advertisements, on packages, and elsewhere, the Federal Trade Commission promulgated guides for environmental marketing claims.[104] These guides outline four general principles that apply to all environmental marketing claims:

1. Qualifications and disclosures should be sufficiently clear and prominent to prevent deception.
2. Claims should make clear whether they apply to the product, the package, or a component of either.
3. Claims should not overstate an environmental attribute or benefit, either expressly or by implication.
4. Comparative claims should be presented in a manner that makes the basis for the comparison sufficiently clear to avoid consumer deception.

The FTC guidelines also address specific categories of environmental claims such as "environmentally friendly," "degradable," and "recyclable." The guides describe the basic elements necessary to substantiate each form of environmental claim and provide examples of specific claims that do and do not provide adequate support. The FTC's document is must reading for any firm considering making a claim about its product's environmental friendliness.[105]

In addition to the guidelines established by the FTC, a task force of attorneys general representing 10 states developed a set of recommendations for environmental marketers. These recommendations provide guidelines for labeling, packaging, and advertising products on the basis of environmental attributes.[106] Marketing communicators are offered four general recommendations for making appropriate environmental claims: (1) Make the claims specific, (2) have claims reflect current disposal options, (3) make the claims substantive, and (4) make supportable claims.[107]

Make Specific Claims. This guideline is intended to prevent marketing communicators from using meaningless claims such as "environmentally friendly" or "safe for the environment." The use of specific environmental claims enables consumers to make informed choices, reduces the likelihood that claims will be misinterpreted, and minimizes the chances that consumers will think that a product is more environmentally friendly than it actually is. In general, it is recommended that environmental claims be as specific as possible—not general, vague, incomplete, or overly broad.

Reflect Current Disposal Options. This recommendation is directed at preventing environmental claims that are technically accurate but practically unrealizable due to local trash-disposal practices. For example, most communities dispose of trash by burying it in public landfills. Because paper and plastic products do not degrade when buried, it is misleading for businesses to make environmental claims that their products are degradable, biodegradable, or photodegradable.

Make Substantive Claims. Some marketing communicators use trivial and irrelevant environmental claims to convey the impression that a promoted brand is environmentally sound. An illustration of a nonsubstantive claim is a company promoting its polystyrene foam cups as "preserving our trees and forests." Another trivial claim is when single-use products such as paper plates are claimed to be "safe for the environment." Clearly, a paper plate is not unsafe to the environment in the same sense that a toxic chemical is unsafe; however, paper plates and other throwaways do not actually benefit the environment but rather exacerbate the landfill problem.

Make Supportable Claims. This recommendation is straightforward: Environmental claims should be supported by competent and reliable scientific evidence. The purpose of this recommendation is to encourage businesses to make only those environmental claims that can be backed by facts. The injunction to businesses is clear: Don't claim it unless you can support it!

Some companies are indeed showing restraint in making environmental claims. Such restraint not only benefits consumers and society at large, but it also supports the long-run interests of businesses themselves. Misleading consumers with false environmental claims is a short-run tactic that provides a company a

Pyrrhic victory at best. A company achieves long-term growth only by developing legitimate product offerings and promoting these offers with honest and supportable claims.

SUMMARY

This chapter examined a variety of issues related to the regulation of marketing communications, ethical MarCom behavior, and green marketing communications. The first major section looked at the regulation of MarCom activities. The regulatory environment was described with respect to both government regulation and industry self-regulation. The Federal Trade Commission's role was explained in terms of its regulation of deception and unfair practices. Self-regulation by the Council of Better Business Bureaus' National Advertising Division (NAD) and National Advertising Review Board (NARB) were discussed, emphasizing the process by which the NAD/NARB regulates national advertising.

The second section examined ethical marketing communications behavior. The ethics of each of the following MarCom activities were discussed: the targeting of marketing communications efforts, advertising, public relations, packaging communications, sales promotions, and online marketing communications. A concluding discussion examined how firms can foster ethical behavior.

In the final section, environmental, or *green*, marketing was described, and implications for marketing communications were discussed. Marketing communicators have responded to society's environmental interests by developing more environmentally friendly packaging and undertaking other communications initiatives. Recommendations provided to marketing communicators for making appropriate environmental claims are to (1) make the claims specific, (2) have claims reflect current disposal options, (3) make the claims substantive, and (4) make supportable claims.

Find more resources to help you study at http://shimp.swcollege.com!

DISCUSSION QUESTIONS

1. What is the distinction between a deceptive and an unfair business practice?

2. In your opinion, should a firm be required to have substantiating evidence (test results or other data) for an advertising claim prior to making the claim? Why or why not? Give examples of products where it is likely that substantiating evidence probably was not available prior to the advertiser making a claim (hint: health and dietary supplements).

3. Give examples of advertising claims that, if found false, probably would be considered material and those that probably would be evaluated as immaterial.

4. What is your opinion of the defense Kraft used in claiming that calcium is an immaterial product attribute?

5. In theory, corrective advertising represents a potentially valuable device for regulating deceptive advertising. In practice, however, corrective advertising must perform a very delicate balancing act by being strong enough without being too forceful. Explain the nature of this dilemma.

6. As noted in the text, the Distilled Spirits Council of the United States voted to lift its voluntary ban on advertising "hard" liquor on television and radio, a self-imposed ban that had been in effect for nearly a half-century. In your opinion, what are the arguments on both sides of the issue regarding the removal of this ban? If you were an executive employed by the Distilled Spirits Council, would you have urged a return to the airways? Is this return to advertising distilled spirits via electronic media unethical or, alternatively, is it a matter of a gutsy business decision by the Distilled Spirits Council that was long overdue?

7. Some nutritionists claim that Gatorade is neither helpful nor harmful to children. If indeed Gatorade for children is little more than an inert substance, is it unethical in your opinion for that company to advertise the product actively?

8. What is your opinion regarding the ethics of product placements in movies targeted to children? Identify the arguments on both sides of the issue, and then present your personal position.

9. What is your opinion regarding the ethics of advertorials in magazines targeted to teenagers? Identify the arguments on both sides of the issue, and then present your personal position.

10. Marketers of malt liquor claim they focus on inner cities because African Americans and Hispanics are the heavy consumers of this product. Is this practice ethical? Identify the arguments on both sides of the issue, and then present your personal position.

11. Advertising is often accused of various ethical violations. The criticisms of advertising mentioned in the chapter include claims that advertising is deceptive, manipulative, offensive, and plays on people's insecurities and fears. Provide evidence from your own personal experience to support any of these claims.

12. What is your view regarding Anheuser-Busch's use in the early to mid 1990s of humorous TV commercials that portrayed animated characters Frank, Louie, and an accompanying cast of lizard and frog characters? Is this form of advertising simply a marvelous creative execution, or is it insidious in its potential to encourage kids to like the concept of drinking beer, and perhaps Budweiser in particular?

13. The *Overview* section of the chapter concluded by asking you to think about the following questions: If you were the manager in this situation, would you have introduced your own brand of degradable trash bag, or would you have been willing to refrain from introducing a falsely claimed degradable trash bag and, consequently, to have suffered lost sales to unethical competitors? Identify marketing alternatives other than *introduce versus don't introduce* that might have been available to the Mobil Chemical Company in the Hefty trash bag situation.

14. During the 2001 holiday season, Philip Morris Companies marketed a new brand called M and promoted it as "A Special Blend for a Special

Season." Convenience stores and other retailers displayed signs with the appearance of gift-wrapping paper in green and red paisley backgrounds and the message "Season's Greetings from Marlboro Country." The president of the Campaign for Tobacco-Free Kids exclaimed that the marketing effort behind M "is selling cancer for Christmas."[108] What are your views on Philip Morris' marketing of M? Is it unethical or a case of smart marketing.

15. Some consumers are more concerned about the physical environment than others. Provide a specific profile of what in your opinion would be the socioeconomic and psychographic (i.e., lifestyle) characteristics of the "environmentally concerned" consumer.

16. The chapter quoted a Harvard Business School professor as claiming that green products would be to the 1990s what "lite" products were to the 1980s. Can you offer any reasons why this assertion may be overstated?

ENDNOTES

1. Quoted on p. 12 of Jennifer Lawrence, "Mobil," *Advertising Age*, January 29, 1991, 12–13. Many of the facts in the following description are based on this article.

2. Jennifer Lawrence and Christy Fisher, "Mobil, States Settle Degradability Suits," *Advertising Age*, July 1, 1991, 4.

3. The interrelation between ethical issues and regulation is discussed by George M. Zinkhan, "Advertising Ethics: Emerging Methods and Trends," *Journal of Advertising* 23 (September 1994), 1–4.

4. Michael B. Mazis, Richard Staelin, Howard Beales, and Steven Salop, "A Framework for Evaluating Consumer Information Regulation," *Journal of Marketing* 45 (winter 1981), 11–21.

5. The following discussion is adapted from Mazis, et al.

6. *Alcohol Beverage Labeling Act of 1988*, S.R. 2047.

7. A thorough review of research pertaining to warning labels is provided by David W. Stewart and Ingrid M. Martin, "Intended and Unintended Consequences of Warning Messages: A Review and Synthesis of Empirical Research," *Journal of Public Policy & Marketing* 13 (spring 1994), 1–19.

8. Janet R. Hankin, James J. Sloan, and Robert J. Sokol, "The Modest Impact of the Alcohol Beverage Warning Label on Drinking During Pregnancy Among a Sample of African-American Women," *Journal of Public Policy &Marketing* 17 (spring 1998), 61–69.

9. For a fascinating history of advertising and regulatory activity in the aspirin/ analgesic industry, see Charles C. Mann and Mark L. Plummer, "The Big Headache," *The Atlantic Monthly*, October 1988, 39–57.

10. Ross D. Petty, "Advertising Law in the United States and European Union," *Journal of Public Policy & Marketing* 16 (spring 1997), 2–13.

11. J. Edward Russo, Barbara L. Metcalf, and Debra Stephens, "Identifying Misleading Advertising," *Journal of Consumer Research* 8 (September 1981), 120. For a thorough review of advertising deception, see also David M. Gardner and Nancy H. Leonard, "Research in Deceptive and Corrective Advertising: Progress to Date and Impact on Public Policy," *Current Issues & Research in Advertising* 12 (1990), 275–309.

12. Public copy of letter dated October 14, 1983, from FTC Chairman James C. Miller III to Senator Bob Packwood, Chairman of Senate Committee on Commerce, Science, and Transportation.

13. For a more thorough discussion of these elements and other matters surrounding FTC deception policy, see Gary T. Ford and John E. Calfee, "Recent Developments in FTC Policy on Deception," *Journal of Marketing* 50 (July 1986), 82–103.

14. Chairman Miller's letter to Senator Packwood.

15. The advertising campaign ran in 1984 and 1985, but the FTC did not file a complaint until 1987.

16. These facts are offered by Jacob Jacoby and George J. Szybillo, "Consumer Research in FTC Versus Kraft (1991): A Case of Heads We Win, Tails You Lose?" *Journal of Public Policy & Marketing* 14 (spring 1995), 2.

17. Ruling of the Federal Trade Commission, Docket No. 9208, January 30, 1991.

18. Jef I. Richards and Ivan L. Preston, "Proving and Disproving Materiality of Deceptive Advertising Claims," *Journal of Public Policy & Marketing* 11 (fall 1992), 45–56; Jacoby and Szybillo, "Consumer Research in FTC Versus Kraft," 1–14; David W. Stewart, "Deception, Materiality, and Survey Research: Some Lessons from Kraft," *Journal of Public Policy & Marketing* 14

(spring 1995), 15–28; Seymour Sudman "When Experts Disagree: Comments on the Articles by Jacoby and Szybillo and Stewart," *Journal of Public Policy & Marketing* 14 (spring 1995), 29–34.

19. For further discussion, see Dorothy Cohen, "Unfairness in Advertising Revisited," *Journal of Marketing* 46 (winter 1982), 74.

20. Dorothy Cohen, "The Concept of Unfairness as It Relates to Advertising Legislation," *Journal of Marketing* 38 (July 1974), 8.

21. Cohen, "Unfairness in Advertising Revisited," 8.

22. The nature of the dispute is clearly played out in alternative positions presented by the president of the American Advertising Federation and the legal affairs director for the Center for Science in the Public Interest. See alternative positions argued by Wally Snyder (AAF) and Bruce A. Silverglade (CSPI) in "Does FTC Have an 'Unfair' Future?" *Advertising Age*, March 28, 1994, 20.

23. Christy Fisher, "How Congress Broke Unfair Ad Impasse," *Advertising Age*, August 22, 1994, 34.

24. For further discussion, see Dorothy Cohen, "The FTC's Advertising Substantiation Program," *Journal of Marketing* 44 (winter 1980), 26–35; and Debra L. Scammon and Richard J. Semenik, "The FTC's 'Reasonable Basis' for Substantiation of Advertising: Expanded Standards and Implications," *Journal of Advertising* 12, no. 1 (1983), 4–11.

25. Cited in the "Legal Developments in Marketing" section of the *Journal of Marketing* 52 (January 1988), 131.

26. Cohen, "Unfairness in Advertising Revisited," 74.

27. Ibid., 75. The rule was later rejected by a court of appeals on grounds that the FTC had failed to define the unfair practices that the rule was designed to remedy.

28. "Kids Ads: To Regulate Or Not?" *Advertising Age*, October 9, 2000, 58–60; Richard Linnett, "Psychologists Protest Kids' Ads," *Advertising Age*, September 11, 2000, 4, 69; Ira Teinowitz, "Hillary Clinton's Kids' Proposal Vexes Ad Groups," *Advertising Age*, October 2, 2000, 2.

29. Ivan L. Preston, "A Review of the Literature on Advertising Regulation," in *Current Issues and Research in Advertising 1983*, eds. James H. Leigh and Claude R. Martin (Ann Arbor: University of Michigan, 1983), 14.

30. The following discussion borrows liberally from the excellent review article by William L. Wilkie, Dennis L. McNeill, and Michael B. Mazis, "Marketing's 'Scarlet Letter': The Theory and Practice of Corrective Advertising," *Journal of Marketing* 48 (spring 1984), 11. See also Gardner and Leonard, "Research in Deceptive and Corrective Advertising."

31. See ibid. for review.

32. See Michael B. Mazis, "FTC v. Novartis: The Return of Corrective Advertising?" *Journal of Public Policy & Marketing* 20 (spring 2001), 114–122; Bruce Ingersoll, "FTC Orders Novartis to Run Ads to Correct 'Misbeliefs' about Pill," *Wall Street Journal Online*, May 28, 1999 (http://online.wsj.com).

33. A study evaluating the effects of a corrective advertising order against STP oil additive determined that corrective advertising action in this case worked as intended: False beliefs were corrected without injuring the product category or consumers' overall perceptions of the STP Corporation. See Kenneth L. Bernhardt, Thomas C. Kinnear, and Michael B. Mazis, "A Field Study of Corrective Advertising Effectiveness," *Journal of Public Policy & Marketing* 5 (1986), 146–162. This article and the one by Mazis in the previous endnote are essential reading for anyone interested in learning more about corrective advertising.

34. Steven W. Colford, "FDA Getting Tougher," *Advertising Age*, April 29, 1991, 1, 53; David Kiley, "FDA Seizes Citrus Hill," *Adweek's Marketing Week*, April 29, 1991, 6–7.

35. Chris Adams, "Xenical Skirts FDA Regulations by Avoiding Unpleasant Effects," *Wall Street Journal Online*, April 3, 2001 (http://online.wsj.com).

36. Paul Harris, "Will the FTC Finally Wake Up?" *Sales and Marketing Management*, January 1988, 57–59.

37. David Kiley, "Candid Camera: Volvo and the Art of Deception," *Adweek's Marketing Week*, November 12, 1990, 4–5; Raymond Serafin and Gary Levin, "Ad Industry Suffers Crushing Blow," *Advertising Age*, November 12, 1990, 1, 76–77; Raymond Serafin and Jennifer Lawrence, "Four More Volvo Ads Scrutinized," *Advertising Age*, November 26, 1990, 4.

38. See Andrew J. Strenio, Jr., "The FTC in 1988: Phoenix or Finis?" *Journal of Public Policy & Marketing* 7 (1988), 21–39.

39. Jean J. Boddewyn, "Advertising Self-Regulation: True Purpose and Limits," *Journal of Advertising* 18, no. 2 (1989), 19–27.

40. Jean J. Boddewyn, "Advertising Self-Regulation: Private Government and Agent of Public Policy," *Journal of Public Policy & Marketing* 4 (1985), 129–141.

41. Martha Rogers, "Advertising Self-Regulation in the 1980s: A Review," *Current Issues & Research in Advertising* 13 (1991), 369–392.

42. For a thorough discussion, see Eric J. Zanot, "Unseen but Effective Advertising Regulation: The Clearance Process," *Journal of Advertising* 14, no. 4 (1985), 44–51, 59. For an insightful treatment of television advertising clearance, see Avery M. Abernethy and Jan LeBlanc Wicks, "Self-regulation and Television Advertising: A Replication and Extension," *Journal of Advertising Research* 41 (May/June 2001), 31–37. For further reading on the advertising clearance process, see Avery M. Abernethy, "Advertising Clearance Practices of Radio Stations: A Model of Advertising Self-Regulation," *Journal of Advertising* 22 (September 1993), 15–26; Herbert J. Rotfeld, Avery M. Abernethy, and Patrick R. Parsons, "Self-Regulation and Television Advertising," *Journal of Advertising* 19 (December 1990), 18–26.

43. Eric J. Zanot, "A Review of Eight Years of NARB Casework: Guidelines and Parameters of Deceptive Advertising," *Journal of Advertising* 9, no. 4 (1980), 20.

44. *Statement of Organization and Procedures of the National Advertising Review Board* (Washington, D.C.: National Advertising Review Board, June 19, 1980).

45. The following discussion borrows from the thorough presentation by Gary M. Armstrong and Julie L. Ozanne, "An Evaluation of NAD/NARB Purpose and Performance," *Journal of Advertising* 12, no. 3 (1983), 19–23.

46. John McDonough, "25 Years of Self-Regulation," *Advertising Age*, December 2, 1996, c1–c2.

47. Jim Guthrie, "Give Self-regulation a Hand," *Advertising Age*, October 15, 2001, 16.

48. O. C. Ferrell and Larry G. Gresham, "A Contingency Framework for Understanding Ethical Decision Making in Marketing," *Journal of Marketing* 49 (summer 1985), 87–96.

49. For interesting discussion of the dysfunctional social effects resulting from implementations of the marketing concept, see Steven H. Star, "Marketing and Its Discontents," *Harvard Business Review* 67 (November/December 1989), 148–154.

50. A provocative and informative discourse on the issue of consumer vulnerability is presented in N. Craig Smith and Elizabeth Cooper-Martin, "Ethics and Target Marketing: The Role of Product Harm and Consumer Vulnerability," *Journal of Marketing* 61 (July 1997), 1–20.

51. Laura Bird, "Gatorade for Kids," *Adweek's Marketing Week*, July 15, 1991, 4–5.

52. For example, "Selling to Children," *Consumer Reports* (August 1990), 518–519.

53. Ibid.

54. Eben Shapiro, "Molson Ice Ads Raise Hackles of Regulators," *The Wall Street Journal*, February 25, 1994, B1, B10.

55. Guideline 8 in the Industry Advertising Code. Published in an undated pamphlet distributed by the Department of Consumer Awareness and Education, Anheuser-Busch, Inc., St. Louis, Mo.

56. Ira Teinowitz, "Congress Quiet on Issue of Liquor Ads," *Advertising Age*, January 21, 2002, 2.

57. For interesting reading on this issue, see Hae-Kyong Bang, "Analyzing the Impact of the Liquor Industry's Lifting of the Ban on Broadcast Advertising," *Journal of Public Policy & Marketing* 17 (spring 1998), 132–138; Arch G. Woodside, "Advertising and Consumption of Alcoholic Beverages," *Journal of Consumer Psychology* 8 (No. 2, 1999), 167–186.

58. Previous FTC chairman Robert Pitofsky acknowledged such limitations in Ira Teinowitz, "FTC Opinion Stirs Advertiser Fears," *Advertising Age*, November 27, 2000, 4.

59. See Ira Teinowitz, "Filmmakers: Give Ad-practice Shifts a Chance to Work," *Advertising Age*, October 2, 2000, 6; David Finnigan, "Pounding the Kid Trail," *Brandweek*, October 9, 2000, 32–38; Betsy Spethmann, "Now Showing: Federal Scrutiny," *Promo*, November 2000, 17.

60. Scott Donaton, "Why the Kids Marketing Fuss? Here's Why Parents Are Angry," *Advertising Age*, October 16, 2000, 48.

61. However, for alternative positions on this issue, see Joel B. Cohen "Playing to Win: Marketing and Public Policy at Odds over Joe Camel," *Journal of Public Policy & Marketing*, 19 (fall 2000), 155–167; John E. Calfee, "The Historical Significance of Joe Camel," *Journal of Public Policy & Marketing*, 19 (fall 2000), 168–182.

62. Brett Shevack, "Ban Joe Camel Campaign? That's Unfair," *Advertising Age*, September 20, 1993, 28.

63. Yumiko One and Bruce Ingersoll, "RJR Banishes Joe Camel, Adds Some Sexy Smokers," *The Wall Street Journal Interactive Edition*, July 11, 1997.

64. For reviews of this research and alternative perspectives, see Jean J. Boddewyn, "Where Should Articles on the Link between Tobacco Advertising and Consumption Be Published?" *Journal of Advertising* 22 (December 1993), 105–107; Lawrence C. Soley, "Smoke-filled Rooms and Research: A Response to Jean J. Boddewyn's Commentary," *Journal of Advertising* 22 (December 1993), 108–109; Richard W. Pollay, "Pertinent Research and Impertinent

Opinions: Our Contributions to the Cigarette Advertising Policy Debate," *Journal of Advertising* 22 (December 1993), 110–117; Claude R. Martin, Jr., "Ethical Advertising Research Standards: Three Case Studies," *Journal of Advertising* 23 (September 1994), 17–29; and Claude R. Martin, Jr., "Pollay's Pertinent and Impertinent Opinions: 'Good' versus 'Bad' Research," *Journal of Advertising* 23 (March 1994), 117–122.

65. "Fighting Ads in the Inner City," *Newsweek*, February 5, 1990, 46.

66. For further reading about these and other controversial cases, see Smith and Cooper-Martin, "Ethics and Target Marketing."

67. Dan Koeppel, "Insensitivity to a Market's Concerns," *Adweek's Marketing Week*, November 5, 1990, 25; "A 'Black' Cigarette Goes Up in Smoke," *Newsweek*, January 29, 1990, 54; "RJR Cancels Test of 'Black' Cigarette," *Marketing News*, February 19, 1990, 10.

68. Laura Bird, "An 'Uptown' Remake Called PowerMaster," *Adweek's Marketing Week*, July 1, 1991, 7.

69. "Fighting Ads in the Inner City."

70. For more discussion of this case, see Smith and Cooper-Martin, "Ethics and Target Marketing."

71. See John E. Calfee, "'Targeting' the Problem: It Isn't Exploitation, It's Efficient Marketing," *Advertising Age*, July 22, 1991, 18.

72. For additional insight on the issue, see Smith and Cooper-Martin, "Ethics and Target Marketing."

73. Pontifical Council for Social Communications, *Ethics in Advertising* (Vatican City: Vatican Documents, 1997). A section in the *Journal of Public Policy & Marketing* 17 (fall 1998) is devoted to analyzing and critiquing the Pontifical Council's report. See pages 313–335 and articles by John P. Foley, Patrick E. Murphy, Gene R. Laczniak, George G. Brenkert, and Debra Jones Ringold.

74. Ronald Berman, "Advertising and Social Change," *Advertising Age*, April 30, 1980, 24.

75. The interested reader is encouraged to review the following three articles for an extremely thorough, insightful, and provocative debate over the social and ethical role of advertising in American society. Richard W. Pollay, "The Distorted Mirror: Reflections on the Unintended Consequences of Advertising," *Journal of Marketing* 50 (April 1986), 18–36; Morris B. Holbrook, "Mirror, Mirror on the Wall, What's Unfair in the Reflections of Advertising?" *Journal of Marketing* 51 (July 1987), 95–103; Richard W. Pollay, "On the Value of Reflections on the Values in 'The Distorted Mirror,'" *Journal of Marketing* (July 1987), 104–109. Professors Pollay and Holbrook present alternative views of whether advertising is a "mirror" that merely reflects societal attitudes and values or a "distorted mirror" that is responsible for unintended and undesirable social consequences.

76. John E. Calfee and Debra Jones Ringold, "The 70% Majority: Enduring Consumer Beliefs about Advertising," *Journal of Public Policy & Marketing* 13 (fall 1994), 228–238.

77. Stephen B. Castleberry, Warren French, and Barbara A. Carlin, "The Ethical Framework of Advertising and Marketing Research Practitioners: A Moral Development Perspective," *Journal of Advertising* 22 (June 1993), 39–46.

78. These issues were identified by Paula Fitzgerald Bone and Robert J. Corey, "Ethical Dilemmas in Packaging: Beliefs of Packaging Professionals," unpublished working paper, West Virginia University Department of Marketing, 1991. The following discussion is guided by this paper. The authors identified a fifth ethical aspect of packaging (the relationship between a package and a product's price) that is not discussed here.

79. For an interesting discussion of perceptual differences among packaging professionals, brand managers, and consumers on the issue of packaging ethics, see Paula Fitzgerald Bone and Robert J. Corey, "Packaging Ethics: Perceptual Differences among Packaging Professionals, Brand Managers and Ethically-interested Consumers," *Journal of Business Ethics* 24 (April 2000), 199–213.

80. Yumiko Ono, "Upfront Ad for Excedrin Touts Different Packages for Same Item," *The Wall Street Journal Online*, April 9, 1998.

81. For an insightful discussion of sales promotion practices and related consumer psychology that result in exaggerated expectations of winning, see James C. Ward and Ronald Paul Hill, "Designing Effective Promotional Games: Opportunities and Problems," *Journal of Advertising* 20 (September 1991), 69–81.

82. Bob Gatty, "Atlanta Woman Guilty of Rebate Fraud," *Promo*, February 1994, 18.

83. A special issue of the *Journal of Public Policy & Marketing* 19 (spring 2000) is devoted to privacy and ethical issues in online marketing. See the articles on pages 1 through 73 by the following authors: George R. Milne; Eve M. Caudill and Patrick E. Murphy; Mary J. Culnan; Joseph Phelps, Glen Nowak and Elizabeth Ferrell; Ross D. Petty; Anthony D. Miyazaki and Ana Fernandez; and Kim Bartel Sheehan and Mariea Grubbs Hoy.

84. Jeffrey P. Davidson, "The Elusive Nature of Integrity: People Know It When They See It, but Can't Explain It," *Marketing News*, November 7, 1986, 24.

85. Ibid.

86. Donald P. Robin and R. Eric Reidenbach, "Social Responsibility, Ethics, and Marketing Strategy: Closing the Gap between Concept and Application," *Journal of Marketing* 51 (January 1987), 44–58. In this context, two additional articles that discuss ethical responsibilities of marketing practitioners are Rhoda H. Karpatkin, "Toward a Fair and Just Marketplace for All Consumers: The Responsibilities of Marketing Professionals," *Journal of Public Policy & Marketing* 18 (spring 1999), 118–122; Gene R. Laczniak, "Distributive Justice, Catholic Social Teaching, and the Moral Responsibility of Marketers," *Journal of Public Policy & Marketing* 18 (spring 1999), 125–129.

87. Based on Gene R. Laczniak and Patrick E. Murphy, "Fostering Ethical Marketing Decisions," *Journal of Business Ethics* 10 (1991), 259–271.

88. Patrick E. Murphy, *80 Exemplary Ethics Statements* (Notre Dame, Ind.: University of Notre Dame Press, 1998), 42, 65.

89. The concept of green marketing has various dimensions beyond this general explanation. For a review of the nuances, see William E. Kilbourne, "Green Advertising: Salvation or Oxymoron?" *Journal of Advertising* 24 (summer 1995), 7–20.

90. Alecia Swasy, "Color Us Green," *The Wall Street Journal*, March 22, 1991, B4.

91. Bob Garfield, "Beware: Green Overkill," *Advertising Age*, January 29, 1991, 26.

92. Stefan Bechtel, *Keeping Your Company Green* (Emmaus, Penn.: Rodale Press, 1990), 1.

93. Jack Neff, "It's Not Trendy Being Green," *Advertising Age*, April 10, 2000, 16.

94. Geoffrey A. Fowler, "'Green' Sales Pitch Isn't Helping to Move Products Off the Shelf," *The Wall Street Journal Online*, March 6, 2002 (http://online.wsj.com).

95. Pratima Bansal and Kendall Roth, "Why Companies Go Green: A Model of Ecological Responsiveness," *Academy of Management Journal*, 43 (No. 4, 2000), 717–736.

96. William J. Holstein, "Green Cars and Red Ink," *U.S. News & World Report*, November 6, 2000, 40–43.

97. This classification is based on Subhabrata Banerjee, Charles S. Gulas, and Easwar Iyer, "Shades of Green: A Multidimensional Analysis of Environmental Advertising," *Journal of Advertising* 24 (summer 1995), 21–32. For additional discussion of the types of environmental advertising claims and their frequency of use, see Les Carlson, Stephen J. Grove, and Norman Kangun, "A Content Analysis of Environmental Advertising Claims: A Matrix Method Approach," *Journal of Advertising* 22 (September 1993), 27–39.

98. "Honda to Use Mr. Clean to Add Muscle to Environmental Claims," *The Wall Street Journal Online*, September 26, 1997.

99. "L'eggs to Scrap Plastic 'Egg' Package," *Marketing News*, August 19, 1991, 20.

100. Bruce Ingersoll, "Got Milk?" *The Wall Street Journal Online*, July 18, 1997.

101. For review of a report on the short-filling problem, see http://www.ftc.gov/opa/1997/9707/milk.htm.

102. Jacquelyn Ottman, "Consider Eco-Labels," *Marketing News*, November 18, 1996, 14.

103. Queena Sook Kim, "Recycling Alliance Wants Symbol with Chasing Arrows Scrapped," *The Wall Street Journal Online*, March 6, 2002 (http://online.wsj.com).

104. Published in the *Federal Register* on August 13, 1992 [57 FR 36,363 (1992)]. These guides also available online at http://www.ftc.gov/bcp/grnrule/green02.htm. See also, Jason W. Gray-Lee, Debra L. Scammon, and Robert N. Mayer, "Review of Legal Standards for Environmental Marketing Claims," *Journal of Public Policy & Marketing* 13 (spring 1994), 155–159.

105. See http://www.ftc.gov/speeches/starek/egstarek.htm.

106. Julie Vergeront (principal author), *The Green Report: Findings and Preliminary Recommendations for Responsible Environmental Advertising* (St. Paul: Minnesota Attorney General's Office, November 1990). The following discussion is a summary of the recommendations in *The Green Report*.

107. The Federal Trade Commission's guidelines are similar in stating that environmental claims should (1) be substantiated; (2) be clear as to whether any assumed environmental advantage applies to the product, the package, or both; (3) avoid being trivial; and (4) if comparisons are made, make clear the basis for the comparisons.

108. Gordon Fairclough, "Philip Morris Launches 'M,' New Holiday Tobacco Blend," *Wall Street Journal Online*, December 4, 2001 (http://online.wsj.com).

A

Ability With reference to marketing, a person's familiarity with message claims and capability of comprehending them.

Account-specific marketing A descriptive term that characterizes promotional and advertising activity that a manufacturer customizes to specific retail accounts; also called *co-marketing*.

Active synthesis The second stage of perceptual encoding, active synthesis involves a more refined perception of a stimulus than simply an examination of its basic features. The context of the situation in which information is received plays a major role in determining what is perceived and interpreted.

Advertising A form of either mass communication or direct-to-consumer communication that is nonpersonal and is paid for by various business firms, nonprofit organizations, and individuals who are in some way identified in the advertising message and who hope to inform or persuade members of a particular audience.

Advertising objective Motive or goal that advertising efforts attempt to achieve. Examples include increasing sales volume, consumer awareness, and favorability of attitudes.

Advertising-sales-response function The amount of sales revenue generated at each level of advertising expenditure.

Advertising strategy A plan of action guided by corporate and marketing strategies which determine the following: how much can be invested in advertising; at what markets advertising efforts need to be directed; how advertising must be coordinated with other marketing elements; and, to some degree, how advertising is to be executed.

Advocacy advertising See **Issue advertising.**

Affective component The emotional component of an attitude.

Affect referral The simplest decision heuristic strategy in which the individual calls from memory his or her attitude, or affect, toward relevant alternatives and picks that alternative for which the affect is most positive.

Affordability method An advertising budgeting method that sets the budget by spending on advertising those funds that remain after budgeting for everything else.

AIO An acronym for *a*ctivities, *i*nterests, and *o*pinions, a combination representing psychographics.

Allegory A form of figurative language that equates the objects in a particular narrative (such as an advertised brand in a television commercial) with meanings lying outside the narrative itself.

Ambushing An activity that takes place when companies that are not official sponsors of an event undertake marketing efforts to convey the impression that they are.

Attention A stage of information processing in which the consumer focuses cognitive resources on and thinks about a message to which he or she has been exposed.

Attitude Represents a general and somewhat enduring positive or negative feeling toward, or evaluative judgment of, a brand or other consumption object such as a store.

Attractiveness An attribute that includes any number of virtuous characteristics that receivers may perceive in an endorser. The general concept of attractiveness consists of three related ideas: *similarity, familiarity,* and *liking.*

Attributes In the means-end conceptualization of advertising strategy, attributes are features or aspects of the advertised product or brand.

Awareness class The first step in product adoption. Four marketing-mix variables influence the awareness class: samples, coupons, advertising, and product distribution.

B

Baby boom The birth of 75 million Americans between 1946 and 1964.

Beliefs Subjective probability assessments regarding the likelihood that performing a certain act will lead to a certain outcome.

Bill-back allowances A form of trade allowance in which retailers receive allowances for featuring the manufacturer's brand in advertisements (bill-back ad allowances) or for providing special displays (bill-back display allowances).

Bonus pack Is a form of sales promotion whereby extra quantities of the product are provided to consumers at the brand's regular price.

Brand Is a company's particular offering of a product, service, or other consumption object. Brands represent the focus of MarCom efforts.

Brand-concept management The planning, implementation, and control of a brand concept throughout the life of the brand.

Brand equity The goodwill (equity) that an established brand has built up over the period of its existence.

Brand lift index This index indicates how in-store P-O-P materials affect the likelihood that customers will buy a product that they had not specifically planned on buying.

Brand image strategy A creative advertising strategy that involves psychological rather than physical differentiation. The advertiser attempts to develop an image for a brand by associating it with symbols.

C

Category management A system established by Procter & Gamble whereby a category manager who has direct profit responsibility manages each product category within a company.

Cause-related marketing (CRM) A relatively narrow aspect of overall sponsorship which involves an amalgam of public relations, sales promotion, and corporate philanthropy. The distinctive feature of CRM is that a company's contribution to a designated cause is linked to customers' engaging in revenue-producing exchanges with the firm.

Cells 1 through 6 Sales promotions are classified into six categories, or cells, based on the manufacturer's objective in using a promotion—whether generating trial purchasing, encouraging repeat buying, or enhancing a brand's image—and the type of reward offered consumers (immediate or delayed).

Cognitive component The intellectual component of attitude. In marketing, it is the consumer's knowledge, thoughts, and beliefs about an object or issue.

Commercial rumor A widely circulated but unverified proposition about a product, brand, company, store, or other commercial target.

Communication Process whereby individuals share meaning and establish a commonness of thought.

Compatibility Is the degree to which an innovation is perceived to fit into a person's way of doing things; in general, a new product/brand is more compatible to the extent that it matches consumers' needs, personal values, beliefs, and past consumption practices.

Compensatory heuristic A choice strategy in which the customer ranks each of the criteria he or she would like a product to meet, decides how well each brand alternative will satisfy these criteria, and integrates this information to arrive at a "score" for each alternative. Theoretically the consumer selects the alternative with the highest overall score. This procedure is likely to be used in risky (high-involvement) circumstances; that is, when a decision involves considerable financial, performance, or psychological risk.

Competitive parity method A budgeting method that sets the advertising budget by basically following what competitors are doing. Also called the match competitors method.

Complexity The degree of perceived difficulty of an innovation. The more difficult an innovation is to understand or use, the slower the rate of adoption.

Comprehension The ability to understand and create meaning out of stimuli and symbols.

Conative component The action component of an attitude; a person's behavioral tendency toward an object. In marketing, it is the consumer's intention to purchase a specific item. Also called *behavioral component*.

Concretizing A marketing approach based on the idea that it is easier for people to remember and retrieve *tangible* rather than *abstract* information.

Consequences In the means-end conceptualization of advertising strategy, consequences represent the desirable or undesirable results from consuming a particular product or brand.

Conspiracy rumors Unconfirmed statements that involve supposed company policies or practices that are threatening or ideologically undesirable to consumers.

Contact Potential message delivery channels capable of reaching target customers and presenting the communicator's brand in a favorable light.

Contamination rumors Unconfirmed statements dealing with undesirable or harmful product or store features.

Contest A form of consumer-oriented sales promotion in which consumers have an opportunity to win cash, merchandise, or travel prizes. Winners become eligible by solving the specified contest problem.

Continuity A media planning consideration that involves how advertising should be allocated during the course of an advertising campaign.

Continuous advertising schedule In a continuous schedule, a relatively equal number of ad dollars are invested in advertising throughout the campaign.

Contribution margin The selling price of a brand minus its per-unit variable cost. When a brand is on deal, its variable cost increases due to the expense of offering, for example, a coupon worth 50 cents. This results in a reduced margin.

Cooperative (Co-op) advertising An arrangement between a manufacturer and reseller (either a retailer or an industrial distributor) whereby the manufacturer pays for all or some of the advertising costs undertaken by the reseller in behalf of the manufacturer's products.

Corporate advertising Advertising that focuses on specific products or brands in a corporation's overall image or on economic/social issues relevant to the corporation's interests.

Corporate image advertising A specific form of corporate advertising that attempts to gain name recognition for a company, establish goodwill for it and its products, or identify itself with some meaningful and socially acceptable activity.

Corrective advertising Advertising based on the premise that a firm that misleads consumers should have to use future advertisements to rectify any deceptive impressions it has created in consumers' minds. Its purpose is to prevent a firm from continuing to deceive consumers rather than to punish the firm.

Coutnerarguments A form of cognitive response that occurs when the receiver challenges message claims.

Coupon A promotional device that provides cents-off savings to consumers upon redeeming the coupons.

CPM An abbreviation for cost per thousand, in which the *M* represents the Roman numeral for 1,000. CPM is the cost of reaching 1,000 people.

CPM-TM A refinement of CPM that measures the cost of reaching 1,000 members of the target market, excluding those people who fall outside of the target market.

Creative brief The work of copywriters is directed by this framework, which is a document designed to inspire copywriters by channeling their creative efforts toward a solution that will serve the interests of the client.

Customer lifetime value The net present value (NPV) of the profit that a company stands to realize on the average new customer during a given number of years.

D

Database marketing Involves collecting and electronically storing information about present, past, and prospective customers. The information is used to profile customers, develop effective and efficient marketing programs by communicating with individual customers, and establish long-term communication relationships.

Data mining Involves the process of searching databases to extract information and discover potentially hidden but useful facts about past, present, and prospective customers.

Deal Refers to any form of sales promotion that delivers a price reduction to consumers. Retailer discounts, manufacturer cents-off offers, and the ubiquitous coupon are the most common forms of deals.

Decoding The mental process of transforming message symbols into thought; consumers' interpretations of marketing messages. See also **Encoding**.

Demographics Variables that are measurable population characteristics, including the age distribution, household living patterns, income distribution, ethnic population patterns, and regional population statistics.

Direct advertising A form of advertising matter sent directly to the person whom the marketer wishes to influence; these advertisements can take the form of letters, postcards, programs, calendars, folders, catalogs, videocassettes, blotters, order blanks, price lists, menus, and so on.

Diverting Occurs when a manufacturer restricts a deal to a limited geographical area rather than making it available nationally, which results in retailers buying abnormally large quantities at the deal price and then selling off, at a small profit margin, the excess quantities through brokers in other geographical areas.

Dual-coding theory The idea that pictures are represented in memory in verbal as well as visual form, whereas words are less likely to have visual representations.

E

Early adopters The second group of people to adopt an innovation. The size of this group is defined statistically as 13.5 percent of all potential adopters. Early adopters are localities, in contrast to innovators, who are described as cosmopolites. Early adopters are well integrated within their communities and are respected by their friends.

Early majority A group of early product adopters known for being deliberate and cautious in their adoption of innovations. This group is slightly above average in education and social status but below the levels of the early adopter group.

EDLP(M) pricing This is a form of pricing whereby a manufacturer charges the same price for a particular brand day in and day out. Rather than charging high-low prices (regular, or "high," prices for a period followed by off-invoice, or "low," prices for a shorter period), EDLP(M) involves charging the same price over an extended period.

Efficient consumer response (ECR) A broad-based concept of business management oriented toward altering industry practices to enhance efficiencies and reduce costs.

Elaboration The mental activity associated with a consumer's response to a persuasive message. Elaboration involves thinking about what the message is saying, evaluating the arguments in the message, agreeing with some, disagreeing with others, and so on.

Elaboration likelihood (EL) Represents the prospect that a message receiver will think about a message and react to it by comparing it with his or her pre-existing thoughts and beliefs regarding the product category, the advertised brand, and perhaps competitive brands.

Elaboration likelihood model (ELM) A theory of persuasion and attitude change that predicts two forms of message processing and attitude change: central and peripheral routes. The former occurs under high involvement and leads to a more permanent attitude change than does the latter.

Elasticity Is a measure of how responsive the demand for a brand is as a function of changes in marketing variables such as price and advertising.

E-mail advertising Is the use of the Internet for sending commercial messages in the form of e-mail messages as an alternative to banner ads, pop-ups, or other forms of rich-media presentations.

Encoding The process of putting thoughts into symbolic form. See also **Decoding.**

Encoding specificity principle A principle of cognitive psychology, which states that information recall is enhanced when the context in which people attempt to retrieve information is the same or similar to the context in which they originally encoded the information.

Encoding variability hypothesis A hypothesis contending that people's memories for information are enhanced when multiple pathways, or connections, are created between the object to be remembered and the information about the object that is to be remembered.

Ethics In the context of marketing communications involves matters of right and wrong, or *moral,* conduct.

Evaluations The subjective value or importance that consumers attach to consumption outcomes.

Event sponsorship A form of brand promotion that ties a brand to a meaningful cultural, social, athletic, or other type of high-interest public activity.

Exceptionist loyalists Consumers who, though loyal to a single brand when all brands in the category are off deal, will make an exception and purchase another, nonpreferred brand when it, but not their preferred brand, is on deal.

Executive-statement release A news release quoting CEOs and other corporate executives.

Exit fee A *deslotting charge* to cover the handling costs for a chain to remove an item from its distribution center.

Experiential needs Needs representing desires for products that provide sensory pleasure, variety, and stimulation.

Expertise The knowledge, experience, or skills possessed by an endorser as they relate to the communications topic.

Exposure In marketing terms, signifies that consumers come in contact with the marketer's message.

External lists Mailing lists bought from other companies rather than being based on a company's own internal list of customers.

F

Feature analysis The initial stage of perceptual encoding whereby a receiver examines the basic features of a stimulus (brightness, depth, angles, etc.) and from this makes a preliminary classification.

Feature article A detailed description of a product or other newsworthy programs that are written by a PR firm for immediate publication or airing by print or broadcast media or distribution via appropriate Internet sites.

Feedback Data that afford the source of marketing communications with a way of monitoring how accurately the intended message is being received and offer some measure of control in the communications process.

Forward buying The practice whereby retailers take advantage of manufacturers' trade deals by buying larger quantities than needed for normal inventory. Retailers often buy enough product on

Off-invoice allowance A deal offered periodically to the trade that literally permits wholesalers and retailers to deduct a fixed amount from the invoice.

On-pack premium Is a premium item that is attached to the package of the brand that offers the free item as a promotional inducement.

Open-ended co-op advertising A cooperative advertising program that involves paying for the portion of the retailer's advertising cost without relating the reimbursement to the amount of product purchased from the manufacturer.

Opinion leader Is a person who frequently influences other individuals' attitudes and behavior related to new products. They inform other people (followers) about new products, reduce followers' perceived risk in purchasing new products, and confirm decisions that followers have already made.

Opportunity A term referring to whether its physically possible for a person to process a message.

Opt-in e-mailing Is the practice of marketers' asking for and receiving consumers' permission to send them messages on a particular topic. The consumer agrees (opts-in) to receive messages on topics of interest rather than receiving messages that are unsolicited.

Outcomes The aspects of brand ownership that the consumer either desires to obtain or to avoid.

Overlay program The use of two or more sales promotion techniques in combination with one another; also called *combination program*.

P

Pay-for-performance programs A form of trade allowance that rewards retailers for performing the primary function that justifies a manufacturer's offering a trade allowance—namely, selling increased quantities of the manufacturer's brands to grocery shoppers.

People Meter A handheld device that automatically records what programs are being watched, how many households are watching, and which family members are in attendance.

Percentage-of-sales method A budgeting method that involves setting the budget as a fixed percentage of past or anticipated (typically the latter) sales volume. See also **Objective-and-task method**.

Perceptual encoding The process of interpreting stimuli, which includes two stages: feature analysis and active synthesis.

Permanent P-O-P display This type of display is used for merchandising products and has an intended use exceeding six months.

Personal selling A form of person-to-person communication in which the seller attempts to persuade prospective buyers to purchase his or her company's (organization's) product or service.

Physical attractiveness Is a key consideration in many endorsement relationships and involves an endorser's beauty, athleticism, and sexuality.

P-mail advertising P-mail, which is structurally equivalent to e-mail and is shorthand for "postal," refers to any advertising matter a company sends via the postal service.

Point-of-purchase (P-O-P) communications Promotional elements, including displays, posters, signs, and a variety of other in-store materials, that are designed to influence the customer's choice at the time of purchase.

Pop-up ads Are a form of Internet advertising in which ads appear in a separate window that materializes on the screen seemingly out of nowhere when a selected Web page is loading.

Positioning Advertising Copytesting (PACT) A set of nine copytesting principles developed by leading U.S. advertising agencies.

Positioning statement The key idea that encapsulates what a brand is intended to stand for in its target market's mind.

Positioning strategy A creative advertising strategy in which an advertiser implants in the consumer's mind a clear understanding of what the brand is and how it compares to competitive offerings.

Preemptive strategy A creative advertising strategy in which the advertiser that makes a particular claim effectively prevents competitors from making the same claim for fear of being labeled a copycat.

Premiums Articles of merchandise or services offered by manufacturers to induce action on the part of the sales force, trade representatives, or consumers.

Price-off promotion Also called cents-off or price packs, this form of sales promotion entails a reduction, typically ranging from 10 to 25 percent, in a brand's regular price.

Proactive MPR A form of marketing PR that is offensively rather than defensively oriented and opportunity-seeking rather than problem solving. See also **Reactive MPR**.

Product release A publicity tool that announces new product, provides relevant information about product features and benefits, and informs interested listeners/readers how additional information can be obtained.

Promotion The aspect of general marketing that promotion management deals with explicitly. Promotion includes the practices of advertising, personal selling, sales promotion, publicity, and point-of-purchase communications.

Psychogalvanometer A device for measuring galvanic skin response that is used as an indicator of advertising effectiveness, specifically by determining whether the consumer's autonomic nervous system is activated by some element in an advertisement.

Psychographic characteristics Aspects of consumers' lifestyles such as activities, interests, and opinions.

Psychological reactance A theory that suggests that people react against any efforts to reduce their freedoms or choices. When products are made to seem less available, they become more valuable in the consumer's mind.

Publicity Nonpersonal communication to a mass audience that is not paid for by an organization. Examples include news items or editorial comments about an organization's products or services.

Pull Marketing efforts directed to ultimate consumers with the intent of influencing their acceptance of the manufacturer's brand. Manufacturers hope that the consumers will then encourage retailers to handle the brand. Typically used in conjunction with *push*.

Push money Cash provided to salespeople by the manufacturer to encourage them to push certain products in the manufacturer's line. Also called *spiffs*.

Push A manufacturer's selling and other promotional efforts directed at gaining trade support from wholesalers and retailers for the manufacturer's product.

R

Rating the proportion of the target audience presumed to be exposed to a single occurrence of an advertising vehicle in which the advertiser's brand is advertised.

Rating points Ratings points are the foundation for concepts such as effective, gross, and target rating points. A single rating point simply represents one percent of a designated group or an entire population that is exposed to a particular advertising vehicle such as a TV program.

Reach The percentage of an advertiser's target audience that is exposed to at least one advertisement over an established time frame (a four-week period represents the typical time frame for most advertisers). Reach represents the number of target customers who see or hear the advertiser's message one or more times during the time period. Also called *net coverage, unduplicated audience,* or *cumulative audience (cume).*

Reactive MPR Marketing undertaken as a result of external pressures and challenges brought by competitive actions, changes in consumer attitudes, or other external influences. It typically deals with changes that have negative consequences for the organization. See also **Proactive MPR.**

Rebate Manufacturers give cash discounts or reimbursements to consumers who submit proofs of purchase when purchasing the manufacturer's brand. Unlike coupons, which the consumer redeems at retail checkouts, rebates/refunds are mailed with proofs of purchase to manufacturers.

Receiver The person or group of people with whom the sender of a communication shares thoughts. In marketing, the receivers are the prospective and present customers of an organization's product or service.

Recency principle Known also as the shelf-space model for media planning, this principle is based on the idea that achieving a high level of weekly reach for a brand should be emphasized over acquiring heavy frequency.

Relative advantage The degree to which an innovation is perceived as better than an existing idea or object in terms of increasing comfort, saving time or effort, and increasing the immediacy of reward.

Repeater class This third stage in the adoption process is influenced by four marketing-mix variables: advertising, price, distribution, and product satisfaction.

Respect Is an endorser characteristic that represents the quality of being admired or esteemed due to one's personal qualities and accomplishments.

S

Sales promotion Marketing activities intended to stimulate quick buyer action by offering extra benefits to customers. Examples include coupons, premiums, free samples, and sweepstakes. Also called *promotional inducements.*

Sampling The use of various distribution methods to deliver actual- or trial-size products to consumers. The purpose is to initiate trial-usage behavior.

Self-liquidating offer Known as SLOs by practitioners, this form of premium requires consumers to mail in a stipulated number of proofs of purchase along with sufficient money to cover the manufacturer's purchasing, handling, and mailing costs of the premium item.

Self-regulation Regulation of advertising by advertisers themselves rather by state or federal government bodies.

Semipermanent P-O-P display This type of display has an intended life span of less than six but more than two months.

Share of market (SOM) Represents a brand's proportion of overall product category sales.

Share of voice (SOV) Represents a brand's proportion of overall advertising expenditures in a product category.

Shelf-space model of advertising Also termed the theory of *effective weekly planning,* a model built on the idea that the first exposure to an advertisement for a brand is the most powerful.

Sign (1) Something physical and perceivable by our senses that represents or signifies something (the referent) to somebody (the interpreter) in some context. (2) Specifically, when both a product/brand and referent belong to the same cultural context.

Similarity Represents the degree to which an endorser matches an audience in terms of characteristics such as age, gender, and ethnicity that are pertinent to the quality of an endorsement relationship.

Simile A form of figurative language that uses a comparative term such as *like* or *as* to join items from different classes of experience (e.g., "love is like a rose").

Single-source data Consist of household demographic information, household purchase behavior, and household exposure to new television commercials that are tested under real world, or in-market, test conditions.

Single-source systems (SSSs) Systems that gather purchase data from panels of households using optical scanning equipment and merge it with household demographic characteristics and, most important, with information about causal marketing variables that influence household purchases.

Slotting allowance The fee a manufacturer pays a supermarket or other retailer to get that retailer to handle the manufacturer's new product. The allowance is called slotting in reference to the slot, or location, that the retailer must make available in its warehouse to accommodate the manufacturer's product.

Source In marketing communications, a source is a person, group, organization, or label that delivers a message. Marketing communications sources influence receivers by possessing one or more of three basic attributes: power, attractiveness, and credibility.

Spam Is an expression used by Internet users that refers to unsolicited and unwanted commercial e-mail messages.

Sponsorship marketing A form of marketing whereby a company invests in special events or causes for the purpose of achieving various promotional and corporate objectives.

Standardized Advertising Unit (SAU) system A system adopted in the 1980s, making it possible for advertisers to purchase any one of 56 standard ad sizes to fit the advertising publishing parameters of all newspapers in the United States.

Stockpiling-exceptionist loyalists A consumer segment that not only makes exceptions by choosing nonpreferred brands, but which also stockpiles quantities of other brand when they are on deal.

Stockpiling loyalists A consumer segment that purchases only the single brand to which it is loyal but which takes advantage of savings by stockpiling when that brand is on deal.

Stockpiling switchers A consumer segment that exploits deal opportunities by purchasing multiple units when any acceptable brand is on deal.

Superstitials Are short, animated Internet ads that play over or on top of a Web page.

Supportive arguments A form of cognitive response that occurs when a receiver agrees with a message's arguments. See also **Counterarguments** and **Source derogations**.

Sweepstakes A form of consumer-oriented sales promotion in which winners receive cash, merchandise, or travel prizes. Winners are determined purely on the basis of chance.

Switchers consumers who, even when all brands in a category are off deal, nonetheless switch among different brands.

SWOT Acronym for the analysis of a brand's strengths, weaknesses, opportunities, and threats.

Symbol A product and referent put together arbitrarily or metaphorically with no prior intrinsic relationship.

Symbolic needs Internal consumer needs such as the desire for self-enhancement, role position, or group membership.

T

Target rating points (TRPs) An adaptation of gross rating points (GRPs), TRPs adjust a vehicle's rating to reflect just those individuals who match the advertiser's target audience.

Temporary P-O-P displays Are point-of-purchase displays designed for short-term use by retailers, typically less than two months.

Three-exposure hypothesis This addresses the *minimum* number of exposures needed for advertising to be effective.

Tie-in The simultaneous promotion of multiple brands in a single sales-promotion effort; also called *joint promotion*.

Trade allowances Also called trade deals, these allowances are used by manufacturers to reward wholesalers and retailers for performing activities in support of the manufacturer's brand such as featuring the brand in retail advertisements or providing special display space.

Trade incentives In contrast to trade contests, trade incentives are given to retail managers and salespeople for performing tasks such as displaying merchandise or selling certain lines of merchandise.

Transformational advertising Brand image advertising that associates the experience of using an advertised brand with the unique set of psychological characteristics that would not typically be associated with the brand experience to the same degree without exposure to the advertisement.

Trialability The extent to which an innovation can be used on a limited basis. Trialability is tied closely to the concept of perceived risk. In general, products that lend themselves to trialability are adopted at a more rapid rate.

Trier class The group of consumers who actually try a new product; the second step in which an individual becomes a new brand consumer. Coupons, distribution, and price are the variables that influence consumers to become triers.

Trustworthiness The honesty, integrity, and reliability of a source.

U

Unfair advertising Is a legal term to define advertising acts or practices that cause or are likely to cause substantial injury to consumers, which is not reasonably avoidable by consumers themselves and not outweighed by countervailing benefits to consumers or competition.

Unique selling proposition (USP) strategy A creative advertising strategy that promotes a product attribute that represents a meaningful, distinctive consumer benefit.

V

Values In the means-end conceptualization of advertising strategy, values represent important beliefs that people hold about themselves and that determine the relative desirability of consequences.

Value proposition Is the essence of an advertisement or other MarCom message and the reward to the consumer for investing his or her time attending the message.

Vehicles The specific broadcast programs or print choices in which advertisements are placed.

Vendor support programs (VSPs) A form of cooperative advertising program initiated by retailers whereby the retailer features one or several manufacturers' products in local advertising media and has the manufacturer(s) pay for the advertising.

VIEW Is an acronym that can be used when evaluating four general features of a particular package: Visibility, information, emotional appeal, and workability.

Voluntary attention One of three forms of attention that occurs when a person willfully notices a stimulus. See also **Involuntary attention** and **Nonvoluntary attention**.

W

Warmth monitor A technique that measures emotional warmth in television commercials.

Wear out Refers to the ultimately diminished effectiveness of advertising over time.